READINGS IN
LINGUISTICS I & II

READINGS IN LINGUISTICS I & II

ABRIDGED EDITION

Edited by Eric P. Hamp, Martin Joos,
Fred W. Householder, and Robert Austerlitz

THE UNIVERSITY OF CHICAGO PRESS

CHICAGO AND LONDON

This volume is a collection of articles drawn from *Readings in Linguistics I: The Development of Descriptive Linguistics in America 1925–56*, fourth edition (1966), edited by Martin Joos, and *Readings in Linguistics II* (1966), edited by Eric P. Hamp, Fred W. Householder, and Robert Austerlitz. There is a new foreward by Eric Hamp.

The University of Chicago Press, Chicago 60637
The University of Chicago Press, Ltd., London
© 1995 by The University of Chicago
Readings in Linguistics I © 1957, 1966 by the American Council of Learned Societies
Readings in Linguistics II © 1966 by The University of Chicago

All rights reserved. Published 1995
Printed in the United States of America
01 00 99 98 97 96 95   6 5 4 3 2 1

ISBN 0-226-41027-7 (pbk.)

Library of Congress Cataloging-in-Publication Data

Readings in linguistics I & II / edited by Eric P. Hamp . . . (et al).
  — Abridged ed.
    p.   cm.
    "A collection of articles drawn from Readings in linguistics I: the development of descriptive linguistics in America, 1925–56, fourth edition (1966), edited by Martin Joos, and Readings in linguistics II (1966) edited by Eric P. Hamp, Fred W. Householder, and Robert Austerlitz."
    Includes bibliographical references.
    1. Linguistics. I. Hamp, Eric P. II. Title: Readings in linguistics I and II. III. Title: Readings in linguistics 1 & 2. IV. Title: Readings in linguistics one & two.
P125.R36   1995
410—dc20   93-40098
                                                  CIP

This book is printed on acid-free paper.

FOREWORD

It is both a mark of the passage of time and a pleasant reminder of their usefulness that *Readings in Linguistics* and *Readings in Linguistics II* have gone out of print. They should, of course, be easily available on library shelves to archivists and retrospective scholars. It is clear that today not all essays included in those two volumes are of equal widespread interest, and that some of them might not be read at all in a priority ranked students' list. Yet it is equally clear that a portion of each volume commands a continuing interest. Some items are of perennial basic value to the fundamental literacy of the field of linguistics; some throw strong and useful light on the development of the modern field; some are proposed as desirable inducements to student reading in areas of current concern but possible neglect; and some, as has been remarked in the Preface to *RIL II*, must be sacrificed to the constraints of space with nostalgia and regret.

Because, therefore, a substantial core of *Readings* and *RIL II* has been judged to fulfill a worthwhile service, it is gratifying that the University of Chicago Press has proposed reprinting an abridgment of those two volumes. In preparing this abridgment three aims have been kept paramount. First, since this volume is meant to be of use to the ongoing business of linguistics and is not intended as an historical archive or bibliophilic museum piece, it should be priced well within the reach of students; this requirement imposes certain features of practicality: size, compression, format, and mode of reproduction. Second, an attempt has been made to conserve something of the flavor of the original volumes. Third, in making selections the needs of students, rather than those of established scholars, have been kept foremost.

As in the case of *RIL II*, the availability of an item in a miscellany in print also guided our exclusions from this abridgment. We must hasten to acknowledge that there were collectanea easily obtainable in 1966 (as well as back files of journals such as *Word*) that are now sadly not widely accessible. It was along these lines that the number and length of the items by Roman Jakobson dictated exclusion from this abridgment. Obviously most of Jakobson is widely accessible in his multivolume *Selected Writings* (Mouton: Berlin/New York/Amsterdam, 1962–88 [copyright 1987]; 8 vols., plus vol. 1, 2d ed., 1971), but few can afford these immensely expensive volumes. Our problem is however solved by his *Russian and Slavic Grammar: Studies 1931–1981*, eds. Linda R. Waugh and Morris Halle (Mouton, 1984), in which *RIL II*'s no. 4 appears in English on pp. 1–14, no. 9 on pp. 59–104, and no. 13 on pp. 151–60. It is to be hoped that this useful Jakobson volume will be kept in print and that scholars will be encouraged to browse, then read more widely in it. In recent years our supply of compact Jakobson anthologies has been greatly enriched. *RIL II* no. 9 is now

available also, with a 1958 Appendix, as no. 22 in L. R. Waugh and M. Monville-Burston, eds., *On Language: Roman Jakobson* (Cambridge: Harvard, 1990), a valuable annotated collection of twenty-nine texts which includes all the Jakobson items in J. Cantineau's Trubetzkoy volume (Paris: Klincksieck, 1949); two (no. 2 and no. 4, appearing, lightly edited, as no. 15) of the *Six Lectures on Sound and Meaning* (Cambridge: MIT 1978, translated from Paris: Minuit 1976, the original 1942–43 French lecture draft); and three (nos. 7, 8, and 22, appearing as nos. 4, 7, and 25) of the twenty-nine annotated essays comprising *Language in Literature: Roman Jakobson*, Krystyna Pomorska and Stephen Rudy, eds. (Cambridge: Harvard, 1987). One can now also consult *Roman Jakobson, 1896–1982: A Complete Bibliography of His Writings [1912–1982]*, S. Rudy, ed. (Berlin: Mouton, 1990).

The selections from the Prague Circle included in this abridgment and in *RIL II* can be supplemented from *A Prague School Reader in Linguistics*, ed. Josef Vachek (Bloomington: Indiana University Press, 1964), on which see also the review by Yakov Malkiel in *American Anthropologist* 68 (1966): 585–88; and *The Prague School: Selected Writings 1929–46*, ed. P. Steiner (Austin: University of Texas Press, 1982). Also helpful is *Etudes phonologiques dédiées à la mémoire de M. le Prince N. S. Trubetzkoy* (= *TCLP* 8, 1939), reissued by Carroll E. Reed (University of Alabama Press, 1964). From N. S. Trubetzkoy see *Principes de phonologie*, tr. by J. Cantineau (Paris: Klincksieck, 1949) *Grundzüge der Phonologie* (= *TCLP* 7, 1939), 3d ed., Göttingen: Vandenhoeck & Ruprecht, 1962; also available as *Osnovy fonologii* (Moskva, 1960), tr. A. Kholodovich, and as *Principles of Phonology* (Berkeley: University of California Press, 1969), tr. Christiane A. Baltaxe. The Cantineau volume includes five reprint articles as well as valuable biographical documentation on Trubetzkoy, and is supplemented by *N. S. Trubetzkoy's Letters and Notes*, ed. R. Jakobson (The Hague: Mouton, 1975). The work of Louis Hjelmslev can now be consulted in *Prolegomena to a Theory of Language*, tr. F. J. Whitfield (Madison: University of Wisconsin Press, 1961); in *TCLC* 5 and *TCLC* 12 (mentioned in *RIL II*); in his *Essais linguistiques II TCLC* 14 (1973); and in his disarmingly lucid book *Language: An Introduction*, tr. Francis J. Whitfield (Madison: University of Wisconsin Press, 1970), originally *Sproget: En introduction* (København: Berlingske, first published in 1963 but written ca. 1943). See also Hans Jørgen Uldall, *Outline of Glossematics, Part I: General Theory*, 2d ed., TCLC 10 (1967, begun in 1936, 1st ed. 1957), with an important introduction by Eli Fischer-Jørgensen. For further work of Daniel Jones see *The Phoneme: Its Nature and Use* (Cambridge: Heffer, 1950), and the review by F. W. Householder, in *IJAL* 18 (1952): 99–105. The collection *Phonetics in Linguistics: A Book of Readings,* ed. W. E. Jones and J. Laver (London: Longman, 1973), drawn from writings by scholars of the British school, embraces phenomena that would be categorized by many as phonological or morpho(pho)nemic. The work of J. R. Firth is well represented by *Papers in Linguistics 1934–1951* (Oxford University Press, 1957) (see the next item for a more accurate list of JRF's publications), and *Selected Papers of J. R. Firth, 1952–1959,* ed. F. R. Palmer (Bloomington: Indiana University Press, 1968), including an illuminating incisive introduction by Palmer, a major scholar in this tradition. In addition to the mentions in *RIL II,* the work of A. Martinet can be surveyed in his *Elements of General Linguistics* (London: Faber & Faber, 1964). The tradition of scholarship claiming direct and local descent from Ferdinand de Saussure[1] (cf. R. S. Wells, *RIL* I, no. 1, excluded with regret here) is represented by *A Geneva School Reader in Linguistics,* ed. Robert Godel (Bloomington: Indiana University Press, 1969); a crucial precursor (1870–1930) to the last, to the Praguian, and to the Copenhagen traditions is admirably represented in Edward Stankiewicz, *A Baudouin de Courtenay Anthology* (Bloomington: Indiana University Press, 1972). For another seminal and relevant precursor to these traditions see *Whitney on Language: Selected Writings of William Dwight Whitney,* ed. Michael Silverstein (Cambridge: MIT Press, 1971), with an introductory essay by Roman Jakobson. An expanded view of R. H. Robins, who somewhat bridges *RIL I* and *RIL II,* may be gained by reading in his *Diversions of Bloomsbury: Selected Writings on Linguistics* (Amsterdam: North-Holland, 1970), and by consulting the list of his publications in *Studies in the History of Western Linguistics: In Honour of R. H. Robins,* ed. Theodora Bynon and F. R. Palmer (Cambridge University Press, 1986), pp. 279–83. It is significant that Robins was invited to deliver the Bloomfield Centennial Address at the meeting of the Linguistic Society of America in December 1987.

Further essays by Benveniste are to be found collected in *Problèmes de linguistique générale* (1966), translated as *Problems in General Linguistics* (Coral Gables: University of Miami Press, 1971) and in *Problèmes . . . II* (1974); one need scarcely mention the well known forerunner collections to Benveniste, those of A. Meillet and J. Vendryes. The work of Jerzy Kuryłowicz is not so well anthologized for our use as one might wish: the collections of his essays on general theory, *Esquisses linguistiques* (1960 and 1974) are not found in all scholarly libraries. The 500-page *Studia językoznawcze* (Warszawa: Państwowe Wydawnictwo Naukowe, 1987) reprints fifty of his articles, two dozen from the time span of our present coverage, overlapping our selections only in one instance; but this entire volume, including the introductory essay, is written in or translated into Polish. Our opportunities to represent the overtly diachronic dimension in the present collection have been limited, and this facet is not so well represented as others; the lacuna can be repaired in part by judicious selection from *Approaches to English Historical Linguistics,* ed. Roger Lass (New York: Holt, Rinehart and Winston, 1969). For questions of language in relation to culture and society for the period of our coverage we refer to the rich annotated collection of *Language in Culture and Society,* ed. Dell Hymes (New York: Harper & Row, 1964); another useful collection is that by Paul L. Garvin and Yolanda Lastra de Suárez, *Antología de estudios de etnolingüística y sociolingüística* (México: Universidad Nacional Autónoma, 1974). For a field such as that now not always called psycholinguistics, including acquisition, it seems that the principle of anthologizing has been entirely different; by the time such miscellanies found a publishing market they were based on mainstream, accessible literature that scarcely reaches into our period of coverage; this presumably says something about obsolescence. An important exception for our literacy resides in the *Collected Works of L. S. Vygotsky,* eds. Robert W. Rieber and Aaron S. Carton, vol. 1, *Problems of General Psychology,* tr. Norris Minnick (New York/London: Plenum, 1987); and L. S. Vygotsky, *Thought and Language,* tr. Alex Kozulin (Cambridge: MIT Press, 1987; 1st ed. 1962). Complementary to some of the above is *Readings in Russian Poetics: Formalist and Structuralist Views,* ed. Ladislav Matejka and Krystyna Pomorska (Cambridge: MIT Press, 1971); one will also find retrospective but relevant issues in *Literary Style: A Symposium,* ed. Seymour Chatman (Oxford University Press, 1971), some of which hark back to the topics of *A Prague School Reader in Esthetics, Literary Structure and Style,* ed. Paul L. Garvin (Washington, D.C.: Georgetown University Press, 1964). It is well recognized that our period of coverage is not rich in semantic studies; useful, well informed works in this area are Stephen Ullmann, *Semantics: An Introduction to the Science of Meaning* (Oxford: Blackwell, 1962), and A. J. Greimas, *Sémantique structurale* (Paris, 1966), translation forthcoming.

There are certain areas of the field which are not covered as well as might be wished in the volumes under abridgment. The readings in syntax can be supplemented in some measure by careful selection from *Syntactic Theory 1: Structur[al(ist)],* ed. Fred W. Householder (Harmondsworth: Penguin, 1972), with a valuable introduction. Another area which failed to surface in the source volumes is represented by *Acoustic Phonetics: A Course of Basic Readings,* ed. D. B. Fry (Cambridge University Press, 1976). The underrepresentation of dialectology in our selection of readings may be somewhat redressed by recalling *Studies in Linguistics in Honor of Raven I. McDavid, Jr.,* ed. Lawrence M. Davis (University of Alabama Press, 1972), and in an allied vein *A Various Language: Perspectives on American Dialects,* ed. Juanita V. Williamson and Virginia M. Burke (New York: Holt, Rinehart and Winston, 1971). Additional indications on this topic may be found in *American Speech* 52 (3–4), 1977 (1981); Hans Kurath, *Studies in Area Linguistics* (Bloomington: Indiana University Press, 1972); and W. Nelson Francis, *Dialectology: An Introduction* (London: Longman, 1983). A further neglected area yielding some items of interest is supplied by *Readings in Applied*

English Linguistics 2d ed., ed. Harold B. Allen (New York: Appleton-Century-Crofts, 1964). It may further be noted that Henry M. Hoenigswald's *Language Change and Linguistic Reconstruction* (University of Chicago Press, 1960) is no longer in print to supplement the selections from *Readings* (*RIL I*).

It seems agreed that this abridgment cannot appear without a selection each from Sapir and Bloomfield drawn from *RIL I*. It is however reassuring that more of Bloomfield can be readily supplied from the abridged edition of *A Leonard Bloomfield Anthology*, ed. Charles F. Hockett (University of Chicago Press, 1987), the unabridged version of which was published by Indiana University Press in 1970, and which has succeeded in retaining the essential items of general purport by deleting those on specifically Algonquian, Germanic, and Tagalog topics. Note additionally, however, Bloomfield's article on Ilocano syntax in Householder's selections on *Syntactic Theory* (93–102) above. Likewise, much of Sapir's oeuvre is available, apart from other isolated reprints, in David G. Mandelbaum, *Selected Writings of Edward Sapir* (University of California Press, Berkeley and Los Angeles, 1949), and the totality is soon to appear as the *Collected Writings of Edward Sapir* (Mouton/De Gruyter, 1990–).

An omission from *RIL I* which is much to be regretted is the total absence of any writing by Kenneth L. Pike. This lacuna can be repaired by resorting to *Kenneth L. Pike: Selected Writings*, ed. Ruth M. Brend (The Hague-Paris: Mouton, 1972), especially the first four reprinted essays (1943–1949). Another unfortunate omission from *RIL I* is the name of George L. Trager, who however appears in *TCLP* 8 mentioned above; but that recognition (or even *Studies in Linguistics in Honor of G. L. T.*, ed. M. Estellie Smith, The Hague: Mouton, 1972) is disproportionately brief for the place that Trager occupied in the period surveyed.[2] There is one important genre which is not represented in *RIL I*: the actual descriptions of grammars, most especially for Native American languages—the languages which played so powerful a part in the development of theory here depicted. The pages of *IJAL* of course offer many examples of that genre; the classic collection of condensed specimens remains *Linguistic Structures of Native America*, ed. Harry Hoijer et al. (New York: Viking Fund, 1946). The last may be supplemented by F. Boas, ed. and author, *Handbook of American Indian Languages* (Washington, D.C.: Smithsonian Institution, Bureau of American Ethnology, 1911, 1922, New York 1933–38; and Norman A. McQuown, ed., *Linguistics*, vol. 5 of *Handbook of Middle American Indians*, ed. R. Wauchope (Austin: University of Texas Press, 1967).

Hockett 1948, of this abridgment, is also to be found as no. 68 of the unabridged *Bloomfield Anthology*, which now presents in a few details the preferred text; it may be noted that the *RIL I* reprinting was not mentioned in the headnote to no. 68.

A large portion of Bloch 1950 has fallen victim to the pressures of space; it is hoped that our excisions, designed to dispense with tedious and technical listing and exemplification of allophones best suited to a lengthy study of Japanese for its own sake, will be found to have left the full argument intact for the more general reader. The complete text of this paper, together with other papers of Bloch's describing Japanese (including *RIL I* no. 17), will be found in *Bernard Bloch on Japanese,* ed. Roy Andrew Miller (New Haven: Yale University Press, 1970), as IV Phonemics, pp. 113–65. That volume also contains a helpful Analytic Index on pp. 179–90, and an informative and documented introduction (pp. ix–xli) by Miller, including the Blochian gem *ooоóóo*, 'let's cover the tail (as of a half-buried fox)'.

Omissions of particular regret from *RIL I* are nos. 23 of Bloch, 26 of Pittman, 6 and 29 of Twaddell, 21 of Hockett, and 19 of Moulton. I have always regretted the absence from *RIL I* of Zellig S. Harris's "Discontinuous morphemes," from *Language* 21 (1945): 121–27, although a sense of the argument may be gained from his Appendix to 12.323–24 on pp. 182–84 of *Structural Linguistics* (University of Chicago Press, 1951 and reprintings), a book reflecting much else in *RIL I*. Interested readers will find articles partly overlapping and partly supplementing the above within the first 350 pages of Valerie Becker Makkai, *Phonological Theory: Evolution and Current Practice* (New York: Holt, Rinehart and Winston, 1972). We have gained an inspiring resource also in *Selected Writings of Gyula Laziczius*, ed. Thomas A. Sebeok (The Hague/Paris: Mouton, 1966).

In lieu of the comments on terms in *RIL I*, pp. 419–21, one may refer to E. P. Hamp, *A Glossary of American Technical Linguistic Usage 1925–1950* (Utrecht/Antwerp: Spectrum, 1963) or *Slovar' amerikanskoj lingvisticheskoj terminologii* (Moskva: Progress, 1964), tr. V. V. Ivanov of first ed. 1957. For similar coverage of Praguian work see J. Vachek, *Dictionnaire de linguistique de l'École de Prague* (Utrecht/Antwerp: Spectrum, 1960), or *Lingvisticheskij slovar' prazhskoj shkoly* (Moskva, 1964).

The comments of Joos in *RIL I* have been retained as far as the economics of reproduction would allow. Cross-references therein which lead to excised items or comment are signalled ( ). One may now recover some of the flavor of Joos on this period in his *Notes on the Development of the Linguistic Society of America 1924 to 1950* (Ithaca, N.Y.: [issued by J M. Cowan and C. F. Hockett], 1986).

Readers desiring encyclopedic treatment of the foregoing topics and persons are referred to Harro Stammerjohann, ed., *Lexicon Grammaticorum* (Tübingen: Niemeyer, 1994), on deceased linguists; and, more generally, R. E. Asher and J. M. Y. Simpson, eds., *The Encyclopedia of Language and Linguistics* (Oxford etc.: Pergamon, 1994); and W. O. Bright, ed., *International Encyclopedia of Linguistics* (Oxford: Oxford University Press, 1992).

It remains only to thank my old friend Howard Aronson for help which sometimes he may not have realized he was giving me, but which he always extends with grace and generosity; Michael Silverstein, whose wit, learning, and friendship gladden countless days; and Geoffrey J. Huck of the University of Chicago Press for his friendly help and patience.

Eric P. Hamp

[1] Ferdinand de Saussure (1857–1913), *Cours de linguistique générale*, Lausanne-Paris: Payot, 1916 [Préface signed Genève, juillet 1915], 2nd ed. Paris: Payot, 1922 [reviewed by L. Bloomfield, *Modern Language Journal* 8 (1923): 317–19 = no. B17, *Bloomfield Anthology* 1970 = 1987 abridged ed., pp. 63–65], 3rd ed. Paris: Payot, 1931, unchanged "4th" ed. Paris: Payot, 1949 (reprint 1955), "5th" ed. 1960 (reprinted since); the entire book synthesized and reconstituted by Charles Bally and Albert Sechehaye, with the collaboration of Albert Riedlinger, from contributed students' notes posthumously assembled from FS's three lecture courses 1906–11; many translations since the Japanese (Tokyo 1928), of which in English tr. Wade Baskin, *Course in General Linguistics,* New York: Philosophical Library, 1959 (London 1960), McGraw-Hill, 1966 [these printings are often referred to by page], rev. ed. (with introduction by J. Culler) London: Fontana, 1974 [see also J. Culler, *F. de S.,* Ithaca NY: Cornell University Press, 1976; rev. ed. 1986]; there are also less satisfactory translations and commentaries; basic text edition: R. Godel, *Les sources manuscrites du Cours de linguistique générale de F. de Saussure,* Genève: Droz/Paris: Minard, 1957; critical edition with textual variants: Rudolf Engler, *Ferdinand de Saussure Cours de linguistique générale,* Wiesbaden: Harrassowitz 1967–68 (3 fascicules) + 1974 (4th fasc.); critical ed. with tr. and commentary originally in Italian (1967, 2nd ed. 1968): Tullio de Mauro, *Édition critique du Cours de linguistique générale de F. de S.,* Paris: Payot, 1972; ed. by Eisuke Komatsu and tr. by Roy Harris, *Saussure's Third Course of Lectures on General Linguistics (1910–1911) from the Notebooks of Emile Constantin,* Oxford etc.: Pergamon, 1993. The literature on Saussure is vast; see, for example, E. F. Konrad Koerner, *Bibliographia Saussureana 1870–1970,* Metuchen NJ: Scarecrow Press 1972.

[2] As this book and foreword go to press I am grateful to be able to call attention to C. F. Hockett's poignant obituary of George Leonard Trager [trɛɪɡɚ], *Lg.* 69 (1993): 778–88, and in particular 784, note 4.

PREFACE
to Volume I

The reissue of this volume by a second publisher, after three printings with progressive removal of misprints but unchanged content, comes in radically altered circumstances. In 1957 a great deal was taken for granted in American linguistics which has been called into question since. This book was first prepared simply because too much was being taken for granted. The tradition which these papers define was three decades old and still growing as rapidly as ever. Hardly anyone who counted on the American linguistic scene seemed to be outside this tradition. It is easy to name important scholars of the same tradition who are not represented in this volume; but there are other reasons for that, especially the limitations of its size.

Descriptive linguistics, as defined by these papers, seemed in 1956 to be without a serious competitor on our scene, with the natural result that too many students were accepting the current techniques without inquiring into what lay behind them. There were even beginning to be teachers of linguistic science who had missed reading some of the basic papers, now that the teachers were being recruited from among the recent students and new departments of linguistics were being set up. Today the Ph.D. in linguistics is granted on more than thirty American campuses, on roughly half of them in departments of that name; in 1940 only a handful of persons held that degree, nearly all the teachers having earned their doctorates in either anthropology or a language and having learned linguistics of the modern kind in the midst of its first strong growth. By the early 1950's, however, linguistics was an autonomous discipline. Textbooks were beginning to appear; students were becoming oriented to the deadening route of using "the book" as if books grew on trees or had been handed down from Mount Sinai. The better teachers could not always send their pupils to the original papers, because some of these were inaccessible outside the largest libraries.

In 1946 it was thought that a volume containing only the least accessible papers would serve the need; page 267 of *Language* (Vol. 22) named eight of them and promised that the Linguistic Society of America would soon issue such a volume. The plan was dropped for lack of response to the invitation to nominate other papers. The Committee on the Language Program of the American Council of Learned Societies (since renamed the Committee on Language Programs) remained aware of the problem and frequently discussed what could be done. By 1954, when I had been a member of the Committee for several years, had developed techniques for preparing such book-pages as the present volume contains, and had edited several books for the teaching of English as a foreign language for the ACLS, the Committee had arrived at a new plan for the content of the needed volume of *Readings in Linguistics*. I was directed to circulate a list of papers for possible inclusion and to ask for the help of scholars in defining the scope and purpose.

From the three dozen useful responses, it appeared that about eight hundred pages would have satisfied the sum of the well-argued demands. The impossibility of that size of book seemed evident. From the responses and the Committee's deliberations, however, a practical solution emerged quite clearly. The theme of the book would have to be the *development* rather than the exemplification of descriptive theory. One consequence was that it would have to exclude any article which reported on a single language without at the same time going beyond adequate statement into restatement via some at least partly new theoretical development. Also, the size limit forbade any further pursuit of the branches that keep leaving the main stem during the development of descriptive linguistics. Examples of such exclusion are acoustic phonetics, perception theory, semantic theory, information theory, the discourse analysis of Zellig Harris—and, since that time, the whole new trend in modern American linguistics which began as ancillary to that work and was known at first as transformational grammar. Finally, the size limit, together with the impossibility of securing permission to reprint certain crucial papers, forced omission of all papers devoted specifically to the phonology of English. This omission does no serious harm, for the lines of theoretical development from the 1920's to 1956 are still clear in the present volume.

During 1955 and 1956, I retyped most of the papers and supplied pedagogical notes to three fourths of them, added the front and back matter, and assembled the volume for the printer's cameras. What I added to the original papers is my personal responsibility; but the selection of them was done by the Committee as a whole, except that from their selection I omitted one paper of my own. All revenues from sales of the volume have gone into the linguistic funds of the American Council of Learned Societies (see page 108).

In 1957 we supposed that such a book would not remain in demand for as much as a decade with unchanged content, and postponed all decisions as to whether to let it go out of print in five years or so or to proceed to successive editions with deletion of some papers and addition of others each time. The pressure of increasing demand has forced unchanged reprinting. Additions and deletions have not been called for by the market, conceivably to some extent because of inertia, but in my belief principally because of an unforeseen factor. Both for intrinsic and for extrinsic reasons, the development of this tradition in descriptive linguistics happened to slacken just at the time when the volume first appeared.

The intrinsic reason is named in the last line of page 418, where the word *reached* was ill-advised: it should have been *touched*. The extrinsic reason is that most of the young men in the profession have turned to a new trend, what is now called generative-transformational grammar, and some of them think of it as a surely victorious competitor to our tradition. At the beginning of page 97 here, Hockett called descriptive linguistics a *classificatory* science; an excellent synonym for this is *taxonomic* linguistics, which certain proponents of the new trend use as a derogatory term. Now when anyone holds that the existence of two kinds of linguistics—taxonomic and, for example, generative-transformational—strictly implies the inferiority or even nullity of one of them, that opinion can only be pernicious no matter which of the two is denigrated. Both extreme views will fade out in due course, especially as each side reads more of what has been published by the other.

Both in such new trends and in the older ones represented in this volume, linguistics has been preeminently a young man's pursuit ever since the 1920's. Only two of our twenty-six authors had died in the thirty years before 1957. A third, Bernard Bloch, died in 1965 at the age of fifty-eight; he had published his crucial contributions by the age of forty-three. Meanwhile, he had been in the middle of it all from the age of about thirty; directly, or in a few cases indirectly, he had strongly influenced some thirty of the thirty-three papers following his first one included in this volume.

It is convenient to take Bloch as the central point for a statement of this sort, but the phenomenon was general: nearly all those same authors strongly influenced him, and they all influenced each other. To this, one detail must be added, and it is of far greater importance than I can hope to make clear. The most significant interactions among all these men were not by way of publication, but characteristically face to face: partly by letter, but mostly in each summer's Linguistic Institute, in local clubs, within working groups (see page 108 again), in social clusters and tête-à-têtes, only partly in annual meetings of the Linguistic Society of America.

Frequently an acute ear can detect all this, when the style of some paper betrays the sociable thinking that gave rise to its publication. But for the most part the origins of the papers in this volume are concealed from us in their printed form. Those origins await historical research; meanwhile, readers of this volume, and especially the younger readers, will be well advised to participate in just such conversations assiduously for several years and thus to gain an understanding of the process. That is likely to be more significant to them than the sum and sequence of the theses presented in the papers.

Here I can do no more than offer a few notes, both long notes at the ends of the majority of the papers and short insertions along the way. These are enclosed in double square brackets resembling the printer's outline-brackets here: 〚 〛. There are also a good many cross-references to other pages within this volume; these are enclosed in doubled round parentheses: (( )).

MARTIN JOOS

PUBLISHER'S NOTE:

The "pedagogical notes" that Martin Joos refers to above have been largely omitted in this abridgment,
as have his "Comments on Certain Technical Terms." Both may be found in *Readings in Linguistics I*,
Fourth Edition, edited by Martin Joos (Chicago: University of Chicago Press, 1966 [Third Impression, 1968]).
At the same time, we have retained to the extent possible the cross-references enclosed in double parentheses
that he inserted at various places; the reader should therefore be aware that these cross-references
(as well as the references to pages 108, 418, and 97 in the Preface immediately preceding) are to pages in
the 1966 edition of *Readings in Linguistics I* and not to pages in this abridged edition.
Joos's preface to the original, 1957 edition was omitted in the 1966 edition and does not appear here.

PREFACE
to Volume II

No anthology can please everyone perfectly, least of all the compilers. It should be difficult for the worst anthology to offend everyone categorically; the more so if they were either devils, druids, or drones—would be sure to find a measure of delight and instruction in such a book. Anthologies, if they are serious and have a closely determined scope, find a rather restricted range in which to excel and demonstrate worth.

Such a collection of writings would seem to be best judged on two principal grounds: the degree to which the scholarly area covered replies to an active or potential need in the field of study, and the relative quality or stimulation found in the items chosen.

We do not shirk our responsibility for the selections made; the decisions, within the limitations of space, are ultimately ours. But we have, so far as possible, taken into account, as part of the data, the judgments and evaluations of our colleagues in the profession at large. And this in two ways: many preliminary selections were made on the basis of documented influence, as evidenced by reference in the later linguistic literature or by content which on inspection turns up, by mention or by argument, in important writings of either later or earlier date. A tentative list of selections was submitted at the time of the 1962 International Congress of Linguists to a broad range of active and distinguished contributors to the field of linguistics. As a result of their comments, subsequently refined in numerous detailed discussions, we were able to make important and extensive changes in the earlier list both by incorporating assessments of value and sensitivity made by broadly learnèd scholars and by reducing our own ignorance somewhat.

If the resulting selections have the excellence and stimulation we think they have, such readings, intended as they are for serious students, have no need of accompanying commentary or apparatus by the compilers.

In 1957 a volume of *Readings in Linguistics*, edited by Martin Joos for the Committee on Language Programs (formerly Committee on the Language Program) of the American Council of Learned Societies, was published by ACLS. Its purpose was to illustrate, exemplify, and typify the development of descriptive linguistics in America from 1925 to 1957. The development represented was a highly cohesive body of doctrine whose practitioners shared a good many points of underlying outlook and a strong *esprit de corps*; the commentary tended to heighten this effect. It is perhaps ironical that *Readings*, intended as a handbook on linguistic theory, has already found wide use as a textbook in the history of linguistics; it may be hoped that *Readings II* will still find a valid place, in some measure, in both roles.

The Committee intended to follow *Readings* with another designed to present other trends in the development of modern linguistics. It should be recalled that in the mid-'fifties general and inclusive volumes on linguistics were still rather rare, and few libraries held really broad basic collections; if some may feel that linguistics has become all too modish nowadays, that was certainly not true then. Like many a committee idea, that plan became displaced for several years by other business. Then, in 1961, it was reactivated. Robert A. Hall, Jr. (Cornell University), Eric P. Hamp (The University of Chicago), and Fred W. Householder (Indiana University) were asked to assume responsibility for the volume.

In the meantime it had been decided that the territory to be covered by such a volume should embrace any areas whatever of modern linguistics outside that abundantly represented in the Joos volume; in principle, excellence and the proper pursuit of knowledge know neither geographic nor national bounds. If the essays in the present volume show a distinctly European provenience, that is the accident of the ground rules which were found useful for selection and not a characteristic of the field.

After the first preliminary work, Robert Austerlitz (Columbia University) was co-opted to replace Hall, who could no longer actively continue because of commitments which were to keep him abroad for an extended period. Hall's excellent help in the early stages should be prominently acknowledged here. He should not be held responsible for any of our subsequent mistakes, and for that reason his name does not appear on the title page. The two remaining editors lost Hall's counsel regretfully; yet in Austerlitz the volume found a valuable new resource with a welcome range of strengths not shared in like fashion by any of the others.

The criteria for selection of the essays were of two sorts, as it was finally and unanimously decided after prolonged reflection. The prime principle for inclusion had to be agreed scholarly quality; objectivity and consensus were aimed at in the manners alluded to above. Another important principle clearly was influence, or pertinence, or centrality with respect to the field as shown by the content of the essay. A further consideration was a fair attempt at representative coverage of the range of facets or aspects that the field offers. Special attention was given to areas often neglected or now atrophied—for example, graphemics. So far as was possible, scholarly literature from all lands was canvassed.

The prime principle for exclusion was chronology: everything before the mid-'twenties; then, for sake of economy, (nearly) everything readily available in print. The latter principle excluded articles in easily accessible cisatlantic journals (*Language*, *Word*, etc.); it also excluded important miscellanies in print or known at the time to be firmly projected (*For Roman Jakobson*, Cantineau's translation *Principes de phonologie*, Hjelmslev's *Essais linguistiques* TCLC 12, the TPS volume *Studies in Linguistic Analysis*, Martinet's *Économie*, and, with deliberate exceptions, Kuryłowicz's *Esquisses linguistiques* and Vachek's *Prague School Reader*). Reluctantly, for reasons of practicality, since it is our purpose and policy to preserve the original language throughout, sources in non-Roman scripts are excluded ; this automatically eliminated, but without prejudice, many languages. And, of course, the tradition represented in the Joos volume was considered as already covered.

Finally, certain eminently desirable items were simply too long to be fitted in ; after all, important books are excluded *a priori*.

Nevertheless, despite the technical savings of space resulting from such systematic exclusions, there was, as one might suspect, easily enough for two volumes this size until we set ourselves to cut back severely—more severely than we could wish. One misses items by Pos, Bühler, Cantineau, Malmberg, Halliday, W. Haas, Milewski, Vogt, Borgstrøm, Lacerda, McIntosh, Alarcos Llorach, and others—this list is a mere excerpt. Every reader can develop his own list of lacunae without thinking very long.

A great many articles were quickly eliminated not at all for their want of excellence but because much of their content was of rather specialized substantive interest.

The attempt has been made throughout to preserve the original text intact. Comparison with the original will show that some minor changes in typographic detail have frequently been introduced ; this, to bring certain Continental conventions into line with habits of the provincial English-language area, since practicality dictates some norms. Some other changes reflect stylistic options in typesetting designed to reduce unnecessary heterogeneity among writings from so many diverse sources. Earlier faults in proofreading have been silently corrected.

Changes in text have been essentially of three sorts : adjustment of footnote numbering and the like to conform to the new pagination occasioned by resetting ; a very few corrigenda kindly supplied by authors, for which we express our sincere gratitude ; an exceedingly small number of silent corrections of faulty grammar or of content or allusion that clearly destroy any possible sense in the passage. Such judgments as the last have always been avoided where irony or some other stylistic rationale could be imputed. To alter these writings in any substantive way would be intolerable for the purpose in view.

It remains to thank the University of Chicago Press for their meticulous care, their patience, and their tasteful execution.

Eric P. Hamp

CONTENTS

CONTENTS

READINGS IN
LINGUISTICS I

SOUND PATTERNS IN LANGUAGE

EDWARD SAPIR
Language 1.37–51—1925

There used to be and to some extent still is a feeling among linguists that the psychology of a language is more particularly concerned with its grammatical features, but that its sounds and its phonetic processes belong to a grosser physiological substratum. Thus, we sometimes hear it said that such phonetic processes as the palatalizing of a vowel by a following i or other front vowel ('umlaut') or the series of shifts in the manner of articulating the old Indo-European stopped consonants which have become celebrated under the name of 'Grimm's Law' are merely mechanical processes, consummated by the organs of speech and by the nerves that control them as a set of shifts in relatively simple sensori-motor habits. It is my purpose in this paper, as briefly as may be, to indicate that the sounds and sound processes of speech cannot be properly understood in such simple, mechanical terms.

Perhaps the best way to pose the problem of the psychology of speech sounds is to compare an actual speech sound with an identical or similar one not used in a linguistic context. It will become evident almost at once that it is a great fallacy to think of the articulation of a speech sound as a motor habit that is merely intended to bring about a directly significant result. A good example of superficially similar sounds is the wh of such a word as when, as generally pronounced in America (i.e., voiceless w or, perhaps more accurately analyzed, aspiration plus voiceless w plus voiced w-glide), and the sound made in blowing out a candle, with which it has often been compared. We are not at the present moment greatly interested in whether these two articulations are really identical or, at the least, very similar. Let us assume that a typically pronounced wh is identical with the sound that results from the expulsion of breath through pursed lips when a candle is blown out. We shall assume identity of both articulation and quality of perception. Does this identity amount to a psychological identity of the two processes? Obviously not. It is worth pointing out, in what may seem pedantic detail, wherein they differ.

1. The candle-blowing sound is a physical by-product of a directly functional act, the extinguishing of the candle by means of a peculiar method of producing a current of air. So far as normal human interest is concerned, this sound serves merely as a sign of the blowing out, or attempted blowing out, itself. We can abbreviate our record of the facts a little and say that the production of the candle-blowing sound is a directly functional act. On the other hand, the articulation of the wh-sound in such a word as when has no direct functional value; it is merely a link in the construction of a symbol, the articulated or perceived word when, which in turn assumes a function, symbolic at that, only when it is experienced in certain linguistic contexts, such as the saying or hearing of a sentence like When are you coming? In brief, the candle-blowing wh means business; the speech sound wh is stored-up play which can eventually fall in line in a game that merely refers to business. Still more briefly, the former is practice; the latter, art.

2. Each act of blowing out a candle is functionally equivalent, more or less, to every other such act; hence the candle-blowing wh is, in the first instance, a sign for an act of single function. The speech sound wh has no singleness, or rather primary singleness, of reference. It is a counter in a considerable variety of functional symbols, e.g. when, whiskey, wheel. A series of candle-blowing sounds has a natural function and contextual coherence. A series of wh-sounds as employed in actual speech has no such coherence; e.g., the series wh(en), wh(iskey), wh(eel) is non-significant.

3. Every typical human reaction has a certain range of variation and, properly speaking, no such reaction can be understood except as a series of variants distributed about a norm or type. Now the candle-blowing wh and the speech sound wh are norms or types of entirely distinct series of variants.

First, as to acoustic quality. Owing to the fact that the blowing out of a candle is a purely functional act, its variability is limited by the function alone. But, obviously, it is possible to blow out a candle in a great number of ways: One may purse the lips greatly or only a little; the lower lip, or the upper lip, or neither may protrude; the articulation may be quite impure and accompanied by synchronous articulations, such as a x-like (velar spirant) or sh-like sound. None of these and other variations reaches over into a class of reactions that differs at all materially from the typical candle-blowing wh. The variation of wh as speech sound is very much more restricted. A when pronounced, for instance, with a wh in which the lower lip protruded or with a wh that was contaminated with a sh-sound would be felt as distinctly 'off color.' It could be tolerated only as a joke or a personal speech defect. But the variability of wh in language is not only less wide than in candle-blowing, it is also different in tendency. The latter sound varies chiefly along the line of exact

1

place (or places) of articulation, the former chiefly along the line of voicing. Psychologically wh of when and similar words is related to the w of well and similar words. There is a strong tendency to minimize the aspiration and to voice the labial. The gamut of variations, therefore, runs roughly from hW (I use W for voiceless w) to w. Needless to say, there is no tendency to voicing in the candle-blowing wh, for such a tendency would contradict the very purpose of the reaction, which is to release a strong and unhampered current of air.

Second, as to intensity. It is clear that in this respect the two series of variations differ markedly. The normal intensity of the candle-blowing sound is greater than that of the linguistic wh; this intensity, moreover, is very much more variable, depending as it does on the muscular tone of the blower, the size of the flame to be extinguished, and other factors. All in all, it is clear that the resemblance of the two wh-sounds is really due to an intercrossing of two absolutely independent series, as of two independent lines in space that have one point in common.

4. The speech sound wh has a larger number of associations with other sounds in symbolically significant sound-groups, e.g. wh-e-n, wh-i-s-k-ey, wh-ee-l. The candle-blowing sound has no sound associations with which it habitually coheres.

5. We now come to the most essential point of difference. The speech sound wh is one of a definitely limited number of sounds (e.g. wh, s, t, l, i, and so on) which, while differing qualitatively from one another rather more than does wh from its candle-blowing counterpart, nevertheless belong together in a definite system of symbolically utilizable counters. Each member of this system is not only characterized by a distinctive and slightly variable articulation and a corresponding acoustic image, but also—and this is crucial—by a psychological aloofness from all other members of the system. The relational gaps between the sounds of a language are just as necessary to the psychological definition of these sounds as the articulations and acoustic images which are customarily used to define them. A sound that is not unconsciously felt as 'placed'[1] with reference to other sounds is no more a true element of speech than a lifting of the foot is a dance step unless it can be 'placed' with reference to other movements that help to define the dance. Needless to say, the candle-blowing sound forms no part of any system of sounds. It is not spaced off from nor related to other sounds—say the sound of humming and the sound of clearing one's throat—which form with it a set of mutually necessary indices.

---

[1] This word has, of course, nothing to do here with 'place of articulation.' One may feel, for instance, that sound A is to sound B as sound X is to sound Y without having the remotest idea how and where any of them is produced.

It should be sufficiently clear from this one example—and there are of course plenty of analogous ones, such as m versus the sound of humming or an indefinite series of timbre-varying groans versus a set of vowels—how little the notion of speech sound is explicable in simple sensorimotor terms and how truly a complex psychology of association and pattern is implicit in the utterance of the simplest consonant or vowel. It follows at once that the psychology of phonetic processes is unintelligible unless the general patterning of speech sounds is recognized. This patterning has two phases. We have been at particular pains to see that the sounds used by a language form a self-contained system which makes it impossible to identify any of them with a non-linguistic sound produced by the 'organs of speech,' no matter how great is the articulatory and acoustic resemblance between the two. In view of the utterly distinct psychological backgrounds of the two classes of sound production it may even be seriously doubted whether the innervation of speech-sound articulation is ever actually the same type of physiological fact as the innervation of 'identical' articulations that have no linguistic context. But it is not enough to pattern off all speech sounds as such against other sounds produced by the 'organs of speech.' There is a second phase of sound patterning which is more elusive and of correspondingly greater significance for the linguist. This is the inner configuration of the sound system of a language, the intuitive 'placing' of the sounds with reference to one another. To this we must now turn.

Mechanical and other detached methods of studying the phonetic elements of speech are, of course, of considerable value, but they have sometimes the undesirable effect of obscuring the essential facts of speech-sound psychology. Too often an undue importance is attached to minute sound discriminations as such; and too often phoneticians do not realize that it is not enough to know that a certain sound occurs in a language, but that one must ascertain if the sound is a typical form or one of the points in its sound pattern, or is merely a variant of such a form. There are two types of variation that tend to obscure the distinctiveness of the different points in the phonetic pattern of a language. One of this is individual variation. It is true that no two individuals have precisely the same pronunciation of a language, but it is equally true that they aim to make the same sound discriminations, so that, if the qualitative differences of the sounds that make up A's pattern from those that make up B's are perceptible to a minute analysis, the relations that obtain between the elements in the two patterns are the same. In other words, the patterns are the same pattern. A's s, for instance, may differ markedly from B's s, but if each individual keeps his s equally distinct from such points in the pattern as th (of think) and sh and if there is a one-to-one correspondence between the distribution of

A's s and that of B's, then the difference of pronunciation is of little or no interest for the phonetic psychology of the language. We may go a step further. Let us symbolize A's and B's pronunciation of s, th, and sh as follows:

A: th   s   sh
B: th₁ s₁ sh₁

This diagram is intended to convey the fact that B's s is a lisped s which is not identical with his interdental th, but stands nearer objectively to this sound than to A's s; similarly, B's sh is acoustically somewhat closer to A's s than to his sh. Obviously we cannot discover B's phonetic pattern by identifying his sounds with their nearest analogues in A's pronunciation, i.e. by setting th₁ = th, s₁ = variant of th, sh₁ = s. If we do this, as we are quite likely to do if we are obsessed, like so many linguists, by the desire to apply an absolute and universal phonetic system to all languages, we get the following pattern analysis:

A: th   s   sh
      /\
B: th₁ s₁ sh₁   —

which is as psychologically perverse as it is 'objectively' accurate. Of course the true pattern analysis is:

A: th   s   sh
B: th₁ s₁ sh₁

for the objective relations between sounds are only a first approximation to the psychological relations which constitute the true phonetic pattern. The size of the objective differences th—s, s—sh, th₁—s₁, s₁—sh₁, th—s₁, s₁—s, s—sh₁, and sh₁—sh does not correspond to the psychological 'spacing' of the phonemes th, s, and sh in the phonetic pattern which is common to A and B.

The second type of variation is common to all normal speakers of the language and is dependent on the phonetic conditions in which the fundamental sound ('point of the pattern') occurs. In most languages, what is felt by the speakers to be the 'same' sound has perceptibly different forms as these conditions vary. Thus, in (American) English there is a perceptible difference in the length of the vowel a of bad and bat, the a-vowel illustrated by these words being long or half-long before voiced consonants and all continuants, whether voiced or unvoiced, but short before voiceless stops. In fact, the vocalic alternation of bad and bat is quantitatively parallel to such alternations as bead and beat, fade and fate. The alternations are governed by mechanical considerations that have only a subsidiary relevance for the phonetic pattern. They take care of themselves,

as it were, and it is not always easy to convince natives of their objective reality, however sensitive they may be to violations of the unconscious rule in the speech of foreigners. It is very necessary to understand that it is not because the objective difference is too slight to be readily perceptible that such variations as the quantitative alternations in bad and bat, bead and beat, fade and fate stand outside of the proper phonetic pattern of the language (e.g., are not psychologically parallel to such qualitative-quantitative alternations as bid and bead, fed and fade, or to such quantitative alternations as German Schlaf and schlaff, Latin āra and ārā), but that the objective difference is felt to be slight precisely because it corresponds to nothing significant in the inner structure of the phonetic pattern. In matters of this kind, objective estimates of similarity and difference, based either on specific linguistic habits or on a generalized phonetic system, are utterly fallacious. As a matter of fact, the mechanical English vocalic relation bad : bat would in many languages be quite marked enough to indicate a relation of distinct points of the pattern, while the English pattern relation -t : -d, which seems so self-evidently real to us, has in not a few other languages either no reality at all or only a mechanical, conditional one. In Upper Chinook, for instance, t : d exists objectively but not psychologically; one says, e.g. inat 'across,' but inad before words beginning with a vowel, and the two forms of the final consonant are undoubtedly felt to be the 'same' sound in exactly the same sense in which the English vowels of bad and bat are felt by us to be identical phonetic elements. The Upper Chinook d exists only as a mechanical variant of t; hence this alternation is not the same psychologically as the Sanskrit sandhi variation -t : -d.

Individual variations and such conditional variations as we have discussed once cleared out of the way, we arrive at the genuine pattern of speech sounds. After what we have said, it almost goes without saying that two languages, A and B, may have identical sounds but utterly distinct phonetic patterns; or they may have mutually incompatible phonetic systems, from the articulatory and acoustic standpoint, but identical or similar patterns. The following schematic examples and subjoined comments will make this clear. Sounds which do not properly belong to the pattern or, rather, are variants within points of the pattern are put in parentheses. Long vowels are designated as a·; ŋ is ng of sing; θ and δ are voiceless and voiced interdental spirants; x and γ are voiceless and voiced guttural spirants; ' is glottal stop; ' denotes aspirated release; ɛ and ɔ are open e and o.

A: a   (ɛ) (e)   i   u   (o) (ɔ)

a·   (ɛ·) (e·) i·   u· (o·) (ɔ·)

'   h   w   y   l   m n (ŋ)

p   t   k

p'   t'   k'

(b) (d) (g)

f   θ   s   x

(v) (δ) (z) (γ)

But B: a   ɛ   e   i   u   o   ɔ

(a·) (ɛ·) (e·) (i·) (u·) (o·) (ɔ·)

(')   h   (w) (y) (l)   m n ŋ

p   t   k

(p') (t') (k')

b   d   g

(f) (θ) s   (x)

v   δ   z   γ

We will assume for A and B certain conditional variants which are all of types that may be abundantly illustrated from actual languages. For A:

1. ɛ occurs only as palatalized form of a when following y or i. In many Indian languages, e.g., yɛ = ya.

2. e is dropped from i-position when this vowel is final. Cf. such mechanical alternations as Eskimo -e: -i-t.

3. o is dropped from u-position when this vowel is final. Cf. 2.

4. ɔ occurs only as labialized form of a after w or u. Cf. 1. (In Yahi, e.g., wɔwi 'house' is objectively correct, but psychologically wrong. It can easily be shown that this word is really wawi and 'feels' like a rhyme to such phonetic groups as lawi and bawi; short ɔ in an open syllable is an anomaly, but ɔ· is typical for all Yana dialects, including Yahi.)

5. ŋ is merely n assimilated to following k, as in Indo-European.

6. b, d, g, v, z, δ, γ are voiced forms of p, t, k, f, s, θ, x respectively when these consonants occur between vowels before the accent (cf. Upper Chinook wa'pul 'night': wabu'lmax 'nights'). As the voiced consonants can arise in no other way, they are not felt by the speakers of A as specifically distinct from the voiceless consonants. They feel sharply the difference between p and p', as do Chinese, Takelma, Yana, and a host of other languages, but are not aware of the alternation p : b.

And for B:

1. Long vowels can arise only when the syllable is open and stressed. Such alternations as ma·'la: u·'-mala are not felt as involving any but stress differences. In A, ma·la and mala are as distinct as Latin 'apples' and 'bad' (fem.).

2. ' is not an organic consonant, but, as in North German, an attack of initial vowels, hence 'a- is felt to be merely a-. In A, however, as in Semitic, Nootka, Kwakiutl, Haida, and a great many other languages, such initials as 'a- are felt to be equivalent to such consonant + vowel groups as ma- or sa-. Here is a type of pattern difference which even experienced linguists do not always succeed in making clear.

3. w and y are merely semi-vocalic developments of u and i. Cf. French oui and hier. In A, w and y are organically distinct consonants. Here again linguists often blindly follow the phonetic feeling of their own language instead of clearly ascertaining the behavior of the language investigated. The difference, e.g., between aua and awa is a real one for some languages, a phantom for others.

4. l arises merely as dissimilated variant of n.

5. p', t', k' are merely p, t, k with breath release, characteristic of B at the end of a word, e.g. ap-a: ap'. This sort of alternation is common in aboriginal America. It is the reverse of the English habit: <u>tame</u> with aspirated t (t'e·ⁱm) but <u>hate</u> with unaspirated, or very weakly aspirated, release (heⁱt).

6. f, θ, and x similarly arise from the unvoicing of final v, δ, and γ; e.g., av-a: af. z and s also alternate in this way, but there is a true s besides. From the point of view of B, s in such phonemes as sa and asa is an utterly distinct sound, or rather point in the phonetic pattern, from the objectively identical as which alternates with az-a.[2]

The true or intuitively felt phonetic systems (patterns) of A and B, therefore, are:

A: a   i   u

a·   i·   u·

'   h   w y l   m n

p   t   k

p'   t'   k'

f   θ   x   s

B: a   ɛ   e   i   u   o   ɔ

h   m n ŋ

p   t   k

b   d   g

s

v   δ z   γ

which shows the two languages to be very much more different phonetically than they at first seemed to be.

[2] If B ever develops an orthography, it is likely to fall into the habit of writing <u>az</u> for the pronounced <u>as</u> in cases of type <u>az-a</u>: <u>as</u>, but <u>as</u> in cases of type <u>as-a</u>: <u>as</u>. Philologists not convinced of the reality of phonetic patterns as here conceived will then be able to 'prove' from internal evidence that the change of etymological v, z, δ, γ to -f, -s, -θ, -x did not take place until after the language was reduced to writing, because otherwise it would be 'impossible' to explain why -s should be written -z when there was a sign for s ready to hand and why signs should not have

The converse case is worth plotting too. C and D are languages which have hardly any sounds in common, but their patterns show a remarkable one-to-one correspondence. Thus:

C: a   ɛ   i   u
        a·   ɛ·

        h   w   y   l   m   n

        p   t   k   q (velar k)
        b   d   g   ġ (velar g)
        f   s   x   x̣ (velar x)

D: ä   e   i   ü
        ä·   e·

        h   v   j[3]   r   m   ŋ

        p'   t'   k'   q'
        β[4]   δ   γ   γ̣ (velar γ)
        f   š   x̣[5]   ḥ (laryngeal h)

Languages C and D have far less superficial similarity in their sound systems than have A and B, but it is obvious at a glance that their patterns are built on very much more similar lines. If we allowed ourselves to speculate genetically, we might suspect, on general principles, that the phonetic similarities between A and B, which we will suppose to be contiguous languages, are due to historical contact, but that the deeper pattern resemblance between C and D is an index of genetic relationship. It goes without saying that in the complex world of actual linguistic

history we do not often find the phonetic facts working out along such neatly schematic lines, but it seemed expedient to schematize here so that the pattern concept might emerge with greater clarity.

An examination of the patterns of C and D shows that there is still a crucial point that we have touched on only by implication. We must now make this clear. We have arranged the sounds of C and D in such a way as to suggest an equivalence of 'orientation' of any one sound of one system with some sound of the other. In comparing the systems of A and B we did not commit ourselves to specific equivalences. We did not wish to imply, for instance, that A's s was or was not 'oriented' in the same way as B's, did or did not occupy the same relative place in A's pattern as in B's. But here we do wish to imply not merely that, e.g., C's p corresponds to D's p' or C's h to D's h, which one would be inclined to grant on general phonetic grounds, but also that, e.g., C's w corresponds to D's v while C's b corresponds to D's β. On general principles such pattern alignments as the latter are unexpected, to say the least, for bilabial β resembles w rather more than dentilabial v does. Why, then, not allow β to occupy the position we have assigned to v? Again, why should D's j be supposed to correspond to C's y when it is merely the voiced form of š? Should it not rather be placed under š precisely as, in C's system, b is placed under p? Naturally, there is no reason why the intuitive pattern alignment of sounds in a given language should not be identical with their natural phonetic arrangement, and, one need hardly say, it is almost universally true that, e.g., the vowels form both a natural and a pattern group as against the consonants, that such stopped sounds as p, t, k form both a natural and a pattern group as opposed to the equally coherent group b, d, g (provided, of course, the language possesses these two series of stopped consonants). And yet it is most important to emphasize the fact, strange but indubitable, that a pattern alignment does not need to correspond exactly to the more obvious phonetic one. It is most certainly true that, however likely it is that at last analysis patternings of sounds are based on natural classifications, the pattern feeling, once established, may come to have a linguistic reality over and above, though perhaps never entirely at variance with, such classifications. We are not here concerned with the historical reasons for such phonetic vagaries. The fact is that, even from a purely descriptive standpoint, it is not nonsense to say that, e.g., the s or w of one linguistic pattern is not necessarily the same thing as the s or w of another.

It is time to escape from a possible charge of phonetic metaphysics and to face the question, "How can a sound be assigned a 'place' in a phonetic pattern over and above its natural classification on organic and acoustic grounds?" The answer is simple.

---

come into use for f, θ, and x. As soon as one realizes, however, that 'ideal sounds,' which are constructed from one's intuitive feeling of the significant relations between the objective sounds, are more 'real' to a naive speaker than the objective sounds themselves, such internal evidence loses much of its force. The example of s in B was purposely chosen to illustrate an interesting phenomenon, the crossing in a single objective phoneme of a true element of the phonetic pattern with a secondary form of another such element. In B, e.g., objective s is a pool of cases of 'true s' and 'pseudo-s'. Many interesting and subtle examples could be given of psychological difference where there is objective identity, or similarity so close as to be interpreted by the recorder as identity. In Sarcee, an Athabaskan language with significant pitch differences, there is a true middle tone and a pseudo-middle tone which results from the lowering of a high tone to the middle position because of certain mechanical rules of tone sandhi. I doubt very much if the intuitive psychology of these two middle tones is the same. There are, of course, analogous traps for the unwary in Chinese. Had not the Chinese kindly formalized for us their intuitive feeling about the essential tone analysis of their language, it is exceedingly doubtful if our Occidental ears and kymographs would have succeeded in discovering the exact patterning of Chinese tone.

[3] As in French jour.
[4] Bilabial v, as in Spanish.
[5] As in German ich.

"A 'place' is intuitively found for a sound (which is here thought of as a true 'point in the pattern,' not a mere conditional variant) in such a system because of a general feeling of its phonetic relationship resulting from all the specific phonetic relationships (such as parallelism, contrast, combination, imperviousness to combination, and so on) to all other sounds." These relationships may, or may not, involve morphological processes (e.g., the fact that in English we have morphological alternations like wife : wives, sheath : to sheathe, breath : to breathe, mouse : to mouse helps to give the sounds f, θ, s an intuitive pattern relation to their voiced correlates v, δ, z which is specifically different from the theoretically analogous relation p, t, k : b, d, g; in English, f is nearer to v than p is to b, but in German this is certainly not true).

An example or two of English sound-patterning will help us to fix our thoughts. P, t, k belong together in a coherent set because, among other reasons: 1, they may occur initially, medially, or finally; 2, they may be preceded by s in all positions (e.g. spoon : cusp, star : hoist, scum : ask); 3, they may be followed by r initially and medially; 4, they may be preceded by s and followed by r initially and medially; 5, each has a voiced correspondent (b, d, g); 6, unlike such sounds as f and θ, they cannot alternate significantly with their voiced correspondents; 7, they have no tendency to be closely associated, either phonetically or morphologically, with corresponding spirants (p : f and t : θ are not intuitively correct for English; contrast Old Irish and Hebrew t : θ, k : x, which were intuitively felt relations—Old Irish and Hebrew θ and x were absolutely different types of sounds, psychologically, from English θ and German x. These are merely a few of the relations which help to give p, t, k their pattern place in English.

A second example is ŋ of sing. In spite of what phoneticians tell us about this sound (b : m as d : n as g : ŋ), no naïve English-speaking person can be made to feel in his bones that it belongs to a single series with m and n. Psychologically it cannot be grouped with them because, unlike them, it is not a freely movable consonant (there are no words beginning with ŋ). It still feels like ŋg, however little it sounds like it. The relation ant : and = sink : sing is psychologically as well as historically correct. Orthography is by no means solely responsible for the 'ng feeling' of ŋ. Cases like -ŋ- in finger and anger do not disprove the reality of this feeling, for there is in English a pattern equivalence of -ŋg- : -ŋ and -nd- : -nd. What cases like singer with -ŋ- indicate is not so much a pattern difference of -ŋg- : -ŋ-, which is not to be construed as analogous to -nd- : -n- (e.g. window : winnow), as an analogous treatment of medial elements in terms of their final form

(singer : sing like cutter : cut).[6]

To return to our phonetic patterns for C and D, we can now better understand why it is possible to consider a sibilant like j as less closely related in pattern to its voiceless form š than to such a set of voiced continuants as v, r, m, ŋ. We might find, for instance, that š never alternates with j, but that there are cases of š : δ analogous to cases of f : β and x : γ; that ava, aja, ara alternate with au, ai, ar; that combinations like -aβd, -aδg, -aγd are possible, but that combinations of type -ajd and -avd are unthinkable; that v- and j- are possible initials, like r-, m-, and ŋ-, but that β-, δ-, γ-, χ- are not allowed. The product of such and possibly other sound relations would induce a feeling that j belongs with v, r, m, ŋ; that it is related to i; and that it has nothing to do with such spirants as š and δ. In other words, it 'feels' like the y of many other languages, and, as y itself is absent in D, we can go so far as to say that j occupies a 'place in the pattern' that belongs to y elsewhere.

In this paper I do not wish to go into the complex and tangled problems of the nature and generality of sound changes in language. All that I wish to point out here is that it is obviously not immaterial to understand how a sound patterns if we are to understand its history. Of course, it is true that mechanical sound changes may bring about serious readjustments of phonetic pattern and may even create new configurations within the pattern (in Modern Central Tibetan, e.g., we have b-, d-, g- : B'-, D'-, G'-,[7] while in Classical Tibetan we have, as correspondents, mb-, nd-, ŋg- : b-, d-, g-; here mb-, nd-, ŋg- are to be morphologically analyzed as nasal prefix + b-, d-, g-). But it is equally true that the pattern feeling acts as a hindrance of, or stimulus to, certain sound changes

[6] Incidentally, if our theory is correct, such a form as singer betrays an unconscious analysis into a word of absolute significance sing and a semi-independent agentive element -er, which is appended not to a stem, an abstracted radical element, but to a true word. Hence sing : singer is not psychologically analogous to such Latin forms as can- : cantor. It would almost seem that the English insistence on the absoluteness of its significant words tended at the same time to give many of its derivative suffixes a secondary, revitalized reality. -er, for instance, might almost be construed as a 'word' which occurs only as the second element of a compound, cf. -man in words like longshoreman. As Prof. L. Bloomfield points out to me, the agentive -er contrasts with the comparative -er, which allows the adjective to keep its radical form in -ŋg- (e.g., long with -ŋ : longer with -ŋg-).

[7] B, D, G represent intermediate stops, 'tonlose Medien.' In this series they are followed by aspiration.

[8] The slight objective differences between English and Spanish θ and δ are of course not great enough to force a different patterning. Such a view would be putting the cart before the horse.

and that it is not permissible to look for universally valid sound changes under like articulatory conditions. Certain typical mechanical tendencies there are (e.g. nb > mb or -az > -as or tya > tša), but a complete theory of sound change has to take constant account of the orientation of sounds in our sense. Let one example do for many. We do not in English feel that θ is to be found in the neighborhood, as it were, of s, but that it is very close to δ. In Spanish, θ is not far from s, but is not at all close to δ.[8] Is it not therefore more than an accident that nowhere in Germanic does θ become s or proceed from s, while in certain Spanish dialects, as so frequently elsewhere, θ passes into s (in Athabaskan θ often proceeds from s)? In English θ tends to be vulgarized to t as δ tends to be vulgarized to d, never to s; similarly, Old Norse θ has become t in Swedish and Danish. Such facts are impressive. They cannot be explained on simple mechanical principles.

Phonetic patterning helps also to explain why people find it difficult to pronounce certain foreign sounds which they possess in their own language. Thus, a Nootka Indian in pronouncing English words with ŋ or 1 invariably substitutes n for each of these sounds. Yet he is able to pronounce both ŋ and 1. He does not use these sounds in prose discourse, but ŋ is very common in the chants and 1 is often substituted for n in songs. His feeling for the stylistic character of ŋ and for the n–1 equivalence prevents him from 'hearing' English ŋ and 1 correctly. Here again we see that a speech sound is not merely an articulation or an acoustic image, but material for symbolic expression in an appropriate linguistic context. Very instructive is our attitude towards the English sounds j, ŋ, and ts. All three of these sounds are familiar to us (e.g. azure, sing, hats). None occurs initially. For all that, the attempt to pronounce them initially in foreign words is not reacted to in the same way. ŋa- and tsa- are naïvely felt to be incredible, not so ja-, which is easily acquired without replacement by dja- or ša-. Why is this? ŋa- is incredible because there is no mba-, nda-, ŋ(g)a- series in English. tsa- is incredible because there is no psa-, tsa-, ksa- series in Eng-

lish; -ts is always morphologically analyzable into -t + -s, hence no feeling develops for ts as a simple phoneme despite the fact that its phonetic parallel tš (ch of church) is found in all positions.[9] But ja- is not difficult, say in learning French, because its articulation and perception have been mastered by implication in the daily use of our phonetic pattern. This is obvious from a glance at the formula:

-j-	-z-	-δ-	-v-
—	z-	δ-	v-

which is buttressed by:

-š-	-s-	-θ-	-f-
š-	s-	θ-	f-

Is it not evident that the English speaker's pattern has all but taught him j- before he himself has ever used or heard an actual j-?

There are those who are so convinced of the adequacy of purely objective methods of studying speech sounds that they do not hesitate to insert phonetic graphs into the body of their descriptive grammars. This is to confuse linguistic structure with a particular method of studying linguistic phenomena. If it is justifiable in a grammatical work to describe the vocalic system of a language in terms of kymograph records,[10] it is also proper to insert anecdotes into the morphology to show how certain modes or cases happened to come in handy. And a painter might as well be allowed to transfer to his canvas his unrevised palette! The whole aim and spirit of this paper has been to show that phonetic phenomena are not physical phenomena per se, however necessary it may be to get at the phonetic facts by way of their physical embodiment. The present discussion is really a special illustration of the necessity of getting behind the sense data of any type of expression in order to grasp the intuitively felt and communicated forms which alone give significance to such expression.

9 Obviously we need not expect -ts and -tš to develop analogously even if s and š do.

10 Needless to say, such records are in place in studies explicitly devoted to experimental phonetics.

A SET OF POSTULATES FOR THE SCIENCE OF LANGUAGE

LEONARD BLOOMFIELD
Language 2.153–64—1926

I. Introductory

The method of postulates (that is, assumptions or axioms) and definitions[1] is fully adequate to mathematics; as for other sciences, the more complex their subject-matter, the less amenable they are to this method, since, under it, every descriptive or historical fact becomes the subject of a new postulate.

Nevertheless, the postulational method can further the study of language, because it forces us to state explicitly whatever we assume, to define our terms, and to decide what things may exist independently and what things are interdependent.[2]

Certain errors can be avoided or corrected by examining and formulating our (at present tacit) assumptions and defining our (often undefined) terms.[3]

Also, the postulational method saves discussion, because it limits our statements to a defined terminology; in particular, it cuts us off from psychological dispute.[4] Discussion of the fundamentals of our science seems to consist one half of obvious truisms, and one half of metaphysics; this is characteristic of matters which form no real part of a subject: they should properly be disposed of by merely naming certain concepts as belonging to the domain of other sciences.

Thus, the physiologic and acoustic description of acts of speech belongs to other sciences than ours. The existence and interaction of social groups held together by language is granted by psychology and anthropology.[5]

Psychology, in particular, gives us this series: to certain stimuli (A) a person reacts by speaking; his speech (B) in turn stimulates his hearers to certain reactions (C).[6] By a social habit which every person acquires in infancy from his elders, A-B-C are closely correlated. Within this correlation, the stimuli (A) which cause an act of speech and the reactions (C) which result from it, are very closely linked, because every person acts indifferently as speaker or as hearer. We are free, therefore, without further discussion, to speak of vocal features or sounds (B) and of stimulus-reaction features (A-C) of speech.

II. Form and Meaning

1. Definition. An act of speech is an utterance.

2. Assumption 1. Within certain communities successive utterances are alike or partly alike.

A needy stranger at the door says I'm hungry. A child who has eaten and merely wants to put off going to bed says I'm hungry. Linguistics considers only those vocal features which are alike in the two utterances, and only those stimulus-reaction features which are alike in the two utterances. Similarly, The book is interesting and Put the book away, are partly alike (the book). Outside of our science these similarities are only relative; within it they are absolute. This fiction is only in part suspended in historical linguistics.

3. Def. Any such community is a speech-community.

4. Def. The totality of utterances that can be made in a speech-community is the language of that speech-community.

We are obliged to predict; hence the words 'can

---

[1] For a clear exposition of this method, see J. W. Young, Lectures on the Fundamental Concepts of Algebra and Geometry, New York 1911.

[2] Cf. A. P. Weiss's set of postulates for psychology, Psychological Review 32.83.

[3] Examples are many. Bopp took for granted that the formative elements of Indo-European were once independent words; this is a needless and unwarranted assumption. The last descendant of his error is the assumption that IE compound words are historically derived from phrases (Jacobi, Compositum und Nebensatz, Bonn 1897; this even in Brugmann, Grundriss II[2], 1, pp. 37–78; cf. TAPA 45.73 ff.). The notion is gaining ground that some forms have less meaning than others and are therefore more subject to phonetic change (Horn, Sprachkörper und Sprachfunktion, Palaestra 135, Berlin 1921); I, for one, can discover no workable definition of the terms 'meaning' and 'phonetic change' under which this notion can be upheld. The whole dispute, perhaps today as unstilled as fifty years ago, about the regularity of phonetic change, is at bottom a question of terminology.

[4] Recall the difficulties and obscurities in the writings of Humboldt and Steinthal, and the psychological dispute of Paul, Wundt, Delbrueck. From our point of view, the last-named was wrong in denying the value of descriptive data, but right in saying that it is indifferent what system of psychology a linguist believes in (Grundfragen der Sprachforschung, Strassburg 1901). The trouble over the nature of the sentence is largely non-linguistic; contrast the simplicity and usefulness of Meillet's definition (adopted below), Introduction à l'étude comparative des langues indo-européennes[3], Paris 1912, p. 339. I am indebted also to Sapir's book on Language, New York 1921, and to de Saussure's Cours de linguistique générale[2], Paris 1922; both authors take steps toward a delimitation of linguistics.

[5] Cf. Weiss, l. c., p. 86: 'The language responses establish the ... social type of organization ...'

[6] Cf. Weiss, Journal of Philosophy, Psychology and Scientific Methods 15.636: 'The significant thing about the speech reaction is that it may be either the adequate reaction to a situation, or it may be the adequate stimulus for either another speech reaction or some bodily reaction.'

be made'. We say that under certain stimuli a French-man (or Zulu, etc.) will say so-and-so and other Frenchmen (or Zulus, etc.) will react appropriately to his speech. Where good informants are available, or for the investigator's own language, the prediction is easy; elsewhere it constitutes the greatest difficulty of descriptive linguistics.

5. Def. That which is alike will be called same. That which is not same is different.

This enables us to use these words without reference to non-linguistic shades of sound and meaning.

6. Def. The vocal features common to same or partly same utterances are forms; the corresponding stimulus-reaction features are meanings.

Thus a form is a recurrent vocal feature which has meaning, and a meaning is a recurrent stimulus-reaction feature which corresponds to a form.

7. Assumption 2. Every utterance is made up wholly of forms.

III. Morpheme, Word, Phrase

8. Def. A minimum X is an X which does not consist entirely of lesser X's.

Thus, if X_1 consists of $X_2 X_3 X_4$, then X_1 is not a minimum X. But if X_1 consists of $X_2 X_3 A$, or of $X_2 A$, or of $A_1 A_2$, or is unanalyzable, then X_1 is a minimum X.

9. Def. A minimum form is a morpheme; its meaning a sememe.

Thus a morpheme is a recurrent (meaningful) form which cannot in turn be analyzed into smaller recurrent (meaningful) forms. Hence any unanalysable word or formative is a morpheme.

10. Def. A form which may be an utterance is free. A form which is not free is bound.

Thus, book, the man are free forms; -ing (as in writing), -er (as in writer) are bound forms, the last-named differing in meaning from the free form err.

11. Def. A minimum free form is a word.

A word is thus a form which may be uttered alone (with meaning) but cannot be analyzed into parts that may (all of them) be uttered alone (with meaning). Thus the word quick cannot be analyzed; the word quickly can be analyzed into quick and -ly, but the latter part cannot be uttered alone; the word writer can be analyzed into write and -er, but the latter cannot be uttered alone (the word err being, by virtue of different meaning, a different form); the word blackbird can be analyzed into the words black and bird and the word-stress ⌐ -, which last cannot be uttered alone (i.e., it differs in form and meaning from the phrase black bird).

12. Def. A non-minimum free form is a phrase.

E.g., the book, or The man beat the dog; but not, e.g., book on (as in Lay the book on the table), for this is meaningless, hence not a form; and not black-bird, which is a minimum free form.

13. Def. A bound form which is part of a word is a formative.*

A formative may be complex, as, Latin verb-endings -abat, -abant, -abit, -abunt, etc., or minimum (and hence a morpheme), as Latin -t of third person.

14. Assumption 3. The forms of a language are finite in number.

IV. Example of a Special Assumption

The phenomena of specific languages will no doubt necessitate further assumptions of form; and these will sometimes modify the general assumptions. The following is an example of such a special assumption.

Assumption S1. A phrase may contain a bound form which is not part of a word.

For example, the possessive [z] in the man I saw yesterday's daughter.

Def. Such a bound form is a phrase-formative.*

This assumption disturbs the definition of phrase above given. Strictly speaking, our assumptions and definitions would demand that we take the-man-I-saw-yesterday's daughter as two words. Convenience of analysis makes an assumption like the present one preferable for English. A similar assumption might be convenient for the Philippine 'ligatures'.

V. Phonemes

15. Assumption 4. Different morphemes may be alike or partly alike as to vocal features.

Thus book : table [b]; stay : west [st]; -er (agent) : -er (comparative). The assumption imples that the meanings are different.

16. Def. A minimum same of vocal feature is a phoneme or distinctive sound.

As, for instance, English [b, s, t], the English normal word-stress, the Chinese tones.

17. Assumption 5. The number of different phonemes in a language is a small sub-multiple of the number of forms.

18. Assumption 6. Every form is made up wholly of phonemes.

These two assumptions are empiric facts for every language that has been observed, and outside of our science are theoretical necessities (Boas, Handbook of American Indian Languages, Bureau of American Ethnology, Bulletin 40, vol. 1, pp. 24 ff.).

*Letter from Bloomfield to John Kepke, April 17, 1934: You are right about the term formative, which in 1926 I used in the value 'a bound form which is part of a word.' At that time I had not the courage to call the-King-of-England's and the like 'one word'. Hence the possessive -'s was here a bound form which was not part of a word. And so for the usual kind of bound forms I needed a special name, and chose 'formative.' Today I call the-King-of-England's and the like 'one word'; hence every bound form will now be part of a word, and the term 'formative' is no longer needed.

Such a thing as a 'small difference of sound' does not exist in a language. Linguists who believe that certain forms resist phonetic change, implicitly reject these assumptions, though, so far as I can see, we could not work without them.

The morphemes of a language can thus be analyzed into a small number of meaningless phonemes. The sememes, on the other hand, which stand in one-to-one correspondence with the morphemes, cannot be further analyzed by linguistic methods. This is no doubt why linguists, confronted with the parallelism of form and meaning, choose form as the basis of classification.

19. Assumption 7. The number of orders of phonemes in the morphemes and words of a language is a sub-multiple of the number of possible orders.

20. Def. The orders which occur are the sound-patterns of the language.

As, English word-initial [st-] but never [ts-].

21. Def. Different forms which are alike as to phonemes are homonymous.

VI. Construction, Categories, Parts of Speech

22. Assumption 8. Different non-minimum forms may be alike or partly alike as to the order of the constituent forms and as to stimulus-reaction features corresponding to this order.

The order may be successive, simultaneous (stress and pitch with other phonemes), substitutive (French au [o] for à le), and so on.

23. Def. Such recurrent sames of order are constructions; the corresponding stimulus-reaction features are constructional meanings.

This expands the use of the term meaning.

24. Def. The construction of formatives in a word is a morphologic construction.

Thus, book-s, ox-en have the construction of formative plus formative and the meaning 'object in number'.

25. Def. The construction of free forms (and phrase formatives) in a phrase is a syntactic construction.

Thus, Richard saw John, The man is beating the dog show the construction of free form plus free form plus free form meaning 'actor acting on goal'.

26. Def. A maximum X is an X which is not part of a larger X.

27. Def. A maximum form* in any utterance is a sentence.

Thus, a sentence is a form* which, in the given utterance, is not part of a larger construction.

*Bloomfield in his review of Ries, Was ist ein Satz? (Lang. 7.209 fn. 6 [1931]): E. A. Esper calls my attention to an error in my English wording of Meillet's definition, Lang. 2.158 [1926]: 'A maximum construction in any utterance is a sentence.' For 'construction' one must, of course, read 'form', since otherwise, the definition, if it meant anything at all, would exclude largest-forms that happened to contain only a single morpheme; e.g. Come! Ouch! Yes.

Every utterance therefore consists of one or more sentences, and even such utterances as Latin pluit, English Fire! or Ouch! are sentences.

28. Assumption 9. The number of constructions in a language is a small sub-multiple of the number of forms.

29. Def. Each of the ordered units in a construction is a position.

Thus the English construction of formative plus formative meaning 'object in number' has two positions; and that of free form plus free form plus free form meaning 'actor acting on goal' has three.

30. Assumption 10. Each position in a construction can be filled only by certain forms.

Thus, in the English construction of formative plus formative meaning 'object in number' the first position can be filled only by certain formatives (noun-stems), and the second only be certain other formatives (affixes of number, such as the plural-sign -s). And in the English construction of free form plus free form plus free form meaning 'actor acting on goal' the first and third positions can be filled only be certain free forms (object expressions) and the second only by certain other free forms (finite verb expressions). This assumption implies the converse, namely, that a given form will appear only in certain positions of certain constructions. Thus, an English noun-stem will appear only in the first position of the construction 'object in number', in the second position of the construction formative plus formative meaning 'object having such an object' (long-nose), and in certain positions of a certain few other constructions. Similarly, an object expression, such as John, the man will appear in the first position of the construction 'actor acting on goal', or in the third, or in certain positions of a certain few other constructions.

31. Def. The meaning of a position is a functional meaning.

That is, the constructional meaning of a construction may be divided into parts, one for each position; these parts are functional meanings. It would be more concrete, but perhaps less useful, if we said: the meaning common to all forms that can fill a given position, when they are in that position, is a functional meaning. Thus, in the English construction of 'object in number' the first position has the functional meaning 'object', or, more concretely, all the formatives (noun-stems) which can occur in this position, have in common, when they so appear, the functional meaning 'object'. And in the English construction of 'actor acting on goal' the first position has the functional meaning 'actor', or, more concretely, all the free forms (object-expressions, such as nouns, noun-phrases, pronouns, etc.) which can occur in this position, have in common, when they so appear, the functional meaning 'actor'. And in this same construction, the third position has the meaning 'goal', or, more concretely, all the free forms (largely the same as those just mentioned) which can appear in this position, have in common, when they so appear, the meaning 'goal'.

32. Def. The positions in which a form occurs are its functions.

Thus, the word John and the phrase the man have the functions of 'actor', 'goal', 'predicate noun', 'goal of preposition', and so on.

33. Def. All forms having the same functions constitute a form-class.

Examples of English form-classes are: noun-stems, number-affixes, object expressions, finite verb expressions.

34. Def. The functional meanings in which the forms of a form-class appear constitute the class-meaning.

Thus, the meanings found in all the functions of the form-class of English object expressions, namely 'actor', 'goal', etc. (§32) together constitute the class-meaning of these forms, which may be summed up as 'numbered object' or in the name 'object expression'.

35. Def. The functional meanings and class-meanings of a language are the categories of the language.

Thus, the above examples enable us to determine the following categories of the English language: from functional meanings: object, number, actor, action, goal; from class-meanings: object, number, numbered object (object expression), predicative action (finite verb expression).

36. Def. If a form-class contains relatively few forms, the meanings of these forms may be called sub-categories.

Thus, the English category of number contains only two meanings, singular-indefinite (egg) and plural (eggs). Hence one may speak of the sub-categories of singular and plural; it is convenient to do so when, as in this case, the sub-categories play a part in the alternation of other forms (see VII).

37. Def. A form-class of words is a word-class.

38. Def. The maximum word-classes of a language are the parts of speech of that language.

VII. Alternation

39. Assumption 11. In a construction a phoneme may alternate with another phoneme according to accompanying phonemes.

As in Sanskrit sandhi: tat pacati, tad bharati.

40. Def. Such alternation is phonetic alternation.

41. Assumption 12. In a construction a form may alternate with another form according to accompanying forms.

As, in English, the plural affixes book-s [s], boy-s [z], ox-en, f-ee-t. Or, verbs: He skates, They skate, according to number of actor.

42. Def. Such alternation is formal alternation.

43. Assumption 13. Absence of sound may be a phonetic or formal alternant.

44. Def. Such an alternant is a zero element.

The postulation of zero elements is necessary for Sanskrit (Pāṇini 1, 1, 61), for Primitive Indo-European (Meillet, Introduction à l'étude comparative des langues indo-européennes[3], Paris 1912, p. 127 f.), and probably economical for English (singular book with affix zero, as opposed to book-s, cf. f-oo-t : f-ee-t).

45. Def. If a formal alternation is determined by the phonemes of the accompanying forms, it is an automatic alternation.

Thus, the alternation of [-s, -z, -ez] in the regular English plural suffix of nouns is automatic, being determined by the final phoneme of the noun-stem. This differs from phonetic alternation since not every [s] in English is subject to this alternation, but only the (four) morphemes of this form. Similarly, Sanskrit tat pacati : tan nayati, since the alternation takes place only in wordfinal (contrast, e.g., ratnam).

The phonetic alternations and the automatic formal alternations of a language allow of a classification of the phonemes, to which the sound-patterns (§20) may contribute. Thus, the regular English plural suffix implies a classification of those English phonemes (the great majority) which may occur at the end of a noun-stem into the classes (1) sibilant, (2) non-sibilant (a, unvoiced; b, voiced). Ordinary phonetics can go no farther than this; phonetics which goes farther is either a personal skill or a science for the laboratory.

46. Def. The classification of phonemes implied in the sound-patterns [§20], phonetic alternations [§40], and automatic formal alternations [§45] of a language is the phonetic pattern.

For the sound-patterns and phonetic pattern see Sapir, Lang. 1.37 ((19)), and cf. Baudouin de Courtenay, Versuch einer Theorie Phonetischer Alternationen, Strassburg, 1895.

47. Def. If formal alternation is otherwise determined, it is grammatical alternation.

As, English plural suffix -en in ox-en alternating with the regular suffix above described; the verb-forms in he skates : they skate.

48. Def. If the accompanying forms which determine one grammatical variant predominate as to number, this variant is said to be regular; the others are irregular.

Thus, -en is an irregular plural suffix.

49. Def. If in a construction all the component forms are irregular, the whole form is suppletive.

If go be taken as the stem of the verb, then the past went is suppletive. Under this definition better as comparative of good would not be suppletive, since the ending -er is regular; a definition that will include such forms can be made only within English (or Indo-European) grammar, after 'stem' and 'affix' have been defined for this language.

50. Def. Whatever has meaning is a glosseme. The meaning of a glosseme is a noeme.

Thus the term glosseme includes (1) forms, (2) constructions, (3) zero elements.

The assumptions and definitions so far made will probably make it easy to define the grammatical phenomena of any language, both morphologic (affixation, reduplication, composition) and syntactic (cross-reference, concord, government, word-order), though I cannot say whether any such further definitions would apply to all languages. Other notions, such as subject, predicate, verb, noun, will apply only to some languages, and may have to be defined differently for different ones,—unless, indeed, we prefer to invent new terms for divergent phenomena.

VIII. Historical Linguistics

The following assumptions and definitions for historical linguistics are added for the sake of completeness. Insofar as they are correctly formulated, they will merely restate the working method of the great majority of linguists.

51. Assumption H1. Every language changes at a rate which leaves contemporary persons free to communicate without disturbance.

The ways in which it changes are described in Assumptions H3 and following.

52. Assumption H2. Among persons, linguistic change is uniform in ratio with the amount of communication between them.

These two assumptions and the assumptions and definitions based on them are necessarily loose, not because the process is too slow for any methods of direct observation that have been used—assumptions could ignore this—but because in historical linguistics it is our purpose to envisage the phenomena as relative. Ultimately no two speakers, and indeed no two utterances, have the same dialect: our assumptions must leave us free to examine the historical process with any desired degree of detail.

53. Def. If linguistic change results in groups of persons between which communication is disturbed, these groups speak dialects of the language.

54. Def. A relatively uniform auxiliary dialect used by such groups is a standard language.

55. Def. If linguistic change results in groups of persons between which communication is impossible, these groups speak related languages.

56. Assumption H3. Phonemes or classes of phonemes may gradually change.

For 'classes of phonemes' see §§45, 46.

57. Def. Such change is sound-change.

This assumption, by naming phonemes, implies that meaning is not involved. Owing to the assumptions that limit the number of phonemes (Assumptions 5 and 6), the change must affect the phonemes at every occurrence and do away with the older form of any phoneme that is changed.

58. Assumption H4. Sound-change may affect phonemes or classes of phonemes in the environment of certain other phonemes or classes of phonemes.

59. Def. This change is conditioned sound-change.

60. Assumption H5. Sound-change preponderantly favors shorter forms.[7]

61. Assumption H6. Linguistic change may substitute sames for differents.

62. Def. This change is analogic change.

63. Def. Analogic change which creates or enlarges a glosseme is contamination.

For example, creation (of a morpheme), pre-Germanic *hweðwōrez 'four', *fimfe 'five' > *f-eðwōrez, *f-imfe. Increase in size (of a morpheme), late Latin gra-ve, le-ve > gr-eve, l-eve (Italian).

64. Def. Analogic change which extends the use of a glosseme is adaptation.

Late Latin reddere > rendere, extending to a new word the morpheme -end- of pr-endere, p-endere, att-endere (v-endere?).

65. Def. Adaptation which replaces one alternant by another is proportional analogy.

English bēc > book-s; the plural affixes vary according to the accompanying noun-stem (grammatical alternation, §41), and now one alternant replaces another. The diagram showing the proportional character is familiar.

66. Def. Analogic change of formatives is formal analogy.

It may of course be contamination, adaptation, or proportional analogy. In a language in which stems and affixes are definable, it is customary to distinguish between 'material' formal analogy (affecting stems) and 'grammatical' formal analogy (affecting affixes).

67. Def. Analogic change of words is semantic change.

It may of course be contaminative, adaptive, or proportional. E.g., English meat 'pabulum' > 'caro'; or home 'Heim' > 'Haus'. Probably proportional:

He left the bones and took the flesh : He left the bones and took the meat :: She cooked the beans with the flesh : She cooked the beans with the meat.

They have a lovely house : They have a lovely home (intensive) :: A fine new house for sale : A fine new home for sale (intensive).[8]

68. Assumption H7. Analogic change predominantly disfavors irregular glossemes and those which diverge from their fellows; it tends to disfavor them in inverse ratio to their frequency of occurrence.

This is necessarily vague, because we know little about replacement and obsolescence through such factors as unusual homonymy, word-tabu, and other deviations of glossemes, that is, about inadequacy of glossemes and its effects. Cf. Gilliéron, Pathologie et thérapeutique verbales, Collection linguistique,

[7] Assumptions H5 and H7 try to embody the results of Jespersen's Progress in Language, New York 1894.

[8] The word 'intensive' is meant merely to describe the meaning of home in its new use (intensive of house), and is not meant as a technical term. Cf. also Kroesch, Lang. 2.35–45 (1926).

vol. 11, Paris 1921.

69. Assumption H8. Whoever speaks a foreign language or dialect may in it substitute resemblant features of his native speech.

70. Def. This is linguistic substitution.

71. Def. Linguistic substitution of phonemes is sound-substitution.

72. Assumption H9. Whoever hears a foreign language or dialect may adopt features of it into his own speech.

73. Def. Such adoption is linguistic borrowing.

74. Def. Borrowed words are loan-words.

75. Assumption H10. The phonemes of analogic forms and loan-words may be changed so as to fit the sound patterns of the language.

Western European peregrinus > pilgrim; German klüppel > knüppel.

76. Def. Such change is sudden sound-change.

77. Assumption H11. Glossemes may go out of use. Compare the comment on Assumption H7, §68.

THE PHONEMIC PRINCIPLE

MORRIS SWADESH
Language 10.117–29—1934

As basic as the phonemic principle is to linguistic science, it is only quite recently that it has had the serious attention of linguists. In studying the phonemes of Chitimacha (an Indian language of Louisiana) I knew of no single source from which I could learn to understand all the phenomena that I observed. There seemed to be a need for an adequate and complete exposition of the phonemic principle including, especially, an account of how it applies to the more marginal and difficult types of phenomena. I at first intended to include this discussion in my paper on the Chitimacha phonemes, but the wider interest of the general discussion makes it more appropriate that it be published separately. The specific treatment of Chitimacha, which can now appear without theoretical digressions, will serve to illustrate many of the points discussed here. I do not attempt to cite previous authors[1] on all of the points treated in this paper, though I recognize fully my dependence on them. On a few points my treatment attempts to avoid weaknesses in previous treatments, and a point or two are perhaps introduced here for the first time. However, the chief ideals of this paper are theoretical comprehensiveness, consistency of treatment, and brevity.

The phonemic principle is that there are in each language a limited number of elemental types of speech sounds, called phonemes, peculiar to that language; that all sounds produced in the employment of the given language are referable to its set of phonemes; that only its own phonemes are at all significant in the given language.

The phonemes of a language are, in a sense, percepts to the native speakers of the given language, who ordinarily hear speech entirely in terms of these percepts. If they hear a foreign tongue spoken, they still tend to hear in terms of their native phonemes. Bilinguals and phonetically schooled individuals hear speech in a language native to them now in terms of the native phonemic system, now in terms of other percepts. If linguists occasionally have difficulty in discovering the phonemes of a language, it is usually when the language is not native to them, unless, indeed, in dealing with their own language, they be confused by some irrelevant or only partly relevant insight (as, for example, the knowledge of etymology or phonetics). At any rate, it is well to realize that one can learn nothing about the phonemes of one language by knowledge of those of another.

If the phonemes are percepts to the native speakers of the language, they are not necessarily percepts that he experiences in isolation. They occur ordinarily as the elements of words or sentences. Phonemes are perceptive units in the sense that the native can recognize as different, words different as to one of the component phonemes, e.g., _bid_ and _hid_ or _bid_ and _bed_ or _bid_ and _bit_. The phoneme is the smallest potential unit of difference between similar words recognizable as different to the native. Given a correct native word, the replacement of one or more phonemes by other phonemes (capable of occurring in the same position) results in a native word other than that intended, or a native-like nonsense word. Other possible or conceivable differences are either not perceived, or are perceived as distortions of proper phonemes, or are chance oral sounds that are not classed as speech sounds at all.

The word sometimes has regular variant forms; in this event, two forms may differ as to one or more phonemes though they are in a sense the same word. Since variants sometimes confuse the phonemic problem, it may be well to point out some of the types of variants:

---

[1] The principal works consulted were:

Bloomfield, Language, Chapters 5–8. New York, Henry Holt, 1933.

Jones, On Phonemes, Travaux du cercle linguistique de Prague 4.74–9; Projet de terminologie phonologique standardisé, op.cit. 4.309–22.

Sapir, Sound Patterns in Language, Lang. 1.37–51 ⟪19⟫; La réalité psychologique du phonème, Journal de psychologie 30.247–55 ⟦58, fn.13⟧.

Troubetzkoy, Zur allgemeinen Theorie der phonologischen Vokalsysteme, Travaux du cercle linguistique de Prague 1.39–66; Die phonologischen Systeme, op.cit. 96–115.

Ułaszyn, Laut, Phonema, Morphonema, op.cit. 4.53–61.

I am most directly indebted to Professor Sapir, as my teacher, for my understanding of the phonemic principle. The present paper has benefited by discussion with him and with my colleagues Dr. Stanley Newman, Dr. George Herzog, and Mrs. Mary Haas Swadesh.

I Free Variants (either variant is equally correct in
    any position)
  A Particular (applying to a single word or a
      limited number of isolated words), e.g.,
      Nootka ?apw'inqis, ?apw'in?is 'in the
      middle of the beach'; Eng. economics
      beginning like eke or like echo
  B General (applying to all words of a given
      class), e.g., Chitimacha words of three
      or more syllables ending in -V?V vary
      with -V as k'ahti?i, k'ahti 'he bites'
II Conditional variants (determined by position in
    the sentence)
  A Particular, e.g. Eng. a, an
  B General
    (a) Phonetically conditioned, e.g., Sanskrit
        punar, punaḥ 'back, again'
    (b) Structurally conditioned, e.g., Tunica disyl-
        labic words of the form CV?V have that
        form only when spoken in isolation; in
        context they become CV as: ri?i 'house',
        context form ri. [2]

Conditional variants may be regular, as the examples given, or may be optional, as the Eng. sandhi
type of as you [az yu, až(y)u], both of which are
sometimes interchangeably employed by the same
speakers.

Characteristics of the Phoneme

A phoneme, as a speech sound type, is defined by
the separate instances of the type. If I say 'Peter
Piper', I have produced three instances of the English phoneme p and every time any one pronounces
these words or others like dip, pit, speed, supply,
further instances of the phoneme are produced. On
the basis of the separate occurrences (or a proper
sampling of them) it is possible to define the type in
terms of a norm and of deviation from the norm.
Each individual has his own norm and range of
deviation, the social norm being a summation of the
individual norms. The description of the phoneme in
terms of norm and deviation belongs to the science
of phonetics.

The norm of the phoneme may be a multiple one.
That is, instead of one norm, there may be two or
more. Such variant norms are ordinarily conditional,
depending on the phonetic surroundings in which the
phoneme occurs. Thus one may distinguish at least
three norms for English p:
  (1) Relatively fortis, aspirated: e.g., in initial
      position, as in pit
  (2) Fortis unaspirated: e.g., medially between
      vowels, as in upper
  (3) Lenis unaspirated: e.g., after s, as in spill.
Positional variants may be even more strikingly different, as, for example the two variants of German

x (ch) in, e.g. Macht, Licht. Positional variants are
unlike phonemes in that to substitute one positional
variant for the other distorts the word, sometimes
beyond recognition, but never changes it into another
native word.

Occasionally one finds free variants, that is, non-
conditional or optional variants. Thus, there are many
people in the Connecticut valley who interchangeably
use either an r or a mid-mixed vowel with or without retroflexion in words like board and far.[3] It
sometimes happens that one of a pair of free variants
coincides with some other phoneme. Thus, Chitimacha
w', y', m', n' may be pronounced with or without a
glottal stricture, coinciding in the latter instance
with the phonemes w, y, m, n. Another instance of
this phenomenon, which may be called phonemic interchange, is the interchange of initial ð with d in
words like the and they in Edgecombe County (near
Rocky Mount), North Carolina.[4] Optional employment
or omission of a phoneme occurs, for example, in
the case of postvocalic r (e.g., barn) in certain sections of New England.[5]

Distribution

In a given language, some phonemes are frequent,
some are infrequent. Sometimes the disparity in
relative frequencies is great indeed, as that between
English s and θ. Sometimes, a phoneme occurs in
only one or a few isolated words; thus g occurs in
Tunica only in the stem -gatci 'mother'.

All phonemes, as a general thing, are limited as
to the positions in which they may occur. Two stops
may not occur together at the beginning of an English
word; yet such clusters do occur in certain other
languages, as Sahaptin (e.g., tkwalwípt 'evening
meal')[6] or ancient Greek. Again, English l does not
occur after d or t at the beginning of a word. Every
phoneme has its positional limitations, so that range
of distribution constitutes a definite characteristic
of each phoneme.

If a phoneme is much more limited as to positions
of occurrence than other comparable phonemes of
the same language, one may refer to it as a defective
phoneme. Such a phoneme is ŋ in English, since it
occurs only after and between vowels and never at
the beginning of a word.

[3] I have this information from Professor Hans
Kurath, director of the Linguistic Atlas of the United
States and Canada.
[4] Observed by Dr. Lowman for the Linguistic
Atlas, and mentioned in his paper Regional Differences in Virginian Speech, read at the tenth annual
meeting of the Linguistic Society of America.
[5] I owe this information to Dr. Lowman. The interchange was observed, for example, in one of his
informants at Rockport, Massachusetts.
[6] See Jacobs, A Sketch of Northwest Sahaptin
Grammar, Univ. of Washington Publications in Anthropology 4.85–292.

[2] Data on Tunica (an Indian language of Louisiana)
were supplied by Mary Haas Swadesh.

Phoneme Classes

English p, t, and k have common phonetic characteristics, relatively analogous positional variants, and relatively similar ranges of distribution; they are relatively different in these three respects from all other phonemes of the language. They therefore constitute a special class of English phonemes. English t, d, and θ have roughly the same articulating position and have distributional features in common, for example, that they occur initially before r but never initially before l. They constitute a class intercrossing with the p, t, k set. On the basis of similarities, all the sounds of a language may be thus classified, sub-classified, and cross-classified. The principal classes are those whose members have the most significant features in common, the sub-classes those that have less significant features in common. The bases of classification are common phonetic, variational, and distributional features. Classes are significant because of the general tendency of these features to occur in correlation.

But even in the absence of variational and distributional similarities, phonetic analogies are significant when they are recurrent. Whenever the phonetic relation of two sounds like English b and p is found to be the same as that of another pair like d and t, it is evident that the relation is not haphazard but systematic. Phonemes tend to occur in more or less consistent patterns.[7]

It is important to distinguish between the phonetic differentiae of phoneme classes and psychologically separable synchronous features. Thus nasalization is the phonetic differentia which in French distinguishes the nasalized vowel phonemes from their non-nasalized parallels; the tone upon which vowels are pronounced in French belongs to the prosody of the sentence and the occurrence of this or that phoneme on this or that pitch does not change its phonemic identity. In addition to patterns of sentence prosody, psychologically separable synchronous phonemes include tonemes in tone languages and tasemes (phonemes of stress) in stress languages, for these features apply to the syllables rather than to any of the phonemes in particular. Syllabic phenomena are necessarily most evident in connection with the vowel, but also apply, where possible, to the consonants. In Navaho n̂s-nè ʔz 'I am tall', the tone of the first syllable is actualized in the syllabic consonant n and not with the consonant s, the tone of the second syllable is carried by the vowel and both consonants.

But prosodic features, often psychologically separable from the sounds with which they occur, do sometimes constitute mere differentiae of phonemes. In Chitimacha ə is distinguished from the other vowels by quality, quantity, and force of enunciation. Thus stress constitutes one of its differentiae.

[7] See the papers of Sapir and Troubetzkoy (fn. 1).

Considerations mentioned above give rise to three fundamental kinds of phonemes, as follows:
1. Sentence phonemes (patterns of sentence prosody)
2. Syllable phonemes (tonemes, tasemes)
3. Self-contained phonemes, phonemes proper
All languages have phonemes of type 3, but may or may not have phonemes of types 1 and 2. English has all three types; French has 1 and 3; Navaho has 2 and 3; Nitinat has only type 3. Of course, it is impossible to speak without prosody, but unless a prosodic feature has some contrastive significance, it is not phonemic. Thus, Nitinat has a very noticeable melody, but there is generally speaking only one melody which then is a concomitant of the sentence. In Navaho, the succession of syllable tones gives the effect of a sentence melody, but this melody has no significance of its own.

Word Structure

Each language has a characteristic word and syllable structure. Some of the limitations of occurrence of phonemes are best accounted for as connected with principles of word structure. Thus in Chitimacha all words begin in a single consonant followed immediately by a vowel. In Nootka a monosyllabic word may end in a consonant or a long vowel, but never in a short vowel. Any language will be found to have a whole set of such rules.

The limits of the word are often marked in special ways. Phonemes may have a special variant for the beginning or end of words. Thus the aspirate stops of Chitimacha are unaspirated at the end of the word; at the beginning of the word they are more fully aspirated than at the beginning of a medial or final syllable. Again, the limits of the word may be indicated by some non-phonemic element like the word accent of Latin or Polish, the initial glottal stop in German, or the aspiration that follows a final vowel in Nitinat. Such elements are not phonemes, but mechanical signs of the limits of the word units.

The sentence too may have characterizing phonetic features. A common mark of the sentence is the pause.

Method

The phonemes of a language can be discovered only by inductive procedure. This going from particular instances to general conception is as characteristic of the unconscious process of a native acquiring his language as it must be of conscious scientific study. But the scientist studying an alien language will make more rapid progress if he understands the essential details of the inductive process involved. A useful set of criteria, which follow from the nature of the phoneme, is given below. It should be remembered that they apply to any single given language, not to all languages taken together.

1. The criterion of consistency of words. Except for word variants (see above, second page) different occurrences of the same word have the same phonemic make-up. If differences are observed in different pronunciations of the same word, these are to be taken as showing the range of deviation of the component phonemes.

2. The criterion of partial identities. By a thorough-going comparison of all sets of words having a phonetic resemblance (e.g., pit–bit, late–latent, etc.), one arrives at a notion of the significant elemental sound types. But in the application of this criterion one must bear in mind the one given next.

3. The criterion of constant association. If a set of phonetic elements only occur together, they constitute a phonemically unitary complex; thus, the stop and the aspiration in English initial p. One or both of the phonetic elements may recur in other complexes without affecting the unitary nature of the complexes; in this event, all the phonemes that involve a given phonetic element constitute a phonemic class.

4. The criterion of complementary distribution. If it is true of two similar types of sounds that only one of them normally occurs in certain phonetic surroundings and that only the other normally occurs in certain other phonetic surroundings, the two may be sub-types of the same phoneme. If the distribution of one type of sound is complementary to that of more than one other, it is to be identified with one rather than the other if there is a more definite phonetic similarity in that direction; an example is the p of English speech whose distribution is complementary to that of the voiced labial b as well as to that of the voiceless labial stop sounds of peak, keep, happen, but goes with the latter rather than the former because of the phonetic similarity. If a sound in a relation of complementary distribution to two sounds is not particularly similar to either of them, it has to be reckoned as phonemically independent.

5. The criterion of pattern congruity. Particular formulations must be congruous with the general phonemic pattern of the given language. Thus, although Navaho i (occurring only after consonants) and y (occurring only before vowels) are complementary in distribution, they are nevertheless independent phonemes because of the fact that Navaho is generally characterized by a sharp distinction between vowel and consonant. (As a matter of fact, any vowel would be found to be in complementary distribution to almost any consonant.) In another language, non-syllabic and syllabic i might be positional variants of the same phoneme.

Throughout the phonemic study of a language, one may frequently employ with profit:

6. The test of substitution. This consists in pronouncing a word with some modification in one of the phonemes. If the modification cannot be perceived by a native, it is within the range of normal deviation. If the modification seems to trouble the native, it is an extreme deviation from the norm, a distortion. If the native definitely hears some other word or feels that one has the word wrong, one may conclude that the modification has amounted to the substitution of one phoneme for another.

Since the phonemic facts may be dependent on position in the word and the sentence, it is necessary always to determine the limits of the word and the sentence and the phonetic and phonemic peculiarities of the word and the sentence as units.

Discovering the phonemes is the first step in the phonemic study of a language. The second step consists in defining the nature of each phoneme in terms of 1) its norm and range of deviation for each position in which it may occur; 2) its positional distribution. One may also study its frequency, though this is somewhat less essential. Finally, it is necessary to study the phonemic system in its totality to find the significant classes, sub-classes, and cross-classes into which the phonemes fall.

Orthography

A phonemic orthography provides the most adequate, economical, and effective method of writing a language. Morphological and grammatical study of a language and the recording of its conclusions looks to orthography as an instrument of fundamental importance. A phonemic alphabet is the only kind that is truly adequate, for it alone represents all the pertinent facts and only the pertinent facts. Each sign in a phonemic alphabet represents one phoneme, and the implicit or explicit definition of each sign is an account of the norms (and deviations) of the phoneme in the various positions in which it may occur. If the writing is entirely in keeping with the phonemics of the language, a mechanical substitution of the values of the signs for the signs will reproduce the recorded forms correctly and completely.

Even in the problem of phonemics itself, orthography is a valuable technique. Indeed, the problem of ascertaining the phonemes of a language may be stated in large part in terms of the devising and defining of a set of symbols that will represent the sounds of the language most adequately and most economically. The test of an adequate phonemic writing is that it be possible for one who does not know the meaning of the words to read them off correctly and without serious distortions (it is assumed in this that the reader has made himself familiar with the key to the system and that he has learned to produce the required sounds). The test of an economical phonemic writing is that it employ as few and as simple signs as possible. However, these tests are insufficient in some details of the choice of signs for sound-types of complementary distribution; this matter is explained above (criterion 4).

Where convenient, the phonemic symbols should be made to reflect the phonemic pattern by having some point of resemblance in the signs for the members of each class of phonemes;[8] such a situation is attained in part when some diacritical mark is used to represent a given feature of differentiation, e.g., Hungarian í, ű, ú, é, ő, ó, á (long vowels),[9] Chitimacha p', t', k', č', c', w', y', m', n', ŋ' (glottalized consonants). Finally, it is important that the symbols be in general accord with those generally in use, except that this consideration is secondary to the two essentials of accuracy and simplicity.

Since the phonemes of different languages are different as to their norms and even more strikingly so as to their positional variants, one might argue that it is necessary to have different symbols for each new language, that the English voiceless labial stop, for example, be written differently from that of French. It is obvious that such a treatment would make linguistic science extremely difficult. It has therefore become conventional to use the same or similar signs in different languages to represent roughly similar phonemes. This method works out perfectly as long as one does not carelessly assume standard or familiar values for given signs wherever they occur.

Normalization

When two or more forms of a word are both correct, two courses are possible, namely, to record the form employed at each given time, or to always write one of the variants. The latter treatment is called normalization. In the case of particular word-variants,[10] normalization would have to be entirely arbitrary and is therefore to be avoided. In the case of optional general variants,[10] it is usually possible to normalize without obscuring the fact of variation. This is possible when one can so define one's symbols that the affected phonemes in such a variation are readable in two ways. For example, one may write äz yu for English 'as you', and indicate as part of the definition of the symbol z that before y it may have the value ž, the y being sometimes then lost; to be complete one may indicate that the variation is usually a function of speed and care of speech, the series being äz yu, äž yu, äžu (not to speak of äžə). Similarly, in the case of phonemic interchange, one may write the distinctive form and mention the interchange in the definition of the phonemic symbol.

8 An ideal working out of this principle would give us a phonemic 'visible speech' in which each phonemic sign would be a composite of elements each of which would represent one of the class, sub-class, and cross-class differentiae or sets of differentiae of the phoneme. However, such an orthography might prove impractical for other reasons.

9 ű and ő represent long ü and ö respectively.

10 See the second page of this paper.

Phonetics

Phonetics (the science of the study of speech sounds) benefits the student of phonemics in two ways. First, it is valuable in the discovery of the phonemes of a foreign language. Secondly, it provides the technique for study and description of the phonemes once they are known.

At the outset of one's study of a foreign language, it is convenient to make a phonetic record based on aural observation and written in terms of a general phonetic alphabet which provides symbols for selected characteristic points in the total range of possible speech sounds. As one continues to work with a language, one replaces the strict phonetic alphabet with a tentative phonemic alphabet which is then corrected from time to time until one arrives at a final, adequate phonemic orthography. A certain number of linguists feel that a phonetic orthography is in itself sufficient, and some even hold that a phonemic orthography is incorrect. However, as I have shown, a phonemic writing (together with its key giving the value of the signs employed) records all the pertinent phonetic facts. A phonetic writing, on the other hand, is lacking in the following ways:

1. It does not indicate the phonetic units that are significant for the given language.
2. It is overly microscopic, complex, and hard to handle.
3. It does not distinguish errors and distortions from normal forms.
4. It is likely to be phonetically inaccurate.

On the last point, I quote Bloomfield (Language 84–5):

Practical phoneticians sometimes acquire great virtuosity in discriminating and reproducing all manner of strange sounds. In this, to be sure, there lies some danger for linguistic work. Having learned to discriminate many kinds of sounds, the phonetician may turn to some language, new or familiar, and insist on recording all the distinctions he has learned to discriminate, even when in this language they are nondistinctive and have no bearing whatever ... The chief objection to this procedure is its inconsistency. The phonetician's equipment is personal and accidental; he hears those acoustic features which are discriminated in the languages he has observed. Even his most 'exact' record is bound to ignore innumerable non-distinctive features of sound; the ones that appear in it are selected by accidental and personal factors. There is no objection to a linguist's describing all the acoustic features that he can hear, provided he does not confuse these with the phonemic features. He should remember that his hearing of non-distinctive features depends upon the accident of his personal equipment, and that his most elaborate account cannot remotely approach the value of a mechanical record.

Furthermore, in the extreme concentration required for minute discrimination of certain features of sound, the phonetician may easily overlook other features that may be of prime importance in the given language.

Some linguists employ a normative phonetic writing in preference to either phonemic or strict phonetic writing. If the interpretation of actual sounds in terms of the norms of the language is correct and if the correction of errors is made without error, a normative phonetic orthography shares some of the advantage of a phonemic orthography. Simplification of the phonetic writing of a given language is also an improvement in the general direction of phonemic writing. As a matter of fact a phonemic orthography is the inevitable result if normalization and simplification are carried out thoroughly, consistently, and correctly.

Historical Phonology

In determining the phonemic system of a language, only phonetic data are relevant. Historical phonology is not relevant. To base one's spelling of a word on the form of the word in a known or reconstructed parent language neither benefits historical study of language nor provides a dependable method of accurate phonemic analysis. Historical etymology in a matter of phonemics is an acceptable aid only when one is dealing with an inadequately recorded non-contemporary language. Of course, phonemes are a historical product and a step in a historical development, but to argue from phonetic law to descriptive fact is discovering the arguments from the conclusion when the procedure should always be the opposite.

The fact that a phonemic system is a step in historical development suggests that one way to understand historical change is to understand phonemics more fully.[11] On the basis of facts pointed out in this paper and on the basis of some simple truths about historical phonetic change, one may make the following suggestions. Phonetic change must consist in the change of the norm of a sound or one of its positional variants. Change in a phonemic norm does not affect the actual phonemic pattern unless the phoneme thereby comes to coincide with some other phoneme or splits up into more than one phoneme. The intermediate step in coalescence of phonemes is the condition of phonemic interchange. The intermediate step in the split-up of a phoneme is the presence of markedly different positional variants; in this situation, if, through analogy or borrowing of foreign words one of the variants comes to be employed in positions other than within its original limits, it takes on the character of an independent phoneme. I shall not illustrate these processes, since the matter is only incidental to my subject; instances are to be found everywhere where we have an actual record of a historical change.

11 This important incidental value of phonemics was called to my attention by Professor Sapir.

Morpho-phonology

Morpho-phonology includes, in addition to the study of the phonemic structure of morphemes, the study of interchange between phonemes as a morphological process. If a given morphologic interchange is sufficiently regular and characteristic, the interchanging phonemes may be regarded as a morphologically unitary set. Examples are Indo-European e/o/ē/ō/zero, English f/v (in, e.g., leaf, leaves). Whether it is a convenient fiction or a true reflection of linguistic psychology, morphological processes are usually described as having a definite order. Leaves is taken to be a secondary formation from leaf, and in consequence v is the mutation of f and not f that of v. But f does not always change to v in the morphological process of plural formation; thus, we have cuff, cuffs. The f of cuff is therefore morphologically different from the f of leaf, though phonemically it is the same entity. Morphologically, we have two f's so that $f_1 : v :: f_2 : f$. Morphologically distinct phonemes are called morpho-phonemes.

A morpho-phoneme is one of a class of like phonemes considered as components of actual morphemes which behave alike morphologically, i.e., have a like place in the same mutation series. The morpho-phoneme is never to be confused with the phoneme as such, even in the event that all instances of a given phoneme are members of the same morpho-phonemic class. One may devise a morphologic writing for use in morphological discussion or in a dictionary, but such a writing is not to be employed in ordinary linguistic records.[12]

The phonemic principle when properly understood provides the only completely consistent and adequate method of understanding the nature of the phonetics of a given language. Phonetics provides the technique of discovering and defining the phonemes. Morphology includes a study of the phonemic structure of morphemes and of morphological interrelations among phonemes as components of morphemes. Historical phonology studies the evolution of phonemes. In these ways phonemics interrelates with other phases of linguistic science, but it does not compete with these other phases. In developing the phonemic principle, its proponents are only bringing into plain view a hitherto imperfectly lighted area in which there has always been a certain amount of stumbling.

12 Of course there are instances where it is desirable to use non-phonemic diacritical marks as a special aid to non-native students.

THE NON-UNIQUENESS OF PHONEMIC
SOLUTIONS OF PHONETIC SYSTEMS

YUEN-REN CHAO

Bulletin of the Institute of History and Philology
Academia Sinica, Vol. IV, Part 4, 363–97—1934

In reading current discussions on the transcription*
of sounds by phonemes, one gets the impression of a
tacit assumption that given the sounds of one language,
there will be one and only one way of reducing them
to a system of phonemes which represent the sound-
system correctly. Since different writers do not in
fact agree in the phonemic treatment of the same
language, there arise then frequent controversies
over the 'correctness' or 'incorrectness' in the use
of phonemes.

The main purpose of the present paper is to show
that given the sounds of a language, there are usually
more than one possible way of reducing them to a
system of phonemes, and that these different systems or solutions are not simply correct or incorrect, but may be regarded only as being good or bad
for various purposes.

I. DEFINITIONS OF A PHONEME

The most comprehensive discussion of the phoneme and related ideas seems to be that by H. E.
Palmer,[1] of which we shall now give a brief summary. Palmer begins by quoting at length Jimbo's
writing on 'The Concrete and Abstract Nature of
Sounds:' 'One concrete sound has one definite quality, one definite pitch, one definite loudness, one
definite length,' in other words, it corresponds to
one particular oscillograph curve or stretch of the
groove of a faithful phonograph record, which is
therefore not the usual object of study for phonetics.
By collecting examples of actual utterances of what
is considered the same word with the same meaning
by speakers of the same language of concrete sounds,
one arrives at 'an abstract sound of the first degree',
such as the first sound in the word army. By comparing different words such as army, archer, art,
argue, one concludes, after due examination, that the
first sound in these words are 'the same', which is
then 'an abstract sound of the second degree'.

Taking Palmer's own system, we note that he
finds it more convenient to replace the term abstract
speech-sound by the term phone. His system of
phones is then as follows:

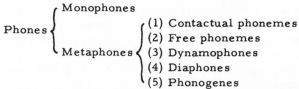

A Monophone is 'any phone of the first or second
degree of abstraction of which the concrete members
are so similar in point of production and of acoustic
effect even when observed by a competent observer,
that it may be regarded as a minimal unit of pronunciation (i.e. practically insusceptible of subdivision).'
(We may add: 'or of further differentiation'.) 'Contrasted with monophones we have metaphones, which
we may define as two or more phones which serve
jointly as units of meaning within the limits of a
given linguistic community.'

(1) Palmer goes on to identify Jones's definition
of a phoneme with his idea of a contactual phoneme:
'A phoneme is a group of sounds consisting of an important sound of the language (i.e. the most frequently
used member of that group) together with others
which take its place in particular sound-groups....
The use of subsidiary members of phonemes is, in
most languages, determined by simple principles
which can be stated once for all, and which can be
taken for granted in reading phonetic texts.'

(2) A free phoneme is like a contactual phoneme
except that it is impossible to say in what phonetic
circumstances' one or another of its members will
be actually used. We can give the apparently random[2]
use of the tip or back of the tongue in the nasal ending of words like 林 [lin ∿ liŋ], 明 [min ∿ miŋ] in
Nanking as an example of free phonemes. This is the
same as Jones's variphone.

(3) A dynamophone is a metaphone which contains
two or more phones differing not only in quality, but
also in regard to the intensity or force of the articulation that produces them. Palmer cites the first
phone in the word as as an example which shades
from the first phone of act to the obscure sound of
the first phone of about, and even to zero value.

It would seem convenient also to include under
this heading those metaphones whose members differ according to conditions of length and intonation
(in which case a term wider than dynamophone will
have to be used). Thus, the vowel in French bette and
bête is a metaphone whose members differ slightly
in quality according to the conditions of length.

---

*Since this was written at a time when the differ-
ences between transcription and phonemicization and
between phonemes and morphophonemes were not as
clear as they are today, the article would have to be
reworded in many places if these differences were to
be taken into account. In this reprint no attempt was
made to make such changes, except to correct minor
errors of fact.—Y. R. C.

[1] H. E. Palmer, The Principles of Romanization,
1931, Tokyo, pp. 52 ff.

[2] That is, determined by psychological or physiological conditions other than those which usually are
considered to be phonetic.

Those who transcribe eat, it as [iːt], [it] are also considering the vowel in these words as forming one metaphone whose members differ in quality according to conditions of length. Again, the vowel in the Foochow words 哥 [kɔ55ː] and 個 [kɔˇ12ː] is a metaphone whose members differ in quality according as the intonation belongs to one or the other of two sets of tones.

Before taking up the next two terms, it will be well to examine a later definition of a phoneme given by Jones: 'Definition of a phoneme: a family of sounds in a given language which are related in character and are such that no one of them ever occurs in the same surroundings as any other in words.' (The term 'language' here means the pronunciation of one individual speaking in a definite style. 'In the same surroundings' means surrounded by the same sounds and in the same condition as regards length, stress and intonation.'[3]) This definition differs from the earlier one quoted above in that it no longer mentions a 'principal member', but specifies that the different members should be 'related in character' and that no two of them should occur 'in the same surroundings as regards length, stress and intonation'. It seems therefore that Jones's conception of a phoneme includes not only Palmer's contactual phonemes, but also some at least of his dynamophones.

(4) The term diaphone is used by Palmer following the usage of Jones: 'The diaphone is a family of sounds heard when we compare the speech of one person with that of another.' Jones cites [oː], [ou], [əu], [ʌu] as members of the diaphone occurring in words like coat, road, home. Similarly, we can cite [ɑu], [ou], [əu], [ɤ], [ɯ], [øy], [ei], [ɪ] as members of the diaphone occurring in words like 歐 'Europe', 狗 'dog', 後 'after'.

(5) The phonogene, a term also proposed by Jones, is 'a given phone together with its ancestral forms,' thus the vowel [ou] in stone, together with [o], [ɔ], [ɑ] form a phonogene. Similarly, [ɚ], [əɹ], [ɻ], [ɹi], [ʑi], [ɲʑi], [ɲi], [ni] form one phonogene in words like 兒 'child', 耳 'ear', 二 'two'.

Bloomfield gives no formal definition of a phoneme. He begins by distinguishing the 'gross acoustic features' of language (Jimbo's 'concrete sounds' or sounds of low degrees of abstraction) and 'distinctive' or 'significant features'. By comparing the partial identities and differences between words like pin, tin, tan, tack, he succeeds in analyzing the distinctive features of words like pin into indivisible units which cannot be analyzed any further (from the standpoint of the language under investigation): each of these units is 'a minimum unit of distinctive sound-feature, a phoneme,'[4] which phrase is the

nearest Bloomfield comes to a formal definition of a phoneme.

Differences of quality conditioned by length are grouped by Bloomfield under the same phoneme, as German Beet [beːt], Bett [bet]. He also writes hatte ['hatə], where the stress on the first syllable indicates sufficiently the weakened and obscure value of the second vowel. Bloomfield's phoneme therefore also includes Palmer's dynamophones.

Bloomfield makes no explicit mention of free phonemes or variphones. In cases like the apparently random use of final [n] and [ŋ] in some Chinese dialects for the same word in the same phonetic surroundings, he would probably consider simple nasality as being the distinctive feature and the place of articulation as among the gross acoustic features. In other words, variphones are also phonemes, except that the choice of the exact shade of the sound used is determined by psychological and physiological factors other than those of phonetic environment. Since, however, whether variation of sounds determined by non-phonetic conditions are wide enough to be called two or more 'different' sounds or simply inevitable small 'accidental' variations depends upon the degree of narrowness of the phonetician's scale of division, Bloomfield is within his rights in neglecting the existence of variphones.[5]

From the preceding, it may seem that Bloomfield has a different conception of the phoneme from that of Jones and Palmer. For Jones and Palmer, a phoneme is a group of sounds, while for Bloomfield it is a sound-feature. If, however, we examine the two ideas more closely, we shall find that they amount to the same thing. Take for example the English phoneme [h]. From one point of view, we may say that it is a group of different sounds [h_i], [h_e], [h_a], [h_u], etc., where the subscripts are an indication of the tongue and lip positions during the pronunciation of the consonant. But from the other point of view we may just as well say that the phoneme [h] is simply the feature of voiceless glottal friction and leave the other non-significant features unspecified. There is therefore no real difference in the use of the term phoneme by those writers, so far as this point is concerned.

For the present discussion, we shall group together Palmer's contactual phoneme, free phoneme, and dynamophone, all under the term phoneme, to be defined as follows:

A phoneme is one of an exhaustive list of classes of sounds in a language,[6] such that every word in the language can be given as an ordered series of one or more of these classes and such that two different

3 Proceedings of the International Congress of Phonetic Sciences, 1932, Amsterdam, p. 23.
4 Leonard Bloomfield, Language, 1933, New York, p. 79.
5 See however III below on the finiteness of the number of distinguishable speech sounds.
6 Taken in the sense of the pronunciation of a homogeneous speech community, such that members of the same community will find absolutely no 'accent' in one another's speech.

words which are not considered as having the same pronunciation differ in the order or in the constituency of the classes which make up the word.

Observations:

(1) This definition presupposes that it is possible to enumerate exhaustively the total number of phonemes for any given language.

(2) It does not exclude the possibility of the same sound belonging to more than one class (Cf. II 2 (f), (g) below).

(3) It is non-committal as to whether given a language, there is one unique way for grouping its sounds into phonemes or there are other possible ways.

(4) It leaves unspecified the scope of the word 'sound' as regards size and kind, i.e. the degree of analysis into successive elements and the degree of differentiation into kinds.

(5) It includes both the cases where, given the phonemes in a word and its phonetic environment, it is possible to determine the actual pronunciation of the word by a set of 'rules of pronunciation' (i.e. to know which member-sounds of sound-classes will actually be used) and those cases where a given word in a given phonetic environment may still contain a phoneme of which one or another member may be used. The former will be a contactual phoneme or a dynamophone and the latter a free phoneme. (This remark, however, would be superfluous if we repudiate the validity of descriptive phonetics, with its narrow transcriptions.)

(6) The clause that every word consists of a series of 'classes' may sound a little strange. But if, as is convenient in the study of languages, we speak of recognizable words consisting of recognizable phonemes, then such phonemes are usually classes of sounds, which a trained ear would distinguish as different sounds. The statement sounds no more strange than that 1, 2, 3, 4 are a series of classes, which is what mathematicians define numbers as.

(7) If each phoneme is written with one definite symbol, then every word will have a definite form of transcription. Homophones, or different words having the same pronunciation, will be transcribed alike. It should be noted, however, that the boundary between a homophone and a word with variations in meaning is often hard to determine.

(8) A phonemic transcription is pronounceable without reference to grammatical or lexical consideration. Thus, the Chinese National Phonetic Script and the National Romanization are phonemic transcriptions in a sense in which English or even German orthography is not.

II. FACTORS WHICH INFLUENCE THE PHONEMIC SOLUTIONS OF PHONETIC SYSTEMS

As the grouping of sounds in a language into phonemes as defined above does not necessarily lead to one unique solution, we shall now consider the various factors which influence the form of the solutions.

1. Size of Unit in Time.

(a) Under-analysis. In the early days of phonetic transcription, the slogan was 'one sound, one symbol'. In these days of phonemic transcription, this has been changed to 'one phoneme, one symbol', so that it is now permissible to represent more than one sound by one symbol.

But there are two aspects to the idea of 'one sound'. From the point of view of differentiation of quality, 'one sound' is one kind of sound, which is what one usually has in mind when using the phrase in discussions about phonemes. But from the point of view of analysis in time, 'one sound' is one piece of sound, such that its quality is homogeneous throughout its duration. Discussions about phonemes do not seem to have been very explicit about the change of quality in time which may be included within the scope of one phoneme. We recall that Palmer defines a monophone 'as a minimal unit of pronunciation (i. e. practically insusceptible of further subdivision)'. All the preceding discussions in the passage quoted have to do with the question of differentiation, but as the words 'minimal' and 'subdivision' can also be taken in the temporal sense, it would seem that a monophone should be both one kind of sound and one piece of sound.

Now if it is convenient to group into classes and call phonemes different kinds of sounds in a language which go together in a certain way, it would also be convenient to join into compounds successive pieces of sounds which act as units in a language. This is by no means new practice. Our point here is only to make it explicit and put it on a par with the differential aspect of phonemes.

All kinetic speech-sounds, diphthongs, affricates, aspirates, and other sounds with their usual glides are compounds which act as units and can be treated as phonemes. Thus, Bloomfield considers the English affricates [č] and [ǰ] as independent phonemes. The English plosives [p], [t], [k] are treated by all writers as single phonemes, although in initial stressed positions they have a slight aspiration and have a larger size than in unstressed positions or after [s] (in [sp-], [st-], [sk-]). In the former case, the inclusion of [č] and [ǰ] is optional, for these could be resolved into the phonemes [tʃ] and [dʒ] respectively. In cases like he cheats [hiː ˈtʃiːts], heat sheets [hiːt ˈʃiːts]; What can each add? [...iːtʃ ˈæd], What can eat shad? [...iːt ˈʃæd], the distinction may either be made by considering [č] and [tš] as different phonemes, as with Bloomfield, or simply by the difference in the position of the minimum point, as with most other writers; that is to say, since the [č] in each add and the [tʃ] in eat shad never occur under the same conditions as regards stress, [č] need not be considered as a separate phoneme. In many Chinese dialects, the initial [k] always occurs before low front vowels or central or back vowels, and initials of the [tɕ] type always occur before high front vowels. The two may therefore be taken as the same phoneme, although the latter is an affricate. Similarly, the [t] in [ta] ㄉ , the [tɕ] in [tɕi] ㄐ and the [ts] in [tsɯ] ㄗ in Japanese may be taken as belonging to one phoneme.

Kinetic sounds of the diphthong type need special consideration. While affricates, aspirates and sounds with characteristic glides can usually be analyzed, if desired, into two or three recognizable elements, kinetic vowels and quasi-vowels are sounds with even more gradual change in quality. The usual method of representing these sounds is simply to indicate the two end-positions of the whole movement, as [ei], or to indicate the open position and the extreme close position even though never actually reached, as [ai] for what is actually never wider than [ae]. In the case of movement not by the most direct line, the turning point is indicated by inserting an additional symbol, as [uei], but not [aou], as [au] means [aou] or [aɔou].

Now by our definition of a phoneme, there is nothing to prevent us from regarding characteristic kinetic open sounds in a language as independent phonemes, which is in fact the practice of the designers of the Chinese National Phonetic Script, who represent [ai], [ei], [ɑu], [ou] by the single symbols ㄞ ㄟ ㄠ ㄡ, and even [an], [ən], [ɑŋ], [əŋ] by ㄢ ㄣ ㄤ ㄥ. It may seem unorthodox to take the National Phonetic Script as serious phonemic transcription, but we should be less sure of ourselves when we come to cases of narrow-range kinetic sounds. There is a real difference in practice, if not of opinion, between Bloomfield's use of [ij] and [uw] for English and other writers' use of [i:] and [u:], as contrasted with [i] and [u]; or of [i] and [u] (with implied relative length) as contrasted with [ɪ] and [ʊ]. Again, in many American dialects, it is a toss-up whether to write bet, bait as [bet], [beit] or as [bet], [be:t], or [bɛt], [bet] (with implied length). The most interesting case of the size-of-unit question is that of the Foochow dialect, where a whole series of vowels in the same words are static or kinetic according to the tone in which each is pronounced. Thus, 氣 [k'ei 12:] 'air', 竹 [tøyk 23:] 'bamboo', 護 [hou 242:] 'protect', take on the following sounds when they are pronounced in the following combinations of tonal environment: 氣壓 [k'i 53: ɑk 23:] 'air pressure', 竹節 [ty 5: žaik 23:] 'bamboo section', and 護兵 [hu 55: ˙viŋ 55:] 'guards' (protecting soldiers), respectively. We have therefore on our hands the question of choice between (1) admitting phonemes of

which some members are static and other members kinetic vowels, or diphthongs, and (2) regarding the static members as forming one phoneme and the corresponding kinetic vowels as two phonemes in succession, thus allowing the same word to have two forms. The presence and absence of the aspiration in English [p], [t], [k] mentioned above is also a similar case, though not so striking.

Another very peculiar case is that of a vowel in a concave circumflex tone in a number of Chinese dialects, such as the yangshaang tone of Hwangyan, Chekiang, where the valley is so low or simply so narrow that the voice is lost into a glottal stop in the middle of the syllable, so that [ɔ 313:] actually becomes [ɔ31: ʔɔ3:]. Phonetically, it sounds like three sounds forming two syllables. But phonemically, it is much more natural to consider it as a form of [ɔ] in a certain tone.

On the whole, the usual practice allows a great deal of latitude in taking kinetic consonants as single phonemes, but is not so free in giving single symbols for kinetic vowels. Bloomfield gives a list of eight diphthongs and one triphthong for English, and calls them 'compound primary phonemes', all their elements occurring also as single primary phonemes. [1955 note: The word 'primary' does not affect this discussion; it was simply Bloomfield's word for our 'segmental' phonemes—the vowels and consonants.]

The chief point we wish to emphasize here is that it is not always advisable or convenient to take the smallest static unit of sound analyzable by the trained ear as the unit of phonemic members ('one piece sound, one symbol'), and that according as we take a smaller or a larger unit for our phonemic members, we sometimes arrive at different forms of phonemic pattern for the same language, which are equally valid, though they may not be equally suitable for this or that purpose.

(b) Over-analysis. The principle of 'one piece sound, one symbol' has yet to allow a class of exceptions in the opposite direction, namely, one piece sound, two or three piece symbols. Jones and Camilli give the following cases where combinations of letters are permitted to represent single phonemes:[7]

a) The affricates [pf], [bv], [ts], [dz], [tʃ], [dʒ], [tɕ], etc.

b) The aspirates [ph], [th], [kh], [tlh], [tʃh], etc., and weak aspirates [p'], [t'], etc.

c) The aspirated [s] or [sh].

d) [t], [d] with lateral explosions: [tl], [dl].

e) The voiceless nasals, [hm], [hn], [hɲ], [hŋ], when these are distinct phonemes.

f) Retroflex vowels, as American [əɹ], or Peiping [ɨɹ]. [[Chao quoted Jones's '[uɹ]'.]]

g) Labiovelar consonants: [kp], [gb].

---

[7] Fondamenti di Grafia Fonetica, by Daniel Jones and Amerindo Camilli, 1933, Aube and London, 11–12.

Of these cases, a) and b) are recognizably compound sounds, which we should consider as two or three piece sounds, for which the use of [tʃ], [dʒ], [ph], [th], etc. would be considered as normal and the use of [č], [ǰ], (or [c], [ɟ]), [p], [t], etc. would be considered as cases of under-analysis. c) and d) may be regarded as borderline cases. e), f), and g) are clear cases of over-analysis, that is, cases of one homogeneous sound represented by two or three piece symbols, each of which represents some aspect or aspects of the sound.[8] Thus, [hm] is a [m]-sound which is breathed (i.e. [h]-ized) or a [h]-sound with labio-nasal articulation (i.e. [m]-ized). It is meaningless to ask which is the substantive and which the adjective, as they are all constituting attributes which together form the sound in question and could be represented by Jespersen's over-analytical analphabetic symbols. Similarly, American [ɚ] is a single vowel formed by the middle of the tongue in the [ə] position with the apex curled back (sometimes transcribed as [ɚ]). The representation of voiceless [w] or [ʍ] by [hw] is another case, which is mentioned by Jones and Camilli under an earlier section in the same pamphlet quoted.[9]

Among the uses of diacritical marks, Jones and Camilli[10] mention 'the saving of a series of new letters,' such as adding ~ to [ɑ], [ɔ], [œ], [ɛ], to form [ɑ̃], [ɔ̃], [œ̃], [ɛ̃] in transcribing French. The reader will recall the great furore which was aroused by Passy's proposal to use [ɑŋ], [ɔŋ], [œŋ], [ɛŋ] for these French vowels in the first post-war issues of Le maître phonétique. He modestly called it orthographic transcription; but if [ɚ] can represent [ɚ], there is no reason why [ɑŋ] cannot represent [ɑ̃]. To object that other French dialects or German actually has [ɑŋ] as two successive sounds is beside the point, as we are talking about phonemic transcriptions and our universe of discourse is limited to one dialect or one language, otherwise we should have to go back to narrow phonetic transcriptions. Not that [ɑŋ] is the only right way or even a good way of representing French [ɑ̃], but there seems to be nothing wrong, so far as usage in other cases goes, with representing one piece sound by two piece symbols.

Jones and Camilli do another thing along the same line. Without mentioning the saving of a series of modified letters under any of the principles, they also use the device of representing one piece sound by two piece symbols in transcribing the Russian palatalized consonants, where the explanatory note says, 'j is used as the sign of palatalization, that is, tj = ţ, nj = ņ, lj = ļ, snj = sņ, tnj = tņ, lnj = lņ,

etc.'[11] This [j] is therefore a significant feature, but it does not necessarily occupy any time of its own.

Another important case is that of the 'voiced h', which plays a very important part in the Wu-dialects in China. These dialects usually have an ordinary [h], which has different values according to the vowel following and may therefore be taken as one phoneme, just as in the case of English or German, so that instead of having $2n$ symbols for h_1a_1, h_2a_2, ... h_na_n (where a_1, a_2, ... a_n are the vowels which may follow the h in the language), we need only $n+1$ symbols for ha_1, ha_2, ... ha_n. But in the case of the voiced h, not only the vowel quality (or the vowel articulation) begins at the very beginning of the breathing, but the breathiness also lasts till the very last moment of the vowel, so as to form one homogeneous breathy vowel, and there is neither question of order of succession nor question of substantive and adjective. If we must have one piece symbol for one piece sound, we should have to have either a series of different voiced h symbols for different vowels, or an extra series of breathy vowels have to be recognized. The only practical thing to do here is to consider voiced h as one phoneme and write the vowel symbols after it as [ɦɑ], [ɦe], [ɦo], etc., although we know that these digraphs represent perfectly homogeneous sounds.

There are also borderline cases where it is open to question whether certain sound-elements are simultaneous or successive. According to ordinary transcriptions, the English word sway is transcribed as [swei] while the Chinese word 歲 'year' is transcribed as [suei], from which it would seem that the first two elements in Chinese 歲 would be separated more clearly than in English sway. As a matter of fact, the contrary is the case. While the [s] in English sway is not at all labialized for most of its duration, the [s] in Chinese 歲 is completely labialized. Moreover, the diphthong [ei] starts almost as soon as the tongue leaves the [s]-position without leaving any appreciable duration for the [u] or [w] to stand alone, so that a narrow transcription might give 歲 as [ʂei] or, as the velar element is rather weak in this type of word, as [σei]. But in similar syllables in other tones or with other initial consonants, there is more independence in the [u]-element. It would be contrary to the spirit of phonemic transcription to write 歲 as [σei] and 對 as [tuei]. Consequently, we must allow as a possible phonemic 'solution' the over-analysis of [σ] into two phonemes [su] or [sw], and so long as our universe of discourse is Chinese (Mandarin) phonemes, we should not be disturbed by the fact that [sw] in English is a succession of two sounds in which [s] is little or not at all [w]-ized.

From the consideration of these cases of under-analysis and over-analysis, we see the great advan-

---

8 G. M. Bolling must have overlooked such cases when he said, 'At least I can recall no example of... a digraph for a non-compound phoneme,' in an editorial note on R. G. Kent's review of Bloomfield's Language in the journal Language, X, 1, 1934, pp. 51–52.

9 Fondamenti, p. 11, section 15.

10 Fondamenti, p. 4, section 3.

11 Fondamenti, p. 17.

tage of Bloomfield's speaking of sound-features instead of sounds. If we consider a sound as made of a number of features, then a phoneme is a combination of certain (simultaneous and/or successive) features, leaving other features unspecified. The English [t]-phoneme, for instance, consists of the features of voicelessness, apico-alveolar articulation of a certain range (eighth, tea, tray), and complete stop of breath, while the exact position of articulation, the force of stopping, the nature of on-glides (heat, hoot) and off-glides (tar, star, tea, two, little, button, but) are left unspecified. The Chinese [u]-phoneme consists of the features of lip-narrowing, a slight velar action, and voice, and as the position of the tip of the tongue is left unspecified, it is perfectly free to form the [s]-articulation while the [u]-articulation is being held, so that we can entertain the idea of two phonemes [s] and [u] being telescoped into one single sound [σ] without necessarily considering the sound [σ] as one new phoneme or as one member of a new phoneme. Similarly, the [ɦ]-phoneme in the Wu-dialects consists of the feature of emitting more air than usual in producing voice, and as it does not specify anything about the oral or nasal features of articulation, the speaker is free to do all kinds of articulatory tricks at the same time with [ɦ],[12] so that there is an [a] type of [ɦ], an [e] type of [ɦ], etc., and even an [m] type of [ɦ], as [ɦm̩] 'have not', as contrasted with [m̩] in [m̩-ma] 'mother', and yet all this does not prevent us from considering the [ɦ] and [a] in [ɦa] as two theoretically separate phonemes.

(c) Zero Symbols.[13] As limiting cases of the variation in size of unit, we have the possibility of using zero symbol for sounds or sound-features and of counting absence of sound as a phoneme or as one member of a phoneme.

Where there are several degrees of significant stress, significant length, or kinds of significant intonation, it is the usual practice to represent one of them by zero symbol. Thus, unmarked syllables in polysyllabic English words are understood to have the low degrees of stress. Vowels without length marks are understood to be short. In most systems

12 There is a trick recitation in one of the dialects near Nanking in the form of a story consisting mostly of phrases like 鵝 對 鴨 [ŋɔ tuei ŋa?] 'goose versus duck', in which a flapped click is made with the front of the tongue each time [ŋ] is pronounced. The effect is that of beating a pair of clapping boards as an independent rhythmic accompaniment to the recitation. In other words, the [ŋ]-phoneme consists of the features of voice, nasality, and articulation with the back of the tongue. The front of the tongue can do as it pleases.

13 Under this heading, we are not including cases like ancient Hebrew, in which the vowels were not written. For in this system of writing, the vowels cannot be deduced from the phonetic environment alone by any set of phonetic rules. The writing is therefore an orthography and not a transcription.

of tone-marking, the first tone in Chinese is 'marked' by not marking it.

In the Chinese syllables [tʂɻ], [tʂʻɻ], [ʂɻ], [ʐɻ], [tsɿ], [tsʻɿ], [sɿ],[14] there is a vowel which is a vocalized prolongation of the preceding consonant, and it is understood to be present when these syllables are written in the standard way, that is with the consonantal symbols standing alone: 出, 彳, 尸, 日, 卩, ち, 厶, in the National Phonetic Script. This is therefore a way of representing actual sounds by zero symbol.

In German stressed syllables beginning orthographically with a vowel, there is normally a glottal stop. Some writers give the symbol [ʔ] for this sound, but others omit the symbol, and in internal positions, as in Verein, a stress mark suffices to indicate the presence of the [ʔ], as [fer'ain]. It would be perfectly possible, though hardly conventional, for us to favor some other phoneme with the saving of a symbol, say [h], and transcribe Hauch as [aux] and auch as [ʔaux].

Readers of Bloomfield's Language who are used to ordinary types of transcriptions of English must have been impressed by forms like these on pages 111, 112, 121, 122:

gentleman	['ǰentl̩mn̩]
atom	['ɛtm̩]
maintenance	['mejntn̩s]
maintain	[mn̩'tejn]
stirring	['str̩iŋ] vs. string [striŋ]
pattern	['pɛtr̩n] vs. patron ['pejtrn̩]
erring	['r̩iŋ] vs. ring [riŋ]
error	['err̩]
butter	['botr̩] on a par with bottle ['batl̩]
bottom	['batm̩] on a par with button ['botn̩]
anatomy	[e'nɛtm̩ij] vs. met me [met mij]

Now Bloomfield systematically avoids the use of the obscure vowel letter [ə], and plays his game admirably well. The e in French le he considers as a short variety of [œ] (p. 106), which agrees more or less with the idea of the French themselves. For German, he lets the difference in stress take care of the difference between [e] and [ə]. For American English, he uses the strong forms where there is no following consonant or where the following consonant is not usually considered to be a syllable-carrier in English, but leaves out the symbol entirely in other cases. Now from the point of view of actual sound, weakened orthographically written vowels either become [ə] or disappear entirely. If we take ordinary deliberate conversation as the style of 'language' to consider, we can say, according to the writer's own observation of Middle Western American speech, that the presence or absence of a vocalized [ə] is about as follows:

14 The symbols ɻ and ɿ are Karlgren's.

[ə] compulsory or preferred	[ə] optional	Absence of [ə] compulsory or preferred
arbor [-bər] vs. club rate	happen [-p(ə)n]	able [-bļ]
upper [-pər] vs. upright	often [-f(ə)n]	simple [-pļ]
gentleman [-mən] vs. autumnal	even [-v(ə)n]	dismal [-mļ]
humor [-mər] vs. am ready	bacon [-k(ə)n]	careful [-fļ]
kingdom [-dəm] vs. bed-mate	Winkum [-k(ə)m]	devil [-vļ]
London [-ndən] vs. kindness	Beauchamp [-č(ə)m]	sudden [-dņ]
under [-dər] vs. shad roe	Gresham [-š(ə)m]	middle [-dļ]
atom [-təm] vs. met me	patron [-tr(ə)n]	colonel [-nļ]
pattern [-tərn] vs. outright	Durham [-r(ə)m]	wiggle [-gļ]
maintenance [-nəns] vs. main news	coral [-r(ə)l]	engine [-ǰņ]
Barnum [-nəm] vs. on me	handsome [-s(ə)m]	cordial [-ǰļ]
corner [-nər] vs. Henry	bosom [-z(ə)m]	luncheon [-čņ]
Helen [-lən] vs. hell no	Bentham [θ(ə)m]	celestial [-čļ]
alum [-ləm] vs. elm (but also [eləm])	fathom [-ð(ə)m]	nation [-šņ]
Keller [-lər] vs. all right	lengthen [-θ(ə)n]	special [-šļ]
finger [-gər] vs. big row	heathen [-ð(ə)n]	vision [-žņ]
teacher [-čər] vs. teach right		listen [-sņ]
pleasure [-žər] vs. rouge-red		tassel [-sļ]
error [-rər] vs. her right		dozen [-zņ]
tracer [-sər] vs. viceroy		hazel [-zļ]
Caesar [-zər] vs. phase-rule		Ethel [-θļ]
ether [-θər] vs. Ruth ran		brothel [-ðļ]
father [-ðər] vs. with rum		

Opinions may differ as to the placing of particular cases under each heading, but there seems to be no doubt as to the presence of [ə] in gentleman [-mən] or its absence in able [-bļ]. Historically, as the orthography indicates, many of these words had clear vowels. Now some of them have an obscure vowel even in deliberate speech, which does not however entirely disappear in some cases. Since the presence, option, or absence of the [ə]-sound are more or less determined by the nature of the sounds preceding and following, and sometimes by conditions of syllabication, we can regard this as one phoneme of which one member is the obscure vowel [ə], a second member is a variphone (or dynamophone) consisting of [ə] and zero, and a third member is zero. Bloomfield has therefore as much right to represent this phoneme by zero symbol as one has to represent German [ʔ] by zero symbol. Apparent ambiguities as in the case of string and stirring may be avoided by marking the syllabication: ['stɻiŋ], which will remind us to explode the [t] before the [r], as it is a case of the first member of the phoneme.

It should be noted that our discussion here is to find a methodological justification for Bloomfield's used of zero symbol for an actual sound. There are other considerations from which this avoidance of the symbol [ə] seems rather inconvenient. Thus, when there is no final consonant like [l], [n], etc., to act as a syllable carrier, as in America, suppose, jealous, he is obliged to use exclusively strong forms like [e'merike] or [ɛ'merika], [so'powz], ['ǰelos], which are rarely heard even in deliberate speech (understanding of course that [o] is the 'short

u'). The definite article the will have to be either [ðij] or [ð], with no middle ground. Those who favor Bloomfield's system for English will find that he is simply carrying the omission of [ə] to its logical conclusion. Those who do not will consider forms like ['stɻiŋ], ['mejntņņs], [e'merika] a reductio ad absurdum.

Under cases of under-analysis, we considered the representation of affricates, aspirates, and narrow-range diphthongs by single symbols. Now if the symbol used is obviously one of the elements in the compound, as [p] for [p'], [c] (instead of [č]) for [cɕ], [ɹ] (instead of [ǰ]) for [ɹʑ], or [o] for [ou], then we can regard that element which is understood but not represented as having zero symbol. For instance, in the Soochow dialect, labials go with [ɯ], velars and dentals go with [əu], and alveolars go with an apical vowel with protruding lips, for which the writer has proposed the symbol [ᶙ],[15] as 布 [pɯ], 故 [kəu], 註 [tɕᶙ]. All these can be considered as members of one phoneme [u], in which case the [ə] in [ə u] would be a sound with zero symbol. Again, in the Foochow vowels [u] ∿ [ou], [i] ∿ [ei], [y] ∿ [øy] according to tone, as cited above, it is common practice to consider the first tone, which goes with [i], [u], [y], as basic, so that it is convenient to write these phonemes as [i], [u], [y], in which case a tone mark would suffice to remind one of the addition of [e-], [o-], [ø-] (by no means weak and parasitic), though these elements still have no symbol to themselves except as implied by the tone.

[15] A combination of Karlgren's [ʅ] and [ᶙ].

(d) Zero Sound. In the cases of over-analysis, as in [ɦα], we had two features representing separate phonemes which together make one single sound. But if we take the series [ʉ], [əu], [ʮ] in Soochow and consider them as varieties of [əu], of which the [ə] is absent after labials and alveolars, then under the latter conditions the phoneme [ə] will have zero as a member. Similarly, if we write in the symbol [ə] for maintenance [-nəns], happen [-pən], button [-tən], all alike, then the [ə] will be a symbol for a phoneme, of which one member (in words of the type in the third column in the preceding table) has the value zero. Again, Bloomfield's use of [ij] and [ow] in unstressed positions may be regarded as cases of [j] and [w] with zero sound. In Passy's 'orthographic' notation referred to above, he spelt out the 'mute e' as [ə] in all cases, letting the 'rule of three consonants' take care of the presence or absence of the actual sound. From our point of view, [ə] would then be a phoneme with zero as a possible member. In the system of Ancient Chinese initials, there are two called yiing (影) and yuh (喻) which have been reconstructed by Karlgren as [ʔ] and smooth vowel respectively. Those are of course only the names of the initials. But Jang Tayyan (章太炎) has devised an alphabet with a symbol for each of the 36 initials, so that his symbol for yuh would be a symbol with zero value, very much like the ' symbol for the smooth ingress of vowels in Greek.

In the theory of sheh (攝) or 'rim-emes' in traditional Chinese phonology, the use of a symbol for zero is extremely useful. Taking again the National Phonetic Script, which is constructed very much in the spirit of traditional phonology, we have the rim-emes ㄟ, ㄡ, ㄣ, ㄥ, which, like the other rimemes, may be preceded by the medials ㄧ, ㄨ, or ㄩ so as to form the following complete finals (i. e. syllables minus initial consonant, if any) which actually occur in words:

without medial :	ㄟ	ㄡ	ㄣ	ㄥ
with medial ㄧ :		ㄧㄡ	ㄧㄣ	ㄧㄥ
with medial ㄨ :	ㄨㄟ		ㄨㄣ	ㄨㄥ
with medial ㄩ :			ㄩㄣ	ㄩㄥ

A simple phonemic transcription in the IPA would be

	əi	ɳu	ən	əŋ
		iɳu	iən	iəŋ
	uəi		uən	uəŋ
			yən	yəŋ

In these twelve finals, the [ə] in [iən], [iəŋ], and [yəŋ] always has zero value (in [yəŋ], the [y] is broken up into an intermediate value between [iu] and [yu]), just like the [ə] in [ba:dən] for German baden.[15a] In the case of [uəi] and [iəu], the [ə] has zero sound in the first and second tones and has some sound in the third and fourth tones, except that in [uəi] not preceded by an initial consonant, [ə] does not entirely

disappear in any tone. In [uən] the [ə] has zero sound in the first and second tones when there is an initial consonant, is fully sounded when there is no initial, and is very weak in other cases. With [uəŋ], the [ə] is sounded only when there is no initial consonant. With [yən], the [ə] is sounded (with the value [ɪ]) when there is a palatal initial or no initial, but has zero sound with other initials. With such a complicated group of facts, where each case is a law unto itself, we should still fail to attain perfect phonetic accuracy by writing something like:

ei	ou	ən	ʌŋ
	iu	in	iŋ
uei		un	uŋ
		yn	iuŋ,

although this may be a useful form of transcription for certain purposes. The paradoxical appearance of a symbol with widely different values, including zero, would disappear if we stuck to the National Phonetic Script or used some non-committal symbol such as 'ɵ' for the phoneme in question, thus:

ɵi	ɵu	ɵn	ɵŋ
	iɵu	iɵn	iɵŋ
uɵi		uɵn	uɵŋ
		yɵn	yɵŋ.

This is of course not the only or even the best phonemic treatment of these finals, but by allowing the possibility of zero members of phonemes, we do gain a number of advantages.[16]

(e) Phonemic Treatment of Conditional End-consonants. In ordinary transcription of French, cases of liaison and elision are spelt as they sound. The word pas then has two forms [pα] and [pαz], le has [lə] and [l], and by the 'rule of three consonants' the word demander has the two forms (vous) [dmɑ̃de] and (pour) [dəmɑ̃de]. Similarly, Southern English sore has the two forms [sɔ:][17] (throat) and [sɔ:r] (eyes). The presence or absence of the sound in question is not distinctive, so that it and zero may be considered as members of the same phoneme. But the difference between saw [sɔ:] and sore [sɔ:] is distinctive, and for the phoneme with the conditional [r], the symbol '*' has been used in dictionaries, though the writer has never seen it used in texts, probably because ordinary transcriptions are not phonemic. From arguments with unsophisticated Frenchmen, who insisted that point did not have the same pronunciation as poing, the writer would think that a special phonemic symbol for these optional sounds would be welcomed by the French, say something like [pαz], [pwɛ̃t], so as to avoid the pitfalls of

15a Bloomfield, Language, p. 113.

16 In this article, we are limiting ourselves to the discussion of phonemes of single languages. If we extend our universe of discourse to diaphones, say about 100 miles south of Peiping, the advantage of the above form will be enormously increased.

17 One type of Southern British English.

the '[pɑtakɛs]' business.[18] Better symbols than these may be devised. Our interest here is in the obvious phonemic nature of these groups [z] ∿ zero, [t] ∿ zero, etc. It may not be necessary to outlaw the writing of two alternate forms for one word. But it would be an advantage not to have to do so.[19]

In this connection, we may mention the so-called 'aspirated h' in French as a consonant phoneme which always has zero sound, but has a very definite 'feature' of its own, and may be conveniently symbolized as [h̲]. The great advantage in regarding this as a consonant phoneme lies in that it greatly simplifies the description of the behavior of other phonemes. We can then say that [-t̲] (liaison t̲) has the sound [t] before vowels, and zero sound before consonants or in end-position. If we refuse existential status to [h̲], we have to say that [-t̲] has the sound [t] before vowels, except before the following exhaustive list of words: [aza:r], [ʒ:z], etc., which is no way of stating the 'rule of pronunciation' for phonemes.

In many Chinese dialects, final consonants like [-n], [-k], [-ʔ] are pronounced very clearly at the end of phrases, but become weakened or disappear entirely when followed immediately by another word. The [ʔ] in Foochow or the Wu-dialects is a phoneme which has zero value before another word. Thus, Soochow 八 [poʔ] 'eight', 八百 [popɑʔ] 'eight hundred', 八百八 [popɑpoʔ] 'eight hundred eight(y)'. The vowel is not even lengthened (as it is in Soochow under certain conditions) to make up for the time of the original [ʔ]. If we write phonemically, we can represent this phoneme with [ʔ] and zero sound as its two members either by (1) zero symbol (and let the symbol for the entering tone, with which it is always associated in these dialects, indicate its presence), or (2) the symbol [-ʔ] or [-ʔ̲] in all cases, whether the glottal stop is articulated or not.

It is not our purpose here to propose purely for the pleasure of perversity either to under-analyze two or more piece sounds and treat them as single phonemes or to over-analyze one piece sounds and treat them as successions of phonemes, nor purposely to write something where there is nothing to write, or to write nothing where there is something to write. We wish only to indicate that all such tricks are actually being done in current transcriptions, and that according to the way in which we treat the time unit of phonemes in a language we may arrive at one or another of various possible solutions for that language.

18 'Puisque ce n'est pat à moi et n'est poins à vous, je ne sais pat à qu'est-ce.' From Passy's Chrestomathie.

19 The case of English a : an is somewhat doubtful. If English never had a system of writing, or if its orthography had come to writing for uncle : fo mother, just like an uncle : a mother, we might then be inclined to treat the indefinite article as one word (as it was) and provide a special phoneme [-n̲] as its second element, a phoneme which occurs only in one word. Cf. II(e) below on word identity.

2. The Grouping of Sounds into Phonemes.

So long as we confine ourselves to the consideration of stock examples like keep, call, cool, our construction of phonemic systems is smooth-sailing. We need only to disregard slight variations of what is generally regarded as 'the same sound' and call it a phoneme. But on many questions of the identification of sounds in a language, we are not favored with such general consensus of opinion. Is the second element of the English 'long i' to be identified with the first element in yes (Bloomfield's [aj]), or with the first element in it ([aɪ] by many writers), or with the final element in very (Palmer's [aɪ]), or with the undistinguished [i] in it [it], eat [i:t], very ['veri] ([ai] by many writers), or with the first element in eight ([ae] in certain 'narrow' transcriptions)? Is the palatal series [tɕ], [tɕ'], [ɕ] in words like 家, 青, 下 (occurring only before high front vowels) to be identified with the velar series [k], [k'], [x] or with the retroflex series [tʂ], [tʂ'], [ʂ] (none of either series ever occurring before high front vowels)? According as we emphasize this or that motive, we should arrive at a different system of organization of elements into phonemes. We may desire to have (a) phonetic accuracy, or smallness of range of phonemes, (b) simplicity or symmetry of phonetic pattern for the whole language, (c) parsimony in the total number of phonemes, (d) regard for the feeling of the native speaker, (e) regard for etymology, (f) mutual exclusiveness between phonemes, (g) symbolic reversibility, and these motives are often conflicting.

(a) A minimum degree of phonetic accuracy is provided for by the 'similar in character' clause contained in Jones's later definition. By our purely logical definition, we should have the possibility of regarding English [h] and [ŋ] as members of one phoneme, which never occur in the same phonetic environment, and we could write forms like [ɦæt], [bi'ɦeiv], [sɔŋ], ['siŋə*] for hat, behave, song, singer, and learn very quickly when to say [h] and when to say [ŋ]. Such practice, however, would not be favored by either the phonetician or the philologist. Now the automaticity of variation within a phoneme has two senses. (1) The variation of [h] of the shades [hₑ], [hₐ], [hə], [hₒ],[20] etc., according to the following vowel is automatic practically in all languages which have these sounds. So is the variation of the [t] in [ts] and [tʃ] in all languages which have these affricates, that is, if we take affricates as successions of two phonemes. But such cases are much rarer than we are inclined to think. (2) In most cases, the automaticity of variation holds only for the particular language in question, although familiarity with the language may give one the impression of its universality. Thus, speakers of one

20 Not to include cases of high vowels, which involve other questions.

language, e. g. Japanese, would find the change of [h] into [ç] before [i] so natural as to be something inherent in the nature of speech sounds, while in another language, e.g. German, [h] can be followed by [i] without becoming [ç], which belongs to another phoneme. The variation of Foochow [a] and [ɛ] 會汇, 'to be able to', according to tonal environment, is so natural to the native speaker that he refuses to admit that he is not pronouncing it always in one and the same way, while in many languages these are widely different phonemes. Since, therefore, the automaticity of variation is mostly of conditional nature, we shall have to allow a good deal of latitude in the interpretation of the 'similar in character' clause. For the sake of phonetic accuracy, it would be an advantage to construct our phonemes with as narrow ranges of variation as possible (though it is never desirable to limit ourselves to universally automatic groups of the type (1) mentioned above), but this one desideratum may have to be sacrificed to some extent for other motives.

(b) <u>Simplicity or symmetry of phonetic pattern</u> is a factor which greatly influences our organization of phonemes. Bloomfield wishes to say that there are no long vowels in English, a statement which, from our standpoint, is neither true nor false, but may be estimated as methodologically desirable or not desirable. He has eight vowels:

i	u
e	o
ɛ	ɔ
a	ɑ

and eight diphthongs or triphthongs:

aj	ɔj[21]	ej	ij	juw
aw	ow		uw	

It would seem that he could gain phonetic accuracy by writing [ai], [ɔi], [ou], even without the addition of special symbols like [ɪ] and [ʊ], but then he could not very well go on and write [ii], [uu], and if he indicated the diphthongal character of these vowels by [ij], [uw], the system would look much less symmetrical. The table would also look less symmetrical if he wrote [i:], [u:], with the American narrow-range [e:] and [o:] lurking around for recognition, while [aj], [aw], and [ɔj] must still remain as diphthongs. The use of the nonce phoneme 'φ' for Chinese (see I (d) above) with zero as a possible member of the phoneme, gives great symmetry to the system. Again, the series ㄢ, ㄧㄢ, ㄨㄢ, ㄩㄢ may be symmetrically rendered as [an], [ian], [uan], [yan] instead of the usual [an], [iɛn],[22] [uan], [yan], which is phonetically more accurate but by no means necessary. When symmetry runs parallel to structural or etymological considerations, so that the phonemes also agree with diaphones or phonogenes, its claim for consideration will of course be greatly increased.

(c) <u>Parsimony of entities</u> in the spirit of 'Occam's razor' is of course the hobby of symbolologists. We have already noted the admission of digraphs for single sounds for the saving of a whole series of new letters. The use of [ij] and [uw] or introduction of length saves the use of the letters [ɪ], [u], and [ʊ] for English. Palmer deplores this 'exaggerated compliance with the principle of symbol economy,'[23] because, among other reasons, the symbol for length, e.g. in <u>although</u> [ɔ:l'ðou] does not necessarily indicate length. The writer can recognize the usefulness of the letters [ɪ], [ʊ], and [ʊ] from motives of phonetic accuracy, but the objection to the length mark does not seem to be fatal, for the symbol [ɔ:] may also be taken phonemically in such a way that it is long in stressed positions, less long before voiceless consonants, and short (without change of quality) in unstressed positions, while [ɔ] can still be considered a separate phoneme. Bloomfield's avoidance of [ə] and his identification of the vowel in <u>son</u> with the first vowel in <u>own</u> (instead of writing the former [ʌ] or [ɤ]) also effects a saving of 'queer symbols'.

The extent to which one could go in the parsimony of symbols can best be illustrated by Liu Fu's numerical code for the Peiping syllables.[24] He used only six symbols in six positions (or 'plus' six positions, if we count positions as part of the set of symbols) as shown by the table on the next page. Thus 光 [kuɑŋ] would be 312241, where 31 stands for [k], 224 is [uɑŋ] and the last figure '1' means the first tone. 000042 would be the nasal interjection meaning 'What did you say?' This system is extremely symmetrical in structure, economical in the number of <u>kinds</u> of symbols used, and very illuminating as to the phonetic pattern of the language, but it can hardly be used as a system of transcription and was never intended to be. It may be noted here that his 'Abdomen No. 1' includes [ɤ], [ʌ], [ɛ], [ɔ], [ɪ], [ə], and zero as members, and corresponds to our 'φ'. In the body of the table, he gave also a somewhat narrow transcription of all the syllables.

---

[21] Regard for 'similarity in character' probably prompted him to identify the first element of <u>oil</u> with the first element of <u>or</u>, rather than the first element of <u>up</u>. He would gain still greater symmetry if he wrote [oj], [ow], or still better [ɔj], [ɔw], as the first element in <u>own</u> is much nearer the first element in <u>or</u> [ɔr] than the first element in <u>up</u> [ʌp] in American English.

[22] Considering ㄣ as the nasal ending counterpart of ㄝ [iɛ].

[23] H. E. Palmer, Principles of Romanization, pp. 68-69.

[24] 'A Table of the Analytical Numbers of the Beeipyng Dialect,' <u>The Kwoshyue Jihkan</u>, III, 3, 1932, pp. 533 ff.

Position / Figure	I. HEAD Place of articulation	II. FACE Manner of articulation	III. NECK 'Medial'	IV. ABDOMEN Principal vowel	V. TAIL Final vowel or consonant	VI. EXPRESSION Tone
0		zero	zero	zero	zero	——
1	labial	unaspirated	i	ə	i	1st
2	dental	aspirated	u	ɑ	u	2nd
3	velar or palatal	nasal	y		n	3rd
4	retroflex	voiceless continuant			ŋ	4th
5	dental advanced	voiced continuant				

(d) The feeling of the native speaker is a factor which is greatly emphasized by Sapir. Where the feeling comes from obvious misconceptions, arising often from orthographic considerations, such as the idea that principal and principle have different pronunciations,[25] or that ng = n + g,[26] we need not take it very seriously. But when there is no question of misconception, but one of preference of choice between alternate manners of organization of phonemes, then the feeling of the native should be given due consideration, though it need not be taken as the deciding factor. Thus, while the phonetician would write Chinese 马,1马,×马,山马 as [an], [iɛn], [uan], [yan], the speaker of the dialect of Peiping feels that they all belong to the same rimeme with different medials. This is further supported by the fact that when the [-n] is dropped when the syllable is amalgamated with a following retroflex vowel, [iɛn] does not become [iɛr], but [iar], as in 一點兒 [i tiɛn ər] > [itiar] 'a little'. Most speakers of the Foochow dialect feel that among the vowels in the following words, 音 iŋ55: 詠 eiŋ242: 鶯 eiŋ55: 限 aiŋ242: 溫 uŋ55: 問 ouŋ242: 恩 ouŋ55: 筬 əuŋ242: those in the same row are tonal variations of the same vowel, while refusing to recognize that the vowels in 詠 [eiŋ242:] and 鶯 [eiŋ55:] or those in 問 [ouŋ242:] and 恩 [ouŋ55:] are the same. As there are very definite rules for the diphthongization of single vowels (or opening of close vowels, as [ɛ] ∿ [a]), it is quite possible to arrange the Foochow vowel phonemes according to the native conception as an alternate and for some reasons a better way of grouping the phonemes. On the ambiguity of the phonemic membership of Peiping 丩, 〈, 丅, the native speaker will also have something to say.

The distribution or patterning of these sounds and related sounds is as follows:

1 丩〈丅   tɕ   tɕʻ   ɕ   always before [i] or [y]
2 巜丂厂   k   kʻ   x   }
3 卩ち厶   ts   tsʻ   s   } never before [i] or [y]
4 出彳尸   tʂ   tʂʻ   ʂ   }

It is therefore possible to identify the series '1' phonemically with any one of the other three series. Wade identifies it partially with '4': he writes ch, chʻ, hs for '1', and ch, chʻ, sh for '4'. The National Romanization identifies '1' with '4' completely by writing j, ch, sh for both. The French system of romanization for Chinese has '2' or '3' according to etymology, which was what '1' came from, and over-zealous adopters of the French system identify '1' with '3' completely, and write forms like Sien Sien for 獻縣, although both belonged to series '2'. Now as to the feeling of the native, the favored series is '2'. For he feels [kə, tɕi, ku, tɕy] or [xə, ɕi, xu, ɕy] to be alliterative series with only different vowels. Moreover, in the system of a secret language which breaks every syllable with initial-final I+F into Iai+kF, (e.g. 北 [pei] > [pai-kei]),[27] the [k] becomes [tɕ] when the final begins with a high front vowel, as 米 [mi] > [mei-tɕi].

(e) Regard for etymology is properly not within the scope of our present study, which is concerned only with the descriptive study of one language of one period. But in the very frequent case of possibility of alternate phonemic treatment, we should certainly be allowed to steal a squint towards extrinsic factors. As a matter of fact, consideration of etymology does have a great weight with many writers. The identification of [tɕ], [tɕʻ], [ɕ] with [k], [kʻ], [x] is etymologically preferable, if only partially, to identifying them with [tʂ], [tʂʻ], [ʂ]. It would, however, cease to be strictly phonemic transcription of the Peiping dialect if we split [tɕ], [tɕʻ], [ɕ] into a velar and a dental series according to derivation, as [xi] for 希 and [si] for 西, for

---

[25] Except when the former is pronounced [prinsiˈpæl], which is merely an abbreviated way of saying, 'the word which ends in -p-a-l.'

[26] Even this is open to question, if we take a broader linguistic (as contrasted with phonetic or phonemic) point of view. Cf. Sapir's discussion on this point in 'Sound patterns in language,' Lang. 1.49 (1925) ((25)).

[27] Y. R. Chao, 'Eight varieties of Secret Language Based on the Principle of Faanchieh,' Bulletin of the Institute of History and Philology, Academia Sinica, II, No. 3, 1931, pp. 320 ff.

then no rule of phonemic membership short of lexical enumeration could tell us when it is [xi] and when it is [si].

It is also of etymological interest to try to secure identity of words by giving them constant phonemic forms. Thus, we can write [sɜ:*] or [sɜ:r] for sir and let the phonetic environment decide when it is to be pronounced [sɜ:r], [sɜ:], [sər], or [sə]. Again, by writing [ɛ:trə] for être, instead of [ɛ:tr] before vowels, [ɛ:trə] before consonants, and [ɛ:tr̩] at the end of phrases, Passy gives the word a constant form, the value of the phoneme [ə], which may be written in italics if desired, to be determined by the 'rule of three consonants', etc. The Foochow word 價 'to be able to' may be given the constant form [a], or a compromise form [æ], and the choice of values between [ɛ] and [a] may be determined by a very simple tonal rule. The identity-of-word interest, however, must not go so far as to cover grammatical considerations, where the rule of pronunciation would have to contain other than purely phonetic conditions. Thus, while we can write French en as [an], understanding that it is to be pronounced [ɑ̃] before consonants (s'en va) and [an] before vowels (s'en aller), we cannot write fin as [fin] in order to provide for the pronunciation of the feminine form [fin]. In such cases, we shall have to consider fin [fɛ̃] (or [fɛn]) and fine [fin] as two separate words, as much as fils and fille.[28]

(f) Mutual exclusiveness between phonemes is another desideratum we wish to consider; that is, the list of phonemes shall not only be exhaustive for the language, but, other things being equal, we should try to make the membership of the classes mutually exclusive. Other things, however, are never equal, and we have in fact already allowed the possibility of over-lapping of membership between phonemes in cases like the Foochow:

one phoneme	[i]	[ei]
another phoneme	[ei]	[ai]
one phoneme	[u]	[ou]
another phoneme	[ou]	[əu],

and in cases of different phonemes each of which contain zero as a member. The treatment of affricates as independent phonemes where their occlusive and fricative element can easily be identified with other phonemes in the same language, such as Bloomfield's [ǰ] and [č] for what many other writers give as [dʒ] and [tʃ], may also be considered as a case of over-lapping of membership. Palmer calls this 'multiple identity',[29] under which he cites a number of examples from Japanese and English. We should note, however, that the 'same sound' which belongs to two or more phonemes may be taken in two senses. In a conditional sense, 'the same sound' never occurs under the same conditions as to contiguous sounds or as to conditions of stress, length, and tone. The [ei] in the Foochow [i]∿[ei] phoneme occurs always in the tones [12:], [242:], [23:], while the [ei] in the [ei]∿[ai] phoneme occurs always in the tones [55:], [53:], [22:], [5:].[30] The English [č] and [ǰ] also occur under different conditions of stress from combinations like heat sheets and and Jeanne. In an absolute sense, on the other hand, Palmer's 'multiple identity' implies that two phonemes will have in common one member identical in all respects. Thus, there is absolutely no difference between the initial in 希 [ɕi] and the initial in 西 [ɕi], discussed above under (e). We could, if we like, put both into the [x] phoneme or both under the [s] phoneme, but if we write 希 [xi] and 西 [si], then the identical [ɕ] would belong to two phonemes under the same conditions. This treatment brings up the question of

(g) Symbolic Reversibility. The use of symbols has two aspects, the aspect of reading, or the determination of the object from the given symbol, and the aspect of writing, or the determination of the symbol from the object. The reading aspect of phonemic symbols is always determinate with respect to the language in question. Given a phonemic symbol, the range of sounds is determined, and the choice within the range is usually further determined by phonetic conditions. It would also be a desirable thing to make this reversible, so as to include the aspect of writing; that is, given any sound in the language, its phonemic symbol is also determined. If phonemes do not overlap, this is obvious. If they overlap, and the common members occur under different phonetic conditions, the reversibility still obtains. For instance, although 電報 is normally pronounced [tiɛmpɑu], so that the m sounds exactly like the m in 門 [mən], yet we can tell that it is only a member of the phoneme n, as the phoneme m never occurs in this position in standard Chinese. Again, in the dialect of Foochow, if we had the symbol A for the [i]∿[ei] phoneme and the symbol B for the [ei] ∿[ai] phoneme, we could still tell whether a given case of the sound [ei] is to be written A or B from the tone.[31] But if the identity of a common member between phonemes is unconditional, as the distinction of 希 [xi] and 西 [si] for the Peiping dialect, then it would be impossible to go from the sound to the symbol even for the native speaker. Strictly, a non-reversible symbolization of sounds based on etymological or other considerations becomes an

---

[28] Cf. Bloomfield's distinction between phonetic alternation and formal alternation, 'A set of postulates for the science of language,' Lang. 3.160 (1926) ((29)).

[29] The Principles of Romanization, p. 151.

[30] A pure phonetician would therefore prefer to take [ei] as one phoneme (or succession of two phonemes) in seven tones, although this would be against the 'feeling of the native'.

[31] This is not as complicated as the description looks on paper. The native speaker is not even aware of the vocalic identity or similarity of the [ei] in the two sets of tones.

orthography and ceases to be a transcription, and the French system of romanization of Chinese, which distinguishes 基, 欺, 希 ki, k'i, hi from 蹐, 妻, 西 tsi, ts'i, si (also favored by Bernhard Karlgren) is a case of this kind. In other words, homonyms should not have different transcriptions. There is, however, a class of intermediate cases, where the common member between two phonemes occurs sometimes under exactly the same phonetic conditions, but at other times becomes differentiated in some way under other sets of identical conditions. Thus, the same [ə] which occurs in mica ['maikə] and in poker ['poukə] before consonants becomes differentiated, for some speakers of English, into [ə] and [ər] respectively before vowels. If we write the former as [ə] and the latter as [ə*] or as [ər], then it will be possible to go from sound to symbol only when the sound in question is followed by a vowel, but not when followed by a consonant. The reversibility is therefore only partial. Usage is by no means uniform in such cases. Sometimes, symbolic reversibility is secured at the expense of word identity, the same word poker appearing in two forms ['poukə] and ['poukər], considered as different sets of phonemes. At other times, identity of word form is secured at the expense of reversibility, the same word Fr. espèce always appearing as [ɛspɛs], where the final [s] is pronounced [z] when followed by a voiced consonant, so that given the final sound [z], one cannot tell whether it is a member of the [s]-phoneme or a member of the [z]-phoneme.

3. Choice of Symbols.

It is one problem to group the sounds of a language into such and such phonemes and another thing to assign such and such symbols or letters to these phonemes. As a phonemic transcription has reference to one language, there is a great degree of freedom in our use of symbols. The freedom, however, is not so unlimited as in the case of mathematics, where the same symbol changes value not only from problem to problem, but also within the same problem. From purely logical considerations, it would seem that once the phonemes themselves are agreed upon, it is only a 'matter of form' as to the symbols used for them, 'What's in a letter?' Who ever heard of one mathematician writing l, m, n and another insisting that the same items shall be written as p, q, r? In phonetic symbols, however, there is tradition, or rather, what is more unfortunate, a number of conflicting traditions in the use of symbols. Consequently, there arise frequent controversies with as much vehemence as about the use of words. We shall feel the importance of the use of symbols when we realize that it often has an influence on our actual organization of phonemes. Some of the factors which influence our choice of symbols run parallel to those which influence the organization of phonemes. Thus, symmetry and simplicity of phonetic pattern corresponds to a certain degree of symmetry and simpli-

city in the symbols. Parsimony in the number of phonemes implies also parsimony in the number of symbols. The feeling of the native as to sound will also apply to the choice of the symbol if the language already has an alphabet, although this is often less dependable than his feeling for the pattern in the abstract. In addition to these, we have following questions especially concerned with the choice of symbols.

(a) The desire to keep within the limits of the ordinary 26 letters of the roman alphabet is such a powerful one that transcribers yield to it at great cost to other considerations. Thus, if a language has [ɑ], [ɔ], or [ɛ] but no [a], [o], or [e], then the latter symbols will be used as a rule.[32] If a language has only [ʀ], but no [r], then [r] would be used, although phonetically it would be taking as much liberty as writing [t] for [k]. Bloomfield's use of [o] in the phoneme [o] and the diphthong [ow] avowedly comes from the desire to avoid 'queer symbols'. So far as parsimony of number of phonemes and symbols is concerned, [ɤ] would do just as well as [o], but would be even more appropriate, as it is more natural to say that the [ɤ]-phoneme is rounded in the diphthong [ɤw], on account of the labial [w], than to say that the vowel [o] in American English is an unrounded vowel except in the diphthong [ow]. This avoidance of queer letters means that while theoretical phonetics tells us that there are such and such sounds, or at least advises us to recognize conveniently such and such distinguishable sounds in the main, yet we feel inclined to identify the phonemes of a language with those sounds which happen to be favored with 'lower case' letters.

(b) Of those symbols which are not the ordinary letters of the alphabet some are considered less 'queer' than others, either on account of old standing or on account of the importance of their position in the scheme of general phonetics. Thus, [ŋ], [ʃ], [ð], [ø], [ɔ] are usually considered much less queer, and less effort is usually made to avoid them than in the case of symbols like [ɕ], [β], [ɯ], [ɤ]. Again, in the abstract scheme of cardinal vowels, a special symbol for the part between [ɛ] and [a] would be of less importance than the eight main positions. And since it is possible to group all the [e]-[ɛ]-region sounds in English under the phoneme [e], the symbol [ɛ] is left free for indicating the phoneme between cardinal [ɛ] and [a], which is what Bloomfield does: using the less queer symbol [ɛ] instead of the symbol [æ], which is 'queer' in that it occupies a less strategic position.

---

[32] Jones and Camilli, Fondamenti, p. 3.

(c) <u>The scale of division</u> into which a variable range of sounds is supposed to be divided will have a great influence on the choice of the symbols. Thus, the traditional triangular scale

```
i                    u
   e            o
           a
```

and the cardinal scale

```
i                    u
   e              o
      ɛ        ɔ
         a  ɑ
```

differ in the number of intervals into which the vowels are divided. The difference would be less confusing if we had non-conflicting symbols in the new scale, something like:

```
              i

   x                    u
      e              p
         y        o
                    q
            z  a  r
```

As a matter of fact, one does find a partiality for using [e] for [ɛ] and [o] for [ɔ] (Cf. (a) above), and, less frequently, [a] for [ɑ], which shows the influence of the prestige of the i-e-a-o-u system. Every transcriber feels that somehow [ɛ] is a variety of [e] and not a variety of [a], [ɔ] is a variety of [o] and not a variety of [ɑ]. If we took our scheme of cardinal vowels seriously, we ought not to have such feelings.[33]

In Karlgren's scheme of vowels, using Lundell's dialect alphabet, the 3-point 2-interval high-vowel scale of $[i(y) - ɨ(ʉ) - ɯ(u)]$ of the IPA is given as a 2-point 1-interval scale of $\underline{i(y) \text{———} ɯ(u)}$. (More accurately speaking, ɯ is placed in Karlgren a little to the front of u.)[34] The Russian и, which on the 3-point scale is nearest to [ɨ], is therefore given as [ɨ] in the IPA,[35] but as ɯ by Karlgren, as it is nearer to the back vowel than to the front i on his 2-point scale.

(d) <u>The avoidance of diacritical marks</u>, which are now reserved for modifiers, also influences our choice of letters. We have already noted that rather than writing [s̯] for the single sound in Chinese , we allowed the modifier to be written

---

[33] The writer once heard a piece of music and interpreted it as being here in major and there in minor and its notes as being <u>do</u>, <u>re</u>, <u>mi</u>, etc., only slightly 'off', but subsequently learned to his surprise that it was a scale of seven equal steps in the octave. The illusion persisted even after he was told. He had forced his own intervals into the new scale, just as we all tend to force the 4-step i-e-a-o-u scale into the 7-step cardinal scale.

[34] Bernhard Karlgren, Études sur la phonologie chinoise, p. 316.

[35] As for instance by Daniel Jones.

---

separately, thus: [suei̯]. Again, if a language has only two series of voiceless plosives, one unaspirated and one aspirated, but no voiced plosives, then either [p, t, k; ph, th, kh] or [b, d, g; p, t, k] would be preferable to [p; t, k; pʻ, tʻ, kʻ] or [ᵬ, ᵭ, g̑; p, t, k].

(e) <u>Consistency with phonemic transcriptions of other languages</u> is a thing that one may keep in mind, but which one must not go out of one's way to obtain. Where our phonemes are of narrow ranges and the symbols given them are the nearest phonetic letter we happen to have, the resulting transcription is not likely to conflict seriously with other transcriptions. But if for one reason or another our phonemes vary within very wide ranges, and if, further, we wish to secure certain symbolic advantages by departing somewhat from the usual range of values of the letters, then the chance of conflict with other transcriptions will be greater.

III. PHONETIC AND PHONEMIC TRANSCRIPTIONS

It is the usual practice to distinguish between phonetic, or narrow, transcriptions and phonemic, or broad, transcriptions. The former express the actual sounds [ɹaɪt], [tɹaɪ], [ˈveɾɪ], [eɪt], [geˑt], [ðɛə], [æt], while the latter only indicate the distinctive classes of sounds [rait], [trai], [ˈveri], [eit], [get], [ðeə], [æt] (or [ɛt]). From the previous discussions, however, we have seen that there is no such thing as <u>the</u> correct phonemic transcription for any given language. According as we emphasize one or another factor in the size of the unit, method of phonemic grouping, and choice of symbols, we arrive at one or another form of phonemic solution. There is nothing in our definition of a phoneme or any other of the definitions quoted that can decide for us, for example, whether the Chinese [ɕ] shall be a member of [x] or [ʂ] or [s], or how the [ɪ] in [aɪ], the [j] in [ij], the [ɪ] in [ɪt], and the [j] in [jes] should be grouped into phonemic classes. The definition <u>permits</u> us to devise ways and means of grouping together distinguishable sounds that are not distinctive with respect to the particular system of phonemic grouping. It also implies that certain sounds in a language are never distinctive in that language by any reasonable manner of symbolic juggling, e.g. the difference between the [k]'s in <u>keep</u>, <u>call</u>, <u>coo</u>, etc., or the [h]'s in <u>heap</u>, <u>hall</u>, <u>who</u>, etc., can never be considered as being distinctive, unless we should do the very unnatural thing of considering all the vowels [i:], [ɔ:], [u:], etc. as non-distinctive members of one vowel phoneme $\underline{X}$, the value to be determined by the nature of the preceding consonant k_1, k_2, k_3, etc., h_1, h_2, h_1, etc., or $zero_1$, $zero_2$, $zero_3$, etc. (i.e. in words like <u>eat</u>, <u>all</u>, <u>ooze</u>). But many sounds in a language are neither distinctive nor non-distinctive per se, but depend upon our particular manner of phonemic treatment. Thus, by writing <u>up</u>, <u>owe</u>, <u>oil</u> as [op], [ow], [ɔjl], Bloomfield considers the difference between the first elements in <u>up</u> and <u>owe</u> as non-distinctive and the difference between elements in <u>owe</u> and <u>oil</u> as distinctive. But precisely the reverse thing will have to be said if we treat the same sounds as [o], [ɔw], [ɔj], a modification which would do no damage to Bloomfield's system as a whole either by way of compromising the parsimony of letters, or by way of introducing queer symbols. Again, in most of the Wu-dialects, in words of the type [tɕⁱɑ], [ɕⁱɑ], [ɲⁱɑ], etc., as against [kɑ], [xɑ], [ŋɑ], the [ⁱ] is so short that it can be considered as a glide of the preceding consonant and can be left out of the transcription, in which case the difference between [k], [x], [ŋ] and [tɕ], [ɕ], [ɲ] would be considered distinctive. On the other hand, if we write the [ⁱ] on the line then we could consider the [tɕ]-series as members of the [k]-series phonemes: [ki], [xi], [ŋi], and it is now the difference between [ɑ] and [iɑ] that is distinctive. In practice, no phonetic transcription is so narrow and concrete as to distinguish between the [h]'s in [he], [hɛ], [hə] in any language, and no phonemic transcription is so broad and so purely abstract as to group English [h] and [ŋ] under the same phoneme [ɧ]. Between these extremes, there are all intermediate proportions of phoneticity and phonemicity. On the whole, we may say that a phonetic transcription is one which makes use of all the usual distinctions which the majority of phoneticians are expected to be familiar with, irrespective of their distinctiveness in the language, and that a phonemic transcription is one which, given a particular set of directions of approach, makes only such distinctions as are necessary in distinguishing words from that particular set of directions.

The reader will notice the unsatisfactory nature of the phrase 'the usual distinctions which the majority of phoneticians are expected to be familiar with.' This comes from the unsatisfactory nature of the actual state of affairs. In the field of descriptive phonetics, there is nothing like the near unanimity of opinion which exists among physicists, either as to the organization of facts or as to the use of symbols for referring to them. Thus, Bloomfield says, 'The phonetician's equipment is personal and accidental; he hears those acoustic features which are discriminated in the languages he has observed... He should remember that his hearing of non-distinctive features depends upon the accident of his personal equipment, and that the most elaborate account cannot remotely approach the value of a mechanical record.'[36] This is all true to a great extent, but in the opinion of the writer, Bloomfield is going too far in saying further: 'Only two kinds of linguistic records are scientifically relevant. One is a mechanical record of the gross acoustic features, such as is produced in the phonetic laboratory. The other is a record in terms of phonemes, ignoring all features that are not dis-

tinctive in the language. Until our knowledge of acoustics has progressed far beyond its present state, only the latter kind of record can be used for any study that takes into consideration the meaning of what is spoken.' We need not, however, be worried if we cannot read or copy the grooves of a phonograph record. The phonograph record is at best an <u>icon</u>, or a picture, not a <u>symbol</u> in the usual sense of something that we can 'read' and 'write'. Nor need we be worried that the number of sounds in human speech is infinite. The number of distinguishable sounds in human speech is relatively small, limited by the condition of <u>oral-auditory transmission of phonemic distinctions from one generation to the next.</u> When the average actual difference falls below a certain finite limen, the distinction becomes unstable, and the two phonemes soon coalesce into one later phonogenic member. We cannot say, as Bloomfield seems to imply, that phonetic transcriptions are mostly subjective and that phonemic transcriptions are mostly objective. We have already seen how phonemic transcriptions are not unique and to that extent subjective. On the other hand, there is also a certain degree of practical agreement as to the non-phonemic use of symbols in general phonetics. For purpose of (1) citation of forms where a feature which is non-distinctive in the language cited is relevant to the point under discussion, (2) giving forms of words or sounds in comparative dialectology, (3) noting incipient or vestigial traces of sound-change, (4) impartial consideration of the gross features of a language before a good phonemic system has been worked out for it, and (5) as a less worthy purpose, for pedagogical use—for all these a narrow phonetic transcription is sometimes very useful and sometimes quite indispensible. One should not do the worst of narrow transcriptions all the time, but one should be prepared for the worst at any time. The dialect alphabet of Lundell, used by Karlgren in his Phonologie Chinoise, both in his main discussions and in the appended dialect dictionary, is a very narrow and non-phonemic transcription. The writer has nevertheless found the system thoroughly usable and understandable, and although for typographical reasons he has changed it into the IPA form in the Chinese translation,[37] he has been able to equate the symbols of the systems with relatively few additions and few doubtful points of classification arising from the number-of-scale-steps problem. In the writer's own experience in the recording of Chinese dialects, he found that besides the matching and comparison of words with related sounds, a very important procedure is to give a reasonably narrow phonetic transcription at the start, so that we have materials to base our decisions upon when we come to questions of choice among alternate treatments.

---

36 Bloomfield, Language, pp. 84–85.

37 中國音韻學研究, 趙元任, 羅常培, 李方桂合譯 Changsha, 1940.

Bloomfield observes rightly that phonetic transcriptions are often inconsistent as to what features to include and what features to neglect. This difficulty can be met in two ways. In the first place, we can lay down as a principle of symbolology that the position of a symbol in its context may be considered to be one constituent of the symbol. Thus, there is no inconsistency in the figure 1 meaning 1 X 10 and 7 meaning 7 X 1 in the form '17', as the symbol 1 is not just '1', but '1 in the second position'. Similarly, there is no inconsistency in the symbol '>' meaning 'greater than' in 19 > 17 and meaning 'changes into' in p > f, or even between the two uses of '>' in a > o according as the formula occurs in an article on phonetics or in one on mathematics.[38] So in discussions on diphthongs, we may need to mention forms like [čaj], [čae], [čæɛ], etc., while in discussions on affricates, we may refer to [tȿai], [tšai], [tɕai], [tʑai], etc., just as Bolling finds it perfectly in order to write Enroughity is coming : The Enroughities are coming, so long as the discussion is about the forms of the plural.[39] But if our discussion should turn on the forms of the indefinite article, it would then be necessary to write [ɛn ˈeg], but [ej ˈdaːbi] (the correct pronunciation of the name Enroughity according to Bolling), as it would not bring out the point at all if we wrote an egg but a Enroughity.

For avoiding too much inconsistency in the citation of forms, both Karlgren and users of the IPA have resorted to the distinction between broad and narrow transcriptions apart from considerations of significant distinction. Karlgren's practice, as carried out in his Phonologie (pp. 260 ff.), is very consistent. He has a set of bold-faced letters for a broad transcription, under each of which he puts a number of the Lundell letters, which are always in italics. Thus, what corresponds to the [ɛ] and [æ] in the IPA are grouped under ä, what corresponds to [ȿ], [ɕ], [ʃ] in the IPA are grouped under š, and so on. There are a few cases of overlapping groups, but on the whole the groups are mutually exclusive. The relation between the two sets is therefore very much like that between phonemes and members except that no reference is made to word distinction. A similar tendency is noticeable among users of the IPA, but no systematic division has ever been made between a narrow and a broad transcription. Nevertheless, there are certain unsystematic traditions among phoneticians which are based, on the whole, on the identity of the letters in the roman alphabet. Thus, r is somehow recognized as a broad form covering [r] and [ʀ], whereas [t] and [ꭓ] are not covered by

any broad form. Similarly [e] and [ɛ] are felt as members of a group of the e-type in a way that [i] and [e] do not seem to be. All this points to a conception which no one consciously recognizes, but which seems to be assumed by many, that there are such things as phonemes in general, apart from reference to any particular language, and that all we need to do either for the study of one language or for comparative work is to use one consistent phonemic transcription for all languages. This would of course be recognized by anyone as an impossible illusion as soon as the situation is thus made explicit, as we may be called upon at any time to make phonemic distinctions between shades of sounds whose differentiation we never anticipated in either our narrow or broad system of phonetic symbols. The existence of the tradition of usage, however, is real. It is true that the existence of only one common letter r for [r] and [ʀ] but two common letters t and k for [t] and [k] (or [ꭓ]) is a matter of historical accident. But we shall see the significance of this accident when we note that as a matter of fact most of the languages which phoneticians, or at least European phoneticians, have studied, do take [t] and [k] as separate phonemes, while [r] and [ʀ] rarely, if ever, occur as separate phonemes. The idea of general phonemes, which we have just proposed and condemned in the same breath, is therefore not entirely baseless. Without entertaining the idea of general phonemes as such, the writer wishes to propose the term typical phoneme, to be defined as those groups of sounds which very often go together to form phonemes in many of the major languages studied by phoneticians. This definition of course makes the idea of a typical phoneme depend again on historical accident, the fact that most contemporary phoneticians are speakers of the Germanic and Romance languages. Thus, for a broad transcription using typical phonemes, a European would group [p] and [pʻ] under one typical phoneme, as against [b],[40] while an unsophisticated Chinese phonetician would most likely group [p] and [b] under one typical phoneme as against [pʻ].

The troublesome part of the transcription problem comes from the inconsistency in using the same symbol sometimes in a general and sometimes in a particular sense. In the citations in this article, the writer has found it hard to do better, and has tried to manipulate the context (taken as part of the symbolic system) in such a way as to eliminate ambiguity. But there is always the danger of slips. When we refer to the English [i], one may not know whether it is narrow [i] or [ɪ] that is meant.[41] This is very similar to the old practice of referring to the ancient

---

[38] In discussions like the present, where there may be a call for 'narrow symbols', one could use '→' for 'changes into' and '>' for 'greater than', thus making peace among mathematics, phonetics, and chemistry.

[39] From an editorial note on R. G. Kent's review of Bloomfield's Language, Lang. 10.50 (1934)

[40] Except speakers of certain German dialects.

[41] On the principle of non-uniqueness of phonemic transcriptions, we cannot prohibit the writing of the vowels in eat, it as [i], [ɪ], and insist on the writing of [iː], [i] or of [ij], [i].

Chinese initials 照, 穿, 牀, 審 in this way:

General names: 照穿牀審

For the apical series: 莊初牀山 [tʂ][tʂʻ][dʐʻ][ʂ]

For the dorsal series: 照穿乘審 [tɕ][tɕʻ][dʑʻ][ɕ]

so that when 照 is mentioned, one is at a loss as to whether it is the 照 in general (including both [tʂ] and [tɕ]) that is meant, or only 照 [tɕ] as against 莊 [tʂ]. He has therefore proposed the following names for the differentiated series, reserving the traditional names for the general sense, incidentally also using an inclusive broad transcription for the general series, thus:

General names: 照穿牀審 [č] [čʻ] [ǰʻ] [š]

For the apical series: 莊初崇生 [tʂ][tʂʻ][dʐʻ][ʂ]

For the dorsal series: 章昌乘書 [tɕ][tɕʻ][dʑʻ][ɕ]

Karlgren's use of a special series of boldfaced types is based on the same principle. Symbols may be as general and inclusive as we may have use for, but must not be vague and ambiguous. An approach to this method of having both general and particular use of symbols is made in connection with the usage of a few symbols in the IPA. Thus, the symbol [ə] is usually understood to be a general form for [ɜ] (half-close) and [ɐ] (half-open). [ʃ] and [ʒ] may be used either for [ʂ] and [ʐ] or for [ɕ] and [ʑ] respectively. This latter, however, is less satisfactory, as in the dialect of Lintzy (臨淄), Shandong, [ʂ], [ʃ], [ɕ], all three exist as separate phonemes, in which the [ʃ] series is intermediate between apical and dorsal articulations of the tongue and is identical with English [ʃ] except that there is no protrusion of the lips. [š] and [ž] would be better general symbols, though they are not properly IPA letters.

SUMMARY

We have proposed a new definition of a phoneme and have endeavored to show that given a language, there is not necessarily one unique solution for the problem of reducing its sounds into elements. We have considered what factors can influence, and have influenced, the phonemic treatment of languages: the variability of the size of the phonemic unit, including the admission of zero symbols and zero sounds, the grouping of phonemic membership, and the choice of actual symbols. Because phonemic solutions are not unique, it is necessary, before arriving at solutions, to have recourse to considerations of descriptive phonetics and the use of phonetic transcriptions. These are also necessary for other purposes, such as the comparative study of dialects. We have also noted that there is a tendency among phoneticians to group together sounds under broad symbols, which form phonemes in a number of languages, and we have called them 'typical phonemes', although there is no consistency in the use of symbols for these. It is hoped that a more consistent system of symbols be devised for indicating both narrow shades of sounds and typical phonemes for the purpose of phonetic and phonemic transcriptions, but for the time being, we have to let the context serve as part of the symbol to inform us as to shade (if particular) or scope (if general). It is not necessary to take serious exception to anyone's transcription so long as it is self-consistent and its interpretation is clear to the extent it is meant for, and so long as it does not claim unique correctness to the exclusion of other possible treatments. Usage may in time become unified, but problems will always vary. Our motto must be: Write, and let write!

PHONETIC AND PHONEMIC CHANGE

ARCHIBALD A. HILL
Language 12.15–22—1936

The theory of phonemes has received a great deal of attention from linguists within the last few years, and the applications of the theory to descriptive linguistics have become reasonably clear, though there still remain problems in need of further study. However, there has been less interest in the theory on the part of students of the history of language, many of whom practically ignore the theory altogether; or assume, on the other hand, that the sound changes which we can prove to have taken place in the past were practically coextensive with phonemic shifts.[1] It seems, therefore, worth while to attempt a tentative examination and classification of the relations between sound change and phonemic change in the hope that the applications of the theory of phonemes to the historic study of language may be to some extent clarified.

In the first place it is clear that the shifts in the pronunciation of a whole set of phonemes, which leave the phonemes as far apart as at the start of the change, involve no shift in the phonemic pattern. This is usually clearly recognized by all scholars, and involves no particular difficulty. A simple example is the fact that most phoneticians who visit the Southern United States for the first time, or after a stay in New England, are struck by the fact that the whole Southern vowel scheme is a notch higher than that of other parts of the country. Aside from individual differences in the pattern of vowel phonemes due to other causes there are, however, no striking differences in phonemic pattern in the two dialects. Historically, also, the first consonant shift from Indo-European to Germanic did not result in extensive phonemic changes, since the three groups of IE sounds remained separate in PGmc., though on a new basis.

Allied to this principle is a second, less often noticed. Phonetic shifts can result in a change in what constitutes the significant element in a phoneme or set of phonemes. This likewise produces no change in the phonemic pattern, though, as in the type of change cited above, the individual phonemes affected are all altered. An example of this type of change is found in the history of English long and short vowels. Originally the long and short vowels of English seem to have had the same quality; thus the significant feature of the two sets must have been length; and that the difference was phonemic is proved by such OE pairs as fullīce 'fully, completely', and fūllīce 'foully, basely'. However, in the late 13th century in the North, and a little later in the Midlands,[2] a change set in in the quality of the short vowels, whereby the natural tendency toward relaxation in short sounds resulted in open quality, eventually giving rise to the distinction that exists between such modern phonemes as [u] and [ʊ]. The gradual result of this sound change has been that quality has replaced quantity as a mark of distinction between phonemes in Modern English. The phonemes remain at equal distance from each other, but the nature of the difference has changed. It is interesting that this change has indirectly contributed to a new treatment of length. Since length has become a non-distinctive feature, the way has been left open for a regrouping of long and short quantities in rigid correspondence with the phonetic situation.[3] In fact I think most of the puzzling changes in the quantity of Modern English vowels can be referred to this general tendency, rather than to elaborate 'laws' describing the treatment of individual long and short vowels in special situations, as was the method of many older grammarians.

A third type of phonetic shift which need not involve phonemic readjustment is combinative sound change. Combinative sound change does not necessarily produce a phonemic shift as long as the sound causing the change remains. The simplest example of this sort of assimilation, not resulting in phonemic difference, is to be found in the almost universal American treatment of the vowels of pat [pæt] and pan [pæ̃n]. In spite of the nasalization of pan, the two vowels are still members of the same phoneme, and it usually requires training in phonetics for an American speaker to perceive the phonic difference. If, however, the two final consonants should disappear, while the nasality persisted, the two vowels [æ] and [æ̃] would then automatically become members of different phonemes.

[1] This seems to be the attitude of Bloomfield, Language, N. Y., 1933. In his chapters on Phonetic Change and on the Comparative Method he makes quite clear that in general the formulae in which historic states of language are summed up indicate historic phonemic rather than narrowly phonetic structure. He does not, however, give any detailed discussion of the exceptions to this rule, or of the relations of the two types of change.

[2] Cf. Luick, Historische Grammatik der Englischen Sprache 374–9, Tauchnitz, Leipzig, 1921.

[3] The best description of the phonetic rules governing NE vowel length is to be found in E. A. Meyer, Englische Lautdauer, Uppsala, 1903.

An almost exactly similar assimilation which does not affect the phonemic pattern occurs in the speech of Spaniards, who often nasalize the first vowel of a word like notario without recognizing any difference between it and the last vowel of the word. A further example is the velarization of the nasal consonant of Spanish cinco [θiŋko], which is still felt to be a member of the n phoneme. Another case is the French unvoicing of the final m of words like rhumatisme [ʁymatism̥].

A more complicated example of the principle that as long as the sound which causes the assimilation remains, the phonemic pattern is not affected, is found in Modern English. Thus in my own speech the Early Modern English open [o] before [r] has resulted in a long [ɔ]-like phone. Since I use this phone in all words of the [o + r] type, and since the [r] is always preserved, I make no distinction between pairs like coarse and course, morning and mourning. This open phone is therefore still a member of the [o] phoneme, though the change which produced the variant phone is of considerable antiquity. In the speech of Virginians and New Englanders who do not pronounce final and preconsonantal r, on the other hand, the loss of the sound which brought about the lowered variant of the phoneme has resulted in the setting up of a new phoneme, since foe and for now contain significantly different sounds, not phonetically controlled variants. In a phonemic transcription of such a type of speech foe and for would have to distinguished by some such symbols as [fo] and [fɔə].

The difficulty of determining whether a historic sound change represents a mere phonic shift, or is one involving phonemic difference, is sometimes considerable. Thus the OE change of 'breaking' is a case in point. OE æ was 'broken' to a diphthong, written ea, and presumably pronounced [æə], before double ll as in [*fællan] > [fæəllan]. The generally accepted cause of this breaking was the development of a glide vowel before a 'dark' variety of l in the same syllable. If the [æə] had continued to occur only before such dark sounds, it would clearly have remained only a subsidiary member of the [æ] phoneme, in spite of the different spelling. There were, however, other varieties of ll, particularly a brighter ll from WGmc. lj, before which breaking often did not take place.[4] The occurrence, however, of occasional forms like Northern sealla from WGmc. *saljan suggests that perhaps the diphthong was carried over to the bright varieties of ll as well, in which case phonemic readjustment of either the vowel or the consonant must have taken place.

Occasionally we are more fortunate in being able to determine the phonemic standing of an ancient sound change. Thus the Gothic lowering of Gmc. u represented in Gothic by the spelling au, occurs only before r, h, and hw. There is, therefore, no evidence that it was not still a member of the u phoneme, since it is obviously phonetically controlled.

Even without the loss of the sound which brings about change in the members of a phoneme placed in its neighborhood, phonemic shifts may, however, occur. Such phonemic shifts nevertheless do not result in the setting up of new phonemes. Their sole result is to bring about a redistribution of already existent phonemes in the words affected. What happens in such a case is that the combinative sound change produces a phone which is closer to a member of some other phoneme than it is to the original phoneme, with the result that attraction sets in, assimilating the aberrant phone to this new close neighbor. This is what has happened in forms like [kæpm̩] for older [kæptən]. On a larger scale it is illustrated by those people who, while still preserving final and preconsonantal r, refer the [o + r] words to the same phoneme as in law, making no distinction between war and wore. An instructive example of phoneme regrouping of this sort is cited by Grammont.[5] He points out that in the French phrase robe courte the final b of the first word is unvoiced, but remains a member of the b phoneme, since it is still a lenis. In obtenu, on the other hand, the following voiceless sound is a constant part of the environment, not a mere accident of the phrase. Here, therefore, the unvoiced b goes completely over to the p phoneme, since it loses its lenis quality.

To turn to phonetic shifts which involve shifts in the phonemic pattern. The most obvious of these is a shift in the direction of some already existent phoneme. Such a change results in the falling together of two phonemes, eliminating one from the total number. A well known example of such a falling together is that of ME [eː] as in [kweːnə] and [ɛː] as in [hɛːθ] which have both given rise to NE [iː] as in queen and heath. A type resulting in an increase of the number of phonemes by means of a split in what was once one phoneme has already been discussed; that is, the splitting of a phoneme because of the loss of a sound which caused a combinative change, as in [fo], [fɔə], above.

Here it is only necessary to add that it is sometimes difficult to determine when the change-causing sound can be called lost. This is particularly true when complete assimilation takes place. Thus it was mentioned that WGmc. lj resulted in a double ll, as in WGmc. *taljan > OE tellan. Can one speak of this j as being lost if the second l is still its representative? The answer should be in the affirmative, since we have essentially one sound, though long, as the representative of the two earlier ones. Moreover it is probable that this ll was different in character (perhaps palatalized?) from the common Germanic ll, since the geminated ll did not produce breaking

4 Sievers-Cook, Grammar of Old English 51, Ginn and Company, N. Y., 1903.

5 Grammont, Traité de Phonétique 186–7, Delagrave, Paris, 1933.

in OE. As long, therefore, as the difference in character persisted, the two ll's constituted separate phonemes.

No less important than these purely phonetic changes are changes in the phonemic pattern resulting from dialect mixture. Thus if a given local dialect shifts a whole phoneme in a new direction (without thereby bringing about a collision with some other phoneme) no phonemic shift occurs. However, if the speakers of that dialect thereafter come in contact with another dialect, or a standard language which they imitate, phonemic changes almost certainly result. If phonemic changes occur, the result may be either the setting up of a new phoneme, or a redistribution of already existent phonemes. The only instance in which such dialect mixture does not produce phonemic changes is when a true variphone is set up, each speaker using either of the dialectically variant phones in all of the words in question. Such cases would seem to be rare. A more common state of affairs is fixation of the variants, either in different ones of the affected words, or in different senses of the same word. An interesting example of the setting up of a new phoneme by fixation of the second type is found in the speech of a subject from eastern Maine. This speaker comes from a region in which the [o] phoneme is strongly centralized, giving a phone which can be written [ɵ]. However, this particular subject belongs to a family in which local dialect has long been abandoned for Standard English. Thus coat has the [ou] phone of the Standard English phoneme. But in the special, and more homely, sense of coat of paint the local phone [ɵ] occurs. Thus there has been a phonemic split, actually in two senses of the same word.

The type of shift which results in the redistribution of already existent phonemes can be exemplified from the speech of many Virginians. The local dialect of eastern Virginia has the [a] phoneme in words of the aunt, dance type. However, the [æ] phoneme characteristic of General American occurs in the special use of aunt or auntie as a title for an old colored woman. It now seems probable that the puzzling divergences in the history of ME [a] and [u], resulting respectively in NE [a] as in father and [æ] as in rather, [ʊ] as in put and [ʌ] as in but, but with fixations in individual words, are the result of dialect mixtures of the types described above; the first resulting in redistribution of existent phonemes, the second giving rise to a new phoneme.

The case of genuine variphones is unknown to me in personal experience of dialect investigation. However, I am acquainted with speakers who vary separate phonemes in a way almost exactly similar. Thus one subject who has lived both in Virginia and the middle Atlantic states uses either [æ] or [a] phonemes in words of the aunt, dance, ask type, according to what sort of speakers he is addressing. Also the border-line cases in which some words occur with either phone, but some are limited to one or

the other, is known to me from subjects in Maine. Thus one speaker can say either [stoun] or [stɵn], but always says [bout]. In such types of distribution it seems closest to the truth to say that there are two phonemes, but that some words can be pronounced with either one.

There remain fairly numerous examples of change in pronunciation where there is a phonemic shift without any general sound change. This is the type of change found in individual words, in which the change is not supported by a similar drift in other words of the same history. An example of this kind of individual change is found in the speech of some localities in Virginia where the single word say has undergone lowering in the stressed position so that it appears with the phoneme of bed. This is in contradiction to the general tendency in this region, which is to raise rather than lower vowels in stressed syllables. Another similar example is found in Maine where at least one speaker says that an ox is driven with a [gɔəd], using the phoneme of board. It is highly improbable that such an individual change, of whatever origin, should result in the setting up of a new phoneme, occurring only once in the speaker's language, since it can usually be assumed that the attraction of existent phonemes will be too strong for a single word to resist it. Only in the more or less isolated and sub-linguistic forms of interjections and similar highly colored words can phones not found in the general phonemic pattern easily maintain themselves. The origin of such individual changes as the two cited above is extremely various, and must always be explained out of a knowledge of the history of the individual word in question. Thus, though I cannot prove it, I suspect that the first change is due to the analogy of the third singular says and the preterite said. As to the second example, the explanation would more probably be found in the existence of the words gore, gored, gourd, which have somehow become blended with goad, always a word of limited application in folk speech. Thus analogy, folk-etymology, and the restoration of worn-down forms all play an important part in such individual changes.

Closely allied to the phenomena of individual phonemic attraction are certain other phenomena that result from closely similar or overlapping phones within two separate phonemes. In English, a characteristic change is the reduction of many unstressed vowels to [ə]. When any of these reduced vowels are restressed, an 'incorrect' form, i. e. not belonging to the original phoneme, may be the result. Such a form is the Louisiana ['pʌkɔn] for pecan. More interesting, and less widely known, however, are cases of individual attraction resulting from contiguity of two whole phonemes. Thus in many parts of New England there are raised and fronted variants of the [a] phoneme, producing a phone, [aˆ], which is very close to the lower limits of the [æ] phoneme. In general the two phonemes are kept quite distinct, but in occasional words attraction between the two phonemes has produced confusion. A clear instance of this kind of confusion is found in the speech of a subject from southern Massachusetts, who pronounces the first syllable of clapboard with the [aˆ] phone, which is a member of the [a] phoneme, not the [æ] phoneme.[6]

From the preceding discussion it seems possible to deduce a few general principles which govern phonemic change in its relation to phonetic change. The most important of these is that when phonetic change brings two phonemes close together, attraction may set in. This attraction may manifest itself more strongly in some words than others, thus appearing at first as a confusion between phonemes of individual words, though the two similar phonemes may elsewhere remain distinct. Later the attraction may extend to the whole group, in which case we say that 'two sounds have fallen together'. Indeed, I think it may safely be assume that no two phonemes ever fall together without passing through such a transition stage, in which the attraction manifests itself sporadically in ever increasing numbers of words.

However, attraction is not the only possibility when phonetic change brings two phonemes close to each other. A second possibility is phonemic repulsion, which results in the selection by the speaker of variants which offer less overlapping, and so tend to increase the distance between the phonemes, rather than to lessen or eradicate it. An instance of phonemic repulsion seems to have taken place in the history of British English in early modern times. We know that at one time some varieties, at least, of London English had a voiced intervocalic t, which we can assume was probably the same phone as the flapped, voiced t so common in America at present.[7]

[6] The pronunciations [kætrɪdʒ] for cartridge, and [pæsl] for parcel, common in New England, are not examples of the reverse confusion, but of early loss of [r] before dentals.

[7] Cf. the spellings collected by Wyld, A History of Modern Colloquial English 312–13, E. P. Dutton, N. Y., 1920.

We also know that at some time, presumably fairly recent, British English must have developed the flapped intervocalic voiced r which is characteristic of Standard British English today. These two phones are extremely close to each other, differing principally only in length. Consequently if they existed as members of separate phonemes at the same time, we should expect confusion to have arisen. Evidence of this confusion, and so of the contemporaneity of the two phones is found in porridge, the by-form from pottage. But at present British English t is unvoiced, and even slightly aspirated, medially, so that there is no longer the slightest danger of confusion with r. I know of no explanation other than habitual selection of variants farther removed from r than is the flapped t to account for this drift.

As to whether attraction or repulsion will result from the overlapping or contiguity of two phonemes, it seems to me that we must resort to the principle of dangerous as against unimportant confusion laid down by the French linguistic geographers to account for the disappearance or preservation of homonymous words. Thus it is demonstrably more important to keep consonant phonemes clear and distinct in English as it is at present organized, than it is to do the same for vowel phonemes. It is thus not strnage that confusion in consonants should be rarer than in vowels, where several ME sounds have been confused in NE.

In conclusion, the theory of phonemic attraction and repulsion, if accepted, should modify considerably our notions of how linguistic change takes place. Where the neo-grammarians held that the individual speaker was without control over sound drift, the theory of phonemes emphasizes that many more things than inexorable phonetic law can control the non-distinctive features of utterance. The selection of those phones within a given phoneme which offer least likelihood of confusion may often spring from a necessity for clearness which has too often been ruled out of court by students of language.

A NOTE ON OLD HIGH GERMAN UMLAUT

W. FREEMAN TWADDELL
Monatshefte für deutschen
Unterricht 30.177–81—1938

It is generally agreed that a group of modifications of vowels and diphthongs known collectively as umlaut occurred in connection with a following palatal element, i, ī, or j; and that the modifications begin to be represented orthographically in MHG, but not in OHG, except for the mutation of short a̲.

A difficulty arises from the fact that, in large measure, the i, ī, or j which 'caused' the umlauting was no longer present in MHG. We are faced with two alternative interpretations: either the umlaut occurred after the disappearance of the condition which caused it—a patent absurdity—or the umlaut occurred in OHG times but for some reason was not recorded orthographically until centuries later.

There is general agreement that the differences caused by umlaut existed in OHG, that however only the umlaut of short a̲ was represented [as e̲] in the writing.[1] And there have been attempts to answer the question: Why, if the umlaut changes occurred in OHG, were they not represented until MHG, except in the case of short a̲? It has been suggested[2] that the phonetic differences due to umlaut were inconsiderable in OHG times, too inconsiderable to call for orthographical representation. This suggestion leaves the essential problem unsolved, for it entails as a corollary the unsupported and inherently improbable assumption that the difference became considerable only after the disappearance of the factor which had caused the original 'slight' differences. A variant of this type of answer is an explanation in terms of a delayed mediate palatalization through intervening consonants: The i, ī, or j is supposed to have palatalized the preceding consonant or consonants, which, having acquired a palatal articulation, subsequently palatalized the preceding vowel. This explanation has several serious weaknesses: It implies that the palatalization of the consonants, originally dependent upon the following i, ī, or j, became an independent phonetic characteristic (though never indicated orthographically), and survived the depalatalization or loss of the following i, ī, or j. The allegedly palatalized consonants would have to retain

their palatalization long enough to palatalize the preceding vowel; and then they would have to lose their palatalization, since the phonetic history of German shows no traces of a differential treatment of palatalized and non-palatalized consonants. This is in itself a highly improbable sequence of combinatory changes. There is the further difficulty of imagining any chain of combinatory changes which involves a succession of regressive palatalizations in trahani, aruzzi, or hawi. The most serious practical objection is of course the complete lack of any evidence for such mediate palatalizations; the only reason why anyone should have thought of such a rationale was the need to explain the delay in orthographical representation of umlaut. It is, in short, an explanation with no basis in objective evidence—a purely ad hoc hypothesis. Another suggested answer[3] is the argument that the Latin alphabet did not supply the required symbols. But the MHG scribes were able to invent symbols; and they knew the same Latin alphabet as the OHG scribes, so far as the number of symbols is concerned. If the Latin alphabet was inadequate in the 9th century, it was similarly inadequate in the 13th; if new symbols were invented in the 13th, they could have been invented in the 9th.

– – – – – – – – –

Let us consider the umlauts which are not regularly indicated in OHG, taking u as a paradigm. We note the following phonetic developments:[4]

$$Uxi — [yxi]$$
$$Uxxi — [uxxi]$$
$$Uxa — [uxa]$$

Then [y] is the phonetic form of sound-type U, when followed by -xi. [y] always represents U before -xi, and never represents any other sound-type. Hence [y] and [u] can never occur in a similar phonetic environment; they are the two complementary repre-

---

[1] Cf.: Behaghel, Gesch. d. d. Spr. (5) §253; Braune, Ahd. Gram. (3) §51; Paul, Mhd. Gram. (10) §40. a 1; Priebsch and Collinson, The German Language II. I B. 8; Prokosch, Outline of Germ. Hist. Gram. p. 51; Schade, Ahd. Gram. §§47,63; Sütterlin, Nhd. Gram. I. 1.5.a. A concise account of the history of investigation is presented by Jellinek, Die Erforschung der indogermanischen Sprachen, II. Germanisch (Streitberg, Michels, Jellinek), 1936, pp. 381–395.

[2] E.g., Braune, Paul, op. cit.

[3] E.g., Behaghel, Schade, op. cit.

[4] A capital letter is used to represent a sound-type, which is that of the stressed vowel to be considered in connection with umlaut. Thus U represents OHG u at the beginning of the divergent developments due to umlaut; x represents a consonant or consonant group which permits phonetic mutation of the preceding vowel; xx a consonant group which inhibits umlaut, temporarily or permanently; -i represents the umlaut-inducing elements i, ī, j; -a represents any other suffixal element. Vowel-symbols in square brackets indicate the actual phonetic form of a given sound-type in a given phonetic environment.

sentatives of the general sound-type U. [y] and [u] represent two aspects of U, dependent upon the phonetic environment. If the phonetic environment is orthographically indicated, the phonetic representative of U (either [y] or [u]) is automatically indicated. When the OHG scribe wrote uxi, the OHG reader had to pronounce the vowel as [y], for the written symbol in this -xi environment had to be interpreted as indicating the fronted variety of U.

It is indeed conceivable that the speaker of OHG was unaware of the phonetic difference between [y] and [u], or at most regarded them as slightly different forms of the 'same vowel', U.

In this earlier phase, the nature of the vowel and the phonetic environment were so correlated that the environment was the determining, primary factor, the independent variable; and the nature of the vowel was secondary, the dependent variable. It was the difference between -xi and -xa which determined the difference between [y] and [u].—This is the definition of the conditions of umlaut.

But when the post-tonic vowels fall together to [ə],[5] then an entirely new set of relations obtains. In this later phase, the old relationships between [y] and -xi, between [u] and -xa, can no longer exist. For both -xi and -xa have been replaced by -xə. We have accordingly arrived at a state in which our three formulae must be represented:

$$
\begin{aligned}
&\text{Uxi} \quad - [yxi] \quad - [yxə] \\
&\text{Uxxi} \quad - [uxxi] \quad - [uxxə] \\
&\text{Uxa} \quad - [uxa] \quad - [uxə]
\end{aligned}
$$

As between the first and third of these formulae, the difference [y/u], which had originally been dependent upon and secondary to the difference [-i/-a], has now become an independent and autonomous difference. In the terminology of the Cercle Linguistique de Prague, the phonetic opposition [y/u] has been 'phonologized'. The result is a new sound-type, Y. Instead of the earlier status, in which [y] and [u] were representatives of two aspects of U, dependent upon phonetic environment, [y] and [u] are now representatives of two different sound-types, Y and U, which occur independently of phonetic environment.

In this phase, then, our formulae must be interpreted as

$$
\begin{aligned}
&[yxə] \quad \text{representing Yxə} \\
&[uxxə] \quad \text{representing Uxxə} \\
&[uxə] \quad \text{representing Uxə}
\end{aligned}
$$

The application to our problem is plain. In the earlier phase, as long as -i [that is: i, ī, j] remained distinct from other suffixal vowels, then there would be no need, indeed no occasion, to record the phonetic difference between [y] and [u]. For, in that phase, the difference between [y] and [u] was not the significant difference; it was a secondary difference, dependent upon and induced by the difference between -i and -a.

As soon as the difference between -i and -a has ceased to be significant, then (and not until then) the difference between [y] and [u] becomes a significant difference, which must be represented orthographically. What is here paradigmatically and over-simply referred to as the dephonologization of the difference -i/-a was in reality of course a series of processes: [-j] was lost or assimilated earlier than the weakening of [-i] to [-ə]; many of the [ī] suffix vowels were long maintained. There must have been a period in which the opposition [y/u] was in part independent (where [-j] had been lost) and in part dependent (where [-i] remained). The failure to record immediately the [y/u] opposition in the former cases was a natural orthographical conservatism, since such cases constituted a minority of the occurrences of [y], and were pretty completely restricted to certain morphological classes and functions,[6] with related forms still displaying [-i]: e.g., infinitive of weak verbs I and related finite forms. Further, the loss of [-j] and the weakening of [-i] occupied appreciable periods of time, and we must assume fluctuations of usage, local, individual, and probably even within the speech of one individual. Not until a considerable majority of the occurrences of [y] were definitely independent of phonetic environment was the phonologization of [y/u] sufficiently valid to call for orthographical representation.

According to this rationale of OHG umlaut, there is nothing surprising about the absence of orthographical representation of [y, ø], etc. in OHG. Indeed, the failure to represent these conditional variants of the sound-types U, O, etc. is entirely natural. To have represented them would have been an act of supererogation, of orthographical pedantry, parallel to an attempt at representing orthographically the various phonetic forms of the sound-type K in modern English or German, or of the sound-type CH in German Frauchen : rauchen.[7]

In following this line of argument, we encounter however one major difficulty, which is the reverse of the usual one. For, if we account for the failure to represent the umlauts of u, o, etc. as above, we are faced with the necessity of accounting for the fact that the umlaut of short a is represented in the OHG orthography.

In dealing with the umlaut of short a, we have to distinguish three lines of development:

$$
\begin{aligned}
&\text{Axi} \quad - [exi] \\
&\text{Axi} \quad - [æxi]^{8} \\
&\text{Axa} \quad - [axa]
\end{aligned}
$$

---

[5] Or, for that matter, to [i].

[6] Similar to the status of ch in Frauchen/rauchen; see L. Bloomfield, German ç and x, Le maître phonétique (1930) 27 f.

[7] A similar phonological process (though with a different orthographical outcome) in Russian is described by Trubetzkoy, Archiv für vergleichende Phonetik 1.144.

[8] x represents such combinations as -ht-, etc.; cons.-vowel-cons.

As between the second and third formulae here, with [æ] and [a], we have a relation analogous to that between [y] and [u]. The difference [æ/a] is merely phonetic in the earlier phase, but is phonologized subsequently, and appears as the so-called 'secondary' umlaut.

With respect to the first formula, Axi, however, a different relation exists. The [e]-aspect of sound-type A was phonetically rather similar to a phonetic aspect [ɛ] of a different sound-type, E. Further, this [ɛ]-representative of sound-type E appeared in another phonetic environment, as in erda. This is the only phonetic environment in which sound-type E can historically be expected, because of the earlier shift of e to i before i, etc.

The phonetic similarity of [ɛ] (from E) and [e] (from A) would then have had a surprising consequence. It must be remembered that the [e] of gesti was a closer vowel than the [ɛ] of erda. The complex of sounds representing the old E and A sound-types would then have assumed this form:

[exi]	from A
[ɛxa]	from E
[æxi]	from A
[axa]	from A

Historically, three of these represented one old sound-type, one represented the other. But the speakers of OHG knew their language functionally, not historically. And functionally, there would have been a neat pairing-off, resulting in a new and symmetrical distribution of sound-types:

[exi]	representing Exi
[ɛxa]	representing Exa
[æxi]	representing Axi
[axa]	representing Axa

The preponderant OHG orthography represents such a new distribution of E and A. The functional unity of the new sound-type E is confirmed by the cases in which OHG [ɛ], occurring exceptionally before -i in new formations, was replaced by [e].[9]

Thus we arrive at a formulation for OHG in which there were two phonetic forms for each of the vowel-types, with the exception of the palatal vowels and diphthongs. But in each case these two phonetic forms are substantially complementary, dependent upon the phonetic environment; and therefore no orthographical representation is called for. Subsequently, when the environmental differentiation is eliminated, the phonetic differences are phonologized. Orthographical evidence of this is found in MHG for every vowel but e; and for e the rime-usage of the poets is conclusive evidence.

It goes without saying that the actual historical shiftings of orthographical usage were often tentative and inconsistent, with all the fumblings that a change in craft tradition can entail. This discussion is not concerned with them, nor with subsequent disturbances of umlaut-relations through operations of analogy. It is presented as a sketch of the main trends of the earlier stages of umlaut in High German, viewed as a phonetic and phonological (therefore orthographical) phenomenon.

[9] Cf. v. Bahder, Grundlagen d. nhd. Lautsystems 132 f.

A PROBLEM IN PHONOLOGICAL ALTERNATION

MORRIS SWADESH and CHARLES F. VOEGELIN
Language 15.1–10 —1939

One may expect to find instances of phonologic (morpho-phonemic) alternation in almost any language. In English there are changes in consonants, vowels, and stress, insertions, and elisions;[1] and many of these are conditioned only by the phonetic surroundings of the morphemes. An example is the possessive suffix, which is -əz (or -ɪz) after a sibilant, -z after a voiced non-sibilant, -s after a voiceless non-sibilant.

In the case cited, the alternation is called regular. It might be more correct to say that the phonologic[2] basis for the alternation is patent, as we may demonstrate by contrasting with this example another one involving 'irregularities'. The plural suffix, otherwise homonymous with the possessive, differs in the case of certain nouns, whose final fricative is voiced.[3] Thus, leaf : leaves contrasts with belief : beliefs (note also leave 'furlough' : plural leaves). An account of plural formation in English may consist of giving the more usual phonology as the rule and then listing the other cases as irregularities. But note the plural formation of leaf is completely consistent with that of sheaf, calf, half, knife, house, and several other nouns. There is, so to speak, regularity within this limited group of 'irregular' words. These cases cease to be irregular if one recognizes that there are two types of voiceless spirant morpho-phonemes, one that is fixed, and one that is subject to voicing on the addition of the plural suffix. If we wish, we may provide different symbols

for the two types of morpho-phonemes, as, for example, *bəlif versus *liF. Different phonologic behavior requires the differentiation of the morphophonemes.

A system of special morpho-phonemic symbols would have little operational efficiency in English, because the instances of non-patent phonology are limited in number and scope. In other cases, one of which we give here in full, the use of special symbols may greatly clarify and objectify an otherwise complicated system of alternations. Before we leave the English examples, let us note that alternations are the result of phonetic history, affected also by foreign borrowings and analogical changes. The most efficient formulation of the synchronic facts is ordinarily not the same as a reconstruction of the actual historical developments, but the process of constructing morpho-phonemic formulae has some resemblance to that of historico-phonological reconstruction.[4]

We give Tübatulabal, a Uto-Aztecan language of California, as a striking illustration of what may be accomplished by recognizing the non-patent in synchronic phonology. In his published account of this language, Voegelin reported a technique of vocalic reduplication accompanied by consonantic changes, contractions, syncopes, and changes in vowel length. For these changes two or three highly productive treatments could be pointed out ('regular principles'), but there remained many less productive treatments ('irregularities'). Again, alternation of length in suffix vowels followed a highly productive treatment, but so many unproductive treatments of stem phonology were found beside this that the only feasible plan seemed to be to list the reduplicated and unreduplicated forms of each stem.[4] Swadesh, having learned the use of formulae in synchronic phonology from Sapir in his work on Nootka,[5] suggested that the morpho-phonemic alternations of Tübatulabal might be effectively treated by this method. In the beginning of our collaboration, Swadesh suggested some hypotheses based on the behavior of a number of stems mentioned in the grammar; then both col-

[1] See Palmer, A Grammar of Spoken English 7–12, Heffer, 1924; Bloomfield, The structure of learned words, A commemorative volume issued by the Institute for Research in English Teaching on the occasion of the tenth annual conference of English teachers 17–23, Tokyo, 1933.

[2] We use the term phonology to refer to alternations (synchronic phonology) or changes (historical, diachronic phonology) in sounds, rather than for the theory of the nature and permutations of the sounds. The latter we call phonemics. Those who use 'phonology' in this sense, probably in imitation of French 'phonologie', deprive themselves of a convenient means of distinguishing two fundamentally distinct subjects.

The phonemic point of view is essential to a proper understanding of the phonology, both synchronic, as will be seen in this paper, and historical, as is nicely shown in W. F. Twaddell's A Note on Old High German Umlaut, Monatshefte 30.177 《85》, 1938.

[3] We omit mention of the irregularity that certain stems use a different formation, as oxen, men,...

[4] Voegelin, Tübatulabal Grammar, University of California Publications in American Archaeology and Ethnology 34.55. See also Voegelin, On Being Unhistorical, Am. Anthropologist 38.344; and Whorf, Notes on the Tübatulabal Language, ibid. 38.341.

[5] See Sapir-Swadesh, Nootka Texts, Linguistic Society of America, 1938, 236–9.

laborators went through Voegelin's lexical files and text material (assembled before the present theory was conceived) to find which morphemes could and which could not be explained on the basis of the first assumptions. This led to a correction and extension of the phonological theory. The theory was counted as finally developed when it accounted for all the phenomena illustrated in the assembled material. The value of the theory is not merely that it is accurate, but that it provides an overlying general pattern (regular principles) to phenomena which, otherwise, could only be presented as a series of distinct, partial, limited patterns (rules and irregularities).

The suffixation vowel

A relatively simple problem is that of the vowels used before different suffixes. Let us compare the infinitive of several stems and themes with the simple imperfective, the causative, and the benefactive.

tək 'to eat'	təkat 'he is eating'	təkinat 'he is causing him to eat'	təkanat 'he is eating for him'
ala·w 'to talk'	ala·wat	ala·winat	ala·wanat
ta·wək 'to see'	ta·wəgat	ta·wəgi·nat	ta·wəga·nat
pohol 'to get blisters'	poholat	poholi·nat	pohola·nat
in 'to do'	inət	ini·nat	ina·nat
hal? 'to sit'	halət	hali·nat	hala·nat
o·l 'to get up'	o·lot	o·linat	o·lanat
mu·yh 'to celebrate'	mu·hyut	mu·hyinat	mu·hyanat
təkilo·k 'to pretend to eat'	təkilo·got	təkilo·ginat	təkilo·ganat
təkiwə·t 'to eat collectively or ravenously'	təkiwə·dət	təkiwə·dinat	təkiwə·danat
pələ·la 'to arrive'	pələ·lat	pələ·linat	pələ·lanat
yə·wu 'to hold'	yə·wut	yə·winat	yə·wanat

Disregarding for the present the length of the suffixation vowel we note that an i is regular in connection with the causative; this is likewise true of several other suffixes, including: -^{i}WkaÑ past habituative, -^{i}Šamā future, -^{i}wa passive, -^{i}ninəMa distributive, -^{i}wə̄də collective intensive, -^{i}baĦa 'to want to ...', -^{i}lōgo 'to pretend to'.[6] The vowel with the benefactive is consistently a; no other suffix is so characterized. The quality of the suffixation vowel for the imperfective element element may be any back vowel, a, o, u, ə (a is by far the most common; e is found in one or two cases), and is determined by the preceding morpheme. Several other suffixes agree with the imperfective -t in their behavior with regard to the suffixation vowel; thus: -H imperative, -maR· exhortative, -puWa 'to seem to ...', -laR 'going', -gima 'coming'. Furthermore, the vowel which a morpheme has before these suffixes is the same as that which it has in final position in the case of those morphemes that end in a vowel in final position. We may therefore take the vowel preceding suffixes of this group to be a part of the preceding morpheme, even though most morphemes lack the vowel in word-final. Suffixes like the causative have the peculiarity of inducing a change of the final vowel to i and the benefactive has the peculiarity of changing it to a.

Since most morphemes lose their final vowel when they stand in final position, it is simplest to mark those that retain it. We may do this by means of the symbol R, e.g. hūdāR 'for the sun to be up' (inf. hu·da).

[6] The reader is asked to disregard capital letters and other special symbols until they are explained later.

Terminal unvoicing

The stops and affricates of certain morphemes alternate between voiced and unvoiced according to whether they stand in medial or terminal position. This is illustrated for final position by ta·wəgat: ta·wək, təki-lo·go-t: təki-lo·k, təki-wə·də-t: təki-wə·t, quoted above. The same is true of initial position, as appears in reduplication, for example, a·dawə·k '(he) saw' (perfective): ta·wək 'to see', ə·bələ·la 'he arrived': pələ·la 'to arrive', u·buw 'he irrigated': puw 'to irrigate'. Now, it is generally true in Tübatulabal that voiced stops and affricates occur only in intersonantic, syllable-initial position, and it is clear that we are dealing with a case of positional alternation: the substitution of voiceless for corresponding voiced takes place in those positions where voiced stops do not (one might say, cannot) occur.

There are, of course, morphemes with fixed voiceless stops, e.g., tək 'to eat' : ətəki-n 'he caused him to eat', pušk 'to blow' : upušk 'he blew'.

Modification of final clusters

Cases like mu·yh : mu·hyut may be accounted for under a rule that clusters of h plus sonorant metathesize in word-final position. Other examples are: a·na·hlət 'he is making it fast' : a?ana·lh 'he made it fast'; ponihwəy 'of the skunk' : poniwh 'the skunk'.

In cases like hal? : halət, the morpho-phonemic formula must be based on the final form, in order to distinguish such cases from others like pohol : poholat. We set up formulae like *hal?ə̄ and the rule that clusters of liquid or nasal plus ? lose the latter except in word-final. Other examples are: gūl?a- 'to play', MoN?mōn?o- 'to boil', Lohōm?a- 'to enter'.

Vowel length

The greatest complexity is found in the matter of vowel lengths. The vowel length of suffixes is determined by the stem, or stem-suffix complex, to which they are attached. The vowel lengths of the stem frequently vary as between unreduplicated and reduplicated forms, and the vowel lengths of the suffixes may differ according to whether the stem is reduplicated or not. Let us take a number of words which illustrate different treatment of vowel lengths, giving the infinitive to show the unreduplicated form, the perfective to show the reduplicated form, except in a few cases where other forms have to be taken. The reduplication consists of repeating the stem-vowel, rather the first vowel of the stem, before the word. The examples are selected to show the nature and complexity of the phonologic problem. Long themes, either primary or involving suffixes, are expressly chosen in order to show the treatment in syllables remote from the initial. Morphophonemic formulae for the stems are given here for convenience, but have yet to be justified.

(1) ta·wəgi·-na-na·-la 'to go along causing him to see' / a·dawə·gina·nala 'he went along causing him to see' / *dawəga
(2) pələ·la 'to arrive' / ə·bələ·la / *bəlālaR
(3) təwəla·-n 'to fix it for him' / ə·dəwəlan / *dəWələ
(4) to·yla·n 'to teach him' / o·do·yla·n / *dōylāR
(5) pay?igə-la 'to go along turning' / a·bay?igəla / *bāY?gə
(6) puwa·-n 'to irrigate it for him' / u·buwa·n / *buwā
(7) poloŋa·-n 'to beat it for him' / opolo·ŋan / *poLoŋa
(8) poholi·-n 'to cause him to get blisters' / opoholin / *poHoLa
(9) či·čwana·bə 'to accompany him' / iči·čwana·bə / *čīžwanābəR
(10) tə?əbinuga?adawa·-n 'to tell a myth for him' / ətə?əbinuga? -adawa·n / *tə̄?binugā?-dawa
(11) tuga?ana-n 'to make it deep for him' / utuga?anan / *tugā?na
(12) togo·y?a-n 'to decoy it for him' / otogo·y?an / *togōy?a
(13) puški-na·-n 'to blow it for him' / upuškina·n / *pǔška
(14) kina-n 'to bring it for him' / iŋgina·n / *giNa
(15) cami·-n 'to burn it' / anʒami·n / *ʒamā
(16) kami·ža-n 'to catch it for him' / akami·žan / *kamīžə
(17) cənənə·? 'to shake it' / əcənənə·? / *cəNənə̄?a
(18) ta·twal 'man' / ata·twa 'group of men' / *tādwaR
(19) ha·ya·-n 'to stir it for him' / a·ha·ya·n / *hāyā
(20) šiwga-n 'he combed his hair' / i·šiwganat 'he is combing his hair for him' / *šīWga
(21) halay?i-n 'to make him wet' / a·halay?in / *halāY?a
(22) hu·da 'for the sun to be up' / uhu·da / *HūdāR
(23) wi·mi·wi·mi·-n 'to cause him to zigzag' / i·wi·mi·wi·mi·n / *wīmīwīmīna
(24) mə·hli·n 'to hurt him' / ə·mə·hli·n / *mōhlīna
(25) ma·ncu?i-n 'to make him tame' / a·ma·ncu?in / *māncū?u
(26) ma·ygi-n 'to make him go ahead' / a·ma·ygin / *māygə
(27) wi·na-gə·m 'to come to give him a present' / i·wi·nagə·m / *wīna
(28) wə·?in 'to pour water' / ə·wə·?in / *wə̄?ina
(29) lu·mi·n 'to take it off' / u·lu·mi·n / *lūmīna
(30) yahna 'to believe him' / a·yahnan / *yāHnana
(31) yə·wa·-n 'to hold it for him' / ə·yəwa·n / *yə?əwūR
(32) ya·yaŋ 'to be timid' / a·yayaŋ / *yayaÑa
(33) yilaho·-la 'to go along happy' / iyilahola / *YiLaHo
(34) nəba? 'to snow' / ənəba? / *Nəbā?
(35) wi·bi-n 'to make him fat' / iwi·bin / *Wībə
(36) wimšini·-n 'to make him move out of the way' / iwimšini·n / *WīMšin
(37) u·di-na·-n 'to untie it for him' / u·?u·dina·n / *?ūda
(38) a·gi-na·-n 'to cause him to open his mouth for him' / a?a·gina·n / *?āga
(39) aya·w 'to grow' / a?aya·w / *Ɨayāwə
(40) əhcaw 'to help him' / ə?əhcaw / *Ɨə̄Hcawa
(41) a·na·hli-n 'to cause him to fast' / a?ana·hli·n / *Ɨana?ahlə
(42) ə·wəni·-n 'to stop him' / ə·?ə·wəni·n / *?ə̄wənə
(43) ina-n 'to do it for him' / ina·n / *?iNə
(44) o·li-n 'to help him up' / o·li·n / *?olo
(45) i·?a-n 'to give him a drink' / i·?a·n / *?i?a
(46) o·wi-n 'to mark it' / o·?owi·n / *?o?owā
(47) kə·?i-n 'to cause him to bite' / ə·gi·n / *gə?ə
(48) šu·?a-n 'to dry it for him' / u·ša·n / *šu?a

We observe that stems beginning in a vowel have ʔ in the reduplication. As will be seen later, it is convenient to assume an initial ʔ to be morpho-phonemically basic in these cases. All stems then begin in a consonant. There is never more than one initial consonant.

Turning to the matter of vowel-length, we note first that the reduplication vowel is always long before a voiced stop or affricate, always short before a voiceless stop or affricate. This correlation must have some connection with a certain fact of phonemic occurrence: in those positions where either a voiced or voiceless stop may occur, only a short vowel ever precedes a voiceless stop; either a short or a long vowel may precede a voiced stop.

Other consonants, which do not have the voiced-voiceless contrast, reduplicate with long vowel for some stems, with short vowel for others. This difference in treatment of vowels established a morpho-phonemic dichotomy extending beyond that of the stops; one class includes all the basic voiced stops and some instances of each of the other phonemes, the other class includes all fixed voiceless stops and some instances of each of the other phonemes. Let us refer to the latter group as shortening consonants, the former as neutral consonants. The classification may be partly extended to the non-initial position by analogy with the stops. All consonants which are preceded, in any of the forms of the morpheme, by a long vowel are neutral. Of those non-stop consonants which are never preceded by a long vowel, some may be vowel-shortening consonants. We may symbolize shortening non-stops by a capital letter; and for the glottal stop, we use Ɪ for capital ʔ.

From examples 14–17 we observe that a nasal after the stem-vowel is included in the reduplication if the initial consonant is a basic voiced stop but not if it is fixed voiceless: iŋgin 'he brought it', anǯam 'it burnt'; but akami·č 'he caught it', əcənə·ʔ 'he shook'. The nasal is assimilated to the consonant. The vowel before the nasal + consonant is short.

Our criteria of consonantal type, though applicable only in some cases, enable us to identify some themes as containing only neutral consonants, and in such themes (1, 2, 4, 6, 15, 19, 23, 24, 26, 28, 29, 31, 37, 42, 44, 45, 46, 47, 48) we can observe the principles of vowel-length as they apply when not interfered with by secondary shortening. We find that some vowels are always long, some vowels alternate between long and short; it is perhaps simpler to speak of 'heavy' and 'light' vowels instead of fixed-long and alternating-length vowels. Except for 31 and 45–48, the actual length of light vowels can be covered by simple rules: (a) in the syllable adjacent to one containing a heavy vowel, a light vowel is always short; (b) otherwise, a sequence of light-vowel syllables alternate in length, the first being long, the next short, and so on. Heavy vowels are illustrated in to·yla·n : o·do·yla·n (4), ha·ya·n : a·ha·ya·n (19), wi·mi·wi·mi·n : i·wi·mi·wi·mi·n (23), mə·hli·n :

ə·mə·hli·n (24), and others. Alternating length of light vowels is shown very well in the first example: ta·wəgi·nana·la : a·dawə·gina·nala. In 37 and 42 we see how a preceding heavy vowel affects the alternation of light vowels by preventing the first following vowel from being long: u·dina·n : u·ʔu·dina·n (stem *ʔūda); ə·wəni·n : ə·ʔə·wəni·n (stem *ʔə̄wənə). In 2 and 6 we have a following heavy vowel preventing a preceding light vowel from being long, but the reduplication, being two syllables removed, is long: pələ·la : ə·bələ·la (stem *bələ̄la); puwa·n : u·buwa·n (stem *buwā).

Examples 31, 44, 45, and 46, although they contain only neutral consonants, seem to show contradictions to the phonological theory already presented. Take example 31, yə·wa·n : ə·yəwa·n. If the base were *yə̄wāna, the reduplicated form should be *ə·yə·wa·n and it is not. If it were *yəwāna, the unreduplicated form should be *yəwa·n. Example 46 is similar. Examples 44 and 45 show no reduplication but only a change in the vowel lengths: o·lin : o·li·n; i·ʔan : i·ʔa·n. The clue to these anomalies is to be found in 47 (kə·ʔi·n : ə·gi·n) and 48 (šu·ʔa·n : u·ša·n), which show that contraction takes place under some circumstances. If o·lin is from *ʔo·lina· (stem *ʔolo), its reduplication would be *o·ʔoli·na; a contraction in the first two syllables would give us the actual form o·li·n. Similarly, i·ʔan : i·ʔa·n are from *ʔi·ʔa-na, *ʔi·ʔi·ʔa·na. yə·wa·n : ə·yəwa·n can then be derived from *yə·ʔəwa·n : *ə·yəʔəwa·n < stem *yəʔəwū. Similarly, the forms of 46 are based on a stem *ʔoʔowā. The rule of contraction is that it takes place between light vowels separated only by ʔ except as between the two syllables of an unreduplicated dissyllabic stem (47, 48) and between the vowels of a certain type of extension of the stem final, illustrated in wə·ʔinat 'he is pouring water' : wə·ʔina·ʔat 'he is pouring lots of water' (stem *wə·ʔina). The quality of the contract vowel is that of the second of the two component vowels, as is seen in u·ša·n (< *u·šuʔa·na), and the quantity is long if one of the components is long, short if both are short. Only two of three light vowels separated by ʔ contract, as in i·ʔa·n < *i·ʔiʔa·na.

If we turn now to words containing shortening consonants, we soon see that a shortening consonant affects only the vowel before it. The phonological effect of the vowel, whether light or heavy, remains the same. In constructing our formulae a vowel, even though followed by a shortening consonant, may be identified as light or heavy according to the behavior of the adjacent vowels, and consonants may be identified as shortening if vowels are short before them under conditions where one would expect a long vowel before a neutral consonant. təki·n : ətəkin points to a stem *tə̄ka-; the heavy vowel is evidenced by the fact that the following vowel is short whether in the second or third syllable of the word. poloŋa·-n : opolo·ŋan points to a stem *poLoŋa- with all light vowels; the actual forms show secondary shortening from *po·Loŋa·n : *o·poLo·ŋan. And the remaining examples can similarly be reduced to adequate formulae.

Word-final vowels insofar as they are retained are shortened. R might thus be called a vowel-shortening consonantal morpho-phoneme. (Indeed, it might be identified with Ḯ, if we could then say that a morpheme-final Ḯ is lost entirely except in word-final position, and that in word-final position it appears only in its effect of retaining and shortening the preceding vowel.)

In addition to the foregoing theory it is necessary to recognize a special V?V group which acts in the length theory like a single heavy vowel (see 5, 10, 11). We may set these up as $\overline{V}Ḯ$ and state the rule that a heavy vowel plus a syllable-final Ḯ is pronounced as V?V, e.g., tə?əbinuga?adawa·n < *tə̄Ḯbinugā̄Ḯdawa-. If a semivowel intervenes between the heavy vowel and the syllable-final Ḯ, as in 5, a high vowel (i or u according to the semivowel) is inserted.

Conclusion

If it has been possible, by the recognition of a non-patent phonology involving two morpho-phonemic types of consonants and two of vowels and a set of mechanical rules, to reduce the apparent irregularity of Tübatulabal phonology to system, this very fact guarantees the truth of our theory. Truly irregular alternations could not be reduced to order.

The value of a phonological theory is in direct proportion to the extent of its application, in inverse proportion to its complexity. Our theory might be called fairly complex, but it applies to a great many words. There are several hundred verb stems attested in Tübatulabal and about a score of suffixes. Not only are the suffixes quite freely added to the stems, but quite a number of different combinations of suffixes are possible. It is probably not an exaggeration to estimate that any particular stem may enter into 300 stem-suffix combinations and that some suffixes occur in 25,000 stem-suffix combinations. These, then, are measures of the value of determining the phonological formula for any given stem or suffix. In presenting the lexicon of the language, the formulae will serve as a shorthand method of indicating the facts for each lexeme.

For other languages we hope our treatment of Tübatulabal may offer some useful methodological suggestions. To linguistic theory Tübatulabal phonology is an instructive instance which can contribute to eventual generalization.

PHONEMIC OVERLAPPING

BERNARD BLOCH
American Speech 16.278-84—1941

The first step in the phonemic analysis of a language or dialect is to group the infinitely varied sounds which make up the spoken utterances of the speech community into a limited number of classes called phonemes. The principles governing this classification do not concern us here;[1] but it is obvious that each phoneme, defined as a class, will include as many actual and objectively different speech sounds as there are utterances containing a member of the class.

We know that the sounds comprising a single phoneme—the allophones, to give them a convenient name—sometimes differ strikingly among themselves. Most writers on the subject have dwelt on this fact, and all readers are familiar with the stock examples offered as illustrations: the different varieties of [k] in keep cool, of [l] in leaf and feel, or of the velar spirant in German ich and ach.[2] To offset this diversity among the allophones, some writers postulate a basic resemblance which unifies the entire class, by defining the phoneme, like Daniel Jones,[3] as a 'family' of sounds clustering around a norm or, like Bloomfield,[4] as a constant feature in the sound waves.

But though writers are agreed that allophones of the same phoneme are often very different phonetically, they appear to be uniformly silent on another aspect of the phonemic interrelation of sounds. I do not know of any published work that has even posed the question—important as it is both in practice and in theory—whether phonemes may intersect: whether a given sound, that is, may belong to two or more different phonemes in the same dialect. If the ques-

tion has ever occurred to writers on phonemic theory, they appear to have treated their answer to it, whatever it may be, as a tacit assumption. It is my purpose here to state explicitly what is usually tacit, and to offer arguments in support of a principle which is usually assumed.

Is the phonemic analysis of a dialect valid if it forces us to assign successive occurrences of the same sound to different phonemes? For the purposes of this discussion, we may define a sound as a recurrent particular combination of sound features (such as labial or alveolar position, stop or spirant or lateral articulation, voicing or voicelessness, aspiration or the lack of it, etc.), of which some are distinctive in the language and some not; and we may agree that two sounds are 'the same' if they represent the same particular combination of such features.[5] The intersection or overlapping of phonemes will be called partial if a given sound x occurring under one set of phonetic conditions is assigned to phoneme A, while the same x under a different set of conditions is assigned to phoneme B; it will be called complete if successive occurrences of x under the same conditions are assigned sometimes to A, sometimes to B.

Our question concerning the possibility of intersection is best answered by examining specific examples. These are all taken from varieties of Midwestern American English, since this is the only dialect for which I have worked out the phonemic analysis at first hand. I shall begin with some cases of partial intersection.

In the speech of many Americans, the [t] phoneme includes as one of its constituent sounds or allophones an alveolar flap (something like the r of London English very), which occurs intervocalically after a stressed vowel, and in this position varies freely with the familiar voiced t and with the aspirated voiceless t, as in butter, betting, kitty (contrast budded, bedding, kiddy). In the speech of some of these persons,

---

[1] For several divergent statements of these principles see Leonard Bloomfield, Language (New York, 1933), chap. 5; Morris Swadesh, The Phonemic Principle, Lang. 10.117-29 (1934) ((32)); W. F. Twaddell, On Defining the Phoneme (Language Monograph No. 16, 1935) ((55)); N. S. Trubetzkoy, Grundzüge der Phonologie (Travaux du Cercle Linguistique de Prague No. 7, 1939).

This paper was read at the 17th annual meeting of the Linguistic Society of America, Dec. 1940. For clarification of my views on phonemic theory I am indebted especially to Professor Bloomfield, Dr. George L. Trager, and Dr. Charles F. Hockett.

[2] See for example Daniel Jones, An Outline of English Phonetics, 3d ed. (Cambridge, 1932), pp. 48-49; John S. Kenyon, American Pronunciation, 6th ed. (Ann Arbor, 1935), pp. 33-35.

[3] Op. cit., p. 48. Cf. also Ida C. Ward, The Phonetics of English (Cambridge, 1931), p. 60.

[4] Language, pp. 78-81.

[5] This statement does not, of course, solve the difficult question of phonetic identity, Since we know from laboratory evidence that no two sounds are exactly alike (and that even one sound is never uniform throughout its duration), but since on the other hand we know that the best-trained ear can distinguish only a small fraction of the objectively different sounds, there would seem to be no solution of the dilemma capable of satisfying both logic and practical necessity. A serviceable rule-of-thumb is to regard two sounds as 'the same' phonetically if an average native speaker, once his attention has been directed to them, cannot tell them apart.

the [r] phoneme includes as one of its allophones the same alveolar flap, occurring after [θ] in words like three, throw, less commonly after [ð] in dissyllabic pronunciation of words like withering, gathering. (The flap after [θ] is often partly or wholly voiceless; but the voiced variety also occurs.) In this dialect of English, then, the [t] phoneme and the [r] phoneme appear to intersect in the alveolar flap; but the intersection is only partial and never leads to uncertainty or confusion: every such flap between vowels belongs to the [t] phoneme, every flap after a dental spirant belongs to the [r] phoneme.

It is a well-known fact, emphasized especially by Menzerath,[6] that in the articulation of any sound in the stream of speech, the speaker normally anticipates part or even all of one or more following sounds. The phenomenon is of course familiar to students of historical grammar as the cause of regressive assimilation. In words like tool, cool, where the initial stop is followed by a rounded vowel, the articulation of the stop often anticipates the lip-rounding of the next sound (contrast the stops in tin, keen). These labialized stops are of course nothing but positionally determined allophones of the [t] and [k] phoneme, and their labialization is non-distinctive. The same kind of lip-rounding appears before [w] in words like twin, queen; but in a rapid and relaxed pronunciation of such words the separate phonetic fraction constituting the [w] may be considerably reduced or even lost altogether, so that this anticipatory lip-rounding of the stops remains as the only trace of its presence. (Forms of twin, tweezers, twist, queen, quick, quiz, and the like with a labialized stop immediately followed by a front vowel are not too common, but they are familiar to observers of the spoken language.) In such pronunciations, then, the lip-rounding of the stop is all by itself an allophone of the [w] phoneme, even though it appears simultaneously with the articulation of another sound, and even though in words like tool, cool the phonetically identical lip-rounding is non-distinctive, a mere positional feature of the allophones of [t] and [k]. The intersection is obvious, but again it is only partial; for the character of the following vowel always distinguishes the two values of the lip-rounding.

My third example of partial intersection, which I owe to a communication from Dr. Charles F. Hockett of the University of Michigan, is more complicated. In Hockett's dialect, and probably in that of many other Midwestern speakers, mints, mince, dents, dense all end either in [-ns] or in [-nts], warmth ends either in [-mθ] or in [-mpθ], length ends either in [-ŋθ] or in [-ŋkθ], finds and fines both end either in [-nz] or in [-ndz]. The facts can be formulated by saying that at the end of a stressed syllable after a nasal, there is free variation between a spirant and a cluster of stop plus spirant (the stop being homorganic with the nasal but voiced or voiceless like the spirant). Now, when the nasal is [n] and the spirant is [š] or [ž],* there is the same free variation between [š] and [tš], [ž] and [dž]: bench ends either in [-nš] or in [-ntš], hinge ends either in [-nž] or in [-ndž]. As Hockett observes, the clusters [ts], [dz] and the unit phonemes [tš], [dž] are phonetically quite comparable, and [tš], [dž] differ from [š], [ž] very much as [ts], [dz] differ from [s], [z]. That [tš], [dž] are unit phonemes and not, like [ts], [dz], clusters of two phonemes each, appears from their patterning elsewhere (their distribution, their occurrence before and after other consonants, etc.); yet at the end of a stressed syllable after a nasal, they behave exactly like ordinary clusters of stop plus spirant. The simplest way to describe the facts, it seems to me, is to posit partial intersection: in all positions except the one here defined, the sounds in question are phonemic units; in this one position they are clusters of two phonemes each, [t] + [š] and [d] + [ž], and alternate in free variation with the corresponding simple spirants [š] and [ž] just as other clusters do.

Similar examples could easily be added, from this and other dialects of English as well as from other languages. Partial intersection, as our illustrations show, can never lead to uncertainty in practice and may therefore be admitted in theory without violating sound phonemic method. The same cannot be said, however, of complete intersection. Examples are rare, and are always the result of an error in the analysis.

The unstressed vowels of English have long been a problem. Some writers, including Jones and Kenyon, treat the unstressed vowel of about, sofa, condemn as a separate phoneme, but regard the unstressed vowels of other words (as adding, city, window, etc.) as belonging to classes that include also stressed allophones. Other writers, notably Bloomfield, classify all unstressed vowels in terms of the vowel phonemes found in stressed syllables. A special problem is created by words that appear in two distinct forms according to the accentual conditions under which they are uttered; thus the word at has the vowel of cat in the phrase where át, but the second vowel of sofa in the phrase at hóme. Since the two vowels in this word always appear under different phonetic conditions and are thus in complementary distribution, it is possible to make out a fairly good case for treating both vowels as allophones of the same phoneme. But against this treatment there are two alternative objections, both involving intersection.

---

6 For instance in P. Menzerath and A. de Lacerda, Koartikulation, Steuerung und Lautabgrenzung (Phonetische Studien, No. 1, Berlin & Bonn, 1933).

*For convenience in typing, this reprint uses [š] and [ž] for the IPA and near-IPA symbols found in the original publication in American Speech.

If the weak vowel of at hóme is a member of the same phoneme as the stressed vowel of where át because it alternates with the latter vowel in complementary distribution, what shall we do with the weak vowels of about, sofa, confess, and many other words, which never alternate with a stressed vowel? Those who agree with Bloomfield, as I do, that stress in English is phonemic (distinctive) and who are therefore unwilling to posit a separate phoneme to accommodate the unstressed vowel of the words just mentioned, will probably class this vowel, on the basis of phonetic similarity and pattern congruity,[7] with the stressed vowel of cut, come, rush. But if the weak vowel of abóut, atóne is thus identified with the vowel of cut, while the weak vowel of at home is identified with the vowel of cat, then successive occurrences of the same sound under the same phonetic conditions have been assigned to different phonemes.

The alternative objection involves intersection on an even greater scale. The same reasoning by which the weak vowel of at hóme is identified with the stressed vowel of where át leads us to identify the weak vowels of such phrases as sée them gó, théy could gó, théy will gó, nót so múch (all phonetically identical in my speech with the second vowel of sofa) with the stressed vowels of the phrases not thém, they cóuld, they wíll, not só, etc. In short, the 'neutral' vowel which appears at the end of sofa would come to function as the unstressed member of nearly all the syllabic phonemes of English; or, to put it differently, all the syllabic phonemes would intersect in their unstressed allophones.

Now it is of course true that such intersection will not seem troublesome if we know in advance which phoneme is represented in a particular occurrence of the ambiguous allophone. Knowing the stressed forms of the words at and them (as in where át, not thém), we are able to assign the identical unstressed vowels of at hóme and sée them gó unhesitatingly to their respective classes. But what if we know only the unstressed form, either because we have not heard the stressed alternant or because such an alternant happens not to exist? Suppose that we are studying a new and unfamiliar dialect of English, and that we have succeeded in pairing the stressed and the unstressed vowels of such words as at, them, could, will, so, and the like: if we now hear a phrase like óut of tówn, with the unstressed vowel of the second word perceptually the same as those which we have already identified with various stressed alternants,

how are we to treat this? We must defer the phonemic analysis until we chance to hear a stressed form of the same word, which may not occur at all in the dialect we are studying, or which, if it does occur, we may fail to recognize as 'the same word.' In the case of English or any other familiar language, such an objection may seem less than academic; but it becomes practically important in working with a new language (especially one that has no written literature), and is theoretically important even for an understanding of the structure of our mother tongue. In short, a system in which successive occurrences of a given sound x under the same conditions must be assigned to different phonemes necessarily breaks down, because there can be nothing in the facts of pronunciation—the only data relevant to phonemic analysis—to tell us which kind of x we are dealing with in any particular utterance.

With this general principle stated, I proceed now to what I regard as my most seductive example of apparent intersection. I observed it first in my own speech, but have noticed it also in the speech of others. Indeed, since my pronunciation agrees rather closely, in its general pattern, with the Chicago dialect described by Bloomfield,[8] the feature may be fairly common in Midwestern English.

The pairs of words bit bid, bet bed, bat bad, but bud, bite bide, beat bead, etc., have respectively the same vowel phoneme, but exhibit a regular and fairly constant difference in the length of the vowel allophones. This difference is summarized in the well-known habit of English pronunciation, that vowels and diphthongs (and also liquids and nasals) are longer before a voiced than before a voiceless consonant. The alternation between longer and shorter allophones runs through the whole phonemic system. The vowel of pot is affected by the same automatic alternation: in the pairs pot pod, cop cob, font fond, the vowel of the first word is regularly shorter than that of the second; and there is nothing, so far, to show that a pair like pot pod is not in every way comparable to bit bid.

In my speech bomb is different from balm, bother does not rime with father, and sorry does not rime with starry: the vowel quality is the same in all these words, but in the first word of each pair the vowel is short (just as it is in pot), and in the second noticeably longer. Since the difference in length cannot be explained as an automatic alternation (like the difference in bit bid), we conclude that bomb and balm, bother and father, sorry and starry have different vowel phonemes; and we naturally indentify the vowel of bomb, bother, sorry with the phoneme

7 On pattern congruity, see Swadesh, 'The Phonemic Principle,' and cf. his article 'The Phonemic Interpretation of Long Consonants,' Lang. 13.1–10 (1937). For the analysis of the weak vowel of sofa on the basis here mentioned, as well as for what I regard as the correct interpretation of the other unstressed vowels, see G. L. Trager and Bernard Bloch, 'The Syllabic Phonemes of English,' Lang. 17.223–46 (1941).

8 'The Stressed Vowels of Chicago English,' Lang. 11.97–116 (1935). The phonemic difference between the vowels of pot and balm, noted below, is attributed to the Chicago dialect (ibid., pp. 97–8); but my pronunciation of the two phonemes and their distribution in my speech both differ slightly from Bloomfield's.

of pot. The vowel of balm, father, starry appears also in alms, palm, pa, star, card. Again there is nothing, so far, to show that the phonemic organization is in any way abnormal. But now comes a hitch.

In the sentence Pa'd go (if he could), the utterance fraction pa'd must be analyzed, according to what we have just said, as containing the phoneme of balm. In the sentence The pod grows, the utterance fraction pod must be analyzed, again according to what we have said, as containing the phoneme of pot. But pod, with a vowel distinctly longer than that of pot (just as the vowel of bid is longer than that of bit), is phonetically identical with pa'd! Two occurrences of x under the same conditions have been assigned to different phonemes.

Approaching the intersection, as we have done, from different directions, and starting each time from a body of data already systematized, the conclusion seems inevitable. But the intersection here, as elsewhere, is inadmissible; for if we start from the facts of pronunciation as we meet them, there is never any clue in the utterance itself to tell us which kind of x we are dealing with. The apparent intersection of the phonemes of pot and balm reveals the fact (which otherwise could scarcely have been suspected) that the analysis we have made is faulty, even though we have proceeded on both sides of the intersection according to sound principles and usually valid methods.

If the fraction pa'd in Pa'd go is identical, under the same conditions, with the fraction pod in The pod grows, then both contain the same phoneme. We must choose between assigning the vowel of pa'd to the phoneme of pot, and assigning the vowel of pod to the phoneme of balm. Our choice will be determined by the validity of the resulting analysis.

If we say that pa'd has the phoneme of pot, bomb, bother, font, and the like, we must necessarily classify the vowels of pa, balm, father, alms, card, and so on in the same way; that is, we must deny the obvious fact that in the dialect here considered bomb and balm are different, and the pairs bother and father, sorry and starry do not rime.

We are left, then, with the other alternative. By classifying the vowel of pod—and consequently also the vowels of rob, nod, bog, fond, and the like—as members of the phoneme of balm, we destroy the neat parallelism of the pairs bit bid, bet bed, bite bide, pot pod: the words in the last pair, instead of exhibiting shorter and longer allophones of the same phoneme, have totally different phonemes. But by sacrificing this symmetry we are able to account for all the facts of pronunciation, which is surely the more important requirement. The resulting system is lopsided; but the classes it sets up are such that if we start from the actual utterances of the dialect we can never be in doubt of the class to which any particular fraction of utterance must be assigned.

SIMULTANEOUS COMPONENTS IN PHONOLOGY

ZELLIG S. HARRIS
Language 20.181-205—1944

1.0 This paper[1] investigates the results that may be obtained when phonemes, or utterances in general, are broken down into simultaneously occurring components: as when the English phoneme /b/ is said to consist of voicing plus lip position plus stop closure, all occurring simultaneously.[2]

1.1 The analysis presented here rests on the fact that two independent breakdowns of the flow of speech into elements are physically and logically possible. One is the division of the flow of speech into successive segments; this is used throughout phonology and morphology, and gives us the standard elements (allophones or positional variants; phonemes; morphemes; words; phrases) of descriptive linguistics. The other is the division of each segment into simultaneous components, as when the single sound ['ɛ́] (high-pitched loud-stressed low mid vowel) is said to be the resultant of three components: high pitch, loud stress, and low-mid vowel articulation. It is this type of breakdown, only little used in phonemics today, that is investigated here.

1.2 This investigation will show that intonations, prosodemes and 'secondary phonemes', pitch and stress morphemes and phonemes, and suprasegmental features in general, can all be obtained as a result of the single operation of analyzing the utterances of a language into simultaneous components. It will show that the various limitations of phonemic distribution, including defective distribution of phonemes, can be compactly expressed by means of the same operation. When this operation is carried out for a whole language, it breaks all or most of the phonemes into new sub-elements (components). Each of the old phonemes will be a particular simultaneous combination of one or more of these new elements; and the total number of different components will be much smaller than the previous total number of different phonemes. It will be possible to select and symbolize the components in such a way as to show immediately the limitations of distribution, and in many cases the phonetic composition, of the phonemes in which they occur.

1.3 It will be seen that the linguistic status of these components varies with their length. Components which are precisely the length of a phoneme, i.e. which represent merely the simultaneous breakdown of each phoneme by itself, enable us to eliminate phonemes of defective distribution and to indicate the phonetic composition of each phoneme (§5.3, 4).[2a] We shall also permit some components to have the length of more than one phoneme, i.e. we shall say that such a component stretches over a sequence of phonemes. When phonemes are written with such long components, we shall be able to know the limitations of distribution of any phoneme by looking at the components of which it is composed (§5.2). Some of these long components will extend over all the phonemes of an utterance or linguistic form. These components will turn out to constitute the intonational or other contours of the language (§5.1).

In the following sections, these three groups of components which differ as to their length will be kept separate.

Present Treatment

2.0 We have then a large number of linguistic situations which, it will turn out, can all be described by means of the analysis into simultaneous components. It will be helpful if we briefly note how these situations are usually treated at present.

2.1 <u>Pitch and Stress</u>. There is a particular group of phonetic features which has customarily been separated from the rest of the linguistic material even though simultaneous with it. This is pitch and stress. The extraction of these features out of the flow of speech is due to the fact that they constitute morphemes by themselves, independent of the rest of the speech, with which they are simultaneous. In You. : You? : Yes. : Yes? we have four different sound-sequences, and four different meanings. These must therefore have four different phonemic compositions. This requirement would be satisfied if we had phonemic /U/ and /E/ as high-pitched vowels contrasting with low-pitched /u/ and /e/. Then we would write /yuw/, /yUw/, /yes/, /yEs/. However, the pitch features which are symbolized by /U, E/

---

[1] I am glad to express here my thanks to Dr. Henry Hoenigswald and the members of the linguistic seminar at the University of Pennsylvania for valuable criticism and for linguistic material. I am particularly indebted to Dr. Roman Jakobson for an interesting conversation on the phonetic breakdown and grouping of phonemes. I owe an exceptionally heavy debt to Dr. Bernard Bloch, who has helped me state many of the more difficult points.

[2] This example of phonetic components is given here only for introductory simplicity. The analysis presented below is primarily distributional rather than phonetic.

[2a] E.g. it is this technique that enables us, in languages which have a phonemic tone on each vowel (Fanti, Chinese, etc.), to extract the tones as separate phonemic elements.

have the specific meaning of interrogation. We therefore wish to consider some part of /yUw/, /yEs/ as the morphemes 'you', 'yes' and another part as the morpheme 'interrogation'. This can be done only if we consider /U, E/ to consist of two simultaneous components /u, e/ and /ˊ/. Then the phonemes /u, e/ are part of the morphemes for 'you' and 'yes'; and the phoneme /ˊ/, or rather the rising pitch which extends over the whole utterance, is the morpheme for interrogation.

In most languages that have been investigated, pitch and stress have been found to constitute the elements of special morphemes (such as phrase and sentence intonation or the English contrastive stress). These elements are pronounced simultaneously with the other morphemes of the language. It would be impossible to isolate the other morphemes without extracting the pitch and stress morphemes that occur simultaneously with them. Perhaps as a result of this, it has been customary to extract pitch and stress features even when they form part of the phonemic make-up of ordinary segmental morphemes (words and parts of words). Thus we do not usually say that a language has ten vowels, five loud and five weak, but rather that it has five vowel phonemes plus two degrees of stress.

2.2 <u>Relations among phonemes</u>, and the limitations of distribution of particular phonemes, are not presented in linguistics as an essential part of the individual phonemes. There exists no method which would enable us to say '/b/ is phonemic everywhere except after /s/' or '/t/ is a phoneme except after initial /k/, etc.' Instead we say that /b/ and /t/ are phonemes, and then tack on statements which correct the phonemic list by pointing out that /b/ does not occur after /s/, i.e. that there is no allophone occurring after /s/ which is assigned to /b/. If a number of phonemes have identical distributions, a single statement is devoted to them all. We say, for example, that morpheme-medial clusters in English hardly ever include both a voiceless consonant and a voiced one which has a voiceless homorganic counterpart: we get /ft/, /ks/ in <u>after</u> and <u>axiom</u>, but not /vt/, etc.[2b] If a phoneme occurs in few positions as compared with other phonemes in the language, as is the case with English /ŋ/, we say that it is defective in distribution. But the writing system which we create does not reveal these limitations. Given the phonemes of a language, a person would not know how to avoid making non-extant sequences unless he kept in mind the distribution statements.

The phonologists of the Prague Circle tried to indicate some of these limitations of distribution by saying that a phoneme which does not occur in a given position is 'neutralized' by one which does,

and that an 'archiphoneme' symbol can be written to represent either phoneme in that position. Thus /b/ and /p/ are neutralized after /s/, and can then be represented by the archiphoneme /P/, which would indicate the 'common element' of both: /sPin/ instead of /spin/. This did not in itself prove to be a productive method of description. In the first place, most cases of 'neutralization' involve not merely two phonemes that directly neutralize each other. Usually several phonemes occur in a given position while several others do not, and 'neutralization' may be said to exist between the two whole classes of phonemes; thus after word-initial /s/ we find /p, t, k, f, l, w, y, m, n/ and the vowels, but not /b, d, g, v, θ, ð, š, ž, s, z, r, ŋ, h/. To select /p/ and /b/ out of the two lists and assign them to a separate archiphoneme /P/ implies some further and hitherto unformulated method of phonemic classification on phonetic grounds. And what shall we do with /θ/ or /š/ or /z/?[3]

Related to these limitations of individual phonemes are other distributional facts. In a particular language, certain positions have the greatest number of phonemic contrasts, and others have the least: in Swahili every phoneme may occur in the position after pause, but only the five vowels ever occur before pause or between consonants. There are also limitations upon clustering: in English, not more than three consonants occur in succession initially, nor more than four or five (depending on the inclusion of foreign names) medially in a morpheme. These clusters may be further limited in the order of the phonemes: /t/ occurs after /p/ and /k/ before word-juncture, but not before them. In our present descriptions, facts of this type are not automatically derivable from any other information given. They must be separately stated, and are not represented in the phonemic writing itself.

A less important point in which our present method of description is inadequate is the phonetic similarity among the allophones of various phonemes. Thus English /p, t, k/ all have identically varying allophones in identically varying positions (strongly aspirated initially, unaspirated after /s/, etc.); /k, g, ŋ/ have identical places of articulation in identical environments (fronted allophones after front vowels, etc.). These similarities are recognized in the grammar when we describe the variation in allophones of all the analogous phonemes in one statement, as we have done above. But the similarities among these phonemes are not explicit in the phonemic inventory or directly marked in the transcription.

[2b] Voiced-voiceless sequences like /rp/ in <u>carpet</u> are not counted here, since /r/ has no voiceless homorganic counterpart.

[3] The Prague Circle more closely approached the technique of dividing elements into simultaneous components, but purely on arbitrary phonetic grounds, when they said that the difference between two phonemes was not a vs. b, but a vs. a + x (where x is is a Merkmal denoting the extra features which differentiate b from a). See N. S. Trubetzkoy, Grundzüge der Phonologie 67 (Travaux du Cercle Linguistique de Prague 7; 1939).

2.3 Breaking an allophone into two phonemes.

Whereas the two previous types of treatment have been fairly clear-cut, there is a group of linguistic facts in which the usual treatment is ambiguous: in some cases simultaneous elements are separated out and in other cases they are not, with no very clear criteria to decide whether the separation is to be performed or not.

It is customary to divide an allophone x into two successive allophones $x_1 x_2$ if we can then assign x_1 and x_2 to two otherwise recognized phonemes whose sequence is complementary to x. Thus we may break up English [č] into two successive phonemes /tš/, considering the retracted [t] as a positional variant of /t/ and the fronted [š] off-glide as a positional variant of /š/. We do this because phonemes /t/ and /š/ have already been recognized in English, but do not (except here) occur next to each other. We therefore consider the two successive parts of [č] as the allophonic values of the two phonemes /t/ and /š/ when they do occur next to each other. Certain accessory criteria influence us in deciding to consider the allophone as a combination of the allophones of two phonemes. The positions in which [č] occurs should be such in which sequences of the same type as /tš/ also occur. The new allophones, back [t] before a palatal spirant /š/, and [š] off-glide after a stop /t/, should have some phonetic similarity to other allophones of the phonemes to which they will be assigned, and should if possible have the same relation to them that analogous allophones have in analogous positions. Finally, the original allophone [č] should have some of the phonetic qualities which characterize a sequence of two phonemes in English (e.g. it should be longer than a single phoneme; or should have the tongue moving not directly from the alveolar stop to the position of the next sound, but going out of its way via the spirant off-glide).

In practice, however, this last criterion is often disregarded. Among speakers who distinguish the initials of tune and tool, many pronounce in tune a simple consonant—a palatalized post-dental blade stop with no recognizable [y] off-glide; nevertheless we consider that allophone to represent the phonemic sequence /ty/. Similarly the nasalized alveolar flap in painting, which contrasts with the alveolar nasal continuant in paining, is not considered a new phoneme occurring only after loud-stressed vowel and before zero-stressed vowel, but is assigned to the sequence /nt/.[4] Analyses of this type constitute an important departure in method, because we are here analyzing a sound segment into two simultaneous parts and assigning one part to one phoneme and the

other to another. In the case of /ty/ we may say that the post-dental occlusion is the allophone of /t/ and the simultaneous palatalization is the allophone of /y/. In the case of /nt/, we may say that nasalization combined with the obstruction of the breath in the dental-alveolar area is the allophone of /n/, and the alveolar flap movement is the normal allophone of /t/ between loud and zero-stressed vowels. In each case we have avoided the introduction of a new phoneme with defective distribution, by assigning the sound to a sequence of previously recognized phonemes.

In all these cases we have an allophone broken up into components each of which we consider an allophone of phonemes which had already been recognized in other positions. As an extension of this analysis we have the occasional setting up of a new suprasegmental phoneme to account for a whole sequence of allophones which always appear together. Thus in Moroccan Arabic a new suprasegmental emphatic phoneme[5] is set up to account for the emphatic allophones. Phonetically, we have [ṣog] 'drive' (with cerebral [ṣ]); [ḍaṛ] 'house' (with cerebral [ḍ] and [ṛ]), but [dær] 'he built'; [lanba] 'lamp' (with low back [a]), but [læbs] 'dressing'. We could write this phonemically by considering [ṣ, o, ḍ, a, ṛ] to be different phonemes from [s, u, d, æ, r] respectively. But we notice that to say this would indicate a greater phonemic distinction than actually exists. In [lanba] ⌒ [læbs], the difference between [a] and [æ] is phonemic; for there is nothing in the neighboring phonemes to indicate that the vowel is [a] in one word and [æ] in the other. But in [ḍaṛ] ⌒ [dær] the difference between [a] and [æ] need not be considered phonemic; for [æ] never occurs next to [ḍ], and we could say that [a] is the positional variant of the [æ] phoneme next to /ḍ/ and other emphatics (i.e. cerebrals). This crux is avoided by breaking each emphatic phoneme into two simultaneous parts: a regular consonant or vowel, and an emphatic component: [ṣ] is analyzed as /s/ plus /'/, [o] as /u/ plus /'/, etc. It is then shown that when this emphatic component occurs after consonants it affects a sequence of phonemes, but when it occurs after vowels it affects only the preceding phoneme: /s'ug/ = [ṣog], /d'ær/ = [dar], /læ'nba/ = [lanba]. But it must be noted that this new phoneme is not inescapable. We could have written each of the Moroccan emphatic sounds as a new emphatic phoneme, and added a statement that in certain positions emphatic phonemes occur with each other to the exclusion of non-emphatic phonemes. However, such a statement would be at least as complicated as the equivalent statement which gives the domain of the single emphatic phoneme, and would leave us with a large number of extra and defectively distributed phonemes instead of the single emphatic /'/.

---

[4] Y. R. Chao gives other 'cases of one homogeneous sound represented by two or three piece symbols, each of which represented some aspect or aspects of the sound' in his article The Non-Uniqueness of Phonemic Solutions of Phonetic Systems, Bulletin of the Institute of History and Philology 4.371 (Academia Sinica; Shanghai, 1934) ⟪38⟫.

[5] Z. S. Harris, The Phonemes of Moroccan Arabic, JAOS 62.309–18 (1942).

Introduction of Simultaneous Components

3.0 The various linguistic situations mentioned in §§2.1–3 can all be compactly described by the use of simultaneous components. In order to introduce these components, all we need do is to permit the segmental elements of our linguistic description to be resolved into any number of simultaneous component sub-elements.

3.1 This is not a new operation in linguistics: it is used implicitly when pitch and stress features are extracted as separate phonemes, and it is used when we analyze English flapped [n] as /nt/. There is no particular reason to admit such analysis in these cases and to deny it in such cases as the Greek aspiration (which, like stress, occurred in most forms only once within a word) or English voicelessness (which, like the Moroccan Arabic emphatic, occurs over a sequence of phonemes). No new methods or postulates are therefore required to extend the analysis of simultaneous components into all the phonemes of a language.

3.2 It may also be noted that this operation involves us in no theoretical difficulties. It does not prevent us from having a statable physical character for our linguistic elements. The traditional phonemes indicate explicit physical events: time-stretches of sound (sound-waves), or sets of simultaneous motions of the 'vocal organs'. The new component elements also indicate explicit physical events: time-stretches of sound-waves,[5a] or motions of particular vocal organs.[6] The only difference is that phonemes are elements which can, in general, occur only after one another, while components are elements which can also occur simultaneously with each other (as well as after each other).

3.3 If we are to permit our segmental elements to be resolved into components, we must bear in mind that there are many different ways in which any elements can be broken down into sub-elements. There are a great many ways in which components—various numbers of them and variously grouped—can be arranged so that every combination of components recognized in the arrangement will yield a particular phoneme. Such expressions of phonemes

in terms of components are not in themselves of value to linguistics. The advantage they offer in reduction of the number of elements may be more than offset if connecting them with the distributional and phonetic facts requires more complicated statements than are required for regular phonemes. We consider the possibility of such analysis into components only because, as will be shown below, we can select the components in a way that will enable us to give simpler statements of the facts about phonemes.

3.4 We can now say in general terms what we must do when we analyze phonemes into components. We take a list of phonemes, each with its phonetic and distributional description; we select a number of components; we select some method for combining these components simultaneously (e.g. not more than three components at a time), in such a way that each combination permitted by the method will identify a phoneme, and that the grammar becomes simpler and briefer when written in terms of the components.

Properties of the Components

4.0 Since the components are to be physical elements (§3.2), we must consider the phonetic values that they can have (§4.1). Furthermore, it will be seen that in special cases a component (or its phonetic value) may extend over more than one phoneme; and it will be important to note what happens when we get such long components (§4.2). The work that a component can do in the description of a language depends on its length. Components whose length is that of one phoneme can be used to describe the phonetic composition of phonemes (§5.4) or the dissection of a single allophone into two or more phonemes (§5.3). Components whose length is that of two or three phonemes (or thereabouts) can be used to indicate the limitations of distribution of any phoneme which contains them (§5.2). And components which can extend over long sequences of phonemes are used in the descriptions of intonational and other contours (§5.1).

4.1 Phonetic values. Since the components are to identify phonemes, or more generally speech sounds, each component must have a stated phonetic value in each environment in which it occurs. As in the case of phonemes, there is no reason to require that its phonetic value be identical in all environments. The component can therefore have different phonetic variants (allophones) in various positions, and the environmental factor which determines the particular allophone may be anything outside the component itself: other components with which it is concurrent, neighboring components or pauses, position of the component within the sequence of segments, etc.

Again as in the case of phonemes, it is not required that components have a constant phonetic value throughout their duration. A component may have a phonetic value which changes in a fixed way in respect to its end-points: e.g. falling tone, increase in nasality, voiceless beginning and voiced ending.

[5a] It is possible, by Fourier analysis, to replace periodic waves by a sum of simpler periodic waves. The original waves (e.g. sound waves) can then be considered the resultants which are obtained by adding together all their component waves.

[6] E.g. vibration of the vocal cords, giving 'voice'. This might be the phonetic value of a particular component in a particular position, whereas the phonetic value of a particular phoneme in a particular position might be, for example, voice plus closing off of the nose plus closing of the lips (English /b/). A phonetic system of this kind without the phonemic limitations is Otto Jespersen's analphabetic system, presented in his Lehrbuch der Phonetik (2d ed. Leipzig and Berlin, 1912) and elsewhere.

Finally, if we are ready to admit partial overlapping among phonemes,[7] we may agree to have different components in different environments represent the same phonetic value. So long as we do not have a component in one environment represent two phonetic values which are not freely interchangeable, or two components or component-combinations in the same environment represent the same phonetic value, we are preserving the bi-unique one-to-one correspondence of phonemic writing. (The term bi-unique implies that the one-to-one correspondence is valid whether we start from the sounds or from the symbols: for each sound one symbol, for each symbol one sound.)

4.2 Length values. Whereas the considerations of phonetic value are comparable for phonemes and for components, we find that in the matter of length there is an important restriction upon phonemes which can be lifted in the case of components. In the operations which lead to the setting up of phonemes, one of the most important steps is segmenting the flow of speech into successive unit lengths, such that every allophone or phoneme consists of exactly one of these lengths.[7a] In analyzing out the components, we make use of this segmentation, because what we break down are phonemes or allophones, not just random parts of the speech flow. However, there is no reason for us to restrict every component to the length of one phoneme. If a component is always common to a sequence of phonemes, we can say that its length is the length of the sequence. This will enable us to describe the limitations of phoneme sequences. When particular phonemes occur next to each other (e.g. English /sp/ in /spin/), while others do not (e.g. /sb/), we will say that the phonemes which occur next to each other all have some one component in common. The length of a component will therefore always be an integral number of phoneme-lengths—1, 2, 3, etc.—but need not be just one.

It follows that just as a component may have different phonetic variants in different positions, so it may have different lengths in different environments. When the Moroccan Arabic emphatic occurs after a vowel, it affects only the preceding vowel; when it occurs after a consonant, it affects a whole neighborhood, including several consonants and vowels.

Obtaining the Components

5.0 The greatest advantage from the analysis into components comes from the components with a length of two or more phonemes. These components enable us to express situations which could not be symbolized by the fixed-length phonemes. We shall investigate

these components first. The first technique we shall use will yield the syntactic contours. The second will yield a way of treating the limitations of distribution of phonemes. The third will yield special cases of segmental phonemes. Finally we shall consider the components whose length is that of only one phoneme.

5.1 Automatic sequences expressed by long components. Our first operation is to extract those components which appear only in fixed patterns.

Intonations. We first consider the case where some connection among particular successive components in successive allophones is readily noticeable to us—that is, where we do not have to conduct a search to find a series of components which we can extract. Since we are assuming that no simultaneous elements have as yet been extracted, we have our language material in the form not of phonemes but of allophones, with each future phoneme, or at least each vowel, represented by many allophones:[7b] loud and middle-pitched [a], loud and high-pitched [a], very loud and middle-pitched [a], soft and low-pitched [a], etc. As a result of our past experience with languages, we may tend to scrutinize particularly the various stresses or pitches of each successive allophone in an utterance. However, we may also happen to note fixed patterns in the sequence of other features in successive allophones: e.g. a decrease in sharpness of articulatory movements from the beginning to the end of English utterances. Or we may notice a fixed pattern composed of several phonetic features of successive allophones: decrease in sharpness plus level tone during most of the utterance, followed by a falling tone at the end, in certain types of English statement.

In any case, we look for successions of phonetic features which recur in various utterances. We note that the occurrence of these features is limited: only certain sequences appear. For instance, we find the relative pitch sequence 1221130 (where 3 = highest and 0 = lowest) in I don't know where he's going. We can't tell when they're coming. etc. Among utterances with the same stress positions we do not find other pitch sequences ending in 30. For utterances with these stresses then, we tentatively count the above pitch sequence as one of the fixed patterns. We then see if we can in any way reduce the number of fixed patterns. We note that before the final 30, the slightly raised pitch 2 occurs wherever a mildly loud stress occurs; we therefore consider pitch 2 to be an allophone of pitch 1 in stressed position. Other

[7] Bernard Bloch, Phonemic Overlapping, American Speech 16.278–84 (1941) ((93)).
[7a] The lengths are not absolute (so many hundredths of a second) but relative. This means that an allophone [p], for instance, is not composed of two shorter allophones 'p-closure' and 'p-release'.

[7b] We will assume that these allophones satisfy all the criteria for phonemes—that is, that complementary allophones have been grouped together—except that allophones having different stress and pitch have been considered different sounds and hence not grouped together under one symbol. It is impossible to obtain the conventional phonemes until intonational components have been extracted from the allophones.

pitch sequences can also be considered special cases of this one: occurrences of relative high pitch 4 at one or more places in such utterances will always be accompanied by a loud contrastive stress (Wé can't tell when they're coming. 4221130), and can therefore also be considered an allophone of pitch 1. As a result of such manipulations a large number of pitch sequences ending in 30 become identical. They are all cases of one fixed sequence: as many relatively low tones as vowels (with slightly raised tones under stress and fairly high tones under contrastive stress) followed by a middling high tone on the last stressed vowel with a drop to zero (lowest) pitch on the vowels or consonants after it.

In English, a number of other sequences will not be reducible to this. For instance, there is the sequence in which every loud-stressed vowel, and every vowel or consonant after the last loud stress, has a higher pitch than the preceding one, while every zero-stressed vowel has the same pitch as the preceding loud-stressed: You're not going over to Philadelphia? 012233333456.

By investigating all these intonations, we obtain a small number of pitch-sequence patterns, occurring over whole utterances or over sections of utterances (phrases, etc.). In phonemics, if we were dealing with a fixed sequence of segmental phonemes as long as these sequences of pitch, we should have to consider it as composed of the observable successive elements; and the fact that only a very few of the possible sequences of these elements occur could only be stated as a limitation upon their distribution. Since, however, components are not restricted as to length, we can say in this case that each of these pitch sequences is a single component whose length is that of a whole utterance or phrase. This is permissible, since the successive parts of the sequence are not independent of each other (e.g. before 30, only 1's occur) and may all be considered parts of one element. And it is advantageous, since we thus avoid having to state limitations of distribution for individual phonemic tones.

The essential operation here is to put two successive sounds or sound features into one unit if they always occur together in a particular environment. This is often done in phonemics, as when we consider the aspiration after initial [p, t, k] to be not a separate phoneme but part of the allophones of /p, t, k/ in that position.[8] Similarly, in these few fixed sequences of pitch or the like, we consider the parts of each sequence to be automatically dependent upon each other, so that the whole sequence is one phonemic element.[9]

[8] This operation is used implicitly throughout phonemics to keep us from breaking sounds down into smaller and smaller segments ad infinitum. We do not consider the lip closing and the lip opening of intervocalic /p/ to be separate phonemes, because they always occur together in that position.

[9] A fuller discussion of the character of these contour components is given in fn. 22a below.

Components of components. If we wish to reduce the number of such dependent-sequence elements, we analyze them in turn into components on the basis of phonetic similarity (since there are no limitations of distribution among them) in the same way that this will be done for segmental phonemes. (see §5.4 below). That is, we break up the sequences into any simultaneous components which seem most convenient, and the combinations of which uniquely indentify each sequence: e.g. the direction of pitch change after the last stressed vowel, the degree of change there, etc.

Stress. An analogous operation is performed when we have word or morpheme junctures phonemically established and note that some feature always occurs exactly once· between each two junctures, or that some phonetic feature has fixed patterns between junctures. Thus we may note that there is never more than one loud stress between word junctures in English, and that the other vowels between these junctures have medium or weak stress, usually in fixed patterns: e.g. 1030 in distribution, independent, etc. Certain facts about the stresses are thus automatic: the number of loud stresses, the occurrence of some of the weak stresses. We therefore mark as phonemic only the remaining non-automatic facts: the place of the loudest stress, and where necessary the place of any secondary stress. In a similar way, English contrastive stress (1040 in distribution, not production) would be discovered, since when it does occur it hardly ever appears more than once between two word junctures. This operation, however, will not discover features which do not appear in a limited number of fixed sequences, e.g. pitch in languages where all sequences occur and where the different sequences cannot be reduced into special cases of one another.

In dealing here with dependent sequences, it has been assumed that the phonetic features comprising the sequences would be readily noticed by the linguist. This is usually the case not only because pitch and stress are so frequently the features concerned, but also because it is relatively easy to notice phonetic features which show recurrent patterns in many sequences of allophones. Nevertheless, the analysis in no way depends upon a lucky finding of these phonetic features. It is possible to discover any fixed sequences methodically by the laborious process of taking each allophone (or each of a class of allophones, e.g. vowels) in many utterances and seeing in what respect the allophone after it is limited: e.g. given a low-pitched, sharply-articulated, weak-stressed vowel at the beginning of various utterances, can we find examples of every grade of pitch, sharpness, and stress in the vowel after it, or do only certain grades occur?

Segmental allophones. The net result of this operation has been not only to produce a number of phonemic sequences of phonetic features (e.g. pitch-sequence phonemes), but also to extract these same phonetic features (e.g. pitch) from the recorded flow of speech. The recurring fixed patterns helped us to notice these phonetic features and gave us the basis for extracting them as a single independent element. But by doing so we are left with the original sequence of allophones minus these features. If we now go back to the allophones, we shall find that the extraction of these dependent-sequence elements (e.g. pitch) has reduced the allophones, which had originally differed in these features, to the conventional phonemes: the variously stressed and pitched [a]'s are now identical /a/, since they no longer represent classes of actual sounds but only features of sounds—namely, all the features except stress and pitch. What we thus obtain out of our original allophones equals the conventional phonemes merely because it has been customary for linguists to extract pitch and stress features, so that our usual phonemes are even now not classes of sounds but classes of sounds minus their pitch and stress features. The original allophones with which we began here were pure classes of freely varying or complementary sounds, and when we extracted the dependent sequences, which in most cases are composed of the pitch and stress features, we obtained the conventional phonemes.

The fact that most of these fixed sequences of sound components have meanings, or correlate with morphological constructions, is a matter apart. This fact is independently recognized by including them in the list of morphemes of the language. Dependent sequences may turn out to be phonemic without being morphemes, e.g. word-stress, varying rhythms and melodies of speech.

5.2 Limitations of distribution expressed by long components. In our second operation we consider the usual type of limitation of distribution, in which a phoneme that occurs in most environments is limited by never appearing in certain positions. Here no solution is possible within the methods of segmental phonemics. The difficulty with the archiphoneme device, and with the statements about distributional relations between phonemes, is that they seek only to find a relation or common factor among the phonemes that can or cannot occur in a given environment. But there also exists a relation between the phonemes which occur in a given environment and the environment itself, namely the fact that they occur next to each other. That relation exists, for instance, between English /ŋ/ and /k/, but not between /ŋ/ and /t/. If we are willing to break phonemes up into simultaneous components, we restate relation as a factor common to /ŋ/ and /k/ but not to /t/; and we say that /ŋ/ and /k/ each contain a certain component (say, back position) and that this component spreads over the length of two phonemes when the first is nasal. /ŋt/ therefore does not occur, nor /nk/, because the component of mouth position always extends identically over both phoneme places. If we mark n̠ for nasal without regard to mouth position, and s̠ for stop without regard to mouth position, and ‾ for alveolar and ‾‾ for velar position, then we say that the latter two marks always have 2-phoneme length when beginning with /n̠/.[9a] Thus /n̠s̠/ = /nt/ and /n̠s̠/ = /ŋk/; there is no way to write /nk/, since ‾ is so defined that it cannot be stopped after the /n̠/.

By the use of components which are defined so as to extend over a number of phoneme places, we thus circumvent the limitation in distribution of the phonemes. This is not merely a trick, concealing the limitations of the phonemes in the definitions of the components. For the components are generalized phonemes: they appear concurrently with each other as well as next to each other, and they may have a length of several phoneme-places as well as of one phoneme-place. And when we write with these components it is natural that various ones will have various lengths; each of them has to have some stated length, and the components symbolized by ‾ and ‾‾ are simply among those that in some situations have 2-phoneme length.

Since we should like our new elements, the components, to have as general a distribution as possible, we try to select them in such a way that the components which occur under (or together with) a two-length component should also occur without it. Thus given English morpheme-medial /sp/ but not /sb/, we say that the component common to /s/ and /p/ is unvoicing, or fortisness, and that its length is that of the cluster in which it is present. /sp/ is then a sequence of sibilant plus stop, with overriding unvoicing. The same sequence occurs with the unvoicing absent: /zb/ in Asbury. As in the case above, /sb/ and /zp/ cannot be written in terms of components, because of our definition of the length of the unvoicing.

[9a] Linguistic forms which are written in components will be set between diagonals, in the same way as forms written phonemically. It is convenient to use identical brackets for these two systems, because many linguistic forms cited in this paper are written partly in phonemes, partly in components: e.g. /t̄sz'r/ 'tree'. We write in components only those parts of a form which are under discussion. This is permissible because phonemics is merely a special case of component analysis; the extension from phonemics into components can be carried out to any degree desired. In the analysis of Moroccan Arabic cited in fn. 5, the phonemes are of the usual kind except for the component /'/ (§2.3 above), which is included among the phonemes.—In some cases, where it is clear that a symbol indicates a component, the diagonals are omitted. The use of non-alphabetic marks like the horizontal bar (§5.2) is not in general desirable; but only such marks can depict on paper the effect of a long component that extends over more than one phoneme.

General formula. The procedure of obtaining these 2-length (and longer) components can be stated generally. If we have a sequence of two phonemes xy, we can select any number of factors which they have in common (both may be oral, both articulated in a certain position, both voiced or both voiceless, both explosive as against implosive, etc.). If one of these two phonemes does not occur with some third phoneme (say xc does not occur), we can then say that xy have significantly that component in common which c lacks. We call this component γ, and say that it has 2-phoneme length. Then x consists of this component γ plus some residue w, and y consists of the same γ plus some other residue u; thus /s/ = unvoicing plus sibilant articulation, /p/ = unvoicing plus lip and nose closing. We try to identify some other sequence of phonemes with these residues, and in particular to have the phoneme c equal the residue u, since the phoneme c is already known as lacking the component γ; in this case such a sequence would be /zb/, where /z/ = sibilant articulation, /b/ = lip and nose closing.[10]

If xy occurs	then xy = γ + (wu)
xu does not occur	x = γ + (w)
wu occurs	y = γ + (u)

Then our new elements are w, u, and the 2-length γ, and all possible sequences of them occur. There is no longer any limitation of distribution: w and u occur alone (intervocalic /z/ and /b/) and together as wu (cluster /zb/), and each of these occurs with γ in the combinations γ + w = /s/, γ + u = /p/, γ + wu = cluster /sp/.[11] If we represent unvoicing by a small circle, we may paraphrase our general formula as follows:

Since /sp/ occurs	/sp/ = ° + (zb)
/sb/ does not occur	/s/ = ° + (z)
/zb/ occurs	/p/ = ° + (b)

Assimilations. In Moroccan Arabic, the clusters /šš/, /žž/, /šž/ all occur, as well as the clusters /ss/ and /zz/; and there are morphemes which contain both /š/ and /ž/, or both /s/ and /z/, not contiguous to each other and in any order. But no morpheme containing /s/ or /z/ ever contains also /š/ or /ž/ anywhere within its bounds, nor does /s/ or /z/ ever occur in a morpheme with /š/ or /ž/. This complete statement of limitations[12] can be eliminated if we extract the feature ↑ as a component and define it as having the length of a morpheme[13] and the pho-

[10] More briefly: Given that xy occurs, we select u such that xu does not occur. Then y = γ + u (where γ has 2-phoneme length, when two phonemes are present), and x = γ + w, where w is selected so that wu occurs.

[11] Note that in this example γ does not occur alone.

[12] Aside from an unrelated limitation between /s/ and contiguous /z/.

[13] Or of a word, except for one enclitic. That is, when ↑ occurs, it extends from one word juncture to the next.

netic value of retracting the tongue when in sibilant position (and as having zero phonetic value when the tongue is not in sibilant position). In doing this we can simply follow the formula above. /š...ž/ occur in one morpheme and represent our xy; /š...z/ do not occur in one morpheme and represent our xc. The factor common to /š, ž/ and absent in /z/ (our γ component) is ↑, a component of morpheme length. Then /ž/ (our y) consists of ↑ (our γ) plus a residue (our u), and we identify this residue with /z/ (our c), which fits in with the fact that /š...z/ does not occur. And since /s...z/ does occur, we consider /s/ to be the residue of /š/ when the ↑ component is extracted: /š/ = ↑ + /s/, /ž/ = ↑ + /z/, /šž/ = ↑ + /sz/, etc. We now have three elements /s/, /z/, and ↑, each with its stated length and phonetic value, and all sequences of them occur:[14] /s/ in /iams/ 'yesterday', /zz/ in /zzit/ 'the olive', /sz/ in /↑sz'r/ (= /šž'r̩/) 'tree', /ss/ and /z/ in /↑ssrzm/ (=/ššržm/) 'the window', etc.

/šš/ occurs	/šš/ = ↑ + (ss)
/šs/ does not occur	/š/ = ↑ + (s)
/ss/ occurs	/s/ = (s)

Note that ↑ has a defined phonetic value when it occurs with some phonemes (the sibilants) and zero phonetic value when it occurs with other phonemes within its length.

Frequently the γ + u and the u, i.e. the phonemes which do and which do not occur next to the γ + w, represent whole classes of phonemes. In Swahili, /t, d, k, g, s, z, l, r, n/ occur after /n/, but the other consonants /p, b, f, v, m, h, θ, ð, γ/ do not.

/nt/ occurs	/nt/ = ‾ + (mp)
/np/ does not occur	/n/ = ‾ + (m)
/mp/ occurs	/t/ = ‾ + (p)

We call /n/ a 2-length component having the value of a dental nasal when occurring by itself, and stated other values (mostly, retarding of the tongue) when occurring simultaneously with various other components. Hence the n-component by itself = /n/. When the n-component is simultaneous with a labial, its value is tongue retarding, so that (n+p) = /t/. Since the n-component has the length of two phonemes, it will always stretch over the p whenever n occurs before it, so that /n p/ = /n (n+p)/ = /nt/. In terms of fixed-length phonemes, the distributional statements seem paradoxical: we are saying that p occurs after /n/, but when it does, it isn't /p/ at all but /t/. This apparent paradox brings out the difference, and the profit, in speaking in terms of components. For in terms of components we have two statements: 1. t = (p+n), d = (b+n), etc.; 2. n has 2-phoneme length when over consonants. Initially, or after m or vowels, we may have the components which constitute /p/, or those which constitute /t/ (i.e. the p components plus the n component): /paka/ 'cat', /tatu/ 'three'. After /n/, the components which

[14] See fn. 12.

comprise /p/ may indeed occur, but they then fall under the length of the n component, and their conjunction with that component yields /t/: /amentizama/ 'he saw me'. If we take an /n/, we can say that the /p/ components may follow it (in which case the n component extends over them); or we may say that the /t/ components follow it, since the segment following /n/ will actually contain precisely the /t/ components (/p/ components plus the n component). It makes no difference which we say, since either statement describes the same situation. This type of description, which cannot differentiate between /np/ and /nt/ in Swahili, corresponds exactly to the Swahili situation where /np/ does not exist phonemically as against /nt/. When we speak in terms of components, therefore, we do not have to make statements of limitation of distribution such as that the phoneme /p/ does not occur after the phoneme /n/.

A component may have a particular length when it occurs in one environment, and another when it is in other positions. In the case of the Moroccan Arabic emphatic (§2.3), we find the following sequences: /tæ/, /ta/ (rare), /ṭa/ (the /ṭ/ being domal unaspirated), but not /ṭæ/ (except across word juncture). We say that /ṭ/ and /a/ each contain a 2-place component ' whose phonetic value in general is to pull consonants and vowels to central position. The lack of /ṭæ/ is explained by that fact that /æ/ does not contain the ' component. We call /æ/ the residue of /a/ after the ' is extracted. Then since /tæ/ does occur, we call /t/ the residue of /ṭ/ after ' is extracted. Now /a/ = ' + /æ/, /ṭ/ = ' + /t/, /ṭa/ = ' + /tæ/, and every combination occurs. We write /mæt/ 'he did', but /gæt'/ for [gaṭ] 'pliers' and /t'æb/ for [ṭab] 'he repented'. However, in this case we also have /ta/ occurring, though rarely, as in [banka] 'bank'. The only way to write it is to restrict our previous statement: ' is a 2-place component only when it appears with a consonant; on the rare occasions when it appears concurrently with a vowel (written after the vowel) it is a one-place component. Now we add /ta/ = /tæ/ + '; we write /bæ'nkæ'/ 'bank'.

/ṭa/ occurs	/ṭa/ = (t'æ)
/ṭæ/ does not occur	/ṭ/ = (t')
/tæ/ occurs	/a/ = (æ')
/ta/ occurs rarely	/ta/ = t(æ')

This situation is repeated for all the vowels and nine of the consonants, and the length of ' when placed after a consonant turns out to be several phonemes, not all contiguous. However, all these additional results can be obtained merely by repeating the investigation sketched above.

The technique of using these components to express limited distribution may simplify the description of morphophonemic alternation. For example, German has (to take only one pair) contrasting /t, d/ before vowels, as in bunte 'colored ones', Bunde '(in the)

group', but only /t/ before open juncture (- or #, and in certain types of clusters). The lack of the sequence /d-/ involves morphophonemic complications, since morphemes ending in /d/ before a vowel, end in /t/ before open juncture: /bunt/, /bunde/ 'group'. The /t-/ is the xy of our formula, and /d-/ is the xc which does not occur. We recognize a 2-place component having the phonetic value of unvoicing (but having zero value on certain phonemes such as /e/) which is common to /t/ and open juncture /-/ but lacking in /d/. If we write this component as $\overline{}$, we can say that open juncture equals $\overline{}$, and /t/ = /d/ + $\overline{}$. Since /e/ does not contain the $\overline{}$ component, /d/ is free to occur before it. However, since we also have /t/ before /e/, we must define $\overline{}$ as having 2-place length only when it occurs by itself (i.e. when it equals open juncture) and as having one-place length otherwise. We now have /bund̄/, /bundē/ = bunt, bunte, and /bund̄/, /bundē/ = Bund, Bunde (where the overhanging $\overline{}$ is the phonemic open juncture). The writing is still phonemic /bund̄/ 'group' and /bund̄/ 'colored' are still identical. But now we need not say that there is a morphophonemic alternation in the word for 'group'. The morpheme is /bund/ in both environments; the unvoicing heard before open juncture is not part of the morpheme /bund/ but is an automatic part of open juncture. This juncture consists of the component $\overline{}$, which is a 2-place component in this position. Note that since open juncture is phonemic, we should have to write it one way or another, if in no other way than by a space. We can equally well write this open juncture with one or more of the new components, so long as the sum of their phonetic values in that position equals the phonetic value of open juncture (and pause). In contrast with this, the morpheme 'colored' is /bund̄/, as in the inflected form /bund̄er/; when it occurs before open juncture the $\overline{}$ component of the juncture and the $\overline{}$ component of the last place in the morpheme coincide, and we have /bund̄/.

/t-/ occurs	/t-/ = $\overline{}$ + (d (+ vowel))
/d-/ does not occur	/t/ = $\overline{}$ + (d)
/d/ + vowel occurs	/-/ = $\overline{}$

In view of the possibilities of a component coinciding with a 2-length component extending over the next place, this case does not eliminate the practical lexical problem: given /bund̄/ we do not know whether the morpheme is /bund/ or bund̄/. But in terms of components we need no longer say that Bund has two forms.

Dissimilations. In all the foregoing cases there has been a physical similarity between the phonemes that occur together, which is not shared by the phonemes that do not occur in such combinations. The matter is somewhat more difficult when it is the dissimilar phonemes that occur together while the similar ones do not.

In classical Greek, only one aspirate occurs in a stem with its affixes, except for a very few morphemes, and there is a morphophonemic alternation between aspirates and non-aspirates, as when an aspirate-initial stem is reduplicated with the homorganic non-aspirate: φύω 'I produce', pf. πέφῦκα. We analyze φ into /p/ plus a component ʿ having the length of a stem plus its affixes, and the phonetic value of aspiration after one of the voiceless stops (which one, to be stated in terms of the phonetic structure of the word) and zero after every other phoneme. It is now possible to write /ʿpépūka/, with the ʿ component written anywhere in the word, and with no need for morphophonemic statements.[15]

In Moroccan Arabic, double consonants are common (e.g. /tt/ in /fttš/ 'he searched', etc.), but no two different phonemes pronounced in the same mouth position (labial, dental, palatal, laryngal) ever occur next each other (with certain exceptions): there is no /fb, bf, td, gx, ɛh/,[16] etc. If we try to pin this limitation upon a component of one of the phonemes, say /f/ among the labials, we must recognize that component in all the other homorganic phonemes— /b/ and /m/—since the limitation applies equally to them. In order to enable the component to have any effect upon the neighborhood of the labial (so as to preclude another labial there), it must be present also in the neighboring position. We are thus faced with the need for a component which occurs in all the labials and in the place next to each labial, and which permitts only a doubling of that labial, or a non-labial, to occur, but no different labial. This can be done by a 3-length component whose phonetic value is defined as follows: in its middle length, labial (so that the component serves to distinguish, say, the labial voiced stop /b/ from the dental voiced stop /d/); in its first and third lengths, labial if the other components are identical with those of the middle length, and laryngal otherwise. If this component is simultaneous in its middle length with the components for voiced stop, it will yield /b/ in that position; and if on either side there are again the voiced-stop components alone, this component will yield with them another /b/; while if the components there are anything else, say voiceless continuant, this component, extending over them, will with them yield a corresponding laryngal voiceless continuant,

15 The morphophonemic alternation of φ for π + ʿ (e.g. in ἀφ' ὧν) can also be avoided, if the ʿ component is written where it is heard. In the few cases of two aspirates within a word, a second ʿ would have to be written over the extra aspirate, and the statement of the length of ʿ would have to be adjusted accordingly. In the case of reduplication there is a real elimination of the morphophonemic statement: the stem initial in /ʿpépūka/ (or /pépʿūka/) is /p/, which is duly present in the reduplication.

16 For the phonetic values of these phonemes see op. cit. in fn. 5.

/ḥ/.[17]

If, as in English, there are no double consonants, we have to say that certain components, one or another of which is present in every consonant, have 3-phoneme lengths and have some stated value in their middle length and some contrary value in their end lengths, if the other components are identical with those of the middle length.

Clustering. Further extensions of our method are necessary when we treat some of the more complicated limitations upon clusters, especially when limitations of order are present, i.e. when certain phonemes occur in one order but not in another. For example, English has morpheme-medial clusters like /rtr/, /ndw/, as in portrait, sandwich, but never clusters like /trt/, with any one of the consonants /r, l, m, n, ŋ, y, w/ in the middle. We cannot say simply that phonemes in the class of /r/ do not occur after stops, because in clusters of two consonants we have /rt, kr, lr, pt/ (curtain, secret, walrus, reptile; but no stop other than /t/ or /d/ after another stop). We require, therefore, a component extending over the length of a cluster and having the following phonetic values: in first position, general consonant value (serving incidentally to distinguish consonants from vowels; this because any consonant may occur here); in second position, continuant or /t, d/ if it follows a stop, otherwise general consonant value; in third position, continuant if it follows a stop (but if the stop is /t, d/, this value only if a continuant precedes it), otherwise, vocalic value. This value of the consonant-component permits any clusters of two except stop plus /p, b, k, g/, and then permits the third place to have continuant value (and to remain a member of the cluster) only if the preceding two are continuant and stop; otherwise the component has non-consonant value and thus changes the third position into a vowel. This statement does not allow for clusters with middle /s/, as in sexton, and omits several details which would be taken care of in the other components for the individual phonemes. However, it is included here to show that even fairly complicated clusterings can be described by single components.

Summary. The net result of this technique is the extraction of 2-length and longer components from all sequences that can be matched against non-occurring sequences (a sequence being an environment and the phoneme that occurs in it); e.g. from English /rtr/ matched against /trt/. These components do part of

17 The laryngal value for the ends of the labial component is not essential, though it seemed most convenient for various reasons. It would also be possible to assign merely a 'non-labial' value to the ends of the labial component, leaving it to the components in the neighboring positions to decide whether they are laryngal, dental, or palatal. They cannot be labial because a 'non-labial' component extends over them.

the work of identifying and phonetically describing the phoneme over which they extend (e.g. the ‛ gives the aspiration component of Greek φ), so that only a residue of the original phoneme is required to accompany them (in this case /p/ to accompany ‛: /‛p/ = φ). This residue in turn can designate another phoneme which occurs without the component (/p/ = π). Meanwhile, the length of the component, covering an environment and the phoneme that occurs in it, takes care of the original limitation in distribution. In the simplest cases this may be just a special limitation between contiguous phonemes, when in a given environment only such phonemes occur as are similar in some respect to that environment: the extracted component then has a single phonetic value throughout its length (so /n̅s̅/ for English /nt/). In other cases, the phonemes which occur in an environment may be no more similar to it than those which do not; in fact, it may be precisely the phonemes similar to the environment that never occur in it: the extracted component will then have different phonetic values in different parts of its length (so the Moroccan labial component). More generally, these components can be set up to express the fact that particular phonemes occur in one order and not in another (English morpheme-medial /pt/ occurs, /tp/ does not), and that only certain types of clusters occur; in such cases the phonetic values of the components may vary according to what phonemes or components adjoin it (just as allophones of phonemes vary in value according to what phonemes adjoin them).

Where two groups of phonemes are completely separated, so that no member of one group occurs with a member of the other, the extracted component always keeps its particular length (e.g. when in Moroccan Arabic neither /š/ nor /ž/ occurs near either /s/ or /z/). Where the separation is not complete (so that Moroccan /ṭ/, for example, occurs with /a/ but not with /æ/, while /t/ occurs with both /a/ and /æ/), the extracted component must have different lengths in different positions: with /ṭ/ it has 2-phoneme length so as to exclude /æ/, but with /a/ it has one-phoneme length so as not to exclude /t/.[18] Where the limitation of distribution operates only between adjoining phonemes, their common component extends only over the sequence in question (i.e. the environment, and the phoneme which occurs in it to the exclusion of some other phoneme): so in English /ŋk/ or in Swahili consonant clusters. Where the limitation operates across unaffected phonemes, or throughout some stated limits such as a cluster or a morpheme, then the extracted component has zero value over those phonemes which happen to occur in its length but are not party to the limitation which it expresses: e.g. the Moroccan limitation on the occurrence of /š, ž/ and /s, z/ is operative

[18] Or we may say that with /t/, absence of that component has one-phoneme length so as to exclude /a/ (which contains the component).

throughout word limits; and the voiced–voiceless separation in English morpheme-medial clusters applies only to phonemes with voiced or voiceless homorganic counterparts and hence does not affect /r, l, m, n, ŋ, y, w/ if they occur in the same cluster (thus /ŋgz/ in anxiety, but /ŋkš/ in anxious; there is no /ŋkz/).

5.3 Defective distribution expressed by simultaneous components. Our third operation is to try to break up into simultaneous components any allophones which cannot be assigned to the existing phonemes and which have a very defective distribution in themselves. This is the case with the nasalized alveolar flap of painting, which occurs only after loud-stressed and before weak-stressed vowels. In this position it contrasts with all the consonant phonemes, so that we would be forced to recognize it as a new phoneme occurring only in this one environment.[18a] Since we cannot set up this restricted allophone as complementary to some single previously recognized phoneme, we ask if it may not be complementary to some sequence of previously recognized phonemes. We find that /nt/ is one of the very few sequences which occur between vowels under other stress conditions without also occurring after loud and before weak-stressed vowels. The nasalized flap is therefore in complementary distribution with this sequence and is analyzed into two simultaneous components, one an allophone of /n/ in this position (V̆–tV) and the other an allophone of /t/.

There is, of course, a morphophonemic consideration: painting can be divided into two morphemes, the first of which would have a morphophonemic alternation between /nt/ and the nasalized flap if we recognized the latter as being anything but /nt/. This consideration is not important here, but might be resorted to in other cases. In any event, it is not essential to such analysis. When we break up the palatalized post-dental blade stop into simultaneous allophones of /t/ before /y/ and of /y/ after /t/ (/tyuwn/ for tune), we have no morphophonemic advantage, since when a morpheme ending with /t/ comes before a morpheme beginning with /y/, we get not the palatalized stop but /č/ (or /tš/) by morphophonemic alternation.

From the point of view of relations between allophones, this operation means that we extend complementary distribution to apply not only to single allophones but also to sequences of allophones. From the point of view of the physical nature of allophones, it means that we no longer require an allophone to be an observable complete sound; we extend the term to include observable components of a sound. The net result is to eliminate some potential phonemes of exceptionally limited distribution.

[18a] Rather than include it in one of the vowel phonemes, which would confuse all the general statements about the distribution of vowel phonemes and their allophones.

5.4 <u>Phonetic similarity expressed by short components</u>. In carrying out the distributional analysis, we shall have extracted components from various phonemes in whatever language we investigate. It may be profitable to continue this extraction until all phonemes have been reduced to combinations of components.

When long components have been set up for all the important distributional limitations, we proceed to analyze those phonemes which have not been broken up, or the residues of the phonemes which have been broken up. Each of these phonemes or residues may be analyzed into simultaneous components so chosen as to distinguish the phonemes phonetically one from the other in the simplest manner. 'Simplest' can be determined with the aid of a few obvious criteria: where possible we should utilize components already recognized in the previous analysis, stating that in this position (or in this combination) the component has only one-phoneme length, since it affects only the phoneme which it identifies phonetically. For example, if in a particular language we have had to recognize front, middle, and back consonants because they follow /m, n, ŋ/ respectively, whereas all vowels occur after each of these three nasals, we may nevertheless use the front, middle, and back components to differentiate vowels, with the proviso that they do not have 2-phoneme length when they occur with vowels, and hence do not preclude the occurrence of a front vowel (say /i/) after a back nasal /ŋ/.[19] This means in effect that the limitations of distribution among certain phonemes are used as a partial guide to show us what phonetic differences among the other phonemes are the relevant ones.

Another criterion is the parallelism of allophones among the different phonemes. If the allophones of English /p, t, k/ are all analogous in that they all have comparable differences of aspiration in identical environments (as [pʰ, tʰ, kʰ] after word-juncture but [p, t, k] after /s/, etc.), we can say that a particular component γ is contained in each of them and that this γ (which may be the combination of the unvoicing and the stop components) is strongly aspirated after word-juncture, unaspirated after /s/, etc.

The physical movements of articulation may also offer certain absolute factors common to various phonemes: /p, t, k/ are generally voiceless, fortis, stopped. Since the components will in the last analysis have to identify articulatory (as well as acoustic) events, it is desirable to reflect these as closely as possible. However, as is well known, the correlation with articulatory events will rarely coincide completely with our other criteria, not even with the criterion of complementary distribution for phonemes. To take the simplest example, there are sounds in the /t/ phoneme which are not stops (in <u>butter</u>, etc.).

Some components which are commonly extracted by linguists merely because they consist of pitch or stress features have no basis for being thus extracted except the phonetic considerations of this section. Such, for example, are the tones in languages where each vowel in a morpheme has an arbitrary phonemic pitch.[20] As far as distributional simplicity goes we could just as well state that a language has not, say, 5 vowels and 3 tones, but 15 vowel phonemes (high /í/, mid /i/, low /ì/ — all of which might differ in quality as well as pitch; high /é/, etc.). If these vowels have not already been completely broken down into components on distributional grounds, we may now extract the tones as components on grounds of phonetic simplicity.

5.5 <u>Manipulating the components</u>. When all the phonemes of a language are completely analyzed into components, various additional problems are met. A set of components which conveniently express certain limitations of distribution (e.g. of the voiced-unvoiced group in English as against /r, l, m, n, ŋ, y, w/) may conflict with a different analysis which results from a different limitation but which involves some of the already-analyzed phonemes of the first group (e.g. /s/ which in certain respects behaves like /r, l, m, n, ŋ, y, w/). Sometimes the only way to resolve such difficulties is to reconsider the phonemic system. This is, of course, permissible, since in grouping allophones together into phonemes there are often alternative ways of grouping within the basic phonemic criteria.[21] We choose one way for our phonemic statement, but a slightly different grouping of some of the allophones may be more convenient for the component analysis. Furthermore, we sometimes obtain an extremely complicated component analysis for the distributional limitations and clusterings of the phonemes throughout the vocabulary of the language, where a much simpler system may be possible if we eliminate from consideration certain morphemes (often borrowed ones) which have a different phonetic structure from the rest.[22] It is often possible to identify phonemically the parts of the vocabulary which we wish to exclude from consideration, and perhaps to give them a separate component analysis. For all these reasons, any attempt at a component analysis of a whole phonemic system requires considerable attention to the detailed facts of the language. No examples of such systems will therefore be presented here. It has been possible, however, to carry out the analysis for a few languages, and to obtain sets of components which had only mildly complicated phonetic values, and which required very few statements about distribution (so that practically every combination or sequence of components occurred).

---

[19] In varying measures, this is the case in English (within a morpheme), Swahili, and Fanti.

[20] E.g. Fanti. See W. E. Welmers and Z. S. Harris, The Phonemes of Fanti, JAOS 62.319 (1942).

[21] Y. R. Chao, op. cit. in fn. 4.

[22] Leonard Bloomfield, The Structure of Learned Words, A Commemorative Volume Issued by the Institute for Research in English Teaching 17–23 (Tokyo, 1933).

Are the Components Usable?

6.1 <u>Their status in descriptive linguistics.</u>
Having worked through specific cases of analysis
into components, we may now ask: What is the status
in linguistic science of the new techniques and the
new elements which they produce? At present the
phonemic elements of linguistic analysis are obtained
by segmenting the flow of speech and calling each
group of mutually substitutable segments ('free variants') an allophone. Now the components described
in this paper are not complete physical events;
therefore, they cannot actually be substituted for
each other to see if any two of them are free variants
or 'repetitions' of each other. First, therefore, we
must move as before from unique sounds to allophones, which in general have the relative length of
a phoneme (that is, are not composed of smaller
segments which in turn are allophones of phonemes).
Only then can we proceed to analyze the allophones
into simultaneous components, producing a new set
of elements instead of the previous allophones. The
operation of complementary distribution can be
performed upon the new elements as well as upon
the old. Theoretically, therefore, we could break the
allophones into components and then do all the complementary grouping upon the components. Actually,
it is more efficient to group the complementary
allophones into tentative phonemes, and to analyze
these tentative phonemes into components. We can
then try to group the components by complementary
distribution in order to get fewer components, each
having wider coverage. If certain limitations of occurrence exist for some components, we may even
try to express their limitations in turn by a second
extraction of components, on much the same grounds
that we used in expressing phonemic limitations by
components, in order to obtain the most general and
least limited set of elements.

We thus obtain for the language a new set of elements, each of which occurs with fewer limitations
than the original phonemes. This is so because each
setting up of a component of more than one-phoneme
length takes care of at least one limitation of phonemic occurrence; this is equally true of the auto-
matic-sequence components (§5.1) which replace the
highly limited distribution of phonemic pitch and
stress.[22a] In some cases the components can be so

selected that practically every possible combination
and sequence of the components actually occurs. Any
combinations and sequences that do not occur will,
of course, have to be stated.

The new elements are still, like the phonemes, in
bi-unique correspondence with speech events: given
the writing we know uniquely what sounds to pronounce, and given the sounds we know uniquely how

---

tures in them. We notice that there are limitations
upon the distribution of these segments. For instance,
after a sequence of segments in which each loud-
stressed segment is higher-pitched than the preceding, we never get a low-pitched segment: after <u>Is
your brother</u> ? we never get a low <u>going</u>, but only a
<u>going</u> which is pitched even higher than <u>brother</u>. And
in <u>Is your brother going?</u> we do not get a low pitched
<u>ing</u>. We express this limitation of distribution by say-
ing that all the segments of the utterance contain a
particular component in common, and that this component has various phonetic values at various parts
of its stretch: low pitch on the first low-stressed
vowel, higher pitch on the next, etc. Exactly this is
what we do with the 2- and 3-place components: We
notice that after /s/ we never have /b/, but only /p/.
We express this by saying that both successive segments have a particular component in common, and
that this component has fortis value throughout its
stretch.

The differences between the two types of long
components are four. First, the phonetic values of
the contour components are usually all pitch and
stress features, which we are accustomed to consider a thing apart, while the phonetic values of the
other components may seem to us to be arbitrarily
extracted from the rest of the segment, as when we
distinguish the closure of /b/ from its lip position.

Second, since the contour components are often
constituents of simultaneous morphemes (e.g. the
question intonation), we often cannot obtain the phonemes of the segmental morphemes (e.g. <u>your</u> or
<u>brother</u>, without regard to intonation) until after the
contour components have been extracted. Therefore
we usually extract the contour components while
working on sequences of allophonic segments, whereas we extract the other long components by working
on sequences of phonemes.

Third, whereas the long components usually
extend over a definite small number of phonemes,
the contour components usually extend over a variable
(and much larger) number—as many as there may
be in a linguistic form or utterance of a particular
type.

Fourth, we usually have many more positional
variants of a contour component than of a 2- or 3-
place component. The 1221130 of I don't know where
he's going. (§5.1) and the 2230 of <u>Bud Clark fumbled.</u>
are positional variants of the 230 in <u>He told him.</u>
The phonemic component environment, which determines the number of 1's and the number and place
of 2's in all these variants, is the simultaneous
sequence of stress contours. The 2- or 3-place
components usually have fewer though more complicated positional variants, as when the Swahili n
component indicates tongue retarding with labial
components, but velar occlusion with h (n + p = t,
n + b = d, n + h = k).

[22a] We have seen that the 2- and 3-place components of §5.2 and the fixed-sequence components of
§5.1 differ in effect, in that the former describe
limitations of distribution and the latter describe
contours. It is of interest to notice wherein these
two types of long components differ structurally and
wherein they are similar.

They are similar in that they are all expressions
for limitations of distribution of different segments.
In the case of the pitch contours, we begin with allophonic segments that contain pitch and stress fea-

to write them.[23] The components are essentially similar to phonemes in that both are distributional symbols with phonetic values. That is to say, the observed physical events are always sounds, and the criteria for classifying them into linguistic elements —whether phonemes or components—are always distributional.

The components are merely generalizations of the phonemes, extending the very development which gives us phonemes out of sounds. In writing allophones we have one distinguishable sound per symbol (hence closely abiding by the physical event); but there are many symbols and each usually has a highly restricted occurrence. In writing phonemes we often have several distinguishable sounds per symbol, usually but not always having considerable phonetic similarity (hence abiding rather less closely by the physical event); but there are fewer symbols with a wider distribution for each. In writing components we usually have more distinguishable sounds per symbol, sometimes with no common feature (hence abiding much less by the physical event); but there are fewer symbols yet, with much wider distribution for each. It follows that analysis into components completes what phonemics can only do in part: the transfer of the limitations of sounds from distributional restriction to positional variation in phonetic value. This is not an argument for the use of components: phonemics is undoubtedly the more convenient stopping point in this development, because it fits alphabetic writing; but we must recognize the fact that it is possible to go beyond it.

6.2 <u>Practical and historical considerations.</u> The use of components will clearly be practicable only within narrow limits. Components which enter into supra-segmental morphemes (e.g. sentence intonations) are now extracted and must be extracted in order to permit isolation of morphemes in general. Components which resolve major distributional limitations, e.g. Moroccan ' or †, can easily be extracted and written among the segmental phonemes. Such components are especially worth extracting if many morphophonemic statements are thereby eliminated.[24] One-length components produce little saving and would not normally be extracted except for cases like vowel tones (§5.4), where the extraction is due chiefly to tradition or is desirable because the tones have morphophonemic alternations under various syntactic pitches.

Analysis into components may be of interest to linguists even where it is not used to simplify the writing system, for components may offer correlations with historical change, and may in a sense quantify the structural importance of various phonemic limitations. The connection with linguistic change derives from the fact that many phonemic limitations are produced by single historical changes[25] or by a related series of them, so that the long components may represent the effect of events in history. The structural quantification derives from the fact that some non-occurrences of phonemes are represented by long components and others merely by the non-occurrence of one component with a particular other component in a position where the first component otherwise occurs. Let us take the non-occurring */sbin/ and */stend/ in English. If the cluster-long unvoicing component is ‾, we may say that spin is /z̄bin/; the sequence /z̄b/ (=/sb/) is impossible since ‾ always extends over the whole cluster in which it occurs. On the other hand the general vowel component contained in /e/ occurs after /st/, but only with the particular quality component of /æ/ and not that of /e/: stand but not *stend. There is no long component excluding the /e/ quality component from the position after /t/ or before /n/ or between clusters, since the /e/-quality component occurs in those positions: tend, spend. Therefore all we have is the fact that while the general vowel component occurs in between /st/ and /nd/, it does not occur there with the /e/-quality component, although it does with that component elsewhere. We may then say that forms like */sbin/ are excluded from the phonetic structure as it is described by our components, while forms like */stend/ are not excluded. True, the same considerations which led us to set up a long component in the first case and not in the second could have led us directly to such a judgment concerning these two forms. But no form of expression creates new information: the only question is the availability and organization which it gives to the information. The difference in terms of components is perhaps more clear-cut than a direct discussion of each form, and in setting up the components we may have used relevant considerations which we should not have thought of in a direct discussion.[26]

[25] See now Henry Hoenigswald, Internal Reconstruction, Studies in Linguistics 1944. [Superseded by Hoenigswald's Sound Change and Linguistic Structure, Lang. 22.138 (1946) (139–41)).]

[26] Various other facts about the phonetic structure also transpire from a component analysis. One can tell, by looking at the combinations of components representing the phonemes, which phonemes ever occur next to each other and which never do (i.e. whether they have a long component in common), which phonemes replace each other in complementary environments (i.e. whether all their one-length components are identical), which phonemes have the smallest number of different phonemes next to them (i.e. the ones that contain the largest number of long components).

[23] If only the first of these were true, we should have morphophonemic writing. We may permit partial overlapping among our components, i.e. the same sound feature may be represented in different environments by different components, but that is no bar to phonemic writing.

[24] This will in general happen only in cases of automatic morphophonemic alternation.

Summary

7. This paper has tried to show that many linguistic facts can be discovered and described by the application of a single operation: the analysis of speech into simultaneous components. Automatic sequences of phonetic features yield intonations, word stresses and the like. Defectively distributed phonemes complementary to sequences of phonemes are broken up into allophones of those sequences. Limitations of phonemic distribution, including neutralization, cluster limits, and certain automatic morphophonemic changes, are resolved by components having a length of more than one phoneme. Phonemes and residues not otherwise broken up are analyzed into components of one-phoneme length on the basis of phonetic considerations. The length of a component can vary in different positions, and can be bounded by phonemic environment or by junctures. The phonetic value of a component can vary in different positions, and can be determined by its concurrent components, or its neighboring components, or the section of the component's length. Whole phonemic systems can be replaced by component systems.

No one technique is essential, but rather the method of attack. Different devices will have to be used in different situations. For each language, it will be necessary to state what system of combination of the components is being used, what the length and phonetic value of each component is, and what limitations of occurrence remain among the components.

It has been shown that this analysis creates a new set of elements out of the original allophones or phonemes, and that these elements have the same status as phonemes and are, indeed, merely generalized phonemes. Analysis into simultaneous parts is the only operation aside from segmentation into allophones that produces usable elements for descriptive linguistics.

FROM MORPHEME TO UTTERANCE

ZELLIG S. HARRIS

Language 22.161–83—1946

1.0. This paper presents a formalized procedure for describing utterances directly in terms of sequences of morphemes rather than of single morphemes.[1] It thus covers an important part of what is usually included under syntax. When applied in a particular language, the procedure yields a compact statement of what sequences of morphemes occur in the language, i.e. a formula for each utterance (sentence) structure in the language.

1.1. At present, morpheme classes are formed by placing in one class all morphemes which are substitutable for each other in utterances, as *man* replaces *child* in *The child disappeared.* The procedure outlined below consists, essentially, in extending the technique of substitution from single morphemes (e.g. *man*) to sequences of morphemes (e.g. *intense young man*). In so far as it deals with sequences, it parallels the type of analysis frequently used in syntax, so that the chief usefulness of this procedure is probably its explicitness rather than any novelty of method or result.

1.2. The reason for a procedure of the type offered here is not far to seek. One of the chief objectives of syntactic analysis is a compact description of the structure of utterances in the given language. The paucity of explicit methods in this work has made syntactic analysis a tedious and often largely intuitive task, a collection of observations whose relevance is not certain and whose interrelation is not clear. Partly as a result of this, many grammars have carried little or no syntactic description. In many of the descriptions that have been written, the lack of explicit methods has permitted the use of diverse and undefined terms and a reliance on semantic rather than formal differentiation.

If we now seek a clearer method for obtaining generalizations about the structure of utterances in a language, it should preferably deal with the simplest observables. These are the morphemes, which are uniquely identifiable and easy to follow. Constructs such as 'morphological levels' may be useful in particular cases, but there is an advantage in avoiding them if we can achieve the same results by direct manipulation of the observable morphemes. The method described in this paper will require no elements other than morphemes and sequences of morphemes,[2] and no operation other than substitution, repeated time and again.

[1] I am indebted to Rulon S. Wells for several valuable discussions of this paper, and to C. F. Voegelin and Bernard Bloch for helpful criticisms. In view of the fact that methods as mathematical as the one proposed here have not yet become accepted in linguistics, some apology is due for introducing this procedure. However, the advantage which may be gained in explicitness, and in comparability of morphologies, may offset the trouble of manipulating the symbols of this procedure. Furthermore, the proposed method does not involve new operations of analysis. It merely reduces to writing the techniques of substitution which every linguist uses as he works over his material. One works more efficiently when one thinks with pencil and paper.

[2] And, of course, phonemic constituents of suprasegmental 'morphemes' (if we wish to call them that), e.g. stress, intonations, and pauses.

THE ELEMENTS

2.0. We assume, then, that we have isolated the morphemes of the language. An exact list of the morphemes is of course required for any description of the language, no matter what method is followed. It is possible to obtain somewhat different lists of morphemes, depending on certain choices made at the start:

2.1. We might say that a particular phoneme sequence represents more than one morpheme: homonyms such as *pair* and *pear*, or *make* in *What make is it?* and *She's on the make.* Alternatively, we may say that the sequence (/peyr/ or /meyk/) constitutes only one morpheme under any circumstances.

2.2. We may say that each morpheme can have only one phonemic form, so that for example the English plural endings /s/, /z/, /əz/ (as in *books, chairs, glasses*) constitute three morphemes, and *am, are* constitute two morphemes. Alternatively, we may include each of these sets in a single morpheme, if we say that different phoneme sequences constitute positional variants of one morpheme when they are complementary to each other.[3]

2.3. We could say, as is usually done, that repeated morphemes express concord, as in Latin feminine -a in *mēnsa parva* 'the small table' or the modern Hebrew article *ha* (and feminine -a) in *haiša haklana* 'the small woman'. Alternatively, we could say that in each of these cases we have not a repeated word-suffix or word-prefix, but rather a single phrase-infix consisting, in the case of the Hebrew article, of the phonemes /ha/ before every noun-morpheme (including adjectives) in a noun phrase. This would mean that instead of our being given a morpheme *ha* and having to state that it occurs only with certain syntactic selections, we are given a morpheme which we may write *ha...ha...* and which has no further limitations of selection, but either occurs or does not occur in a phrase, just as do the other morphemes. If the phrase contains the morpheme for 'man' and 'small', it is *haiš hakatan*; if it also contains the morpheme for 'feminine', it is *iša ktana*; if it contains both, it is *haiša haklana*.[4]

[3] The conditions may be phonemic or morphological.

[4] In effect, such a treatment of concord takes some of the features of selection, e.g. the fact that all nouns in the Hebrew phrase agree as to the article, and puts these facts into the phonemic form of the repeated morpheme. As a result, not only the physical recurrence of a repeated phoneme, but also its special position (e.g. before every noun of the phrase), is now given when we describe that morpheme. Such treatment permits a simpler syntactic statement, because the information about the recurrence of the repeated morpheme would otherwise have to be given somewhere in the course of the syntactic description. The syntactic equations to be offered below will suffice to describe what morphemes occur together and in what order, but will not be able to describe conveniently the agreements among the morphemes in a sequence. To do so would require various devices; e.g. instead of writing *NN* (*N* for noun), we would have to write something like $_haN_haN$, meaning that we can have either *NN* or *haN haN* but not *haNN*. Hence it is preferable to get as much of this information out of the way as possible before we attack the sequences. Not only the obvious cases of repeated morphemes but also more complicated types of agreement can be stated as being merely the special forms of particular morphemes. For further discussion of this treatment of repeated morphemes as single morphemes, see LANG. 21.121-7 (1945).

2.4. In the alternatives presented in §§2.2-3 above we find that in each paragraph the first method yields phonemically simple morphemes about which statements of selection remain to be made. Thus, we would have to say somewhere that the plural morpheme /s/ occurs only after morphemes ending in a voiceless consonant; that *am* occurs only after *I*; that when *parv-* is in one phrase with *mênsa* it always has *-a* following; and that whenever *ha* occurs with one noun it will also occur with all other nouns in the phrase. The second method in each case offers phonemically more complicated morphemes which have fewer special limitations of selection as distinguished from other morphemes.

Each method clearly has its advantages and its uses. The syntactic procedure to be indicated below can be carried out regardless of the method followed in setting up the morphemes. However, as will be seen, the fewer limitations of selection we have to deal with, the simpler will be this syntactic procedure. Therefore, in the examples used in this paper it will be assumed that the morpheme list for the language concerned has been constructed by the second method, i.e. that we have included in the phonemic form and definition of the morpheme as many of its limitations of selection as we could.

THE OPERATION

3.0. The procedure to be indicated below consists essentially of repeated substitution: e.g. *child* for *young boy* in *Where did the — go?*. To generalize this, we take a form A in an environment C — D and then substitute another form B in the place of A. If, after such substitution, we still have an expression which occurs in the language concerned, i.e. if not only *CAD* but also *CBD* occurs, we say that A and B are members of the same substitution-class, or that both A and B fill the position C — D, or the like.

The operation of substitution is basic in descriptive linguistics. Not only is it essential in phonemics, but it is also necessary for the initial setting up of morphemes, for the recognition of morpheme boundaries.

3.1. MORPHEME CLASSES. The first step in our procedure is to form substitution classes of single morphemes. We list, for the language concerned, all single morphemes which replace each other in the substitution test, i.e. which occur in the same environments (have the same selection). If any of them do not occur in the same order, they are placed in a special sub-class. Thus, Moroccan Arabic *n-* 'I will' and *-t* 'I did' are mutually substitutable, although they occur at different points in the order of morphemes: *ana nmši ld'aru* 'I'll go to his house', *ana mšit ld'aru* 'I went to his house'.

3.2. In making these substitution classes of morphemes we may be faced with many problems. In some languages, relatively few morphemes occur in exactly the same environments as others: *poem* occurs in *I'm writing a whole — this time*, but *house* does not. Both morphemes, however, occur in general in *That's a beautiful —*. Shall we say that *poem* and *house* belong in general to the same substitution class, or that they have some environments in common and some not?

It will be seen that the method proposed in §§3.5-9 below can be used no mat-

ter how this problem is met.[5] However, in order to keep the examples of §§4-6 as simple as possible, it will be assumed here that morphemes having slightly different distributions are grouped together into one class if the distributional differences between their environments correspond to the distributional differences between the morphemes. That is, if *poem* and *house* differ distributionally only in the fact that *poem* occurs with *write* and *house* with *wire*, and in comparable differences, and if *write* and *wire* in turn differ only in that *write* occurs with *poem* and *wire* with *house*, and in comparable differences, we put *poem* in one class with *write*, and simultaneously put *write* in one class with *wire*.

3.3. Other differences of environment are less easily handled. English *cover* occurs after both *un-* and *dis-*, while *dress* occurs only after *un-*, *connect* only after *dis-*, and *take* after neither (but *connected* occurs also after *un-*). On the other hand, *cover, dress, connect*, and *take* all occur before *-ing*, and in environments like *Let's not — it just now*. Here again, shall we group these into the same morpheme class, or into four different classes? That is, should the classes to be used in our method below be set up on the basis of relation to *-ing*, or on the basis of relation to *un-*? We find that the selections which these four have in common (their occurrence before *-ing* and in *Let's not — it just now*) differentiate them from other large substitution classes, such as *India, child*, or *to, from*, which do not occur in these positions. On the other hand, the selections in which they differ do not differentiate or equate morphemes in a way that is useful in analyzing many utterances. Although *un-* occurs before some of the morphemes which occur before *-ing*, we also find *un-* before a few of the morphemes which occur not before *-ing* but in the *the — man*: e.g. *just, true*.[6]

As in the case of §3.2, the method to be described below is applicable regardless of the definition of morpheme class that we select. If we put *cover, dress, connect*, and *take* into four different classes on the basis of relation to *un-*, we will be able to group the classes together later on the basis of their relation to *-ing*. And if we treat them as members of one class on the basis of *-ing*, we will have to note that they differ distributionally (as sub-classes) with respect to *un-*. For brevity, we will here consider them as members of one morpheme class.

3.4. In some cases of morphemes having one environment but not another in common, both the similarity and the difference are relevant for utterance structure. Thus *cover, note, find* all occur in *-ing, We'll — his path*, as well as

[5] If *poem* and *house* are placed in one class N, overlooking the difference in their distribution, then *write* and, say, *wire* (*I'm writing a whole house this time*) would be placed together in a class V since the distributional difference between them corresponds to that between *poem* and *house*. We would then obtain a statement connecting N and V. If we kept *poem* and *house* in separate classes, and *write* and *wire* in separate classes, we would obtain two statements, one connecting *write* and *poem*, and another connecting *wire* and *house*. These two statements together would equal the one statement about N and V.

[6] The criterion which decides for *-ing*, and against *un-*, as the relevant environment in determining substitution classes is therefore a criterion of usefulness throughout the grammar, a configurational consideration. It will be seen below that the classes defined on the basis of *-ing* can be replaced by certain sequences of classes, which in the case for any classes based on the *un-* environment. Special statements will have to be made later about the selection of *un-*, which in part will run across the boundaries of the classes set up on the basis of *-ing*, etc.

in —*s* ('plural'), *You can have my* —. But *think* occurs only in the first two types of environment, and *child* only in the last two.[7] In general, practically all morphemes which occur in —*ing* also occur in many environments like *We'll* — *his path.* Similarly, almost all morphemes which occur in —*s* ('plural') occur also in many environments like *You can have my* —. We will therefore recognize these two sets of positions as being diagnostic, and will say that every morpheme which occurs in several environments of one of these two sets is a member of the substitution class which is identified as occurring in that set of positions. There will be two such classes: *cover, note, find, think*; and *cover, note, find, child.* The fact that many morphemes occur in both classes is not relevant at this point, since some do not.[8]

3.5. MORPHEME SEQUENCES. The chief novelty in the procedure which is offered here is the extension of substitution classes to include sequences of morphemes, not merely single morphemes. We now ask not only if *A* and *B* each occur in the environment *C — D* but also if *AE* together, or *FGH*, also occur in that environment. If they do, then *A, B, AE, FGH* are all substitutable for each other. We may say that they are all members of one substitution class, which is now not merely a class of morphemes but a class of morpheme sequences. The single morphemes in the class are merely the special cases where the sequence consists of one.

Thus we note that in *Please put the book away* we can substitute for *book* not only other single morphemes like *bottle* or *brandy* but also sequences of two and more morphemes like *books, bank-book, brandy bottle, bottle of brandy, silly green get-up.* These sequences differ in various respects: in *brandy bottle* each of the component morphemes could have been substituted singly for *book*; in *books* only the first could; in *silly green get-up* no one of the morphemes could (in most utterances) have alone been substituted for *book.* These differences, however, are not relevant to the essential criterion of our present procedure, which is merely whether or not the sequences are substitutable for each other.

3.6. In the case above, and in most applications of this procedure, we have single morphemes for which the sequences can be substituted. That means that the sequences of morphemes do not yield new classes; we simply group them with various morpheme classes which we have already obtained in the usual manner described in §3.1. We may say that in any such application of our procedure, we reduce sequences to the status of single morphemes (or of environmental classes of single morphemes).

However, there may be sequences of morphemes which occur in environments where single morphemes do not occur, i.e. where they cannot be replaced by any single morpheme. Such sequences may or may not be useful as elements of the utterance structure. For example, Semitic roots plus verb patterns occur in environments in which no single morpheme occurs. They occur before verb suffixes, after verb prefixes, and in various sentence positions such as (in early Semitic) before an accusative noun (presumably with command intonation): thus, in classical Arabic, root *ftḥ* 'open' and pattern (*i*)-*a*- 'command' in *iftaḥ ilbāba* 'open the door!'. In all these environments we always find the sequence of some root plus some pattern; we never find a single morpheme here. We may consider this sequence to constitute an element in the utterance structure, calling it, say, verb stem.

3.7. Since our procedure now permits us to make any substitutions of any sequences, it may become too general to produce useful results. For example, we might take the utterance *I know John was in* and substitute *certainly* for *know John*, obtaining *I certainly was in.* This substitution conceals the fact that the morphemes of *I know John was in* can be said as two utterances instead of as one, if we make the single change of pronouncing its intonation twice, over the first two words and again over the last three, instead of once over all five. That is, it conceals the fact that *I know John was in* can be described as two sentences strung under one sentence intonation. It further conceals the fact that *certainly* may also occur in a different place in the sentence: *I was certainly in*, whereas *know John* would occur only in the one position. And it conceals the concord of *was* with *John*: for if we substituted *we* for *I*, we would still have *was* in *We know John was here*, but *were* in *We certainly were here.* All this suggests that substitution of sequences be so carried out as to satisfy all manipulations of that environment which forms the frame of the substitution.[9]

3.8. In the following sections (§§4, 5), this procedure will be carried out, in a very sketchy manner, for English and for Hidatsa, a Siouan language of North Dakota. There will of course be no attempt to approach even remotely a complete analysis for either language. The purpose of these descriptions is only to show the general lines of the procedure; countless details, as well as some of the types of utterance in each language, will be omitted.

3.9. Equations will be used to indicate substitutability. *BC = A* will mean that the sequence consisting of a morpheme of class *B* followed by a morpheme of class *C* can be substituted for a single morpheme of class *A.* In cases where unclarity may arise, we shall write *B + C* for the sequence *BC.* When we

---

[7] With variant *-ren* plus vowel change for plural *-s.*

[8] This would give us a class *V* including *cover, note, find, think*, and a class *N* including *cover, note, find, child.* It would permit individual morphemes to be members of more than one class. Alternatively, we could put *cover, note, find* into a class *G, think* into *V, child* into *N.* Then each morpheme could only belong to one class, and morphemes having wider distributions, or having the distributions of two classes, would find themselves in a new class. Bernard Bloch uses yet another solution in his analysis of Japanese. He would regard the noun *cover*, which occurs in positions of *N*, and the verb *cover*, which occurs in positions of *V*, as two independent morphemes whose homonymy is syntactically irrelevant. That is, he uses class membership as a necessary condition for morpheme identity. Any of these methods of classification can be followed rigorously, and may be advantageous for particular purposes. Any one of them can be used in the method discussed below without affecting the final result.

[9] Such substitutions as *certainly* for *know John* can be precluded by analyzing the utterance into immediate constituents. However, the analysis into immediate constituents requires a technique different from that used in this paper, a technique based on comparing the apparent structures of utterances and parts of utterances. In this paper, on the other hand, we seek to arrive at a description of the structure of an utterance, without having any prior way of inspecting these structures or of saying whether two utterances are equivalent in structure. Therefore, the analysis into immediate constituents is not used here, and we must state other methods of excluding such substitutions as *certainly* for *know John.*

want to say that A substitutes for B only if C follows, we shall write $AC = BC$.

ENGLISH

4.1. THE MORPHEME CLASSES. For the purposes of the English examples, we shall set up the following classes of morphemes, on the criterion that for each class there are particular sentence positions which can be filled by any member of that class and by these alone.[10]

N: morphemes which occur before plural -s or its alternants, or after the or adjectives: *hotel, butter, gain, one,*[11] *two.*

V: before -ed past or its alternants; before -ing; after N plus *should, will, might,* etc: *go, gain, take, think, will* ('desire'), *have, do.* We may distinguish several sub-classes such as those listed below, while V without any subclass mark will be used to indicate all the sub-classes together.

V_b: *be, appear, become, get, keep, stay,* etc. (but not *have*).

V_c: verbs which occur between N and V -ing: *stop, try, be* in *Mac will — walking.*

V_a: the transitive verbs which occur before N: *make, buy, want* (but not *go, sleep*) in *I'll — butter.*

V_i: intransitive verbs which do not occur before N: *go, sleep.*

V_f: verbs which occur before two independent N's: *make, consider, want* (but not *buy, go*) in *I'll — this book a best seller.*

V_e: verbs (often causative in meaning) which occur before NV (a noun phrase followed by a verb phrase): *make, let, see* (but not *consider, buy, go*) in *I'd like to — newcomers try it.*

V_h: verbs which occur before N to V: *cause, teach, dare, want* (but not *make, go*) in *The other kids — Junior to do it.*

R: between N and V (the V lacking -ing, -ed); NRV occurs initially, or after a list of V including *think, guess* (*I think the boy can win it*): *will, do, shall, can, may, must, ought* (but not *to*). The -s of 3rd-person-singular concord does not occur with these, nor does -ing. *Should* can be considered as *shall* + -ed, and so on.

have, be: appearing in R positions and in some other positions. These two have the -s, -ed, and -ing occurring after them. After *have* the V is followed by -en (if that particular member of the class V ever has -en, it has it also after *have*), and after *be* by -en or -ing: *we are going, we have taken,*[13]

as compared with *we did go.* When a position is discussed below in which R, *had, be* can all occur equally, the abbreviation R_a will be used to indicate all three.

A: between *the* and N, never before plural -s: *young, pretty, first.*

D: between *the* and A, but not between *the* and N: *rather, very, now, nol.* Many of these, e.g. *now,* occur in various positions in the utterance (after V: *Don't look now*; before V: *He now wishes it weren't*; at the beginning of an utterance, with a level /,/ intonation: *Now, what's up?*). Some adverbs, e.g. *very,* do not occur in most of these positions. When we wish to indicate only the more widely-occurring ones, to the exclusion of *very* and the like, we write D_a. In more detailed analysis, many more sub-classes of D would be necessary.

T: before N, or A, or DA, but not before V (unless -ing or -ed or -en follow it): *a, my, some.* These may all be considered as substituting for *the* and so forming an article-class. Here we must include *all, which,* in addition to occurring in the above positions also occurs before T (*all the very good people* as well as *all very good people*); also the cardinal numbers, which occur not only in T position but also after T (*my two very uncertain suggestions* as well as *the two very new suggestions, two very new suggestions,* parallel to *the very new suggestions*).

I: before or after V, after *from, before,* but not after A or T or before plural -s: *it, all, some, now, here.*[14] Some morphemes in this class do not occur after *from, before,* etc., or after utterance-initial V: *he, I.* Others do not occur before V unless NV precedes them: *me.*

P: before N, T, A, D, I, and before V only if -ing follows: *of, from.* Several morphemes in this preposition class also occur after certain V; when they are in this position we mark them P_b: *up, off, over* (*walk off, beat up*). Some prepositions (marked P_c) sometimes alternate with zero when an N which precedes P_cN is placed after the $(P_c)N$: *to, for* in *They're giving a present to the boss, They're buying a present for the boss,* are replaced by zero in *They're giving the boss a present, They're buying the boss a present.* This does not occur with *from* as in *He's receiving a raise from the boss.*

-Nn: After N and before anything which follows N: -let, -eer, -er, -ess, (*playlet, engineer, Londoner, lioness*).

-Vv: After V and before anything which follows V: past -ed, 3rd person singular -s (*rowed, rows*).

-Aa: After A and before anything which follows A: -er, -est, -ish (*older, oldest, oldish*).

-Nv: After N and before anything which follows V:[14] -ize, -(i)fy (*colonize, beautify*).

-Na: -ful, -ish, -th, -'s (*beautiful, boyish, sixth, parent's*).

-Vn: -ment, -tion, -er, -ing (*atonement, abolition, writer, writing* in *Writing is just what he hates*).

---

[10] This does not mean that every member of the class occurs in all the positions in which any other member occurs (fn. 5). A particular morpheme may occur in several classes (fn. 8). Some morphemes occur in two or more classes in the list below; cf. class-cleavage in Leonard Bloomfield, Language 204 (New York, 1933). The statement of the environments of each morpheme class given here is far from complete, and is merely sufficient to identify the class.

[11] In such expressions as *the one I saw, a good one.*

[12] If subdivisions are not recognized here they will have to be dealt with as special types of selection (§7.6).

[13] We may include *have* and *be* in R in some environments, e.g. in relation to *not*: *have not taken* parallel to *will not take* as against *don't get going.* Note that when *do, have,* or *be* have -ing after them they are in the position of V, not of R.

[14] There are special utterances like *the here and now,* but in general these limitations hold.

-Va: -able, -ing, -ed, -en (likable, a shining light, the cooked meal, his shaven head).

-An: -ness, -ty (darkness, cruelly).

-Av: -en, -ize, (darken, solemnize).

-Ad: -ly (really).

Nv-: before N, and after anything which precedes V:[15] be-, en- (bedevil, enshrine).

Xd'-: before morphemes of several classes, chiefly N or A. The combination, consisting of these morphemes plus Xd'-, may be marked D'. It occurs chiefly after V (often with intervening N, etc., as in Are you asleep?): a- (astray, afresh, asleep, ashore). D' is used here to indicate the adverbs which occur in this post-V position, since it is a position in which both D_a and A occur. D' sometimes occurs after N: A day ashore.

Av: en- (enlarge).

Na: pre-, anti-, pro- (pre-war, anti-war, pro-war).

Ap: be- (below, behind).

Xz-: before any morpheme class or sequence, and after anything which preceded that same morpheme class. The environment of the morpheme which follows is not affected by the addition of the Xz- morpheme, except that it now contains that addition itself: dis-, re-, pre- (disorder, recall, preview).

S: stems which occur only next to affixes, i.e. next to the 16 classes -Nn to Xz- immediately preceding. These stems cannot be assigned to any of the preceding classes N, V, A, D, etc., except by seeing if they occur with the same affixes as N, etc. Thus, in society, social, it would have been possible, instead of considering soci- as S (as we do here), to consider it as A when it occurs before -ety and N when it occurs before -al (compare superiority, A -An and communal N -Na). However, what is nat- in native? It could be either N or V before -ive, since -ive is both -Na and -Va: massive, adoptive. We therefore put all such morphemes in the class S. Many of the affixes in the classes above occur not only next to A, N, or V, but also next to S.

&: conjunctions between any two sequences: and, but (I wanted to go, but couldn't make it.) In some environments (e.g. in the example above) the member of & is preceded by /,/ intonation; in other environments the /,/ intonation does not occur (e.g. war and peace without /,/).

B: in -NV /,/ NV or in NV /,/ NV: if, since, as, while (If you go, I won't). The last subordinative and sometimes also the others lack the preceding /,/ intonation when they are in the middle of the utterance: We fix it while you wait. Some members of this class occur after A or N, etc., before NV, VN (Little as there is of it, —. Man though he is, —.) These will be marked B_a.

Finally, there remain various independent morphemes, some of which occur almost anywhere in utterances, often set off by /,/: then, now, thus. Others are set off either by /,/ or by quote-intonation, or have /,/ by themselves: yes, no. Others usually have /!/ intonation by themselves: hello, oh.

4.2. We now consider sequences of these thirty-odd morpheme classes, to see what sequences of morphemes can be substituted for single morphemes.

Sequences of morpheme classes which are found to be substitutable in virtually all environments for some single morpheme class, will be equated to that morpheme class: $AN = N$. If we write $DA = A$ (quite old for old), then DA can be substituted for man anywhere.[16] If we write $DA = A$ wherever A appears, e.g. in $AN = N$ (old fellow for man, where we can substitute quite old for old, and obtain quite old fellow $DAN = AN = N$).[17] There is nothing to prevent us from substituting DA for A even in the equation $DA = A$. We would then obtain $DDA = A$: really quite old for old.

If, however, it proves impossible to substitute the equivalents of a symbol for that symbol in some of its occurrences, we distinguish those occurrences by giving the symbol a distinctive raised number. For instance, $N -s = N$: paper $+$ $-s =$ paper; and papers can be substituted for paper in most environments. However, we cannot substitute $N -s$ for the first N in this very equation: we cannot substitute papers for the first paper and then add -s again (papers $+$ -s), as this equation would seem to indicate. We therefore write $N^1 -s = N^2$ and state that wherever N^2 occurs we can substitute for it any N^1 or another N^2, while for N^1 we can only substitute any member of N^1 (never N^2). Then it becomes impossible to construct a sequence papers $+$ -s, since papers is N^2 and -s is added only to N^1.

The procedure in assigning these raised numbers which indicate uni-directional substitutability is in essence as follows: we assign raised ^{1} to each class symbol, say X, when it first appears. Next time the X appears in an equation, we assign it the same number ^{1} if the equivalents of this X can be substituted for X^1 in every equation which has so far been written. If the new X cannot be substituted for all the preceding X^1 we number it X^2. If we later obtain an X which cannot be substituted for all the preceding X^1 or X^2, we will number it X^3, and so on. If some symbols never go above ^{1} we can dispense with the raised number for them and merely write the symbol without numbers.

On the left-hand side of the equations, each raised number will be understood to include all lower numbers (unless otherwise noted). Thus in $TN^2 = N^3$ we have not only the men (N^2) equalling N^3, but also the man (N^1). Any N^1 can be substituted for the N^2 on the left side. On the right-hand side, however, each raised number indicates itself alone: N^3 on the right can only substitute for another N^3, and $N^{1,2}$ for an N^1 or an N^2.

[16] This is true only within the broad limits of what utterances frequently occur in the culture. There are also limitations when man is preceded by an adjective A (e.g. young man). There would then be two adjectives, the A of good boy, and the A of young man, which together should yield young good boy ($A A N = A N = N$). The conditions under which the two adjectives would occur next to each other in this way are mentioned in §4.32.

[17] The standard procedure being as follows: since $D A = A$ permits us to substitute $D A$ for A wherever A appears, we write $D A$ in place of the first A in this very equation: if $D A = A$, then $D D A = A$, i.e. $D D A = D A = A$.

4.3. Morpheme sequence equations for English now follow.

4.31. Equations involving N^1, V^1, A^1 are almost all cases of word formation, i.e. of adjoining morphemes within one loud-stress unit.

$N^1 - Nn = N^1$: e.g. for *engineer* we can substitute *engine* in *I saw the —*.
$A^1 - An = N^1$: *darkness* for *smell* in *I don't like the — here*.
$V^1 - Vn = N^1$: *abolition* for *bread* in *We demand —*. Note that *abolition* ($V^1 - Vn$) is N^1 and can be followed by *-Nn*: *abolitionist*.
$N^1 - Nv = V^1$: e.g. *colonize* for *conquer* in *The French Government —ed North Africa*.

$Nv - N^1 = V^1$: *enchant* for *scare* in *He —s them*.
$A^1 - Av = V^1$: *sharpen* for *break* in *Don't — the knife*.
$Av - A^1 = V^1$: *enlarge* for *print* in *Do you want to —it*?
$A^1 - Ad = D$: *beautifully* or *really* for *well* in *It's —finished*.
$Ap - A^1 = P$: *below* for *at* in *It fell — the dividing line*.

$D_a V^1 = V^1$: *cordially despise* for *like* in *I — him* (this applies if there is no /,/ or /!/ after D_a; $P N$ for D_a is rare in this position).
$Xd' +$ any class (chiefly N^1 or A^1) $= D'$, where D' represents a class of words which occur almost always after V, though not always immediately after: *asleep* in *He is —, He fell —, He is fast —; ashore* in *A day ashore*.
$Xx +$ any class $=$ that class: e.g. *dislike* for *like* in *He really —s it*.
$S +$ any affix $=$ the class indicated by the second letter in the affix mark: e.g. $S - Vn = N^1$: *nature* for *life* in *He loves —*.
$all + T = T$: *all my* for *some* in *We lost —books*. When *all* is not followed by T, it may itself be a member of T: *all for the* in — *assertions are arbitrary*.
$T +$ cardinal number $= T$: *Which two* for *which* in — *really modern composers?* When cardinal numbers are not preceded by T, they may themselves be members of T: *two* for *the* in the sentence above.

As a result of these equations, we may consider affixes not as distinct elements in the sentence structure, but merely as elements altering the substitution class of the neighboring morphemes. The affix classes will no longer appear in our picture of the sentence structure (except for special cases of selection), since any structure into which they enter can also be composed of $N, V, A, D,$ and P morphemes.

4.32. We next obtain equations in which A^2 is necessary, though N^1 is still adequate.

$A^1 - Aa = A^2$: e.g. *oldish* for *old* in *Aren't they a bit —?*.
$V^1 - Va = A^2$: *likeable* for *oldish* in *My — uncle*. Note that the V^1 can be obtained from $N^1 - Nv$: *A heartening* ($N^1 - Nv - Va$) *thought*.
$D A^2 = A^2$: *completely false* for *false* in *That's a — statement*. (D here from A $-Ad$).

$A^2 N^1 = N^1$: *peculiar fellow* for *Senator* in *Isn't he a —*.[18]

$A^2 A^2 N^1 = A^2 N^1$: Two adjoining A in a particular order, which we will call the 'usual' (e.g. as between *ambitious* and *young*, *ambitious* is first in the usual order), will be stressed $ÁA$ (reduced loud, medial).[19] *ambitious young, pretty dark*, substitutable for *funny* in *She is a — girl*. If the adjectives are not in the usual order, or if they are in the usual order but with greater note given to the second A, or if no usual order obtains between them, or if the second A is composed of $D A$, the pattern is $Á$ / / $Â$: *pretty, dark; dark, pretty; young, ambitious; ambitious, very young* in *She is a — girl*.[20]

4.33. Equations involving N^2 and N^3 develop the noun-phrase.

$N^1 - s = N^2$: *papers* for *paper* in *I'll get my — out*.
$N^2 - Na = A^2$: e.g. *parents'* for *big* in — *day at school*.
$Na - N^2 = A^2$: *pro-war* for *big* in *a — industrialist*.
$N^2 N^2 = N^{1.2}$: *family heirloom* substitutable for *boy* in *It's a —*. — *Albert Einstein* for *Jim* in — *was here*.

Any sequence including one loud stress and one or more reduced loud (or medial) stresses $= N^{1.2}, V^1,$ or $A^{1.2}$, according to which of these may be substituted for the sequence. Most of these $= N^1$: *blackbird* (AN), *by-pass* (PN), *get-up* (VP_b), *our third motor-boat crash* (NNN). Some ending in $A^2 = A^{1.2}$: *air-minded* ($N^1 A^2$, the A^2 being a sequence of $V^1 - Va$). Others $= V^1$: *They by-passed it; They'll railroad* ($N^1 N^1 = V^1$) *the strike leader* ($N^1 N^1 = N^1$; N^1 from $V^1 - Vn$).
$T N^2 = N^3$: *the orchestra* or *these pointless, completely transparent jokes for butter* in *I don't like —*.
$T A^2$ (with no N following) $= N^3$: *The longer* or *the uncertain* in — *is what interests us more*. The *-s* 'plural' does not occur after this N^3 substitute, except in special cases.
$N^3 PN^4 = N^3$: *This piece of junk for the book* in *Who brought — here?*. The occurrence of $N^3 PN^3$ in the position of N^3 or N^4 in the equations below is restricted by various special selections for particular P. Repetition is not frequent except when P is of: *This piece of junk of my mother's* = $N^3 PN^3 PN^3 = N^3 PN^3 = N^3$ (*my mother's* is $T N - Na = T A^2 = N^3$).

4.34. Equations requiring V^2 to V^4 develop the verb phrase.

also sometimes A^2: e.g. we see whether among the sequences having the same environment as *senator* we have not only *peculiar fellow* but also *older fellow*. The other procedure is to set up equations as working hypotheses, on the basis of whatever data we have, and then try various substitutions for each symbol in our equations, until we discover which symbols are mutually substitutable. Thus on the basis of *He's a peculiar fellow* we may write tentatively $A N^1 = N^1$. Then we would test to see if A is A^1 or A^2 by seeing if we can substitute *older* for *peculiar* and still get an English utterance. The two procedures are, of course, epistemologically equivalent.

[18] We determine that it is A^2 rather than A^1 in this equation by testing whether *peculiar* (A^1) can be replaced by *older, oldish* (A^2). In constructing all these equations we may use either of two working procedures. One is to obtain a large amount of data, including many sequences which have the same environment as N^1; we may then sort out, from among these, those sequences which consist of A followed by N, and see whether the A is always A^1 or

[19] See George L. Trager and Bernard Bloch, The Syllabic Phonemes of English, LANG. 17.228 (1941).

[20] When we have the stress pattern `` the medially-stressed morpheme is in class D: *pretty young* is $D A$ in *She's a pretty young girl to be out this time of night*. It parallels *very young* in *He's a very young fellow*. The addition of emphasis stress, and other changes in the environment, complicate these stress statements. Exact statements will be necessary, however, since various morphemes (e.g. *first*) occur in both A and D.

R_a not $= R_a$: *will not* or *have not* or *was not* for *will* or *have* or *was* in *I will go.*; *Has he gone?*; *I was going.*

$R_a N$ not $= R_a N$: *did he not* for *did he* in *But — attempt it?*.

have V^1-en $= V^2$: *have eaten* for *know* in *I — it.*; *I will — it.*

$V_c^1 V^2$-ing $=$ have V_b^1-en V^2-ing $= V^2$: *be eating* or *stop eating* or *have stopped eating* for *know* in *I — it now.*

$V_b^1 A^2 =$ have V_b^1-en $A^2 = V_c^2$: *is gone* or *has been gone* or *seems neat* or *is grayish* for *comes* in *He — now.* Note that A^2 on the left-hand side represents both *neat* (A^1) and *grayish* (A^2).

$R V^1 = R = V^2$: *will go* or *will* for *go* in *We — today.*

$R N^4 V^2$? $=$ have $N^4 V^1$-en ? $=$ be $N^4 V^1$-en ? $=$ be $N^4 V^1$-ing ? $= R_a N^4$? $= N^4 V^2$?: *Did you talk* or *Haven't you gone* or *Are you taken* or *Are you going* or *Were you in — with him?*.

$V^2 P_b = V^2$: *walk off* (V^1) or *have walked off* (V^2) for *escape* in *We'll — before them.* The appearance of V^2 on both sides of the equation means that we can also obtain $V^2 P_b P_b = V^2$: etc. This occurs in *walk on over* or *fly on up* for *go* in *Let's —*. However, the selection and number of these sequences of P_b is highly restricted, and detailed equations would have to be given to indicate the selections which actually occur.

$V_d^2 N^4 = V_e^2$: *take it* for *go* in *I'll — now.* When V^2 includes P_b, there are certain V, P_b, and N for which the order is VNP_b (*I'll knock your opponent down.*), while for others the order is VP_bN (*I'll take over my father's estate.*). The N^4 will be identified below.

$V_e^2 N^4 N^4 = V_c^2$: *make Harding President* for *vote* in *We're going to —.*

$V_g^2 N^4 V^3 = V^3$: *make him vote* for *vote* in *We'll — your way.*

$V_b^3 N^4$ to $V^3 = V^3$: *force him to vote* for *vote* in *We'll — your way.*

$V_d^2 N_1^4 P_c N^4 = V_d^2 N^4 N_1^4 = V^3$: For P_c and certain N, we find both the first sequence (e.g. *I'll make a party for my husband.*), and the second (e.g. *I'll make my husband a party.*). The N_1 with the subscript is used only to identify the N in its two positions. The first sequence is identical with the usual order, as in *I'll get a nickel from my dad.*

$V_d^2 N^4 V^4$ (all under one sentence intonation) $= V_d^2 N^4 = V_c^2$: *know he is* for *know it* in *I — now.* The $N^4 V^4$ is thus the object of the V_d^2. The V^4 indicates a full verb phrase, e.g. *was* as well as *is* in the example above.

V^3 to $V^3 = V^3$: *try to escape* or *kill the guard to avoid getting caught* in *Let's — here.* Note that *avoid getting caught* is $V_c^1 V_b^1$-ing V^1-en $= V_c^1 V_b^1$-ing $A^2 = V_c^1 V^2$-ing $= V^2$.

V^3 -$Vv = V^4$: *walked* or *walked off* or *had eaten* or *tried to escape* for *walk* or *have eaten* in *I — alone.* The -Vv is added to the first V or R of the whole V^3 phrase.

$V^4 D_a = V^{3,4}$: *travel smoothly* for *go* in *We'll — in this place.*

$V^4 P N^4 = V^{3,4}$: *travel in this place* for *go* in *Let's — today.* For certain $P N$ and D_a the order is $V^3 D_a P N$; for others it is $V^3 P N D_a$; compare the two examples above.

4.35. The noun phrase is completed with the introduction of N^4. $N^3 N^4$

$V_d^4 = N^3 N^4 V_e^4 P = N^4$: *The clock he fixed* or *The house he slept in* for *The clock in — is all right now.* The second N in the sequence usually has reduced stress, while the first N^3 and the end of the V^4 phrase (if it is not sentence-final) usually have a level tone. The sequence $N^3 N^4 V^4$ here is therefore distinguished formally, as well as in its environment, from the sequence $N^3 N^2 V^4 = N^3 V^4$ (with $N^3 N^2 = N^3$, since we have seen that $N^2 N^2 = N^2$ and this can be built up into an N^3 by completing the noun phrase before the first N^2): *The family heirloom broke.*

Since $V_d^2 N^4$ (*fixed it*) $= V_e^2$, and since V_e^2 occurs in this equation only if P follows, we see that $V_d^2 N^4$ (without P) is excluded from this sequence. We may have $N^3 V_d^2 N^4$ (*He fixed it.*), and we may have $N^3 N^4 V_d^2$ (*the clock he fixed*); but we never have the first N^3 and the last N^4 together in one sequence (there is no *the clock he fixed it*). We may therefore say that the first N^3 replaces the last N^4. This indicates the semantic connection between these two noun phrases, since each of them represents the object of V_d^2.

$I = N^4$: *it* for *the room* in *Was — very hot?* For each morpheme here we can substitute a whole noun phrase, including I, i.e. anything equalling N^3.

$N^4 A^2 P N^4 = T A^2 N^2 V^1$-Va $= V^3$-ing $= N^4$: *strawberries fresh from the field* or *the best drinks obtainable* or *having you all* substitutable for *hope* in *It was only — that kept me going.*

$PN^4 = D_a = D'$: These three classes, represented by *in a moment* or *eventually* or *ashore*, all occur *We'll do these things —.* and less freely in *—, we'll do these things.* However, since style and selection features differ markedly for PN and D_a, detailed statements would be needed to specify in each equation which is more frequent.

N^3 :/,: $= P N^4$ /,/: *Some day*, for *in a moment*, in the utterances above. This applies only to particular N^3; detailed statements of selection or equations involving particular sub-classes of N would be necessary.

Quoted material $= N^4$ (with special quote-intonation); "*Not today, thanks.*" or "*wanted*" for *this* in *He said — in a loud voice.*

4.36. Subordinations and Coordinations.

$A^2 B_a = N^4 B_a = B$: *Little as* or *Child though* or *Since in — he is, I like him.*

$B N^4 V^4 = P N^3 N^4 V^4 = N^4 V^3$-ing $= V^3$-ing $= P N^4$: *If he goes home* or *In the event that he goes home* or *Everyone having left* or *Being at home* are all substitutable for *At night in —, he'll lock up the house.*

any class $+ \, \& \, +$ same class = same class: *records and new needles* ($N^2 \, \& \, N^2$) for *records* (N^2) in *I have — for you today.*

V^4 /,/ $\& V^4 = V^4$: *found it but lost it again* for *found it* after *We.*

4.37. Equations involving whole utterances.

$P N^4$, $N^4 V^4 = N^4 V^4$, $P N^4 = P N^4 N^4 V^4 = N^4 V^4 P N^4$: *At night, it's too hard.*; *It's too hard, at night.*; *At night it's too hard.*; *It's too hard at night.* The morpheme /,/ before or after $P N^4$ or any of its substitutes underscores the conditional meaning.

$\& \, +$ any utterance = that utterance: *But John!* for *John!*; *And I know that too.* for *I know that too.* Only a few conjunctions occur frequently in this position.

$N^4 V^4$ /./, /&/ & $N^4 V^4 = N^4 V^4$: For any $N^4 V^4$ utterance we may substitute two $N^4 V^4$ sequences with a conjunction between them, and with reduced loud stress on the second: *I know, but I can't tell.* for *I know.*

4.4. A check of the preceding equations will show that all morpheme classes and all sequences of morphemes, except the independent ones in the last paragraph of §4.1, occur in positions where they can be replaced by N^4 or V^4. We can therefore state in terms of these classes what sequences of morphemes occur in English utterances. The great majority of English utterances are a succession of the following forms:

$N^4 V^4$ with /./, /?/, or other intonations; with N^4 (= $PN^4 = D_a$), independent morphemes, and successive repetitions introduced by &, set off by /,/. Independent morphemes and almost all others except affixes (classes -Nn to Xx in §4.1), occurring singly or with affixes, with /./, /?/, /!/, and other intonations: *Yes;, Why?; No!; Come!; John!; English.; Here.*

HIDATSA

5.1. A particularly brief sketch will be given for Hidatsa, which is of interest here because its structure is very different from that of English. For the most part, Hidatsa consists of morphemes which are not in themselves nouns, verbs, etc., but which combine with affixes of nominal, verbal, or other meaning.

Most morphemes of Hidatsa may be grouped into the following classes on the basis of substitutability:

S: stems, which occur with any affixes or with no affix (or zero), and next to other stems: *ika·* 'look' in *ika·c* 'he looks', *ika·s* 'watcher', *ika·ʔi·s* 'the one who always watches', *ikako·wiha·k* 'finishing to look'; *ko·wi* 'end', *ko·wic* 'it is the end', *ko·wihe·c* 'he finished'.

P: prefixes, which occur before almost any stem and with each other. There are special selections and relative order among them, as also among the suffixes: *ki·suus'* in *ki·ka·k* 'looking at their own'; *aru-* 'place or object, future' in *aruʔika* 'something to look at'.

Pr: a group of mutually exclusive personal prefixes: *w-* 'I', *r-* 'you', *i-* (or zero, etc.) 'he', in *wiru·hic* 'I stand up', *riru·hi·ʔi* 'do you stand up', *iru·hic* 'he stands up'.

Inst: about 70 stems occur in most cases only with instrumental prefixes: *-saki-* 'split' in *pasakic* 'he split with a stick', *rusakic* 'the split with the hand', *kasakic* 'the split by pounding'.

Pinst: about 6 prefixes which occur only with Inst stems: see above.

U: utterance-final suffixes which occur at the end of (as well as within) stretches of speech: *-c* 'it is', vowel repetition 'ʔ': *wahkuc* 'he is here' *wahkuʔu* 'is he here?'.

F: clause-final suffixes which can be substituted for U if the utterance continues: *-k* '-ing', *-wa* 'when', in *wuʔusiak* 'we arriving, . . .', *wuʔusiʔawa* 'when we arrived' (cp. *wuʔusiʔac* 'we arrived'). In the equations below, F will be taken to include U, since no statements are needed for F that do not apply also to U.

N: non-clause-final suffixes. Some of these are final in the stress-group (word) and others are not, but none of them normally occur at the end of a sequence of words such as have U or F at their end: *-s* 'naming suffix' in *waʔahkuʔas* 'the skulls'; *-se* 'by', *-aʔa* 'several' in *aˑtaʔase* 'by their several houses'.

Post: a few postpositive morphemes which occur after word-final affixes (sometimes at the end of an utterance): *isa* 'again' in *waˑhacisa* 'we go again'.

Ind: a very few stems which occur with no affixes, as calls or whole utterances: *ho·* 'yes', *riskare* 'friend'.

5.2. We proceed to state what sequences of morphemes can be substituted for single morphemes of the classes named above.

$S^1 S^1 = S^2$: *risʔi* 'dance' and *hiri* 'make' in *waʔoˑriˑsʔihirak* 'making a dance' (*o·* is nominalizing prefix, member of P).

Pinst Inst = S^2: we can substitute *rusaki* 'split by hand' for *aciwi* 'follow' in *wa·—c* 'I did —'.

Pr $S^2 = S^3$: *wa* 'I' + *aciwi* 'follow'; *wi* 'I' or *i* 'he' + *ru·hi* 'stand up'.

$PS^3 = S^3$: *hiru* 'bone', *aruhiru* 'skeleton'. There is considerable limitation of selection for individual members of P and for sub-classes.

$S^3 = S^3$: *ika·* for *ikako·wi* in *—c* (see under S in §5.1). Substitution of Pr S^2 and PS^3 from the preceding equation for S^3 permits sequences like $P S^1 P S^1 = S^3$, or $Pr S^1 P Pr S^1$ as in *wahku·ciwa·wa·ha·ʔac* 'we want to get': *wah-* '1st person', *kuci* 'get', *wa-* 'something' (a prefix of the second stem), *wa-* '1st person', *he* 'want', *-aʔa* 'severally', i.e. plural', *-c* 'verbalizer'.

$S^3 N = S^4$: *ikahke* 'he caused to look', substitutable for *ika* in *wiʔika·c* 'he looked at me', *wiʔikahkec* 'he makes me look'. Substitution from the preceding equations gives us results like this: $S^3 S^3 N = S^4$, $P S^3 P S^3 N = S^4$; see the example in the equation above, where the *-aʔa* plural applies to both stems with their prefixes. Here too there are some individual members and sub-classes of N which have restricted distribution.

$S^4 S^4 F = S^4 F$: we can substitute *araxe·xak* 'holding' or *ika·k* 'looking' or *ika·c* 'he looked' for *ixpase araxe·xak* 'holding by the wing' (*ixpa* 'wing', *-se* 'by').[22]

$S^4 S^4 U = S^4 F S^4 U = S^4 U$: *haruk kara·k re·wa·re·c* 'thereupon running he went, they say'[23] can be replaced in context by *re·wa·re·c* 'he went, they say', or by *re·c* 'he went' alone, but not by any single morpheme. Similarly, *taheˑruk aruʔisiak hapˑehsahic* 'If he kills, him it will be bad. It will be dark.'[24] can be replaced in its context by *aruʔisiac* 'It will be bad'.

[21] V! can substitute for N V in many utterances: *Come into the house!* for *He came into the house.* Therefore V! can be considered as equalling N V, with the morphemic intonation ! substituting syntactically for N. This cannot be done for N!, since the stretch of speech immediately following N! has the complete intonation of an independent minimum utterance: *John, why don't you come!* Therefore N! too must be taken as an independent minimum utterance.

[22] The position of this phrase in the sentence may be seen in II 5, p. 205, of R. H. Lowie, Z. Harris, and C. F. Voegelin, Hidatsa Texts (Indian Historical Society, Prehistory Research Series 1.6, May 1939), from which volume most of the Hidatsa examples given here have been taken. The analysis in §§5.1-3 is tentative.

[23] Ibid. II 31, p. 207.

[24] Ibid. I 49, p. 195.

5.3. In terms of the classes of morpheme sequences, we can now say that most utterances in Hidatsa, in the style of talking summarized here, consist of S^4 U (representing stretches of speech of any length), or S^4 N (= S^4 representing usually a single stress-unit, e.g. a person's name uttered by itself), or *Ind* (again a single word occurring as an utterance with its separate intonation). *Post* occurs in several positions in $S U$ utterances, and we may say that its syntactic value within the $S U$ formula is zero: $Post\ S U = S U\ Post = S U$.

DISCUSSION

6.0. Having sketched how our procedure could be applied in two languages, we may now ask what kind of description it has given us. The following sections attempt an interpretation of the linguistic status of this analysis, and a summary of the kind of results that it yields.

6.1. POSITION ANALYSIS. The procedure begins by noting the environments of each morpheme and by putting in one class all those morphemes that have similar distributions. However, in many cases the complete adherence to morpheme-distribution classes would lead to a relatively large number of different classes: *hotel* would be N, *think* would be V, and *take* would be in a new class G since it has roughly the distribution of both *hotel* and *think*. In order to avoid an unnecessarily large number of classes, we say that *take* is a member of both N and V. This means that we are no longer studying the morpheme *take* or *think*. We are studying the positions, Bloomfield's 'privileges of occurrence', common to both *take* and *think*, or those common to both *take* and *hotel*.[25]

This means that we change over from correlating each morpheme with all its environments, to correlating selected environments (frames) with all the morphemes that enter them. The variables are now the positions, as is shown by the fact that the criterion for class membership is substitution. The element which occurs in a given class position may be a morpheme which occurs also in various other class positions. We merely select those positions in which many morphemes occur, and in terms of which we get the most convenient total description.[26]

6.2. STOPPING POINT. One might ask how we can tell where to stop the analysis. This is answered by the nature of the work. All we do is to substitute one sequence for another in a given context. When we have the formula for English utterances with assertion intonation, we find that all we can substitute for it is another utterance, with the same or another intonation. When more work has been done on sentence sequences and what is called stylistics, we may find that in certain positions within a sequence of sentences only N V / /, say, ever occurs, to the exclusion of V / /. When we have such informa-

tion, we will be able to extend the substitution procedure to sentences and sequences of utterances (whether monologs or conversations).

6.3. RESULTANT CONSTRUCTION FORMULAE. The final result, for each language which can be analyzed in this manner, takes the form of one or more sequences of substitution classes ('utterance constructions', 'sentence types'). The formulae tell us that these are the sequences which occur. The final formulae therefore give us the limitations upon the freedom of occurrence of morphemes in the language, for they imply that no sequence of morphemes occurs except those which can be derived from the formula.[27]

The utterance formulae are thus rather like the formulae for the phonetic structure of a language, and even like phonemic writing: all of these are formulae showing what occurs in the language. The signs used in the utterance formulae have value: N has the values A N, T A N, T A, etc.; and each of these has specific morphemes as values. Supplying morpheme values for the signs of the formula will give us expressions in the language.

This is not quite the whole story, for there are further limitations of selection among the morphemes, so that not all the sequences provided by the formulae actually occur.[28] Individual limitations of selection cannot be described in these formulae; at best, the more important among them can be stated in special lists or in the dictionary. Limitations applying to various groups of morphemes in each class can, however, be included if we give our formulae the form of charts. The second dimension which the chart provides enables us to state selections among sub-groups in the several columns (each column representing a position, i.e. a class), by placing along one horizontal line the sequences of sub-groups that actually occur.

6.4. The procedure outlined here could be paralleled by a series of substitutions beginning with the whole utterance and working down, instead of beginning with single morphemes and working up. In that case we would have to find formal criteria for breaking the utterance down at successive stages. This is essentially the difficult problem of determining the immediate constituents of an utterance.[29] It is not clear that there exists any general method for successively determining the immediate constituents, when we begin with a whole utterance and work down. In any case, it would appear that the formation of

---

[25] This is also done, in essence, by Bloomfield's class cleavage (Language 204), and by his functions of form classes (ibid. 196), which in essence provide for the syntactic equivalence of words and sequences of words (phrases). Needless to say, the whole procedure described here owes much to Bloomfield's method.

[26] It may be necessary to point out that this positional analysis is strictly formal, as compared with form-and-meaning analyses like the one in Otto Jespersen's Analytic Syntax (Copenhagen, 1937).

[27] Of course, from the formula N V we derive many sequences that occur: e.g. T A N V (*The old order changeth*) since T A N = N, and so on.

[28] Some of these limitations can be included by giving the signs more than one alternative value depending on the value of the other signs, somewhat as phonemic letters are given various allophonic values. We could say that after N^4, English V^4 has two values: simple V^4, and $V^4 N^4$. The utterance sequence N V could represent both N V and N V N (see §4.4). The more limitations of selection we wish to indicate by these equations, the more raised numbers we may need. This may not always be the case; but if we wished for example to indicate that noun stems occur with which -Nn suffixes we would require a long list of equations, involving several numerically differentiated resultant N^4s, before the first $N^1 \cdot N_n = N^1$ equation of §4.3.

[29] Bloomfield, Language ch. 13. Note also Kenneth L. Pike, Taxemes and Immediate Constituents, LANG. 19.65–82 (1943); and the method of analysis used for Japanese by Bloch, Studies in Colloquial Japanese II, LANG. 22.200–48 (1946). ((154))

substitution classes presents fewer theoretical difficulties if we begin with morphemes and work up.

IMPLICIT IN THE FORMULAE

7.0. We have seen the application and the interpretation of the procedure outlined here. This is perhaps all that is required of a procedure. However, in order to fit it into the rest of the description of a language we should find out how much of the information which we expect from syntactic description is derivable from this procedure.

7.1. SUPRASEGMENTAL FEATURES. The intonational and other suprasegmental features, as well as the pauses, are generally included in the equations. When one sequence is substitutable for another in an utterance, it is understood that the intonations, pauses, etc. of the utterance remain unchanged under the substitution. If the substitution is associated with a change in intonation, as in *Who* for *John* in — *got lost*, we state that fact. Some substitution groups may require not only particular sequences but also particular suprasegmental features; e.g. any English sequence with loud stress followed by reduced loud stress may equal N (§4.33). The domains of suprasegmental features often coincide with the sequences which we recognize in our substitution equations; e.g. /·/ and slight-pause separating adverbial phrases in certain positions in English.

In general, therefore, the formulae are based not only on the sequences involved but also on the suprasegmental features of the sequences substituted and of the utterances in which they are substituted. The formulae may thus correlate with phonemic junctures which express the limits of suprasegmental features.

7.2. MORPHOLOGIC BOUNDARIES. The formulae also correlate with non-phonemic (structural) junctures, such as may be set up to mark the boundaries of intervals which serve as elements of the utterance structures.

7.3. MORPHOLOGIC RELATIONS. Many of the relations between a morpheme class and other morpheme classes, or the interval or utterance in which it occurs, can be derived from the formulae, although they are not explicitly stated there for their own sake. The formulae show what morpheme classes (or sequences) are syntactically zero, like X_1- prefixes and -Aa suffixes in English (§4.31); we can even learn from them that in English most prefixes, but relatively few suffixes, are syntactically zero.

The formulae show which morpheme classes occur by themselves in utterances, and which classes are bound not to other morpheme classes (as are most affixes) but to constructions, i.e. to sequences of classes: e.g. English & is limited to any class or extant class sequence; English T is bound to a following noun phrase as a sort of phrase prefix (§4.33); Hidatsa suffixes operate on the whole preceding word, whereas prefixes operate usually only on the immediately following stem (§5.2). The fact that English -Vv suffixes (-*ed*) are best added not to V^1 (verb morphemes) but to V^3 (verb phrases including object, etc.), shows that -*ed* may best be regarded as a suffix of the whole verb phrase. In general,

a class may be considered as bound to the level indicated by the number with which it is associated; i.e. it is bound to whatever is substitutable for the symbol-and-number combination that accompanies it in the equations.

We can also learn from the formulae which morpheme classes are the heads and which are the closures of the sequences in which they appear: the closure is the class which always appears last; and the head is the class which can always substitute for the sequence, e.g. an N morpheme for an N-phrase sequence. The formulae can thus show which sequences are endocentric (e.g. $A N = N$) and which are exocentric (e.g. $T A = N$).

It goes without saying that adequate information about the morpheme classes can be derived not from sketchy examples of the equational procedure such as we have given, but from detailed analyses of all the mutually substitutable sequences of the language.

7.4. ORDER. The formulae are devised in part on the basis of the order of classes in each sequence, and can therefore be used to show it explicitly or by means of the raised numberings.

7.5. ALWAYS OR SOMETIMES. They also enable us to indicate if certain classes occur always or only sometimes in a given sequence. If we write $D A = A$ and $A N = N$, and are free to apply or not to apply the results of one equation in the other, then we can derive from these equations the fact that N, $A N$, and $D A N$ all occur.

7.6. SELECTION. Some of the features of selection, the restrictions on particular morphemes which occur only with particular other morphemes, are indicated in these formulae, or derivable from them. Some selection, such as that between *I* and *am* as against *he* and *is*, is included in the list of variant forms of the morphemes. Selections of concord are listed as special domains of the morpheme in question (§2.3 above).

We can also consider selections and order among sub-classes, e.g. the fact that certain Hidatsa stems are always the last stem in the word, or that *ought* alone among English preverbs usually has *to* after it. This can be expressed by the formulae if they are allowed to become more complicated in form, and especially if they are made into two-dimensional diagrams. Lastly, the formulae in themselves are statements of selection, saying for instance that $N V$ sequences occur, but not $N T$.

7.7. MEANING. The formulae can be used as a source of information on the grammatical meaning of the morpheme classes symbolized in them. To do this, it is necessary to say that morpheme classes or class sequences which replace each other in various equations, i.e. which occur in identical morpheme-class environments, have similar functions or grammatical meanings. Thus the N^3 of $N^3 N^4 V_d^4$ (§4.35) is shown to replace the N^4 which is otherwise found after V_d; both of these represent the object of the V_d.

7.8. COMPARABILITY OF LANGUAGE STRUCTURES. The nature and number of the morpheme classes that have to be set up for a particular language, the forms and number of the equations, and the number of levels which have to be differentiated by raised figures for some of the class symbols, all permit comparisons between the descriptions of one language and another. Such comparisons must not be made too lightly, since considerable choice remains in the setting up of equations for any language. In particular, there may be room for ingenuity in keeping the raised numbers of certain symbols—say N, V, S—at a minimum for each language; so that of two sets of equations for a language, one might reach up to N^8 while the other does not go beyond N^4. Undoubtedly, the procedures of setting up equations and assigning the raised numbers can be made more explicit and, if desired, standardized for greater convenience in structural comparative research. An analysis of this type for Moroccan Arabic comes out rather similar to the English, ending up with $N^5 V^3$ and $N^4 N^4$ for the former as against $N^4 V^4$ for the latter, while the Hidatsa equations are very different, ending with $S^4 U$. This fits in with the general similarity between Indo-European and Semitic structure as against Siouan.[30]

7.9. TESTING MORPHOLOGICAL CRUCES. In §6.1 it was seen that the values of the symbols in the equations are not morphemes but positions, indicating whatever morphemes occupy these positions (irrespective of what other positions these morphemes may occupy in other equations). Therefore, when we wish to know the analysis of a particular utterance, it is impossible merely to replace each morpheme by its class symbol since many morphemes may be members of several classes. W. F. Twaddell has suggested[30a] that such analyses of utterances be carried out by repeated substitution tests on the basis of the equations, in what he has termed 'experimental substitution at all levels'. To carry this out, we would ask what substitutions are permitted by the equations for each morpheme or morpheme sequence of our utterance, in the class environment which it has in that utterance. This is repeated until we know unambiguously to what class each occurrence of each morpheme in our utterance belongs.

We take, for example, the utterance *She made him a good husband because she made him a good wife.* We know that there is a difference in meaning between the two occurrences of *made*; and since we know this without any outside information beyond hearing the sentence, it follows that indication of the difference, in meaning and in construction, can be derived from the structure of the utterance. We proceed to analyze the utterance, going backward along the equations as far as may be necessary to reveal this difference. First, we know that the utterance is an instance of $N^4 V^4$ & $N^4 V^4 = N^4 V^4$. At this stage we know that the two halves of the sentence are still identical in structure. Each V^4 has the structure V^2 (*make*) N^4 (*him*) N^4 (*a good husband/wife*) $+ -Vv$ (*-ed*). The equations show the two cases of this sequence (§4.34): $V_2^2 N^4 N^4 = V_2^3$ (*making President*) and $V d^2 N^4 N^4 = V_2^3$ (*make my husband a party*). We cannot tell which of these applies to each of our V^4, or whether both go back to the same one, because *make* is equally a member of V_a and V_f.[31] We find, however (§4.34), that $V_2^2 N^4 N_1^4 = V d^2 N_1^4 P_e N^4$ (where the subscript number merely identifies

the N which has different positions in the two sequences). We try now to discover whether either V^4 in our utterance has the structure $V d^2 N^4 N^4$, by applying to each V^4 the substitution which is possible for $V d^2 N^4 N^4$. To do this we interchange the two instances of N^4 and insert between them an instance of P_e. In the first V^4 we get a meaningless utterance which would practically never occur: *she made a good husband* (N_1) *for* (P_e) *him* (N) in place of *she made him* (N) *a good husband* (N_1). In the second V^4, however, the substitution gives us an equivalent and not unusual utterance: *she made a good wife* (N_1) *for* (P_e) *him* (N) in place of *she made him* (N) *a good wife* (N_1). Clearly, then, the second V^4 in our utterance is analyzable into $V d^2 N^4 N^4 + -Vv = V_e^3 + -Vv$. Since the first V^4 can not be analyzed in this way, it can equal only the one remaining $V N N$ construction, namely $V_2^2 N^4 N^4 + -Vv = V_e^2 + -Vv$.[32]

We have thus found that the two halves of the original utterance are formally different in the substitutions which can be performed upon them. The whole analysis could of course have begun with morphemes. We could have assigned class symbols to each morpheme, and upon reaching the two occurrences of *made* would not have known whether to indicate each of them by $V a$, V_f, or any one of several other symbols. We would then have had to decide the question by carrying out on the $N N$ following them the very substitutions attempted above.

EXCLUDED FROM THE FORMULAE

8.0. Having seen what syntactic facts can be derived from the formulae, we now ask which ones cannot be included in them and must be found by separate investigations and expressed in separate statements.

8.1. The great bulk of selection features, especially those that distinguish between individual morphemes, cannot be expressed except by very unwieldy formulae. Although it may be of theoretical interest to know that two-dimensional diagrams of such detailed selections are conceivable, in practice this information can only be given in lists and statements appended to the formulae.

8.2. This is true also of such relations among morphemes as the families of mutually replacing English suffixes, e.g. *-id*, *-or* in *squalid: squalor, candid: candor*, etc.[33]

8.3. The formulae also cannot in themselves indicate what meanings may be associated with the various positions or classes.

---

[30] Cf. also a comparable brief analysis of Kota in LANG. 21.283-9 (1945), based on the data supplied in M. B. Emeneau, Kota Texts, Part I (Berkeley and Los Angeles, 1944).

[30a] In a private communication.

[31] All members of V_f are also members of V_a: V_a are verbs which occur before N (as well as before N). Cf. §4.1.

[32] We can check this by noting that if in the first V^4 we substitute a verb which is not a member of V_f, we get a sequence which hardly ever occurs, and whose meaning is not changed by the substitution of $N^4 P_e N^4$: *She bought him a good husband*: *She bought a good husband for him* would not differ in meaning (if it occurred) from *She bought a good husband for him*. But if we try another member of V_f, for instance *think*, we find again that the substitution gives a 'meaningless' (non-occurring) utterance, or in any case one with a greatly altered meaning: *She thought him a good husband* as against *She thought a good husband for him*. Verbs in V_f are therefore verbs which involve obvious change in meaning when the $N_1 P_e N$ substitution is imposed upon them; verbs not in V_f do not involve any reportable change in meaning under that substitution. Therefore the *made* in *made him a good husband* functions as a member of V_f.

[33] Such families of morphemes came to my notice in Stanley Newman's and Morris Swadesh's material on English.

Thus, in Hidatsa, of two formally equivalent words (with noun suffixes) before the clause-final word (which ends in a verbalizing *F*), the first will normally indicate the subject and the second the object: *ruwac·iri istacu rux·iak* 'one of them his eye opening (when one of them opened his eye)'. Such information about the meaning of positions and constructions have to be given in separate statements accompanying the formulae.[34]

8.4. The formulae will also fail to give information about the complete distribution of any one morpheme, which may occur in various classes (§3.4), or about the frequency of morphemes or classes, or about the phonemic structure of various classes (e.g. the fact that Hidatsa *F* or various English affixes are unstressed).

9. We have seen that by extending the term substitution class from single morphemes to sequences of morphemes, we arrive at formulae equating various sequences which are substitutable for each other in all or certain utterances of the language in question. We have seen further that when the setting up of equations is continued until no new results are forthcoming, we obtain succinct statements for the sequences of morphemes which constitute the utterances of the language. The procedure of constructing these equations has here been investigated in order to see what syntactic information it gives or fails to give.

It is clear that the usefulness of this procedure will vary from language to language, the more so in view of the fact that many languages (e.g. to some extent Hidatsa) reveal comparatively little difference between the structure of all utterances and the structure of minimum utterances, and in view of the fact that some languages have great freedom in the distribution of minimum utterances within all utterances.

[34] See, for example, Edward Sapir, Language 86 ff. (New York, 1921).

IMMEDIATE CONSTITUENTS

RULON S. WELLS
Language 23.81–117—1947

We aim in this paper[1] to replace by a unified, systematic theory the heterogeneous and incomplete methods hitherto offered for determining immediate constituents (hereafter abbreviated IC, plural ICs). The unifying basis is furnished by the famous concept of patterning, applied repeatedly and in divers special forms.

I. Expansion

§1. Zellig S. Harris, in his article From Morpheme to Utterance,[2] makes explicit an operation of substituting one sequence of morphemes for another; by somewhat elaborating this operation, and defining some auxiliary terms, we arrive at a concept of expansion. This characterizes one special variety of patterning: two sequences of morphemes, insofar as one is an expansion of the other, pattern alike.

§2. Morphemes are assigned to morpheme-classes on the basis of the environments in which they occur. Each environment determines one and only one morpheme-class, namely the class of all morphemes occurring in that environment. To the morpheme-class determined by the environment ( )ly (adverbial) belong slow, near, quaint, and many other morphemes; but not dead, because the ly of deadly is not the adverbial ly; not pick, because pickly does not occur, and not unhesitating, because unhesitating is not a morpheme.[3] A morpheme A belongs to the

morpheme-class determined by the environment ( )X if AX is either an utterance or occurs as part of some utterance. Thus man occurs in the environment a ( ) are, i.e. the morpheme-sequence a man are occurs; witness the utterance The sons and daughters of a man are called his children. This example shows how it can happen that a morpheme occurs in an environment only if that environment, together with the morpheme itself, occurs in a certain larger environment (the phenomenon called 'grammatical agreement'); it was selected to show also that some morpheme-classes are trivial, and in practice ignored by the grammarian. The fact is that certain morpheme-classes wholly or nearly coincide. The morpheme-class determined by the possessive singular morpheme is very nearly the same as the one determined by the plural morpheme, both classes being called 'nouns' in common parlance. It is such clusters of roughly coincident classes on which the grammarian focuses his attention. Also, some classes are included in others; e.g., all single-morpheme proper nouns are single-morpheme nouns, but not conversely.

§3. Besides morpheme-classes, the grammarian sets up classes of other expressions; we will call these sequence-classes, since every expression is a sequence of one or more morphemes. Given a sequence S, a sequence-class to which S belongs is defined as the class of all sequences whose first morpheme belongs to the same morpheme-class as the first morpheme of S, whose second morpheme belongs to the same morpheme-class as the second morpheme of S, and so on; it follows that all members of a given sequence-class contain the same number of morphemes. Given blackbird, redcoat belongs to the same sequence-class; for black belongs to the same morpheme-class as red, bird belongs to the same class as coat, and the stress-pattern, here treated

---

[1] The central importance of the problem of immediate constituents was driven home to me in many valuable conversations with Zellig S. Harris, who also let me read a number of his manuscripts, of which not all have yet been published. Subsequently it was my privilege to acquire a minute acquaintance with Bernard Bloch's fine and well-balanced description of Japanese. Extensive viva voce discussion yields an insight into nuances, the weighing of alternative possibilities, and the far-reaching implications of any assumption that no written account can achieve.

I am indebted to Bloch, to Elizabeth F. Gardner, and to Henry M. Hoenigswald for pointing out ways in which two earlier drafts of this paper needed revision.

The present study is part of a project sponsored by the American Council of Learned Societies, whose support I gratefully acknowledge.

[2] Lang. 22.161–83 (1946) ((142)).

[3] Farly does not occur in actual utterances. The grammarian must decide whether this non-occurrence is accidental—because farly would have no meaning, or because the meaning which it would have is expressed by some other, current expression, or because (like brownbird; cf. blackbird, bluebird) it describes an object or a situation which people never have occasion to talk about—or whether,

on the other hand, farly is grammatically impossible, like pickly or kindlily. To demarcate what is grammatically impossible (ungrammatical) from what does not occur merely for some stylistic or semantic reason is a difficult problem. We do not deal with it here because it is irrelevant to the theory of ICs, which takes as its data all those utterances known to occur, and analyzes them.

In citing environments, we use a pair of parentheses to indicate the position of morphemes or morpheme-sequences that occur in a given environment. Thus, the parentheses in ( )ly, above, indicate the position of such morphemes as slow, near, quaint before the morpheme ly.

as a morpheme or morpheme-sequence (cf. §70), is identical in the two words. The two-word sequence black bird belongs to a different sequence-class, however, because the stress-pattern is different. Even when contrastive stress is applied—It's a black bird, not a red one—black bird is phonemically and morphemically the same as blackbird (§§67, 72, 75) but constructionally (§38) different; in other words, black bird and blackbird are in this environment homonymous.

A sequence belongs to more than one sequence-class whenever at least one of its component morphemes beongs to more than one morpheme-class—which is usually the case. Since city is both a common noun and a noun, city-bred belongs to at least two sequence-classes; London-bred, containing the proper noun London, belongs to one of the sequence-classes but not the other.

Let us repeat that by 'sequence' we shall understand not only a sequence of two or more morphemes, but also a sequence of a single morpheme, that is, the morpheme itself, so that all morphemes are sequences but not conversely. It follows that every morpheme-class is a sequence-class, but not every sequence-class is a morpheme-class. The purpose of this use of terms is to avoid the cumbersome phrase 'morpheme or sequence', which we should otherwise very often have to employ.

§4. Now the simple but significant fact of grammar on which we base our whole theory of ICs is this: that a sequence belonging to one sequence-class A is often substitutable for a sequence belonging to an entirely different sequence-class B. By calling the class B 'entirely different' from the class A we mean to say that A is not included in B, and B is not included in A; they have no member sequences in common, or else only a relatively few—the latter situation being called 'class-cleavage'. For instance, Tom and Dick is substitutable for they, wherever they occurs; They wanted me to come is a grammatical sentence, and so is Tom and Dick wanted me to come.[4] They did it because they wanted to is grammatical, and Tom and Dick did it because Tom and Dick wanted to is equally grammatical, being uncommon for stylistic reasons only. Similarly, The stars look small because they are far away and The stars look small because Tom and Dick are far away are both grammatical, the second sentence being uncommon (or not used) for semantic reasons only.

We may roughly express the fact under discussion by saying that sometimes two sequences occur in the same environments even though they have different internal structures. When one of the sequences is at least as long as the other (contains at least as many morphemes) and is structurally diverse from it (does not belong to all the same sequence-classes as the other), we call it an expansion of that other

[4] The converse does not hold. For instance, they is not substitutable for Tom and Dick in the sequence I met Tom and Dick downtown.

sequence, and the other sequence itself we call a model. If A is an expansion of B, B is a model of A. The leading idea of the theory of ICs here developed is to analyze each sequence, as far as possible, into parts which are expansions; these parts will be the constituents of the sequence. The problem is to develop this general idea into a definite code or recipe, and to work out the necessary qualifications required by the long-range implications of each analysis of a sequence into constituents.

§5. A preliminary example will give an inkling of how the method works. The king of England opened Parliament is a complete sentence, to be analyzed into its constituent parts; we ignore for the time being its features of intonation. It is an expansion of John, for John occurs as a complete sentence. But it is an expansion of John only in this special environment, the zero environment—not in such an environment as ( ) worked [John worked]. It helps the IC-analysis to show that the sequence being analyzed is an expansion, but only if it is an expansion of the same shorter sequence in all, or a large proportion, of the environments where the shorter sequence occurs. For the sequence taken as an example, The king opened, or The king waited, or John worked will serve as shorter sequences. (It is not necessary, in order for A to be an expansion of B, that A should contain all the morphemes of B and in the same order. This is only a special case of expansion, called by Bloomfield 'endocentric'. Moreover, the king of England is an endocentric expansion of a queen—insofar as a and the belong to the same morpheme-classes—just as much as of the king.)

§6. Our general principle of IC-analysis is not only to view a sequence, when possible, as an expansion of a shorter sequence, but also to break it up into parts of which some or all are themselves expansions. Thus in our example it is valuable to view The king of England opened Parliament as an expansion of John worked because the king of England is an expansion of John and opened Parliament is an expansion of worked. On this basis, we regard the ICs of The king of England opened Parliament as the king of England and opened Parliament.

The king of England is in turn subject to analysis, and John is no help here because it is a single morpheme. The king will serve; the king of England is an expansion of the king and, in turn, king of England is an expansion of king. The king of England is accordingly analyzed into the and king of England (cf. §20). The reasons for analyzing the latter into king and of England (rather than king of and England) will be given later.

As for the second half of the sentence, opened Parliament, besides the obvious analysis into opened and Parliament there is another, instantly rejected by common sense but yet requiring to be considered, into open and -ed Parliament. The choice between these two analyses is dictated not by the principle of expansions as stated and exemplified above but by two other principles of patterning, equally fundamental for English and very probably for other languages: the principle of choosing ICs that will be as independent of each other in their distribution as possible, and the principle that word divisions should be respected. The first of these principles is stated in §18, the second in §40 and §47.

§7. Let us call the ICs of a sentence, and the ICs of those ICs, and so on down to the morphemes, the constituents of the sentence; and conversely whatever sequence is constituted by two or more ICs let us call a constitute. Assuming that the ICs of The king of England opened Parliament are the king of England and opened Parliament, that those of the former are the and king of England and those of the latter are opened and Parliament, and that king of England is divided into king and of England, of England is divided into the morphemes of and England, and opened is divided into open and -ed—all of which facts may be thus diagrammed:* the[king[of[[England]open[[ed[Parliament—then there are twelve constituents of the sentence: (1) the king of England, (2) the, (3) king of England, (4) king, (5) of England, (6) of, (7) England, (8) opened Parliament, (9) opened, (10) open, (11) -ed, (12) Parliament. And the six constitutes in the above sentence are those five of the constituents (nos. 1, 3, 5, 8, 9) that are not morphemes, plus the sentence itself. According to this analysis the sequence the king of, for instance, or England opened, is in this sentence neither a constituent nor a constitute. And in terms of this nomenclature the principle relating words to IC-analysis may be stated: every word is a constituent (unless it is a sentence by itself), and also a constitute (unless it is a single morpheme). But if opened Parliament were analyzed into open and -ed Parliament, the word opened would be neither a constituent nor a constitute.

§8. What we view as the correct analysis of The king of England opened Parliament has now been stated, but it remains to consider why other analyses of it were rejected. For an IC-analysis is never accepted or rejected on its own merits. Our procedure aims only to tell, given two or more mechanically possible dichotomies (whose number is always one less than the number of morphemes in the dichotomized sequence), how to decide in favor of one of them. Assuming that all the words in The king of England opened Parliament except opened are single morphemes (the possibility of analyzing England and Parliament into two morphemes each being neglected here as irrelevant), there are six analyses to be evaluated one against the other; the analysis into the king of England and opened Parliament has the same advantage over all the other five, and therefore it will suffice to consider exhaustively only one of these five: the analysis into the king and of England

*For typing convenience, this reprint combines brackets instead of duplicating the conventional bars and clusters:][>[for],]][> [[for ‖, etc.

opened Parliament. A common-sense response would be to say that analysis into the king and of England opened Parliament violates the meaning. This is true, but it is possible in our exposition to leave the factor of meaning out of account until much later (Part III), meanwhile going as far as possible on formal grounds alone.

§9. Several more sophisticated arguments based on formal patterning might be advanced. One could argue that of England opened Parliament is not an IC of the whole sentence because it is a sequence that could not be found anywhere except after a noun-phrase. But while this argument is sufficient ad hoc, it is too weak to exclude other analyses which one would regard as wrong, e.g. the king of[England opened Parliament. For there is no question about England opened Parliament, and the king of can be found in such other environments as I wonder what country he's the king of.

Or again: there is an actor-action pattern in English, and whatever occurs as an actor or as an action in an actor-action sentence also occurs as a sentence by itself (i.e. accompanied by nothing but a sequence of pitch morphemes). Thus: [Who opened Parliament?] The king. [What did you say the king of England did?] Opened Parliament. This consideration certainly cuts out the king[of England opened Parliament, but it does not preclude either the king of[England opened Parliament or the king of England opened[Parliament; to deal with these one must revert either to meaning or to supplementary formal principles. And in the second place, the consideration that we have mentioned is available only at a later stage of grammatical description than we are taking for granted at this point. For the principles delineated in this paper are intended to be used not only in deciding to which of the known constructions or patterns of the language any given sentence belongs, but also as part of the means for ascertaining those very patterns themselves. If they are adequate they will suffice, for example, when applied to the data of English, to establish the existence of the general actor-action pattern itself.

§10. An argument might be based on economy or simplicity: the constituents of a sentence should be those units in terms of which the sentence is most easily described.[5] Now other sentences such as I saw the king of England alongside of I saw John,

[5] Leonard Bloomfield, Language 212 (New York, 1933); Kenneth L. Pike, Taxemes and Immediate Constituents, Lang. 19.65–82, esp. §4.19 (1943).

One particular version of simplicity which someone might propound but which must be rejected would call for the totality of analyses that requires the minimum number of sequence-classes to be defined. The proposal is sound in itself but inadequate to exclude all wrong analyses, such as the king of[England. Note that the king of must be described as a constituent in certain other occurrences, e.g. What country is he the king of?

and he opened Parliament alongside of he came, require us to treat the king of England and opened Parliament as units, but no sentence (unless, circularly, those of the very type under consideration) constrain us so to treat of England opened Parliament.

It will be noted that this argument does not exclude all wrong divisions, as for instance the king of[England opened Parliament (see above). However, perhaps we cannot expect that any one principle should be completely sufficient. Be that as it may, a more powerful and satisfactory version of this argument, and the one which we shall adopt as a fundamental principle of IC-analysis, is stated in terms of expansions, and a fuller definition of expansions is necessary than the preliminary one already given in 84.

811. Every sentence may be divided into focus and environment. The focus is any sequence that is viewed as replaceable by other sequences; correlatively, the rest of the sentence is the environment of such a sequence. In practice it is often possible to narrow down the focus-plus-environment from a whole sentence to some shorter part of it. As a rule, that shorter part turns out to be a constituent in the technical sense. Thus, we can investigate what sequences may function as focus (may fill the blank) in the ( ) of England, without considering the wider environment of which the sequence the ( ) of England is itself the focus. In such cases there is a relevant environment smaller than the total environment. When a whole sentence is considered as focus, the environment is zero.[6]

The class of all sequences substitutable for a given focus in a given environment may be called the focus-class relative to that environment. Now every focus is a sequence (of one or more morphemes). If we analyze our sentence as The‖king‖‖ of‖‖England[open‖ed‖Parliament so that the main break comes after England, we can explain the constituents as expansions down to the following point: the king of England is an expansion of the king (which in turn is an expansion of a proper noun, say John) because king of England is an expansion of king; opened Parliament is an expansion of a past-tense intransitive verb like worked. The whole sentence, therefore, is an expansion of John worked, which is of a fundamental sentence-type because it is not an expansion (except in a very few environments, such as the zero-environment) of anything shorter; but John worked and John works, each containing three morphemes, may be regarded as expansions of each other.[7] Thus the search for expansions leads us to the actor-action sentence-type; we do not need to take it for granted.

But if, on the other hand, we analyze our sentence as the king]of England opened Parliament, then no matter what further analysis we make, of England opened Parliament is not an expansion of anything shorter than of England worked or of England works. Thus it compares unfavorably with opened Parliament. And the other half has no compensating advantage, because the king of England can be construed as an expansion just as well as the king. Therefore the principle of expansion conclusively favors the analysis the king of England]opened Parliament. It cannot strictly be said to confirm or corroborate common sense, although it agrees with it; for it is precisely one of the reasons on which the common-sense judgment is based, although of course common sense alone would never be able to formulate it.

812. Some implications of our procedure need to be made explicit. Expansion was defined relative to an environment. If two sequences belong to all the same sequence-classes, then each is an absolute equivalent of the other, in the sense that each occurs in all the environments where the other occurs and nowhere else. However, it is rare, if it happens at all, that one sequence is an absolute equivalent of a sequence belonging to an entirely different sequence-class. On this account our interest centers in non-absolute expansions, and the problem is to find expansions that approximate as closely as possible to being absolute.

813. It is frequently the case that one sequence occurs wherever a certain other one occurs but not conversely. This asymmetry is typical of endocentric expansions. Wherever the expansion oldish occurs, the model old occurs also, but the converse is not true; for instance, old occurs in oldish, but oldishish is grammatically impossible. (It may be that there are also cases of the opposite sort where the expansion occurs wherever the model occurs but not conversely.) A much more frequent case, given any two sequences chosen at random, is that there are some environments in which both the first and the second occur, some in which only the first occurs, and some in which only the second occurs. Both boy and boys occur in the environments I saw the ( ) and the ( ) saw me. But only boy occurs in I saw that ( ) and the ( ) sees me, and only boys in I saw those ( ) and the ( ) see me. It is because of the former environments that there is a class of nouns, and because of the latter that this class is divided into singulars and plurals.

---

[6] In the sequel, we shall often speak loosely of a sequence as occurring in the zero-environment when we mean that its total environment is the pitch-morpheme of the sentence. Cf. fn. 34.

[7] This statement is made on the assumption that worked consists morphologically of only the two

morphemes work and -ed. If, as some would consider, the proportion they work : John works = they worked : John worked is perfect, so that worked includes also a zero-alternant of the 3rd-singular morpheme -s when it has a singular subject, then John works is indeed shorter than John worked (since it lacks the past-tense morpheme -ed), and furnishes a simpler example of the fundamental sentence type.

14. It is easy to define a focus-class embracing a large variety of sequence-classes but characterized by only a few environments; it is also easy to define one characterized by a great many environments in which all its members occur, but on the other hand poor in the number of diverse sequence-classes that it embraces. What is difficult, but far more important than either of the easy tasks, is to define focus-classes rich both in the number of environments characterizing them and at the same time in the diversity of sequence-classes that they embrace. Actor and action (or in the older terminology subject and predicate) are such focus-classes. Another (less grand) example is the focus-class of verbs and verb-phrases; subsumed under this, as a subclass, is the focus-class of third singular present verbs and endocentric phrases containing such a verb as their head. Again, the pronouns he, she, it, this, that, and one; all singular proper nouns; and all singular noun phrases beginning with the, a, this, that, any, each, every, together form a focus-class whose diversity of membership is as we have just specified and which occurs in a large number of environments —environments which are not themselves unified by all belonging to a major focus-class. The traditional parts of speech are focus-classes, not morpheme-classes or other sequence-classes.[8] Thus the class of English nouns includes compounds and derivatives as well as single morphemes. (Paradigms, including all the inflected forms of a given stem, are yet another kind of class, unless it should happen that there are one or more environments in which all the inflected forms occur. Cf. fn. 14.)

15. An instructive formula summarizing the contrast between sequence- and focus-classes is in terms of external and internal grammar. The internal grammar of a sequence is the class of all sequence-classes to which it belongs; the external grammar is the class of all focus-classes to which it belongs. If two sequences have the same internal grammar, they must have the same external grammar, but the converse does not hold true; this is why the method of expansion is possible. If two sequences are similar in external grammar, but internally different, then by definition one of them is an expansion of the other. The contrast between internal and external grammar makes precise what is sometimes meant by the contrast between form and function.

16. In choosing the major focus-classes that will be used in dividing any utterance into constituents, it is necessary to consider the whole system which these focus-classes, taken collectively, form with each other. This is why an analysis is not pronounced good or bad of itself, but only better or worse than some other.

17. Judged by this criterion of over-all consequences, the analysis the king of England [opened

Parliament is better than the king] of England opened Parliament, because there is a focus-class to which opened Parliament belongs, embracing more sequence-classes and occurring in more environments than any focus-class to which of England opened Parliament belongs. It is true that there are some environments, such as the king of Scotland and ( ), where the latter sequence but not the former occurs; it is also true that a focus-class to which of England opened Parliament belongs includes some sequence-classes not included in the focus-class of opened Parliament—for instance, the class to which by marriage runs a bank belongs in my cousin [by marriage runs a bank. In fact, the example makes it clear that wrong analyses into ICs tend to support each other, just as right ones do.[9] But right analyses are ultimately supported from without by the method of regarding them as expansions of shorter sequences, whereas wrong analyses lack this ultimate extraneous support. And right analyses turn out to relegate more sequences to larger focus-classes (larger both in diversity of membership and in the number of characterizing environments) than those to which wrong analyses would relegate them. Opened Parliament occurs, thus differing from of England opened Parliament, after adverbs and also in zero environment (i.e. as a sentence by itself).

18. This is the fundamental aim of IC-analysis: to analyze each utterance and each constitute into maximally independent sequences—sequences which, consistently preserving the same meaning, fit in the greatest number of environments and belong to focus-classes with the greatest possible variety of content.

19. Another way of stating the basic utility of expansions is that they furnish a way of proceeding from the simple to the complex, from the established to the not yet established, from that whose analysis is transparent to that whose analysis is obscure. But a difficulty is that, given a complex constitute to be analyzed, a number of different models (§4) seem to offer themselves. We turn now to the problem of how to choose between these.

20. For instance, shall the king of England be analyzed as the [king of England or as the king] of England? Our principle directs us to analyze into constituents which are expansions; but at first sight the advantages of the alternatives appear to be about equal. King of England is an expansion of king, but the king is an expansion of John.[10] In respect of their other ICs, the [king of England is better than the king] of England, since the is a single morpheme while

---

[8] So are Bloomfield's 'form-classes'; cf. his Language 185 top, 190 top, 194 second paragraph, etc.

[9] We call an IC-analysis wrong when there is another possible analysis of the same sequence that is better, and right when there is none.

[10] That the king of England is itself an expansion of John is relevant in determining the king of England to be a constituent of any longer sequence in which it occurs, but not relevant in determining its own constituents.

of England is neither a morpheme nor yet an expansion. But this is too slight to figure in the decision. As before, it is necessary to see how close to equivalence is the reciprocal substitutability of king of England with king, and of the king with John. It turns out that while the relation of king of England to king is almost absolute equivalence, the environment poor ( ) —poor being here replaceable by any other non-pronominal adjective—differentiates John from the king, for there is no poor the king. Rather, and instead, there is the poor king. But if the better analysis the|king of England were for some reason excluded, the fact that the king is in some environments an expansion of John would support the king| of England in comparison with the other possibility, the king of|England; for the king of is not an expansion of anything in very many environments.

II. Further methods

§21. Having tentatively settled upon the|king of England as the best analysis of that phrase, we proceed to draw out its consequences by checking how it harmonizes with other analyses. King of England and (for example) English king belong to a focus-class in common; therefore it is desirable, unless other considerations weigh against it, to treat one of them as a constituent and a constitute if the other is so treated. The pair of analyses the|king of England and the|English king is the only pair achieving this result; no other pair does so.[11]

§22. A further step is now possible. The two sequences king of England and English king belong to a certain focus-class, and they contain a part in common, namely a noun. The former belongs to the class of sequences composed of noun plus following modifier, the latter to the class of sequences composed of noun plus preceding modifier. We define a noun modifier as whatever is either a preceding modifier or a following modifier;[12] it will be seen that the class of noun modifiers is neither a sequence-class nor a focus-class. So far from the two kinds of noun modifiers occurring in the same environment, they are, in a sense, in complementary distribution to each other.[13] We unite the two classes of modifiers (each of which is, by itself, a focus-class) into a new type of class, which we may call an associative group. The grammatical reason for doing so is that we thus create a common structure for two sequence types (modifier + noun; noun + modifier) which are included in the same focus-class. This construction obviously

does not imply that the two types of modifier-and-noun phrases are completely identical in structure; it only points out one common feature—a feature which proves, as formal features often do, to correlate with modification in the semantic sense.

The constructability of associative groups does not argue for one analysis rather than another. The English, an English, many a, more than one, all the are sequences of diverse internal grammar (§15) that belong to a common focus-class; and there is a sequence-class of which some member (a, the, one) is a subsequence of each of these sequences. Therefore English, many, more than and all belong to an associative group. But this is not the reason for regarding the English, an English, many a, more than one, and all the as constituents. No IC-analysis will recognize all the focus-classes there are, nor all the associative groups; an analysis results from determining some focus-classes and some associative groups to be more important (more major) than others. And the associative groups worth defining are those that harmonize with the IC-system.

§23. Another variety of patterning argument is based on paradigms. King and kings belong to the same paradigm;[14] therefore, derivatively the king of and the kings of would be expected to relate to each other as king and kings relate to each other. Accordingly, if the king of England were analyzed the king of|England, then the kings of England should be analyzed the kings of|England, and the king of England and Scotland should be analyzed the king of|England and Scotland. But the latter analyses are to be rejected not only for reasons similar to those invalidating of England opened Parliament, but also for the additional reason that the king of and the kings of do not pattern like modifiers. More exactly expressed, the associative group 'modifiers' that we have set up could not be augmented by the focus-class of the king of, the kings of, etc., without radically altering its defining properties. Any sequence consisting of singular noun plus modifier 'patterns like' (is an expansion of) singular nouns, and any sequence consisting of plural noun plus modifier is an expansion of plural nouns. This is not true of the king of, the kings of; for the king of England and Scotland is singular, and the kings of England is plural. This same fact differentiates them from pronominal modifiers like this, these, which indeed are themselves inherently singular or plural but which grammatically agree, in respect of number, with what they modify. Thus sequences like the king of, if treated as modifiers, stand isolated in a focus-class of their own, and since there is another analysis of the king of England not suffering from this undesired consequence, the analysis the king of|England is rejected.

---

[11] Until we admit discontinuous constituents. See Part V of this paper.

[12] The circularity is only apparent. What is assumed as previously defined is the whole phrase 'preceding modifier' and the whole phrase 'following modifier'. A third type of modifier is discussed in §56.

[13] Cf. Moroccan Arabic n- 'I will' and -t 'I did', in nmši 'I will go' and mšit 'I went' (Harris, op.cit. §3.1).

[14] And also to a number of focus-classes in common. But it is always a coincidence when a paradigm is also a focus-class; it may be that some paradigms in some languages have no environment characteristic of all their members.

824. Further examples will at the same time illustrate the principles already stated, and occasion the introduction of some additional principles.

Taking for granted that I will be ready should be analyzed I|will be ready, let us inquire into the further analysis of the second IC. Assuming each of the three words to be a single morpheme, the two possibilities are will|be ready and will be|ready. Each analysis recognizes important focus-classes, so that it would be hard to decide between them on this basis. Like will be pattern not only must be, could be, may be, etc., and will become, will seem, will appear, will look, etc., but also more complex sequences like will pretend to be and less complex ones like am, is, are, was, were.[15] Like be ready pattern become ready, seem ready, look ready, as well as go, wait, read a book, etc. The solution lies in comparison with certain other sequences, e.g. was ready. Even if was be regarded morphologically as be + past-tense morpheme + third-singular morpheme, the principle (840, 847) that every word is a constitute leaves was|ready as a better analysis than any other. Now since will be is in many environments an expansion of was, the analysis will be|ready comports well with the analysis was|ready.

But why not argue, on the same basis, that since will wait must be analyzed will|wait, and be ready is in many environments an expansion of wait, the analysis of will be ready should be will|be ready?— Because in any environment where will be is not an expansion of was, it is an expansion of were; whereas in the environments where be ready is not an expansion of wait, it is not an expansion of anything. This is an instance of how paradigms play a part in determining ICs—was, were, will be all belong to the same pardigm. Paradigms are valuable in IC-analysis when they occur in pairs, standing in agreement relations with each other. Here, for example, the pairs consist of nouns and pronouns on the one hand and verbs on the other: I agrees with am, and he, she, it, etc. with is. Thanks to this feature we are able to show that is and are together are absolute equivalents of will be, so that will be|ready is an analysis superior to will|be ready.

825. Another example: infinitives. Shall we analyze want to|go or want|to go? Want to is in some environments an expansion of can, must, will, should, etc.[16]

[15] But a focus-class to which only one of the three sequences am, is, are belongs is characterized by more environments than one to which two or all three of them belong, because of the grammatical agreement which these words require with their subject or actor.

[16] But not, for example, in the environment he ( ) go. Here the expansion of can is wants to. Want to and wants to are paradigmatically related, like want and wants, so that if want to is treated as a constituent, it is desirable to treat wants to in the same way. And if, on other grounds, it has been decided to treat them both as constituents, then they will conjointly support the analysis of any sequence of which they are conjointly either an expansion or a model.

On the other hand, to go is in some environments an expansion of a proper or collective noun; thus, both to go and food occur in the same environment ( ) is pleasant, I wanted ( ), ( ) is better than ( ), etc. There are other environments that differentiate the two—environments, that is, where one but not the other occurs; thus, only the infinitive occurs in it is pleasant ( ) [synonymous with ( ) is pleasant], I tried not ( ), I want him ( ), it's good for you ( ), while only the noun occurs in I'm waiting for ( ), this kind of ( ). The method of expansion as we have stated it so far is therefore not suited to decide between want to|go and want|to go.

826. In the sequence to go is easy, the two ICs are to go and is easy; this is demonstrated by the considerations that establish the actor-action construction in general. Since to go is a constituent in this environment, it is desirable that it be treated as a constituent wherever it occurs with the same meaning; on this ground we choose the analysis want|to go.

827. The principle just stated is an exceedingly important one, but it has two equally important exceptions. A continuous sequence treated as a constituent in one environment should be treated as a constituent in any other environment where it occurs, unless (1) there is some longer sequence of which it is both a part and a model (in other words, some endocentric expansion of it) and which is treated as a constituent, or (2) it bears a different meaning.[17] The fact that want to is a constituent in the sentence I go there because I want to does not entail that want to should be treated as a constituent in want to go, for to (in want to at the end of a clause) is a model for to go; therefore the analysis want|to go is compatible with the analysis of want to as a constituent when it occurs at sentence-end. Similarly, the occurrence of the king as a constituent of I|saw|the king does not entail treating it as a constituent in I|saw||the||king of England.

This exception to the general principle is necessary, since otherwise almost every constitute would be subject to conflicting analyses. The sequences I saw the king and John of England would entail the king|of England, while he became king of England would entail the|king of England. But even with the exceptions noted above, the principle is a very powerful and valuable one, playing a somewhat analogous role to that played in Euclid's geometry by the axiom that one figure may be moved around and superimposed on another while remaining constant in shape and size.

828. A subsidiary and related principle is that if a given sequence occurring with the same meaning in two environments is treated in both environments

[17] For the purposes of stating this principle, we assume that every sequence has a meaning, though actually it is in general much more difficult to define the meaning of non-constituents—especially when they are discontinuous—than of constituents.

as a constitute (therefore also as a constituent, un-less it is a complete utterance), it must in both oc-currences receive the same analysis into ICs. This principle, like the preceding, is valuable in allowing us to establish a consistent system by checking and testing our analyses one against the others. Another such principle (indispensable but so obvious as to need no discussion) is that if two sequences belong to exactly the same sequence-classes (§3), they must be identically analyzed. If one of them, occurring with a certain meaning in a certain environment, is analyzed in such-and-such a way, then the other, when it occurs with the same meaning in the same environment, must be analyzed in the same way.

§29. One IC-analysis involves others; its sound-ness is not tested until its most far-reaching effects on the system have been explored. Ultimately, what is accepted or rejected is not the analysis of a single sentence but what we may call the IC-<u>system</u> of the language, an entire set or system of analyses, com-plete down to the ultimate constituents, of all the utterances of the language. Since every constitute is wholly composed of constituents, every proposal to regard such-and-such a sequence as a constituent entails that every other constituent of the sentence in which it occurs shall wholly include it or wholly exclude it or be wholly included in it. The analysis <u>the king of⟨England opened Parliament</u> is obviously excluded if <u>of England</u> is a constituent of that sen-tence; conversely, if <u>the king of⟨England opened Parliament</u> is the accepted analysis, it is impossible that <u>of England</u> should be a constituent. Hence errors, as well as right analyses, compound each other.

For this reason, we do not propose our account as a mechanical procedure by which the linguist, starting with no other data than the corpus of all the utterances of the language and a knowledge of the morphemes contained in each one, may discover the correct IC-system. For any language, the number of possible IC-systems is very large; but in practice it is easy to see that most of the possibilities are neg-ligible. Just as when working out the phonemics, the practicing linguist will discover many shortcuts.

Because of the systematic interlocking of one IC-analysis with others, both of the same sentence and of other sentences of the language, it is not possible to demonstrate conclusively upon one or a few selected examples that, all things considered, such-and-such analyses are the best. All we can do is to delineate the proof and to show how far-reaching the conse-quences of any one particular IC-analysis may be.

III. Constructions

§30. In §8 we remarked that a theory of ICs could be developed up to a certain point without a consider-ation of meaning; that point has now been reached. We have, indeed, several times used the phrase 'with the same meaning' (§§18, 26, 27, 28), but without ex-plaining why the proviso is necessary. Very simply, it is necessary because there are many instances

of a sequence which in some occurrences has one meaning and in other occurrences has another, and which, moreover, has different analyses into ICs ac-cordingly. An example is the sequence <u>old men and women</u>. In one meaning this is nearly synonymous with <u>old men and old women</u>; in another, with <u>women and old men</u>. One of the prime functions of analysis into ICs is to reveal a formal difference correlated with the semantic one. In the former meaning, the sequence is <u>old⟨men and women</u>; in the latter, <u>old men⟨and⟨women</u>.[18]

Again, <u>the king of England's people</u> has two mean-ings, and correspondingly two IC-analyses: (1) <u>the⟨king⟨⟨of England's people</u> means 'the king of a certain people, viz. the English'; (2) <u>the king of England⟨⟨'s⟨people</u> means 'the people of a certain king, viz. the king of England'.

§31. This sort of equivocation, if not found in every language of the globe, is certainly widespread. Its import for grammar is very great. For it means that the grammarian must include among his data some-thing more than morphemes and their sequences. Grammatical 'order' is something more than mere sequence. To this 'something more' we propose to give the name <u>construction</u>.[19]

§32. <u>The king of England's people (1)</u> and <u>the king of England's people (2)</u> as defined above are the same sequence of phonemes, yet they have two different meanings. How is the difference to be accounted for, how localized? It cannot plausibly be ascribed to the morphemes taken severally; it is not like the homo-nymy of of 'effected by' and of 'effected upon' in <u>the conquest of Pizarro</u> : <u>the conquest of Peru</u>. Nor is it like <u>It's father</u> (e.g. in answer to <u>Who is it?</u>) and <u>Its father</u> (e.g. in answer to <u>Who is the man holding that baby?</u>), where two morpheme-sequences having the same sound belong to different sequence-classes. The only remaining factor to which the dif-ference in meaning between (1) and (2) can be ascribed is the arrangement of the morphemes (the taxis).

It has long been recognized that the order in which morphemes are arranged is often a bearer of mean-ing; as <u>John hit Bill</u> vs. <u>Bill hit John</u>. But although in the pair before us, (1) and (2), the meaning-differ-ence is ascribable to the arrangement of morphemes in some sense, it is obviously not ascribable to their order. Therefore, as stated above, order does not exhaust arrangement.

§33. Preparatory to defining constructions, we distinguish between sequences and occurrences (or instances) of sequences.[20] The sequence <u>he writes</u>

---

[18] We shall justify in §54 the analysis of a noun phrase <u>A and B</u> into three ICs, <u>A⟨and⟨B</u>.

[19] The reader must constantly bear in mind that our definition of this term is not the same as Bloom-field's (Language 169), although both are generaliza-tions of what is meant in traditional grammar by such expressions as 'the ablative absolute construction'.

[20] Cf. Y. R. Chao, The Logical Structure of Chinese Words, Lang. 22.5 (1946).

pages and pages contains six morphemes: he, write, -s (3rd singular), page, -s (plural), and; but eight morpheme-occurrences, since the morphemes page and -s (plural) each have two occurrences. Likewise he writes pages and pages is the same sequence as the first underlined sequence of this paragraph, but a different occurrence of that sequence. Sequences are universals; occurrences are particulars.[21]

34. Now a construction is a class C of occurrences, subject to the following conditions: (1) there is at least one focus-class which includes all the sequences of which the members of C are occurrences; (2) all these occurrences have a certain meaning in common; and optionally (3) all these occurrences occur in a certain total environment or in all of a certain class of total environments. Note that while a sequence may occur in more than one environment, a given occurrence of a sequence occurs in just one occurrence of an environment.

We have given above a broad definition of the term construction; it admits as constructions a great many classes that are of no interest in the theory of ICs.[22] But it is easy enough simply to ignore these uninteresting cases, and thus to avoid a complicated and cumbersome definition. When the verb run occurs with the pitch morpheme of an indicative sentence $/24/$[23] as its total environment (i.e. as a sentence) and with the meaning of command, the construction to which it belongs is different from the construction of the same verb with the same pitch phonemes occurring as a sentence with the meaning of statement (e.g. in answer to the question Which would you rather do—walk or run?); and both of these constructions are different from the respective constructions of come in the sentences Come here, I'm coming, and I'll try to come (with whatever intonation and what-

ever meaning). But there are several constructions (clause, declarative sentence, imperative sentence, etc.) which include both the sequence come here occurring with the pitch morpheme of an indicative sentence as its total environment, and the single morpheme come occurring in the same environment.

Our definition of the term construction allows an occurrence to belong to more than one construction. Thus we may say that Come here (as a sentence, accompanied by the pitch morpheme of an indicative sentence) belongs at the same time to the clause construction and to the declarative or imperative sentence construction, whereas in the sequence Come here and I'll tell you it belong only to the clause construction. Similarly, in The king of England opened Parliament, the sequence the king of England belongs simultaneously to the noun-phrase construction and to the subject (actor) construction. There is no conflict in this, because the meaning of the one construction is compatible with the meaning of the other, and sometimes a part of it.

But there is conflict in the cases of old men and women and the king of England's people. An occurrence having one of the meanings does not have the other; therefore, while old men and women, meaning 'old men and old women', may belong to several constructions at once, there are some constructions to which it does not belong and to which the same sequence with the other meaning 'women and old men' does belong.

35. We have assumed (fn. 17) that every sequence has at least one meaning; hence every one of its occurrences has the same meaning or meanings, and belongs to at least one construction. Now the meaning of the king of England is compounded of a number of lesser meanings: (1) the meanings of the several

---

[21] Therefore, the statement 'pages and pages contains three morphemes but five morpheme-occurrences' is only a loose way of saying 'pages and pages contains three morphemes and every occurrence of pages and pages contains five morpheme-occurrences'. When we said, in **3**, that two members of the same sequence-class must contain the same number of morphemes, we meant that these members, or more strictly any pair of occurrences of them, must contain the same number of morpheme-occurrences.

A sequence might be defined as a class of occurrences; then the statement 'the sequence A occurs in the environment B' could be explained as meaning 'some members of A occur in some members of B'.

[22] For instance, if no condition of type (3) is imposed, every sequence-class is also a construction.

[23] The four English pitch phonemes are designated by the numerals from 1 (highest pitch) to 4 (lowest pitch), following Kenneth L. Pike, The Intonation of American English (Ann Arbor, 1946). In a phonemic transcription, each pitch phoneme is written as a superior numeral before the syllabic which it accompanies; when a succession of two pitch phonemes accompanies a single syllabic, the two appropriate numerals are written before the appropriate letter.

The absence of a superior numeral before one or more successive syllabics means that those syllabics bear the same pitch phoneme as the last syllabic preceding them on which a pitch is indicated; see fn. 56. But we write, for example, I won't go pronounced emphatically as $/^3$ayw^{2}ôwnt-g^{24}6w$/$, where the practice described above would lead to confusion with $/^3$ayw^{2}ôwnt-g^{4}6w$/$; see **79**. It is often convenient (e.g. in **54**) to write a mixture of standard orthography for the segmental phonemes and phonemic transcription for the pitch phonemes; in this mixed notation, the stress phonemes (see **66** ff.) are sometimes indicated and sometimes not, depending on their relevance.

Pitch morphemes, like segmental morphemes, are generally identified by citing one of their alternants—the alternant of a pitch morpheme being a sequence of one or more pitch phonemes. The alternant of the pitch morpheme contained in the first pronunciation of I won't go mentioned above would be written either as $/32(24)/$ the parentheses indicating that the last two pitch phonemes accompany the same syllabic) or—with a deliberately ambiguous cover notation—as $/324/$, which indicates what pitch phonemes occur and in what order, but not how many syllabics there are in the phrase.

morphemes; (2) the meaning of the sequence <u>the king</u>; (3) the meaning of the sequence <u>of England</u>; and (4) the meaning of the sequence compounded of <u>the king</u> and <u>of England</u>. Or, alternatively, (1) the meanings of the individual morphemes; (2) the meaning of <u>of England</u>; (3) the meaning of the sequence compounded of <u>king</u> and <u>of England</u>; (4) the meaning of the sequence compounded of <u>the</u> and <u>king of England</u>. Clearly, since by our assumption every occurring sequence has a meaning, the meaning of every sequence of three or more morphemes can be described in terms of the meanings of any two sub-sequences into which it is divided, plus the meaning of the sequence compounded from them. The two sub-sequences need not be the ICs of the sequence.

However, the two meanings of <u>old men and women</u> are most readily accounted for in the following way. In the meaning 'women and old men', the sequence[24] belongs to that construction (noun or noun-phrase + <u>and</u> + noun or noun-phrase) which has the meaning of conjunction; the first noun-phrase belongs to the construction modifier + noun or noun-phrase. But in the meaning 'old men and old women', the sequence belongs to the construction modifier + noun or noun-phrase; the noun-phrase in turn belongs to the construction noun or noun-phrase + <u>and</u> + noun or noun-phrase.

The point is that although these are not the only constructions in terms of which the two meanings of <u>old men and women</u> could be accounted for, they are nevertheless the most efficient ones. If, for example, we switched the explanations given above and accounted for <u>old men and women</u> in the meaning 'women and old men' as an instance of modifier + noun or noun-phrase, we could do it, in view of our postulate that every sequence has a meaning; but the meaning would be enormously involved: the class 'modifier + noun or noun-phrase' with this meaning would be by definition a different construction from the same class with the usual meaning, and the resulting construction would be a very uncommon one, supported only by other wrong analyses. But no consistently carried out system of wrong analyses will be as efficient as a set of right analyses; indeed, it is precisely this fact which is the criterion of a right analysis.

§36. Now—and this is the relevance of constructions in the theory of ICs—the IC-analysis should reflect the construction. Consequently, when the same sequence has, in different occurences, different meanings and therefore (provided that the meaning-difference cannot be ascribed to the morphemes taken separately) different constructions, it may have different IC-analyses.[25] The IC-analysis of a sequence

often reflects the semantic analysis of what the sequence means, but the meaning needs to be considered in making the analysis only when two occurrences of the same sequence (or of two sequences belonging to all the same sequence-types) have meanings incompatible with each other.

§37. Such cases exhibit <u>homonymous constructions</u>, analogous to homonymous morphemes. Perhaps the most current meaning of the word 'homonym' is that two morphemes (or two sequences in general) are homonyms if they are phonemically identical but different in meaning. A narrower definition is that two morphemes are homonymous if they differ in meaning alone. It follows that two morphemes cannot be homonymous in this narrower sense unless they belong to all the same morpheme-classes, for otherwise they would be grammatically as well as semantically different.[26]

§38. Homonymy of constructions is similar in that there are sequences such that two occurrences of a given sequence will contain the same morphemes, belong to all the same sequence-classes, and yet have different meanings solely because they belong to different constructions. The difference between homonymy of morphemes and homonymy of constructions is that constructions may be only partly homonymous. Two constructions are <u>wholly homonymous</u> if every sequence that in some occurrences belongs to the one construction, in other occurrences belongs to the other; they are <u>partly homonymous</u> if some but not all sequences meet this condition. The two constructions exhibited by <u>old men and women</u> are only partly homonymous, because <u>old men</u> belongs to the same construction as old⌉men and women, but not to the same construction as old men⌉and⌉women; whereas <u>men and women</u> belongs to the latter construction but not to the former.[27]

§39. As an example of wholly homonymous constructions in English, consider compounds that are stressed on the prior member. One construction whose members are of this form ÁB has the mean-

So also we treat the cases where others would recognize a solitary IC (cf. §52) and the cases of wholly homonymous constructions (fn. 30).

[26] Special cases are presented by morphemes that have more than one morpheme-alternant. Thus, the four alternants of the English 3rd-singular morpheme /-z, -s, -ez, -0/, as in <u>reads</u>, <u>writes</u>, <u>teaches</u>, <u>can</u>, are respectively homonymous with four alternants of the plural morpheme, as in <u>dogs</u>, <u>cats</u>, <u>horses</u>, <u>sheep</u>, but not with the alternants that appear in <u>oxen</u>, <u>children</u>, <u>geese</u>, etc. But such cases do not concern us here.

[27] There are other constructions to which both (A) old⌉men and women and (B) old men⌉and⌉women belong, such as the noun-phrase construction; but these constructions are not responsible for the difference in meaning between A and B, and hence do not interest us here. Both the special construction of A and the special construction of B are compatible with all the more general constructions to which both A and B belong.

[24] More strictly, every occurrence of it has that meaning.

[25] But there is also the case where two sequences, even of three or more morphemes each, have different constructions but the same analysis into ICs; e.g. go⌉to⌉the⌉store (a) as a command, and (b) in answer to the question <u>What are you going to do?</u>

ing 'a B which is identical with or has the property of being (an) A'; examples: lady-friend, he-goat, postoffice-building.[28] A homonymous construction has the meaning 'a B of or connected with (an) A'; examples: birthday, name-plate, lady-killer. Since friend and killer belong to a number of focus-classes in common, and there is a compound lady-friend 'friend who is a lady', there should be a grammatically possible compound lady-killer 'killer who is a lady', homonymous with lady-killer 'killer (in a metaphorical sense) of ladies'.[29] If no such compound actually occurs, this fact is without grammatical significance.[30] Similarly, in actual occurrences old men and children generally has the meaning 'children and old men', since one does not speak of 'old children'. An analogue in homonymy of morphemes is that although steak and stake belong to all the same morpheme classes, /əjûwsiy-stéyk/ very seldom means 'a juicy stake'; the meaning of the morpheme stake, and the resulting meaning of juicy stake, exclude it.

It remains to note that just as there is often doubt whether to relegate a number of morpheme-occurrences to one morpheme with two meanings or to two homonymous morphemes, there may also be the same practical doubt with respect to constructions.

IV. Words

§40. People of some grammatical sophistication feel that there is something 'funny' about a phrase like the president of the bank's daughter. We have already (§6), in anticipation of the present section, formulated the principle which is the basis for this feeling: every word should be a constituent, and bank's, generally regarded as a word, is certainly not a constituent here.

Three solutions of the paradox are open to the grammarian: (1) abandon or qualify the principle; (2) maintain that bank's is a constituent; (3) admit that bank's is not a constituent but maintain that, in this occurrence, it is not a word either.

We do not flatly assert that the second alternative is absurd, but we do not envisage any plausible theory of ICs which would allow it to be true.

The third alternative admits of a subdivision. On the one hand, the president of the bank could be regarded as a sort of compound word, so that presi-

dent-of-the-bank's, a derivative thereof, is also a single word. Bank's, therefore, is only a fragment of a word, like writer's in typewriter's. This solution is embraced by Bloomfield.[31] The other recourse is to regard the possessive morpheme 's as a separate word. Both alternatives offend common sense. Both views, as well as alternative (1) above, presuppose a clear definition or set of criteria for the word.

§41. Since the publication of Bloomfield's Language, the best general treatment of the word known to me is Nida's.[32] Nida distinguishes two kinds of criteria for determining what the words of a given language are: phonemic and grammatical. Juncture is a common marker of word-boundaries, though perhaps there is no language where every sequence that one would want to regard as a word is marked off, in every occurrence, by the occurrence of a juncture both at its beginning and at its end. It is also common, in languages possessing junctures, that those junctures occur not only at word-boundaries but in the interior of certain words (e.g. English night-rate /náyt-rêyt/). In many languages certain phonemic patterns signify the presence or (more commonly) the absence of a word-boundary; for instance, Japanese has an accent phoneme whose non-automatic occurrences in any one word are at most one. It is a prevailing fact that these phonemic indices of word-boundaries are incomplete; even in a language that includes a number of such signals, not every word-boundary in every occurring sentence is signalized by means of some combination of them.

§42. It must be borne in mind that wherever we have said that not every word is marked off in such-and-such a way, we have meant that not every sequence that one would want to consider a word is so marked. The grammarian, undertaking to characterize the words of a certain language, starts with a certain common-sense working conception of what a word in that language is, based largely on his conception of what a word is in his native language and in any others that he may have studied. He sets about to formulate his criteria explicitly, to modify them in case they conflict, and to supplement them if they are insufficient to decide, for any given occurrence of any sequence, whether it is a word or not.

§43. Because of their insufficiency, the phonemic criteria of a word must be supplemented, for every or nearly every language, by criteria of the second kind remarked by Nida, the grammatical. In some languages, indeed (apparently French is an example),

---

[28] Assuming these and our other examples to be compounds rather than word-sequences.

[29] Unless we choose to assume that there is no such word as lady-killer 'killer who is a lady', and conclude therefore that in this respect friend and killer belong to different focus-classes.

[30] In this example, as in all wholly homonymous constructions that have come to my notice, the IC-analysis is the same regardless of which construction the sequence belongs to. If a given sequence is to have different analyses into ICs according to the different constructions to which it belongs, it must necessarily contain at least three morphemes.

[31] Language §11.5 end. Also by Eugene A. Nida, Morphology 149–50 (Ann Arbor, 1946); Bloch and Trager, Outline of Linguistic Analysis 67 bottom (Baltimore, 1942).

[32] Chapter 7 of his Morphology (cf. fn. 31). Also noteworthy are Bloch's characterization of the Japanese word (Studies in Colloquial Japanese II: Syntax, Lang. 22.202–6, §§1.3–6 [1946]) and Chao's characterization of the Chinese word (op.cit. our fn. 20).

phonemic criteria are quite lacking. Classical Greek and Latin, as well as the other predominantly inflecting Indo-European languages, exhibit par excellence the word as a grammatically characterized unit: the majority of their words terminate in one of a small class of endings, verbal or substantival. Moreover, in Greek and Latin the order of morphemes within a word is rigid, but the order of words relative to each other is somewhat variable. This is not to say that word order in these languages is free or indifferent. There are standard orders in prose both colloquial and literary; verse too has factors — and not only meter —that determine the arrangement of words. But the prose orders are rather different from the verse orders, while the order of morphemes within a word is identical in all styles. Whether or not two orders of the same words have different meanings, they serve to emphasize words as shiftable units; whereas order within the word (excepting compounds) is meaningless precisely because it is automatic. This justifies a contrast between morphology and syntax, a contrast fortified by the phonemic, especially the accentual properties of the grammatically characterized words.[33]

In fact, the word is most solid as a unit in those languages where phonemic and grammatical criteria reinforce each other. Bloomfield's definition of a word as a minimal free form involves both criteria: considered as a phoneme-sequence, a word occurs in a phonemic zero-environment; considered as a morpheme-sequence, it occurs in a morphemic zero-environment.[34] The corollary that a word must be pronounceable in isolation likewise contains both criteria, for an 'unpronounceable' form may be so either because of its phonemic composition (e.g. the possessive 's by itself) or because it is a bound form (e.g. -ness with weak stress). A linguist would regard five and fif (as in fifty, fifth) as alternants of the same morpheme; but from the common-sense point of view it is alternants, not morphemes as such, that are pronounceable or not. And unpronounceability of both kinds is a partial reason why the possessive

33 The term grammar is here used in the narrower sense, as coordinate with phonemics, rather than including it. In this narrower sense, grammar is commonly divided into morphology and syntax: the former treating the internal grammar of words (§15), the latter their external grammar and the sequences of words; but the division does not apply to languages that lack words as a distinct kind of unit. Harris (op. cit. our fn. 2) shows how it is possible to ignore the distinction between morphology and syntax even in other languages (cf. §45). The term taxemics has been suggested to me to cover the narrower sense of grammar; I have not adopted it, because it rests on Bloomfield's unclearly defined term taxeme.
34 See fn. 6 and Bloomfield, Language 168–9. Bloomfield's definition must be suitably modified if the sentence-intonations and certain stresses (§66) of such a language as English are regarded as morpheme-sequences rather than (op.cit. 163, 169) as modulation, one of the four 'ways of arranging linguistic forms'.

's of England's is regarded by common sense as not being a word.

§44. When the phonemic and the grammatical criteria do not confirm each other, they may sometimes be used to supplement each other. If certain sequences belonging to a particular sequence-class are phonemically marked as single separate words, then we may consider all members of this sequence-class to be words whether or not they are phonemically marked.

§45. One of the points implied in Harris's article From Morpheme to Utterance is that in describing what utterances occur in that language, the distinction between morphology and syntax may be dispensed with; that the word is not a necessary, perhaps not even a useful unit of grammar. This is not to deny that at some point in the description of a language one should state whatever correlations may obtain between phonemic and grammatical features of morpheme-sequences, nor that for some languages this statement is most efficiently cast in the form of a definition of a word. It is only to propose that in doing one part of the task of grammar, namely describing the utterances of the language in question, the division into a morphological phase and a syntactic phase of this description may be given up.

§46. We do not here offer any opinion on this proposal. The task of IC-analysis is the task not of describing what utterances occur, but of describing, after these utterances have been given, what their constituents are. In practice, the grammarian studying a language will prosecute both inquiries at once, and will have made up his mind about both before he expounds either; but this fact of procedure does not concern us. Nor do we mean, when we say that all the grammatically possible utterances of a language are presupposed as data for the IC-analysis, that only a complete characterization of them is presupposed—a characterization which may well be in terms of the constituents of those utterances. This is circularity of exposition, but it is not vicious, nor is it avoidable except by basing the grammatical description, including the IC-analysis, on a finite sample of text. The distinction between methods of discovery and methods of proof (or more generally, methods of exposition), and between the order in which certain facts are discovered and the order in which they are expounded, is familiar to logicians. In descriptive linguistics, discovery consists in finding the best scheme in terms of which to describe the facts; it is not strictly part of the exposition to show that that scheme is the best.

§47. But the word is a relevant unit in IC-analysis. Many analyses can be made without taking word-boundaries into account; but many others are left undetermined. In such cases, if a consideration of word-boundaries and the principle that every word is a constituent will decide the analysis, it seems to us reasonable to consider word-boundaries and to invoke this principle. In other words, the word is not a dispensable unit in the present theory of IC-analysis.

§48. Harris also says (178–9) ((150–1)): 'The procedure outlined here could be paralleled by a series of substitutions beginning with the whole utterance and working down, instead of beginning with single morphemes and working up. In that case we would have to find formal criteria for breaking the utterances down at successive stages. This is essentially the difficult problem of determining the immediate constituents of an utterance. It is not clear that there exists any general method for successively determining the immediate constituents, when we begin with a whole utterance and work down. In any case, it would appear that the formation of substitution classes [in our terminology, focus-classes] presents fewer theoretical difficulties if we begin with morphemes and work up.'

But the major purpose of this paper is to show that expansions and focus-classes, the very concepts developed in Harris's paper, furnish the basic apparatus necessary for a theory of ICs. And a theory of ICs is not necessarily bound to the order of 'working down'. Regardless of whether the exposition of the descriptive grammar works up or works down, the constituents of any utterance will be the same. As for the order of discovery, which is what Harris has in mind, 'working up' will systematically determine the focus-classes of a language; but we have pointed out that a complete set of IC-analyses must rest on more than the focus-classes: it must also rest (a) on the importance of each focus-class, in respect of diversity of members and in respect of the number of environments characterizing it, and (b) on the constructions.

§49. There are instances where the pattern of the language opposes treating every word as a constituent. In Japanese, the suffix -rasíi 'has the appearance of' forms compounds with nouns (kodomorasíi 'looks like a child'), noun phrases (kodomo norasíi 'looks like a child's' [cf. kodomo no 'of a child']), verbs (tabetarasíi 'appears to have eaten') and certain other sequences. Now kodomorasíi, norasíi, tabetarasíi (orthographic abbreviations for kodómórásíi, norásíi, tabétárásíi, where the acute marks a high-pitched syllable) are to be regarded as single words, because if -rasíi (i.e. -rásíi) is regarded as a separate word (1) it will be the only word in the entire language accented on both the first and the second syllables; (2) in no other case is a word with accent on the final syllable immediately followed by one with accent on the first syllable.[35] On the other hand, purely syntactical considerations favor the IC-analysis kodomo no⌷rasíi, etc.

Instead of proclaiming, therefore, that every word in every language must be a constituent of any

sequence in which it occurs as a part, the most we may say is that every word should be so regarded unless it engenders a conflict or complication in the description of the language.

§50. In Japanese itself the principle is useful, and even enables us to treat the class of particles as a word-class.[36] Sequences such as ano hito wa 'as for that person', ano hito ni 'to that person', ano hito kara 'from that person' are undoubtedly to be analyzed ano hito⌷wa, ano hito⌷ni, ano hito⌷kara; this is shown very easily by the method of expansion, since ano hito 'that person' is an expansion of hito 'person', but hito wa 'as for the person', hito ni 'to the person', and hito kara 'from the person' are not expansions of anything. The phonemic criteria (in Japanese, occurrence as a minimum pause-group, and the accent) do not determine the particles wa, ni, and kara either to be words or not to be words; and since none of the other particles ever has an accent except in phonemic environments that leave its status as a word indeterminate, we derive no help from the principle that a given sequence is a word if and only if every other member of the same sequence-class is a word (see §44). But if hito wa were one word (so that ano hito⌷wa would be two words), the principle that every word is a constituent would be needlessly contravened; therefore we regard the particles as separate words.

V. Multiple and discontinuous constituents

§51. Up to this point we have proceeded as though every IC-analysis divides a constitute into two ICs, each a continuous sequence. We have now to consider other possibilities of analysis and the circumstances under which they may reasonably be resorted to.

First, are there sequences which are best analyzed into fewer or more than two ICs?

Second, is it ever useful to recognize constituents that are discontinuous?[37]

For example, should not the sequence men, women, and children be analyzed into three coordinate ICs: men,⌷women,⌷and children? And should not the sequence Call your friend up be analyzed into the continuous constituent your friend and the discontinuous constituent call ... up ?

§52. In our system, no constitute has only one IC. (It will be recalled that single morphemes are not called constitutes.) Anything that has ICs at all, has two or more. Other systems, however, allow solitary

---

[35] Bloch, op.cit. [our fn. 32] §1.5 and fn. 7. Cases where one would expect this result are rare; and when they do occur (perhaps in personal names?) the prior word morphophonemically loses its accent (Bloch, op.cit. fn. 5).

[36] Bloch, op.cit. §1.5.

[37] Bloomfield recognizes the possibility of solitary constituents (Language, 218) and of multiple constituents (194, lines 10–11; 227, line 6). He is followed by Pike, Taxemes and Immediate Constituents, Lang. 19.70, line 1 and §4.1. Bloch and Trager (op.cit. [our fn. 31] 67) recognize 'usually ... two and only two immediate constituents'. The same view seems to be taken by Nida (Morphology 81; Syntax §2.5.3 et passim [Ann Arbor, 1946]). Pike further admits discontinuous constituents (op.cit. §§4.12–4).

constituents. Thus Bloch[38] describes every Japanese sentence as consisting of one or more clauses; if there is but one clause, it is the sole IC of the sentence, though it may have, as a clause, two ICs of its own. Again, in line with Bloomfield's handling of modulation, one might describe the Japanese verbal noun yasumí 'vacation' as derived from the infinitive yasúmi 'rest' by applying the taxeme of modulation (here a shift of accent). Then the infinitive would be the sole IC of the noun, though consisting, in turn, of the two ICs yasúm- (the verbal base) and -i (the infinitive ending).[39]

The system that we have set up does not ignore the facts, it only treats them in a different way: in terms of constructions. When a clause is a sentence by itself, it participates in the sentence construction as well as in the clause construction; but (like the English example come here, see §34 and fn. 25) its ICs are the same whether it participates in both constructions or only in the one. The noun yasumí, on the other hand, we would describe as containing the infinitive yasúmi plus a morpheme, or else as replacing a morpheme contained in yasúmi by some other —depending on how the accent-phoneme is handled morphologically. Whatever the details, the Japanese accent-phoneme, like any phoneme of any language, would always be assigned to some morpheme, either by itself or as part of a phoneme-sequence, and not to a 'grammatical process' of modulation (cf. fn. 34).

§53. We propose to recognize multiple (three or more) ICs only under one definite condition. Given a constitute consisting of three continuous sequences A, B, and C, then, if no reason can be found for analyzing it as AB|C rather than A|BC, or as A|BC rather than AB|C, it is to be analyzed into three correlative ICs, A|B|C. Similarly, four ICs may be recognized when no analysis into two and no analysis into three ICs is recommended, and so on.

§54. A possible example is furnished by English noun-phrases of the type A and B. A and never occurs as a constitute except before a noun (or noun-phrase) B; and B never occurs as a constitute except (a) after a noun A and (b) as a separate clause. Now the latter occurrence is not an argument for the analysis A|and B. And women occurs as an independent sentence, and its ICs there are and and women. But its focus-class is of the structure and + clause: the same basic structure as in and|I saw it myself or and|then we'll go home. Correspondingly, the basic

constructional meaning of and|women is that of a clause, not of a noun-phrase. When and women occurs at the beginning of a clause, it is never a constitute: and|women were lined up hours ahead of time, not and women|were lined up etc. Thus it is perfectly clear that the sentence and women does not support the analysis men|and women. So the theory of IC-analysis developed in this paper gives no basis for choosing between men|and women and men and|women; consequently, we adopt the tripartite analysis men|and|women.

With conjunctive clauses it is different. He huffed and he puffed is undoubtedly to be analyzed he huffed |and he puffed; each of the two constituents has great freedom of combination, including occurrence as a separate sentence. When and he puffed occurs as a separate sentence it participates in the sentence construction, which of course it does not when preceded by he huffed. But there are some constructions common to it in both occurrences (the clause construction, for instance); whereas there is no single construction in which the two occurrences of and women —(a) as a separate sentence and (b) in men and women —participate.

But when there are three or more clauses connected by and, the number of ICs is the same as the number of clauses. There is no reason to analyze (A) H^{3}e h^{2}uffed (B) ^{3}and he p^{23}uffed (C) ^{3}and he bl^{2}ew the house d^{24}own (with a pause before each and) into AB|C rather than into A|BC, or conversely; therefore the three clauses are three correlative ICs of the sentence.

Should a detailed study of English reveal some here unnoticed reason for analyzing men|and women rather than men and|women, or conversely, then of course the phrase would simply cease to be an example; the proposal stating when we must recognize three or more ICs would not thereby be impugned.

§55. The same basic rationale that leads to the proposal discussed above prescribes the conditions for discontinuous constituents. Analysis of the English king into English and the ... king yields constituents of much greater independence and mobility than the analysis into the and English king. Moreover, the pattern of poor|John and English|literature would be better imitated. But if the admission of multiple and of discontinuous constituents were subject to no other restriction than yielding maximally independent constituents, IC-analysis would become a tremendously intricate affair. The possibilities requiring investigation would be enormously multiplied. A more orderly and manageable procedure is to extend the IC-system as far as possible on the basis of two continuous ICs for each constitute; and then to supplement this system and revise it where revision is called for by admitting the more complex kinds of analysis. In order to keep the revision at a minimum, we have proposed a restricting condition for multiple

---

[38] Bloch, op.cit. §2.4. For a similar case in morphology, see Bloch, Studies in Colloquial Japanese III: Derivation of Inflected Words, JAOS 66.305, §1.3.

[39] For the factual data, see Bernard Bloch and Eleanor H. Jorden, Spoken Japanese, 135, Note 5.15, and 504, Note 16.18 (New York, 1945–46). Bloch no longer insists on this way of describing the derivation.

ICs, and we propose now the following for discontinuous ICs: A discontinuous sequence is a constituent if in some environment the corresponding continuous sequence occurs as a constituent in a construction semantically harmonious with the constructions in which the given discontinuous sequence occurs. The phrase 'semantically harmonious' is left undefined, and will merely be elucidated by examples.

§56. English noun-modifiers are of three sorts: those that precede, those that follow, and those that partly precede and partly follow the noun or noun-phrase that they modify. Examples are: (1) [a] very interesting [book], only [the finest quality], too expensive [a choice], such [a method], [a] mere [boy]; (2) [a scholar] second to none, [a contract] signed by the manager, [a possession] more priceless than jewels; (3) [a] better [movie] than I expected, [the] best [friend] in the world, [an] easy [book] to read, too heavy [a box] to lift. Of the examples of type (3), all but best ... in the world satisfy the proposed condition for being discontinuous constituents: the corresponding continuous sequences all occur after a copula; thus (4) [this movie is] better than I expected, [this book is] easy to read, [this box is] too heavy to lift. And the constructional meaning of these predicates (better than I expected, etc.) is harmonious with—is in fact almost or quite the same as—the meaning which the corresponding discontinuous constituents bear in the examples under (3): in each case a certain property is meant, whether the larger construction into which it fits is that of modification (3) or of predication (4).

§57. Best ... in the world is chosen as an example of a discontinuous modifier that perhaps does not qualify as a constituent. At least it does not occur in the environment (4).[40] The nearest approximation is [as a friend, he's] the best in the world. Predicates of the type the + adjective or adjective-phrase are limited; generally the adjective (if singular) is either a comparative or superlative or else an ordinal. In these sequences, it seems that a noun is always 'understood', e.g. friend after best in he's the best in the world, or day after fifth in the fifth of January. If so, the construction of best (and a fortiori of best in the world) in he's the best is different from that of easy or easy to read in this book is easy to read, and consequently best ... in the world is not a constituent of the best friend in the world.

§58. The clause this possession⌷is⌷ more priceless than jewels, analyzed as shown, justifies admitting the corresponding discontinuous constituent in a more priceless possession than jewels —provided that the constructional meanings are harmonious in the required sense. By harmonious we mean, approximately, identical except insofar as there is a necessary reason for difference. If the predicate I: more priceless than jewels is harmonious in this

40 Usages such as [Washington was] first in the hearts of his countrymen are not regular or free.

sense with the discontinuous modifier II: more priceless ... than jewels, then what is its relation to the continuous modifier III: [a possession] more priceless than jewels? We are committed to recognizing at least a potential difference of meaning between II and III. (1) It may be that I has two distinct senses, in one of which its constructional meaning definitely corresponds to that of II, in the other to that of III. If so, there is no problem. Or (2) it may be that I has only one sense, which definitely corresponds to that of II rather than of III, or to that of III rather than of II, insofar as the senses of III and II differ from each other. In this case, again there is no problem; it is merely a fact that the distinctive sense of II (or of III) is not expressed by an adjective phrase used in predicate rather than in modifier position. But (3) I may have a unitary sense, and yet at the same time the difference of meaning between II and III may be so tenuous that neither the distinctive meaning of II nor the distinctive meaning of III can be detected in the meaning of I. This possibility is troublesome. Perhaps an adequate definition of harmony could be devised according to which the meaning of I is harmonious with the meanings of both II and III, even though the meanings of II and of III are not harmonious with each other.

§59. Besides modifiers, there is another important type of discontinuous constituent: a clause interrupted by an intrusive phrase, as in the sentence His father, according to John, is the richest man in Scarsdale. These interrupted clauses meet the proposed test, since the intrusion can simply be dropped and then what was discontinuous becomes continuous, with practically the same constructional meaning.

§60. Verb phrases of the type verb + prepositional adverb (up, away, through, etc.) may seem to deserve being treated as constituents even when they are discontinuous; wake up your friend and wake your friend up are almost synonymous. But there are other pairs like see through your friend 'discern your friend's sham or false front' and see your friend through 'aid your friend through to the completion of his project' where a difference in meaning stands out.[41] The meaning-difference here can be accounted for in several ways. (1) Perhaps different meanings of through are involved. (2) Perhaps the construction of see through your friend does not bear the same semantic relation to that of see your friend through as the construction of wake up your friend bears to that of wake your friend up, and the difference reflects itself in the IC-analysis as follows: see⌷your friend⌷through vs. see through⌷your friend. In other words, perhaps see ... through is not a constituent. Or (3) the analysis may be see...through⌷your friend but the discontinuous constituent see...through participates in a construction that is different in mean-

41 Note that see through him occurs, often bearing the emphatic morpheme on through; but wake up him does not, no matter how accented.

ing from that of the continuous constituent see through and not harmonious with it; the difference in the constructional meanings of see through and see...through would account for the difference in meaning between see through your friend and see your friend through.

§61. Pike (op.cit. §4.14) suggests analyzing the noun-phrase the large books, the important papers, the new pens as 'a complex endocentric phrase with head and attribute alike consisting of noncontiguous members', viz. the large...the important...the new + books...papers...pens. By our proposed criterion, books...papers...pens could be a discontinuous constituent, but the large ... the important ... the new could not. And indeed no reason is apparent why the above noun-phrase should not be analyzed as a 'co-ordinative endocentric' sequence (Bloomfield 195) of three ICs, each IC being a 'subordinative endocentric' sequence (ibid.).

§62. Analysis of the English king into English and the ... king satisfies our proposed condition for discontinuous constituents. If this analysis be accepted, then the analysis of the king of England needs reconsideration. For one of the arguments in favor of the⌡king of England was its basic conformity with the⌡English king. The identical argument, applied to the new analysis English + the ... king, would equally tolerate the king⌡of England, which after all seems to be the analysis favored by common sense. The noun-preceding modifier English and the noun-following modifier of England belong then to about the same focus-classes, as do the king (conjointly with its discontinuous counterpart the ... king) and proper names like John. The English king and poor John would then have corresponding analyses: English + the ... king, poor + John.

There is much to be said for this proposal to admit discontinuous phrases as well as (§56) discontinuous noun-modifiers. We here merely point out the possibility, and the fact that it is compatible with our suggested criterion of §55.

VI. English Juncture, Stress, and Pitch

§63. Most of our examples in this paper have been drawn from English, though not even a hint of a comprehensive IC-system for English has been given. However, one topic is so central that at least brief attention must be paid to it: the topic of the prosodic morphemes, juncture, stress, and pitch. Our treatment applies, mutatis mutandis, to a number of other languages, but we shall not point out the parallels.

The English phonemes—and, by extension of sense, the morphemes—of juncture, stress, and pitch, are called prosodic, modulational, or suprasegmental.[42]

Applied to stress and pitch, these terms mean that the simple linear or one-dimensional order of segmental morphemes[43] is complicated into a two-dimensional one by the occurrence of stresses and pitches. In the sentence What is it? /hw^{3}àt-^{2}íz^{4}it/, we may consider the stress phoneme / ´ / and the pitch phoneme /2/ as occurring simultaneously with the first occurrence of the vowel phoneme /i/.[44] Now since a linear series is the easiest to deal with, we may try to convert What is it? into a strictly linear series like the following: /hw3`at-2´iz4it/. But the sequence of phonemes /324/ constitutes (an alternant of) one single morpheme; by converting the two-dimensional order of phonemes to one dimension, certain morphemes (e.g. /324/) have been made phonemically discontinuous which were continuous before the conversion (cf. §88 and fn. 52). This is the difficulty: this is why one distinguishes between segmental phonemes and morphemes on the one hand, and suprasegmental ones on the other. Juncture is reckoned as suprasegmental instead of segmental, in spite of its not being simultaneous with anything else, for the grammatical reason that in its distribution and in its meaning it resembles stresses and pitches more than vowels and consonants.

We do not flatter ourselves that the following treatment will satisfy anyone. The disagreement will reflect the small amount of widespread discussion that the subject has received. Because of the exploratory nature of our proposals, we have aimed at a system which is conservative at the expense of being cumbersome, preferring this to one that is economical but liable to be scuttled by the discovery of some irreducible fact that it cannot embrace.

§64. Juncture. The validity of juncture phonemes is open to grave doubts on phonetic grounds. Linguists find themselves tempted to institute 'junctures' simply as notational devices for reducing the number of phonemes. For instance, what phonetic warrant is there for saying that night-rate differs from nitrate by /t-r/ vs. /tr/ rather than by /Tr/ or /tR/ vs. /tr/? Strictly, ought we not to say that night-rate differs phonemically from nitrate either in containing a different single t-like phoneme before the /r/ or else a different r-like phoneme after the /t/?

We assume that these questions can be answered somehow and that the English juncture phoneme can

---

[42] Bloomfield, Language 163; George L. Trager, The Theory of Accentual Systems, Language Culture and Personality 131-45 (Sapir Memorial Volume; Menasha, Wis., 1941); Bloch and Trager, op.cit. 41. For further references see R. S. Wells, The Pitch Phonemes of English, Lang. 21.28 fn. 10 (1945).

[43] A morpheme is called segmental if each of its one or more morpheme-alternants consists either of one or more vowels and consonants (with or without stresses / ´ / or / ` /), or else of nothing at all (a zero-alternant).

[44] Bloomfield (Language 113) proposes to phonemicize the contrast between a name and an aim in terms of stress rather than of juncture: /ə ńeym/ vs. /ən éym/ rather than /ənéym/ vs. /ən-éym/. This is a good suggestion, but since the cases of contrast in English between ĆV and CV́ are relatively few, we retain here the more customary notation.

be salvaged.[45]

Whether pause at the beginning and at the end of an utterance may be regarded as an allophone of juncture, and whether more than one juncture should be recognized in some dialects and styles of English, are minor questions in the present discussion. Pause, and as many junctures as there are, all behave alike in IC-analysis and all have generically similar meanings.

§65. There are pairs of phrases differing phonemically only in that one contains, the other lacks, a juncture; e.g. thank you /θǽŋkyùw/ and /θǽŋk-yùw/, at your leisure /ǽtyurléžər/ and /ǽt-yurléžər/. There is some discernible difference of meaning between the two members of each pair, if we understand 'meaning' in a very wide sense that includes stylistic overtones such as meticulousness of speech, etc. It is reasonable to say, therefore, that the juncture here contributes to the meaning of the whole phrase, hence that it has a meaning, and hence that it is a morpheme.

In night-rate it is less apparent that the juncture has a meaning. There is no /náytrêyt/ containing the morphemes night and rate with which night-rate is in minimal contrast. But it is a valuable principle of linguistics that every phoneme in a given utterance belongs to one and only one morpheme. So the juncture of /náyt-rêyt/ belongs either to /nayt-/ or to /reyt-/ or to a morpheme by itself. General considerations make the third way of considering it seem wisest: juncture, wherever it occurs, is a morpheme —though often with no detectable meaning.

§66. Stress. The stress symbolized / ´ / is here considered to constitute a morpheme by itself, wherever it occurs, with the generic meaning of emphasis. Every sentence contains at least one occurrence of / ´ /, and therefore at least one occurrence of the emphatic morpheme.[46]

[45] In order to preclude extravagances, one might adopt the requirement that every phoneme have at least one allophone consisting of an actual segment of sound, or else of a silence between or before or after such segments. This would involve assigning some segments simultaneously to more than one phoneme—e.g. assigning the first i of What is it? simultaneously to the vowel phoneme /i/, to the pitch phoneme /2/, and to the stress phoneme / ´ /. See R. S. Wells, op.cit. fn. 7. If we could reckon the silence at the beginning and end of an utterance as one allophone of juncture, we would be justified in positing another allophone, a zero-allophone, which occurs for example in night-rate.

[46] Except perhaps short sentences in which a normal occurrence of / ´ / is replaced by an occurrence of the contrastive stress /i/; see §70.
The system of stress-phonemes assumed in this paper is the one described by Bloch and Trager, Lang. 17.226–9 and Outline of Linguistic Analysis 47–8; but we differ from Bloch and Trager in regarding their phoneme of weak stress as simply the absence of a stress phoneme. The remaining three stress-phonemes are written as accents over vowel letters: /á/ = Bloch and Trager's 'loud stress', /â/ = 'reduced loud stress', /à/ = 'medial stress'.

§67. Whereas the stress / ´ / is 'skimmed off' from the segmental morphemes, the other two stress-phonemes / ˆ / and / ` / remain as parts. This treatment gives rise to systematic sets of morpheme-alternants. In a blackbird /əblǽk-bə̂hrd/, bird occurs in the alternant /bə̂hrd/, but black occurs in the alternant /blæk/, because the / ´ / belongs to a different morpheme. But in a black bird /əblǽk-bə̂hrd/, bird occurs in the stressless alternant /bəhrd/, and black occurs in the alternant /blǽk/. The stress / ´ / is treated differently from / ˆ / and / ` /, in spite of its phonetic relationship, because its grammatical and semantic roles are different.

§68. The alternants of each morpheme may be conveniently classified into ranks according to the stresses they contain. Those of the first rank contain / ˆ /; those of the second rank contain / ` / but not / ˆ /; those of the third rank contain no stress-phonemes. Each rank may be subdivided according to the other stress-phonemes that enter into the alternants of that rank. Thus the morpheme Balaclava has two alternants of the first rank: /bæ̂ləklǽvə/ (as in B. helmet) and /bæ̂ləklævə/. The latter occurs in the presence of the emphatic morpheme; the phonemic result of combining these two morphemes is /bæ̂ləklǽvə/. When the morpheme-alternant that occurs in the presence of the emphatic morpheme contains two or more unstressed syllabics, there is no way of knowing, from inspection of that alternant alone, which of these the stress / ´ / of the emphatic morpheme will coincide with—unless one of the syllabics occurs, when preceded or followed by particular non-syllabics, only in conjunction with / ´ /, / ˆ / or / ` /.[47]

§69. When a morpheme has alternants differing in their segmental phonemes, each of these may have stress-alternants. Thus clear has altogether five

I am especially indebted to Bloch for supplying the phonemic transcriptions of English in Part VI, which reflect his own dialect. To get a system of English phonemes that will apply, with modifications, to as many different dialects as possible, it has seemed wise to take as a descriptive basis a more complicated dialect like Bloch's, rather than a less complicated one like mine, which does not distinguish, for instance, between 'reduced loud' stress and 'medial' stress.

[47] Of course it is easy to design a notation that will show which syllabic potentially bears the stress, e.g. /bæ̂ləklævə/. This use of italics, like the leaving of a space between words in most phonemic transcriptions, has no phonemic status whatever; it is purely a mnemonic device equivalent to the statement that the stress / ´ / (belonging to the emphatic morpheme) occurs—when it occurs at all in conjunction with a given segmental morpheme—on such-and-such a syllabic of that morpheme. Moreover, simply to cite the phonemic result of juxtaposing the segmental and the stress morpheme (e.g. /bæ̂ləklǽvə/, the result of juxtaposing /bæ̂ləklævə/ and / ´ /) conveys the same knowledge; and so does a comparison of alternants like /bæ̂ləklævə/ and /bæ̂ləklǽvə/.

alternants: /klîhr, klihr, klǽr, klèr, klær/, occurring respectively in clêar úp, it's cléar (accompanied by the emphatic morpheme), clârify thís, clàri-
ficátion, and clárity (again accompanied by the emphatic morpheme). In general, for every alternant
containing one or more occurrences of /ˆ/, there is
an otherwise identical alternant in which one of these
occurrences is lacking.[48] But many morphemes
have no alternant containing /ˆ/; and those containing /ˋ/ do not in general alternate with otherwise
identical ones lacking /ˋ/. Thus, /èyt/ as in rotate
and calculate has no corresponding alternant /eyt/.[49]

§70. Contrastive stress is of two sorts: (1) the
stress /ˊ/ is placed on a syllabic where /ˊ/ and
/ˆ/ do not normally occur; (2) a contrastive stress
phoneme /i̦/, distinct from /ˊ/, either (a) replaces
/ˊ/ or (b) is placed on a syllabic where /ˊ/ and
/ˆ/ do not normally occur.[50] Cases (1) and (2b) involve morpheme alternants additional to the ones
recognized above. Every morpheme without exception, provided that at least one of its alternants contains a syllabic, is subject to this kind of alternation;
moreover, if it has more than one syllabic, /ˊ/ and
/i̦/ may fall on any of them.

There is often concomitant alternation within
the syllabic itself. Thus, when the first syllabic
of allusion is contrastively stressed (to distinguish
the word, say, from illusion), the result is either
/ǽillúwžən/[51] or /ǽllûwžən/. Abstracting the contrastive and emphatic morphemes leaves /ǽlluwžən/
or /ǽllûwžən/, both different from the alternants
/əlûwžən/ and /əluwžən/ normally encountered—
the latter only in the presence of /ˊ/ and perhaps
/i̦/, yielding /əlúwžən/ and /əluwi̦žən/ respectively. When contrastive stress is applied to a syllabic of a morpheme other than the one on which the
ordinary emphatic morpheme /ˊ/ normally falls, we
may consider either that the morpheme is used

hypostatically or that it has a special complex of
hypostasis and primary meaning together. In our
present account, it is sufficient to deal with /ˊ/
and /i̦/ as they combine with segmental morphemes
in non-hypostatic uses; the simplification affects
only the details, not the principles.

§71. In phonetic and phonemic fact, the emphatic
and contrastive morphemes always occur simultaneously with some segmental morpheme. It is easy to
treat them conventionally as being themselves segmental, so that we have only one string of morphemes
to deal with—a string in which every morpheme either
precedes or follows, immediately or mediately, every
other morpheme. There are, indeed, two possibilities, between which the choice is indifferent: to consider that emphasis and contrast always precede, or
that they always follow the morpheme with which they
are phonetically and phonemically simultaneous.[52]
But the conventional order of conversion must be
rigidly uniform, even when it is inconvenient; otherwise we should be not merely rearranging the order
of the morphemes but trying to improve upon it.

§72. The temptation is apparent in treating derivatives and compounds. Suppose that we consider emphasis and contrast as always following the modified
morpheme. Then the sequence He speaks clearly
/h³iyspîyks-kl²îhrl⁴iy/ consists, in morphological
terms, of the following sequence of morphemes (each
morpheme being cited, as in fn.52, in the alternant
that actually occurs in the sequence to be described)
hiy + spîyk + s + juncture + klihr + emphatic stress
+ liy + 324. Common sense would want to say that it
is the whole word clearly, not only the morpheme
clear, that is 'affected' or 'modified' or 'governed'
by the morpheme of emphatic stress—in short, that
the whole word is emphasized.

[48] Exceptions are morphemes like the loom in
heirloom /éhr-lûwm/, which accidentally occur only
in compound words.

[49] The verbs alternate /óhltərnèyt/, degenerate
/dijénərèyt/, etc. might be regarded morphologically
as derived from the adjective alternate /óhltərnət/,
degenerate /dijénərət/, etc. by addition of a morpheme; or the adjectives might be regarded as derived from the verbs in the same way. If so, the
morpheme /èyt/ has an alternant /ət/. Moreover,
the nouns alternation, degeneration, etc. exhibit the
alternants /êyš/ and /eyš/ of the same morpheme.
But even so, the verb as a word by itself never
shows an alternant /eyt/ or /ət/ or /eyš/.

[50] Bloch and Trager posit 'contrasting intonation
/i̦/, involving both a distortion of the normal sentence tone and an extra-loud stress' (op.cit. 52). But
we may equally well view the stress, rather than the
pitch, as the non-automatic feature. This allows us
to group the phoneme /i̦/, (now renamed 'the contrastive stress phoneme') with the phoneme /ˊ/,
which it resembles (1) in always constituting a morpheme by itself, namely the contrastive morpheme,
and (2) in its meaning and grammatical patterning.

[51] According to Bloch's oral statement.

[52] It would be possible to make emphasis and contrast phonemically as well as morphologically segmental, in the manner suggested in §63: what we now
write as /hw³àt-²íz⁴it/ would become, say, /hw3ˋat
-2ˊiz4it/. Applying this procedure to all utterances
would result in two types of discontinuity: (1) discontinuous morphemes and (2) discontinuous sequences.
The morphemes would be discontinuous not in the
sense treated by Harris (Discontinuous Morphemes,
Lang. 21.121-7 [1945]), but in the sense in which
the Arabic morphemes a...a...a 'past tense, 3rd person singular' and k...t...b 'write' are each discontinuous in the word kataba 'he wrote'. The sequences
would be discontinuous in the sense discussed in
Part V above; cf. §88. When an alternant of one morpheme phonemically intrudes into or interrupts an
alternant of another morpheme, it is convenient in
morphology to consider that one of the morphemes
wholly precedes the other—e.g. that ktb, in the example just given, wholly precedes or wholly follows
aaa. The reason is the one already mentioned: that
a perfectly linear sequence of units is the easiest to
deal with. Accordingly, the sequence /hw3ˋat-2ˊiz4it/
would be morphologically described, say, as follows
—using plus-signs to separate single morphemes in
the alternants that occur in the sentence What is it?:
hwˋat + juncture + iz + ˊ + it + 324.

Again, blackbird is blæk + emphatic stress + juncture + bə̂hrd in some environments, e.g. It's a ( ); but blæk + juncture + bə̂hrd in others, e.g. a ( ) pie. In the latter environments, it is homonymous with the two-word sequence black bird. One might want to say that blackbird, wherever it occurs, contains some morpheme that allocates the potential emphatic stress to the first morpheme of the compound rather than to the second, and that thus blackbird is everywhere distinguished from black bird. Further, one might want to implement this notion by setting up a zero-alternant of the emphatic morpheme; and this morpheme would then be present equally in (A) [It's a] blackbird and in (B) [It's a] blackbird [pie].

873. The latter proposal can be dismissed at once, because / ´ / can occur simultaneously with black in (C) [It's a] blackbird [pie]. (So also can / i /; in this environment, both / ´ / and / i / would be called instances of contrastive stress.) Therefore, in this environment, the alternant / ´ / and the proposed zero-alternant would contrast.[53]

This suggests a retrenchment. Instead of supposing a zero-alternant of the emphatic morpheme, suppose a morpheme with no phonemic shape, whose sole meaning or rather function is to signify whether the first or the second member of the compound potentially bears the emphatic morpheme; compare hóusebrŏken and hêartbrŏken. Housebroken might be described morphologically as house + broken + ‹- ; the fact that broken is itself a derivative—brok (alternant of break) + en—complicates the picture because heart + brok + en + ‹- is an ambiguous notation. We must punctuate, perhaps, like this: (heart) + (brok + en) + ‹- .

874. The objections against the morphemes ‹- and -‹ are twofold. In the first place, as a check against extravagant and merely ingenious analyses, it is wise to observe the requirement that every morpheme have at least one alternant consisting of a phoneme or phoneme-sequence. This principle, parallel to the phonemic principle mentioned in connection with juncture, rules out zero-morphemes, that is, morphemes whose presence is known solely by their effect on other morphemes or by the presence of a certain meaning. But it sanctions a zero-alternant of a morpheme, provided the morpheme has other alternants besides. The proposed morphemes ‹- and -‹ would be zero-morphemes, i.e. having phonetic zero as their only alternant, and are therefore excluded by the requirement just mentioned. It might be thought that the phoneme / ´ / is one of their alternants, but it is not; for one phoneme, in

any given occurrence, belongs to one and only one morpheme. Accordingly, if / ´ / is ever assigned to the morpheme ‹- or -‹, it cannot in that occurrence belong to the emphatic morpheme. One last possibility is to say that each of the three morphemes ‹-, -‹, and the emphatic has a zero-alternant: the zero-alternant of ‹- and -‹ appears when the emphatic is absent, and the zero-alternant of the emphatic appears when either ‹- or -‹ is present (these two morphemes being present only at the end of compound words). But / ´ /, as the non-zero alternant of the emphatic, appears when both ‹- and -‹ are absent, and / ´ /, as the non-zero alternant of ‹- and of -‹, appears when the emphatic morpheme is present. By this juggling, the first objection is circumvented; ‹- and -‹ are then free to proceed to their doom in breaking against the second.

875. The supposed morphemes ‹- and -‹ are figments. It is a fact that blackbird never occurs with stress / ´ / on bird, but sometimes with / ´ / on black. But this fact is not conveyed by any morpheme contained in blackbird, any more than the fact that blackbird is sometimes found before the plural s but never before the superlative est. It is simply a fact about the external grammar (cf. 815) of the word blackbird. If ‹- and -‹ be regarded not as the names of morphemes but as symbols of environments analogous to such writings as it's a ( ) and the ( )est thing I ever saw, then it is true to say that blackbird occurs in the (partial[54]) environment ‹- but not in the environment -‹, just as it is true to say that blackbird occurs in the environment it's a ( ) but not in the environment the ( )est thing I ever saw. Having decided to treat the two-dimensional array of morphemes ÁB as the one-dimensional array A´B, we must accept the result that AB becomes a discontinuous sequence A...B. However, this A...B passes our proposed test for discontinuous constituents. So we may say that the sequence black + emphatic stress + juncture + bird contains the ICs (1) black + juncture + bird and (2) emphatic stress; for elsewhere—viz. in the absence of emphasis—the sequence black + juncture + bird occurs as a continuous sequence. The problem could not be solved simply by considering the emphatic morpheme to precede rather than follow what phonetically it coincides with, since in that case the exactly analogous difficulty would be presented by those compounds that occur in the environment -‹, e.g. hêartbrŏken.

876. It is, as we have said, a fact of the external grammar of blackbird that it occurs in the environment ‹- but not in -‹ ; a fact, let us add now, tied up with the construction. A nearly minimal pair like hóusebrŏken and hêartbrŏken clearly shows the meaning-difference between compounds of the structure A´B and those of the structure AB´.

---

[53] Though not minimally; for when blackbird is contrastively stressed with / ´ /, pie appears in the alternant /pây/, unaccompanied by the emphatic morpheme. All the sentences (A), (B), and (C) contain the same pitch-morpheme, though in different alternants.

[54] See 811.

The basic unsoundness of regarding ´- and -´ as morphemes is that it involves placing different occurrences of these morphemes in different relative segmental positions, even though in all the occurrences their suprasegmental phonemic position is the same. Suppose two sequences of morphemes ÁBC and DÉF, and suppose further, to free the case from complications, that each of the morphemes from A to F contains a single syllabic; and finally, suppose that ABC is a two-word sequence of the compound AB and the simple word C, while DEF is a single compound word consisting of the simple word D and the derivative word EF (night-watchman or the like). Then in terms of ´-, ÁBC would be regarded as A + B + ´- + C, but DÉF would be regarded as D + (E + F) + ´-.

For this inconsistency or lack of parallelism there is no justification. Phonemically, the proposed morpheme ´- occurs simultaneously with the first morpheme of each sequence; in converting or translating the two-dimensional phonemic order to a one-dimensional morphemic order, there is no warrant for embellishing the original order by translating it differently in extrinsically different cases. But, when this privilege is denied to ´- and -´, their main usefulness as morphemes is lost.

§77. Even a last vestige of apparent utility must be stripped away. One might grant that the emphatic morpheme must always be assigned a segmental position in the same mechanical way, and yet hold that it should be distinguished into several (or an indefinite number of) homonymous morphemes E_1, E_2, E_3 ..., each one governing a different scope. Thus ÁBC of the above example would contain the morphemes $A + E_1 + B + C$, in that order, and DÉF would contain $D + E_2 + E + F$. The morphemes E_1 and E_2 would both have /´/ as their phonemic value, but E_1 would signify that the preceding and the following morpheme together make a compound word, whereas E_2 would signify that the preceding morpheme is the first member and the two following morphemes together are the second member of a compound (E_1 and E_2 etc. would have zero-alternants in the absence of the emphatic morpheme, and the emphatic morpheme would have a zero-alternant in their presence, just

like ´- and -´ as formulated above.) The function of E_1, E_2, etc. would be threefold: (1) to identify compound words, (2) to show whether it is the first or the second member that potentially bears the accent, and (3) to show the scope of the emphatic morpheme when the latter is present—that is, to show how extensive a sequence is emphasized. (The scope is, in each case, the entire compound word.)

Our answer to this proposal is that it is not the business of linguistic analysis to invent morphemes that fulfill functions of this sort. These three pieces of information are conveyed by the constructions in which the morphemes A, B, C, etc. and the emphatic morpheme participate, not by some other morpheme additional to all of these. If the morphemes E_1, E_2, etc. were phonemically distinguished so that their existence and distinctness were indisputable, there would be no question and no difficulty about admitting them; but it is not a sufficient ground for positing a certain morpheme that it would be convenient to have it.

§78. Such is the line of reasoning that dissuades us from ever assigning /´/ to any but the one emphatic morpheme. The fact that a certain sequence is a compound word is dealt with in our system, like the fact that this or that sequence is a word of any sort, by assigning it to a certain construction. If the sequence /blǽk-bȯhrd/ is a single word in some occurrences and a two-word sequence in others, then it belongs in the two occurrences to different constructions, and there is no need to create an invisible morpheme present in the one and lacking in the other.

§79. Pitch-morphemes and their sequences need less extensive discussion than stress because they have already been worked out in considerable detail by Kenneth L. Pike.[55] Each occurrence of a pitch-morpheme has a scope—i.e. a sequence of segmental morphemes with which it is coincident and which, in general, it semantically modifies or 'modulates'; and each pitch-morpheme has an indefinite number of alternants, varying according to the number of syllabics in their respective scopes. Another conditioning factor is the position of the emphatic morpheme. The following examples illustrate a few of the alternants of the most common pitch-morpheme, that of the indicative sentence:

(a) He bought a book.   /h³iybȯht-əb²⁴úk/; alternant /333(24)/.
(b) He bought a book.   /h³iybȯht-²éy-b⁴ûk/; alternant /3324/.
(c) He bought a book.   /h³iyb²óht-⁴əbûk/; alternant /3244/.
(d) He bought a book.   /h²íy-b⁴ȯht-əbûk/; alternant /2444/.

All of these alternants involve four syllabics; the cover symbol for the first three is 324, for the fourth 24 (cf. fn. 23 end). The parentheses in the first alternant indicate that the two pitch-phonemes /24/ occur on the same syllabic; this happens only when the last syllabic in the scope of a pitch-morpheme coincides with the stress /´/ or /ǰ/.[56] In phonemic transcription and in citing alternants of pitch-morphemes (as for instance in §34), it is convenient to record only the first of a series of occurrences of the same pitch-

55 The Intonation of American English; cf. fn. 23.
56 An alternative notation would be to ascribe two occurrences of pitch-phonemes to every syllabic. Then the pitch-phonemes of (a) would be written /33333324/, which would indicate four syllabics. This is cumbersome, because each numeral in an even-numbered position would always be identical with the numeral immediately preceding it, unless it accompanies the last syllabic in the scope (the fourth, in our example) and furthermore this last syllabic bears the stress-morpheme /´/ or /ǰ/.

phoneme—e.g. as in example (a) above, instead of writing /h^{3}iyb^{3}ôht-^{3}əb^{24}úk/—because such iterations are extremely common.

   (e) H^{3}e bought a new b^{24}ook; alternant /3333(24)/.
   (f) H^{3}e bought a handsome b^{24}ook; alternant /33333(24)/.
   (g) H^{3}e bought an expensive b^{24}ook; alternant /333333(24)/.
   (h) H^{3}e sl^{2}ipped ^{3}and f^{3}ell d^{24}own; alternant /3233(24)/.

The last alternant /3233(24)/ occurs instead of /3333(24)/ when there are two occurrences of the stress-phoneme /´/ in the sentence, one on the second syllable and one on the last.

§81. In this alternant /3233(24)/, the indicative-sentence pitch-morpheme is homonymous, except for its lack of pause between the two successive occurrences of the pitch-phoneme /3/, with the two-morpheme sequence consisting of the non-final pitch-morpheme (one of the pitch-morphemes orthographically symbolized by a comma) + the indicative-sentence pitch-morpheme, when these occur in the alternants /323/ and /324/ respectively. An example of this two-morpheme sequence is

   (i) ^{3}If h^{2}é c^{3}ân, th^{3}èn ^{2}Í c^{4}ân.

If, as sometimes happens, this sentence is pronounced without pause between the two clauses, then it contains not two pitch-morphemes but one, exactly like (h) above. In this case, the construction alone shows that the sentence contains two clauses; but in sentence (i), the existence of two clauses is further shown—is reinforced—by the internal pause and by the pitch-morphemes that precede and follow it.[57] Such reinforcement or over-characterization is very widespread in language. Another example of it is the fact that in English yes-or-no questions the interrogation is usually signified both by the word-order and by the pitch-morpheme, though less commonly each of these occurs without the other.

§82. As the preceding discussion has implied, the scope of a pitch-morpheme is always taken to be a pause-group, a sequence of morphemes bounded at both ends, but not interrupted, by pauses.[58] In other

§80. Some further alternants of the same pitch-morpheme of the indicative sentence are shown in the following examples:

words, every pause-group contains one and only one pitch-morpheme. Presumably, an internal pause in an utterance should be regarded as a phoneme (symbolized /#/),[59] and hence, like every other phoneme, should be assigned, in each of its occurrences, to one and only one morpheme. We may consider that pause, like juncture, belongs to a morpheme by itself. The sequence of pitch-phonemes /323/ is a separate morpheme when followed by /#/, as in sentence (i) above: /^{3}ifh^{2}íy-k^{3}ǽn # ð^{3}èn-^{2}áy-k^{4}ǽn/, and perhaps also when followed by the juncture phoneme /-/; otherwise the same sequence /323/ is part of a longer pitch-morpheme, as in sentence (h).

§83. It remains to state how juncture-, stress-, and pitch-morphemes function in IC-analysis.

One can be sure that any segmental morpheme which ends the scope of a pitch-morpheme also ends a constituent (or else the whole utterance); but it is not always true that the beginning of the scope of a pitch-morpheme similarly coincides with the beginning of a constituent (or of the utterance). If, in our orthography, we marked a parenthetical expression by placing a closing parenthesis) at the end but no corresponding opening parenthesis (at the beginning, we should have a parallel to the manner in which the beginning and end of the scope of a pitch-morpheme may be said to mark the limits of a constituent. In the sentence They served me a nice, juicy steak /ð^{3}ey-sə̀hrvdmiy-ən^{2}âys #j^{2}ûwsiy-st^{24}éyk/, the scope of the pitch-morpheme 32 is they served me a nice; but the analysis of the sentence into ICs must be into (1) the indicative-sentence pitch-morpheme 24 and (2) all the remaing morphemes of the sentence. These, in turn, divide into the 'actor' constituent they and the 'action' constituent served me a nice, juicy steak. The 'action' consists of me and the discontinuous constituent served...a nice, juicy steak; the latter, obviously, has the ICs served and a nice, juicy steak. The analysis of the remaining sequence, as it occurs in this sentence, shown by the following diagram:

   ə⟦nâys⟧32⟦#⟦jûws⟧iy⟧2⟦juncture⟧steyk⟧

The constituent with which the pitch-morpheme is paired is not its whole scope in the sense that we have defined, but only the one word nice. The same morpheme 32 occurs a second time in the same sentence (in the alternant /2/), and is there paired with the word juicy.

---

[57] How to distinguish whether a given sequence of pause + A + pause + B + pause is one utterance with internal pause or two utterances, is a difficult question. Here we assume outright that the distinction is tenable.

[58] Two sequences A + B and A + pause + B may be very similar in meaning or quite indistinguishable; Bloomfield (Language §12.3) even calls the difference non-distinctive. However, for reasons stated in connection with juncture, it is unwise to say that pause—supposing that it has the status of a morpheme—exhibits a zero-alternant in the sequence A + B. The two sequences A + B and A + pause + B are close in meaning; but they are no more identical morphemically than I ate dinner there once and I ate a dinner there once. Nevertheless, facultative pause as defined by Bloch (Lang. 22.202) is useful in IC-analysis, because it is more fruitful to define words initially as minimum facultative pause-groups than as minimum free forms.

[59] Distinct from juncture, because there are environments in which both occur; e.g. after came in the sentence When he came I left.

884. We conventionally assign to a pitch-morpheme the position immediately following the last morpheme of its scope. It must not be thought that this is merely a symbolic gesture aimed at simplifying the IC diagrams. If we wrote our symbols in one line but regarded the morphemes as nevertheless arrayed in a two-dimensional order, we should still have to deal with this order. By reducing the order of the morphemes themselves, and therewith the graphic order of their symbols, to a single dimension, we eliminate these complexities.

885. It is the construction that reveals how many of the morphemes preceding a pitch-morpheme make up the partner with which it is paired. In the example of 883, the indicative-sentence morpheme 24 is paired with the entire remainder of the sentence, whereas the morpheme 32 (appearing as /32/ and /2/), in each of its occurrences, is paired with only a single word. We now take up another sentence. Line A gives the phonemic transcription; line B shows the sequence of morphemes as conventionally reduced to a single dimension; line C is a diagram of the analysis of the whole sentence into ICs.

(A) <u>He said so, but I doubt it.</u> /h^{3}iys^{2}éd-s^{3}ôw $\#$ b^{3}ətayd^{2}áwt^{4}it/

(B) hiy + se + $'$ + d + juncture + sôw + 323 + $\#$ + bət + ay + dawt + $'$ + it + 324

(C) hiy Ⅲ se... Ⅲ ...d Ⅲ $'$ Ⅲ juncture Ⅲ sôw Ⅱ 323 Ⅰ $\#$ Ⅰ bət Ⅲ ay Ⅲ dawt Ⅲ $'$ Ⅲ it Ⅱ 324

886. The same information about the IC-analysis of the sentence is conveyed less compactly but more explicitly by the following set of statements:

The ICs of the entire sentence are (1) hiy + se + $'$ + d + juncture + sôw + 323;

(2) $\#$;

(3) bət + ay + dawt + $'$ + it + 324.

The ICs of (1) are (4) hiy + se + $'$ + d + juncture + sôw; (5) 323.

The ICs of (3) are (6) bət + ay + dawt + $'$ + it; (7) 324.

The ICs of (4) are (8) hiy; (9) se + $'$ + d + juncture + sôw.

The ICs of (6) are (10) bət; (11) ay + dawt + $'$ + it.

The ICs of (9) are (12) se + $'$ + d; (13) juncture; (14) sôw.

The ICs of (11) are (15) ay; (16) dawt + $'$ + it.

The ICs of (12) are (17) se ... d; (18) $'$.

The ICs of (16) are (19) dawt + $'$; (20) it.

The ICs of (17) are (21) se; (22) d.

The ICs of (19) are (23) dawt; (24) $'$.

887. This, then, is an exhaustive IC-analysis of the sentence <u>He said so, but I doubt it.</u> (To list the constructions in which the morphemes and the constitutes participate is a further task, not undertaken here). Needless to say, the analysis is tentative; we particularly call attention to the fact that at two different points it involves multiple constituents—in the analysis of the sentence as a whole into (1), (2), and (3), and in the analysis of the constitute (9) into (12), (13), and (14)—and once a discontinuous constituent—in the analysis of the constitute (12). An alternative possibility that especially deserves investigation is to divide the sentence as a whole into two ICs only: (1) the initial sequence ending with and including the pause $\#$, and (2) all that follows the pause. If detailed investigation of English syntax should reveal both of these analyses to be untenable, a third possibility would be to divide the sentence into the morpheme 324 on the one hand and everything else on the other (like the example of 883).

For the treatment of juncture and pause as coordinate with the sequences that precede and follow them, compare the analysis of <u>men and women</u> into three ICs (854).

888. The matter of dimensions calls for one further remark. In the sentence <u>He said so, but I doubt it</u>, the pitch-morphemes 323 and 324 form a continuous suprasegmental sequence. In conventionally accommodating them in a one-dimensional segmental sequence, we lose this continuity: 323 + 324 now become 323 + ... + 324. As we have already pointed out (884; cf. 863 and fn. 52), the difficulty is not simply notational: if we give up the two-dimensional order, we must give up its advantages as well as its defects. However, as it happens, it is no loss to let the sequence of pitch-morphemes become discontinuous; for we never wish to regard this sequence as a constitute.

If A and B are segmental sequences separated by a pause $\#$, and S and T are pitch-morphemes having A and B as their respective scopes, then the analysis of the sentence

$$\begin{matrix} S & & T \\ A & \# & B \end{matrix}$$

presents no difficulties. The fundamental criterion of independence pronounces decisively in favor of AS Ⅰ $\#$ Ⅰ BT (or perhaps AS$\#$Ⅱ B Ⅰ T), not A$\#$B Ⅰ ST.

PROBLEMS OF MORPHEMIC ANALYSIS

CHARLES F. HOCKETT
Language 23.321-43—1947

I. Introductory

1. This paper develops further the theory of morphemic analysis presented by Zellig S. Harris in 1942.[1] Morphemic analysis is the operation by which the analyst isolates minimum meaningful elements in the utterances of a language, and decides which occurrences of such elements shall be regarded as occurrences of 'the same' element.

This operation does not constitute all of grammatical analysis: when it is completed, there remains the task of describing the arrangements in which the minimum meaningful elements occur, and—where the same elements are observed to occur in more than one arrangement with a difference in meaning— the features other than morphemes (the 'tagmemes') that are involved. For this latter phase, I have proposed the term 'tactics'.[2]

The fact that John hit Bill and Bill hit John have different meanings,[3] or that old men and women is sometimes approximately the same as 'old men and old women', sometimes rather comparable to 'women and old men',[4] proves that features other than morphemes have to be recognized—unless, of course, we wish to redefine 'morpheme' to cover features of this type too. There is other evidence: a graduate student in a hurry to prepare himself for a French reading exam, or a scholar deciphering a dead language written in a non-phonetic or semi-phonetic orthography, may achieve good control of the tactics and semantics of the language, but remain in almost total ignorance of anything submorphemic. To do this he needs some mnemonically satisfactory device for keeping morphemes apart. The device probably consists of speech sounds;[4a] but these may be purely private. Thus a western sinologist may know Confucius backwards and yet stumble in passing the time

of day with any speaker of a modern Chinese dialect.

Although, then, morphemics and tactics are both necessarily involved in grammar, we nevertheless have considerable range of choice in drawing the line between them.[5] Faced with a language of a certain degree of complexity, we may prefer to describe it with simple morphemics and complicated tactics, or conversely, or somewhere in between. The language is not disturbed by our choice; its complexities remain whether itemized in one part or another of our description. But the resulting descriptions may vary a great deal in the clarity with which they depict the situation. Presumably we should try to obtain that distribution of data between morphemics and tactics which produces the greatest clarity. In this paper we assume, without steadfast conviction, that this end is achieved by the simplest possible tactics, whatever submorphemic complications may be necessitated.

2. The same assumption was apparently involved in Harris's formulation of 1942. Yet Harris realized that this cannot stand as the only assumption. We must have, also, a set of principles on the basis of which we identify, or refuse to identify, different stretches of speech as morphemically the same. The great value of Harris's paper lies in this: that although he does not add any individual method of morphemic identification to those currently used, he demonstrates how all the superficially diverse methods can be regarded as cases of one general procedure. This general procedure we outline herewith, with such minor modifications of terminology as will be useful to us:

Step 1. The utterances of a language are examined.[6] Recurrent partials with constant meaning (ran away in John ran away and Bill ran away) are discovered; recurrent partials not composed of smaller ones (-way) are alternants or morphs.[7] So are any partials not recurrent but left over when all recurrent ones are accounted for. The citable case most nearly approaching this is the cran- of cranberry, which does indeed recur, but always with berry following. By definition, a morph has the same phonemic shape in all its occurrences. Because we

[1] Zellig S. Harris, Morpheme Alternants in Linguistic Analysis, Lang. 18.169-80 (1942) ((109)).

[2] Review of Eugene A. Nida, Morphology: the Descriptive Analysis of Words, Lang. 23.273-85 (1947).

[3] Leonard Bloomfield, Language §10.4 (New York, 1933).

[4] Rulon S. Wells, Immediate Constituents, Lang. 23.81-117, esp. 93 ff. (§§30 ff.) (1947).
It would be possible to say that this ambiguity of old men and women was grammatically irrelevant; but features of order of the type involved in John hit Bill versus Bill hit John cannot be ignored. This being so, Bloomfield's term 'tagmeme' for a feature of meaningful arrangement is useful.

[4a] This is a reasonable assumption because of man's million years or so of natural selection, in which ability in aural memory and oral mimicry has been a factor making for survival.

[5] Cf. Zellig S. Harris, From Morpheme to Utterance, Lang. 22.161-83, esp. 162-3 (§2) (1946) ((142-3)).

[6] Obviously not all of them, but a sampling which we hope will be statistically valid. By working with successively larger samplings, and by predicting on the basis of each what else will occur, we approach, at least asymptotically, a complete description.

[7] A convenient term, because it (1) eliminates the lengthy expressions 'morpheme alternant' and 'morpheme unit', and (2) suggests a valid analogy (allo)phone : phoneme = morph : morpheme.

operate with whole utterances, morphs are not always composed of continuous uninterrupted stretches of phonemes,[8] but they are always composed of phonemes. Every utterance is composed entirely of morphs. The division of a stretch of speech between one morph and another, even if the two are simultaneous, overlapping, or staggered, we shall call a <u>cut</u>.

Step 2. Two or more morphs are grouped into a morpheme if they '(a) have the same meaning, (b) never occur in identical environments, and (c) have combined environments no greater than the environments of some single alternant in the language',[9] e.g -<u>en</u> in <u>oxen</u>, /z/ in <u>cows</u>, and various others, all meaning 'noun plural', with combined environments, or <u>range</u>, paralleling the range of zero with meaning 'noun singular'.[10]

Step 3. The differences in the phonemic shape of alternants of morphemes are organized and stated; this constitutes <u>morphophonemics</u>. Morphophonemic statements may involve morphophonemes—that is, the symbols used for phonemes, plus supplementary ones, with special definitions as to phonemic value under varying circumstances—or they may not; often lists are more convenient, and sometimes they are unavoidable. But regardless of the methods used in describing them, such alternations are morphophonemic.

3. In several ways a rigorous adherence to Harris's system as here stated is troublesome.

(1) Sometimes we are confronted with a set of alternants with apparently identical meaning which are almost, but not quite, in complementary distribution. So with the two alternants meaning 'noun plural' in <u>hoofs</u> and <u>hooves</u>, or <u>laths</u> with /θ/ and with /ð/. These would forbid the tactically desirable conclusion that there is but one noun-plural morpheme in English.

(2) Sometimes a set of alternants with identical meaning and completely in complementary distribution have to be kept apart because we can find no single alternant whose range parallels that of the given group. In Latin, for instance, there is no case-number combination represented after all noun stems by the same suffix; therefore we may not legitimately (by Harris's criteria) speak of a single 'nominative-singular' morpheme, or a single morpheme for any other case-number meaning.

(3) Sometimes a stretch of speech may be cut at

either of two places, so as to produce equally satisfactory—and equally unsatisfactory—morphs. In Menomini, when an element ending (otherwise) in a consonant precedes, in the same word, an element beginning (otherwise) in a consonant, an /e/ appears between them. Do we cut before or after this /e/? Either cut will do; either choice is arbitrary. Harris proposes that we cut in both places, and regard /e/ as an alternant of /-/ 'morpheme juncture'.[11] In this proposal he does not adhere to his own rules, for morpheme juncture has no meaning, and is not a morpheme; yet any Algonquianist will say that his solution is correct, and the problem is to readjust the rules so that the interpretation does not violate them.

(4) Since there is no way in which French /o/ 'to the (masc.)' can be cut, we must take it as a single morph. But the tactical survey suggests rather that it be taken as two successive morphemes, <u>à</u> 'to' plus <u>le</u> 'the (masc.)'. There is at present no way in which the latter conclusion can be reached without doing violence to our criteria.

(5) As we perform step 1 of Harris's procedure, only morphs of overt phonemic content turn up. It is suggested that the definition of morph be extended to cover also the following: minus-features, such as that which added to French <u>bonne</u> 'good (fem.)' produces <u>bon</u> 'good (masc.)'; replacement features, as <u>man</u>: <u>men</u>; zero features, as in <u>sheep</u> (sg.): <u>sheep</u> (pl.); and combinations of these, such as the difference between <u>child</u> and <u>children</u>. This is a difficult maneuver, however desirable; Harris (within the scope of his paper) tells us neither under what conditions it is called for nor how to perform it.

The items just listed are not criticisms, but points on which improvement is clearly possible within Harris's general framework. The first two difficulties are easily handled; the remaining three are more serious, but respond to a single modification in plan of attack.

Many of the problems of morphemic identification met with in dealing with any language are trivial. Before turning to the full-scale discussion of the five difficulties listed above (in Parts III and IV below), we attempt to show how the more trivial problems can be solved quickly and easily, in a fashion that sheds light on the more intricate questions to which one must eventually turn.[12]

[8] The possibilities are investigated by Harris, Discontinuous Morphemes, Lang. 21.121–7 (1945)—but the added complication of this is avoided in the examples of the present paper.
[9] Harris, Morpheme Alternants §7.1.
[10] The zero element with meaning 'noun singular' is one of Harris's parallels (Morpheme Alternants §2.2). Such a morpheme has very dubious status, having no alternant of other than zero shape (see fn. 37 and reference cited there). Harris lists also the parallel -<u>ful</u>; given the modification of criteria proposed in §13 of this paper, one could add also '<u>s</u> 'genitive'.
[11] Harris, Morpheme Alternants §4.2.
[12] We propose to say both 'the morph x occurs in such-and-such an utterance', and 'the morpheme x occurs in such-and-such an utterance'. By our definition, a morpheme is a class of morphs, so that the latter type of expression, without further qualification, is logically invalid. We render it valid by stating that an expression of the form 'the morpheme x' shall be taken in some cases as a class-name, in other cases as a variable indicating the appropriate though unspecified member of the class, depending on what the context requires. No ambiguity results; this is customary usage in linguistics; but it is a point on which more care is needed than is usual.

II. Preliminary Normalization

4. Let us assume that we have before us a display of a large number of utterances of a language, in a phonemic notation. As we begin the search for recurrent partials, we may discover that a phonemic notation other than the one we have used—for there are always several mutually convertible possibilities—would simplify the task.

In Yawelmani,[13] for example, the point of syllable division is phonemic. One way to write Yawelmani is to use a hyphen for syllable juncture; then the phonemic content of syllables can be indicated with a relatively small number of vowel and consonant letters. If our display of utterances is in this notation, we find such obviously related forms as /gʔadsʔ/ 'obsidian' : /gʔadsʔ-ni/ 'obsidian (dative)' : /gʔa-dsʔa/ 'obsidian (accusative)'. The second form contains a stretch identical with the first, plus /-ni/ 'dative'; the third form contains, before /a/ 'accusative', a stretch identical with the first part of the other two save for an inserted hyphen. If we are to identify the non-identical stretches /gʔadsʔ/ and /gʔa-dsʔ/ as being morphemically the same (whether one morpheme or more is another matter), and make similar identifications in other cases where the presence or absence of a hyphen is the phonemically differentiating factor, then we must handle this evanescent hyphen in our morphophonemic statements.

Yawelmani can also be written phonemically without the hyphen. If we want to write it so, we must use unit symbols for certain consonants which otherwise might be interpreted either as belonging wholly to a single syllable or as being divided between two: for example, /VgʔV/ would be an ambiguous notation for both /V-gʔV/ and /Vg-ʔV/; but if we replace /gʔ/ in a single syllable by /kʼ/, the ambiguity is removed.[13a] With all such changes as are necessary, we reach a notation which does not write the point of syllable division with a separate symbol, but which nevertheless indicates it unambiguously: when a single consonant symbol stands between two vowel symbols, a point of syllable division falls before the consonant symbol; when two consonant symbols stand between two vowel symbols, a point of syllable division falls between them.

In this notation, the forms given above appear as /kʼac'/ : /kʼac'ni/ : /kʼac'a/. The partial /kʼac'/ appears to be identical in all three forms. Phonemically, of course, it is not; but the only phonemic difference has been relegated to a status of notational predictability, and can be ignored in our further manipulations. There are so many intricate problems

in Yawelmani morphemics that any advantage of this kind that we can obtain is greatly to be desired.[14]

5. A notation is phonemic if it indicates, in every position, only those phonemic contrasts which occur in that position, but indicates all of them. Once one has found the morphemically most desirable phonemic notation, one can often handle certain additional simple morphemic problems by modifying it in such a way that, in addition to indicating unambiguously all the phonemic contrasts occurring in a position, it also indicates in certain positions contrasts which are not there phonemic.

If our display is of Navaho utterances,[15] we notice, sooner or later, that vowel symbols do not occur before pause (P). The sequence /VhP/ (with V for any vowel symbol) does occur. When we examine the display for recurrent partials, we find certain stretches with constant meaning that end in /Vh/ both before P and elsewhere, others that end in /Vh/ before P but without the /h/ elsewhere. Thus /bìtàhP/ 'among them' : /bìtàh níhP/ 'among them, he says', but /dòˑdàhP/ 'not' : /dòˑdà níhP/ 'he says no'. The morphemic identification of /dòˑdàh/ (P) and /dòˑdà/ (no P) is elementary, as are other such cases. So we modify our notation throughout the display, by erasing certain pre-pause h's—namely, those at the end of stretches that occur medially with the same meaning but without the /h/. In our notes we enter the memorandum: both V and Vh before pause represent phonemic /Vh/. Thereafter, save when reading off our transcription with Navaho speech sounds, we ignore the memorandum; the new /dòˑdà/ now has the same shape, to the eye, before P and elsewhere.[16]

Or suppose that we are dealing with Latin. We find pairs like ars : artis, noks : noktis, urps : urbis,

---

13 Stanley S. Newman, The Yokuts Language of California (New York, 1944). The phonemicity of the point of syllable division is my conclusion from the evidence he gives.

13a In this notation the letter k and the apostrophe ' are meant to constitute one symbol together. Similarly c and ' below.

14 The second notation is that used by Newman. It may be wondered why anyone would be led to investigate the potentialities of our first notation, the one that we decided to reject. But in Southern Athabascan (see citations in fn. 15) an entirely similar problem arises, and Hoijer chooses an orthography comparable to our first Yokuts orthography, not to our second. The complexity of morphophonemic statement which results is considerable, and could be rendered measurably easier if a phonemic notation were used in which syllable division is marked indirectly instead of overtly.

15 Harry Hoijer, Navaho Phonology, University of New Mexico Publications in Anthropology I (Albuquerque, 1945); a similar phenomenon in Chiricahua Apache: Harry Hoijer, Chiricahua Apache, Linguistic Structures of Native America 55–84 (New York, 1946).

16 Hoijer's working notation incorporates this normalization, though he calls the contrast between 'constant' pre-pause h and the evanescent type phonemic instead of morphophonemic. A similar normalization leads to the writing, within word borders, of phonemes both of the s-series and of the š-series, although, at least in rapid speech, only those of a single series occur within the stretch bounded by word junctures; see Zellig S. Harris, Navaho Phonology and Hoijer's Analysis, IJAL 11.239–48 (1945).

re·ks : re·gis, niks : niwis. The semantic and morphemic difference between ars and artis recurs with other pairs, but the difference in phonemic shape between the members of a pair is not so constant from one pair to another. Whatever may be our ultimate morphemic conclusions (e.g. that artis is ars plus something, or that ars and artis are both art plus something), they will be more easily reached if we can make the difference in shape to the eye parallel the morphemic difference.

This can be done. From phonemics we know that the sequences rts, kts, rbs, gs, gws do not occur before word juncture,[17] and that gw does not occur intervocalically. We may therefore rewrite the forms with precisely these non-occurrent sequences: arts : artis, nokts : noktis, urbs : urbis, re·gs : re·gis, nigws : nigwis. We note that in the modified orthography, rts and rs (before word juncture) are both representations of phonemic /rs/, and so on.[18] In the new notation, the second form of each pair differs from the first only in the presence of an i before the final consonant.

6. Sometimes it helps to perform this type of normalizing operation more than once.

In Potawatomi, a first normalization introduces, at certain points within utterances, a mark (say a space) indicating potential pause. Then we examine the stretches between successive points of potential pause to see which ones recur in various positions (relative to actual pause, or to adjacent stretches of varying structure) with the same meaning and the same or almost the same phonemic shape. Neither preceded nor followed by (actual) pause, we find kak 'porcupine', k·we 'woman', muk· 'beaver', k·uk· 'bucket'. Preceded but not followed by pause, we find rather kak, kwe, muk·, kuk·. Followed but not preceded by pause, the forms with the same meanings are kak, k·we, muk, k·uk. Both preceded and followed by pauses, the forms are kak, kwe, muk, kuk.

Now observation shows that the phonemes /p·/, /t·/, /č·/, /k·/ occur neither directly after nor directly before pause. Therefore we normalize all such forms as those itemized above, in all positions in which they occur, to kak, k·we, muk·, k·uk·, with the necessary memorandum that when either preceded or followed by pause, both k and k·, both p and p·, etc., represent phonemic /k/, /p/, etc.

This same normalization also accounts for all other alternations turning on the presence or absence of pause. When we have retranscribed our entire display of forms, we look further, and discover such

pairs as nkutšuwe 'he wins a race' : nnuktušwe 'I win a race', kwtumočke 'he's fishing' : nkwutmočke 'I'm fishing', pmos·e 'he's walking' : npums·e 'I'm walking', msunʔukun 'paper' : nmusnuʔkun 'my paper'. If we want to, we can begin at this level to cut our forms up into smaller recurrent partials. Clearly n means 'I, my'; the remainder of the first form, nuktušwe, presumably means 'win a race', but is not the same morph as nkutšuwe '(he) win(s) a race', because of the difference in phonemic shape. For that matter, each of these may be more than one morph. Whatever comes of this, our morphophonemic statements are going to have to be complicated at every stage by an alternation of the positions in which vowels appear.

So instead of continuing our comparison and cutting, we can try first to make a further notational normalization that will take care of the alternating vowels, or many of them. We do this by rewriting the original forms, writing a vowel in both forms of a pair whenever it appears in either form, and in a few other places for good measure: nŪkUtUšUwe : nUnUkUtUšUwe, kwUtUmočUke : nUkwUtUmočUke, pUmOs·e : nUpUmOs·e, mUsUnUʔUkUn : nUmUsUnUʔUkUn. Our memorandum this time states how these graphs are to be interpreted, not directly into a phonemic notation, but into the supraphonemic notation achieved by the previously applied normalizations: the first and each alternate one of a series of capitalized vowel symbols counts as zero, unless it precedes a final consonant.[19]

The second form of each pair now consists, to the eye, of nU (presumably 'I, my') followed by something that is identical with the first form of the pair. All the remaining problems of morphemic isolation and identification are rendered simpler.

7. There is no real drawback to counter the advantages of this kind of preliminary notational normalization, but there is a caution which must be observed. Our notational changes make morphs of differing phonemic shape look alike—indeed, that is why we make them. But the ultimate problem of the grouping of such morphs into morphemes is one which must be solved in a manner consistent with our handling of less patent cases—that is, on the basis of Harris's criteria (Step 2, §2) or of some other set. Performed as we have here suggested, notational regularizing is not apt to obscure more desirable morphemic identifications; but in extensive work with any specific language, one needs to check back over such preliminary operations from time to time to make sure.

[17] Though it is not clear what word juncture is in Latin; it may be a non-phonemic matter introduced by a previous notational normalization.

[18] Full phonemic information is still given, since such a graph as rts before word juncture stands always for phonemic /rs/, never anything else. In the new notation we have multiple writings for certain phonemic sequences, but only one phonemic sequence for each writing.

[19] We are forced to use capitals or some other device for evanescent vowels, because other vowels, phonemically the same, are not evanescent. This fact marks these alternations as non-automatic. Where no extra symbols are needed—where the symbols already used phonemically are merely extended to positions in which they do not phonemically occur—the alternations are automatic.

III. Revision of the Grouping-Requirements

8. In step 2 (§2) are stated Harris's three grouping-requirements—the three conditions which must be met by two or more morphs if they are to be regarded as belonging to the same morpheme. Some of the troubles itemized in §3 result from the particular way in which these grouping-requirements are formulated. The first of them, involving meaning,[20] is obviously the most difficult to handle. We attempt no revision of it here, and any choices dependent on it under the Harris procedure will remain in the present scheme. The second and third requirements are purely distributional, and more easily subject to analysis and modification.

Preliminary to our proposal for a modification of the second grouping-requirement we define non-contrastive distribution. Two elements of the same kind (i.e. both allophones, both morphs, or the like) are in non-contrastive distribution if either (1) they are in complementary distribution, or (2) they are in partial complementation, and in those environments in which both occur, they are in free alternation. By free alternation is meant (a) that one cannot predict, save perhaps statistically, which form will occur in a particular instance, and (b) that the occurrence of one, rather than of the other, does not produce an utterance different in meaning.

In phonemic analysis, non-contrastive distribution is often used as a criterion permitting the grouping of two or more allophones into a single phoneme. Thus the unaspirated [t] of stick and the aspirated [t'] of tick are both found at utterance-final and in certain other positions: He's in the skit may end with [t] or with [t']. But this utterance is 'the same' utterance whether the aspiration is present or not; similarly with any other pair differentiated only in this respect. The occurrence of both allophones in certain environments does not deter us from classing both in the same phoneme, /t/.

We propose, then, to revise the second grouping-requirement from 'never occur in identical environments'—which is another way of saying 'are in complementary distribution'—to read 'are in non-contrastive distribution'.[21]

The examples which follow (§§9–11) will demonstrate both the way in which this change increases the efficiency of our analysis, and also a danger inherent in it.

[20] In a manuscript not yet published, Harris demonstrates how, at least in theory, this criterion can be eliminated, thus appealing to semantic considerations at only one step of the whole process of descriptive analysis: the step at which one must decide whether two utterances, as historic events, are 'the same' or not (Bloomfield's fundamental assumption of linguistics, Language §5.3, §9.5). The first grouping-criterion (same meaning) thus becomes a practical shortcut; as such it is used here.

[21] In Yokuts Structure and Newman's Grammar, IJAL 10.196–211 (1944), Harris makes explicit use (§6) of the second grouping-requirement as modified, but without theoretical discussion.

9. In Modern West Armenian[22] a number of morphs occur with meaning 'genitive singular': /o/ and /0/ with one stem of preceding noun, /van/, /u/, /an/, and /i/ with other stems. The environments in which these occur can be differentiated in terms of the nouns which immediately precede, and such nouns fall into a series of classes (of purely morphophonemic importance) by virtue of the morph or morphs of this meaning which follow them. One occurs only with /o/ and the oblique stem: /asdəvaʒ/ 'God' : /asduʒ.o/ 'of God'. Some occur only with /0/ and the oblique stem: /kuyr/ 'sister' : /kəroč/ 'of sister, sister's'. Some occur only with /i/ and the singular stem; this is the most common pattern: /atoř/ 'chair' : /atoř.i/. Most of those which occur with /van/ and the singular stem, for example /irigun/ 'evening' : /irig.van/, are also observed to occur with /i/: /irigun.i/. The same is true for most of those which occur with /u/ or with /an/: /meg/ 'one' : /meg.u/ or /meg.i/; /axčig/ 'girl' : /axčəg.an/ or /axčig.i/.

The morphs meaning 'genitive singular' are thus not in complementary distribution, and by the original form of the second grouping-requirement could not be combined into a single morpheme. However, there is no observable difference in meaning between, say, /axčəgan/ and /axčigi/; nor is the speaker's choice of one or the other of these on any particular occasion predictable, save perhaps statistically. Therefore, within the limits of semantic judgment available to us at present, the various morphs in question are indeed in non-contrastive distribution, and by the modified second grouping-requirement—providing the third grouping-requirement is also met—are classifiable as a single morpheme.

10. In Peiping Chinese there are, as the elementary texts usually put it, two words for 'two': èr and lyǎng. The latter graph, by a preliminary normalization that need not concern us here, subsumes two distinct forms, lyǎng and lyáng. Unit numerals (those for 'one' through 'nine') occur in Chinese in the following positions: before a measure; after a group numeral ('ten' etc.); before a group numeral; after an ordinal demonstrative (dì 'the ...th'); preceded and followed by unit numerals (in counting 'one, two, three,...'). Sān 'three' appears in all these positions with a single phonemic shape. Èr occurs in the second, third, fourth, and fifth positions, lyǎng in the first and third. In the third position, before a group numeral, only èr occurs before shŕ 'ten', but either may occur before bǎi 'hundred', chyǎn 'thousand', and wàn 'ten thousand' and its multiples. The choice here is free. Èr also occurs in position one, to the exclusion of lyǎng, before the measure lyǎng 'tael, ounce'; and before a few other measures either èr

[22] Information and forms were kindly supplied by Gordon H. Fairbanks. It does not matter for the present discussion whether the stem differences are submorphemic within the stem or are part of the suffix. Some other complications, which do not alter the picture materially, are omitted here. In the cited genitive forms, a dot separates stem from ending.

or lyǎng may be found, with no difference in meaning.

This statement of distribution is not quite exhaustive, but a completely exhaustive one reveals the same facts. Clearly, èr and lyǎng cannot be regarded as a single morpheme under the old form of the second grouping-requirement, but can under the new form.

The case of èr and lyǎng is unique in Chinese; most other sets of morphs differing in phonemic shape but classed nevertheless as belonging to single morphemes have at least some phonemic feature in common. If this factor is to deter us in grouping èr and lyǎng together, then some additional grouping-requirement, not mentioned by Harris, and apparently quite difficult to formulate in a strict fashion, must be involved. We mention this possibility because we feel the Chinese example 'instinctively' to be somewhat different in nature from the Armenian.

11. As indicated in §3 (1), Harris's example of English noun-plural morphs will not hold by a strict application of his criteria, because of such pairs as hoofs : hooves. One of the more interesting of such pairs is brothers : brethren. Cases like hoofs : hooves present no difficulty under the modified second grouping-requirement because the morphs involved (hoof and hoove-, /s/ and /z/) are in non-contrastive distribution: hoofs and hooves do not differ in meaning. This is not true of brothers and brethren.

There are several possible ways of handling the problem. One way, which fits both versions of the second grouping-requirement but seems not too pleasing, is to group the /z/ of brothers, along with most other morphs meaning 'noun plural', into a single morpheme, but to exclude from this morpheme the morph found in brethren, both because it is not in free alternation with /z/ in this environment and because it has a different meaning: 'plural, with semantic specialization, producing a form of address for fellow lodge- or church-members of the male sex'.

Another solution is to postulate two distinct, though homophonous, morphemes brother : brother₁ 'male child of same parents', and brother₂ 'fellow lodge- or church-member of the male sex'. The plural of brother₁ is brothers; that of brother₂ is either brothers or brethren, in free alternation. The morphs meaning 'plural of noun' in these two cases, together with others of the same meaning, are now in non-contrastive distribution, and can be grouped into a single morpheme.

This breakdown of brother into two homophonous morphs, in order to achieve a greater differentiation of the environments in which various morphs meaning 'noun plural' occur, may seem artificial; but if one starts with the plural forms and then works to the singular, it seems less so. For brethren occurs in larger environments in which brothers also occurs, whereas brothers occurs in some larger environments in which brethren does not occur, e. g.

I want you to meet my ( ), John and Bill. If one groups the cases in which both may occur, and contrasts the non-linguistic environment of these cases with that of the cases in which only brothers occurs, the semantic difference is fairly clear. Extension by analogy to the singular forms then seems justified. The source of difficulty here, as often, lies of course in the complexity of manipulating any type of semantic criterion.

12. The proposed revision of the second grouping-requirement leads rather clearly to simpler tactics; but it raises a problem for which I have no answer.

There is a generally accepted working assumption in descriptive analysis to the effect that while there may be homophonous morphemes, there are no exactly synonymous ones.[23] No matter how subtle the difference in meaning may be between, say, twenty and score,[24] the difference in phonemic shape implies non-identity morphemically. Now the revised version of the second grouping-requirement implies that we will violate this working assumption when the evidence leads us to believe that the violation is desirable. But I can make no statement as to the formal conditions under which the principle should be suspended. In every case of not quite complete complementation, we have to examine the positions in which more than one morph of the set appears, and decide whether in these positions they are in free alternation or not. In every case, this decision seems to turn on semantic considerations. If this is true, then for a long time to come such decisions are going to be partly a matter of individual taste. This need not deter us; for in any such case we need only suspend judgment, state both or all the alternative analyses, and indicate that our choice of one for further analytical purposes is only tentative.

13. The modification of Harris's third grouping-requirement that we propose is somewhat simpler; cf. §3 (2). Instead of requiring that the morphs to be grouped 'have combined environments no greater than the environment of some single alternant in the language', we require that they have a total range which is not unique. The range of a morpheme is the class of all environments in which the member morphs of that morpheme occur. Our revised requirement still stipulates that a morpheme obtained by grouping several morphs together shall have a range identical with (or paralleling) that of some other morpheme, but no longer requires that the second morpheme (the test morpheme) shall consist of a single morph.

The tactical advantage to be gained by either form of the requirement is that we thereby avoid the need to list separately the ranges of individual morphemes; we prefer to handle them in terms of classes having identical or closely parallel ranges. With either form

23 Bloomfield, Language §9.5.
24 Harris, Morpheme Alternants §2.2.

of the requirement, there may remain morphemes containing only a single morph, which have unique ranges; but this we cannot handle in the present connection.[25] For those morphs which perhaps can be grouped into complex morphemes, the tactical advantage is worthwhile.

The revised form of the requirement enables us to gain this tactical advantage in cases where it is impossible under the older form. Latin case-endings are a clear example. Since no single case-number category is represented after all noun stems by the same morph, it is impossible under the old form of the requirement to group all the morphs of any single case-number combination into a single morpheme. Under the new requirement, we may do so for one case-number combination, providing we also do so for at least one other case-number combination; the natural conclusion is to do so for every such combination. The set of eight or ten case-number morphemes can now be handled tactically as a class: they occur after noun stems; and a noun stem occurs before a case-number morpheme.

IV. Morph and Morpheme

14. We now attempt to remove the source of the remaining difficulties mentioned in §3 (3–5). This we do by a single rather fundamental alteration of the relationship between morph and morpheme.

Both before and after this alteration, an utterance consists wholly of morphs: every bit of phonemic material in an utterance is part of one morph or another. Before the alteration, every morph belongs to one and only one morpheme, so that there are as many morphemes in an utterance as there are morphs. After the alteration, the number of morphs in an utterance and the number of morphemes therein may not be identical: some of the morphs, and hence some bits of phonemic material, of some utterances, are morphemically irrelevant. How this change is brought about, and with what utility, will be demonstrated presently. In making it, we must conform to a principle which Harris does not state but which he adheres to rigorously: the principle of total accountability. Every morph, and every bit of phonemic material, must be determined by (i.e. predictable from) the morphemes and the tagmemes (if any) of which the utterance is composed.[26]

[25] In his unpublished material [see now his Methods in Structural Linguistics 202 (Univ. of Chicago Press, 1951)] Harris shows how this can be handled. His example is English /tuw/ (to, two, too), which in the absence of semantic criteria first appears as a single morph.

[26] No defect of many older grammars of less-well-known languages is more marked than the confusion, or at best fuzziness, which results from a neglect of the principle of total accountability. Of course we do not condemn their writers for being 'men of their times rather than of ours'; for one thing, this doctrine could hardly be stated explicitly until the phonemic principle had been discovered.

Two morphemic analyses of an utterance are tactically equivalent if they give the structure of the utterance in terms of the same morphemes and tagmemes—whatever the differences in the handling of submorphemic matters. For example, according to one analysis, Fox[27] poonimeewa 'he stops talking to him' consists of the morphs pooni 'cease', m 'act by speech on an animate object', and certain succeeding elements which do not concern us. A different analysis breaks the form into poon and im, with the same meanings. These two analyses are tactically equivalent. By the first one, the morpheme 'cease' has form poon before morphs beginning with a vowel, form pooni before those beginning with a consonant, and the morpheme 'act by speech on an animate object' has everywhere form m. By the second analysis, 'cease' has everywhere form poon, and the second morpheme has the two forms m and im, depending on what precedes. In either case, the sequence of morphemes involved can be indicated as {poon} + {m} ; it is only below the tactical level that there is any difference.

If, on the other hand, we divide the given form into poon 'cease', i, and m 'act by speech etc.', and consider each of these a morpheme as well as a morph, the analysis will not be tactically equivalent to the first two. For in this case the sequence of morphemes must be indicated as {poon} + {i} + {m} —there are more morphemes in the word than by the first two analyses. It is easy to see also why this analysis is tactically inferior to the first two: the statement as to the occurrence of the morpheme i—to which no meaning can be assigned—will have to operate in terms of submorphemic (phonemic) properties of environments, whereas on the tactical level we should like to be able to state environments of occurrence and non-occurrence of classes of morphemes in terms of other classes of morphemes, without regard to submorphemic matters.

But can we find any valid basis for preferring the first of the above alternative treatments to the second, or vice versa? Clearly, there can be no tactical reason for choosing any one of two or more tactically equivalent analyses. If any reason at all is discoverable, it will be within the submorphemic realm: a matter of patterning, or perhaps simply of greater convenience. And although convenience is a legitimate basis for a choice, we must recognize such a criterion as different in kind from others, and as more open to disagreement. A more convenient analysis tells us nothing more about a language than a less convenient one that is otherwise equivalent; but what it does tell it tells more clearly.

[27] I choose Fox rather than Menomini because the examples are a bit easier to cite; the same principles apply. The Fox forms are from Leonard Bloomfield, Notes on the Fox Language, IJAL 3.219–32, 4.181–226 (1924–7), and from the same writer's Algonquian, Linguistic Structures of Native America 85–129 (New York, 1946).

15. The alteration by which the number of morphemes in an utterance fails in some cases to coincide with the number of morphs consists of recognizing two special kinds of morphs: empty morphs, which have no meaning and belong to no morpheme; and portmanteau morphs, which belong simultaneously to two (or, theoretically, more) morphemes, and have simultaneously the meanings of both.

If for some submorphemic reason (patterning or convenience), the breakup of Fox poonimeewa into poon + i + m (+) is to be preferred to either of the two alternative procedures outlined in §14, this breakup can be made tactically equivalent to the latter two, rather than to the analysis which requires the occurrence of i to be taken care of on a tactical level, by calling i an empty morph. Total accountability is maintained because we say, on the submorphemic level, that when a morph ending in a consonant is followed in the same word by one beginning with a consonant, the empty morph i appears between them.

The simplest example of a portmanteau morph is French /o/ 'to the (masc.)' (§3). If this be taken as a single morpheme, tactical difficulties ensue. What other morpheme has a range of positions of occurrence parallel to the range of this one? On the other hand, since /o/ is a single phoneme, it is hardly possible to make a cut and produce two morphs. But if we interpret it as a portmanteau morph, the representative of the morpheme sequence {à le}, we not only eliminate a forlorn morpheme, but round out the distribution of {à} and of {le}, both otherwise somewhat defective. For à 'to' parallels to a great extent the distribution of sur 'on', après 'after', and other morphs, but—unless the proposed interpretation is accepted—does not occur in one important position where the others occur: before le 'the (masc.)' when the following noun begins with a consonant. Similarly, the suggested treatment of /o/ makes the parallelism between le and la 'the (fem.)' much neater. The case is so clear-cut that there is nothing remarkable in the fact that au has been traditionally so interpreted.

It is to be noted that our morphemic expansion of /o/ to {à le} involves not only the morphemes {à} and {le}, but also a specific order thereof: /o/ is not morphemically {le à}. This specific order, like the morphemes themselves, is given not by the portmanteau as such, but by its distribution and that of the morphs to which we propose to relate it. Choice of the order {à le} leads to the parallelism indicated above; choice of the reverse order leads to nothing at all.

16. The simple examples just given speak, it is believed, for the naturalness of this approach; but as yet we have given no formal statement of the conditions under which an empty morph or a portmanteau morph is to be set up.

Because of the possible importance of submorphemic patterning, it will be necessary to consider the typical phonemic shapes, or canonical forms, of morphs. It is a well-recognized fact that in any particular language, if we examine and classify those cases of morphs which do not patently involve the questions here being raised, we find that many different morphs have much the same general phonemic shape.[28] Fijian affords an elementary example.[29] A large number of morphs have the shape $\#C_1V_1C_2V_2(C_3)$, where $\#$ is word juncture, the C's indicate any consonant (or none), the V's any vowel, and C_3 is lacking when word juncture or a consonant follows: koro 'village' (C_3 = zero), sala 'path', dina 'true, truth', selev 'cut, knife', ðabet 'go up', kaðiv 'call, announce'. A second, much smaller, group have the shape $\#C_1V_1C_2V_2C_3V_3(C_4)$: taŋane 'man, male', yalewa 'woman, female'. A third group have the shape V or V_1CV_2: a 'transitive with common object', as in ðabeta 'go up (a hill)', raiða 'to see (a child, etc.)'; i 'transitive with proper object', as in raiði 'to see (John, me, etc.)'; aka 'transitive indirective', as in ðabetaka 'carry (someone) upwards'. Lastly, there is a group of structure $\#CV\#$, occasionally $\#C_1V_1C_2V_2\#$: na 'the (common)', as in na koro 'the village'; ni 'of the (common)', as in na yaða ni koro 'the name of the village'; i 'that connected with the act of', as in na i sele 'the knife'; ko 'the (proper)', as in ko viti 'Fiji' or ko ðei 'who?'.

In some languages the variety of canonical forms is far greater than in Fijian, but in every language the total number—however assessed, for there is some choice in the process of abstraction from specific phonemes to symbols like C and V—is relatively small. In English many morphs have the shape of a single syllable with $\#$ preceding[30] (girl, act); others consist of a single consonant, or of a single syllable with initial vowel, with no preceding $\#$ (-s, -ing, -ed, -or). In both Fijian and English, and probably generally, some canonical forms can be expressed as the 'sum' of certain smaller ones: Fijian $\#CVCVCV(C)$ as $\#CVCV(C)$ plus V; the English type of author as the type of act (or watch) plus the type of -or (or -ing). Moreover, in these cases the 'sums' occur as sequences of several morphs (actor) as well as in single morphs (author). Those canonical forms which cannot be so expressed may conveniently be called minimum.

[28] A point discussed in detail by Benjamin L. Whorf in various unpublished material, and orally.

[29] C. Maxwell Churchward, A New Fijian Grammar (1941).

[30] This avoids the risky complications which result from calling word-juncture a morpheme, as Rulon S. Wells does in his Immediate Constituents §64 (see fn. 4). The semantic contrast between Thank you with word juncture and the same without it means that word juncture is morphemic, but in such cases it might just as well be concluded—I think, a little better so—that absence of word juncture is the morpheme.

17. If in analyzing the morphemics of a language we make a preliminary classification of canonical forms, based only on those morphs whose status is perfectly clear, this classification can serve as a guide in handling the less obvious cases.

Multiplicity of analytical choice turns on two things: the location and number of cuts to be made in certain utterances; and the classification of the resultant morphs as ordinary, empty, or portmanteau. When faced with alternatives, we base our decision, wherever possible, on the relative desirability of the resulting tactics. It is on this account that the treatment of French /o/ 'to the (masc.)' as a single morpheme, or of Fox connective i as a morpheme, is rejected. When this factor cannot play a part, we turn next to morphophonemic simplicity. Morphemes of constant phonemic shape are simplest; when we cannot find these, we look next for sets of morphemes showing similar alternations in phonemic shape, since then we can describe the alternations of many different morphemes at once. When this also is not decisive, we turn to canonical forms, and prefer that analysis which produces morphs most closely conforming to the canonical forms already established— if possible, to minimum canonical forms. It may be that the second and third of these considerations should be assigned the other order of priority; apparently they are not often in conflict.

When we are confronted with three tactically equivalent alternatives for Fox poonimeewa (pooni|m, poon|im, and poon|i|m with i as an empty morph), we need only proceed to the second consideration to reach an answer. If we make either the first or the second choice, one of the morphemes involved will have two alternants (poon and pooni, or else im and m). If we make the third, both poon and m become morphemes of constant phonemic shape. If this were not enough, the third criterion would show us that failure to set up i as an empty morph would force us to recognize some morphs, beginning or ending in i, of canonical forms not otherwise required (though not in the case of the elements in the particular word poonimeewa), whereas the decision to set up the i by itself produces only morphs of shapes necessary anyway.

Likewise in the French case: tactical considerations rule out a monomorphemic interpretation of /o/, but do not decide whether we must take it as a single (portmanteau) morph or may cut it further. Now by a criterion mentioned in §2 under Step 1, a morph must have overt phonemic content. In order to cut /o/ into two morphs, we must break up the phoneme /o/ into two components, say mid-back tongue position and lip-rounding. Neither of these components fits into any otherwise necessary canonical form of morphs in French (though in some other languages some morphs do have a shape definable in components rather than in phonemes). On the other hand, /o/ taken as a single morph fits into a canon-

ical form, represented by such clear cases as /o/ 'water', /e/ 'and', /u/ 'or', /a/ 'to'. The vote is clearly for the interpretation as a portmanteau morph.

In the succeeding sections of Part IV we give further examples in which these same principles call for the recognition of empty or portmanteau morphs.

18. In Nootka[31] a word consists—submorphemically, as we shall show—of a stem plus one or more suffixes. (This statement is circular: a stem is a morpheme which begins with word-juncture, a suffix one which does not; but it will suffice for orientation.) Certain suffixes, which we may call location suffixes, occur both after ordinary stems and after a stem hina-, hin-, hita-,[32] which Sapir and Swadesh label an empty stem.

Thus ƛiḥ- 'red' + -(q)oˑʸ(ƛ) = ƛiḥoˑƛ 'red on the face'; sixʷ- 'sores, pox' + the same suffix = sixoˑƛ 'having sores on the face'; but hina- + the same suffix = hinoˑƛ 'on the face, being on the face'. Similarly, ƛiḥ- 'red' + -(ʔ)akso(ƛ) = ƛiḥaksoƛ 'red at the lips'; hap- 'hair, fur' + the same suffix = hapaksoƛ 'having a moustache'; but hina- + the same suffix = hinaksoƛ 'at the lips or mouth, being at the lips or mouth'. Finally, maƛ- 'tied' + -aḥoˑp 'cause momentarily to be in front' = maƛaḥoˑp 'ties in front'; but hina- + the same suffix = hinaḥoˑp 'places in front'.

The empty stem has no meaning. Our tactics are just as well suited, and our morphophonemics are not complicated, by interpreting each form of the empty stem as an empty morph. The remaining stems constitute a class of morphs which begin with #. Suffixes other than the location suffixes constitute a class of morphs which do not begin with #. When a location suffix is preceded by a stem, neither # nor any other phonemic material intervenes. When a location suffix is not preceded by a stem, it is preceded instead by the appropriate (predictable) form #hina-, #hin-, #hita-, which in any case is meaningless and tactically irrelevant. The principle of total accountability is not violated; and the empty morphs conform to canonical forms. The alternative of taking #hina- etc. as a stem (a morpheme) is undesirable because of the meaninglessness of this element. The alternative of taking hinaḥoˑp as an alternant going with -aḥoˑp, and similarly for every other such combination, produces a greater complication of canonical forms.

31 Edward Sapir and Morris Swadesh, Nootka Texts (Philadelphia, 1939), esp. Part III, The Primary Structural Elements of Nootka; Morris Swadesh, Nootka Internal Syntax [sic], IJAL 9.77–102 (1936–8). The specific examples were generously supplied by Swadesh.

32 The alternation among these three shapes of the element will not concern us; it is covered by statements on a lower level of morphophonemic treatment.

19. In most of the central Algonquian languages occurs a phenomenon which we shall here illustrate with Potawatomi examples. Nouns appear in both unallocated and allocated forms: wUkUma 'chief' : nUtOkUmam 'my chief' or kUtOkUmamwa 'your (pl.) chief'. Some nouns, however, appear only in allocated forms; so nos· 'my father', kos· 'your (sg.) father'. A noun in an allocated form contains a personal prefix before the noun stem, and after the noun stem one or more of several suffixes (including, in the allocation is plural, a personal suffix) and various inflectional endings. Some of these nouns which occur in both unallocated and allocated forms contain, after the noun stem in an allocated form, a morph m, Um, im, om; so, for example, the forms for 'my chief' and 'your chief' above. Other such nouns appear sometimes with a morph of this shape, sometimes without it, but with no semantic contrast —the presence and absence of the morph are in free alternation. Still others, including all nouns which appear only in allocated forms, never occur with the m element.

The m elements are more satisfactorily regarded as morphs than as parts of the preceding morphs, particularly since the choice among the various forms of the m element depends on the environment in much the same way as does the choice among the alternants of the morpheme {k} 'locative' and (though with less similarity) among the various alternants of a number of other suffix morphemes. But the m elements are meaningless, even where forms appear both with and without one of them, and it is tactically convenient to eliminate them from the picture before tactical discussion begins. So we take them to be empty morphs.

20. The English interjections written conventionally as hm!, eh?, and the like, consist phonemically of an intonation-sequence, a stress, and a segmental 'carrier' for these features. In my dialect, this segmental component may have any vocalic quality (whether this occurs elsewhere or not), or any oral closure or closures, but it must be nasalized. Such a segmental structure is atypical in its wide range of nondistinctive variation, but the articulatory feature involved distinctively—nasalization—is one which does recur in more typical segmental structure, for example as that which distinguishes /m/ from /b/, /n/ from /d/.

If we compare the utterance hm (intonation 32)[33] with yes(32) and with hm(24), we see that the meaning of hm(32) is that of yes(32) minus the meaning of the intonationless abstraction yes; between hm(32) and hm(24) there is no semantic similarity. Hm itself, then, apart from the intonation which it serves to carry, has no meaning at all.

33 Following Pike (The Intonation of American English; Ann Arbor, 1946), and Wells (Immediate Constituents §79) in the assignment of figures, and numbering the four levels from top down.

We may conclude that the hm part of such interjections is an empty morph. The intonational morphs which accompany it are also found spread through such morphs or morph-sequences as yes, I know, maybe, he didn't come, and so on. Accountability is maintained: if an utterance consists morphemically of an intonational morpheme alone, the empty morph hm will be present; otherwise hm is absent.

The tactical implications are interesting: the only free morphemes of English, in Bloomfield's sense of 'free', are intonational morphemes, and the only monomorphemic utterances of the language are those consisting of such a morpheme.

21. In certain Spanish verb forms there appears, between the stem and the endings, an element often called a conjugation vowel: the á, é, and í of amar 'to love', beber 'to drink', vivir 'to live'; the áb, í, and í of amábamos 'we loved', bebíamos 'we drank', vivíamos 'we lived', etc. Which vowel (or in one case vowel plus consonant) appears, depends on the stem and on the ending: the infinitive ending r, for example, requires á after a stem of the first conjugation, é after one of the second, and í after one of the third. The three conjugations are classes of stems, in fact, based precisely on this feature of behavior.

The conjugation vowels have no meaning. The meaning of amar is that of the two component morphemes, stem am 'love' and the infinitive ending, whether we treat the latter as ár in this case, alternating with ér and ír elsewhere, or simply as r. The latter alternative relegates the á, and all other such conjugation vowels, to the status of empty morphs.

Not all the post-stem vowels which occur in Spanish verbs have this status. The a of amas 'thou lovest', for example, is the only thing which distinguishes this form from ames 'that thou love' (subjunctive). Here the a is no empty morph, but an ordinary morph with meaning 'present indicative'. In one possible analysis of Spanish verbs, which would perhaps be the simplest from the morphophonemic standpoint, distinctions such as that between a 'present indicative' and the meaningless á of amar are not made. But this somewhat greater morphophonemic ease is outweighed by more complicated tactics.

22. Our first additional example of a portmanteau morph comes from Yokuts.[34] In the Yawelmani dia-

34 See fn. 11. The capital letters at the beginning of cited suffixes are components of the vowels in the part of the word which precedes the specific phonemes of the suffix. Thus the stem me·k'i 'swallow' contains two consonants and parts of two vowels: after the first consonant, the vowel components high-front and long, and after the second consonant, the vowel components high-front and short. When this stem occurs with the suffix FRit 'passive aorist', the component F merges with the first group of vowel components in the stem to give e·, and the component R merges with the second group of vowel

lect there are about a dozen morphemes which occur after a verb stem and before a finite or gerundial suffix. One of these is WZa·la· (with alternants WZla·, FRla·, WW'e·, WLe·, FZWZla·, ila·, la·, WSla·, variously apportioned among different types of preceding element, but in non-contrastive distribution) 'cause someone to x': tisa·la·hin '(he) caused (it) to come out, (he) took (it) out', with stem tisi 'come out' and finite suffix hin 'aorist'. Another is WAda· (with variants da·, R = reduplication) 'x often or repeatedly': sodoxdoˀ 'will throw him repeatedly', with stem sodox 'throw' and final suffix ˀ 'future'.

In some cases two of these elements occur in succession, within the position of occurrence stated above. Indeed, the alternant R of the morpheme 'x repeatedly' occurs followed by the alternant FZWZla· of the morpheme 'cause to x': muhmuhlat 'was made to dive repeatedly', with stem muhu 'dive' and final suffix t 'passive aorist'. But other alternants of the morpheme 'x repeatedly' do not occur before any alternant of the morpheme 'cause to x'. No semantic gap results, however, for there is an element WE·lsa· ᔕ WE·sa· of the same positional class, meaning 'cause to x repeatedly': nine·lsa·hin 'got him to keep still several times', with stem nine· 'keep still, become quiet', and final suffix hin 'aorist'.

It is far from convenient, within the morphophonemic economy of Yokuts, to cut WE·lsa· ᔕ WE·sa· into smaller morphs; each alternant subsumed by this notation is best taken as a single morph. The distribution and meaning lead one to interpret each of these morphs as a portmanteau representative of the sequence of two morphemes 'x repeatedly' + 'cause to x'.

23. In finite forms of the Spanish verb the tense-mode is usually indicated by one morph, and the person-number by another, in that order: amáb|a|mos 'we loved', ama|ré|is 'you (pl.) will love'. In a few cases, it is difficult or impossible to separate the element meaning a tense-mode from that meaning a person-number; in these cases, we may regard the undivided endings (after any conjugation vowel that may occur) as portmanteau morphs: o 'present indicative + first person singular', as in amo 'I love', é (with verbs of the first conjugation) ᔕ í (with those of the second and third conjugations) 'preterit indicative + first person singular', and ó (first conj.) ᔕ ió (second and third conj.) 'preterit indicative + third person singular'. This treatment, combined with the empty-morph interpretation of conjugation vowels, reduces all finite Spanish verb forms to a uniform structure: stem + tense-mode morpheme + person-number morpheme.[35]

24. In Fijian there is a construction consisting of any of certain particles followed by a noun or pronoun: na sala 'the path', na ᵭava '(the) what?', ni koro 'of-the village', ko viti '(the) Fiji', vei au 'to me'. One of the particles is vei 'to, with, of', as in the last example above and in vei keda 'with, to, of us', vei Joni 'with, to John'. One of the pronouns is koya 'he, she', as in ko koya '(the) he, she', nei koya 'of him, of her'. But the specific combination of vei and koya seems not to occur.[36] Where semantically it would be expected, one finds, instead, the portmanteau morph vuaa 'with, to, of him or her', as in au na vosa vuaa na ŋone 'I future speak-to-him the child' = 'I shall speak to the child'.

25. We may best approach a consideration of the fifth difficulty of §3 by examining some English cases. On the tactical level, it is certainly desirable to consider men as consisting of the morpheme man plus the morpheme s 'plural'. When cutting utterances containing men into morphs, we will not be led to men into smaller pieces; it fits a canonical form and if broken further the smaller fragments do not. So one solution, and certainly the most obvious one, is to regard men as a single portmanteau morph, representing the morpheme sequence {man} + {s}.

It is true that there is a phonemic similarity between man and men—the identity of initial and final consonants—which we do not want to lose sight of. This places men in a different category from French /o/, Yokuts WE·(l)sa·, Spanish o, or Fijian vuaa, for in the latter cases the resemblance of the portmanteau to other alternants of either of the constituent morphemes is negligible. Even if men were an isolated case in English, this resemblance would be worthy of mention. But it is, of course, far from isolated; we have also mouse : mice, foot : feet, woman : women (if woman is a single morpheme), slide : slid, sing : sang, and many others.

The portmanteau interpretation of such bimorphemic forms need not obscure the phonemic resemblance of which we are speaking. In our morphophonemics we have to mention all portmanteaus. By assembling, in one section of our description, all portmanteaus which have this feature of partial phonetic identity with one of the constituent morphemes, and by organizing them into groups on the basis of the specific phonemic difference, we give ample attention to the matter.

Some may nevertheless prefer to reinterpret portmanteaus as bimorphic as well as bimorphemic, even though to do so one must extend the definition

---

components in the stem to give zero; the resulting form is me·k'it 'was swallowed'. With a different set of components contributed by the suffix WAˀan 'durative present', the resulting form is mik'a·ˀan 'is swallowing'. For the details of this, see Zellig S. Harris, Yokuts Structure and Newman's Grammar, IJAL 10.196–211 (1944).

[35] The 'irregular' verbs present more complex cases of both portmanteau and empty morphs, but are tactically quite the same, save where one or another form is missing.

[36] Churchward is not entirely clear on the matter: he says (op.cit. I.24.3) that vei koya is 'unusual'. If it does indeed occur, then the interpretation proposed is wrong; rather vei koya is like English with it and vuaa like therewith.

of 'morph' to cover elements of other than overt phonemic content. If this is considered desirable, then in the notion of portmanteau we have at least achieved a more rigorous way of extending the coverage of the term 'morph' in such a manner, as follows:

In our initial cutting of utterances, we obtain only morphs of overt phonemic content. Further examination, along the lines detailed in this paper so far, reveals the possibility that certain of our morphs are portmanteaus; but for our present purpose we may call them rather tentative portmanteaus. We then examine each tentative portmanteau and compare its phonemic shape with that of the other alternants of the constituent morphemes. If we find that the tentative portmanteau has some phonemes (or components) in common with one of the non-portmanteau alternants of one of the constituent morphemes, we may set up the entire non-portmanteau alternant as one constituent morph of the form which has tentatively been regarded as a portmanteau, and the alternation from this shape to that of the tentative portmanteau as the other constituent morph. Alternatively, we may set up the tentative portmanteau, as a whole, as an alternant of that constituent morpheme which it resembles phonemically, and set up a zero morph as an alternant of the other constituent morpheme.[37] For example, our initial cutting produces men, which does not look like more than one morph. The sequence man plus s does not occur. Men fills the tactical place which one might expect to be filled by the sequence man plus s. Men is therefore morphemically { man } + { s }. But—so runs the argument that would set up alternation morphs—men and man resemble each other in phonemic shape, both containing m-n. So men is not a portmanteau. One morph in men is man. The other is the alternation a ⌣ e. Or—arguing now for a zero morph—men is not a portmanteau, but consists of an alternant men of { man } plus an alternant /0/ of { s }.

If a language contains only a few isolated instances of this kind, probably everyone would agree to reject the last steps of the above argument and return to the portmanteau interpretation, relying on the organization of one's morphophonemic statements to put the matter of partial phonemic resemblance into clear relief. But if the language contains a sufficient number of such cases that one is warranted in setting up a canonical form for morphs like a ⌣ e, or like /0/, then some may prefer the extension.

Somewhat similar considerations apply to French

bon 'good (masc.)' and to English sheep (pl.). In the course of examination, the portmanteau interpretation is that which first presents itself; from it we may proceed to the recognition of morphs of other than overt phonemic content if we find factors comparable to those in the case of men. It is to be emphasized that when portmanteaus are eliminated in this way, the new definition of 'morph' is no longer that with which we began; perhaps, therefore, it would be advisable to distinguish terminologically between, say, 'primary morphs' (those of overt phonemic content) and 'extended morphs' (including primary ones and morphs of the zero, replacement, or subtraction types).

English children, however, remains recalcitrant. Obviously it is morphemically { child } + { s }; so that whatever submorphemic interpretation we chose, the tactical picture is clear. The first part of children resembles child, and the last part is identical with one of the alternants of { s }, namely the -en of oxen. The alternative analyses are (1) child|ren, (2) childr|en, (3) child|r|en, (4) child + vowel change and -ren, and (5) no cut, i.e. portmanteau. The first gives a morph /čild/, the difference between which and child recurs in other contexts, e.g. slide : slid, bite : bit; but then the morph -ren is unique. The second gives a morph -en which recurs; but then the difference between /čildr/ and child is unique. The third has the merits of each of the first two, without the defects, but involves an empty morph r, which is not observed to recur and therefore requires a special statement for this occurrence. The fourth produces a morph (vowel change and -ren) which fits no canonical form, unless the vowel-change-plus-en of bitten, hidden, and others is grouped with it from the point of view of shape. Apparently this is one of the cases in which all our preferential criteria (§14) fail, and nothing remains but a resort to convenience.[38]

38 The unsolved case of children is discussed in detail for a reason. There is no merit in an analytical procedure which 'eliminates' all but one of a set of alternative analyses simply by fiat—by saying that when such-and-such types of alternative present themselves we shall accept the one which has certain characteristics and reject the others. Our aim is to achieve the most accurate and clearest picture possible of the workings of a language, on all levels —phonemic, morphemic, and tactical; in some cases this is attained not by giving a single treatment, but precisely by indicating the alternatives. For in some cases a range of choice is determined not by our approach, but by the nature of the language; and when this is so, the existence of a range of choice in a particular portion of the language is one of the facts about the language that ought to be portrayed in our description. In one sense, any method of description which conforms to the principle of total accountability is correct; if we nevertheless discuss the relative merits of one procedure or another within this fundamental framework, the purpose is to attain greater mutual intelligibility among the writers of grammars and, in terms thereof, more accurate pictures of the languages we describe.

37 This second alternative is that proposed by Bernard Bloch, English Verb Inflection, Lang. 23.399 –418 (1947). Bloch rejects all alternation or subtraction morphs, and interprets all tentative portmanteaus as an alternant of one of the constituent morphemes plus a zero alternant of the other. One special criterion is introduced for dealing with zero alternants: no morpheme is postulated which has only a zero alternant.

V. Conclusions

26. We now summarize the procedure of morphemic analysis worked out in the course of our discussion, and end with an example from English which illustrates several of the points that have been made. Our summary of the procedure is given in steps, as in §2; but in actually working with a particular language one has to skip back and forth, operating by trial and error.

Step 1. We assemble the utterances of the language before us, recorded in some phonemic notation. If preliminary examination reveals that a different (also phonemic) notation would make the task simpler, we retranscribe them all. If further preliminary examination shows that some normalization of notation, maintaining all phonemic distinctions but adding thereto, would further simplify the task, we retranscribe again, and perhaps again. As we proceed to other steps, we check back from time to time to be sure we have not involved ourselves in contradictions.

Step 2. The utterances are now examined in the notation finally chosen. Recurrent partials with constant meaning are discovered; those not composed of smaller ones are morphs. So are any partials not recurrent but left over when all recurrent ones are accounted for; therefore every bit of phonemic material belongs to one morph or another.[39] By definition, a morph has the same phonemic shape in all its occurrences; and (at this stage) every morph has an overt phonemic shape, but a morph is not necessarily composed of a continuous uninterrupted stretch of phonemes. The line between two contiguous morphs is a cut.

Step 3. Omitting doubtful cases, morphs are classed on the basis of shape and the canonical forms are tentatively determined.

Step 4. Two or more morphs are grouped into a single morpheme if they fit the following grouping-requirements: (a) they have the same meaning; (b) they are in non-contrastive distribution; (c) the range of the resultant morpheme is not unique. Some morphs, however, may be assigned to no morpheme at all, and some may be assigned simultaneously to two (or more) morphemes. An empty morph, assigned to no morpheme,[40] must have no meaning, and must be predictable in terms of non-empty morphs. A portmanteau morph must have the meanings of two or more morphemes simultaneously, and must be in non-contrastive distribution with the combination of any alternant of one of the member morphemes and any alternant of the other (usually because no such combination occurs).

[39] We say 'phonemic' for simplicity's sake; if our notation has been normalized, then more accurately this should read 'every bit of orthographic material'.

[40] All the empty morphs in a language are in complementary distribution and have the same meaning (none). They could, if there were any advantage in it, be grouped into a single empty morpheme— but one which had the unique characteristic of being tactically irrelevant.

Step 5. Where there are alternative possibilities, choice is based on (a) tactical simplicity, (b) morphophonemic simplicity, and (c) conformity to canonical forms, in this order of priority.

Step 6. The differences in the phonemic shape of morphs as alternants of morphemes are organized and stated; this (in some cases already partly accomplished in Step 1) constitutes morphophonemics. In particular, portmanteaus are compared with the other alternants of the morphemes involved, and if resemblances in phonemic shape and the number of cases warrant it, morphs of other than over phonemic content are recognized, some of the portmanteaus being thus eliminated.

27. Our final example is the system of personal pronouns in English (including who, whom, whose).

At least in certain dialects, the morphs I and me (and similarly we and us, he and him, etc.) are in non-contrastive distribution; in some dialects, indeed, the complementation is probably complete. We may suspect that if it were not for the Latinizing school tradition, the complementation would be complete for most speakers: I initially except in isolation, me directly after a verb or a preposition and in isolation. Actual exceptions to this are either on the Latin pattern (It's I, or Who's there?—I, instead of Me), or are overcorrections (between you and I). For many speakers whose usage of I and me does not put them in complete complementation, there is no contrast between, for example, It's I and It's me. In other dialects and styles, on the other hand, the forms are in contrast: literary English, school-teachers' on-duty English, and certain whimsical styles.[41] The remainder of this discussion applies only to a dialect in which the distribution is non-contrastive.

My and mine (and similarly our and ours, your and yours, etc.) are in complete complementation: my occurs when a noun follows without pause, mine otherwise.

If the above statements are to hold, we must split the occurrences of her into those which parallel those of his and those which parallel those of him; the former, her$_1$, is morphemically identical with hers, while her$_2$ is morphemically identical with she.

Paralleling John in John came, Bill saw John, John's book, the book is John's, and virtually every other utterance containing the morpheme John, we have I came, Bill saw me, my book, The book is mine, etc. John's is two morphs and two morphemes; we conclude that my and mine are two morphemes each, though each is only a single morph.

[41] For example, that style in which one says 'me, myself, and I' as if the reference were to three people. This is not unrelated to a style which obviously has to be excluded, both here in the discussion of English pronouns and in any other discussion of morpheme alternants: the style of the discussion itself, in which such forms as me and I contrast because they are are used as names of particular morphs.

We conclude, therefore, that the English personal pronouns have the following morphemic structure:

{I} I, me   {she} she, her₂
{I} + {s} my, mine   {she} + {s} her₁, hers
{we} we, us   {it} it
{we} + {s} our, ours   {it} + {s} its
{you} you   {they} they, them
{you} + {s} your, yours   {they} + {s} their, theirs
{he} he, him   {who} who, whom
{he} + {s} his   {who} + {s} whose

The forms it, its, and whose are the same morphically and morphemically; the others illustrate one or more of the grouping-requirements that we have discussed. Together, the twenty-six forms are analyzed into only nine different morphemes.[42]

42 We might go further, interpreting we, us as {I} + pluralizing {s}, with a similar treatment for

The tactical implications are considerable. Except for the category of number, the pronouns are now exactly like any proper noun in their tactics, and can be classed as a subdivision of proper nouns. There is no longer any justification for speaking of case in English; for the distinction between subjective and objective 'cases' (under whatever name) disappears as soon as I and me, etc., are shown to belong to the same morpheme. A form with added -'s is not a case-form either, but simply a form with added -'s: the -'s is simply another morpheme, with a statable range of positions in which it occurs.

the other plural pronouns. We are deterred from this step not because plural you is identical with singular you (since after all sheep and other nouns manifest this property), but because {he} + {s}, {she} + {s}, and {it} + {s} would all add up to they, them.

IMPLICATIONS OF BLOOMFIELD'S ALGONQUIAN STUDIES

CHARLES F. HOCKETT
Language 24.117–31—1948

It is generally known[1] that one of Leonard Bloomfield's life works is the descriptive and comparative study of Algonquian.[2] It is also generally conceded that his work in this field is of considerable importance.[3] But most of those who are quite willing to admit this do so on indirect evidence: since Bloomfield's other work proves him a sound scholar, his Algonquian studies must be sound too. Algonquian, after all, is an out-of-the-way language family, and few have concerned themselves with it. In view, particularly, of Bloomfield's endeavors in this field, this neglect is unfortunate. To the writer the following points seem beyond dispute: (1) careful study of Algonquian as Bloomfield has described it can be a fascinating, enlightening, and rewarding experience even for established comparatists and historical linguists; (2) for the newcomer to linguistics, a reading of Bloomfield's Algonquian works is one of the finest indoctrinations into the best of linguistic method.

In a sense, any body of data on any group of languages can serve in both these roles. But if, for example, the would-be linguist attempts to learn the elementary principles of comparative method in terms of Indo-European, or even of Germanic or Romance, the external difficulties are great: the material is widely scattered and bulky, some of it is old and hard to interpret, some of it is excellent but some is extremely bad. On the other hand, even though the Algonquian languages are 'exotic' (whatever that may mean), they are phonetically simple, not too widely divergent from the familiar Indo-European languages in structure—remarkably similar, in some ways, to older Germanic—and Bloomfield's treatment is compact, uniform in approach, and uniformly excellent.[4]

Most of the lessons which can be learned from Bloomfield's Algonquian are apparent to anyone who reads, with suitable diligence, his Sketch.[5] There are, in addition, a few important points which are not apparent from that paper alone, nor even necessarily from that paper together with his other writings in this field, save to someone who has had some independent first-hand contact with the extant Algonquian languages and with earlier efforts, mainly by missionaries, to describe this or that language of

---

[1] Many of the non-Algonquian references given in the footnotes of this paper were found with the assistance of Robert A. Hall Jr. For my understanding of the 'almost mystical' version of the drift theory (see §8), I am indebted to Gordon H. Fairbanks (who is not a proponent of this version of the theory). All of my colleagues at Cornell have participated in instructive discussion of this paper, and to all of them I express my thanks.

[2] Bloomfield's publications on Algonquian are listed here, approximately in order of publication. They will be referred to hereafter as 'Ref. 1' and so on, except that the third and twelfth items will be termed, respectively, the Sound System and the Sketch. The latter includes a bibliography of Algonquian which is complete save for a few items which have appeared since 1941.
  (1) Review of The Owl Sacred Pack of the Fox Indians, by Truman Michelson, AJP 43.276–81 (1922).
  (2) The Menomini Language, Proceedings of the Twenty-first International Congress of Americanists 336–43 (The Hague, 1924).
  (3) On the Sound System of Central Algonquian, Lang. 1.130–56 (1925).
  (4) The Word-Stems of Central Algonquian, Festschrift Meinhof 393–402 (Hamburg, 1927).
  (5) Notes on the Fox Language, IJAL 3.219–32 (1924), 4.181–219 (1927).
  (6) A Note on Sound Change, Lang. 5.99–100 (1928).
  (7) The Plains Cree Language, Proceedings of the Twenty-second International Congress of Americanists 427–31 (Rome, 1928).
  (8) Menomini Texts, Publications of the American Ethnological Society, Vol. 12 (New York, 1928).
  (9) Sacred Stories of the Sweet Grass Cree, Bulletin 60, National Museum of Canada (Ottawa, 1930).
  (10) Plains Cree Texts, Publications of the American Ethnological Society, Vol. 16 (New York, 1934).
  (11) Proto-Algonquian -iit- 'Fellow', Lang. 17.292–7 (1941).
  (12) Algonquian, in Linguistic Structures of Native America 85–129 (Viking Fund Publications in Anthropology, Number 6; New York, 1946).

[3] 'A remarkable contribution', says Sturtevant of Bloomfield's Sketch, Lang. 23.314 (1947).

[4] Bloomfield has noted the resemblance to older Germanic several times in conversation but not, so far as I know, in print; in Ref. 5, 4.191, the comparison is rather with Indo-European as a whole. Needless to say, the attempts of Rider T. Sherwin, The Viking and the Red Man (4 vols. to date; New York, 1940–46), to establish a genetic connection between Algonquian and Germanic are entirely misguided.

[5] See fn. 2.

the group. It is our purpose here to list those principles and procedures of historical and comparative linguistics which seem to emerge with especial clarity and force from Bloomfield's Algonquian studies. It is the writer's hope that this listing and discussion will serve to focus more attention on the work dealt with, and to be of some assistance to the person who does undertake the study recommended.[6]

We shall discuss the following points:

(1) Description and history
(2) The evaluation of written records'
(3) The use of phonemic notation
(4) Preliminary internal reconstruction
(5) Assumptions about directions of linguistic change
(6) The assumption of regular phonemic change
(7) The Wörter-und-Sachen technique
(8) Drift
(9) The significance of starred forms
(10) Negative lessons

On each of these there has been, and is, disagreement among those who occupy professional posts in which they purport to deal with language. On each point (save the last) Bloomfield's Algonquian material unambiguously indicates one answer, to the exclusion of the various alternatives that have been proposed.

1. Description and History. There are still extremists who say that descriptive linguistics is balderdash,[7] and a few, equally extreme, who scorn the comparative method in historical linguistics as irrelevant antiquarianism and, at best, guess work.[8] Some of the disagreement is genuine, but some stems simply from the insufficient complexity of our terminology for different types of linguistic operation. In order to see the genuine issue we must clear away the terminological obscurities.

A synchronic analysis describes the speech habits of an individual or a relatively homogeneous group at a particular time.[9] It ignores what interpersonal differences may be known, and makes no mention of changes in habits that take place during the period from which the evidence dates. A contrastive study compares the speech habits of different individuals or groups and tallies the similarities and differences

—regardless of the relative position of the speakers or groups in space or time.[10] A diachronic analysis states the changes in speech habits in a single community from one point in time to a later period. Occasionally one can observe marked personal differences even in a small community, or clear instances of change of habit during a very short span of time; when such observations are included in a monograph which is mainly synchronic, that does not necessitate any change in the definition of 'synchronic', but simply means that the content of the monograph is not purely synchronic. This comment should not be interpreted as an objection to the practice, which is often valuable.[11]

In the gathering of information, for synchronic, contrastive, or diachronic, purposes, there are several different methods. The contact method consists in first-hand observation of the speakers. The philological method consists in the interpretation of written records. The comparative method extrapolates backwards from the earliest evidence available (or the earliest used) from two or more dialects or languages which seem to be related. Between these methods there is no sharp line of demarcation. The field worker, though he uses the contact method, later studies his own notes and in so doing involves himself in a kind of philological method; another linguist may read the notes, or the completed report, of the first, and so places himself in a position somewhat analogous to that of the interpreter of written records which date from earlier generations. The close intertwining of the philological and comparative methods is obvious.[12]

The extraneous sources of argument about 'description' and 'history' stem from the ambiguity in the use of those two terms (or of others used in place of them). 'Description' sometimes refers to synchronic analysis; sometimes to contact method. 'History' sometimes means diachronic analysis,

---

[6] The principles itemized in this paper are by no means intended to constitute a complete canon of historical or comparative linguistics. The choice is based on the nature of the Algonquian material, not on a general analysis of linguistic method.

[7] Classical Philology 38.210–11 (1943), 39.218–22 (1944); also the implications of the review in Lang. 16.216–31 (1940).

[8] Acta Linguistica 2.1–22 (1940–1); IJAL 10.192–3 (1944); and see Robert A. Hall Jr., Bàrtoli's 'Neolinguistica', Lang. 22.273–83 (1946).

[9] The terms 'synchronic' and 'diachronic' date at least from Ferdinand de Saussure, Cours de Linguistique Générale (Lausanne, 1916).

[10] 'Contrastive' is Whorf's proposal (I cannot find the reference), made because the more natural term 'comparative' is already pre-empted for a different technical use. [[I can't find the reference either.]]

[11] Good illustrations of the value of mixed synchronic and diachronic discussion are Ref. 4, 401— which includes also some extremely penetrating remarks on the relation between the synchronic and diachronic points of view—and Bloomfield's paper Literate and Illiterate Speech, American Speech 2.432–9 (1927).

[12] This three-by-three categorization of types of linguistic activity is more general in its application than here indicated: it applies, as a matter of fact, to all the subject-matter of cultural anthropology, of which linguistics is logically a subdivision. This is clearly indicated in Sapir, Time Perspective in Aboriginal American Culture (Ottawa, 1916) [now more accessible in Selected Writings of Edward Sapir..., ed. David G. Mandelbaum, Univ. of California Press, 1949]. There are doubtless some types of fruitful and valid investigation, of language or of culture as a whole, not subsumed in the classification.

sometimes philological or comparative method or both. With the more narrowly defined terms, the logical interrelationships are easy to see:[13]

(a) Synchronic analysis may be based on any of the three methods, or on combinations of them. Synchronic analysis of a language no longer spoken, obviously, cannot involve the contact method; that of a language for which there are no direct records has to be based on the comparative method. In this sense, 'description' is not logically prior to 'history'.

(b) Either diachronic or contrastive analysis involves prior synchronic analysis. In this sense, 'description' is logically prior to 'history'.

(c) The comparative method has to involve comparison of something. The data to which the comparative method is applied consist of bodies of synchronic descriptions of related languages. The assumptions which underlie the comparative method are distilled from diachronic analyses of bodies of synchronic material, all of which are based, in turn, on a method other than the comparative method.[14]

These interrelations are complex. The virtue of Bloomfield's Algonquian studies on this score is that the interrelations not only are perfectly clear to Bloomfield, but are made equally clear to his reader. His Sketch, for example, is at one and the same time all of the following: (1) a brief synchronic outline grammar of four Algonquian languages still extant;[15] (2) a brief synchronic outline grammar of their parent; (3) a contrastive analysis of the four modern languages and the parent language; (4) an outline of the diachronic analysis of the continuum from the parent to each of the modern languages; and (5) a

demonstration of the application of the comparative method to the modern data for the reconstruction of the parent language. The Sketch does not take up these problems one by one, but rather gives a composite picture. A single careful reading produces an accurate and realistic general impression of Algonquian structure. A subsequent reading with special attention to any one of the facets listed above can give more detailed information. In such successive readings, one is never at a loss to know the range of application of each individual statement: it applies just to F, or just to the development of F from PA, or just to PA, or to all the languages, and so on.

Bloomfield's Sketch, then, is a model useful to anyone who faces the task of organizing information about a family of languages into an arrangement that makes synchronic, diachronic, and contrastive sense.

2. The Evaluation of Written Records. The documentary material on which Bloomfield bases his Algonquian analysis is of several types: (1) his own field records of M and C, made with full benefit of phonemic theory; (2) F records from William Jones, a native speaker of F who was trained under Boas and Michelson in phonetics, but not in phonemics;[16] (3) O records from the same person; (4) earlier records by missionaries and traders, without benefit of either phonetics or phonemics, and with English or French as native language, but with the advantage of long residence with the Indians and constant practical use of the languages. Since Bloomfield's first publications, others trained under him or within his sphere of influence have recorded F and O,[17] and Bloomfield himself has recorded O. We thus have a check on the accuracy of older reports, except for the negligible extent to which speech patterns may have changed between missionary times and the present.

Jones's F materials are overloaded with superfluous diacritics, indicating evanescent distinctions or subphonemic differences, but in general no phonemic contrast is omitted. O materials from the same observer have the same unnecessary indication of minutiae, but in addition obscure certain phonemic contrasts which are of considerable comparative importance — for example, the contrast between sk and šk. Certainly there is a relationship between these facts and Jones's background. F does not have the contrast sk : šk; it is not surprising that as a native speaker of F, Jones missed the contrast when

---

[13] The methodological points or 'principles' drawn from the discussion are lettered serially through the paper, from (a) to (p).

[14] That is, we derive our notions of linguistic change in the first instance from the history of those languages, such as English, French, and German, for which there is documentary evidence over a considerable span of time. We then make a comparative analysis of some group of languages whose common ancestor is known to us independently — for example, Romance — assuming the kinds of linguistic change discovered by the first operation, and comparing our reconstruction with the documentary evidence for the parent. Since our inverted predictions in such cases have a considerable degree of accuracy, we feel confident of at least statistically accurate results when the same comparative method is applied to a group of languages for whose parent there is no other evidence. It is true that linguistic science in the 19th century did not follow this course in its chronological development; but this does not invalidate the logical statement. Until the logical interrelationships had clearly emerged, the statements of historical linguistics were somewhat more tentative than afterwards.

[15] That is, Fox (F), Cree (C), Menomini (M), and Ojibwa (O). The abbreviations indicated will be used in the rest of this paper, together with 'PA' for Proto-Algonquian, the reconstructed parent (but see §10).

[16] For references see the Sketch. Later contributions by Michelson use approximately the same notation. It is not clear whether this notation was a joint product of Jones and Michelson, or was worked out by one and passed on to the other.

[17] F: at least J M. Cowan, Carl F. Voegelin, and the present writer; O: the latter two, J. A. Geary (other dialects), F. T. Siebert Jr., and — in the summers when O was the language studied in the field-methods course at the Linguistic Institute — a good many others.

listening to the rather similar O. His phonetic training, without phonemics, led to the overly minute recording of what he had happened to be trained to hear; his native control of F prevented omission of contrasts that were relevant there.[18]

As might be expected, the missionary records are much less satisfactory. Some of them consistently fail to indicate such important features as vowel length; some of them write subphonemic distinctions heard at one time or another, because those distinctions were present phonemically in French or in English; sometimes certain contrasts are recorded irregularly. As a result of the last, when one desires to check on some feature of a particular word, one often finds that the missionary recording is unreliable on that point.[19]

We may distil from this the following methodological observations:

(d) The extent to which one can use written records made by an untrained person can only be determined by direct observation of the language by a trained person. For a language no longer spoken, this is of course impossible.

(e) When a direct check is impossible, records made by a native speaker are more trustworthy than those made by a foreigner; those made by a person with some training (as Jones's training in phonetics to the exclusion of phonemics) are more trustworthy than those from a person with no training at all; obviously, records from a person with long practical contact, other things being equal, are more trustworthy than those from a casual passer-by.

3. The Use of Phonemic Notation. If one compares Bloomfield's Sketch with a recent paper by Geary[20] one difference is striking. All forms cited in Bloomfield's paper are phonemicized, and the choice of symbols for each language is such as to render the switch from one language to another as easy as possible for the reader. Geary could not validly do this; for his object was to cull from all sources, including

the missionary records, forms which are evidence for a particular PA consonant cluster; of necessity he cites each form from an older record in the graphic shape in which it was found. Anyone can read Bloomfield; only an Algonquianist can really read Geary.

Further scrutiny of these two papers, and of some of the older records, shows that the close relationship of the Algonquian languages is immediately apparent from the missionary records; but it would be almost impossible to attempt the reconstruction of PA on the basis of the missionary records alone. On the other hand, once something is known of the structure of PA many of the missionary records can be used, though sometimes with uncertainty, to find additional cases of this or that correspondence.

This further supports points (d) and (e), and suggests the following:

(f) Written records are a means to an end, and there is no justification for holding them in high esteem, or even in reverence (as is sometimes the case) except as indirect evidence for what one is trying to discover.[21]

(g) When his only evidence consists of written records, the analyst should attempt a phonemic interpretation of the material. He can achieve accuracy in his synchronic description, in his diachronic deductions, and in his use of the material for comparative purposes, only to the extent that the phonemic interpretation of the written records is feasible without ambiguity.[22] Furthermore, he should make his phonemic interpretation clearly recognizable to his readers, by including for every form cited, explicitly or by implication, a possible phonemicization.[23] Failure to do the former impairs his own results; failure to do the latter hampers his readers.

Some of the undue esteem in which written records are held has probably been supported by the following additional principle, which is not deducible from Bloomfield's Sketch, but does appear in some of his earlier writings and quite clearly in Geary's paper:

(h) When the interpretation of written records cannot be completely free from ambiguity, the graphic shape actually occurrent in the source should be included along with the attempted phonemicization—or, when more convenient, a transliteration of the original graphic shape. The reader is then in the best possible position to re-examine the evidence and draw his own conclusions.

---

[18] It would be tempting to generalize as follows. If a native speaker of a language is trained in phonetics in such a way that he will hear, in any language, at least all those contrasts which are distinctive for his own speech, and will have the symbols easily at hand to record them, he will, in recording his own language, sometimes include subphonemic contrasts, but will never omit contrasts that count. But this statement is far from obviously true. Suggestions of this kind were made by Sapir in Sound Patterns in Language, Lang. 1.37–51 (1925) ((19)), and more elaborately in La réalité psychologique des phonèmes, Journal de Psychologie 30.247–65 (1933) [see now Selected Writings..., op. cit. in fn. 12 here, for the original English of this], but Twaddell's discussion, On Defining the Phoneme 8–16 ((56–9)) (LSA Monograph 16 [1935]), raises serious doubts.

[19] Some such cases are discussed in J. A. Geary, Proto-Algonquian çk: Further Examples, Lang. 17.304–10 (1941).

[20] See fn. 19.

[21] Lang. 22.256 (1946); French Review 17.168–70 (1944).

[22] Disagreements about methods of phonemicization are another matter. If 'phonemic solutions' are non-unique, as seems likely to me at the present moment, any alternative one will do. There is a gain in clarity and simplicity if each of a set of languages to be compared is phonemicized by the same principles, but if this is not done reconstruction is still perfectly feasible. Against phonemics of any kind: Archivio Glottologico Italiano 31.159 (1940)—one instance of many.

[23] Bloomfield, Language §5.10 (New York, 1933).

4. Preliminary Internal Reconstruction. The statement made above that in Bloomfield's Sketch all forms are phonemicized now has to be modified. His notation for O, and possibly for M and F, deviates from the phonemic 'ideal' in being somewhat more than phonemic.

In Southern O occur three varieties of vowels: long /ii ee aa oo/, short /i a o/, and ultra-short /ə u/. Within the limits of a word, the distribution of short and ultra-short vowels is almost, but not quite, predictable in terms of environment. Since the predictability is not complete, the distinction is phonemic: one must write /i a o/ and /ə u/ as they are heard. Bloomfield does not do so: he writes only ii ee aa oo and i a o, e.g. mittik instead of məttik 'tree'. For most Southern O dialects, one cannot tell whether the vowel in the first syllable—an ultra-short one—is /i/ or /a/, and phonemically one would have to use a special symbol /ə/; the same symbol would have to be used in a completely phonemic transcription of what Bloomfield transcribes as akkikk 'kettle', rather than the initial a of that form. O itself, and the diachronic analysis of the continuum from PA to O, are treated by Bloomfield in terms of this normalized notation. Can this procedure be justified?

The answer is yes. Bloomfield's notation is based on the preliminary internal reconstruction[24] of an O dialect-type that must have preceded the current dialects by only a relatively short period of time. The reconstruction is internal, not based on comparison of dialects, since the earlier stage can be postulated with validity on the basis of the data for any one dialect. If one compares phonemic /məttik/ 'tree' with /nəmittəkoom/ 'my tree', and /əkkikk/ 'kettle' with /nəntakkəkkoom/ 'my kettle', one observes that /ə/ alternates (under statable conditions of word-rhythm) with both /i/ and /a/. There are a few cases in which no larger form can be found of the right rhythmic pattern to determine whether the alternation is with /i/ or with /a/, and in most of the dialects there are a few cases in which ultra-short vowels have disappeared altogether. Even in a synchronic description of O, however, the restoration of /i/ and /a/ rather than /ə/ in all such cases, with statements on the reduction of short vowels in words of each rhythmic pattern, is a necessary step for efficient treatment. One's working notation then becomes morphophonemic rather than purely phonemic; from the graphs /mittik/, /nimittikoom/, /akkikk/, /nintakkikkoom/, and the statements, one can infer the actual phonemic shape with very little difficulty.

In other words, what Bloomfield does in the case of O is to use a morphophonemically regularized notation instead of a straight phonemic transcription.

There is evidence of such regularization in M and F too. F forms are given with intervocalic /w/ and /y/, which are morphophonemically correct and which must have been phonemically correct in a slightly earlier stage, rather than with the curious alternation and evanescence that those morphophonemes now exhibit.[25] M is cited with five short and five long vowels, though Bloomfield himself has said that in actual pronunciation the three-way distinction of /i/ : /e/ : /ɛ/ is partly obscured.[26]

We deduce the following principle:

(i) Before comparative analysis is undertaken, each body of synchronic data should be examined carefully to see whether there are not internal clues, mainly morphophonemic, to the structure of the language at a slightly earlier stage. When there are, any possible internal reconstruction should be undertaken, since it will dispose of later innovations in each language, getting them out of the way for a clearer view of the deeper time-perspective of external comparison.

5. Assumptions about Directions of Linguistic Change. Bloomfield's description of Proto-Algonquian reveals it as a language of approximately the same degree of complexity as any one of the modern languages. Each of the modern languages has retained some of the features of the parent, lost some, and developed some new ones. F has the vocalic system of PA; C and O have one vowel fewer than PA; M has two more. The number of individual consonants in PA (excluding first members of clusters, §9) is greater than in any of the modern languages; it seems highly probable, however, that θ and s, and similarly t and č, which stand in close morphophonemic relation in PA, were at a slightly earlier stage allophones of single phonemes—perhaps, indeed, this was true even in PA times. The larger number of consonants in PA, then, was a temporary matter, the result of certain phonemic and analogic changes, and the number was later reduced in each line of development. The modal systems of verbs in the daughter languages correlate exactly only in a few cases. One suspects that some of the modes present in PA have split in some of the modern languages, and have been lost in others; certainly the

---

[24] H. M. Hoenigswald, Internal Reconstruction, SIL 2.78–87 (1944); Sound Change and Linguistic Structure, Lang. 22.138–43 (1946) ((139)).

[25] Obvious from Jones's texts; observed by the present writer in the Kickapoo and Sauk dialects of Fox.

[26] Ref. 8, xiv: 'The texts are here recorded as they struck my ear. Analysis shows that this record (and therefore, if I heard aright, the actual pronunciation) largely obscures the distinction between three short front-vowel phonemes, which here appear as i and e.' Since Bloomfield became a fluent speaker of Menomini (a fact which he does not admit, but which is fairly obvious from his discussions), his recording is probably accurate. Nowadays we would cast his statement in the terminology of morphophonemics rather than phonemics, but the fact stated would not be altered.

total number of modes in PA did not exceed the rather large number in present-day F.[27]

(j) In undertaking a reconstruction, there is no justification for any of the following a-priori assumptions: (1) that the parent language was simpler than the descendants; (2) that it was more complex than the descendants; or (3) that it manifested about the same degree of complexity as the descendants.

The first of these a-priori assumptions is the old theory of the 'primitiveness' of 'early' language, and of contemporary languages spoken by 'simple' peoples.[28] The second is the inversion of the first brought about primarily by Jespersen's discussion.[29] More concrete suggestions, akin to one or the other, are also found.[30] All such theories derive from a hope which a hundred years ago was legitimate: that comparative linguistics might in time push our perspective on the history of language appreciably nearer the beginnings of human speech. Now that we realize how old human speech is, and what a scratch on the surface of that depth is our deepest reconstruction, the hope must be abandoned.

Bloomfield's PA reconstruction speaks not only against assumptions (1) and (2), but against any a-priori assumption of this kind whatsoever. In his paper of 1925 (Ref. 3), Bloomfield postulated two more vowels and one more consonant for PA than are included in the Sketch. Since then he has discovered the analogical bases, in certain of the individual languages, for the complications that had earlier led him to assume these additional phonemes. The first, more complex system was not set up because Bloomfield thought than an older language 'should be' more complex; nor did he later simplify the picture through any conviction that an older language 'should not be' more complex. In each case the assumed degree of complexity was simply an inference from the facts known about the modern languages.

6. The Assumption of Regular Phonemic Change. One story in the slow development of our understanding of PA is worth telling in detail, even though it is already perhaps the most generally known phase of Algonquian linguistics.

In his Sound System (Ref. 3) Bloomfield postulated the PA cluster çk (F O šk, C M hk) on very slim evidence. There was only one stem, meaning 'red', to be found which showed just this correspondence in the extant languages, and each of those languages had the cluster in question also as a reflex of one or more other PA clusters. Yet there seemed to be no analogical basis in any of the languages whereby a reconstruction could be made with a better attested PA cluster, and borrowing seemed unlikely in view of the meaning of the stem. There were a few other sets of apparently related words showing unique correspondences of clusters—'spoon' has F C hk, O kk, as though from PA hk, but M has sk instead of the hk which would arise from the latter. But these other cases are in morphologically isolated words, whereas the PA stem 'red' underlies many derivatives in every language.

A year or so later, it was discovered that Swampy Cree, a dialect from which records had not earlier been available, had in words containing this stem not hk but htk, a cluster not found in Swampy Cree as the reflex of any other PA cluster so far set up. Here was not merely an exceptional correspondence between usual clusters, but an extant dialect in which the postulated PA cluster is kept separate from all others. Bloomfield published a note giving this as evidence for the productivity of the assumption of regular phonemic change.[31] Sapir cited the case, together with a similar one from his own Athabascan work, in an article on the comparative method as one of the methods of social science.[32]

But the story did not end there. New investigators discovered that Jones had consistently misheard the O forms: the O words with this stem have sk, not šk, and this sk is not found as a reflex of any other PA cluster.[33] Swampy Cree no longer stood as the only extant dialect to keep PA çk separate; O was now known to do so too. Geary examined the missionary sources and discovered a number of other cases of the same correspondence, so that the stem for 'red' was no longer isolated—even though PA çk still seemed to be relatively rare. In his Sketch, Bloomfield includes a footnote: 'The fuss and trouble behind my note in Language [see above]...would have been avoided if I had listened to O, which plainly distinguishes sk (< PA çk) from šk (< PA šk); instead, I depended on printed records which failed to show the distinction.'[34]

---

[27] Sketch §33.

[28] Max Müller's myth of speakers with vocabularies of only a few hundred words is related. W. von Humboldt, Die Verschiedenheit des menschlichen Sprachbaues §19, gives three stages in the history of language: 'growth' before IE, a 'state of perfection' in IE, and 'decay' since then; for other early references see Lang. 12.101 (1936) and Italica 18.145–54 (1941). Later survivals of these older notions: the subject of review in Lang. 11.154–60 (1935); Emérita 3.257–76 (1935), esp. 272, 274–5; Alf Sommerfelt, La langue et la société (Oslo, 1938).

[29] Otto Jespersen, Progress in Language (London, 1894); cf. also his Efficiency in Linguistic Change (Copenhagen, 1941), and the review in Lang. 17.350–3 (1941). Bernhard Karlgren, in reconstructing ancient and archaic Chinese, posits extremely complex phonological structure for those stages of Chinese, and seems (though without explicit reference) to justify this greater complexity for the older stage in terms of Jespersen's theory; see his Philology and Ancient China, esp. 16–18 (Oslo, 1926).

[30] See more recent references in fn. 28.

[31] Ref. 6.

[32] Edward Sapir, The Concept of Phonetic Law as Tested in Primitive Languages by Leonard Bloomfield, Methods in Social Science 297–306 (ed. Stuart A. Rice; Chicago, 1931). Also Bloomfield, Language §20.8 (end).

[33] See fn. 17, and Geary, loc. cit.   [34] Sketch, fn. 10.

It should be clear that the wording of Bloomfield's note detracts in no way from the importance of the sequence of events outlined above as evidence for the productivity of the assumption we are discussing. After the publication of the Sound System, events might conceivably have taken a different turn. Instead of discovering additional cases of the same correspondence, Jones's error, and the special reflex in Swampy Cree, Algonquianists might have found an analogical basis or an opportunity for borrowing whereby PA çk could be eliminated. This turn of events would also have proved the fruitfulness of the assumption.

For what we mean in this case by 'productivity' or 'fruitfulness' is just what Bloomfield states in his book Language (§20.5): residual forms, not accounted for at a particular stage in the history of the reconstruction of a particular parent language either by well-attested sound change or by analogical formations or borrowing, or accounted for by postulated changes for which there is very little evidence—such residual forms stimulate further investigation. As a basis for further investigation, the linguist sets up hypotheses to explain what might have been the past history of certain forms. Many such hypotheses remain unproved, because additional investigation reveals no additional evidence; others are disproved by new evidence that is uncovered. But some of them are proved right. Slowly but surely the stock of residual forms is reduced, though it may never be exhausted. The contrary fundamental assumption—that sound changes proceed at random—produces nothing at all, because there are never any problems: given any form that won't fit the sound changes so far observed, one simply assumes a sporadic change of a different sort.

(k) We must assume regularity of phonemic change.

7. The Wörter-und-Sachen Technique.[35] Bloomfield reconstructs PA paaškesikani 'gun' and eškoteewaapoowi 'whisky', both on the basis of perfectly normal correspondences between whole words in the extant languages. The items named by these terms, of course, are post-Columbian. The forms are compound; Bloomfield says in a footnote to the first that 'here, as in some other examples, the meaning is modern, but the habit of formation is old.'[36]

If only this is to be ascribed to pre-Columbian times, then each of the modern languages concerned has coined new terms for the new items of material culture, using identical (cognate) morphemes according to identical patterns of formation, in such a way that the phonemic correspondences between the whole words are perfect. But it might also be that the terms themselves date from PA times, and that since the introduction of whisky and guns by Europeans the semantic shifts have been parallel in the va-

35 Bloomfield, Language §18.14, and his references.
36 Sketch, fn. 13.

rious languages. Or, as European influence spread, the forms may have been invented by the speakers of one language and then borrowed by loan-translation into the other languages.[37]

It does not matter, for our present purpose, which of these alternatives is true. The fact that from well-attested modern forms one can reconstruct PA forms with meanings that were obviously impossible for PA is a clear indication of danger in the Wörter-und-Sachen technique. We deduce the following composite principle:

(1) Attempts to infer the culture of the speakers of a reconstructed parent language wholly from the forms and meanings of the daughter languages are always dangerous. The danger is less, though probably still considerable, if the forms compared are morphologically simple than if they are compounds.

8. Drift. There are two versions of the theory of drift. One is almost mystical: in a particular linguistic continuum the same sound shifts may happen over and over again; there is something in the genius of the language which leads to these sound shifts rather than to others.[38] The other is realistic, and fairly simple: when a speech community has split, inherited speech habits are for a while fairly similar, and may lead to the independent analogical development of forms which look like inherited cognates. If at a later date the descendant languages are compared with a view to reconstruction of the parent, some such pseudo-cognates may be falsely ascribed to the parent language.[39] The Algonquian words for 'gun' and 'whisky', in all probability, are illustrations of this, though we cannot be absolutely sure.

(m) Any individual reconstructed form is suspect because of the possible influence of drift (in the second sense). In comparative linguistics one may achieve only statistical accuracy.

9. The Significance of Starred Forms. There have been two theories of reconstructed forms.[40] The so-

37 The English expression fire-water may be a loan-translation from Algonquian; if the former is older, then one or more Algonquian languages may have loan-translated the English.
38 E. Prokosch, A Comparative Germanic Grammar, esp. 34 ff. (Philadelphia, 1939).
39 The discussion in Sapir's Language, chapters 7–8 (New York, 1921), is sufficiently broad to justify (apparently) either interpretation; for the realistic theory, see 184–5 in particular.
40 Cogently discussed by C. D. Buck, Some Questions of Practice in the Notation of Reconstructed IE Forms, Lang. 2.99–107 (1926). Buck says (102): the purpose of reconstructions 'is not to furnish a picture of the parent speech for its own sake, but as a background of the historical relations.' This is in part an answer to the charge of 'irrelevant antiquarianism' sometimes levelled at the comparative method; even so, we should say that 'a picture of the parent speech for its own sake', to the degree attainable, is also a legitimate aim.

called 'realistic' theory holds that in reconstructing the phonemic pattern of a parent language, one should try to arrive at a set of phonemes bearing a relation to each other of the kind that is known to exist in languages more directly observed. The 'formula' theory, on the other hand, holds that reconstructions are simply short notations representing sets of correspondences.

Bloomfield's Algonquian reconstructions show clearly the circumstances under which the first practice is possible, and those under which the second is necessary. The vowel system postulated for PA is certainly phonemically realistic, being identical with that of one modern language, F. The fundamental consonant system is also: p t č (possibly an allophone of t) k s θ š (possibly an allophone of θ) h l m n w y (the last two possibly allophones respectively of o and i). Of these, l m n (w y) were in all probability voiced; the others may have been voiced or voiceless, or perhaps were sometimes one and sometimes the other, without phonemic distinction.[41] θ may have been a voiceless lateral rather than an interdental spirant, or, again, perhaps both, depending on dialect or on environment.[42] The phonetic details are naturally obscure; it is the phonemic pattern which we claim to be 'realistic'.[43] The only type of doubt which could be raised as to the status of these elements as the actual phonemes of PA would be purely logistic: if, for example, every daughter language had, independently, changed PA m to n and PA n to m, no one could be the wiser. One could even claim that such a change would be subphonemic; in any case such possibilities need not disturb us.

When it comes to medial clusters, the situation is different. Medial clusters consist of two members; the second is always clearly identifiable as one of the ordinary consonants; but the multiplicity of correspondences requires the postulation of a somewhat larger number of purely arbitrary elements as prior members.[44] Thirty-one different medial clusters are attested; no one of them has identical reflexes in all four of the modern languages.[45]

In this case all one can do is to choose for the prior members a set of symbols which will have, if possible, some mnemonic value; e.g. PA mp nt nč

nk ns nš nθ nl for clusters which in O have a nasal as first element, especially since such clusters in O occur only as reflexes of this set in PA.

Similarly, instead of writing çk for the PA cluster which gives F šk, C M hk, O sk, one could write sk, which is not otherwise used. It may well be that the PA clusters customarily written mp, nt, etc. actually had a nasal as first element. It may also be that PA çk was phonemically sk, the first element being phonemically identical with the independently occurring PA s. But the use of these notations for mnemonic reasons is not evidence for such a phonemic interpretation: one may attain a spurious appearance of realism, but the actual phonemic nature of the first members of the clusters is still as obscure as before.

That the number of medial clusters in PA was larger than the number in any descendant language is surprising only to one who is not familiar with aspects of Algonquian linguistics other than phonology. In most of the modern languages there is a sandhi habit whereby an element ending in a consonant, when due to be followed in the same word by one beginning with a consonant, is separated therefrom by a non-morphemic i.[46] This habit existed in PA times, but was then apparently rather new. The new habit prevented the re-formation of many clusters that had formerly existed; but compounds surviving from an earlier stage retained the more complex consonantism. The trend towards simplification of the cluster system was a characteristic of PA which continued in the various separate dialects after their split, but the details varied from one dialect to another. Some of the pre-PA compounds are reconstructible from the modern languages, giving an essential clue to the statements just made; most, however, remain obscure.[47]

Thus it is quite possible that Algonquian research may in time produce evidence that will make the interpretation of the prior members of PA consonant clusters less purely algebraic. Only a deeper time-perspective, achieved by more detailed comparisons with Algonquian languages not of the Central Algonquian type, can do this. In the meantime, to underscore the point, 'realism' in this phase of the reconstruction of PA can only be spurious.

(n) Reconstruction should be phonemically realistic whenever possible.

(o) When realistic reconstruction is not possible, arbitrary indices of correspondences must be used. The fact that they are arbitrary, and the reasons which necessitate this arbitrariness, should be clearly stated. This practice will prevent a spurious impression of realism on the reader, and will obviate futile speculation on his part as to what the arbitrarily symbolized elements may 'really' have been.

---

41 Sketch, §6.

42 Loc. cit.

43 In several recent papers (Lang. 20.84–6 [1944], 23.34–42 [1947]), Herbert Penzl has demonstrated, in connection with problems of early English, the difference between phonemic realism and what might be meant by phonetic realism.

44 Sketch, §7.

45 Since the phonemic systems of the modern languages are different, 'identical' must be interpreted relatively: since F and O š and k are elements in differing sets of contrasts, F šk and O šk are not in any absolute sense 'identical'.

46 Sketch, §16.

47 Sketch, §17.

10. <u>Negative Lessons</u>. This paper could not serve its purpose fully without mentioning a few points on which, in the present writer's opinion, Bloomfield's Sketch can be misleading.

(1) Bloomfield labels his reconstructed prototype 'Proto-Algonquian'. It is based mainly on the comparison of F, C, M, and O; eastern Algonquian and the three groups of Plains languages are not often brought into the picture. Indeed, it would be difficult to include more mention of them in the present state of our knowledge. In feeling that the PA reconstructed in his Sketch will take care of the Plains languages, Bloomfield gives Michelson's work in the comparative analysis of the latter languages more credit than it deserves.[48] The course of wisdom for the reader of Bloomfield's Sketch is to replace 'PA' everywhere by 'PCA', standing for 'Proto-<u>Central</u>-Algonquian', and to withhold judgment on the status of the eastern and Plains languages until a good deal more of descriptive and comparative work has been done.

(2) Bloomfield says, 'before syllabic vowels, PA i, o are nonsyllabic; we write y, w.'[49] The phonemic status of y and w is another point on which judgment is best reserved. Bloomfield's notation (with all four symbols i o y w) is good; his statement seems hasty.

(3) Bloomfield cites Penobscot forms from Siebert, following Siebert's orthography except that accent marks are omitted. This conceals the fact that a number of the eastern languages of the family have an accentual system, more or less complex but definitely phonemic; these accentual systems have to be taken care of in the reconstruction of anything that can be called Proto-Algonquian. Exact citation of Siebert's forms, including the accent marks (perhaps with a footnote), would have been more in line with the general principles on which Bloomfield's work is based.

Point (3) turns on the discussion of §2 and §3 in this paper. Point (2) is connected with the content of §9. From point (1) we derive our last principle:

(p) A parent language reconstructed from the comparison of a certain set of daughter languages can be regarded as the parent only of the languages so used. Information from languages not previously used may change the reconstruction, deepen the time-perspective with a new reconstruction of an earlier stage, or demonstrate that the reconstruction already made is capable of handling the new data also.[50]

<u>Conclusion</u>. The sixteen principles which have been listed in the course of our discussion are not new or startling; indeed, by this time each of them ought to be so generally agreed upon that any mention of them, save in the most elementary textbooks of linguistics, would be ridiculous. We have unhappily not yet reached such uniformity of opinion about fundamentals. Yet if, for any one of the sixteen, Bloomfield's Algonquian evidence stood alone—if there were no comparative Germanic, comparative Romance, comparative Indo-European, comparative Semitic, and so on—that isolated support for the principle would still be persuasively solid.

[48] Sketch, §2, referring to T. Michelson, Phonetic Shifts in Algonquian Languages, IJAL 8.131–71 (1935). The implication here is not that Michelson's study is not 'brilliant', as Bloomfield terms it, but that the synchronic information on Plains Algonquian available to Michelson was unsatisfactory.

[49] Sketch, §4.

[50] Thus Potawatomi is probably historically analyzable on the basis of Bloomfield's P(C)A without modification thereof (C. F. Hockett, The Position of Potawatomi in Central Algonkian, Papers of the Michigan Academy of Sciences, Arts, and Letters 28.537–42 [1942]); but Delaware is probably not (C. F. Voegelin, Proto-Algonquian Consonant Clusters in Delaware, Lang. 17.143–7 [1941]).

THE PRINCIPAL STEP IN COMPARATIVE GRAMMAR

HENRY M. HOENIGSWALD
Language 26.357–64—1950

[Reconstruction by the comparative method (as distinct from internal reconstruction based on alternations between phonemes in a paradigm) is essentially a problem in phonemics, in which the place of allophones is taken by sets of sound correspondences that are partially alike (share one component) and in complementary distribution. The principle is illustrated by the IE dental and labial stops as reconstructed from Sanskrit and Germanic, by IE *s in Greek and Latin, and by the IE aspirates in Italic.]

Theorists of comparative grammar have concerned themselves a great deal with the reality of our reconstructions: whether they are phonetically concrete and fixed in time and space, or merely formulas for observed correspondences, lacking chronological depth. The question is, of course, important. But surprisingly little has been done about a much humbler task, namely that of rigorously describing the procedure used in reconstruction. The reason is no doubt that the matter has been considered too humble even to require formulation. The great tradition in comparative linguistics is teaching by example: if the examples are taken from languages with which the student is familiar because he is also a student of texts, they can be relied upon to build up a sound feeling for the workings of the comparative method. There is much to be said for this pedagogical approach, and even more against mere discussion of methodology as contrasted with the development of new methods implicit in the treatment of concrete new problems as they arise. On the other hand, generalizations are essential, both in discussing our science with investigators from other fields and, within our own domain, in weighing the merits of alternative reconstructions. Characteristically, some of the best efforts to put reconstructive procedures into words are found in polemic writings, where criteria are needed to prove oneself right and one's opponent wrong.

We assume that when two or more languages are compared (in the technical sense) the initial hypothesis, namely that of genetic relationship, has been made, and lists of corresponding morphemes or longer forms have been drawn up. We also assume that the task of weeding out material which is not directly inherited has somehow been accomplished. Some of the procedures used to this end are well known. Thus, in discarding analogical new formations one follows, roughly, a hierarchy of trustworthiness in which phonemes in morphologically isolated forms come first; then phonemes in paradigms where they alternate with other phonemes (because many alternations result from conditioned sound change); and finally phonemes in regular paradigms (because the regularity may be due to leveling). Or, to guard against the effects of secondary developments in daughter languages, we may refer to Meillet's rule that in reconstructing the vocabulary of a proto-language we need the testimony of three, rather than two, independent witnesses.[1] For many other purposes, however, reconstruction from more than two witnesses may well be viewed as a mere extension of the fundamental operation involving only two.

From the material thus restricted, we abstract sets of correspondences. Considering, for instance, (Vedic) Sanskrit and Germanic, we find a great many sets; among them are the following:[2]

	1	2	3	4	5	6	7	8	9	10	11	12
Sanskrit:	t	t	t	d	d	dh	p	p	p	b	b	bh
Germanic:	t	d	þ	d	t	d	p	b	f	b	p	b

Examples: 1 ásti : ist 'is'; 2 pitár- : fadar 'father'; 3 bhrátar- : broþar 'brother'; 4 dehí- 'wall' : deigan 'knead'; 5 véda : wait 'I know'; 6 mádhya- : midjis 'middle'; 7 spáç- 'watcher' : OHG spehōn 'look out'; 8 lip- '(stick,) smear' : bi-leiban '(stick,) stay'; 9 see 2; 10 bódhati 'awakes, is attentive' : ana-biudan 'bid, charge with'; 11 rámbate 'hangs down' : MG lampen 'droop'; 12 see 3.

---

[1] Introduction à l'étude comparative des langues indo-européennes[5] 340 (Paris, 1922).

[2] Germanic forms quoted are Gothic unless otherwise identified; with respect to the crucial features, the dialects used agree among themselves and with proto-Germanic. The list is in no way exhaustive: it does not include Skt. t = Gmc. s (in clusters from IE t before t) or any reflex of the IE voiceless aspirates; nor does it include sets that involve Gothic specifically, such as where Gmc. b has been unvoiced to f in Gothic.

The components of the various sets are phonemes, obtained by descriptive analysis of phonetic records in the case of living languages or by interpretation of written sources in the case of dead languages. Since alphabet records are often in effect phonemic, we are mostly in the dark about subphonemic differences in earlier stages of a language. In the light of the discussion below, such knowledge, where we have it, may be helpful, though perhaps never crucial. For instance, it is helpful to know that the allophones of Gmc. b were spirants in the positions where set 8 occurs.

The sets are now classified according to the relations that exist between them. There are two criteria. First, certain sets are partially alike in that they share either their Sanskrit component (e.g. 2 and 3) or their Germanic component (e.g. 2 and 4). Second, certain sets are so distributed with respect to the sets which precede and follow them in the etymologies considered that they occur only in mutually exclusive environments (e.g. 2 after Skt. unaccented vowel and Gmc. vowel, 3 after Skt. accented vowel and Gmc. vowel or after pause in both languages, but not conversely), while other sets are found to be in contrast with each other in at least one environment (e.g. 3 and 9: both, say, after pause and before r, as in tráyas : þreis 'three', pra- 'fore' : fra- prefix).

The following sets are partially alike:

1	2	3						share Skt. t
			4	5				share Skt. d
					7 8 9			share Skt. p
						10 11		share Skt. b
	2		4		6			share Gmc. d
						8	10 12	share Gmc. b
1				5				share Gmc. t
					7		11	share Gmc. p

Only some of these partially like sets, however, are taken to be continuations of one and the same phoneme of the proto-language. Thus, 4 and 6 are thought to derive from one IE phoneme, written *dh, which remained a single phoneme (d) in Germanic, but split in Sanskrit, by conditioned sound change, into two phonemes (d if the following syllable begins with an aspirate, otherwise dh). On the other hand, 2 and 6, though they share Gmc. d, are interpreted as representing two different IE phonemes, written *t and *dh, of which the first was affected in Germanic by a conditioned sound change in such a way that some of its occurrences merged with the second. In other words, although sets 2, 4, and 6 all share Gmc. d and are different only in their Skt. members, the difference between 4 and 6 is taken to be a recent development while the difference between 2 and 6 is taken to be original. (The relation between 2 and 4 will be dealt with later.)

What is it that enables us to infer these particular historical events? Clearly it is the manner in which the sets are distributed in our comparative material. Set 4 (Skt. d = Gmc. d) occurs when the next syllable begins with Skt. h = Gmc. g, Skt. dh = Gmc. d, or a few other sets; set 6 (Skt. dh = Gmc. d) does not occur in these environments. Set 2 (Skt. t = Gmc. d) occurs only after Skt. unaccented vowel = Gmc. vowel with or without certain consonants intervening; set 6 occurs in this environment also, as well as in others.[3]

[3] Of course, IE was not reconstructed from Vedic Sanskrit and Germanic alone. Actually, scholars made use of the fact that the other major IE languages are apt to show one and the same phoneme

These examples illustrate a fundamental assumption of comparative grammar: partially like sets occurring in mutually exclusive environments are taken to be continuations of one and the same phoneme of the proto-language.[4] The assumption has one important corollary: if, after the reconstruction has been made, we describe the relations between the phonemes of the proto-language and those of only one of the two or more daughter languages (ignoring the rest), our statements constitute the historical phonology of this language in terms of sound changes. Examples can be found in the preceding paragraphs.

Possible applications of our assumption may, however, be in conflict. Let us examine the entire table of partially like sets (given above) for the distribution of the sets in various environments. Sets 4 and 5, as well as 10 and 11, are in contrast; for in the few surroundings where 4 and 10 are found (before h = g, dh = d, and a few other sets in the following syllable), 5 and 11 occur also. The same is true, as has been shown, for sets 2 and 6, and equally for sets 8 and 12, whose distribution is parallel to that of 2 and 6. No contrast can be established between any other partially like sets: they are all more or less obviously in complementary distribution. This leaves the following choices. Set 1 may be grouped together with 3 (and possibly 2; see the next statement), which would amount to reconstructing a single source for all the occurrences of Skt. 5; but also with 5, which is one of the sources of Gmc. t. Set 2 may be grouped with 1 and 3 (all sharing Skt. t), but also with 4, though not with 6 (both Skt. d). Set 3 is grouped with 1 and perhaps 2 (see above). Set 4 cannot, as we have seen, be grouped with 5 (Skt. d), hence it can only be grouped with 6 or perhaps 2 (Gmc. d). Set 5 can only belong with 1 (Gmc. t), provided 1 is not rather linked with 3 (and 2), in which case 5 would stand alone. Set 6 goes with 4, but not with 2. The relationships among sets 7–12 are parallel to those among sets 1–6; in what follows sets 7–12 will not be specially noted.

in 4 and 6 (not Greek, which has, roughly, t t t t d th from 1 to 6; see note 6 below) but two different ones in 2 and 6. Still, such multilateral comparison may be viewed as a system of bilateral ones. This is important since it becomes increasingly clear (and not only for Romance; see R. A. Hall Jr., Lang. 26. 24 ((313))) that some of the well-known difficulties about the setting up of family relations between languages disappear as soon as these relationships are interpreted in terms of successive bifurcation rather than simultaneous, multiple split.

[4] In terms of surrounding sets. Instances where two partially like sets differ in language A, but the environments appear as mutually exclusive only because they are different in language B, are the particular triumphs of the comparative method. Sets 2 and 3 differ only in Germanic, under conditions that are revealed only in Vedic Sanskrit (and, if we compare Germanic with other IE languages, only where the IE accent has left direct traces, as in Greek); hence the startling effect of Verner's discovery.

The principal criterion to decide among these choices is economy. If we were not concerned with economy, we could be content with reconstructing as many phonemes for the proto-language as there are sets of corresponding phonemes in the daughter languages—a frequently criticized flaw in poor comparative work. Examining the possibilities, we find that two different choices will each result in three reconstructed phonemes for sets 1–6 (and three more for 7–12); no choice will yield fewer than three, and several others will yield more. The two possibilities of grouping sets as reflexes of only three phonemes in the proto-language are these: either 1 and 5, 2 and 3, 4 and 6; or else 5 by itself, 1 and 2 and 3, 4 and 6. In other words, the only question still unsolved is whether set 1 (t = ṭ) should be derived from the common source of 2 (t = d) and 3 (t = þ), or from the source of 5 (d = t), i.e. from *t or from *d. We note that set 1 occurs only after s = s, p = f, etc. (set 7 probably only after s = s).

It may sometimes be irrelevant to decide the status of such a set as 1. In some instances of ambiguity, both possible reconstructions may be equally effective. However, for set 1 (though not for 7) we can go a step further. It is true that 1 (t = t) nowhere contrasts with 2 and 3, or with 5, since 2, 3, and 5 do not occur in the same environments as 1 (say after s = s). But it is also true that 5 (d = t) occurs in at least one environment where 2 and 3 do not: after y = s, as in Skt. meda- 'fat' : MG Mast 'fattening'. (Here Skt. y is seen in the second element in long e.) Upon further examination the set y = s is in turn found to occur only in positions from which s = s is barred; there is an equation st = st (ásti : ist) and an equation yd = st (meda-: Mast), but there is no sd = st and no yt = st. Consequently the choice between the two possible assignments of set 1 (t = t) will affect also the status of the set y = s. As soon as set 1 is grouped with 5, i.e. derived from *d, the sets s = s and y = s must be said to contrast with each other before *d of the proto-language, and we must reconstruct something like *sd for ásti : ist and *zd for meda-: Mast. But if set 1 is grouped with 2 and 3, i.e. derived from *t, we need to reconstruct only *st and *sd. The former grouping requires the reconstruction of a new IE phoneme *z, of very limited distribution; the latter grouping requires only such IE phonemes as have been reconstructed already on the basis of other evidence, and at the same time gives them a more complete distribution (both *t and *d now occur after *s).[5]

[5] In this case, then, the criterion of mutually exclusive environments solely in terms of surrounding sets must be to some extent implemented by saying that if the structure of the environments has been reinterpreted through reconstruction or phonemicization, the distribution of the set in question must be reexamined in terms of the newly described environments. The general theory involved here is an interesting problem in itself. (Brugmann's *zd is unnecessary in any case.)

Thus, considerations of economy have again decided the dilemma. On the strength of the general parallelism between the dentals and the labials, set 7 (p = p) will now be grouped with 8 and 9 rather than with 11.

To sum up, we have obtained the following reconstructions and sound laws: IE *t for sets 1, 2, and 3; IE *dh for sets 4 and 6; IE *d for set 5; IE *p for sets 7, 8, and 9; IE *bh for sets 10 and 12; IE *b for set 11; Verner's law for sets 2 and 8; Grassmann's law for sets 4 and 10; and the treatment of *t and *p after a Gmc. spirant for sets 1 and 7. Incidentally we have also decided against the reconstruction of IE *z.

The next application of our basic assumption points up some limitations of a strictly bilateral comparative procedure. In the comparison of Latin and Greek we observe, among others, the following sets of correspondences:

	13	14	15	16
Latin:	s	s	r	r
Greek:	s	h	0	r

Examples: 13 genus: génos 'family'; 14 sequ-: hep- 'follow'; 15 generum: genéōn 'of families'; 16 ferō: phérō 'I bear'.

Sets 13 and 14, as well as sets 15 and 16, are partially alike in sharing their Latin component. As for distribution, set 16 is in contrast with the other three: set 14 occurs after pause before a vowel, 15 occurs between vowels, 13 occurs in other environments; 16 occurs in all these surroundings (vowel prothesis aside). Distributionally, sets 13 and 14 can of course be derived from a single phoneme of the proto-language, say IE *s, with a conditioned sound change in Greek. But set 15 cannot be connected with sets 13 and 14 by distribution alone, since the criterion of partial likeness is absent: set 15 shares no component with the other two.[6] The realization that set 15 is also a reflex of IE *s is reached by other means or on the basis of other data.

Aside from a presumption which arises from the defective distribution of the Greek phoneme h (it is barred from precisely those positions where 0 appears in our sets, i.e. between vowels), and aside

[6] This peculiar result is of course due to the fact that IE *s has been reassigned to different entities (Lat. r, Gk. 0) under what happen to be identical conditions. In a comparison between Greek and Sanskrit, the set Gk. t = Skt. d, corresponding to set 4 above, would be in a similar relation with th = dh (corresponding to set 6) as is 15 with regard to 13 + 14, reflecting the two independent dissimilations of aspirates in the two languages (see above, note 3). In the case of 15, we have reason to assume that IE *s between vowels was h at one time in Proto-Greek before it was lost entirely. If we had to reconstruct IE from that stage, we would find ourselves in a somewhat better position: 13 and 14 (sharing Lat. s), and 14 and 15 (sharing early Greek h) are partially alike, though 13 and 15 are not.

also from certain additional evidence which, in effect, merely adds further sets to the ones already listed (and which is here ignored for the sake of the argument), set 15 can be referred to IE *s only by two methods: (a) by recourse to material from other IE languages, or (b) by internal reconstruction, in Greek and Latin separately, on the basis of the morphophonemic behavior of the set in question. Thus, in Latin, the r of set 15 (but not the r of 16) is found to alternate with the s of 13, as in gener(um) ∿ genus, ger(it) 'he conducts' ∿ ges(tus) 'conducted'; in Greek, the 0 of set 15 alternates similarly with the s of 13, as in génos ∿ gené(ōn)—i.e. gené0(ōn).

By the same kind of internal reconstruction, the derivation of Gmc. t (of set 1) and þ (of set 3) from the same phoneme of the proto-language finds support in the alternating forms of the past participial morpheme: (haf)t(s) ∿ (salbo)þ(s). Such considerations are entirely valid in themselves, but they have nothing to do with the comparative method.

Where the distribution of sets is simple to state, the application of comparative procedure can be condensed into a two-dimensional arrangement. This is here illustrated by a comparison of parts of the Latin and the Osco-Umbrian consonant system. The reconstructed phonemes based on this material may be regarded either as proto-Italic or as (provisionally) Indo-European, according as one accepts or rejects the assumption of a historical proto-Italic unity.

The Osco-Umbrian phonemes in question are here ordered on the horizontal axis, the Latin phonemes on the vertical axis:

OU:	b	d	f	v	Lat.:
					b
					d
					f
					v

An entry at the intersection, say, of the Osco-Umbrian b column and the Latin v row will mean that a set OU b = Lat. v has been abstracted from the material compared (as in U berus [abl. pl.]: Lat. verū 'spear'). If the entry at this point reads 'I', it will mean that the set occurs initially, 'M' that it occurs medially, 'IM' that it occurs both initially and medially. These two symbols and their combination happen to be sufficient for a simplified presentation of the problem.

We have eight sets, denoted by the symbols I, IM, and M in the following table:

OU:	b	d	f	v	Lat:
	IM		M		b
		IM	M		d
			I		f
	IM		M	IM	v

Entries in the same vertical column are alike in their Osco-Umbrian component; entries in the same horizontal row are alike in their Latin component.

Distribution among mutually exclusive environments is shown in the OU f column: the set OU f = Lat. f must be grouped with f = b, or with f = d, or with f = v; the choice is probably irrelevant. We can arbitrarily group this set with f = b on the basis of greater phonetic plausibility. The sets f = d and f = v remain, then, as representatives of defectively distributed phonemes occurring only in medial position. Each of the other entries reflects a separate phoneme of the proto-language. Choosing the traditional alphabetic symbols, we reconstruct as follows:

OU:	b	d	f	v	Lat:
	*b		*-f-		b
		*d	*-þ-		d
			*f-		f
	*gᵂ		*-xᵂ-	*w	v

Here *f- stands for the phoneme *f in initial position, *-f- for the same phoneme in medial position.

This is as far as the comparative method itself will take us, on the basis of Osco-Umbrian and Latin alone. It does not tell us, for instance, that the set f = f < *f- is the reflex of four originally contrasting IE phonemes (*bh-, *dh-, *gᵂh-, and *s before r), of which three parallel the medial entries in the Osco-Umbrian f column; nor that the set f = b < *-f- similarly represents a merging of several sources (IE *-bh-, *-dh- in some environments, and *-s- before r). These additional facts are perhaps suggested, though not clearly shown, by certain limitations upon the distribution of the reconstructed phonemes: *þ only medial, and not in the particular environments where IE *dh > Lat. b rather than d; *s before most consonants but not before *r; and *xᵂ only medial. The same facts can also be recovered by internal reconstruction on the basis of such alternations as Lat. con-dere 'found' (with d) ∿ fēcī 'I made' (with f), representing an IE morpheme *dhē/dhə with and without a prefix. But such facts cannot be revealed by simply applying the comparative method to the sounds of the Italic dialects.

If the formulation here proposed for the principal procedure in comparative reconstruction sounds unfamiliar to historical linguists (who have nevertheless consistently used the procedure), it clearly reminds us of certain formulations in descriptive phonology. Phonemes have been defined as classes of sounds which are phonetically similar and not in contrast—i.e., chiefly, in complementary distribution.[7] The second criterion is matched in historical work, while the first is paralleled, not too incongruously, by the criterion of partial likeness. Phonemic problems that arise from lack of symmetry in the distribution of sound segments have led investigators to look for additional criteria of patterning to decide between alternative arrangements; such a criterion was used in the reconstruction for set 7 (Skt. p = Gmc. p)

[7] E. g. B. Bloch and G. L. Trager, Outline of Linguistic Analysis (Baltimore, 1942).

above. Economy is an avowed goal of phonemic analysis (however controversial the means of achieving it may be); it is the same in comparative work. The sets of correspondences play the role of positional allophones. In short, when we use the reconstructive method of the nineteenth-century scholars we are in fact describing the phonemic system of the proto-language—on the basis, to be sure, not of a minutely diversified phonetic record but of the results of phonetic changes preserved in the daughter languages.

It is trivial to say that only the assumption of regular sound change makes reconstruction possible, and unnecessary to inquire into the implications of that assumption. But if the question be asked why the results of sound change should behave like allophones, we answer that it is through positional allophones that sound changes take place. This is usually expressed by saying that a sound change is conditioned by the phonemic environment. If Early Latin s between vowels becomes r (i.e. falls together with the old r phoneme), we have no difficulty in picturing the change as a reassignment of the particular allophone of s

that appeared between vowels—something like [z], as we have reason to believe. Comparison of two related languages reveals such allophones of the parent language as happened subsequently to change their phonemic status in certain ways.

The phonemic principle was implicit in the neogrammarian assumption of regular sound change; formal syntactic definitions of meaning were implicit in Paul's statement of semantic change. The fundamental unity of diachronic and synchronic thinking is beyond doubt.[8] But it is useful, and somewhat surprising, to realize how directly and how concretely that unity is reflected in scholarly practice, once it has been described in detail.

[8] Some doubt it. J. Lohmann, in an otherwise very valuable discussion of Steinitz' reconstruction of the Finno-Ugric vowel system on the basis of phonemic interpretation, declares (DLZ 70.201) that here 'Trubetzkoy's phonologie' has undergone its first (!) historical test, and adds that if it proves successful, all our earlier reconstructions, including the traditional work in Indo-European, will be worthless: a sorry misunderstanding of the continuity of linguistics and of the reviewer's own position.

PEIPING MORPHOPHONEMICS[1]

CHARLES F. HOCKETT
Language 26.63–85—1950

Morphophonemics, as the term is used here, subsumes every phase of the phonemic shape of morphemes: the typical shapes of alternants, the types of alternation, and the various environmental factors (phonological or grammatical) which elicit one alternant or another of those morphemes which appear in more than one shape. This usage is broader than some which have recently been described, for instance by Bloch and by Wells.[2]

Every language has morphemes, and so every language has morphophonemics. In the conceivable limiting case, the morphophonemic section of a description would list the typical shapes, and then would consist of a single statement: each morpheme appears, wherever found, in one and only one phonemic shape. Probably no such language exists. Chinese has been thought to approximate this state, and indeed it does, if we compare it with Yokuts or Navaho, or even with Spanish or Japanese. Nevertheless, the Chinese of Peiping has a respectable number of morphemes which appear in more than a single shape. In this paper we survey and classify the alternations involved; in some cases it is necessary to give relevant portions of the morphemic and tactical analysis.

[1] This paper continues the discussion of the structure of Peiping Chinese begun in Peiping Phonology (cited hereafter PP), JAOS 67.253–67 (1947) ((217)). The approach is essentially that developed by Zellig S. Harris, with the minor modifications outlined in the writer's Problems of Morphemic Analysis (cited PMA), Lang. 23.321–43 (1947) ((229)). The terminology of these two papers is here used without new definition.

In the course of the investigation letters of inquiry were addressed to Yuenren Chao and to Fangkuei Li, both of whom graciously answered in considerable detail. For their advice—which, it must be confessed, has not in all instances been followed—I wish to express my sincere thanks.

[2] Bernard Bloch, Lang. 23.414 ((251)): 'Morphophonemics is the study of the alternation between corresponding phonemes in alternant shapes of the same morpheme.' This implies a limitation of the term to cover only alternations, rather than shapes and alternations, and, furthermore, to subsume only alternations between shapes that are more or less comparable phonemically (knife and knive-s), so that one can pick out which phoneme of one shape corresponds to which in another shape. We want also to cover such cases as go and wen-t. Also Rulon S. Wells, Lang. 25.100 (fn. 5): '[the differences between alternant shapes of morphemes are] only a part of a more general class of facts, the facts about the phonemic shapes of morphs in general in the language in question.' Wells limits the term 'morphophonemics' to the narrower class of facts.

0. Notation. As a point of departure we must have a phonemic analysis, and a notation that accurately reflects it. Any analysis which takes care of all the relevant facts will do, since we can revise it if need arises. For the most part, these prerequisites are supplied by the discussion in PP. Even to start with, however, we shall find it convenient to revise the notation of that paper in a few respects; also, unfortunately, there are some errors of fact incorporated into PP which must be dealt with before we can proceed.

The modifications of notation are these:

(1) Slant lines will be used only when needed for clarity.

(2) Microjuncture (PP §2) will be transcribed with /#/ instead of with a space during the first part of the discussion, to direct attention to its occurrence in certain places. The other junctural symbols, /,/ and /;/, defined in PP to stand respectively for simultaneous microjuncture and mesojuncture and for simultaneous microjuncture, mesojuncture, and macrojuncture, are to be interpreted here as mesojuncture and as that plus macrojuncture, without the simultaneous microjuncture in either case.

(3) Nuclear stress (discussed in PP §4 but not supplied with a symbol) will be written /˘/.

(4) The symbols /p ph t th c ch k kh/ of PP will be replaced by /b p d t z c g k/ respectively.

The discussion in PP was in error in the following respects:

(1) As indicated in addendum (3) of PP, simultaneous /i/ and /u/ must be written with a unit symbol (here /y/), because the graph /iu/ must be used for those two elements in succession. /iu/ stands in contrast with /ieu/ at least with tone /2/ and quiet or zero stress: #ᵢiu²#ᶦzing³ 'oil well' : #ᵢieu²#ᶦzing³ 'there are wells'. As a matter of fact, even apart from cases such as this (involving the type of tonal sandhi discussed in §6 below), the sequences /iu/ and /ieu/ seem to constitute two distinct points in the phonological pattern. There are speakers who will say consistently #iu² for 'oil', but who will fluctuate between that and #ieu² for 'postal', or even consistently use the latter form. The contrast carries very little functional burden, true enough; but it is there. It is possible that /ui/ and /uei/ must be similarly distinguished, but this is not yet clear, and no effort is made to do so in this paper.

(2) The choice between /ien/ and /ian/, mentioned in PP §9.55, is not so arbitrary as is implied there. There are speakers who say #bien¹ 'side' (and, with the retroflex suffix, #ᶦbieir¹#srang⁴ 'on the edge'),

but #dian³ 'bit' (#i⁴#'diair³ 'a little').³ It may be that for such speakers the choice of /ien/ or /ian/ correlates with tone—the former with tones /1/ and /2/, the latter otherwise—but even if so it seems preferable to keep the two apart.

(3) The statement in PP §10 precluding a sequence of two microsegments both with tone /3/, or both with tone /5/, within a single <u>macrosegment</u> ought rather to bar these sequences within a <u>mesosegment</u>. Furthermore, one does indeed find a sequence of two /3/'s within a single mesosegment, providing that the first microsegment carries contrastive stress: one may say either #"biau³#,hau³ or #"biau⁵#,hau³ 'watches are better'. Phonetically, the first microsegment in such a sequence has the terminal rise in pitch characteristic of tone /3/ preceding a pause.

With the above revisions, the analysis and notation of PP will serve us as we begin our present investigation. Two classes of phonemically relevant phenomena are intentionally omitted. The first is tempo, the discussion of which is postponed to §9.

1. The <u>Problem</u>. We begin with a display of several typical utterances:

a) #ue³#de#'sie², #,tai⁴#˘siau³#le; #ni²#,gei⁵#ue³#˘zrang⁴#i#,zrang⁴.
'My shoes are too small; stretch them for me.'

b) #'bu⁴#srang#de, #,nei⁴#kuai#,iu²#˘dian³#z; #iung⁴#,ning²#meng²#'zrl#z, #i⁴#,cal#zieu⁴#˘mei²#le.
'If you put lemon juice on the cloth, that grease spot will come out.'

c) #taml#bu²#˘huei⁴, #,hua⁴#'huar⁴. 'They don't know how to draw pictures.'

d) #'sye⁴, #,cung²#'srangl#keu³, #˘liu²#cru#,lai. 'Blood flowed from the wound.'

Our morphemic analysis must account for all the phonemic content of these utterances (or any others) —the junctures and stresses as well as the vowels, consonants, and tones. However, this accounting may be fairly complex if we find it desirable, for the sake of simpler tactics, to make it so. That is, we may, if we wish, regard one and the same group of phonemes as morphemic under some conditions, nonmorphemic under others, or as comprising alternants of different morphemes under different conditions, providing that the various conditions involved can be stated in terms of the morphemes we recognize, their phonemic shape, and their arrangements.

The requirement of total accountability turns out to be most easily and realistically met if we recognize three main types (canonical forms) of morphemes: (1) junctural, (2) accentual, and (3) segmental— composed phonemically, for the most part, of juncture phonemes in the first case, stresses in the second, and vowels, consonants, and tones in the third. We shall take up these types in the given order; in due time the third type will be further subdivided.

The other is intonation, which merits some discussion here.⁴

Our chief reason for leaving out intonation is ignorance of details, and yet even if the intonational picture were clear a good case could be made for setting it aside. One does not expect to find, in Chinese or English, any morphemes composed partly of intonation phonemes and partly of phonemes of other kinds. One expects rather that intonation phonemes will cluster into intonation morphemes, produced simultaneously with the stream of non-intonational morphemes. If this is true, then the eventual analysis of intonation will not call for major reformulation of the results achieved here. In English and Chinese—and perhaps in all languages—a speaker transmits two messages simultaneously, one intonational and one composed of vowels, consonants, and the like.⁵ Both messages reach the same destination; the intonations constitute, as it were, a running commentary on the rest, without which, in some cases, the latter is unintelligible.

2. <u>Juncture Morphemes</u>. We deal first with the junctural phenomena symbolized /,/ and /;/; microjuncture can best be handled in another connection.

Our morphemic accounting is extremely simple. We recognize /,/ as one and the same morpheme wherever it occurs, and /;/ as another. These two, formally and semantically, are morphemes of a special variety which we may call <u>structural signals</u>:⁶

³ I had missed this point completely during over six years of work with Chinese, until finally it was called to my attention by Henry C. Fenn Jr.

⁴ Considerable information on intonation is given in Yuenren Chao, Mandarin Primer (Cambridge, 1948).

⁵ There may be other messages as well—tone-quality variations indicating emotional attitudes or identity of speaker or the like. Such matters, however, either stand outside the realm of language, or else have not yet received the kind of study which would reveal their linguistic nature. Kenneth L. Pike is fond of discussing them; see in particular The Intonation of American English, Ch. 7 (Ann Arbor, 1946).

⁶ The notion of structural signals was proposed by David L. Olmsted, specifically for the 'conjugation vowels' of Spanish and Portuguese. Instead of treating these as empty morphs (PMA §21), we may take them as morphemes, the meaning of which is something submorphemic in the structure of the language: a particular conjugation vowel tells us 'the verb stem just spoken belongs to such-and-such a morphophonemic class in its inflection'. Structural signals are then like Bloomfield's substitutes in that their meaning is definable within the structure of language, rather than in terms of the practical world; indeed, while this is by definition true of structural signals, there is some doubt as to whether it really holds for the forms Bloomfield calls 'substitutes'.

their meaning is the grouping, of morphemes of other types, which their occurrences serve to establish. For instance, in sample sentence (a), the /;/ divides the string of other morphemes into two portions, which are the immediate constituents of the whole; the occurrence of /,/ in the first of these two portions marks the structure of that portion as likewise bipartite. The position of each structural signal tells us which of the morphemes of other types go together as a constituent, but the structural signals themselves stand outside the hierarchical structure of immediate constituents. Of course not every set of immediate constituents, occurring in sequence to form a constitute, is marked in this way; but when the marking is there, the structure is as indicated.

We may argue for the realism of this interpretation by a demonstration of the effect of longer pauses (of uncertain phonemic status) in English. Bloomfield points out that an ordinary English utterance such as 'two plus three times five plus four' is ambiguous: it may represent forty-five, twenty-one, twenty-nine, or several other numbers.[7] In writing, we keep these apart by graphic indications of scope: $(2+3) \cdot (5+4)$, $2+(3 \cdot 5)+4$, $[(2+3) \cdot 5]+4$, and so on. Using pauses as we speak, these can be differentiated fairly well as follows: two plus three (pause) times (pause) five plus four; two (pause) plus three times five (pause) plus four; two plus three (pause) times five (longer pause) plus four. The pauses thus serve as markers of scope, as indicators of what goes with what. The forms grouped and separated by the Chinese structural signals are not necessarily mathematical (indeed, they are mathematical only if some of the morphemes involved happen to have mathematical meanings), but their role is quite similar. Although it would not be easy, a sufficiently exhaustive search would reveal Chinese utterances differing only in the location of structural signals, and with different meanings as a result of the different groupings of constituents.

3. Accentual Morphemes. The morphemic status of the phonemes of stress is considerably more complicated than that of the junctures. Any occurrence of a given stress phoneme is either a morpheme, or else is morphemically irrelevant (and predictable from the surrounding morphemic material);[8] we shall not recognize any occurrence of any stress phoneme as part of a morpheme which includes also vowels, consonants, or tones. But for our discussion of the stresses we must anticipate a distinction to be made later among segmental morphemes: most of the

latter are tonic, in that they occur on occasion with stress /ˇ/, /ˊ/, or /ˌ/; a few, however, are atonic, occurring with zero stress or with /"/ but not with any intermediate level. In the case of segmental morphemes longer than a single microsegment, the tonic−atonic contrast applies to the various portions one microsegment long.

Contrastive stress (") is morphemic wherever it occurs. In sample utterance (d), we could place /"/ on any of the segmental morphemes (each, in this case, one microsegment long) except possibly the last, obtaining the following meanings: 'blood flowed from the wound', 'blood flowed from the wound', 'blood flowed from the wound', 'blood flowed from the opening of the wound', 'blood flowed from the wound', and 'blood flowed out from the wound'.

Loud stress (ˊ) is a morpheme when it is followed in the same mesosegment by a quiet stress (ˌ). Thus #ˌziau⁴#ˊcai⁴ 'order food (in a restaurant)' and #ˌziau⁴#ˊcai⁴#le 'ordered food' do not contain a morphemic loud stress, but #ˊziau⁴#ˌcai⁴ 'order food' does contain one.

Nuclear stress is a morpheme if it falls in a nonterminal mesosegment. Utterance (d) thus contains no morphemic nuclear stress; but if we interchange the loud stress of #ˊsrang¹ 'wound' and the nuclear stress of #ˇliu² 'flow', we add one morpheme to those in the utterance, and change the meaning by adding a slight emphasis to 'out of the wound'.

Zero stress is nonmorphemic when it occurs with an atonic morpheme or morpheme-part. Thus in sentence (a), the zero stress accompanying segments #de (attributive particle) and #le (completive particle) is not morphemic. We also regard zero stress as nonmorphemic when it occurs with certain tonic morphemes in certain fixed tactical positions, where the accompanying stress level is limited to zero and contrastive. For example, when #i¹ 'one, a, an', a tonic morpheme, occurs directly after an active verb and before a measure, as in the last part of utterance (a), #ˇzrang⁴#i#ˌzrang⁴ 'stretch a bit', it either bears no stress, as in this case, or contrastive stress, and the former we regard as morphemically irrelevant.

Except in cases of this kind, zero stress is morphemic. In fact, we recognize two morphemes of this shape. One has the meaning 'de-emphasis', contrasting semantically with the other stress morphemes so far itemized. The first segmental morpheme of utterance (a) (#ue³ 'I', a tonic morpheme) is accompanied by this morpheme. The other is a marker of one kind of compound, and occurs on the second of two successive tonic morphemes. #mei³ 'beautiful' and #gue² 'country', both tonic morphemes, can stand together (though the particular combination is rare) as #ˌmei³#ˊgue² 'beautiful country'; this contrasts with #ˊmei³#gue², where the compound-marking morpheme just mentioned is also present, and which means 'America'.

7 Leonard Bloomfield, Linguistic Aspects of Science (International Encyclopedia of Unified Science 1.4; Chicago, 1939).

8 In this paper, instead of using the term 'empty morph' (see PMA), we simply classify certain phonemic material as nonmorphemic or as morphemically irrelevant.

With these interpretations of zero, loud, nuclear, and contrastive stress, quiet stress becomes everywhere nonmorphemic. We have, then, five accentual morphemes: /"/ 'strong emphasis'; /˘/ in other than a terminal mesosegment 'emphasis on the meaning of the segmental morphemes of the mesosegment'; /'/ if a quiet stress follows in the same mesosegment 'emphasis on the meaning of the segmental morpheme covered' (but less emphasis than with /"/); and two morphemes of zero stress shape, 'de-emphasis' and 'compound-marker'.

Our decision to treat /'/ and /˘/ as morphemic only in certain positions is based on the following considerations. An utterance which has /˘/ within the last mesosegment of each macrosegment, and /'/ not followed by /ˌ/ within any mesosegment, is, so to speak, the most 'colorless' way of saying anything. The speaker can emphasize the content of the terminal mesosegments only by using contrastive stress, or by arranging the segmental morphemes in some different way; he can emphasize the meaning of a segmental morpheme which bears loud stress in the 'colorless' form, similarly, only by raising the stress level to contrastive or by rephrasing. But, with few exceptions, occurrence of loud or nuclear stress in other than these 'colorless' positions does serve to emphasize the segmental material so marked. In the exceptions, we have an analytical choice. In the segmental construction consisting of single-microsegment verb plus #i¹

'one, a, an' plus measure R_m (see §12), the verb regularly receives /'/ and the measure /ˌ/; we can again cite as an example the form #'zrang⁴#i #ˌzrang⁴ 'stretch a bit'. In the segmental construction consisting of verb plus negative element #bu⁴ plus the same verb, e.g. #'iau⁴#bu#ˌiau⁴ 'want or not want?', /'/ regularly falls on the first occurrence of the verb, /ˌ/ on the second. In such cases we can either say that the stress pattern, being regular and predictable, is nonmorphemic, or we can say that the morpheme of 'displaced' primary stress is regularly present as part of the construction.

We have now to pose and answer two questions. (1) Is it feasible to modify our notation in the direction of writing only the morphemically relevant stresses? (2) If this is feasible, can we revise our phonemic analysis so as to render the changed notation phonemic instead of morphophonemic?

If we accept every displaced /'/ and /˘/ as morphemic (thus accepting the second analytical alternative in the cases mentioned just above), we can modify our notation so as to write non-zero stresses only where they are morphemic. We cannot manage to write only the morphemic zero stresses without leading to ambiguity. Suppose we leave quiet stress unmarked; indicate zero stress by a preposed dot /·/ instead of with no mark; and indicate morphemic loud, nuclear, and contrastive stress with /'/, /˘/, and /"/. With these conventions, our four sample utterances will appear:

a) #·ue³#·de#sie², #tai⁴#siau³#·le; #·ni²#gei⁵#·ue³#'zrang⁴#·i#zrang⁴.

b) #bu⁴#·srang#·de, #nei⁴#·kuai⁴#iu²#dian³#·z; #·iung⁴#ning²#·meng²#zrˡ#·z, #·i⁴#caˡ#·zieu⁴#mei²#·le.

c) #·tamˡ#·bu²#˘huei⁴, #hua⁴#huar⁴.

d) #sye⁴, #cung²#srangˡ#·keu³, #'liu²#·cru#lai.

In the first macrosegment of (a), we know that the nuclear stress falls within the second mesosegment, because no mark is present to indicate its displacement. We know furthermore that it falls on #siau³, since that is the last microsegment not marked with /·/ for zero stress, and there is again, within the mesosegment, no mark of displacement. In the first mesosegment, there is necessarily a non-zero stress on #sie², and since the nuclear stress of the whole macrosegment does not fall within this mesosegment, that non-zero stress must be loud. The second macrosegment of the utterance contains but one mesosegment, and so the nuclear stress will fall wherever the loud stress does, and will in fact be identical with it.[9] The loud stress is marked; the other non-zero-stressed microsegments by definition bear quiet stress.

[9] See PP §4. The differentiation of loud and nuclear stress is meaningful only when a macrosegment includes more than one mesosegment. It is terminologically convenient to say that when a macrosegment includes but one mesosegment, loud and nuclear stress coincide.

The reader who must interpret this notation into Chinese speech sounds has to remember more complex rules than with the earlier transcription; but for purposes of further grammatical discussion, the revised notation is clearly more convenient, whether or not we can also make out a case for the phonemic, rather than morphophonemic, status of the revision.

But such a case can be made out, thus answering our second question affirmatively. For the revised notation still indicates unambiguously, and without reference to either morpheme boundaries or morpheme identities, the phonemically relevant material and its arrangement. The underlying phonemic analysis would be as follows. We recognize the contrast between zero and non-zero stress, and call the former a phoneme. We then examine the sequences of non-zero stresses in mesosegments. If a contrastive stress is present, all the microsegments which neither bear the contrastive stress nor the zero stress are approximately equal as to level; we recognize the contrastive stress as a phoneme and can thus indicate all the levels which contrast in such circumstances. We are left with mesosegments which contain no contrastive stress. If the one, two, or more non-zero stresses within a mesosegment form throughout a non-diminuendo series, we take this to be the normal state of affairs and recognize no new phonemes. But if anywhere in such a series a diminuendo sets in, the loudest point constitutes a phoneme to be written $/\prime/$. Similarly, within the macrosegment, we examine the sequence of loudest stresses of each constituent mesosegment. If a contrastive stress (or more than one) is present, the phonemes already recognized take care of the situation. If not, and the sequence constitutes a non-diminuendo series throughout, we once again take that to be the normal situation and recognize no new phonemes. But if somewhere in the series a diminuendo sets in, the point at which it begins constitutes a phoneme to be written $/\smile/$.

We have been led to this rephonemicization through grammatical considerations; but once discovered the new analysis is established purely on phonological grounds.[10]

Although the new analysis and notation are tactically preferable to the old, there will be points in the remainder of our morphophonemic discussion where the older analysis is more useful. We shall retain the new notation, and where it does not matter whether a particular microsegment bears a particular stress phonemically or automatically by the new analysis, we shall refer to zero, quiet, loud, nuclear, and contrastive stress levels.[11]

4. Classification of Segmental Morphemes. The early western students of Chinese, and the Chinese themselves until quite recently, perceiving the language through a haze of characters, saw utterances as rows of bricks, of uniform size and shape, each a single syllable and a single 'word', immutable, subject to no influence (or almost none) from the preceding and following bricks. Now that we have set intonation aside, have provided for the opener junctures, and have lifted off and dealt with the stresses, the material that still confronts us begins to resemble more closely this earlier picture. We have now

only microsegments to deal with — composed of vowels, consonants, and tones, and held apart (or cemented together?) by microjunctures. But we must proceed cautiously; our fundamental precaution will be to speak of morphs for the present instead of morphemes, reverting to the latter term only as morphs are classed together, or kept separate, in the course of the analysis.

The constant occurrence of microjunctures has been underscored by representing them, so far, with a positive mark $/\#/$ rather than merely by a blank spot on the page, because they must indeed be accounted for; we cannot simply count on their turning up 'naturally'. How shall we take care of them morphemically?

One alternative would be to treat them, like $/,/$ and $/;/$, as structural signals. We could regard microjuncture initially and finally in the mesosegment as automatic, and say that when a microjuncture occurs medially in a mesosegment, it marks a boundary between successive segmental morphs. The trouble is that this is not always the case. Some medial microjunctures separate microsegments which are parts of a single morph: #bue[1]#·li 'glass', #ning[2] #·meng[2] 'lemon'. We should have to accept some medial microjunctures as structural signals of the kind indicated, but regard others as simply parts of segmental morphs. Such a solution is of course possible, but a better answer should be sought.

A second alternative would be to treat all microjunctures, medial in the mesosegment as well as initial and final, as automatic, save for those few referred to above which occur within, and as part of, a segmental morph. We could then say that when two segmental morphs stand in succession within a mesosegment, microjuncture automatically occurs between them. But this also is not universally true: #huar[4] 'picture' is two segmental morphs, not one, and no medial microjuncture separates them. We should therefore have to specify the circumstances under which two successive segmental morphs are separated by microjuncture, and the circumstances under which they are not. This too is of course possible.

But a third alternative seems to combine the merits and avoid the defects of both of the above. This is to regard all microjunctures as parts of segmental morphs.[12] If we do this, then segmental morphs are of the following canonical forms as regards length:

I. Morphs beginning with a microjuncture but containing none internally: #sie[2] 'shoe', #siau[3] 'small', #gei[3] and #gei[5] (two different morphs) 'give; for', #zrang[4] 'stretch', #·de (attributive particle), #·le (completive particle), #·z (nominal suffix), and many more.

---

[10] This is a statement of historical fact. Since the discovery of the possible rephonemicization obviously came about before this paper was ready for publication, it would have been possible to introduce it before, rather than after, the discussion of morphophonemics. But it seemed worthwhile to retain the ordering of matters as above, as a fairly elaborate demonstration of the way in which grammatical considerations can serve as clues for phonological analysis without implying that the latter is logically built on the former; there are still no grammatical 'prerequisites' for phonemic analysis.

Compare the similar view expressed by Bloch, Lang. 26.92–3 and fn. 16 ((332)), and the argument by which he supports it in §9 of his paper ((347–8)).

[11] With the present discussion of stress may profitably be compared that in Yuenren Chao, op.cit. 26, and that in John de Francis, Beginning Chinese 5–6 (New Haven, 1946). De Francis devises a notation for stress very much like our revised notation.

[12] Compare the handling of $/\#/$ in Fijian (PMA §16) and Nootka (PMA §18), and contrast the handling of English $/\#/$ by Rulon S. Wells in Immediate Constituents, Lang. 23.107–8, §64 (1947) ((201–2)).

II. Morphs beginning with microjuncture, and containing one or more internally: #bue^l#·li 'glass', #ning^2#·meng^2 and #ning^2#·meng (two different morphs) 'lemon', #sran^l#·hu 'coral', #dung^l#·si 'thing'.

III. Morphs containing no microjunctures: the /r/ of #huar^4 'picture' or #huar^l 'flower' (the preceding sequence in each case constitutes a morph of type I); the /me/ of #sreme^2 'what' or #zeme^3 'how'; the /m/ of #tam^l 'they'. Most, but not quite all, microsegments ending in the phoneme /r/ contain a morph of this type; all ending in /m/ do; almost all dissyllabic microsegments do.

IV. In one and only one case, it seems advisable to recognize a zero morph—one having no phonemic shape at all. This is classed as segmental because of its morphemic assignment (see §9).

V. Similarly, in just one case we recognize a negative morph—one consisting of less than no phonemic material at all, a significant absence (§14). Here also we call the morph segmental because of its morphemic assignment and the tactical class of the morpheme to which it belongs.

Whether a segmental morph is preceded by microjuncture or not now becomes a meaningless question, since the microjuncture is part of the morph itself. Whether a segmental morph is followed by microjuncture or not now depends entirely on the structure of the following segmental morph, or the following structural signal or end-of-utterance.

Intersecting the classification by length is that mentioned briefly in §3 into tonic and atonic. Type I segmental morphs are, as wholes, tonic or atonic; those listed above with /·/ (for zero stress) are of the latter category, and occur only as indicated or with contrastive stress, while the others may occur with any stress level. Type II segmental morphs have one constituent microsegment, usually the first, which is tonic in this sense, while the other constituent microsegments (marked /·/ in the examples above) are atonic. The contrast does not apply to type III morphs, which are always less than a microsegment, nor of course to types IV and V.

Having chosen this interpretation for microjuncture, our symbol /#/ can henceforth safely be omitted. So long as a tone-mark or a stress-mark is present between the vowel-and-consonant letters of two successive microsegments, we will not henceforth insert any mark to indicate the location of a microjuncture; in the few cases where neither such mark is present, we retain the sign /#/. In citing morphs of type III, which involve no initial microjuncture, the absence thereof will be indicated by a preposed hyphen; thus /-r/, /-me/, /-m/.

5. Morpheme Shapes. Our working assumption for segmental morphs will be that morphs of different shapes are morphemically different until proved otherwise. As the classification into morphemes is made, it will be possible to group morphemes into the canonical forms (of length and tonicity) given

above for morphs; expressions of the shape 'type III morpheme' will therefore appear in due course. This does not imply, as might seem to be the case, that morphs of different canonical shapes are never taken to constitute alternants of the same morpheme, although this is in general true. But the few exceptions (§9) do not require the setting up of additional canonical types for morphemes.

6. General Tonal Alternation. The four type I morphs hen^3, hen^5, hen^2, and hen^l all mean 'quite, very'. They occur in a distribution which is partly complementary. Factors in the environment limiting the privileges of occurrence of the four forms are the level of stress on the morph itself, and the tone of the following microsegment, if any, within the same mesosegment.

With contrastive stress, both hen^3 and hen^5 occur before a microsegment with tone /3/, but only hen^3 otherwise. Thus "hen^{3}hau^3 or "hen^{5}hau^3 'very good', but only "hen^{3}gau^l, 'very tall'.

With stress-level /ˇ/ or /ˈˈ/, only hen^5 occurs before a microsegment with tone /3/, and only hen^3 otherwise. Thus 'hen^{5}hau^3 'quite good', but 'hen^{3}gau^l 'quite tall'.

With stress-level /ˌ/, both hen^5 and hen^2 occur before /3/, both hen^3 and hen^2 before /5/, otherwise only hen^3. Thus hen^{5}hau^3 'quite good', hen^{2}ma^5·fan or hen^{3}ma^5·fan 'quite annoying', but hen^{3}gau^l 'quite tall'.

With zero stress, both hen^2 and hen^l occur before /3/, any of the three hen^3, hen^2, or hen^l (though more often one of the latter two) before /5/, but only hen^3 otherwise. Thus bu^4·hen^{2}hau^3 or bu^4·hen^{l}hau^3 'not very good', bu^4·hen^{3}ma^5·fan, bu^4·hen^{2}ma^5·fan, or bu^4·hen^{l}ma^5·fan 'not very annoying', but bu^4·hen^{3}gau^l 'not very tall'.

In the position defined above in which more than one of these morphs occur, the choice is non-contrastive. The distribution of the four morphs parallels the distribution of the single morph tai^4 'too, excessively'. We can therefore take the four tonally different forms as alternants of a single morpheme.

We might still not choose to do so if this set were isolated. But there is supporting evidence. In the first place, a microsegment with tone /3/ does not occur (unless it bears contrastive stress) before another in the same mesosegment also bearing tone /3/. Furthermore, almost every type I tonic morph bearing tone /3/ is matched, as is hen^3, by three others, respectively with tones /5/, /2/, and /1/, with the distribution we have found above. In fact, even if a microsegment happens to be bimorphic instead of constituting a single morph, the same alternations hold: thus uem^3, uem^5, uem^2, and uem^l 'we, us' have the same distribution as do the four forms discussed, though each is two morphs (type I tonic plus type III). Therefore we choose, in every such case, to treat the members of the set as alternants of a single morpheme or morpheme sequence.

We may normalize our notation in accordance with this decision by writing, in each case, just one of the four forms, and allowing the environment to be the indication of which shape is called for or, in the cases of free alternation, which choices can be made without affecting the morphemic structure. It is not possible, for this purpose, to generalize the form with tone /5/, /2/, or /1/, since in each case there are other morphs with the tone in question which do not participate in alternating sets of four.[13] But we can generalize the form with tone /3/ without ambiguity. This revision of notation is morphophonemic, not phonemic, and cannot be matched by a revision of the phonemic analysis, since we shall now be writing one and the same tone sometimes one way, sometimes another, depending on morpheme identity. That is, what we hear as hai^{2}hau^3 'still good' will be so written, but what we hear on occasion as hen^{2}hau^3 'quite good' will be written rather hen^{3}hau^3; when we hear such a /2.–3/ sequence we know whether to write /2/ or /3/ on the first microsegment only if we know what shape the morpheme takes in other environments.

Only one of our four sample utterances is affected by this revision. Sentence (a) now appears as:

·ue^3·de#sie^2, tai^{4}siau^3·le;
·ni^{3}gei^3·ue^3'zrang^4·i#zrang^4.

7. Specific Tonal Alternation. There are a few specific morphemes which appear in shapes differing only in tone, depending on tonal environment, but which can be described only by listing—not by a covering statement, as in §6.

(1) The forms i^1, i^2, and i^4 'a, an; one' are distributed as follows: before mesojuncture, i^1; before a microsegment bearing tone /4/, i^2; otherwise i^4. Thus li^3·bai^{4}i^1 'Monday', i^{2}kuai^4 'a hunk', but i^{4}tian^1 (some speakers i^{4}tien^1) 'a day', i^{4}nian^2 (i^{4}nien^2) 'a year', i^{4}bei^3 'a cupful'. If the following microsegment is toneless, the shape of this morpheme depends on the tone which the following microsegment would have if it had one (see §8 below for alternation between presence and absence of a tone); thus i^2·ge 'a, one', where the second type I tonic morph, when not accompanied by a morpheme of absence of stress, is ge^4.

(2) The forms ba^1, ba^2 'eight', and ci^1, ci^2 'seven', are somewhat similar to the foregoing in their distribution: the form with /1/ appears in all environments; the form with /2/ appears only when the following microsegment has (or, like ge^4, in other positions would have) tone /4/. In the latter positions, then, both members of each pair occur, but without contrast. Thus ba^{1}tian^1 'eight days', ba^{1}nian^2 'eight years', ba^{1}bei^3 'eight cupfuls', but either ba^{1}kuai^4

or ba^{2}kuai^4 'eight hunks' and either ba^1·ge or ba^2·ge 'eight'; similarly with 'seven'. due^1 'how, how much, so' is said to alternate similarly with due^2.

(3) The forms bu^1, bu^2, and bu^4 'not, don't, doesn't' match the distribution of i^1 in all details except that before mesojuncture one finds either bu^1 or bu^4, more often the latter.

In each of these cases we recognize a single morpheme with several alternants. Here no notational normalization is possible if we are to retain freedom from ambiguity when working from notation to phonemes. In a practical orthography, of course, one could select one or another of the forms in each case and write it everywhere, counting on the reader's familiarity with the morphemes involved (rather than just his ability to follow rules—phonemic and automatic morphophonemic definitions—in translating marks into sounds) to lead to the choice of the right form for each context.

8. Alternations Conditioned by Stress. The two accentual morphemes that consist phonemically of zero stress have different effects on the segmental morphemes that they accompany.

If we add the morpheme of de-emphasis to the first segmental morpheme of gen^{1}bie^2·de 'with others' and cung^{2}ner^4 'from there', we get freely alternating pairs of forms: ·gen^{1}bie^2·de and ·gen^{2}bie^2·de in the first case, ·cung^{1}ner^4 and ·cung^{2}ner^4 in the second. In each case the alternate shape with tone /1/ is rather more common. We take the form which appears when no /·/ is present as basic, and normalize the notation accordingly.

This is the source of the alternation between shapes with tones /1/ and /2/ of morphemes which basically have tone /3/ (§6).

If we add the morpheme of compound-marking to a segmental morpheme having any tone whatever, we get freely alternating sets of forms: free alternation between the basic tone and no tone at all if the basic tone is /3/ or /4/, free alternation between /1/, /2/, and no tone at all if the basic tone is /1/ or /2/. Thus one has feil^1·cru^1, feil^1·cru^2, and feil^1·cru 'fly out'; zrung^1·gue^2, zrung^1·gue^1, and zrung^1·gue 'China'; sue^5·i^3 and sue^5·i 'therefore'; sr^2·heu^4 and sr^2·heu 'time'. We can without ambiguity write everywhere feil^1·cru^1, zrung^1·gue^2, sue^5·i^3, and sr^2·heu^4. Here, as with the morpheme of de-emphasis above, replacement of basic /2/ by /1/ is somewhat commoner than replacement of basic /1/ by /2/; but replacement by no tone at all is commonest.[14]

An atonic part of a segmental morpheme of type II either is subject to the same variation, e. g. ning^2·meng^2, ning^2·meng^1, and ning^2·meng 'lemon', in which case we can write one of the forms with a

---

[13] Some speakers have no such independent occurrences of /5/. For them, the distinction between [3] and [5] is subphonemic, and the statements of alternation made here can be simplified.

[14] This may depend partly on which tone the morpheme has basically. Loss of tone /3/ seems to be relatively rarer than loss of the other tones.

tone on the second microsegment, or else never appears with a tone, as sran^1·hu 'coral'. In the case of 'lemon', it would not matter whether we generalized the form with tone /1/ or that with tone /2/; we have hit on the latter purely because the character usually used for the second microsegment carries tone /2/ in other contexts.

When zero stress occurs nonmorphemically on a tonic morpheme in a specified tactical position (§3), the tone seems to be regularly lost. Thus, in addition to the three alternants of i^1 'a, an; one' and of bu^1 'not' listed in §7, one also has toneless i and bu in 'kan^4·i#kan^4 'take a look', 'man^4·i#diair^3 'a little slower', and 'iau^4·bu#iau^4 'want or not'.

9. Alternations Conditioned by Tempo. Like other people, the Chinese speak at varying rates. Certain features of segmental and junctural structure differ when 'the same' utterance is spoken fast or slow. We wish to codify these differences and regard them as determined by the speed of speech, rather than as constituting, individually, morphemically different structures. One way to do this is to set up varying rates of speech as themselves morphemic; but since what we call morphemes are composed, in one way or another, of phonemes, this necessitates also setting up varying rates of speech on the phonological level as phonemic.

It turns out to be sufficient to recognize two tempo phonemes: fast and slow. Any utterance begins with one of these two, which continues, simultaneous with the flow of other phonemes, either through the entire utterance or to some medial macrojuncture (or, possibly, mesojuncture), where it may be replaced by the other. That is, every piece of an utterance falls within a domain of one of the two tempo phonemes. Each tempo phoneme constitutes a single morpheme. Alternatively, of course, we could regard one of the tempo phonemes as morphemic, the other as not—presumably we would take the fast phoneme as nonmorphemic, since fast speech is more common —but the difference between these views seems slight. Meanings can be assigned, even if a bit vaguely, to the two tempo morphemes: the fast one means 'this speech is natural and conversational'; the slow one means 'this is careful emphatic speech for extra clarity'.

Now since, phonetically, there are an infinite number of possible rates of speech, the problem arises, as we consider successively faster stretches of speech, how to tell just when the 'slow' phoneme ceases to operate and the 'fast' one comes into play. It turns out, as will be shown, that this question answers itself whenever it is relevant.

In the discussion that follows, we specify the presence of the fast or the slow phoneme in each case, but supply no special notations for them.

One type of alternation conditioned by tempo is illustrated by the following:

Slow	Fast	
bu^2·sr^4	busr^2	'isn't'
sie^4·sie^4	siesi^4	'thanks'
da^4·me#zr^3	dam^4#zr^3	'thumb'
pi^4·gu, pi^4·hu	pigu^4, pihu^4	'buttocks'[15]

The slow form is in each case two microsegments, of which the second may bear a tone; the first is stressed, the second unstressed. The fast form is in each case a single microsegment, dissyllabic or monosyllabic; its tone is the same as that of the first microsegment of the two-microsegment slow form. In addition, there is a terminal /e/ in the slow alternant of the second and third examples, missing in the fast alternant.

This type of alternation takes place most often with certain forms, but from time to time one hears it with others which in slow speech have essentially the structure of the slow alternants listed above.

A second, though closely related, type of alternation is illustrated by the following (the examples are exhaustive or almost so):

Slow (or fast before /,/)	Fast (otherwise)	
ue^3·men^2	uem^3	'we'
ni^3·men^2	nim^3	'you (pl.)'
ta^1·men^2	tam^1	'they'
zan^2·men^2	zam^2	'we (inclusive)'
due^1·me, dueme^1	duem^1	'how, how much, so'
sreme^2	srem^2	'what'
zeme^3	zem^3	'how'
neme^4	nem^4	'so, that way'
zeme^4, zreme^4	zem^4, zrem^4	'so, this way'

Here some of the slow alternants are single microsegments, though dissyllabic; the -men or -me terminal in the slow alternant is replaced by bare -m in the fast alternant.

In forms of the two types cited above we see morphs of different canonical forms grouped into single morphemes: sr^4 and -sr, sie^4 and -si, and so forth, the first alternant in each case a type I tonic morph, the second a type III morph. In all such cases, we class the morpheme as type I tonic, rather than setting up a special canonical form; for apparently any type I morpheme in the proper setting might be replaced in this way by a type III alternant in fast speech, and the phenomenon has simply been easier to observe in the cases listed.

[15] In PP it was stated that consonants medial in dissyllabic microsegments are voiced. The fast alternant pihu^4 had not been heard when PP was written. If the PP statement holds, the /h/ in this form should be a voiced velar spirant—and so it is. In a small way, this illustrates how one can make an extrapolation beyond one's data, and how verification of this by later observation can test the validity of the analysis. On such matters, see IJAL 14.269-71. (1948) ((279)). ⟦See now also the editorial comment on page 80 of the present volume, especially at the end of the first column and the following sentences.⟧

A third alternation dependent on tempo involves the only zero morph which we find it necessary to recognize. Between an active verb and a measure, the form i[1] 'a, an', with nonmorphemic zero stress, appears phonemically in slow speech, but is replaced by zero in fast speech. Thus (slow) 'kan[4]·i#kan[4] 'take a look' but (fast) 'kan[4]·kan[4]. (The zero stress on the measure, in the fast alternant, is also automatic.) Since, except for the difference in meaning between the two speeds, the two forms have identical meaning, and since the position for the zero alternant of i[1] is well defined, we regard the fast-speech form, with no phonemically present /i/, as morphemically identical with the slow-speech form in which it appears overtly.

We can now define the speed at which the slow morpheme (and phoneme) is inoperative and the fast morpheme (and phoneme) takes effect. Any rate of speech which is fast enough to involve the alternants labelled 'fast' in the above discussion is structurally fast; any rate of speech which is slow enough to involve the alternants labelled 'slow' in the above is structurally slow. This means that some fast speech, structurally speaking, is phonetically slower than some structurally slow speech. So long as an utterance contains at least one of the forms listed, or some other form in which microjuncture can be present or absent, this does not matter; we have a way of telling whether the fast phoneme and morpheme or the slow ones are involved. In utterances that contain no such form, we cannot tell whether the speech is structurally fast or slow. Perhaps in this case we should say that the utterance involves neither the fast phoneme nor the slow phoneme; in this case our original statement that every segment of every utterance is in the scope of one of the two would have to be modified.[16]

---

[16] Admittedly this treatment is circular. Not until after the analysis had been devised did it occur to me, however, that the circularity may be vicious in that we may be introducing a grammatical criterion for the phonemic analysis. If we are, then the treatment certainly has to be rejected. But we can still save the essential procedure of regarding the 'fast speech' forms as consisting of the 'slow speech' morphemes plus an additional morphemic constituent (or vice versa). We simply recognize the same segmental morphemes in each matching pair, but extract from one set (say the fast forms) an additional morphemic long component not present in the other set, without trying to identify which part of the phonemic material of each fast form constitutes this component. Speech of speech then reverts to nonphonemic status. The procedure is expounded in Zellig S. Harris, Componential Analysis of a Hebrew Paradigm, Lang. 24.87–91 (1948) ((272)). It might be useful also for the problem solved otherwise in Bernard Bloch, English Verb Inflection, Lang. 23.416–8, §8 (1947) ((252–4)).

Bloch has offered the following two highly relevant comments on this section. (1) If we set up tempo phonemes at all, one is enough; it can be present in certain stretches, absent in others. (2) The semantically

---

10. The Final Particle Ce.

We find a set of elements, terminal in utterances, with the shapes ·e, ·a, ·ie, ·ia, ·ye, ·ya, ·ue, ·ua, ·ne, ·na, ·nge, ·nga, ·re, and ·ra. The alternations between the shapes with /e/ and those with /a/ is entirely free (PP §9.54) and can be predicted by assuming the shapes with /e/ as basic.[17] The alternation between the various consonants and semivowels is determined by the shape of the preceding microsegment: shape ·ne after microsegment-final /n/, ·nge after /ng/, ·re after /r/, ·ie after /i/, ·ue after /u/, ·ye after /y/. If the preceding microsegment ends in a vowel, there is free alternation between shapes ·e and ·ie, the latter predominating. The forms carry various meanings, depending on context, but the variations in meaning do not correlate with the differences of shape, even where there is shape alternation in a single environment. We therefore take them all as alternants of a single morpheme ·Ce.

This morpheme then falls into a small class of sentence-final particles, including also ·me (interrogative for 'yes-no') and ·be (peremptory or suggestive).

Certain occurrences of utterance-final ·ne or ·na are not cases of the morpheme ·Ce, but rather instances of a different particle, of shape ·ne or ·na

---

preferable solution is certainly to set up only one tempo morpheme, the slow one, with the meaning 'deliberateness, emphasis, etc.'

[17] A confusing note is introduced by the relative frequency of forms with /e/ and forms with /a/ in such cases as this. The particles ·Ce, ·me, and ·be all have /a/ much more frequently than /e/; the particle ·ne, and terminal vowels of dissyllabic microsegments of the right shape, all have /e/ more commonly than /a/. Yet we cannot set the former morphemes up with basic /a/ instead of /e/, since there are some (e. g. guai[1]·da 'pat, spank lightly') which always have /a/. If relative frequency is a criterion, then we must recognize three distinct morphophonemic types.

Chao (op. cit.) eliminates the alternation in initial consonantism by a different phonemicization. This particle is recognized as one of the few forms with initial vowel. Elsewhere where our phonemic analysis recognizes an initial vowel (e. g. ai[4] 'to love, like' or en[4] 'to press down'), Chao sets up a consonant, phonetically sometimes glottal stop, sometimes weak voiced velar spirant (almost high back unrounded semivowel). The initial consonant of this particle is then simply the final consonant of the preceding microsegment, ambisyllabic when between two vowels. Chao's analysis also eliminates microjuncture, the occurrence of which is rendered automatic and nonphonemic. The difficulty with Chao's analysis is that it does not provide for forms like sreme[2] and zeme[3], where one has an intervocalic consonant with syllabification quite different from that between the second and third syllables of lau[3]fang[2]·nge 'Hey, Old Fang!' To take care of all the facts, microjuncture has to be introduced, together with the distinction between syllables and microsegments; and this implies the greater morphophonemic complexity of the particle here under discussion.

in all positions, with the meaning of hesitation, indecision of choice between alternatives, or continuing action. This particle is not final, but prefinal, since it occurs also with ·me or ·be after it; but when no final particle follows, and the preceding microsegment ends in /n/, it is sometimes difficult to decide which morpheme is present.

11. The Suffixes /-r/. Most forms with a terminal /r/ match similar forms without /r/ and with a somewhat similar meaning. The shapes before /-r/ are sometimes identical with the matching shapes without /-r/, and sometimes not.

The shapes are identical with and without /-r/ if the microsegment ends with /a e u y ei ai eu au eng ang ung iung/: fa2 : far2 'method'; ue1 : uer1 'nest'; ie4 : ier4 'leaf'; and so on.

If the preceding microsegment, without /-r/, ends in /ing/, this is replaced by /ieng/ before /r/: bing3 : biengr3 'cake'.

If the preceding microsegment ends otherwise in /en an yn in/ or in /i/ not preceded by a vowel, before /-r/ the final /n/ is lost, a syllabic /i/ is replaced by /ie/, and an /i/ is inserted before the /-r/: uen1 : ueir1 'essay'; zin1 'this' : zieir1 'today'; di3 : dieir3 'bottom'; bien1 (for some speakers) or bian1 (for others) : bieir1 or biair1 'side, edge'.

If the preceding microsegment has the segmental shape /r cr zr sr c z s/, /ei/ is added before the /-r/: z4 : zeir4 'word'.

When the shape before /-r/ is different from the shape without /-r/, it is of course quite irrelevant where we cut between the two morphs. In the above statements we have assumed the suffix morpheme throughout to consist simply of the /r/, all that precedes constituting an alternant of the other morpheme involved. We could just as well set up the suffix as sometimes /-r/, sometimes /-ir/.

/-r/ is one of a small class of nominal suffixes, including also ·z as in fang2·z 'house'. There are, however, certain tactical problems. A very small number of verbs end in the phoneme /r/, particularly uair2 'to play (with)'. This form resembles a morpheme uan2 with similar meaning, and the difference in shape is in accordance with the statements made above for the nominal suffix /-r/. We may choose among three procedures: (1) assume a single suffix /-r/, usually occurring in nouns but rarely also in verbs; (2) assume two different suffixes /-r/, homophonous and with identical morphophonemic effect, one nominal and one verbal; (3) assume that verbs like uair2, very few in number anyway, are simply monomorphemic, as are, for example, er4 or air4 'two' and er2 'son, child'. Alternatives (2) and (3) keep the tactical picture clear; alternative (1) does not. Alternative (3) obscures the similarity between verbs ending in /r/ and morphemes not ending in /r/ that parallel them and are similar in meaning. Alternative (2) seems slightly artificial. Even so, if

no further alternative is available, the second choice seems perhaps the best.

A different case of suffixed /-r/ will be discussed below in §12 (4). The morphophonemics are the same, but the tactical position is so clearly different and the meaning is so distinct that there is no problem involved in setting up another homophonous morpheme.

There are a few cases of the nominal suffix /-r/ where the morphophonemics are not in accord with the statements given above. Thus 'flower' is sometimes huar1, expected with underlying hua1, but for some speakers it is more often huair1. These irregular forms can be handled only by listing.[18]

12. Chameleons. In several cases it is tactically convenient to regard a segmental morph which matches, with statable differences, the phonemic shape of some nearby morph, as an occurrence of a reduplicative or 'chameleon' morpheme rather than as a second occurrence of the morpheme whose shape it matches. We recognize four such chameleons; possibly one should also establish others.

(1) R_d (R for 'reduplication', d for 'demonstrative') occurs before a measure, rarely before a noun, and has the meaning 'distributive plural'.[19] The segmental shape and tone of R_d are those of the following measure. R_d fits into a class of morphemes which we call demonstratives, including zrei4 'this', nei4 'that', nei3 or nai3 'which', and mei3 'every'; mei3 and R_d have very similar meanings. Examples: 'zrei4·tian1 'this day', 'nei4·tian1 'that day', 'nai3·tian1 'which day', 'mei3·tian1 'every day', and with R_d, 'tian1·tian1 'every day, daily'; zrei4·ge#ren2 'this man', and with R_d, ge4·ge#ren2 'each man, every man'; similarly 'nian2·nian2 'every year, yearly'; 'zian4·zian4 'item by item, section by section (as of a document)'; directly before a noun: 'ren2·ren2 'everyone, everybody'.

(2) ·R_n ('n' for 'noun') occurs after certain bound nominal morphemes, producing a free form; the meanings are generally kinship terms or items of childhood culture. ·R_n assumes the segmental shape of the preceding bound morpheme, but is atonic and toneless. ·R_n is one of a small class of nominal suffixes, including also ·z, -r, and ·teu2—differential glosses for which are almost impossible. Examples: ba4·ba 'papa', ma1·ma 'mama', ge1·ge 'older brother', di4·di 'younger brother', zie3·zie 'older sister', mei4·mei 'younger sister', gue1·gue (or gue1·guer, with /-r/ added too) 'large green cricket', cy1·cyr 'cricket (another kind)'; wa2·wa 'doll'.

[18] Some speakers have far less differentiation phonemically in microsegments with terminal /r/; for their speech the morphophonemic patterns are actually a bit more complex.

[19] Other demonstratives also occur most usually before a measure, but sometimes directly before a noun with no intervening measure: zrei4·ge#sr2·heu4 or zrei4sr2·heu4 'this time'.

(3) R_m ('m' for 'measure') occurs after certain monosyllabic verbs, with intervening i^1 'a, an' (in its zero form if not overtly present); it means, essentially, 'for a short while, a bit, a while'. R_m has the segmental and tonal shape of the verb. R_m falls into a small class of measures which typically occupy this position; like some but not all of the others, it occurs only with the numeral i^1 'one'. Others of the class are c^4 'time, occasion', $bian^4$ 'number of times through' (some action that involves performing a string of smaller actions in a prescribed sequence, as in singing a song), $huei^2$ 'occurrences, times'. Examples of R_m: $^{1}kan^4·i\#kan^4$ 'take a look, examine for a minute'; $^{1}tan^2·i\#tan^2$ 'converse for a while, chat'; $^{1}ting^1·i·i\#ting^1$ 'listen a bit, take a listen'; $^{1}siang^3·le·i\#siang^3$ 'thought for a minute'. If the mesosegment ends with R_m, the verb, as indicated, bears a displaced loud stress; if more material follows, the stress is often not displaced, thus $tan^2·i\#tan^2huar^4$ 'carry on for a bit speech = have a chat'.

(4) R_a ('a' for 'adverb') occurs before almost any monosyllabic stative verb, with meaning 'intensive, much so, greatly'. R_a has the segmental and tonal structure of the following stative verb. The stative verb itself, however, in position after R_a, has tone /1/ regardless of its tone in other contexts. R_a falls into the class of adverbs, and into a subclass thereof which occur before stative verbs: hen^3 'quite, very', tai^4 'too much so', $zren^1$ 'truly', $zuei^4$ 'most', and others. The sequence beginning with R_a normally has an /-r/ suffix added to the stative verb; this is a different /-r/ suffix, though with the same morphophonemics, from those of §11. The combination is limited to occurrence with following particle ·de, a limitation not generally found with other combinations of adverb plus stative verb. Examples: $hei^1heir^1·de$ 'extremely black'; $bau^2baur^1·de$ 'very thin'; $hau^3haur^1·de$ 'extremely good'; $man^4mair^1·de$ 'very slowly'.

Since one also hears $hau^3haul·de$, the /-r/ suffix must be taken as a separate morpheme, rather than as a separate part of R_a itself.

Some stative verbs consisting of two microsegments are bimorphemic, the separate morphemes standing in the relation 'A and B'. With these, R_a takes the shape of a microsegment before each of the constituent morphemes of the compound stative verb, and the stress pattern and tonal relations are different: $rung^2·i^4$ 'easy' : $rung^2·rung^2i^4i^4·de$ 'very easy indeed'; $ming^2·bai^2$ 'clear' : $ming^2·ming^2bai^2 bai^2·de$ 'very clear(ly) indeed'.

In each of these four cases we have the problem of deciding which of the two similarly shaped morphs in a context is the chameleon, which is the background to which the chameleon has adapted itself. (If there were no such problem, the term 'chameleon' would of course be inappropriate.) We decide on the basis of similar structures not involving chameleons.

Since $ge^4·ge$ 'every' is like $zrei^4·ge$ 'this', we call the first syllable of the former the chameleon; similarly in the other cases, as indicated by the analogies given for each.[20]

There are several other types of 'repeating' or partial repeating which we might choose to provide for with chameleons. The decision not to do so at present is tentative; the main difficulty is a lack of sufficient evidence. Some of these cases we itemize herewith.

(a) Certain verbs of greater than one microsegment length (normally two in slow speech) are habitually uttered twice. Thus one may merely say $sie^4·sie^4$ 'thanks', but often enough thanks consist of the utterance $/˘sie^4·sie, sie^4·sie./$. 'Let's take a stroll' may be $/·uem^3{}^{1}liul·da\#liul·da·be./$; the verb $liul·da$ occurs more often doubled than single. The alternative to chameleon treatment is to analyze such constructions as the same sequence of segmental morphemes spoken twice — as implied by the phrasing of the descriptions just given.

Different both from the construction of verb plus R_m, and from the construction just described in which a verb is spoken twice, is the apparently doubled occurrence of kai^1 'to open' in such a sentence as $ba^3men^2, kai^1·kai^1$ 'open the door'. Both occurrences of kai^1 are occurrences of the same morpheme, but the construction is not that of doubling; rather the first occurrence is comparable to the occurrence of the same morpheme in kai^1wan^2 'to open completely', and the second occurrence is comparable to the occurrence of the same morpheme in $da^3·kai^1$ 'strike open', $lal·kai^1$ 'pull open', $tuei^1·kai^1$ 'push open', and many others. This construction is the <u>resultative</u> construction of two verbs, in which the first specifies the manner in which the action is brought about and the second specifies the resulting action. It just happens that kai^1 'open' occurs both as first member and as second member in this construction, in either case with various accompanying members, and it just happens that one possible case of the construction has kai^1 as both first and second member. The apparent reduplication is therefore quite accidental.

(b) A number of two-microsegment free forms, with stress on the first, the second toneless, of obscure morphemic status (quite possibly single morphemes of type II) are matched by four-microsegment free forms as follows: $gal·da$ 'knot (in string or wood), bump (on skin)' : $gal·li\#galdal·de$ 'rough, bumpy (of a surface)'; $hu^2·tu$ 'muddled' :

---

[20] Chao (op. cit.) handles some of these forms as instances of the 'grammatical process' of reduplication, though noting (39, fn. 7) the possibility of the chameleon treatment. But the Romanization he uses in his course implies the chameleon solution, since 'x' is used for 'preceding syllable repeated', and 'vx' for 'the two preceding syllables repeated' (333, 332).

hu^2·li#hu^{2}tu^2 'fuzzy-wuzzy';[21] with some distortion ga^l·la 'corner, angle' (cf. ga^l·la#bar^4 or ge^l·le#bar^4 'knee') : zi^l·li#ga^{l}lar^2 'in every nook and cranny'. One could set up a chameleon consisting of preposed duplication of the shape of the underlying form, but with the substitution of the microsegment ·li for the second microsegment of the underlying form; the last instance cited would still call for special treatment.

(c) There are a number of two-microsegment free forms in which the second microsegment begins with /l/ or with /s/, and is otherwise like the first: ba^l·la 'scar, pockmark'; hu^2·lu 'to brush or stroke with the hand'; hu^2·lu 'gourd'; gu^l·lu 'to roll something along'; gu^2·lu 'wheel'; ha^l·la 'rancid'; tu^2·lu 'to drag on (floor); to lose one's grip'; du^l·lu 'bunch of (keys), cluster of (grapes)'; with /s/, due^l·sue 'to shake, quiver, shiver, tremble'; ma^l·sa 'to smooth out with the hand, rub, massage'; and others. We could set up postposed chameleons for these two sets. In some cases the underlying forms occur elsewhere, or can at least be suspected of being identical with similarly shaped morphs in other environments; in some cases, however, setting up the form as bimorphemic would necessitate recognizing unique constituents.

In (c), and perhaps in (b), we may have reached that difficult borderline represented in English by sets of words like crash, bash, smash; flip, flap, flop.

13. Suppletive Alternations.
There are a number of cases in which morphs (or sets of morphs already grouped together by the various criteria discussed above) of different shapes seem to be in noncontrastive distribution and identical in meaning, tempting us to class them in single morphemes. The forms er^4 and air^4 'two' are probably free alternants wherever both are found in the speech of a single individual. The case of these versus liang^3 'two' was described briefly in PMA §10. Similarly, in addition to crang^3 'a spell of' there is a form crang^2 with identical meaning, occurring freely in any environment in which any alternant of crang^3 would be called for. Both bue^2 and bau^2 mean 'thin (in dimension), weak (of human relationships)', and the two are superficially in free alternation. 'Blood' is variously sie^3, sye^3, and sye^4.

In such cases as these, there is no systematically recurrent phonemic difference between the alternants, and the distribution is never complementary, always involving at least some cases of apparent free alternation in a single environment. Without devices for measuring the reactions of speakers of a language to the forms they hear, far more accurate than any now available, we can never be sure that the stylistic connotations of the differing forms are not considerable, however easy it may be to supply all the members of a set with a single English gloss to cover their most obvious meaning. In the case of 'blood',

there is clear evidence that such stylistic differences exist: sye^3 is rather literary, sie^3 and sye^4 are more colloquial. The course of wisdom is undoubtedly to keep the members of such sets apart. I would now do this even with er^4 and liang^3 'two', contrary to PMA §10.[22]

14. Minus Morphemes.
The ordinary forms for 'two' and 'three' are respectively liang^3 and san^1. There are also, however, two forms lia^3 and sa^1 which seem to have (save for stylistic differences) the same meanings. By the decision we have just reached (§13), lia^3 and liang^3 cannot be taken as morphemically identical, nor can sa^1 and san^1. In order to determine the status of the shorter forms, we must examine their distribution.

Numerals occur before measures (as well as in some other positions), and a group of numeral plus measure may occur before a noun: liang^3·ge 'two' : liang^3·ge#ren^2 'two people'. The forms lia^3 and sa^1 do not occur before a measure, but rather directly before a noun; and in other positions where a numeral-plus-measure combination might occur, we find just lia^3 or sa^1: lia^3·ren^2 'two people'; lia^{3}sreu^3 'two hands'; lia^{3}er^3·deu 'two ears, both ears'; lia^{3}ian^3·zing 'two eyes, both eyes'; lia^{3}meir^2 'two (paired) doors'; uem^{3}lia^3 or uem^{3}lia^3·ren^2 'we two'; sa^1·ren^2 'three people'; uem^{3}sa^1 or uem^{3}sa^1·ren^2 'we three'.

[22] In the case of alternations from one speaker to another, or within a single speaker's dialect but of the same general nature as those which for the most part are from one speaker to another — e.g. tien^1 versus tian^1 for 'day', or iu^2 versus ieu^2 for 'postal' (see §0) — the same principle ought in theory to apply. If in practice we do not apply it, it is because of the great difficulty in making sufficiently precise observations. We are here at the thin edge between synchronic and diachronic linguistics. If a single speaker says sometimes iu^2 and somes ieu^2 for 'postal', it is ultimately because he has picked up both forms from others, and there has presumably been some first individual to acquire and use both. The two forms then differ at least in the subtle connotations they have due to the specific life-history circumstances accompanying the acquisition of each. [[Each of us learns his language from his community, readily admitting that he falls short by learning less than the community teaches him; what is seldom recognized is that he also learns more than what he is taught by over-valuing fluctuations in the presentation of the models to him. Thus a student of mine thought that there were two English words spelled ego, respectively /íygòw/ and /égow/, with different meanings which he fluently explained to me; on prolonged cross-questioning it turned out that he had learned the word exactly twice, from two persons whom he was able to name... We each of us have our quota of similarly acquired private distinctions, which we do not know to be private and hence automatically offer as models to all around us. Most of them fail to prosper; occasionally one of them prospers and establishes a doublet-pair like sleek and slick.]] To make a blanket statement of this kind is easy; to try to cover all such cases in a description of a language or dialect is totally impossible.

[21] Chao, op. cit. 41.

Since the positions occupied by lia^3 and sa^1 are positions open also to a combination of numeral plus measure, we may suspect that these two forms also should be interpreted as a numeral plus a measure.

lia^3 is then structurally two morphemes, respectively $liang^3$ and this measure, and sa^1 similarly. To interpret them in this way, we must recognize one morpheme which appears only in the shape of this truncation of the 'preceding' morpheme, since no measure of overt phonemic shape occurs with which we can identify this one. The similarity in shape of $liang^3$ and lia^3, of san^1 and sa^1, and the parallelism of difference in shape (absence of final consonant in each case) apparently force us to this conclusion. If it be disallowed, then the only alternative is to take lia^3 and sa^1 as single morphemes, thus ignoring their resemblance in shape and meaning to $liang^3$ and san^1, and complicating the tactics since the morphemes lia^3 and sa^1 would then have to constitute a tactical class of their own.

15. Small-Scale Resemblances. We have almost completed our survey; the remaining cases of possible morphemic identity are in general quite problematical. This may of course reflect a defect in method, or in the breadth of the information on which the discussion is based. But it is also possible that there is something in the nature of the language —or perhaps in the nature of all languages—to produce the dilemmas: perhaps morphemic analysis must always choose between being neat but not quite complete, or else more nearly complete but not quite neat.

Without prejudice to our ultimate decisions, we shall tentatively call the forms about to be discussed 'morphemes'.

Atonic morphemes of type I, and type II morphemes, are not of minimal canonical forms. If we compare $fang^2·z$ 'house' and $ming^2·z$ 'name', or $buel^1·li$ 'glass' and $sing^2·li$ 'baggage', we see why this is so. The $·z$ of 'house' is a type I atonic morpheme; but the $·z$ of 'name' is a type I tonic morpheme z^4 'character, word' accompanied by the compound-marking zero-stress morpheme. Thus the atonic morpheme is seen to resemble in its phonemic shape such a combination of two morphemes. 'Glass' is a single morpheme of type II, but it resembles 'baggage' in shape, though the latter consists of two successive type I tonic morphemes, with the compound-marking zero-stress morpheme accompanying the second; so 'glass' looks like such a trimorphemic form. With every form that we suspect of being a single morpheme of a nonminimal canonical form, the problem therefore arises whether further analysis may not be possible and desirable.

Thus 'glass' and $liu^2·li$ 'glaze' have similar meanings and end similarly. Instead of taking each to be a single type II morpheme, we might segregate the recurrent $·li$ as a morpheme in itself. This would require us to recognize $buel^1$ and liu^2 as unique constituents, and it is this that deters us; but since there are some indisputable cases of unique constituents in the language, perhaps it should not.

The other major area of ambiguity is in sets of morphemes resembling each other somewhat in sound and in meaning. In a few cases it is very clear that analysis must go further. There is a set of forms involving microsegment-initial $/n/$ and tone $/4/$ with a distal-demonstrative sense: na^4 'that (abstract); therefore' : nei^4 'that (concrete)' : $neme^4$ 'so, in that case, that kind of' : ner^4 'there'. There is another set involving initial $/n/$ and tone $/3/$, with interrogative-indefinite sense: na^3 'whence, how come, in what way' : nei^3 or nai^3 'which (concrete)' : $neme^3$ (rare) 'how, in what case' : nar^3 'where'. There is a third such set, with initial $/zr/$ or $/z/$ and tone $/4/$, with proximal-demonstrative sense: $zrei^4$ 'this (concrete)' : $zeme^4$ (rarely $zreme^4$) 'so, in this case, this kind of' : $zrer^4$ 'here'. And there are two isolated forms, both interrogative, one with initial $/z/$ and tone $/3/$: $zeme^3$ 'how, how come'; and one with initial $/sr/$ and tone $/2/$: $sreme^2$ 'what'. Except for this last form, it is clear that the difference between tone $/4/$ and tone $/3/$ accompanies the semantic difference between non-interrogative and interrogative-indefinite. With tone $/4/$, it is equally clear that the difference between initial $/n/$ and initial $/zr/$ or $/z/$ parallels the semantic difference between distal and proximal. Other partial similarities in sound and meaning can easily be spotted— for example, the terminal $/r/$ with a locative sense.[23]

If we find it more convenient to regard these forms as single morphs, we must at least take them to be portmanteaus, and not completely arbitrary ones, since as has been demonstrated we can identify within their phonemic structure portions which correlate with portions of the whole meanings.

---

[23] Probably tactical considerations must lead us to take $neme^4$, $neme^3$, $zeme^4$ or $zreme^4$, $zeme^3$, and $sreme^2$ as bimorphemic, an alternant of a demonstrative (itself perhaps subject to further analysis as sketched in the text) plus a measure -me, and ner^4, nar^3 and $zrer^4$ similarly as an alternant of a demonstrative plus a measure -r. But these forms have somewhat special tactical statuses, and the answers are not clear.

The measure -r, if we so analyze, is a different morpheme from the noun-suffix -r and the other morphemes of that shape discussed in earlier sections. Historically it is probably to be related to the type I tonic (bound) morpheme li^3 'in, inside': earlier $na^4·li^3$, $na^3·li^3$ and $zre^4·li^3$, with loss of the microjuncture in rapid speech and accompanying loss of the terminal $/i/$, then with the $/l/$ changed to $/r/$ 'because' $/l/$ is not habitual in microsegment-final position. But the two-microsegment forms have been reintroduced, analogically or from writing or in both ways, and now stand beside the one-microsegment forms, as more elevated and literary alternants, so that the -r of the short forms can no longer be identified morphemically with any element occurring elsewhere.

Other cases are far less clear. There are many sets such as the following: zrung[1] (bound form) 'middle; China' : zrung[4] 'in the center, in the bull's-eye, square' (da[3]zrung[4] 'to hit the bull's-eye, to succeed in an examination'); zrang[3] 'to grow, to spread' : crang[2] 'long' : zrang[4] 'wide, spread out' (as of water in flood time); dau[3] 'to turn upside down or on one side; to fail (of a business)' : dau[4] 'to be inverted, turned upside down; to drive (a car) backwards'; hau[3] 'OK' : hau[4] 'to like to (do something)'. In each case there are obviously similarities of phonemic shape and of meaning. Actually, sets such as crang[3] and crang[2] 'spell of' (§13). where it is hard to find any semantic difference at all, are simply limiting cases of this phenomenon of partial resemblance. At the other extreme one has forms so different in form or in meaning, or both, that the problem of possible morphemic relationship simply does not arise.

One common solution to the problem presented by such sets is to follow the identifications given by the characters with which the forms are traditionally written. Since Chinese characters constitute essentially a morphemic writing system, they also represent a centuries-old, slowly but constantly evolving folk-analysis of the language. In this characterization, the term 'folk' is not to be read with a sneer; all morphemic analysis is in a sense folk-analysis, and one might suspect that the identifications thus arrived at would be as valid as any the modern analyst might discover. If one does this, then one says that zrang[3] 'to grow' and crang[2] 'long', for example, are related forms, and one devises the necessary morphophonemic machinery to handle the relationship. On the other hand, one does not identify zrang[3] 'to grow' and a homophonous and grammatically identical zrang[3] 'to rise and spread (as water in flood time)', because these are written with two different characters. And when one discovers that this procedure would require an interpretation of dung[1]·si 'thing' as consisting of dung[1] 'east' plus si[1] 'west' plus compound-marking zero stress—leaving the burden of the semantic difference to be borne entirely by the last-named constituent—then certainly one must reach the conclusion that the characters are helpful, if at all, only as clues, not as answers.

When that conclusion is reached, it appears that the same caution is advisable in the cases treated here as for those treated in §13, where there was no discernible difference in meaning and grammatical function accompanying the difference in phonemic shape. That is, since there is no <u>systematic</u> parallelism between the differences in meaning and the differences in shape from one set to another, we had better leave each form of such a set intact, a separate and distinct morpheme.[24]

---

[24] Chao (op. cit. 40) reaches essentially the same conclusion: 'Although [the examples he gives] are pairs of cognate words (and often written with the same characters), they should, for practical purposes, be learned as separate words.' 'Cognate', of course, is a historical term, not a descriptive one.

STUDIES IN COLLOQUIAL JAPANESE IV

PHONEMICS

BERNARD BLOCH

Language 26.86-125—1950

0. Introductory. In earlier papers of this series,[1] Japanese forms are cited in a transcription that purports to be phonemic; the system that underlies the transcription is briefly outlined in the footnotes.[2] On closer examination that system proves to be untenable. Instead of being purely phonemic, it is heavily influenced by unformulated morphophonemic considerations, and even, to some extent, by the traditional representation of Japanese in roman letters.[3] There is room, then, for a new and more careful study of Japanese phonemics, based solely on the sounds that occur in Japanese utterances and on their distribution. Such a study is the object of the present paper.[4] The dialect to be investigated is the modern standard colloquial, defined as the speech of educated persons native to Tokyo.

0.1. The presence of recent loanwords in Japanese, as in many other languages, complicates the analysis; but there is no purely descriptive test by which they can be identified, and no valid excuse for excluding them—so far as the analyst can recognize them through his accidental knowledge of other languages—from the total vocabulary. The view set forth by Fries and Pike,[5] that loanwords may constitute a separate phonemic system coexisting with one or more other systems in the same dialect, is unacceptable. What we are able to discern as the phonemic system of a dialect is necessarily single, not multiple: the total network of relationships among all the sounds that occur in the dialect; and the analyst's task is to describe the system in a way that is correspondingly single, in a coherent set of general statements which will enable him to predict the phonetic shape of utterances that have not yet occurred.[6] All the details that make up a language have an equal claim to be used as evidence for the system; whatever occurs in the utterances of those who speak the language is for that reason a part of the total structure.[7] The question how to treat loanwords can have only one answer: treat them as words.

remains always on the lowest phonetic level. The sounds of Japanese, for Mori (as for practically all the other scholars who have described them), are mere noises, without structural organization or any sort of interrelations except in their physical properties.

[5] Charles C. Fries and Kenneth L. Pike, Coexistent phonemic systems, Lg. 25.29-50 (1949). The crucial illustration in this article is taken from Mazateco, an Indian language of Mexico. In Mazateco words of native origin there are two dental stops: after [n] only [d], elsewhere only [t]. This situation by itself would call for a single phoneme with two allophones. But there is also a word [siento] hundred, a loan from Spanish, with [t] after [n]. Fries and Pike regard this [t] as belonging not only to a different phoneme but to a different phonemic system from that which includes the [t]s and [d]s of native words. But the presence of [siento] necessarily affects the treatment of all dental stops in the language: it contributes no less than other utterance-fractions to the total analysis. The cultural evidence adduced by Fries and Pike against this view, that monolingual speakers of Mazateco learn to read the [nd] of native words more easily in the spelling 'nt' than in the spelling 'nd', whatever its ultimate explanation may be, is not a cogent reason for setting aside the phonetic and distributional data.

Certain other cases of so-called coexistence are easily accounted for by traditional methods. Thus whispered utterances are utterances without pitch phonemes, singing is a non-linguistic use of linguistic material. Differences in tempo and style must probably be treated as differences in dialect, at least until a more fruitful approach can be worked out. For a phonemic interpretation of tempo differences see now Charles F. Hockett, Peiping morphophonemics §9, Lg. 26.74-7 (1950). ((315))

[6] See the admirable short statement by Charles F. Hockett, A note on 'structure', IJAL 14.269-71 (1948). ((279))

[7] This does not mean that every noise made by a speaker in speaking must be accommodated in the phonemic system. Sounds that occur in a completely unrestricted set of environments (before and after all other sound types without exception), such as hiccups, coughs, and sniffles, can be excluded from the relevant material at once. Sounds that never combine with other sound types in an utterance, such as the alveolar 'click of commiseration' in English and the polite indrawn hiss in Japanese, can be similarly excluded, or else treated as an organically separate part of the system (though not as part of an independent system coexisting with the main one). Note that the sounds here listed for exclusion are identified by their distribution.

[1] This paper is the fourth in a series of articles under the general title Studies in Colloquial Japanese (abbr. SCJ). The earlier papers in the series are I. Inflection, JAOS 66.97-109; II. Syntax, Lg. 22.200-48; III. Derivation of inflected words, JAOS 66.304-15 (all 1946). For an acknowledgment of the help that I received from the American Council of Learned Societies, from several Japanese informants, and from my colleagues, see SCJ I, fn. 1 (JAOS 66.97), or SCJ II, fn. 1 (Lg. 22.200). ((154))

[2] In SCJ I, JAOS 66.98 fn. 4; in SCJ II, Lg. 22.200-1 fn. 3, 203-4 (§1.4). ((154))

[3] It was the neat and systematic National Romanization (Kokutei Rômazi), promulgated by a decree of the Japanese cabinet in 1937, that especially influenced my transcription, rather than the so-called Hepburn Romanization of 1885. Yet the latter—unsystematic and cumbersome as it seems to be—is the one that turns out to be closer to a phonemic notation. (On these two systems of romanization see Denzel Carr in JAOS 59.99-102 [1939] and Edwin O. Reischauer in JAOS 60.82-9 [1940].)

[4] So far as I know, all other attempts by American linguists to work out the phonemic structure of Japanese are open to the same objections as mine. I have seen unpublished analyses by George A. Kennedy (ca. 1942) and A. M. Halpern (ca. 1944), as well as the published account in Joseph K. Yamagiwa, Modern conversational Japanese 1-9 (New York and London, 1942). All these, like my own earlier version, overlook phonemic contrasts and rely heavily on morphophonemic data. But since their main purpose was pedagogical (again like that of my own earlier version), their morphophonemic tinge is a merit rather than a reproach.

* In writing this paper I have had the benefit of several suggestions by Rulon S. Wells and Eleanor Harz Jorden. Masako Yokoyama has kindly checked the examples for me. Most of the examples are drawn from my own files; but where these did not contain illustrations of particular sequences, I consulted Kenkyusha's New Japanese-English dictionary (Tokyo, 1938). All examples taken from this source were submitted to qualified informants before being transcribed.

Several accounts of Japanese pronunciation have been published in English, but none that approaches the subject from a structural (phonemic) point of view, or that presents more than crude phonetic data, undigested and naive. The most useful (or least useless) of the works that have so far appeared in English is Masatoshi Gensen Mori, The pronunciation of Japanese (Tokyo, 1929); others are listed by Borton, Elisséeff, and Reischauer in A selected list of books and articles on Japan 74-5 (Washington, 1940). Mori's treatment is detailed and exhaustive, in the best tradition of the London school of phonetics; but it

Yet this answer does not wholly settle the problem of loanwords in Japanese, especially of those recently taken from English. Speakers of standard Japanese agree, within a fairly narrow range of personal variation, on the pronunciation of nearly all the words they use—except precisely these. In their treatment of English loans the variation from speaker to speaker is considerable. Some, who speak no English, confine themselves in these loans to sound types and combinations that occur also in longer-established words; others, with some command of English, use sound types and combinations not found elsewhere in their speech; still others are intermediate in the degree to which they assimilate English words to the rest of their vocabulary. It is clear that these different idiolects (personal dialects) cannot all be analyzed in the same way: phonemic distinctions that exist in one are absent from another; sounds that occur in one man's speech as allophones of a single phoneme belong to separate phonemes in the speech of his neighbor. In short, standard colloquial Japanese is not one dialect but several, which differ from each other, greatly or little, in their treatment of English loans.

A complete solution would be to describe separately each of the several dialects of standard Japanese; this paper will attempt only a partial solution. Only two dialects will be described: that in which English loanwords have been fully assimilated to the pronunciation of other words; and that at the other extreme (spoken chiefly by persons with a good command of English), in which these loanwords are characterized by a maximum number of special sound types and combinations. The two dialects will be referred to as the CONSERVATIVE and the INNOVATING respectively. In each dialect, the style to be described is that of normal conversation, ranging in tempo from moderately fast to moderately slow, but excluding the extremes of tempo at both ends of the scale. (The conservative dialect is treated in §§1–7, the innovating dialect in §8.)

0.2. Definitions of a few basic terms will clarify the description.[8]

A PHRASE is an utterance or part of an utterance bounded by successive pauses (interruptions of speech activity, regardless of length).[9] A phrase may be preceded or followed, or both preceded and followed, by other phrases in the same utterance, with pauses intervening; but no phrase contains a pause within itself.

A QUALITY is any aurally distinguishable single component of the total auditory impression made by some part of a phrase—a particular vowel color, the effect of a particular consonantal position or movement or manner of articulation, palatalization, oral or nasal resonance, voice or voicelessness, a particular level of loudness or pitch, and so on. Qualities are identified by ear; but in linguistic works they are traditionally defined in terms of their assumed production by the vocal organs.

A PHONE is any continuous fraction of a phrase that is heard as coextensive with a given quality; very often a phone is defined by several qualities at once, beginning and ending together. Phones are of two kinds: a SEGMENT is a minimum phone, one that contains no smaller phone; a SPAN is a phone composed of two or more segments that have a quality or a combination of qualities in common. The order of phones in a phrase is successive, simultaneous, or overlapping: segments occur only in succession; but spans, which are coextensive with qualities common to a train of several segments, occur simultaneously with the segments that compose the train, and may overlap with other spans. Every phone is a unique event. The segmentation of a phrase into phones is accomplished by ear; but in linguistic works, again, it is traditionally described in terms of the assumed movements and positions of the vocal organs.

Successive qualities are THE SAME if no difference can be heard between them; otherwise they are DIFFERENT. Two or more phones are THE SAME if they contain the same qualities and no others; otherwise they are DIFFERENT. Sameness and difference are thus determined impressionistically by ear.[10]

Two or more phones are PHONETICALLY SIMILAR if they contain a quality or a combination of qualities that is absent from all other phones in the utterances of the same dialect. (It follows that if two or more phones are the same they must be phonetically similar, but not conversely.) Under this definition phonetic similarity has an absolute, not a relative meaning.

The ENVIRONMENT of a phone is the discontinuous sequence of phones that precede and follow it in the phrase (or, if it is initial or final, the sequence of phones that follow or precede it). For most purposes the relevant environment of a phone consists only of the immediately preceding and the immediately following phone. Environments of two or more phones are THE SAME if they consist wholly of the same phones in the same order. Phones occurring in the same environment are said to have the environment IN COMMON.

If different phones have none of their environments in common, they are IN COMPLEMENTARY DISTRIBUTION; if they have in common only a phonetically or phonemically definable set of environments, they are IN OVERLAPPING DISTRIBUTION; if one phone shares all the environments of another, they are IN FREE VARIATION.[11] Different phones that are in complementary or overlapping distribution or in free variation are NON-CONTRASTIVE.

---

[8] These definitions are restated, with additions and with a pervading shift of emphasis, from my article A set of postulates for phonemic analysis, Lg. 24.3–46 (1948); they were presented, in a preliminary version, before a meeting of the Linguistic Society in New York, 30 December 1948. The restatement is intended to meet the objections of Martin Joos, Acoustic phonetics 8 fn. 9 and 120 fn. 85 (Language Monograph No. 23, 1948), by establishing the theory of phonemic analysis on an auditory instead of an articulatory basis.

[9] In SCJ II, Lg. 22.202 ff., this unit is called a pause-group, in order to avoid confusion with the use of the term 'phrase' for syntactic units. ((155)) It might be argued that PAUSE, the interruption of speech activity, should be distinguished from mere SILENCE, the absence of speech activity that precedes and follows a whole utterance; the two could be distinguished by assigning to pause an arbitrary upper limit of duration—say ten seconds. Such a distinction would complicate the definition of a phrase, and would appear to serve no particular purpose; but any reader who favors it can safely make for himself the small adjustments that would result from its adoption. All the pauses marked in this paper (except in §7) occur internally in utterances.

[10] Whenever two or more phones are mentioned in these definitions, it is understood that they are phones occurring in utterances of a single dialect.

[11] This statement is meant to cover both the situation where two phones P and Q have all their environments in common, and the more usual situation where P shares all the environments of Q but occurs also in environments where Q does not occur.

If different phones have some but not all of their environments in common, and if their common environments do not form a phonetically or phonemically definable set, they are IN CONTRAST. Two classes of phones are in contrast if every member of one class is in contrast with some member of the other.

A PHONEME is a class of non-contrastive and phonetically similar phones. Together, the phonemes of a dialect accommodate all the phones that occur in the utterances of the dialect; and every phoneme, as a class, is in contrast with at least one other phoneme in at least some of the positions where its members occur. Each phoneme is defined by the quality or combination of qualities present in all its members and absent from all other phones of the dialect; and every phone that contains such a quality or combination belongs to the phoneme which is defined by it. A phone that contains two or more such qualities or combinations accordingly belongs to two or more phonemes at once.

Not all the qualities that are common to the members of a phoneme are necessarily relevant in defining the phoneme. If a give phone P contains two qualities or combinations of qualities a and x (whether it contains other qualities or not), such that x occurs in other phones unaccompanied by a but a does not occur in any phone without x, the quality or combination x is DETERMINED in the phone P, and is not properly part of the definition of the phoneme to which P belongs.

A quality or combination of qualities that occurs in some but not in all members of a phoneme, and does not by itself define any other phoneme, is CONDITIONED by the environments in which it occurs.

A quality or combination of qualities that is neither determined nor conditioned is DISTINCTIVE.[12]

An ALLOPHONE is a subclass of a phoneme, composed of phones that are the same. In this paper the term 'phone' will be used ambiguously in two senses: strictly, to designate a unique event; and loosely, to designate a class of phones that are the same. In the latter meaning, the term 'phone' is a shorter equivalent of 'allophone'. The context in each case will make it clear which meaning is intended.

A PHONETIC TRANSCRIPTION is a record either of a single utterance by one speaker (PHONIC transcription) or of a class of utterances composed of the same phones in the same order (ALLOPHONIC transcription). A PHONEMIC TRANSCRIPTION is a record of a class of utterances whose constituent phones belong respectively to the same phonemes in the same order.

1. Syllables. The most striking general feature of Japanese pronunciation is its staccato rhythm. The auditory impression of any phrase is of a rapid patter-

[12] The term 'quality' is used in this paper as the auditory correlate of what I called aspects and components in my article on postulates (cited in fn. 8 above).

ing succession of more-or-less sharply defined fractions, all of about the same length. In any one utterance, or indeed in any one conversation or style of discourse, the perceived relative duration of successive phrases can be adequately compared in terms of these fractions: two phrases containing the same number of fractions are heard as equal in duration; a phrase containing twice or three times as many fractions as another is heard as lasting just twice or three times as long. The phrases [to-ko-ro]13 *place* and [ha-ko-bu] *carries* contain three fractions each; [no-ri-mo-no] *vehicle* and [to-ki-do-ki] *sometimes* contain four fractions each; [so-no-ko-do-mo-no-ki-mo-no] *that child's clothing* and [yo-ko-ha-ma-no-mi-na-to-de] *in the Yokohama harbor* contain nine each.

In the examples given so far, each fraction consists of a single consonantal segment and a vowel; but fractions of other types occur also. Some fractions consist of two consonantal segments and a vowel, as in [ma-tši] *town*, [kʲa-ku] *guest*, [nʲo-dži-tsu-ri] *true to life*; some consist of one or two consonantal segments and a voiceless vowel, as in [su-su-mu] *advances*, [ki-ta] *came*, [ha-tsu-ši-mo] *first frost of the year*; some consist of a vowel alone, as in [o-mo-u] *thinks*, [i-e] *house*, [a-o-i] *blue*; some consist of a long nasal consonant alone, as in [hõ-ŋ'] *book*, [kõ-n-do] *this time*, [kõ-m-bã-n'] *tonight*; and some consist of one or two long voiceless consonants alone, as in [s-te-ru] *throws away*, [i-p-pa-i] *full*, [ts-tši] *soil*. All these fractions are heard as having the same time value; the perceived relative duration of successive phrases depends only on the number of fractions that they contain, not on their type.

Because the affricates [ts, tš, dž] occur in the same positions and with the same time value as [t, k, s], and other single segments, they will be regarded as unitary consonants, not as sequences of two consonants. But combinations

13 Phonetic transcriptions in this paper, enclosed in square brackets, are allophonic; they have been simplified as much as possible, so as to avoid the use of too many special characters. The hyphen that appears in the transcriptions of §1 is merely a graphic device for showing the number of equivalent fractions in a phrase; it has no phonetic or phonemic significance. For the meaning of the phonetic terms in the following descriptions see Bloch and Trager, Outline of linguistic analysis, ch. 2 (Baltimore, 1942).

Consonant symbols for the most part have their traditional values. [p, b, m] are bilabial, but [f] is bilabial or labiodental in free variation; [t, d, n] are dental, [ts] is dental or denti-alveolar, [s, z, r, l] are alveolar; [tš, š, dž, ž] are prepalatal; [k, g, ŋ] are mediovelar. [y] is a voiced prevelar semivowel, [ɣ] is the corresponding voiceless sound. Italic letters denote palatalized sounds. The term 'palatalized' is here used to include on the one hand labial, dental, and glottal sounds pronounced with simultaneous raising of the tongue toward the hard palate ('palatalized' in the usual sense), and on the other hand prevelar sounds, pronounced with contact between the tongue and the forward part of the soft palate.

A raised dot after a consonant indicates that the sound has the time value of a full syllable.

Vowel symbols depart in some respects from their traditional meanings. [i] is high front; [e] is mean-mid front, like the vowel in English *bet*, not upper-mid; [a] is low back (slightly advanced toward central position), not low front; [o] is mean-mid back, approximately like the vowel of German *Gott*, not upper-mid; [u] is high back, often somewhat advanced toward central position, unrounded or weakly rounded. Capital letters [I, A, O, U] denote voiceless vowels.

Glosses are printed in italics, without quotation marks. A gloss is meant only to identify the cited form, not to provide an exhaustive account of its meaning.

with [ɤ] or [y] as the second member will not be so regarded, since the two parts are not homorganic (not formed by the same vocal organ).

An apparent exception to the regular train of equal fractions is the presence of long vowels, with or without preceding consonants, as in [ki·-ta] *heard*, [te-bu-ru] *table*, [o-ba·-sã-n·] *grandmother*, [šo·-sa] *major*, [gyu·-nyu·] *cow's milk*. In duration, each long vowel is equal to two fractions of the ordinary kind: [ki·-ta] is a match for [to-ko-ro], [gyu·-nyu·] for [no-ri-mo-no]. It is especially significant that a long vowel has the same duration as a sequence of two unlike vowels: [ko·] *thus* is a match for [ka-o] *face*, [ki·-ta] for [ka-i-ta] *wrote*. For these reasons, long vowels will be treated as sequences of two fractions (two like vowels) each, and will be written with double symbols: [ki-i-ta, te-e-bu-ru, o-ba-a-sa-n·, šo-o-sa, gyu-u-nyu-u].

All these fractions, of whatever type, will henceforth be called SYLLABLES.[14]

2. Qualities. What we hear in listening to the utterances of a speaker is a flow of interwoven, continually changing qualities. These qualities are the irreducible atoms from which all higher units in a phonemic description of the speaker's dialect must be formed. Whether the analyst prefers a description in terms of components[15] or one in terms of phonemes, his data consist ultimately of the qualities that he has heard in the stream of speech, and of nothing else. In the grouping of qualities to define phonemes, there may sometimes be a choice between alternative possibilities: a phone that contains two or more qualities may be regarded as belonging to a single phoneme defined by all the qualities together, or as belonging simultaneously to two or more phonemes defined respectively by the several qualities (or by smaller combinations within the total number); and in deciding a choice of this kind there is no theoretical objection to using morphological or even syntactic arguments.[16] If different phonemic descriptions

of a dialect account with equal accuracy and completeness for all the qualities that occur in the dialect, and invoke no other criteria, there is nothing to choose between them on the phonemic level; at most, one of them may lend itself more conveniently than the others to morphological and syntactic statements.[17] But no phonemic description is valid if it fails to account, explicitly or implicitly, for any of the qualities in a dialect, or if these qualities are not the sole basis on which it is built.

2.1. In addition to the four distinctive levels of pitch to be described in §3.1, Japanese utterances are heard as containing sixteen qualities, which occur in 67 different combinations. These qualities will be defined in terms of their assumed production by the vocal organs; but it must be borne in mind that they are isolated and identified wholly by ear. The articulatory terminology is used only because a usable auditory terminology has not yet been developed.[17a]

In the following list, the first six qualities (denoted by capital letters) are referred to different places of articulation; the next seven (denoted by numerals) are referred to different kinds of articulation or degrees of aperture. This means that such an entity as labial closure (present in [p, b, m], etc.) is taken to be composed of two separate qualities, labialness and closure.[18]

combinations defining phonemes. Cf. Charles F. Hockett, Problems in morphemic analysis §§4–7, Lg. 23.324–7 (1947)((231–2)); Peiping morphophonemics §3, Lg. 26.69–70 and fn. 10 (1950)((319)).

An illustration from English. The phones [f] and [v], [θ] and [ð], [s] and [z] are of course phonemically different. Traditionally, each of them is assigned to a single phoneme contrasting as a unit with all the others; but this interpretation proves to be awkward in dealing with certain morphological relations. In such pairs as *belief : believe, safe : save, wreath : wreathe, use* (noun) *: use* (verb), it would be convenient to regard the verb as consisting of two morphemes: one that appears by itself as a noun or an adjective, the other a verb-deriving suffix; but if /v, ð, z/ are unitary phonemes, there is no phoneme present in these verbs that could be taken as a suffix. An alternative and equally accurate interpretation of the phones [v, ð, z] would be to regard the quality of voice (at least when accompanied by the quality of constriction) as defining a separate phoneme /V/, so that each of the phones [v, ð, z] would belong simultaneously to two phonemes: to /f, θ, s/ respectively, and to /V/. This treatment, like the traditional one, is based solely on the qualities observed in English utterances; but by providing a phoneme /V/ to serve as a verb-deriving suffix, it greatly simplifies the exposition of the morphology.

[17] In any case, such descriptions are always mechanically convertible into one another, and are therefore scientifically equivalent.

[17a] For an interesting but not (I think) wholly successful attempt to use an auditory terminology see R. Jakobson and J. Lotz, Notes on the French phonemic pattern, Word 5.151–8 (1949). In this article the phonemes of French are defined in terms of six auditory oppositions or contrasts: vowel/consonant, nasal/oral, saturated/diluted, grave/acute, tense/lax, and continuous/intercepted. The following statement (151) is especially to be noted: 'Our basic assumption is that every language operates with a strictly limited number of underlying ultimate distinctions which form a set of binary oppositions. These opposite features occur either solely as terms of a single relation (*pure* opposition) or they can occur together as complexes.'

[18] That such a division into qualities of position and qualities of articulation is in accord with acoustic reality has been demonstrated in the laboratory, most plainly in work with the acoustic spectrograph. See Martin Joos, Acoustic phonetics (Language Monograph No. 23, 1948), esp. ch. 4.

---

[14] The number of syllables in a phrase is therefore not found by counting peaks of sonority or chest pulses, but only by counting the temporally equal fractions contained in it, or by comparing its duration with that of another phrase in which the number of such fractions is known. In short, the Japanese syllable is a unit of duration. Such a unit is often called a mora; but the term 'syllable' is better established in descriptions of Japanese.

It is worth noting, as a cultural correlate of the linguistic structure, that a speaker of Japanese is just as ready as a speaker of English to state the number of syllables in any phrase, though neither one, without special training, can state the number of segments. Since the two speakers count different kinds of units, they will not always agree on the number of syllables in a given phonetic continuum. In the English word *asks*, pronounced with a long vowel and distinctly released consonants, a Japanese will hear five syllables; in the Japanese word [gyuunyuul], a speaker of English will hear only two. (The Japanese speaker's 'feeling' for the number of syllables in a phrase is no doubt partly due to his knowledge of how the phrase is written in the native syllabary; but the syllabary, in turn, must reflect the speakers' naive structural analysis of their language.)

[15] For a theoretical discussion see Zellig S. Harris, Simultaneous components in phonology, Lg. 20.181–205 (1944)* For one type of application see Charles F. Hockett, Componential analysis of Sierra Popoluca, IJAL 13.259–67 (1947), and Peiping phonology, JAOS 67.253–67 (1947). ((217)) *((124))

[16] Morphological and syntactic criteria must not be used to influence the basic analysis leading to the discovery of distinctive qualities and their distribution; but they are often helpful in deciding how to group these qualities, once they have been discovered, into

L labial position	3 constriction
D dental or alveolar position	4 flap movement
P prepalatal position	5 small aperture
F prevelar (front) position	6 medium aperture
B mediovelar (back) position	7 wide aperture
G glottal position	N nasalization
1 closure	V voicing
2 affrication[18a]	Q syllabic quantity

A number of combinations require special comment:

L1: bilabial stop; L3: bilabial or labiodental spirant, without distinction; L5: weak lip-rounding.

D1: dental stop; D2: dental or denti-alveolar affricate; D3: dental or alveolar spirant, always with groove-shaped aperture (i.e. sibilant); D4: alveolar flap. A variety of flap movement in which there is a lateral opening at the moment of contact (resulting in 'flapped l') is denoted by the symbol D4a.

P1, P2, P3: stop, affricate, and spirant produced with contact between the blade or front of the tongue and the forward part of the hard palate.

F1, F3: stop and spirant produced with contact between the back of the tongue and the forward part of the soft palate; F5: high front vowel and semivowel, or front vowel.

B1: stop produced with contact between the back of the tongue and the middle part of the soft palate; B5: high back vowel and semivowel; B6, B7: mid and low back vowels.

G1: glottal stop; G3: strongly pulsed voiceless onset of a following vowel or semivowel, slightly fricative ('h').

2.2. N, V, Q are qualities of a different kind from the rest. Each of these is one term of a dichotomy that divides the entire body of phones into halves of comparable magnitude: every phone in Japanese contains one of the two opposite qualities in each dichotomy, but in each dichotomy only one term is provided with a symbol. Accordingly, the absence of any of the three symbols N, V, Q implies the presence of the corresponding opposite: absence of N implies oral resonance; absence of V implies voicelessness; absence of Q implies the lack of syllabic time value (quantity).

A segment that contains the quality Q is described as long; a segment that lacks this quality is described as short. A long segment is one that constitutes a syllable by itself; a short segment is one that does not. The number of syllables in any phrase, therefore, is equal to the number of long segments that occur in it. As applied to consonants, the terms 'long' and 'short' have the meanings generally attached to them in phonetic works; but as applied to vowels they have special meanings different from their usual ones. A short vowel, in this paper, is a segment with vowel qualities but without syllabic time value—in other words, a segment with vowel qualities and a semivowel; a long vowel is a segment with vowel qualities and with syllabic time value—in other words, what is elsewhere usually called a short vowel. (What is elsewhere called a long vowel, i.e. a vowel of greater-than-average duration, is here called a double vowel; cf. §1.)

3. Pitch. The phones defined in Japanese by qualities of relative pitch vary in length from one segment to a dozen or more. In the phrase [aoi] *blue*, each of the three vowels is on a separate pitch level: [a] is low, [o] is higher mid, [i] is low again; in the phrase [kimonoɲaʏoꜜoreta] *the clothes got dirty*, the initial [k] has no quality of relative pitch, the segment [i] is low, the span [monoɲaʏoꜜore] (comprising twelve segments) is lower mid, the [t] again has no pitch quality; and the final [a] is low.

Continual reference to the fact that voiceless phones have no pitch qualities will henceforth be obviated by adopting the following conventions. If two voiced phones with the same pitch are separated by one or more voiceless segments, the whole sequence (including the voiceless interrupting element) is regarded as a single span, defined by a single occurrence of a pitch quality. If two voiced phones with different pitches are separated by one or more voiceless segments, the latter are regarded as belonging to the following voiced phone and forming with it a single span defined by the pitch quality of its terminal part. Similarly an initial voiceless segment is regarded as part of the first span in the phrase defined by pitch.

3.1. For a complete account of the observable pitch variations in Japanese, four phonemically different levels are necessary and sufficient. Not all utterances contain all four levels; indeed, the highest level is relatively rare, and the lowest is rare except on the first and the last syllable of a phrase. But even when only one or two of the levels are heard in a given phrase, it is usually not hard to identify them.

The four pitch phonemes of Japanese will be designated by numerals as follows:

/1/ highest pitch: the highest level reached in normal conversation; near the upper limit of the speaker's voice range;

/2/ higher mid pitch: near the middle of the speaker's voice range; slightly lower on the last syllable of a phrase than elsewhere;

/3/ lower mid pitch: about three tones below /2/; slightly higher on the last syllable of a phrase than elsewhere;

/4/ lowest pitch: near the lower limit of the speaker's voice range; slightly lower on the first syllable of a phrase than on a medial syllable, and lower still on the last syllable—here often well below the normal speaking-range.

The members of these pitch phonemes, as of any phonemes, are phones: continuous fractions of utterance heard as coextensive with various audible qualities—in this case various levels of pitch. In other words, each of the four pitch phonemes includes as members (allophones) all the sequences of vowels or consonants or both—from one to a dozen or more—that are heard as having a particular pitch. In the phrase [kimonoɲaʏoꜜoreta], the segment [k] belongs to some consonant phoneme, [i] to some vowel phoneme, [m] again to some consonant

[18a] The reason for treating affrication as a single quality rather than a succession of two qualities (closure plus constriction) has been stated in §1.

phoneme, and so on: each segment belongs to some phoneme by virtue of the qualities present in it as a segment; but beyond this, the span [ki] belongs to pitch phoneme /4/, the span [monopayoɲore] belongs to pitch phoneme /3/, and the span [ta] belongs to /4/ again. In the phrase [aoi], each of the three vowels belongs to some vowel phoneme; and in addition, each one belongs also to some pitch phoneme: [a] to /4/, [o] to /2/, [i] to /4/ again. This illustrates the statement in §0.3 that a phone which contains two phoneme-defining qualities or combinations belongs to both phonemes at once.

In citing short phrases pronounced with statement intonation (as in §3.2 and §4.1), it is enough to distinguish members of pitch phoneme /2/ by writing an acute accent on the vowel letter of each syllable with higher mid pitch (and on the letters denoting the long nasals when they have this pitch). Unmarked initial and final syllables belong to pitch phoneme /4/; unmarked medial syllables belong to pitch phoneme /3/.[19] In citing longer utterances pronounced with more varied intonations (as in §7), it will be necessary to adopt other graphic devices.

Variations in loudness are of course also observable in Japanese utterances; but these turn out to be predictable in terms of pitch phonemes. In general, greater loudness correlates with higher pitch: syllables with pitch /1/ are usually louder than those with /2/, syllables with /3/ are usually still softer, and those with /4/ are least loud. When two or more syllables in succession have pitch /2/, the last syllable in the sequence is louder than the rest.

3.2. Although minimally different pairs are not necessary to prove that a given phonetic difference is distinctive in a particular language, they illustrate such differences more strikingly than other examples. Accordingly, a number of phrases are presented here which differ only in pitch.

The sequence [soodes·ka] contains five syllables. With pitch /2/ on the first, /3/ on the next two, and /4/ on the last, it means *Is that so?*; with /2/ and /3/ as before but with two pitches, /3/ and /1/, on the last syllable, it means *Is that really so?* (expressing great interest or surprise); and with /1/ on the first syllable, /3/ on the next two, and either /4/ or /31/ on the last, it means *Oh so that's it!*.[20]

In each of the following pairs, the second member contains pitch /2/, contrasting with /3/ or /4/ in the first member: [atsusa, átsusa] *thickness, heat*; [bán, bán·] *night, inning*; [hawa, háwa] *as for the leaf, as for the tooth* (but [ha] both *leaf* and *tooth*); [its·ka, its·ka] *five days, some time*; [kaeru, káeru] *changes, returns*; [kama, káma] *iron pot, sickle*; [kau, káu] *buys, raises (animals)*; [kiru, kíru] *wears, cuts*; [oku, óku] *puts, hundred million*; [sakán·, sákán·] *plasterer, field officer*; [yome, yóme] *bride, read it!*; [atsui, atsúi] *thick, hot*; [hanawa, hanáwa] *as for the nose, as for the flower* (but [hana] both *nose* and *flower*); [mikata, mikáta] *allies, way*

of looking; [omoi, omói] *heavy, a thought*; [s·tawa, s·táwa] *as for the place beneath, as for the tongue.*

In each of the following pairs, both members contain pitch /2/, but differently placed: [hašide, hašíde] *with chopsticks, at the bridge*; [kámiwa, kamíwa] *as for God, as for the paper (or hair)*; [súmide, sumíde] *in the corner, with India ink.*

4. Phones. The following list includes every type of phone observed as a regularly recurring unit[21] in utterances of the dialect to be described, except spans defined by qualities of pitch. Some of these types are limited in their use, being rare or even non-occurrent in the speech of some persons; but all the types here listed are found in the utterances of at least some speakers of the dialect.[22]

4.1. Each paragraph in the list contains the following: a phonetic symbol to designate the phone, or rather the class of perceptually identical phones (= allophone); a phonetic description in physiological (articulatory) terms, intended to convey the auditory effect of the phone; in parentheses, a record of the qualities present in the phone, represented by the symbols explained in §2.1; a full statement of the environments in which the phone occurs, in terms of immediately preceding and following phones; a reference, where necessary, to other phones with which the phone is in free variation, showing the phone in various typical environments. Not all the environments in which every phone occurs are illustrated. In a few cases, the list of immediately preceding and following phones includes one or more environments in which the phone has not actually been observed, but which are inferred, from the distribution of other phones, to be at least theoretically possible.

The pause that occurs (by definition) at the beginning and end of every phrase is listed as a phone because its presence internally in an utterance cannot be predicted from anything else in the utterance. Note the following utterances, which differ only by the presence or absence of an internal pause: [mádooake-tenemás·ta] *I went to bed with the window open*: [mádooakete ✳ nemás·ta] *I opened the window and went to bed.* Pause may be regarded as a kind of zero phone, characterized by a complete lack of qualities.[23]

[✳] pause (no qualities): before [i, e, a, o, u, ts·, tš·, s·, š·, f·, x·, m·, n·], and all short consonants except [ʔ, ʊ, ʏ, ž, ɤ]; after [i, e, a, o, u, ?, ts·, tš·, s·, š·, n·, n·,

---

[19] Some of the forms cited in this paper with no pitch higher than /3/ are paralleled by otherwise identical synonymous forms with pitch /2/ on all syllables but the first, when followed without pause by one or more syllables with lower pitch. Thus the word for *room* is cited in §4.1 as [heya] (with pitch /4/ on both syllables), but occurs with pitch /2/ on last syllable in the phrase [heyáwa] *as for the room.*

[20] This example is restated from SCJ II, Lg. 22.200-1, §1.1 ((154-5)).

[21] The expression 'regularly recurring unit' is meant to exclude the sound types mentioned in fn. 7.

[22] In the strictest sense of the word 'dialect' (as defined, for instance, in Lg. 24.8, §3.2), the phones listed below represent a mixture of slightly different dialects. But they can just as well be regarded as representing a kind of average among idiolects too similar to merit individual treatment.

[23] Although pause is here called a zero phone, it is not zero in the sense of having no extension in time. Pauses occur, and have duration, like other phones. They are zero only in being characterized by the total absence of qualities rather than by the presence of one or more.

ʊ·, ɣ·].²⁴ Examples: [⋕isu⋕] chair, [⋕éki⋕] station, [⋕áme⋕] rain, [⋕oka⋕] hall, [⋕úso⋕] lie, [⋕ts·tsúimu⋕] wraps, [⋕tš·kára⋕] strength, [⋕s·teru⋕] throws away, [⋕š·kata⋕] way of doing something, [⋕f·tóru⋕] grows fat, [⋕x·tóts·⋕] one, [⋕m·rna⋕] horse (beside [⋕uma⋕]), [⋕n·⋕] yeah, [⋕hatš·⋕] eight (in rapid speech), [⋕arimas·⋕] there is, [⋕pán·⋕] or [⋕páŋ·⋕] bread, [⋕bín·⋕] or [⋕bíɣ·⋕] bottle. Hereafter the presence of a pause will be taken for granted at the beginning and end of every cited phrase, and the symbol [⋕] will no longer be written there.

[p] short voiceless bilabial stop (L1): before [e, a, o, u, ʌ, O, ʊ]; after [⋕, i, e, a, o, u, ɪ, ʌ, O, ʊ, v, p·, m·]; slightly aspirated except after [p·]. Examples: [pén·] pen, [pán·] bread, [pôm·pu] pump, [pakurito] in one gulp, [pOkét·to] pocket, [ippai] full, [ippúku] one sip.

[p·] long voiceless bilabial stop (L1 Q): before [p]; after [i, e, a, o, u, ɪ, ʌ, O, ʊ]; unreleased. Examples: [ip·pai] full, [tep·poo] gun, [kap·pa] or [kʌp·pa] raincoat, [kop·pu] or [kOp·pu] glass tumbler, [up·pún·] resentment, [kip·pu] ticket, [sup·pái] sour.

[pʲ] short voiceless bilabial stop, palatalized (L1 F5): before [i, ɪ, ɣ]; after [⋕, i, e, a, o, u, ɪ, ʌ, O, ʊ, p·, m·]; slightly aspirated except after [p·]. Examples: [pʲín·] pin, [ip·pʲiki] or [ip·pʲiki] one (animal), [pʲuuto] whizzing, [kím·pʲin·] gold and other valuables.

[pʲ·] long voiceless bilabial stop, palatalized (L1 Q F5): before [i, ɪ, ɣ]; before [p]; after [i, e, a, o, u, ɪ, ʌ, O, ʊ]; unreleased. Examples: [ipʲ·pʲiki] one (animal), [hapʲ·pʲaku] eight hundred.

[t] short voiceless dental stop (D1): before [e, a, o, ʌ, O]; after [⋕, i, e, a, o, u, ɪ, ʌ, O, ʊ, t·, ts·, tš·, s·, š·, f·, x·, n·]; slightly aspirated except after [t·]. Examples: [te] hand, [ta] rice field, [to] door, [tʌkái] high, [tOkoro] place, [tta] board, [geta] wooden clogs, [hata] flag, [botan·] button, [buta] pig, [kɪta] came, [kutábíréru] gets tired, [it·tóo] one (horse), [máts·to] if one waits, [kats·toosu] wins through, [s·teru] throws away, [š·ta] tongue, [f·tats·] two, [x·tóts·] one, [hôn·too] truth.

[t·] long voiceless dental stop (D1 Q): before [t, ts, s]; after [i, e, a, o, u, ɪ, ʌ, O, ʊ]; unreleased. Examples: [it·too] one (horse), [mát·te] waiting, [kɪtto] surely, [kut·taku] trouble, [it·tsui] one (document), [otót·sán·] dad (only example of [t·s]).

[tʲ] short voiceless dental stop, palatalized (D1 F5): before [y]; after [⋕]. Only example: [tʲuũn·de] since one says that (beside [tšuũn·de] and [toyruunode]).

[tʲ·] long voiceless dental stop, palatalized (D1 Q F5): before [tš]; after [i, e, a, o, u, ɪ, ʌ, O, ʊ]; unreleased. Examples: [itʲ·tšaku] one (suit), [mát·tši] match, [pɪt·tšaa] pitcher (in baseball).

[k] short voiceless mediovelar stop (B1 Q): before [e, a, o, u, ʌ, O, ʊ]; after [⋕, i, e, a, o, u, ɪ, ʌ, O, ʊ, k·]; slightly aspirated except after [k·]. Examples: [ke] hair, [bʌka] fool, [ikôo] let's go, [roku] six, [kʌkéru] hangs it, [kOkóro] heart, [kutsu] shoe, [kék·koo] splendid, [hats·ka] twenty days, [mats·kara] from the town, [s·kóši] a little, [š·kata] way of doing something, [f·kuro] bag, [x·kúi] low, [sáŋ·káŋetsu] three months.

[k·] long voiceless mediovelar stop (B1 Q): before [k]; after [i, e, a, o, u, ɪ, ʌ, O, ʊ]; unreleased. Examples: [ik·ko] one (piece), [kek·koo] splendid, [pik·koro] piccolo.

[k] short voiceless prevelar stop (F1): before [i, ɪ, ɣ]; after [⋕, i, e, a, o, u, ɪ, ʌ, O, ʊ, k·, ts·, tš·, s·, š·, f·, x·, ɣ·]; slightly aspirated except after [k·]. Examples: [ki] tree, [kɪta] came, [kyúu] nine, [ip·pki] or [ip·piki] one (animal), [hak·kíri] clearly, [kutš·ki] decayed wood, [uɪš·ki] whisky, [f·kimáš·ta] bleu, [míx·ki] two (animals), [géŋ·ki] health.

[k·] long voiceless prevelar stop (F1 Q): before [k]; after [i, e, a, o, u, ɪ]; unreleased. Examples: [hak·kíri] clearly, [ik·kyuu] one class.

[ʔ] short glottal stop (G1): before [⋕]; after [i, e, a, o, u]. Examples: [to?] so saying, [tše?] ugh!, [kóra?] hey!.²⁵

[ts] short voiceless dental or denti-alveolar affricate (D2): before [⋕, i, e, a, o, u, ɪ, ʌ, O, ʊ, t·, ts, tš, ts·, tš·, s·, f·, x·, n·]; unaspirated. Examples: [tsuri] fishing, [átsusa] heat, [kutsu] shoe, [it·tsui] one (document), [ts·tsúmu] wraps, [ts·tsúidžo] good order, [s·tsúrei] rudeness, [f·tsuuno] regular, [x·tsudži] sheep, [sán·tsuu] three (documents).

[ts·] long voiceless dental or denti-alveolar affricate (D2 Q): before [⋕, t, k, ts, tš], after [⋕, i, e, a, o, u]; released but unaspirated. Examples: [ts·tsúmu] wraps, [máts·to] if one waits, [hats·ka] twenty days, [ts·tši] soil, [x·tóts·] one.

[tš] short voiceless prepalatal affricate (P2): before [i, e, a, o, u, ɪ, ʊ]; after [⋕, i, e, a, o, u, ɪ, ʌ, O, u, ɪ, ʊ]; unaspirated. Examples: [tši] blood, [tšék·ku] bank check, [tše?] ugh!, [kutši] mouth, [tšisei] topography, [it·tšaku] one (suit), [ts·tši] soil, [tš·tši] father, [s·tšimu] steam, [š·tši] seven, [f·tšidži] government of an urban prefecture, [x·tšoo] flying bird, [bân·tši] house number.

[tš·] long voiceless prepalatal affricate (P2 Q): before [⋕, t, k, ts, tš]; after [i, e, a, o, u]; released but unaspirated. Examples: [tš·kára] strength, [kats·toosu] wins through, [tš·tsúidžo] good order, [tš·tši] father, [hatš·] eight (in rapid speech).

[s] short voiceless alveolar (groove) spirant (D3): before [e, a, o, u, ʊ]; after [⋕, i, e, a, o, u, ɪ, ʊ, t·, s·, n·, ʋ·]. Examples: [sên·soo] war, [susumu] advances, [kɪsóona] seeming to come, [otót·sán·] dad (only example of [t·s]), [mas·súŋu] straight, [bín·sén·] writing-paper.

[s·] long voiceless alveolar (groove) spirant (D3 Q): before [⋕, t, k, ts, tš]; after [⋕, i, e, a, o, u, ɪ, ʊ]; unreleased before [s]. Examples: [arimas·] there is, [s·teru] throws away, [sóodes·ka] is that so?, [s·tšimu] steam, [mas·súŋu] straight, [kɪs·soo] good news, [kus·setsusuru] refracts.

[š] short voiceless prepalatal (groove) spirant (P3): before [i, e, a, o, u, ɪ, ʊ, š·, ʋ·]. Examples: [šašin·] photograph, [šŋsei] municipal government, [šusei] alcohol, [kɪša] train, [zaš·ši] magazine, [šân·šin·] peace of mind.

[š·] long voiceless prepalatal (groove) spirant (P3 Q): before [⋕, t, k, k·, ts, tš, š]; after [⋕, i, e, a, o, u, ɪ, ʊ]; unreleased before [š]. Examples: [s·koš·] a little,

²⁴ In these statements of distribution, the nasalized vowels are not separately enumerated. In general, any phone that occurs before or after an oral vowel occurs also before or after the corresponding nasalized vowel. (But nasalization of vowels is indicated in the transcription of the examples).

²⁵ The distribution of this phone is unique in type: it occurs only before pause, and only in a few expressions (mostly interjectional).

(in rapid speech), [š·kata] *way of doing something*, [š·kimono] *carpet*, [arĭmáš·ta] *there was*, [š·tsúrei] *rudeness*, [š·tši] *seven*, [zaš·ši] *magazine*, [keš·šte] *never*, [kúš·šón·] or [kúš·šón·] *cushion*.

[f] short voiceless bilabial or labiodental spirant (L3): before [u, ʋ]; after [✻, i, e, a, o, u, ɪ, ʋ, n·]. Every phrase containing [f] is paralleled (though rarely) by an otherwise identical synonymous phrase containing [h] instead. Examples: [furúi] *old*, [fúufu] *married couple*, [fusuma] *light opaque sliding door*, [ifu] *dread*, [sofu] *grandfather*, [xífu] *contribution*, [sáň·fúráň·šis·ko] *San Francisco*.

[f·] long voiceless bilabial or labiodental spirant (L3 Q): before [✻, i, e, a, o, u]. Examples: [f·tóru] *grows fat*, [gof·kuya] *drygoods store*, [f·tsuuno] *regular*, [f·tšidži] *governor of an urban prefecture*, [nif·ku] *two nurses*.

[x] short voiceless prevelar spirant (F3): before [i, a, o, u, ɪ]; after [✻, i, e, a, o, u, ɪ, ʋ, n·]. Every phrase containing [x] is paralleled by an otherwise identical synonymous phrase containing [hy] instead, or [h] before [i, ɪ]. Examples: [xima] *leisure*, [xaku] *hundred*, [xoobán·] *fame*, [xuuto] *with a zip*, [xffu] or [xɪfu] *skin*, [koóžii] *coffee*, [séý·xaku] *one thousand one hundred*.

[x·] long voiceless prevelar spirant (F3 Q): before [t, k, k, ts, tš]; after [✻, i, e, a, o, u]. Examples: [x·to] *person*, [x·kúi] *low*, [x·tsudži] *sheep*, [x·tšoo] *flying bird*, [nír·ki] *two (animals)*.

[h] short voiceless glottal spirant, i.e. a strongly pulsed and slightly fricative voiceless onset of a following vowel or semivowel (G3): before [e, a, o, u, ʋ]; after [✻, i, e, a, o, u, n·, ɴ·]. Every phrase containing [h] before [u] or [ʋ] is paralleled by an otherwise identical synonymous phrase containing [f] instead; the sequences [hu, hʋ] are less common than [fu, fʋ], and in the speech of many persons do not occur at all. Examples: [hébi] *snake*, [ha] *leaf*, [hón·] *book*, [hurúi] *old* (beside [furúi]), [góhán·] *cooked rice*, [f·táhako] *two boxfuls*, [džúusáŋ·háǹ·] *thirteen and a half*.

[h] short voiceless glottal spirant (as above), palatalized (G3 F5): before [h] or [hy] and [x] see the paragraph on [x]. Every phrase containing [h] before [i, ɪ] is paralleled by an otherwise identical synonymous phrase containing [f] instead; ... Examples: [hima] *leisure*, [hyaku] *hundred*, [hyoobán·] *fame*, [hyuuto] *with a zip*, [hífu] *skin*, [hɪfu] or [hɪfu] *skin*, [koóhii] *coffee*, [séý·hyaku] *one thousand and one hundred*.

[b] short voiced bilabial stop (B1 V): before [e, a, o, u]; after [✻, i, e, a, o, u, m·]. Examples: [kabe] *wall*, [kooba] *factory*, [booši] *hat*, [buta] *pig*, [kóm·bán·] *tonight*.

[b] short voiced bilabial stop, palatalized (L1 V F5): before [i, y]; after [✻, i, e, a, o, u, m·]. Examples: [bǐn·] *bottle*, [byookí] *illness*, [hébi] *snake*, [sǎm·byaku] *three hundred*.

[d] short voiced dental stop (D1 V): before [e, a, o]; after [✻, i, e, a, o, u, n·]. Examples: [fude] *writing brush*, [dóko] *where?*, [hidari] *left (side)*, [kón·do] *this time*.

[g] short voiced mediovelar stop (B1 V): before [e, a, o, u]; after [✻, i, e, a, o, u, n·]. Some phrases containing [g] not preceded by [✻] are paralleled by otherwise identical synonymous phrases containing [ŋ] instead. Examples: [gekidžoo] *theater*, [gak·koo] *school*, [góhán·] *cooked rice*, [dónogurai] *about how much?*, [agaru] *rises*, [mago] *grandchild*, [sonogo] *after that*, [sǎŋ·gén·] *three (buildings)*.

[g] short voiced prevelar stop (F1 V): before [i, y]; after [✻, i, e, a, o, u, ɴ·]. Some phrases containing [g] not preceded by [✻] are paralleled by otherwise identical synonymous phrases containing [ŋ] instead. Examples: [gíǹ·] *silver*, [gyuunyuu] *cow's milk*, [hyuugyuu] *milch cow*, [kagi] *key*, [árugiǹ·koo] *a certain bank*, [kíǹ·giǹ·] *gold and silver*, [niǹ·gyoo] *doll*.

[dž] short voiced prepalatal affricate (P2 V): before [i, e, a, o, u]; not preceded by [✻]. Some phrases containing [dž] not preceded by [✻] are paralleled (though rarely) by otherwise identical synonymous phrases containing [ž] instead. Examples: [džišiǹ·] *earthquake*, [džerii] *jelly*, [džari] *gravel*, [džotšuu] *maid servant*, [džúu] *ten*, [kídži] *newspaper article*, [kádži] *conflagration*, [sǎǹ·džuu] *thirty*.

[z] short voiced alveolar (groove) spirant (D3 V): before [e, a, o, u]; after [✻, i, e, a, o, u, i, e, a, o, u, n·]. Examples: [zaš·ši] *magazine*, [kaze] *wind*, [kázoku] *family*, [mizu] *water*, [bǎn·zai] *hurrah*.[26]

[ž] short voiced prepalatal (groove) spirant (P3 V): before [i a o u]; after [✻, i, e, a, o, u, n·]. Most phrases containing [ž] are paralleled by otherwise identical synonymous phrases containing [dž] instead; [ž] is less common than [dž], and in the speech of many persons does not occur at all. Examples: [mižɪkái] *short*, [nížuu] *twenty*, [sǎn·žuu] *thirty*.

[r] short voiced alveolar flap (D4 V): before [e, a, o, u]; after [✻, i, e, a, o, u, n·]. Some phrases containing [r] before [e] or [o] are paralleled (though rarely) by otherwise identical synonymous phrases containing [l] instead. Examples: [roku] *six*, [kore] *this*, [hara] *belly*, [iru] *he is*, [séń·rop·pyaku] *one thousand six hundred*.

[l] short voiced alveolar lateral flap (D4a V): before [e, o]; after [✻, i, e, a, o, u]. Every phrase containing [l] is paralleled by an otherwise identical synonymous phrase containing [r] instead; [l] is far less common than [r], and in the speech of many persons does not occur at all. Examples: [loku] *six*, [kole] *this*.

[r] short voiced alveolar flap, palatalized (D4 F5): before [i, y]; after [✻, i, e, a, o, u, n·]. Examples: [riku] *land*, [arimas·] *there is*, [kǐri] *gimlet*, [ryokoo] *journey*, [bén·rina] *convenient*.

[m] short voiced nasalized bilabial stop (L1 V N): before [e, a, o, u]; after [✻, i, e, a, o, u, m·]. Examples: [mame] *beans*, [momo] *peach*, [gímu] *duty*, [sǎm·mari] *too much*.

[m·] long voiced nasalized bilabial stop (L1 V N Q): before [p, b, m]; after [✻, i, e, a, ǒ, ǔ]. Examples: [m·ma] *horse* (beside [uma]), [gúm·pǔku] *uniform*, [kóm·bán·] *tonight*, [sǎm·mari] *too much*.

[m] short voiced nasalized bilabial stop, palatalized (L1 V N F5): before [i, y]; after [✻, i, e, a, o, u, m·]. Examples: [mimi] *ear*, [myóonit·ši] *tomorrow*, [kami] *paper*, [kǒm·myóonit·ši] *today and tomorrow*.

[m·] long voiced nasalized bilabial stop, palatalized (L1 V N Q F5): before [p, b, m]; after [✻, i, e, a, ǒ, ǔ]. Examples: [sǎm·byaku] *three hundred*, [kǒm·myóo-nit·ši] *today and tomorrow*, [m·mi] *sea* (beside [úmi]).

[26] A very few speakers of standard Japanese (but many speakers of other dialects) use a short voiced dental or denti-alveolar affricate [dž] beside or instead of [z], most commonly before [u], as in [midzu] *water*. In view of its rareness, this phone has been excluded (perhaps arbitrarily) from consideration in the present paper.

[n] short voiced nasalized dental stop (D1 V N): before [e, a, o, u, n·]. Examples: [neru] *goes to bed*, [hana] *nose*, [óno] *ax*, [inu] *dog*, [káɴ·na] *carpenter's plane*.

[n·] long voiced nasalized dental stop (D1 V N Q): before [✳, ẽ, ã, õ, ũ, t, ts, s, h, d, z, r, n]; after [✳, i, ẽ, ã, õ, ũ]. Examples: [n·] *yeah*, [ip·púɴ·] *one minute*, [nihóɴ·é] *to Japan*, [hán··ái] *philanthropy*, [péɴ·ó] *pen* (as goal), [hóɴ·too] *truth*, [sán·tsuu] *three (volumes)*, [sén·soo] *war*, [džúusán·hán·] *thirteen and a half*, [kóɴ·do] *this time*, [bán·zai] *hurrah*, [sén·rop·pyaku] *one thousand six hundred*, [káɴ·na] *carpenter's plane*.

[ṇ] short voiced nasalized dental stop, palatalized (D1 V N F5): before [i, y]; after [✳, i, e, a, o, u, n·]. Examples: [niku] *meat*, [gyuuɴyuu] *cow's milk*, [kóɴ·nitši] *today*.

[ṇ·] long voiced nasalized dental stop, palatalized (D1 V N Q F5): before [✳, i, y, tš, š, h, dž, ž, r, ɲ]; after [i, ẽ, ã, õ, ũ]. Examples: [bíɴ·] *bottle*, [téɴ·iɴ·] *salesman*, [háɴ·i] *extent*, [hóɴ·ya] *book-seller*, [báɴ·tši] *house number*, [sén·šuu] *last week*, [sáɴ·džuu] or [sáɴ·žuu] *thirty*, [béɴ·rina] *convenient*, [kóɴ·nitši] *today*.

[ŋ] short voiced nasalized mediovelar stop (B1 V N): before [e, a, o, u]; after [i, e, a, o, u, ɥ·]. Every phrase containing [ŋ] is paralleled by an otherwise identical synonymous phrase containing [g] instead. Examples: [káɲe] *shadow*, [aŋaru] *rises*, [maŋo] *grandchild*, [mas·súɲu] *straight*, [sáɲ·ɲéɴ·] *three (buildings)*.

[ŋ·] long voiced nasalized mediovelar stop (B1 V N Q): before [✳, ẽ, ã, õ, ũ, k, h, g, ɡ, w]; after [i, ẽ, ã, õ, ũ]. Every phrase containing [ŋ·] before a vowel or [✳] is paralleled by an otherwise identical synonymous phrase containing a voiced frictionless nasalized mediovelar spirant instead of the nasalized stop; but this sound, which is everywhere in free variation with [ŋ·], is not separately listed. Examples: [ip·púɲ·] *one minute*, [nihóɲ·é] *to Japan*, [háɲ·ái] *philanthropy*, [péɲ·ó] *pen* (as verbal goal), [sáɲ·káɲetsu] *three months*, [džúusáɲ·háɲ·] *thirteen and a half*, [sáɲ·ɡéɴ·] or [sáɲ·ɡéɴ·] or [sáɲ·ɲéɴ·] *three (buildings)*, [hóɲ·wa] *as for the book*.

[ɲ] short voiced nasalized prevelar stop (F1 V N): before [i, y]; after [i, e, a, o, u, ɥ·]. Every phrase containing [ɲ] is paralleled by an otherwise identical synonymous phrase containing [ɡ] instead. Examples: [kaɲi] *key*, [ɲyuuɲyuu] *milch cow*, [kíɲ·gyóo] or [níɲ·gyoo] *doll*.

[ɲ·] long voiced nasalized prevelar stop (F1 V N Q): before [✳, i, y, k, h, x, x·, ɡ, ɲ]; after [i, ẽ, ã, õ, ũ]. Every phrase containing [ɲ·] before a vowel or [✳] is paralleled by an otherwise identical synonymous phrase containing a voiced frictionless nasalized prevelar spirant instead of the nasalized stop; but this sound, which is everywhere in free variation with [ɲ·], is not separately listed. Examples: [bíɲ·] *bottle*, [téɲ·iɴ·] *salesman*, [háɲ·i] *extent*, [hóɲ·ya] *book-seller*, [ɡéɲ·ki] *health*, [máɲ·néɲ·x·tsu] *fountain pen*, [kíɲ·giɴ·] or [kíɲ·ɲiɴ·] or [kíɲ·ɲiɴ·] *gold and silver*, [kíɲ·ɲyin·] *gold and silver*, [níɲ·gyoo] or [níɲ·ɲyoo] *doll*.

[ɣ] short voiceless prevelar (front) vowel, i.e. semivowel (F5): before [a, o, u]; after [p, k]. Examples: [hap·pyaku] *eight hundred*, [pyuuto] *whizzing*, [kyaku] *guest*, [kyóo] *today*, [kyúu] *nine*.

[y] short voiced prevelar (front) vowel, i.e. semivowel (F5 V): before [a, o, u]; after [✳, i, e, a, o, u, t, h, b, ɡ, r, m, n, n·, ŋ, ɲ·]. Examples: [yáɲi] *goat*, [yoko] side, [yuka] *floor*, [omiyaɲe] *souvenir*, [heya] *room*, [ayamaru] *apologizes*, [oyu] *hot water*, [fuyu] *winter*, [tyuuɴ·de] *since one says that* (only example of [ty]), [hyaku] *hundred*, [byooki] *illness*, [gyuuɴyuu] *cow's milk*, [ryokoo] *journey*, [myóo-nitsi] *tomorrow*, [hóɴ·ya] or [hóɲ·ya] *book-seller*, [ɲyuuɴyuu] *milch cow*.

[w] short voiced mediovelar (back) vowel, i.e. semivowel, weakly labialized (B5 V L5): before [a]; after [✳, i, e, a, o, u, ɥ·]. Examples: [warúi] *bad*, [iwanai] *doesn't say*, [sewa] *assistance*, [kawa] *river*, [kowásu] *breaks it*, [kuwa] *hoe*, [hóɴ·wa] *as for the book*.

[i] long[27] voiceless prevelar (front) high vowel (F5 Q): after [tš, š, x, h] and before [s, š, f] or any long voiceless consonant; or after [p, k] and before any voiceless consonant, long or short. Every phrase containing [i] is paralleled, especially in slow or careful speech, by an otherwise identical synonymous phrase containing [i] instead. Examples: [hatšisén·tši] *eight centimeters*, [hatši-fúráɴ·] *eight francs*, [uts·kúšisa] *beauty*, [šis·šoku] *unemployment*, [xisomeru] or [hisomeru] *conceals*, [sik·kéɴ·] *judgment*, [sít·ta] *knew*, [pitšapitša] *splash*, [kiša] *train*, [dekíta] *was possible*, [kít·to] *surely*, [kip·pu] *ticket*.[28]

[A] long voiceless mediovelar (back) low vowel (B7 Q): after [p, t, k] and before [p, p·, p, t, t·, t, k, k·, k, k·][29] in rapid speech only. Every phrase containing [A] is paralleled by an otherwise identical synonymous phrase containing [a] instead; [A] is less common than [a]. Examples: [pakurito] *in one gulp*, [tAkái] *high*, [kakéru] *hangs it*, [kap·pa] *raincoat*, [kat·te] *kitchen*, [tak·kyuu] *pingpong*.

[O] long voiceless mediovelar (back) mid vowel, weakly rounded (B6 Q L5): after [p, t, k] and before [p, p·, p, t, t·, t, k, k·, k, k·][30] in rapid speech only. Every phrase containing [O] is paralleled by an otherwise identical synonymous phrase containing [o] instead; [O] is less common than [o]. Examples: [pOkét·to] *pocket*, [tOkoro] *place*, [kOkóro] *heart*, [kOt·tši] *this direction*, [kOp·pu] *glass tumbler*.

[u] long voiceless mediovelar (back) high vowel, weakly rounded (B5 Q L5): after [ts, tš, š, f, h] and before [s, š, f, x, h] or any long voiceless consonant; or after [p, k] and before any voiceless consonant, long or short. Every phrase containing [u] is paralleled, especially in slow or careful speech, by an otherwise identical synonymous phrase containing [u] instead. Examples: [átsusa] *heat*, [susumu] *advances*, [susai] *supervision*, [fusuma] or [husuma] *light opaque sliding door*, [hatsušímo] *first frost of the year*, [sup·pái] *sour*, [fut·tei] *scarcity*, [ip·puku] *one sip*, [kutsu] *shoe*, [kusa] *grass*.

[i] long voiced prevelar (front) high vowel (F5 V Q): before pause, all voiced vowels, and all consonants except the long nasals and [ɾ, ɣ]; after pause, all voiced vowels, and all consonants.

[27] The reader should bear in mind that 'long' has a special meaning in this paper, as already noted in §2.2. A 'long' vowel is a vowel of ordinary duration, constituting a syllable alone or in combination with one or two preceding 'short' consonants.

[28] No instances of voiceless [ɛ] have been observed, but the sound type may nevertheless occur in the dialect, perhaps with a distribution similar to that of voiceless [A].

[29] According to this statement voiceless [A] occurs only between voiceless stops; but it perhaps occurs also between voiceless consonants of other types, though I have no record of such instances.

[30] Voiceless [O] is here described as having the same distribution as voiceless [A]. Like [A] (see fn. 27), it may occur also between other voiceless consonants.

or [kǎŋ·ðŋ·] *gratitude*. When [ð] follows a long nasal, there is often a very brief nasalized glide sound [ʋ] between the two phones.

[u] long voiced mediovelar (back) high vowel, weakly rounded (B5 V Q L5): before pause, all voiced vowels, and all consonants except the long nasals and [t, ʏ]; after pause, all voiced vowels, and all short non-palatalized consonants except [t, d, w]. For the alternation between [u] and [ʊ] see the paragraph on [ʊ]. Examples of [u] before and after vowels: [nůide] *taking off (clothes)*, [ue] *top*, [buai] *percentage*, [uo] *fish*, [gyuunyuu] *cow's milk*, [šiutši] *attitude*, [meuma] *mare*, [kau] *buys*, [omóu] *thinks*; other examples above.

[ů] long voiced mediovelar (back) high vowel, weakly rounded, nasalized (B5 V Q L5 N): before [m·, m·, n·, n·, ɲ·, ʋ·] and after the same phones as [u]; or before long nasals. Examples: [ip·pům·] or [ip·púɲ·] *one minute*, [gům·púku] *uniform*.

4.2. In general, the auditory effect of a sequence of two or more segments can be inferred from the description of the individual segments in the foregoing list. Except as implied or expressly stated in the list itself, there are no assimilations or intervening glide sounds.[31] But the effect of consecutive vowels requires a brief comment.[32]

(1) Two different consecutive vowels are pronounced without interruption but without fusion; each vowel is part or all of a separate syllable. Examples already given are [ie, miaŋeru, šio, šiutši, eisei, deát·ta, komêo, meuma, hái, máe, kao, kau, kói, kóe, oaši, omóu, nůide, ue, uo].

(2) Three or more consecutive vowels, including no sequence of two like vowels, are similarly pronounced without interruption but without fusion; each vowel, again, is part or all of a separate syllable. Examples: [deåu] *encounters*, [aói] *blue*, [šiai] *game*, [buai] *percentage*, [niou] *smells*.

(3) Two like vowels in succession are pronounced as a phonetically overlong[33] vowel, equal in duration to two vowels of normal length (§1). But if the second vowel in such a combination is followed by a long nasal, or if it is higher in pitch than the immediately following syllable, there is a diminution in loudness between the two vowels (sometimes accompanied by a slight glottal constriction) and a renewed pulse of expiration on the second.[34] Examples: [kiita] *heard*,

[31] Compare the statement concerning nasalized [ĩ, ẽ, õ] in §4.1. What are sometimes described as assimilations—phones partaking of the character of certain neighboring phones—are here treated as distinct phones, with distributions of their own.

[32] In this comment no distinction is made between oral and nasalized vowels. But note that in a succession of two or more vowels preceded or followed by a long nasal, only the one vowel contiguous to the nasal is nasalized.

[33] The term 'overlong' is used here with the meaning usually attached to 'long' (i.e. perceptibly greater in duration than other syllabic vowels) in order to avoid confusion with the special use of 'long' in this paper (cf. fn. 27).

[34] The diminution in loudness (accompanied by glottal constriction) between certain consecutive vowels in rapid or moderately slow speech is not a phoneme of 'open juncture' or the like, but an automatic phenomenon, predictable in terms of the phonetic environment. A similar diminution in loudness, equally predictable, occurs in rather slow speech between a long nasal and an immediately following vowel.

In very slow or very careful speech (excluded from the scope of this paper), such diminutions in loudness between consecutive vowels are not limited to the environments described

vowels, and [p, k, tš, š, x, h, b, g, dž, z, r, m, n, ŋ]. For the alternation between [i] and [ɪ] see the paragraph on [ɪ]. Examples of [i] before and after vowels: [kiita] *heard*, [ie] *house*, [iie] *no*, [miaŋeru] *looks up*, [šio] *salt*, [šiutši] *attitude*, [eisei] *sanitation*, [hái] *yes*, [kói] *come!*, [nůide] *taking off (clothes)*; other examples above.

[ĩ] long voiced prevelar (front) vowel, nasalized (F5 V Q N): before [m·, n·, n·, ɲ·]; or before the same phones as [i] and after [n·, ɲ·]; or between long nasals. Examples: [kim·pin·] *money and goods*, [bíɲ·] *bottle*, [tén·in·] or [téɲ·iɲ·] *salesman*. When [ĩ] follows a long nasal, there is often a very brief nasalized glide sound [ʋ] between the two phones.

[e] long voiced prevelar (front) mid vowel (F6 V Q): before pause, all voiced vowels, and all consonants except the long nasals and [t, ʏ]; after pause, all voiced vowels, and all short non-palatalized consonants except [ts, š, f, ž, ʏ, w]. Examples of [e] before and after vowels: [eisei] *sanitation*, [teeburu] *table*, [deát·ta] *encountered*, [komêo] *rice (as verbal goal)*, [meuma] *mare*, [ie] *house*, [máe] *front*, [kóe] *voice*, [ue] *top*; other examples above. Some phrases containing [ee] are paralleled by otherwise identical synonymous phrases containing [eij] instead; and conversely.

[ê] long voiced prevelar (front) mid vowel, nasalized (F6 V Q N): before [m·, m·, n·, n·, ɲ·, ʋ·] and after the same phones as [e]; or before the same phones as [e]; or between long nasals. Examples: [sêm·méɲ·ki] *sink (for water)*, [pén·] or [péɲ·] *pen*, [tén·in·] or [téɲ·iɲ·] *salesman*, [sân·ên·] or [sâɲ·êɲ·] *three yen*. When [ê] follows a long nasal, there is often a very brief nasalized glide sound [ʋ] between the two phones.

[a] long voiced mediovelar (back) low vowel (B7 V Q): before pause, all voiced vowels, and all consonants except the long nasals and [t, ʏ]; after pause, all voiced vowels, and all short non-palatalized consonants except [ts, f]. For the alternation between [a] and [A] see the paragraph on [A]. Examples of [a] before and after vowels: [hái] *yes*, [máe] *front*, [obåasân·] *grandmother*, [kao] *face*, [kau] *buys*, [miaŋeru] *looks up*, [deát·ta] *encountered*, [oaši] *cash*, [buai] *percentage*; other examples above.

[ã] long voiced mediovelar (back) low vowel, nasalized (B7 V Q N): before [m·, m·, n·, n·, ɲ·, ʋ·] and after the same phones as [a]; or before the same phones as [a] and after [n·, ɲ·, ʋ·]; or between long nasals. Examples: [hãm·bín·] *half*, [pãn·] or [pãɲ·] *bread*, [hån·i] or [hấɲ·i] *extend*.

[o] long voiced mediovelar (back) mid vowel, weakly rounded (B6 V Q L5): before pause, all voiced vowels, and all consonants except the long nasals and [t, ʏ]; after pause, all voiced vowels, and all short non-palatalized consonants except [ts, f, w]. For the alternation between [o] and [O] see the paragraph on [O]. Examples of [o] before and after vowels: [kói] *come!*, [kóe] *voice*, [oaši] *cash*, [hóoboo] *here and there*, [omóu] *thinks*, [šio] *salt*, [komêo] *rice (as verbal goal)*, [kao] *face*, [uo] *fish*; other examples above.

[õ] long voiced mediovelar (back) mid vowel, weakly rounded, nasalized (B6 V Q L5 N): before [m·, m·, n·, n·, ɲ·, ʋ·] and after the same phones as [o]; or before the same phones as [o] and after [n·, ɲ·, ʋ·]; or between long nasals. Examples: [kõm·bán·] *tonight*, [hõn·] or [hõɲ·] *book*, [kôn·šuu] *this week*, [kãn·ôn·]

[nîisân·] *older brother*, [tšîisǽi] *small*, [ēe] *yes*, [teeburu] *table*, [kareeda] *dried twigs*, [aayat·te] *like that*, [obǽasân·] *grandmother*, [depǽato] *department store*, [koo] *thus*, [hóoboo] *here and there*, [dóozo] *please*, [gyuunyuu] *cow's milk*, [nuu] *sews*, [kíuki] *air*; but with a diminution of loudness between the two vowels [gîin·] *council member*, [goōn·] *Chinese pronunciation* (of a written character), [mizíuumi] *lake*.

[p·, p, t·, t, k·, k·] (1 Q). Note that these phones appear also in the preceding three sets: the long voiceless stops are in complementary distribution with each other and with the corresponding short stops. The latter—[p, p], [t, t], [k, k]—are of course in contrast with each other.

	labial	labial, palatalized	dental or alveolar	dental, palatalized	prepalatal	prevelar (front)	mediovelar (back)	glottal	glottal, palatalized
short voiceless stops	p	p·	t	t·		k·	k·	ʔ	
long voiceless stops	p·	p·	t·	t·		k·	k·		
short voiced stops	b	b	d			g	g		
short voiceless affricates			ts		tš				
long voiceless affricates			ts·		tš·				
short voiced affricates			dz		dž				
short voiceless spirants	f		s		š	x		h	h
long voiceless spirants	f·		s·		š·	x·			
short voiced spirants			z		ž				
short voiced nasals	m	m	n	n·		ŋ	ŋ		
long voiced nasals	m·	m·	n·	n·		ŋ·	ŋ·		
short voiced flaps			r,l	r					
short voiceless semivowels						ɾ	w		
short voiced semivowels						y	w		
(long) voiceless high vowels						ɪ	ʊ		
(long) voiced high vowels						i,ï	u,ü		
(long) voiceless mid vowels							O		
(long) voiced mid vowels						e,ɛ̈	o,ö		
(long) voiceless low vowels							ʌ		
(long) voiced low vowels							a,ä		

TABLE 1. THE PHONES OF THE CONSERVATIVE DIALECT

(4) If a succession of two or more vowels includes a sequence of two like vowels, the latter is pronounced as a phonetically overlong vowel; the unlike vowel precedes or follows without interruption but without fusion. Examples: [kooatsu] *high voltage*, [tooi] *distant*, [kaoo] *let's buy it*, [kooióo] *let's say it this way*, [miziuumi] *lake*.

(5) Three like vowels in succession are pronounced either as a prolonged vowel equal in duration to three vowels of normal length, or as a normal vowel followed by a phonetically overlong vowel of the same color, with a diminution of loudness between them and a renewed pulse on the second part. But if the last of three consecutive like vowels is followed by a long nasal, the sequence is pronounced instead as an overlong vowel plus a vowel of normal length, again with a diminution of loudness between them. Examples: [kooosuru] *acts in unison*, [kooootsu] *gradation*, [nomíii] *easy to drink*; but with a diminution of loudness [kooōn·] *great obligation*, [gooōn·] *signal*.[35]

5. Contrast. The list in §4.1 comprises 68 phones; these are shown (except for the zero phone, pause) in a phonetic arrangement in Table 1. As appears from the statement of their distribution, not all the phones are in contrast with each other. Some are in complementary distribution, some in free variation, some in overlapping distribution. The following sets and pairs of non-contrasting phones share one or more qualities (indicated in parentheses).

5.1. Phones in complementary distribution:

[p, p·, p, p·] (L1).
[t, t·, t, t·] (D1).

[k, k·, k, k·] (F/B1). Since F means prevelar (front) and B means mediovelar (back), the notation F/B means velar in general, without specifying the part of the velum against which the contact is made.

in the text. In that style of speech, [koo] *child* (as verbal goal) and [kareeda] *dried twigs* are often distinguished from [koo] *thus* and [kareeda] (beside [kareida]) *it is splendid* by a diminution in loudness between the two vowels, again with glottal constriction. (The diminution occurs only at morpheme boundaries.) In a description of extra-slow or extra-careful speech, it would therefore not be possible to account for the diminution in loudness as an automatic function of the environment; the diminution would have to be referred to a separate phoneme. In view of the glottal constriction that accompanies it, it would be most suitably accommodated in the same phoneme as the phrase-final glottal stop. (I owe this suggestion to Samuel E. Martin.)

[35] Successions of four or more like vowels are extremely rare. An example is [oóóo] *let's cover it* (presumptive form of the verb [oou] *covers*), which is pronounced as two phonetically overlong vowels with a diminution of loudness between them. It is possible to construct even longer sequences: [oooóo] *let's cover the tail* (as of a half-buried fox). Such an oddity is of course not intelligible to Japanese speakers at first hearing; but when it has been explained to them, they can both understand and repeat it.

[ʔ, p], [ʔ, t], [ʔ, k] (1). That is, the glottal stop is in complementary distribution with all the other stops; but these are in contrast with each other. Since the quality common to these pairs (1) is present also in other phones, and since the assignment of [ʔ] to the same phoneme with [p] or [t] or [k] would be wholly arbitrary, it is necessary to posit a separate phoneme for [ʔ] in spite of its complementation with other phones.

[tš, tš·] (D2).
[tš, tš·] (P2).
[s, s·] (D3).
[š, š·] (P3).
[f, f·] (L3).
[x, x·] (F3).
[h, h] (G3).
[b, b] (L1 V).

[g, ǵ] (F/B1 V). For the notation F/B see above on [k] etc.

[r, r̄] (D4 V).

[m, m̓; m·, m̓·] (L1 V N).

[n, n̦] (D1 V N).

[ŋ, ŋ̄] (F/B1 V N).

[m·, m̓·; n·, n̄·] (L/D1 V N Q). The notation L/D (labial or dental) can be interpreted as meaning non-velar. Theoretical justification of such a quality is not required, since no use will be made of it in what follows.

[m·, m̓·; ŋ·, ŋ̄·] (L/F/B1 V N Q). The notation L/F/B (labial or prevelar or medievelar) can be interpreted as meaning non-dental; this quality also will not be used in what follows. Note that the phones [m·] and [m̓·] are in complementary distribution with each other and with each of the three pairs [m, m̓], [n·, n̄·], and [ŋ·, ŋ̄·]; but short [m, m̓] are in contrast with the other two pairs.

[r, y] (F5).

[i, i̠] (F5 V Q).

[e, e̠] (F6 V Q).

[a, a̠] (B7 V Q).

[o, o̠] (B6 V Q L5).

[u, u̠] (B5 V Q L5).

5.2. Phones in free variation:

[f, h] (L/G3). All the environments of [f] are shared by [h]; but [h] has environments not shared by [f]. The notation L/G (labial or glottal) can be interpreted as meaning not dental or prepalatal or velar—in a word, non-lingual. Although the quality L/G is disjunctive (involving alternatives and the exclusion of one or more intermediate qualities), it can be justified on the principle—adopted ad hoc—that the recognition of a disjunctive quality is valid in phonemics provided the set of intermediate qualities excluded by the disjunction is not itself disjunctive. The set of qualities D, P, F, and B (dental, prepalatal, prevelar, and medievelar), intermediate in position between L and G, is not disjunctive because all its members are subdivisions of one class, the lingual.

[r, l] (D4 V). All the environments of [l] are shared by [r], but [r] has environments not shared by [l].

[i, i] (F5 Q). All the environments of [ɪ] are shared by [i], but [i] has environments not shared by [ɪ]. As noted in §5.1, [i] (and hence [ɪ] also) is in complementary distribution with [i]. Similar comments apply to the three pairs that follow.

[ʌ, a] (B7 Q).

[O, o] (B6 Q L5).

[U, u] (B5 Q L5).

5.3. Phones in overlapping distribution:

[x, h] (F/G3). According to the ad-hoc principle adopted for [f, h], the notation F/G (prevelar or glottal) designates a disjunction that cannot be legitimately used as a criterion in phonemic analysis. Note that [h] is non-contrastive with [h] and [x], [h] is non-contrastive with each other.

[n·, v·; y·] (D/F/B1 V N Q). The first two of these phones, as already shown, are in complementary distribution; similarly the last two. It is the two pairs of phones, [n·, v·] and [ɣ·, y·], that are in overlapping distribution. Both pairs occur before pause, all vowels, and [h, y]; but only [n·, v·] occur before dental and alveolar consonants, and only [ɣ·, y·] occur before velar consonants. In their common environments, the pairs [n·, v·] and [v·, y·] occur interchangeably. The notation D/F/B (dental or prevelar or medievelar) is a valid disjunction, since it includes all lingual nasals, excluding only the labial; but it will not be necessary to make use of it in the final classification.

5.4.
In three pairs of phones—[g, ŋ], [ɡ, ʋ], [dʒ, ʒ]—the members are in partially free variation with each other, but must nevertheless be kept apart. Nearly all phrases containing [ŋ], [ʋ], and [ʒ] are paralleled, especially in slow or careful speech, by otherwise identical synonymous phrases containing respectively [g], [ɡ], and [dʒ] instead. But there are many phrases containing the latter three phones that are not paralleled by phrases containing the former; and these phrases are not marked by any phonetic or phonemic peculiarities. Both phones occur in [aŋaru, agaru] rises, [maŋo, mago] grandchild, [mas·sŭgu, mas·sŭgu] straight; [kaŋi, kaɡi] key, [nʲuuɲyuu, nʲuuɡyuu] milch cow, [niŋ·gyoo, niŋ·gyoo] doll; [miʒikái, midʒikái] short, [nízuu, nídʒuu] twenty, [sáɴ·ʒuu, sáɴ·dʒuu] thirty. But there is no such alternation in [sonoɡo] after that, [dónoɡurai] about how much?, [árugak·koo] a certain school; [konoɡyuunyuu] this (cow's) milk, [nihóɴ·noʄkai] the Japanese Diet, [árugiŋ·koo] a certain bank; [kídʒi] newspaper article, [óokina-dʒiśiɴ] a great earthquake, [utśinodʒotśnu] our maid servant. Since the alternations between [g, ɡ, dʒ] and [ŋ, ʋ, ʒ] respectively are limited to certain phrases only, and since their common environments do not form a phonetically or phonemically definable set, the three pairs of phones must be treated separately in the phonemic analysis.

5.5.
Different phones that are not in complementary or overlapping distribution or in free variation belong to different phonemes. In formulating the relations among such phones, it is not necessary to show that each one is in contrast with all the others. If two phones have no qualities in common, or share only such qualities as are present also in other phones, they cannot be grouped in the same phoneme in any case: thus [t] and [y], with qualities D1 and F5 V respectively, will belong to different phonemes whether it is possible to prove contrast between them or not; pairs like [toko] bed : [yoko] side add nothing to the evidence. It will be enough, therefore, to show contrast between phonetically similar phones or groups of phones, which might otherwise be thought to belong to the same phoneme.

In the following list, phones that have already been established as non-contrastive are grouped together. A contrast between any members of two such groupings is taken to prove contrast between the groupings as a whole.

[n, n]: in contrast with [d], as in [neta, détai]; with [m, m], as in [kane] metal, [káŋe] shadow; with [ŋ, ʊ], as in [yaku] ignites, [waku] boils; with [ɪ, i, i], as in [kawanai] [kanei] crab, [hán·i] extent.

[ŋ, ʊ]: in contrast with [g, g], as in [háruŋakíru, árugak·koo]; with [n, n], as in [káŋe, kane]; with [m·, m·, n·, n·, ʊ·, y·], as in [maŋo] grandchild, [káŋ·óŋ·] gratitude.

[m·, m·, n·, n·, ʊ·, y·]: in contrast with [m, m], as in [kán·ón· ~ káŋ·óŋ·, kama]; with [n, n], as in [hán·i, kani]; with [ŋ, ʊ], as in [káŋ·óŋ·, maŋo].

[ɾ, y]: in contrast with [w], as in [yaku] ignites, [waku] boils; with [ɪ, i, i], as in [kyoku] office, [kiots·kéru] pays attention.

[w]: in contrast with [ɾ, y], as in [waku, yaku]; with [ʊ, u, ū], as in [waku, yaku] doesn't buy, [kauabura] oil that one buys.

[ɪ, i, i]: in contrast with [ɾ, y], as in [kiots·kéru, kyoku]; with [e, ē], as in [ike] go], [éki] station; with [ʊ, u, ū], as in [itái] painful, [utau] sings.

[e, ē]: in contrast with [ɪ, i, i], as in [éki, ike]; with [a, a, ā], as in [éki], [áki] autumn; with [O, o, ō], as in [éki], [ōkíta] woke up.

[a, a, ā]: in contrast with [e, ē], as in [áki, éki]; with [O, o, ō], as in [akai] red, [oka] hill.

[O, o, ō]: in contrast with [a, a, ā], as in [oka, akai]; with [ʊ, u, ū], as in [otšíru] falls, [utši] home; with [e, ē], as in [ōkíta, éki].

[ʊ, u, ū]: in contrast with [w], as in [kauabura, kawanai]; with [O, o, ō], as in [utši, otšíru]; with [ɪ, i, i], as in [utau, itái].

6. Phonemes. The phonetic and distributional evidence makes it an easy matter to group the sixty-eight phones into phonemes. For all but two of the groupings it is enough to proceed on the double basis of non-contrastive distribution and phonetic similarity. In the two instances where these criteria fail to decide between alternative groupings, a simple appeal to patterning gives the answer.

6.1. As noted in §5.1, the long voiceless stops [p·, p·, t·, t·, k·] are in complementary distribution with each other and with the corresponding short stops [p, p, t, t, k, k]; but the latter (grouped in three pairs of non-contrasting phones) are mutually in contrast. In the two instances where these criteria fail to decide ... Two groupings of the long stops are possible. (1) They can be separated from the corresponding short stops and grouped all together in a single phoneme, say /q/, with a total distribution as follows: before [p, p, t, k, ts, tš, š], after [i, e, a, o, u, ɪ, ʌ, O, ʊ]. (2) The three pairs of long stops—[p·, p·], [t·, t·], [k·, k·]—can be assigned respectively to the same phonemes as the corresponding three pairs of short stops, with total distributions as follows: /p/ before [i, e, a, o, u, ɪ, ʌ, O, ʊ, p, p, ʏ], after [#, i, e, a, o, u, ɪ, ʌ, O, p·, p·, m·, m·]; /t/ before [e, a, o, ʌ, O, t, ts, tš, s, y], after [#, i, e, a, o, u, ɪ, ʌ, O, ʊ, t·, ts·, tš·, š·, f, x·, n·]; /k/ before [i, e, a, o, u, ɪ, ʌ, O, ʊ, k, k·]; /k/ before [i, e, a, o, u, ɪ, ʌ, O, ʊ, k, k, y], after [#, i, e, a, o, u, ɪ, ʌ, O, ʊ, k, k·, x·, ʊ·, y·].

The distribution of the proposed phoneme /q/ would be unique in type: no other phoneme is limited to positions between a vowel and a consonant. On the other hand, the distributions of the three phonemes /p, t, k/ (each including both short and long stops as members) are precisely parallel in type to the distribu-

[p, p·, p·]: in contrast with [t, t·, t·, t·], as in [pḗŋ·ki] paint, [tḗŋ·ki] weather; with [k, k·, k·, k·], as in [pén·] pen, [kén·] prefecture; with [f, f·], as in [puro] pro-letarian, [furo] bath; with [b, b], as in [pán·] bread, [bán·] inning.

[t, t·, t·, t·]: in contrast with [p, p·, p·, p·], as in [tḗŋ·ki, pḗŋ·ki]; with [k, k·, k·, k·], as in [ta] rice field, [ka] mosquito; with [ts, ts·], as in [mát·te] waiting, [máts·to] if one waits; with [s, s·], as in [otót·sán·] dad, [tos·sa] instant; with [d], as in [tóo] copper.

[k, k·, k·, k·]: in contrast with [p, p·, p·, p·], as in [kén·, pén·]; with [t, t·, t·, t·], as in [ka, ta]; with [x, x·, h], as in [kiru] puts on (clothes), [xiru] or [hiru] daytime; with [g, g], as in [ko] child, [go] five.

[ts, ts·]: in contrast with [t, t·, t·, t·], as in [máts·to, mát·te]; with [tš, tš·], as in [máts·to] if one waits, [matš·to] town and (country, etc.); with [s, s·], as in [ts·tsú-mu] wraps, [susumu] advances.

[tš, tš·]: in contrast with [ts, ts·], as in [katš] victory, [katši] conflagration.

[tš, tš·]: in contrast with [t, t·, t·, t·], as in [katši] victory; with [dž], as in [katši] conflagration.

[s, s·]: in contrast with [t, t·, t·, t·], as in [tos·sa, otót·sán·]; with [ts, ts·], as in [susumu, ts·tsúmu]; with [š, š·], as in [séi] stature, [žéi] tax.

[š, š·]: in contrast with [tš, tš·], as in [ši, tši]; with [s, s·], as in [šuu, suu]; with [ž], as in [naži] pear, [onaži] same.

[f, f·]: in contrast with [p, p·, p·, p·], as in [furo, puro]; with [s, s·], as in [nifún·] two minutes, [nisún·] two inches; with [x, x·, h], as in [f·tóru] grows fat, [x·tótsu] one.

[x, x·, h]: in contrast with [k, k·, k·, k·], as in [xiru ~ hiru, kiru]; with [š, š·], as in [x·tótsu, f·tóru].

[x, x·, h]: in contrast with [š·to] person, [š·ta] tongue; with [f, f·], as in [x·tótsu, f·tóru].

[h, h]: in contrast with [k, k·, k·], as in [ha] leaf, [ka] mosquito; with [s, s·], as in [hako] box, [sake] rice wine.

[b, b]: in contrast with [p, p·, p·, p·], as in [bán·, pán·]; with [d], as in [bóku] I, [dóko] where?; with [m, m], as in [boo] stick, [moo] already.

[d]: in contrast with [t, t·, t·, t·], as in [dóko, tóo]; with [b, b], as in [dóko, bóku]; with [g, g], as in [déta] went out, [geta] wooden clogs; with [n, n], as in [déta], [neta] went to sleep.

[g, g]: in contrast with [k, k·, k·, k·], as in [go, ko]; with [d], as in [geta, déta]; with [ŋ, ʊ], as in [árugak·koo] a certain school, [háruŋakíru] spring comes.

[dž]: in contrast with [tš, tš·], as in [kádži, katši]; with [d], as in [džerii] jelly, [déru] goes out; with [ž], as in [ʔookinadžišín·] a great earthquake, [onaži] same.

[ž]: in contrast with [s, s·], as in [žéi, séi]; with [ž], as in [sén·zo] ancestor, [sén·žoo] (beside [sén·džoo]) battlefield.

[ž]: in contrast with [š, š·], as in [onaži, naši]; with [dž], as in [onaži, ʔokina-džišín·]; with [z], as in [sén·žoo, sén·zo].

[r, l, r]: in contrast with [d]: [róol] prison, [dóo] copper.

[m, m]: in contrast with [b, b], as in [moo, boo]; with [n, n], as in [make] de-feat, [naku] cries; with [m·, m·, n·, n·, ʊ·, y·], as in [kama] iron pot, [kán·ón·] or [káŋ·óŋ·] gratitude.

tions of several other phonemes—especially, as one might expect, of those which include as members the several voiceless affricates and spirants. (The total distributions of these latter phonemes are obtained by adding together the distributions of [ts] and [tš], [tś] and [tś·], [s] and [s·], [š] and [š·], etc., as shown in §4.1 and restated in §6.2.)

If, in spite of its unique distribution, the phoneme /q/ made the over-all description of Japanese phonemics more compact or more economical—that is, if the recognition of /q/ resulted in fewer and more general statements—it would be legitimate to disregard the facts of patterning and accept the first of the two groupings proposed above. But the adoption of /q/ would not have such a result. The members of /q/ would be in contrast with all the remaining long voiceless consonants, as these are in contrast with each other. The phoneme /q/ could not include the phones [ts·, tš·, s·, š·, f·, x·]; each of these is clearly to be grouped in a single phoneme with the corresponding short consonant. The effect of adopting /q/ would be to make the descriptive statements more numerous and less general.

The argument from patterning, then, is not offset by any counterargument from economy. It is the second of the two possible groupings that must be accepted: the three pairs of long stops must be assigned respectively to the same phonemes as the corresponding three pairs of short stops.

The other case where phonemic similarity and lack of contrast are not enough to decide the phonemic grouping is that of the nasals. The three pairs of short nasals—[m, m̩], [n, n̩], [ŋ, ŋ̩]—are in contrast with each other; but the six long nasals are mutually non-contrastive. Furthermore, the short and long bilabial nasals are in complementary distribution; but the short dental and velar nasals are in contrast with the corresponding long phones. These facts lead at once to the establishment of four phonemes: /m/, including [m, m̩] as members; /n/, including [n, n̩]; /ŋ/, including [ŋ, ŋ̩]; and /ñ/, including [n·, ɲ·; ɲ̩·]. The problem is where to place [m·, m̩·], since these phones are in complementary distribution with the members of both /m/ and /ñ/.

Total distributions are as follows: /n/ before [i, e, a, o, u, y], after [# , i, e, a, o, u, n·, n̩·]; /ŋ/ before [i, e, a, o, u, y], after [i, e, a, o, u, ŋ·, ŋ̩·]; /m/ without [m·, m̩·] before [i, e, a, o, u, y], after [# , i, e, a, o, u, m·, m̩·]; /m/ with [m·, m̩·]; /ñ/ without [m·, m̩·] before [i, e, a, o, u, m·, m̩·]; /ñ/ without [m·, m̩·] before [# , i, ē, ã, õ, ũ]; /ñ/ with [m·, m̩·] before [# , i, ē, ã, õ, ũ, t, k, ǩ, ts, tš, s, š, x, x·, h, h, b, b, d, g, g, dž, z, ž, r, r, m, n, n, ŋ, ŋ, ū, p, p, t, k, ǩ, ts, tš, s, š, x, x·, h, h, b, b, d, g, g, dž, z, ž, r, r, n, n, ŋ, ŋ, ū, p, p, t, k, ǩ, ts, tš, s, š, x, x·, h, h, d, g, g, dž, z, ž, r, r, m, n, n, ŋ, ŋ, y, w], after [# , i, ē, ã, õ, ũ].

It is obvious that the distribution of /m/ with the phones [m·, m̩·] included is radically different in type (with respect to the phones before which its members occur) from the distributions of /n/ and /ŋ/, to which—in view of the phonetic parallelism—one would expect it to be similar. The distribution of /ñ/ is unique in type whether the phoneme includes [m·, m̩·] or not; but so also is its membership, which consists wholly of long consonants. Accordingly, though uniqueness of distribution type was used as an argument against the recognition of a phoneme

/q/ and in favor of an alternative grouping, the argument has no force when applied to the phoneme /ñ/, since there is no possibility of grouping [n·, n̩·, ɲ·, ɲ̩·] with the corresponding short nasals.

Again the conclusion is unambiguous: the long bilabial nasals [m·, m̩·] are to be grouped with the other long nasals in a phoneme /ñ/.

6.2. The conservative dialect of standard Japanese has twenty-nine phonemes, in addition to the four pitch phonemes already described: five vowels, one long nasal, ten voiceless consonants, two semivowels, and pause. In the list below, each phoneme symbol is followed by one or more phonetic symbols (in square brackets) denoting the allophones of the phoneme, and by an indication of the qualities which define it. Determined qualities of each phoneme are added in parentheses.[36]

i	[i, i·, ī]	F5 Q
e	[e, ē·]	F6 (Q V)
a	[A, a, ā·]	7 (Q B)
o	[O, o, ō·]	B6 (Q L5)
u	[ʋ, u, ū·]	B5 Q (L5)
ñ	[m·, m̩·, n·, n̩·, ɲ·, ɲ̩·, ŋ·, ŋ̩·]	N Q (1 V)
p	[p, p·, p̄, p̄·]	L1
t	[t, t·, t̄, t̄·]	D1
k	[k, k·, k̄, k̄·]	F/B1
?	[ʔ]	G1
c	[ts, ts·]	D2
č	[tš, tš·]	P2
s	[s, s·]	D3
š	[š, š·]	P3
x	[x, x·]	F3

h	[f, f, h, h]	L/G3
b	[b, b]	L1 V
d	[d]	D1 V
g	[g, g]	F/B1 V
j	[dž]	P2 V
z	[z]	D3 V
ž	[ž]	P3 V
r	[r, l, ɾ]	4 (D V)
m	[m, m̩]	L N (1 V)
n	[n, n̩]	D N (1 V)
ŋ	[ŋ, ŋ̩]	F/B N (1 V)
y	[y, ɥ]	F5
w	[w]	B5 (V L5)
#	[#]	None

The following paragraphs give a formal definition of each phoneme, together with the distribution of its allophones, restated from §4.1 in phonemic terms.

/i/ the class of long (syllabic) high front vowels: [ɪ] after /č, š, x, h/ and before /s, š, h, pp, tt, tc, tč, tč, kk/, or after /p, k/ and before /p, t, k, c, č, s, š, x, h/, in free variation with [i]; [i] before or after /ñ/; [i] elsewhere.

/e/ the class of mid front vowels: [ē] before or after /ñ/; [e] elsewhere.

[36] The convention explained in §2.2 concerning the use of the symbols N, V, Q must be modified for the purposes of this list. Here the absence of any of the three symbols N, V, Q implies the presence of the corresponding opposite quality as a necessary part of the definition of a phoneme only if the remaining qualities occur in the list accompanied by the omitted symbol. Thus, in the definition of the phoneme /p/, namely L1, the absence of the symbol V implies the presence of voicelessness as a distinctive (non-determined and non-conditioned) quality because the combination L1 V occurs as the definition of /b/; but in the definition of /y/, namely F5, the absence of V implies nothing, since there is no combination F5 V defining any other phoneme. In short, the absence of N, V, or Q in this list is distinctive only if the combination from which it is absent is otherwise identical with an occurring combination in which it is present.

/a/ the class of low vowels: [A] in rapid speech before /p, t, k/ and after /p, t, k/, in free variation with [a]; [ä] before or after /ñ/; [a] elsewhere.

/o/ the class of mid back vowels: [O] in rapid speech before /p, t, k/ and after /p, t, k/, in free variation with [o]; [ö] before or after /ñ/; [o] elsewhere.

/u/ the class of long (syllabic) high back vowels: [U] after /c, č, s, š, h/ and before /s, š, x, h, pp, tt, tc, tč, kk/, or after /p, k/ and before /p, t, k, c, č, s, š, x, h/, in free variation with [u]; [ü] before or after /ñ/; [u] elsewhere.

/ñ/ the class of long (syllabic) nasals: [m·] before /p, b, m/ not followed by /i, y/; [m·] before /pi, py, bi, by, mi, my/; [n·] before /t, c, s, d, z/, and /r, n/ not followed by /i, y/; [n·] before /č, š, j, ž, ri, ry, ni, ny/; [ŋ·] before /w/, and /k, g, ŋ/ not followed by /i, y/; [ŋ·] before /x, ki, ky, gi, gy, ŋi, ŋy/; [n·] or [ŋ·] when not preceded by /i/; [w·] or [y·] before /i, y, hi, hy/, and /#/ when preceded by /i/.

/p/ the class of voiceless labial stops: [p] before vowels except /i/; [p·] before /t, c, s/; [p·] before /pi, py/.

/t/ the class of voiceless dental stops: [t] before /e, a, o/; [t·] before /t, c, s/; [t] before /y/; [t·] before /č/.

/k/ the class of voiceless velar stops: [k] before vowels except /i/; [k·] before /t, k, c, č, s/; [k·] before /ki, ky/.

/?/ the class of glottal stops: [?] before pause. (Cf. fn. 32.)

/c/ the class of voiceless dental or denti-alveolar affricates: [ts] before /u/; [ts·] before pause and /t, k, c, č/.

/č/ the class of voiceless prepalatal affricates: [tš] before vowels; [tš·] before pause and /t, k, c, č/.

/s/ the class of voiceless alveolar spirants: [s] before vowels except /i/; [s·] before pause and /t, k, c, č, s/.

/š/ the class of voiceless prepalatal spirants: [š] before vowels except /e/; [š·] before pause and /t, k, c, č, š/.

/x/ the class of prevelar spirants: [x] before vowels except /e/; [x·] before /t, k, c, č/.

/h/ the class of non-lingual spirants: [f] before /u/, in free variation with [h]; [f·] before /t, k, c, č, h/; [h] before vowels except /i/; [h] before /i, y/.

/b/ the class of voiced labial stops: [b] before /e, a, o, u/; [b] before /i, y/.

/d/ the class of voiced dental stops: [d] before /e, a, o/.

/g/ the class of voiced velar stops: [g] before /e, a, o, u/; [g] before vowels.

/j/ the class of voiced prepalatal affricates: [dž] before vowels.

/z/ the class of voiced alveolar spirants: [z] before vowels except /i/.

/ž/ the class of voiced prepalatal spirants: [ž] before vowels except /e/, in free alternation with /j/.

/r/ the class of flaps: [r] before /e, a, o, u/; [l] before /e, o/, in free variation with [r]; [r] before /i, y/.

/m/ the class of short (non-syllabic) labial nasals: [m] before /e, a, o, u/; [m] before /i, y/.

/n/ the class of short (non-syllabic) dental nasals: [n] before /e, a, o, u/; [n] before /i, y/.

/ŋ/ the class of short (non-syllabic) velar nasals: [ŋ] before /e, a, o, u/; /ŋ/ before /i, y/.

/y/ the class of short (non-syllabic) high front vowels, i.e. semivowels: [r] after /p, k/ and before /a, o, u/; /y/ elsewhere.

/w/ the class of short (non-syllabic) high back vowels, i.e. semivowels: [w] before /a/.

/#/ the class of pauses: [#] before all phonemes except /?, ŋ, ž/, after /i, e, a, o, u, ñ, ?, c, č, s, š/.

6.3. The total distribution of these twenty-nine phonemes, with respect to the phonemes that immediately precede and follow them in phrases, is shown in Table 2. Each horizontal row shows all the two-phoneme combinations in which a given phoneme appears as the prior member; each vertical column shows all the combinations in which a given phoneme appears as the second member. Hence each row contains all the phonemes that follow a given phoneme, and each column contains all the phonemes that precede it.

Phonemes are listed in this table in a descending order according to their freedom of distribution. The following tabulation shows for each phoneme the number of phonemes that precede it (Prec.), the number of those that follow it (Foll.), and the total number of combinations in which it appears.

Phoneme	Prec.	Foll.	Totals	Phoneme	Prec.	Foll.	Totals
a	27	29	56	h	7	10	17
o	26	29	55	p	8	7	15
u	25	29	54	x	7	8	15
e	22	29	51	b	7	6	13
i	21	29	50	g	7	6	13
*	11	25	36	r	7	6	13
ñ	6	27	33	m	7	6	13
č	14	10	24	n	7	6	13
t	14	8	22	ŋ	6	6	12
k	14	7	21	j	7	5	12
c	14	6	20	z	7	4	11
y	17	3	20	d	7	3	10
s	9	10	19	ž	5	4	9
š	8	10	18	w	7	1	8
				?	5	1	6

The text in §7 contains only slightly more than 2000 phonemes; it is too small a sample to yield significant statistical information. But a tabulation of the frequencies with which the several phonemes occur in this text may be useful as a model for the more extensive investigation of relative frequency that must some day be undertaken.

Phoneme frequencies in the text range from 296 for /a/ to 2 for /x/; two phonemes, /p/ and /ž/, do not occur at all. In the tabulation, relative frequencies

(R) are expressed in terms of occurrences per 10,000 phonemes (i.e. the actual percentage of its occurrences multiplied by 100). The columns I, M, and F show for each phoneme the percentage of its occurrences in initial, medial, and final position respectively.[37] The figures for /#/ refer to positions in the utterance as a whole; the figures for all other phonemes refer to positions in the phrase: 'initial' means preceded by /#/; 'final' means followed by /#/; 'medial' means neither preceded nor followed by /#/. Numerals in the first column designate pitch phonemes.

	R	I	M	F
a	1333	2.4	83.1	14.5
o	1081	8.3	84.2	7.5
3	774	0.6	76.2	23.2
i	734	2.4	92.0	5.6
2	729	21.5	62.3	16.2
t	617	5.8	94.2	0.0
#	581	23.2	53.6	23.2
4	559	52.4	22.6	25.0
e	464	0.0	70.0	30.0
k	418	9.9	91.1	0.0
m	351	6.4	93.6	0.0
n	347	7.8	92.2	0.0
u	297	6.0	92.4	1.6
r	265	1.7	98.3	0.0
s	252	17.8	82.2	0.0
š	189	4.8	95.2	0.0
ñ	139	0.0	93.6	6.4
d	130	3.4	96.6	0.0
ŋ	130	0.0	100.0	0.0
h	94	52.4	47.6	0.0
b	94	0.0	100.0	0.0
w	94	4.8	95.2	0.0
y	72	6.3	93.7	0.0
j	59	0.0	100.0	0.0
č	54	25.0	75.0	0.0
l	27	16.6	16.6	66.8
c	22	0.0	100.0	0.0
z	22	20.0	80.0	0.0
?	13	0.0	0.0	100.0
g	13	0.0	100.0	0.0
x	9	0.0	100.0	0.0
p	0	—	—	—
ž	0	—	—	—

6.4. In spite of the striking auditory effect produced by the equal duration of Japanese syllables (§1), syllabic structure seems to have only a very minor place, if any, in the phonemic structure as a whole. Subject to the limitations of occurrence shown in Table 2, phonemes occur[38] in utterances simply as phonemes,

[37] Some light is thrown on the relative INITIAL frequency of certain phonemes by the number of dictionary entries beginning with various letters (interpreted phonemically). Such a count, in which every dictionary word figures once, regardless of its frequency in speech, is of course different in kind from the running count tabulated above. (On the difference between list frequency and text frequency see Martin Joos, Lg. 18.33 [1942].) The following figures denote the number of PAGES occupied by words with various initial phonemes in Kenkyusha's New Japanese–English dictionary (total 2263 pp.).

k 416	n 105	d 68	x 41
h 225	i 102	b 62	u 39
t 185	y 101	g 60	z 25
s 168	j 76	r 55	e 24
š 148	o 76	č 50	w 17
m 139	a 72	c 41	p 7

[38] On the logical error involved in saying that phonemes occur, and on the way in which the expression can be justified, see Lg. 24.36, §53.3 and fn. 30.

The 41 pages shown for /x/ are included among the 225 shown for /h/; that is, there are 41 pages of words that begin with /x/ or /h/ in free alternation.

	a	o	u	e	i	#	ñ	č	t	k	c	y	s	š	h	p	x	b	g	r	m	n	ŋ	j	z	d	ž	w	?
a	aa	ao	au	ae	ai	a#	añ	ač	at	ak	ac	ay	as	aš	ah	ap	ax	ab	ag	ar	am	an	aŋ	aj	az	ad	až	aw	a?
o	oa	oo	ou	oe	oi	o#	oñ	oč	ot	ok	oc	oy	os	oš	oh	op	ox	ob	og	or	om	on	oŋ	oj	oz	od	ož	ow	o?
u	ua	uo	uu	ue	ui	u#	uñ	uč	ut	uk	uc	uy	us	uš	uh	up	ux	ub	ug	ur	um	un	uŋ	uj	uz	ud	už	uw	u?
e	ea	eo	eu	ee	ei	e#	eñ	eč	et	ek	ec	ey	es	eš	eh	ep	ex	eb	eg	er	em	en	eŋ	ej	ez	ed	ež	ew	e?
i	ia	io	iu	ie	ii	i#	iñ	ič	it	ik	ic	iy	is	iš	ih	ip	ix	ib	ig	ir	im	in	iŋ	ij	iz	id	iž	iw	i?
#	#a	#o	#u	#e	#i		#ñ	#č	#t	#k	#c	#y	#s	#š	#h	#p	#x	#b	#g	#r	#m	#n		#j	#z	#d		#w	
ñ	ña	ño	ñu	ñe	ñi	ñ#		ñč	ñt	ñk	ñc	ñy	ñs	ñš	ñh	ñp	ñx	ñb	ñg	ñr	ñm	ñn	ñŋ	ñj	ñz	ñd	ñž	ñw	
č	ča	čo	ču	če	či	č#		čč	čt	čk	čc																		
t	ta	to		te				tč	tt		tc	ty	ts																
k	ka	ko	ku	ke	ki					kk		ky																	
c			cu			c#		cč	ct	ck	cc																		
y	ya	yo	yu																										
s	sa	so	su	se		s#		sč	st	sk	sc		ss																
š	ša	šo	šu		ši	š#		šč	št	šk	šc			šš															
h	ha	ho	hu	he	hi			hč	ht	hk	hc	hy																	
p	pa	po	pu	pe	pi							py				pp													
x	xa	xo	xu		xi			xč	xt	xk	xc																		
b	ba	bo	bu	be	bi							by																	
g	ga	go	gu	ge	gi							gy																	
r	ra	ro	ru	re	ri							ry																	
m	ma	mo	mu	me	mi							my																	
n	na	no	nu	ne	ni							ny																	
ŋ	ŋa	ŋo	ŋu	ŋe	ŋi							ŋy																	
j	ja	jo	ju	je	ji																								
z	za	zo	zu	ze																									
d	da	do		de																									
ž	ža	žo	žu		ži																								
w	wa																												
?						?#																							

TABLE 2. DISTRIBUTION OF PHONEMES IN THE CONSERVATIVE DIALECT

one after another, without being obviously grouped in any larger structural units except the spans defined by phonemes of pitch.[39] Some phonemes (as /i, ñ/) have only 'long' members, and hence constitute a phonetic syllable wherever they appear; some phonemes (as /b, n/) have only 'short' members, and hence never constitute a phonetic syllable; and some phonemes (as /t, s/) have 'long' members in certain environments, 'short' members in others.

Nevertheless, it is useful to state the correlation between phonetic syllables and phoneme sequences. Each of the following single phonemes and phoneme sequences constitutes one phonetic syllable:

Group 1: /i, e, a, o, u, ñ/, when preceded by a member of the same group or by pause

Group 2: /p, t, k, c, č, s, š, x, h/, when not followed by a member of Group 1

Group 3: /i, e, a, o, u/ together with one immediately preceding phoneme, provided the latter is not pause or a member of Group 1 and is not /y/ preceded in turn by a consonant

Group 4: /a, o, u/ together with two immediately preceding phonemes, provided the first is not pause or a member of Group 1, and the second is /y/

The pause phoneme is not included in any syllable. Pitch phonemes have no effect on the number of syllables in a phrase.

Though syllables appear to have little structural importance, they furnish a convenient basis for statements about the distribution of phonemes. In any syllable that contains more than one phoneme, the order of phonemes is unalterable and therefore non-distinctive: /ka/ and /kya/ are actually occurring syllables, but /ak, yak, kay, aky, ayk, yka/ are not (though all these except the last two are actually occurring sequences). It is therefore enough to enumerate the phonemes contained in a syllable, without making any statement about their order.[40] The total distribution of phonemes can be described by listing the syllables that occur and by stating the limitations on their occurrence in terms of preceding and following syllables. The units involved in such a description (syllables instead of phonemes) will be more numerous than in the treatment adopted above, but the statements about them will be fewer.[41] The following formulation may be compared with §6.3.

Syllables are grouped in five types, designated V, ?, N, K, S:

Type V: the syllable ends with or consists of a vowel; total 119: see Table 3.

Type ?: the syllable ends with a glottal stop; exact number not known; see §4.1.

Type N: the syllable consists of a long nasal consonant; total 1: /ñ/.

Type K: the syllable consists of a voiceless stop; total 3: /p, t, k/.

Type S: the syllable consists of a voiceless affricate or spirant; total 6: /c, č, s, š, x, h/.

TABLE 3. SYLLABLES OF TYPE V

i	pi	ki	či	ši	xi	hi	bi	gi	ji	ji	ži	ri	mi	ni	ne	ŋi	
e	pe	ke	če	se	he	be	de	ge	je	ze		re	me	ne	ne	ŋe	wa
a	pa	ka	ča	ša	xa	ha	ba	da	ga	ja	za	ža	ra	ma	na	na	ŋa
o	po	ko	čo	šo	xo	ho	bo	do	go	jo	zo	žo	ro	mo	no	no	ŋo
u	pu	ku	ču	su	xu	hu	bu		gu	ju	zu	žu	ru	mu	nu	nu	ŋu
ya	pya	kya				hya	bya		gya				rya	mya	nya	nya	ŋya
yo	pyo	kyo				hyo	byo		gyo				ryo	myo	nyo	nyo	ŋyo
yu	pyu	kyu				hyu	byu		gyu				ryu	myu	nyu	nyu	ŋyu

The distribution of these syllable types is shown in Table 4. In this table, V* denotes a syllable of type V that begins with a voiceless stop (the same stop that constitutes the preceding syllable of type K); V** denotes a syllable of type V that begins with a voiceless consonant of any kind. The distribution of syllables of type S is indicated only in general terms; for the details see Table 2.

	after /*/	after V	after N	after K	after S
before /*/	V N	V ? N S	V	V*	V**
before V	V N	V N K S	V	V*	V**
before N, K, S	V	V	V (?) / V̥	V* (?) / V̥*	V** (?) / V̥**

TABLE 4. DISTRIBUTION OF SYLLABLE TYPES

7. Text. The following text is written in a strictly phonemic transcription; all morphophonemic, morphemic, and merely orthographical considerations are disregarded. The four pitch phonemes are indicated by inferior numerals from 1 (highest) to 4 (lowest); each numeral applies to the whole sequence of one or more phonemes that follows it, until canceled by another numeral or by the pause phoneme. Two numerals written together (as 31) denote a succession of two pitch phonemes coinciding with a single vowel. The pause phoneme is here written with a space instead of the symbol / # /; the substitution is only graphic, intended to make the reading of the text easier. Every space—before and after an utterance as well as internal—can be replaced by the overt symbol. Separate utterances (sentences) are numbered.[42]

(1) $_4$mu$_3$kašimuka$_2$ši $_{23}$arutokoro$_3$ni $_4$o$_3$jiisañto $_4$o$_2$ba$_3$assañ$_3$ŋa $_4$a$_2$rima$_3$šta

(2) $_{23}$aru$_3$hi $_4$o$_3$jiisañwa $_4$ya$_2$ma$_3$ekareedaohiroini $_4$de$_2$kakema$_3$šta

(3) $_4$so$_3$no$_3$atode $_4$o$_2$ba$_3$asañ$_2$mo $_4$te$_2$nuŋuioka$_2$butte $_4$ha$_2$dašini$_2$natte $_4$ka$_2$wa$_2$esentakuni$_2$kima$_3$šta

(4) $_4$se$_2$ntaku$_2$a$_2$su$_3$ñde $_4$ka$_2$ero$_3$otosuru$_2$to $_4$ka$_2$wakamikara $_2$o$_2$okinamomo$_2$ŋa $_4$na$_2$ŋa$_2$retekima$_3$šta

(5) $_1$nañtoyuu $_2$o$_2$okinamomoda$_2$ro$_2$o

[39] The impression that there is some structural unity in a sequence like /ka/ but not in /ak/ rests in part on the phonetic prominence of syllables, as noted in §1, and in part also on the traditional Japanese orthography, in which /ka/ but not /ak/ is written with a single character.

[40] Cf. Joos, Acoustic phonetics 80, §3.38.

[41] Each row and each column in Table 2 is a statement, though not explicitly verbalized.

[42] The text is a new version of the passage transcribed (on the basis of a different analysis) in SCJ II, Lg. 22.238–48 ((177–84)). Particulars concerning its provenience, as well as an English translation, will be found in that place.

servative. Where no difference is specified, the two dialects are to be understood as having the same features.[43]

The innovating dialect differs from the conservative in three ways: (1) certain of its phonemes have a wider distribution, entering into combinations that are foreign to the conservative dialect; (2) it exhibits a phonemic distinction between two sound types which in the conservative dialect are allophones of a single phoneme; and (3) it contains one sound type, constituting a new phoneme, which is not present in the conservative dialect at all. As a result of these differences, the innovating dialect has two more phonemes than the conservative (thirty-one instead of twenty-nine, in addition to phonemes of pitch), and is characterized by a somewhat greater freedom of distribution.

Phonemes of the innovating dialect will be enclosed between double diagonals, thus //a//. Letters shown between single diagonals represent phonemes of the conservative dialect.

8.1. The conservative phoneme /t/ has an allophone [t] before /e, a, o/, and an allophone [ł] before /y/ (as well as other allophones in other positions); it does not occur before /i/. The innovating phoneme //t// has the same allophones; but here [ł] occurs not only before //y// but also before //i//, as in [vaniłi] *vanity case*, [yuutiritii] *utility*, [s·keetiŋ·ŋu] *skating*, i.e. //vaniti, yuutiritii, skeetiŋŋu//.[44]

The conservative phoneme /d/ has a single allophone [d], occurring before /e, a, o/. The innovating phoneme //d// has in addition the allophone [d], occurring before //i//, as in [kʸadii] *caddy* (in golf), [hǎn·dikʸappu] *handicap*, [diizeru] *Diesel engine*, i.e. //kʸadii, haṅdikʸappu, diizeru//.[45]

The conservative phonemes /b, d, g/ have only short allophones. The innovating phonemes //b, d, g// have also long allophones, which occur before certain voiced consonants. [b·] and [dž·] occur before [b] and [g] respectively, [d·] occurs before [d] and [dž], as in [mob·bu] *mob*, [béd·do] *bed*, [piramíd·do] *pyramid*, [ed·džiŋ·ŋu] *edging*, [kared·dži] *college*, [hóg·gu] *hog* (in engineering), i.e. //mobbu, béddo, piramiddo, edjiŋu, karedji, hóggu//.[46]

The conservative phoneme /w/ occurs only before /a/. The innovating phoneme //w// occurs also before //i, e, o//, as in [weetaa] *waiter*, [wiŋ·ŋu] *wing* (of an airplane), [woomiŋ·ŋuap·pu] *warming up* (in baseball), i.e. //weetaa, wiŋŋu, woomiŋŋuappu//.[47]

8.2. The conservative phoneme /h/ has an allophone [h] before /e, a, o, u/,

[43] The material of this section was discussed from the diachronic point of view in a paper presented before a meeting of the Linguistic Society in Chicago, 30 December 1946. The same point of view is implicit in Sanki Ichikawa, The pronunciation of English loan-words in Japanese, A grammatical miscellany offered to Otto Jespersen on his seventieth birthday 179–90 (Copenhagen, 1930). Ichikawa has gathered a wealth of material, but makes no attempt to arrive at a phonemic or other structural interpretation.

[44] /baniči, yuučiricii, skeetoiñŋu/ in the conservative dialect.

[45] /kʸaji, haṅjikʸappu, jiizeru/ in the conservative dialect.

[46] Theoretically /mobu, bédo, piramido, ejiñŋu, kareji, hógu/ in the conservative dialect; but these forms seem not to occur.

[47] /ueetaa, uiñŋu, uoomiñŋuappu/ in the conservative dialect.

8. The innovating dialect of standard colloquial Japanese, like any form of speech, is worth describing in full, without reference to other varieties of the language; but since it coincides at most points with the conservative dialect, a full description would be largely a repetition of what has already been said, with only a few departures and additions. It will be more convenient, therefore, to describe the innovating dialect wholly in terms of its differences from the con-

---

(6) ₄konoto₂šiniŋa₃ruma₂de ₄koɸina₁o₅okinamomowa ₂miʳtakotoŋa₂na₄i

(7) ₄čo₂odo₂ii

(8) ₄hiʳrotteiₐtte ₄o₂jiʳisaῆnoomiyagenišiyo₄o

(9) ₂to₂xtorigotooinaŋa₂ra ₄to₂ro₃otoši₂maʳštaₐŋa ₂teₐŋato₂dokimase₄ñ

(10) ₂naₐnikaboowaₐnaₐiₐka

(11) ₂to? ₂ho₂oboomiₐmawašima₃šta₂ŋa ₄ainiku ₂na₂nimoa₂rimase₂ñka₂ra ₄o₂ba-asaῆ₂wa ₂₂arukuhuuoka₂ῆŋ₂ete ₄to₂oimizuwani₂ŋa₂i₄zo ₂oῆka₂imizuwaamai₄zo ₄amai₂ho₂oeyotteoide₂to ₄uₐtainaŋₐ₂ra ₂te₂ota₂takima₄šta

(12) ₄so₂osuruto ₄huₐšiŋ₂niₐmo ₄mo₂mowadaῆdaῆnaₐŋaₐretekiₐₐte ₄o₂ba-asaῆno- ₂maₐedeto₂marima₄šta

(13) ₄o₂ba-asaῆwa ₄iₐso₂ide₅o₂reohiₐroiaₐŋeₐte ₄seῆtakumonotoiššoni ₄uₐčie- ₄moₐttekaₐerima₄šta

(14) ₄so₂ošte ₂haₐyakuo₂jiʳisaῆŋaₐkaₐettekureba₂ii

(15) ₂to? ₂maₐttei₂maₐsto ₄hiₐŋaɓakurerukoro ₄o₂jiʳisaῆwa ₄kaₐreedaoyamano- ₂yo₂onišo₂tte ₂kaₐettekima₄šta

(16) ₂kyo₂onoaₐcuₐikoₐto

(17) ₂aₐsebi₂ššoₐriₐda

(18) ₄o₂jiʳisaῆno₂ko₂eo₄kiₐaₐte ₄uₐčino₂naₐkakara ₄iₐso₂ide₄deₐtekima₄šta

(19) ₄oₐkaerinasaₐttaₐka

(20) ₄waₐtašiwa ₂haₐyakuo₂kaerinasaₐaₐrebaₐaitoo₂moₐtte ₂zuₐibuῆ₂maₐtteiₐta- ₂nodesuₐyo

(21) ₂ruₐsuni ₂naₐnikaoₐkoₐttano₂ka

(22) ₄iₐie

(23) ₂So₂oiaₐaₐrimaseₐñ₂ŋa ₂iₐimonoₐŋaₐaₐruno₂de ₂haₐyakuₐo₂jiʳisaῆniₐo₂menika- ₂keₐtakutte

(24) ₂Seₐakkačačino₂o₂baₐasaῆwa ₄aₐšioaratte ₄uₐčiniaŋattaₐbaₐakarino₄o₂jiʳisaῆno- ₂maₐeni ₂saₐkkino₂o₂okinamomooka₂kaetekiₐma₄šta

(25) ₄čo₂odo₂o₂nakamo₂suₐiteiₐruₐkara ₄oₐyuwaₐaₐtonište ₄saₐassokugo₂čisoo- ₂ninaₐro₂o

(26) ₄o₂ba-asaₐñ ₄maₐnaitaₐto₂ho₂oč̆oo₄moₐtteoide

(27) ₄o₂jiₐisaῆwa ₄mo₂mooₐmaₐnaitaₐnoueni₂ŋo₂sete ₂htacuni₂nišiyootoši₂maₐsto ₂naₐkakara ₄o₂jiₐisaῆ ₂č̆o₂tto₂maₐtteto? ₄kaₐwaiaₐkoₐeŋakikoeₐte ₄mo₂moŋaₐma- ₂htacuni₄waₐrema₄šta

(28) ₄so₂ošte ₂htoₐtta₂kiₐreina ₂hcuunokotowa₄maₐrude₂iŋauₐaₐkaῆboo₂ŋaₐto- ₂bidašima₄šta

(29) ₄o₂jiₐisaῆto₂o₂baₐasaῆwa ₄šiₐbaₐrakuₐaₐitakučiŋaₐhuₐaŋaranaihodo ₄o₂doro- ₂kimaₐštaŋa ₂šiₐjuuₐkoₐdomoŋaₐxtoₐriho₂šiₐitoo₂moₐtteitatokoro₂deₐskaraₐ ₂taₐisoo- ₄yo₂rokoₐῆde ₄so₂nokooso₂dateₐrukotonišiₐma₄šta

(30) ₄mo₂mono₂naₐkakaraₐuₐmaretaₐnode ₄mo₂mo₂tarootoyuunaₐo₂ckemaₐšta

and an allophone [f] before /u/ which is in free variation with [h] (as well as other allophones in other positions). The same sound types are present in the innovating dialect, but here they are in contrast with each other: [f] occurs not only before //u// (where it is still in free variation with [h]) but also before //e, a, o//; and there is a palatalized labiodental spirant [f] that occurs before //i, y//. Accordingly the phones [h] and [f, f] in the innovating dialect must be assigned to separate phonemes: the phoneme //h// (qualities G3) has the allophones [h] and [h]; the phoneme //f// (qualities L3) has the allophones [f, f], and [f]. Examples: //firumu, figyua, feea, fauru, kafeteria, fairu, fañburu, fooku, foñto, fyuuzu, maffu// *film, figure* (in skating), *fair* (ball), *foul* (ball), *cafeteria, file* (for letters), *fumble, fork, font* (in printing), *fuse, muff*.[48]

8.3. The phone [v], a short voiced labiodental spirant (with qualities L3 V), occurs only in the innovating dialect, where it constitutes a separate phoneme. Examples: //verañda, vañpu, vaniti, vaioriñ, voodoviru, ravu// *verañda, vamp* (movie siren), *vanity case, violin, vaudeville, love* (in the movies or in tennis).[49]

8.4. The distribution of the thirty-one phonemes of the innovating dialect (exclusive of pitch phonemes) is shown in Table 5. The arrangement here follows the same plan as in Table 2. The order in which phonemes are listed is again determined by their relative freedom of distribution, as indicated by the following tabulation; compare the similar tabulation in §6.3.

Phoneme	Prec.	Foll.	Totals		Phoneme	Prec.	Foll.	Totals
a	29	31	60		p	8	7	15
o	29	31	60		x	7	8	15
u	27	31	58		b	8	7	15
i	26	31	57		g	8	7	15
e	25	31	56		d	8	6	14
⋕	11	27	38		h	7	6	13
ñ	6	29	35		r	7	6	13
č	14	10	24		m	7	6	13
t	14	9	23		n	7	6	13
y	19	3	22		v	7	6	13
k	14	7	21		j	8	5	13
c	14	6	20		ŋ	6	6	12
f	8	11	19		z	7	4	11
s	9	10	19		w	7	4	11
š	8	10	18		ž	6	4	10
					ʔ	5	1	6

9. A note on orthography. Only one kind of written record, according to Bloomfield,[50] is scientifically relevant: 'a record in terms of phonemes, ignoring

[48] /hirumu/ or /huirumu/, /heea/ or /hueea/, /hairu/ or /huairu/, /hooku/ or /huooku/, etc., in the conservative dialect.

[49] /berañda, bañpu, baniči, baioriñ, boodobiru, rabu/ in the conservative dialect.

[50] Leonard Bloomfield, Language 85 (New York, 1933).

	a	o	u	i	e	⋕	ñ	č	t	y	k	c	f	s	š	p	x	b	g	d	h	r	m	n	v	j	ŋ	z	w	ž	ʔ
a	aa	ao	au	ai	ae	a⋕	añ	ač	at	ay	ak	ac	af	as	aš	ap	ax	ab	ag	ad	ah	ar	am	an	av	aj	aŋ	az	aw	až	aʔ
o	oa	oo	ou	oi	oe	o⋕	oñ	oč	ot	oy	ok	oc	of	os	oš	op	ox	ob	og	od	oh	or	om	on	ov	oj	oŋ	oz	ow	ož	oʔ
u	ua	uo	uu	ui	ue	u⋕	uñ	uč	ut	uy	uk	uc	uf	us	uš	up	ux	ub	ug	ud	uh	ur	um	un	uv	uj	uŋ	uz	uw	už	uʔ
i	ia	io	iu	ii	ie	i⋕	iñ	ič	it	iy	ik	ic	if	is	iš	ip	ix	ib	ig	id	ih	ir	im	in	iv	ij	iŋ	iz	iw	iž	iʔ
e	ea	eo	eu	ei	ee	e⋕	eñ	eč	et	ey	ek	ec	ef	es	eš	ep	ex	eb	eg	ed	eh	er	em	en	ev	ej	eŋ	ez	ew	ež	eʔ
⋕	⋕a	⋕o	⋕u	⋕i	⋕e		⋕ñ	⋕č	⋕t	⋕y	⋕k	⋕c	⋕f	⋕s	⋕š	⋕p	⋕x	⋕b	⋕g	⋕d	⋕h	⋕r	⋕m	⋕n	⋕v	⋕j		⋕z	⋕w		
ñ	ña	ño	ñu	ñi	ñe	ñ⋕		ñč	ñt	ñy	ñk	ñc	ñf	ñs	ñš	ñp	ñx	ñb	ñg	ñd	ñh	ñr	ñm	ñn	ñv	ñj	ñŋ	ñz	ñw	ñž	
č	ča	čo	ču	či	če	č⋕		čč	čt		čk	čc																			
t	ta	to		ti	te			tč	tt	ty		tc		ts																	
y	ya	yo	yu																												
k	ka	ko	ku	ki	ke					ky	kk																				
c			cu			c⋕		cč	ct		ck	cc																			
f	fa	fo	fu	fi	fe			fč	ft	fy	fk	fc	ff																		
s	sa	so	su		se	s⋕		sč	st		sk	sc		ss																	
š	ša	šo	šu	ši		š⋕		šč	št		šk	šc			šš																
p	pa	po	pu	pi	pe					py						pp															
x	xa	xo	xu	xi				xč	xt		xk	xc																			
b	ba	bo	bu	bi	be					by								bb													
g	ga	go	gu	gi	ge					gy									gg												
d	da	do		di	de															dd						dj					
h	ha	ho	hu	hi	he					hy																					
r	ra	ro	ru	ri	re					ry																					
m	ma	mo	mu	mi	me					my																					
n	na	no	nu	ni	ne					ny																					
v	va	vo	vu	vi	ve					vy																					
j	ja	jo	ju	ji	je					jy																					
ŋ	ŋa	ŋo	ŋu	ŋi	ŋe					ŋy																					
z	za	zo	zu		ze																										
w	wa	wo		wi	we																										
ž	ža	žo	žu	ži																											
ʔ						ʔ⋕																									

TABLE 5. DISTRIBUTION OF PHONEMES IN THE INNOVATING DIALECT

all features that are not distinctive in the language'—and ignoring also, if the record is to be strictly phonemic, all features that are distinctive but not immediately observable in the stream of speech, such as morpheme boundaries, word structure, and morphophonemic relations.[51] Such a record is the only safe and adequate basis for further investigations of linguistic structure; the analyst who attempts to study the morphemes or the grammatical constructions of a language in terms of a transcription that is either less or more than phonemic—a raw phonetic transcription on the one hand, or on the other a transcription that tacitly relies on non-phonetic evidence—will either be lost in a confusion of irrelevant details or overlook significant correlations between the phonemic structure and the structure of other linguistic levels. This does not mean (though it has now and then been misunderstood[52]) that the analyst should shut his eyes to all morphemic and grammatical facts until he has completely worked out the phonemics of a new language. Facts of all kinds come to his attention from the very beginning of his first interview with an informant, and should be filed away as they appear, even if some of them cannot be immediately accommodated in a larger system. But though the analyst acquires bits of information about the language piecemeal and in a random order, he cannot fully organize what he has learned about morphemes until he has codified the phonemes, or what he has learned about grammatical constructions until he has codified the morphemes. Finally, when he comes to write down his description of the language so that others may see the structure that he has discovered, he must group the many facts to be presented (since he cannot present them all at once) into separate compartments or levels, each one organically distinct from the others; and here the requirements of good method and good style demand that the statements made on any given level be as independent as possible of those made at other levels—in particular, that they assume as known only what has been said earlier, nothing that is to be said later.

It is also legitimate, in the interests of a neat-looking and easily printed orthography, to represent single phonemes by combinations of letters, even of letters that denote other phonemes in the same language, provided such a representation introduces no ambiguity. Thus it is possible to represent the Japanese phoneme /š/ by the letters *sy*, since the phonemes /s/ and /y/ do not occur in sequence.

The transcription of Japanese used in the first three papers of this series (§0), though it is not strictly phonemic, can be justified as a normalized orthography.[54] The phonemes of the conservative dialect—the only dialect treated in the earlier papers—are represented in part by the same letters as in the present paper, in part by special morphophonemic symbols or combinations. The departures from a purely phonemic representation are shown in the following list.

/p/ before /p/	q		/š/ before /t, k, c, č/	si
/t/ before /t, c, č/[55]	q		/š/ before /š/	q
/k/ before /k/	q		/x/ before /i/	h
/c/ before /u/	t		/x/ before /a, o, u/	hy
/c/ before /t, k, c, č/	tu		/x/ before /t, k, c, č/	hi
/č/ before /i/	t		/h/ before /t, k, c, č, h/	hu
/č/ before /e, a, o, u/	ty		/j/ before /i/	z
/č/ before /t, k, c, č/	ti		/j/ before /e, a, o, u/	zy
/s/ before /t, k, c, č/	su		/ž/ before /i/	z
/š/ before /s/	q		/ž/ before /a, o, u/	zy
/š/ before /i/	s		/ḍ/ everywhere	g
/š/ before /a, o, u/	sy			

Pause is indicated by any of four marks of punctuation, which at the same time denote the pitch of the phrase-final syllable: a period means pitch /4/, a question mark /31/, an exclamation point /1/, and a comma /3/ or /43/ if the preceding syllable has pitch /1/ or /2/, otherwise /3/ or /2/ in free alternation.[56] An acute accent denotes pitch /2/ on the syllable marked and on every preceding syllable within the word, except the first. (Word boundaries are shown by spaces.) An unmarked initial syllable has pitch /4/, other non-final syllables have /3/.

In this orthography certain phonemic distinctions are ignored—for instance between /t/ and /c/ and /č/, between /x/ and /h/, between /j/ and /ž/, between /ḍ/ and /g/. But the phonemes that are thus graphically confounded are all in free or in morphophonemic alternation with each other: in the context in which the orthography was used, the distinctions between them are unimportant.

However, it does not follow that a rigorously phonemic transcription must be retained throughout all the levels of a descriptive treatment, or that forms cited near the end of the work in the exposition of syntax must be written in the same way as those cited in the exposition of morphemes near the beginning. Once the transcription has been used in the study of morphemes (in particular, of morphophonemic alternations), it may be legitimately modified, elaborated, or normalized on the basis of new facts now first made fully available to the reader. A normalized notation, still firmly based on the phonemic analysis but incorporating the most common or the most important morphophonemic relations—especially those that are automatic[53]—and such grammatical features as word boundaries and pitch morphemes, approaches the character of a practical orthography. It is usually far better adapted to the discussion of morphology and syntax than a wholly unmodified transcription; when used for the writing of connected texts it reveals more of the linguistic structure; and those who already know the language find it easier to read.

---

[51] The reshaping of a phonemic transcription on the basis of morphological and other criteria, mentioned in §2 and fn. 16—what Hockett calls preliminary normalization of the orthography—does not, or at any rate need not, affect its purely phonemic character.

[52] Cf. Kenneth L. Pike, Grammatical prerequisites to phonemic analysis, Word 3.155–72 (1947).

[53] As defined by Rulon S. Wells, Automatic alternation, Lg. 25.99-116 (1949).

[54] Even though the normalization was not intended, and is now justified a posteriori.

[55] But /t/ before /s/ is *t*.

[56] These descriptions of the four pitch morphemes, denoted in the orthography by marks of punctuation, do not wholly agree with the statement in SCJ II, Lg. 22.200–1 ((154 f.)). They are based on the description given by Eleanor H. Jorden in her doctoral dissertation, The syntax of modern colloquial Japanese (Yale University, 1949).

KOREAN PHONEMICS

SAMUEL E. MARTIN

Language 27.519-33—1951

1. The phonemes of Korean are here analyzed in three ways: in terms of articulatory components, of auditory qualities, and of distinctive oppositions.[1] A detailed phonetic description is provided in §2 and §2.1. The language analyzed is standard colloquial Korean, ideally represented by educated speakers native to Seoul. Like many standard languages, standard Korean consists of not one but many dialects.[2] This analysis attempts to include all linguistic patterns other than those which seem to be partially assimilated borrowings from English.

1.1. Sixteen distinctive articulatory components are found: two pitch components, five vowel components, and nine consonant components. These components (represented by upper-case letters, except for pitch) occur in four types of sequence: coextensive, overlapping, successive, and interrupted. Five criteria of phoneme classification are used; the results of these are extended to the auditory and oppositional analyses in §3 and §4. With the exception of the pitch components, which receive a separate analysis, (1) a coextensive sequence of components or component clusters[3] is considered ONE PHONEME; (2) an overlapping or successive sequence is considered MORE THAN ONE PHONEME; and (3) an interrupted sequence is considered to include the phoneme of PAUSE /#/.[4] An exception to the use of these criteria is the treatment of a coextensive sequence which occurs in free variation with an overlapping sequence: if (4) the free variation of such a sequence is limited to certain environments, the sequence is considered one phoneme; if (5) it is not so limited, the sequence is considered two phonemes. (Examples are /ia/ and /wi/; see §131.)

1.2. The pitch components are RAISING ($\uparrow$) and LOWERING ($\downarrow$). In a syllable bounded on at least one side by pause, the component consists of a rise (or fall) of pitch within the syllable; in other positions, the component represents the pitch level of the syllable relative to the preceding syllable. (On syllables see §2.1.) When both components occur together within a sequence bounded by pause, the pitch range is widened. Some examples (the component symbol is here arbitrarily inserted in the phonemic writing BEFORE the syllable in which the component begins): /#nu↑ka#wa↑sqəm↓ni↓kqa#/ 'Who came?'; /#nu↑ka#wa↑sqəmni↑kqa#/ 'Did someone come?'; /#pak↑sonseŋi↓sici↑o#/

---

[1] This paper was begun as a research project in a graduate seminar at the University of California. To Mary R. Haas I owe special gratitude for developing my interest in descriptive linguistics. I have benefited from discussions of this paper with Bernard Bloch, Elinor Clark Horne, and especially Rulon S. Wells.

[2] Cf. B. Bloch, Lg. 26.87-8 (1950). I have heard the speech of three informants from Seoul: Miss Young Sook Chang, Mrs. Blanche C. Lim, and Mrs. Sang Soon Yun; and of two informants from Phyongyang: Mr. Frank Lee and Mr. Eung Pal Yun; as well as that of Miss Pauline Kim, of a Korean family living in China. (Since this article was written I have heard the speech of two more informants from Seoul: Mr. Sung Un Chang and Mr. Peter H. Lee.)

I have benefited from the studies made by Elinor Clark Horne, Introduction to spoken Korean, 2 vols. (New Haven, 1950-1), and by Fred Lukoff, Spoken Korean, 2 vols. (New York, 1947), as well as from unpublished studies by Rulon S. Wells.

A partial bibliography of other secondary sources consulted: Cosono Hakhwe [Korean Language Society], Cosono phyocunmal moam [Outline of standard Korean language] (Seoul, 1939). Id., Cosono mal khan sacon [Unabridged Korean dictionary], Vol. 1, (Seoul, 1947). Id., Vol. 2 (Seoul, 1949), through Korean letter *m*. P. A. Eckardt, Koreanische Konversations-Grammatik (Heidelberg, 1923). H. H. Figulla, Prolegomena zu einer Grammatik der koreanischen Sprache, Berlin-Universität Mitteilung des Seminars für orientalische Sprachen 38.101-21 (1935). J. S. Gale, A Korean–English dictionary (Seoul, 1897). Id., Korean grammatical forms (Seoul, 1894). Sun-Gi Gim (= Sunki Kim), Korean, Le maître phonétique III.15.21-2 (1937). M. Haguenauer, Système de transcription de l'alphabet coréen, Journal asiatique 222.145-61 (1933). Hison I (= Hison Li), Hankəl nonkoŋ [Articles on Korean linguistic research] (Seoul, 1947). Kəŋno I (= Kəklo Li), Silhom tohe cosono əmsoŋ hak [A study of Korean phonetics, with diagrams] (Seoul, 1947). Yunee I (= Yunee Li), Phyocun coson mal sacon [Dictionary of standard Korean] (Seoul, 1947); Insub Jung, Romanization of Korean, Actes du 4° congrès international de linguistes 210 (Copenhagen, 1936). A. A. Kholodovich, O latinizacii korejskogo pis'ma, Sovetskoje Jazykoznanije 1.147 ff. (1935). Pyəŋce Kim, Hankəl macham pop hesəl [An exposition of Korean orthographic rules] (Seoul, 1946). G. M. McCune and E. O. Reischauer, The romanization of the Korean language, Transactions of the Korean Branch of the Royal Asiatic Society (Seoul, 1939). Sinpei Ogura, The outline of the Korean dialects, Memoirs of the Research Department, Tōyō Bunko 12 (1940). Id., Tyoosengo-hoogen no kenkyuu [Research on Korean dialects], 2 vols. (Tokyo, 1944). Id., Tyoosengogaku-si [A history of Korean language study] (Seoul, 1921). E. W. Pae, Conversational Korean (Washington, D. C., 1944). K. D. Park, Oral Korean for beginners (Honolulu, 1945). E. D. Polivanov, Glasnye korejskogo jazyka (Petrograd, 1916). G. J. Ramstedt, A Korean grammar, Mémoires de la Société Finno-ougrienne 82 (Helsinki, 1939). James Scott, A Korean manual² (Seoul, 1893). H. W. Sunoo, A standard colloquial Korean text book for university students (Seattle, 1944). Tyoosengo-Daiziten [Unabridged Korean-Japanese dictionary] (Seoul, 1920). H. G. Underwood, An introduction to the Korean spoken language² (Seoul, 1914).

The romanization systems appearing in these works are many and diverse; the most consistent are those in the manuals of Horne and Lukoff. All of the systems are somewhat influenced, as for teaching purposes they should be, by morphophonemic considerations.

I am indebted to Thomas A. Sebeok for calling my attention to a lengthy bibliography of works mostly pertaining to Korean historical linguistics; this appears in a review of Ramstedt's grammar by Andrej Rudnev, Finnisch-Ugrische Forschungen, Anzeiger 27.55-68 (1941).

[3] A component cluster is itself a coextensive sequence of components which is under consideration with respect to its sequential relation with still other components.

[4] In other words, pause is defined as a phoneme uniquely characterized by the absence of distinctive components and perceived as the interruption of a componental sequence. Many instances which other analysts might consider 'open juncture' are thus included as occurrences of the pause phoneme. For example, the expression meaning 'both' (literally 'two all') is pronounced sometimes as /#tul*ta#/ and sometimes as /#tulta#/; it is also pronounced as /#tultqa#/. The occurrence or non-occurrence of pause in a given utterance or set of utterances—like the occurrence of any other phoneme—is a problem of morphophonemic description. Some analysts seem to perceive pause only when the sequential interruption is accompanied by some pitch change, usually described as 'intonational'; this is encouraged by the frequent interrelation of pause and pitch phonemes on the morphophonemic level (where the analysis of intonations is usually appropriate). On pause as a phoneme, cf. Bloch, Lg. 26.97 fn. 23.²³On individual variation in pause perception, cf. J M. Cowan and B. Bloch, An experimental study of pause in English grammar, American speech 23.89-99 (1948). *((334))

'You're Mr. Pak, aren't you?'; / ＊co↑sɔnsa↑lam ＊chin↑kuhansala↑mi ＊so-↑u↑le ＊i↑sqem↓ni↓ta ＊/ 'I have a Korean friend in Seoul'. The possibility that these components may constitute phonemes (pitch levels or contours) has not been investigated; it is convenient to proceed directly from the components themselves to the intonation morphs. This is a part of the morphophonemic analysis, to be presented in a separate paper.

1.3. There are five vowel components:

```
high tongue position   I        front tongue position   Y
mid tongue position    E        lip rounding            W
low tongue position    A
```

1.31. The vowel components occur in the following coextensive sequences. (Coextensive sequence of components is indicated by simple juxtaposition, and overlapping or successive sequence by a hyphen.)

```
          IY   I    IW
    WEY   EY   E    EW
          AY   A
```

For some speakers, the coextensive sequence WEY is in free variation with the successive sequence W-EY; for other speakers the two are in contrast.

Successive sequences of vowel components are:

```
W-IY
W-EY   W-E    Y-EY   Y-E    Y-IW
W-AY   W-A    Y-AY   Y-A    Y-EW
```

Note that neither W-I nor Y-I occurs.

The phonemes formed by these sequences are eleven in number. (The symbols are chosen for convenience. A phonetic description is given in §2 and §2.1.) There are nine vowel phonemes:

```
/i/    /ə/    /u/
/e/    /ɔ/    /o/
/ε/    /a/
       /ö/
```

and two semivowel phonemes occurring before vowels as follows:

```
/wi/                 /yu/
/we/   /wɔ/   /ye/   /yɔ/   /yo/
/wε/   /wa/   /yε/   /ya/
```

For many speakers, the phoneme /ö/ does not exist, corresponding to some (in fact most) of the occurrences of the sequence /we/. For most of these speakers, the successive sequence W-EY is everywhere in free variation with the coextensive sequence WEY. For speakers who distinguish /ö/ from /we/, the two contrast in such examples as these: / ＊we↑eniili↑o ＊/ 'What's the matter?', / ＊ö↑öncqoke ＊i↑sqem↓ni↓ta ＊/ 'It's to the left'.

For most speakers the successive sequence W-IY occurs everywhere in free variation with the coextensive sequence WIY. These two cases—WEY for some speakers in free variation with W-EY = /we/; WIY for most speakers in free variation with W-IY = /wi/—are examples of the fifth criterion of phoneme classification mentioned in §1.1.

The components Y and W of coextensive vowel sequences are in free variation with overlapping components when followed by another vowel; e.g. IY-A or IY-YA. Because of the limited environment (preceding another vowel), these sequences are not considered to include occurrences of the phonemes /y/ and /w/; the intercalated semivowels are simply ignored as free variants of the phonemic sequences /ia, ua/, and the like. This is covered by the fourth criterion in §1.1. An example is in the phrase / ＊mi↑a↑nham↓ni↓ta ＊/ 'I'm sorry'. The morphophonemic implications are outside the province of the phonemic analysis.

The syllabicity of the vowels proper /i, e, ö, ε, ə, ɔ, a, u, o/ and the non-syllabicity of the semivowels /y, w/ is considered a conditioned, non-distinctive feature.

Examples of vowel and semivowel-vowel sequences:

```
pi 'rain'                           swi 'soon'
ince 'now'       yemul 'gift'       kqwɛ̂nta 'binds'
                                    kqö 'wits'
pe 'ship'        yɛ̂ki 'story'       we 'why?'
nəl 'always'
tɔ 'more'        pyɔl 'star'        ilwɔn 'one Won'
paŋ 'room'       yaŋmal 'socks'     wansoŋ 'completion'
mul 'water'      yuli 'glass'
onəl 'today'     yoli 'cuisine'
```

1.32. Long vowels occur in contrast with short vowels, and are treated as dyads of like vowels, by analogy with dyads of unlike vowels, which occur freely. For some speakers there are few contrasts of long and short vowels; for others there are many. In view of the variation, it is convenient to indicate those vowel lengths which are variable for a given utterance by a circumflex accent (as /yɛ̂ki/ in the list above). This notation is not completely morphophonemic, since only utterance variants—not morpheme alternants—are fully subsumed; the notation may be considered at least partly diaphonic (subsuming dialect variants). It is a morphophonemic fact that variable vowel length usually occurs only within the boundaries of a morph; vowels which are long for all speakers usually include a morph boundary.

Examples of common contrasts for each vowel follow:

SHORT FOR ALL SPEAKERS	LONG FOR SOME SPEAKERS
il 'one'	il 'work'
ince 'now'	cɛ̂tö 'system'
tek 'your house'	tɛ̂hak 'university'
ɛnhɛŋ 'bank'	ɛ̂msik 'food'
som 'rice-straw sack'	sôm 'island'
pam 'night'	pâm 'chestnut'
nun 'eye'	nûn 'snow'
son 'hand'	tôn 'money'

1.4. There are nine consonant components:

Labial closure	P	Heavy aspiration	H
Dental closure	T	Glottal tension	Q
Alveolar or prepalatal affrication	C	Nasality (velic opening)	N
Sibilance (grooved friction)	S	Lateral opening	L
Velar closure	K		

1.41. The components H and Q are listed as consonant components; yet each of these overlaps both a preceding consonant and a following vowel (making the vowel respectively breathy or unusually tense). Since these components always occur in overlapping sequence, they are considered separate phonemes (the second criterion in §1.1).

1.42. The consonant components occur in nineteen coextensive and successive sequences, represented by the resulting phonemes and phoneme sequences in Table 1. (Two letters indicate a sequence of two phonemes.) The phoneme of pause, which has no components, is included in the table.

	P	T	C	S	K	—
	p	t	c	s	k	#
H	ph	th	ch		kh	h
Q	pq	tq	cq	sq	kq	
N	m	n			ŋ	
L		l				

TABLE 1

In the environments /mw, mu, mo/, the nasal component sometimes ends slightly before the lip closure is replaced by lip rounding, resulting in a momentary voiced stop: [mᵇ]. Since this stop is in free variation with zero in a limited environment, the fourth criterion of §1.1 is applicable: [mᵇ] and [m] are free variants of /m/ before /w, u, o/. Examples: /mû/ 'turnip', /mwə/ or /mwət/ or /muət/ 'what', /mom/ 'body'. In a similar way, the phoneme /n/ is occasionally [nᵈ] before a front vowel; examples: taninta 'goes back and forth', nê 'yes'.

Some examples of consonants, and of consonant sequences in initial position after pause:

pap 'cooked rice'	namu 'tree'	koki 'meat'
pha 'onion'	cosɔn 'Korea'	kho 'nose'
pqalli 'fast'	chôn 'village'	kqot 'flower'
mal 'horse'	cqocham 'pursuit'	paŋ 'room'
tâ 'all'	san 'mountain'	he 'sun'
thanta 'rides'	sqal 'uncooked rice'	salam 'person'
tqaŋ 'land'		

2. Before proceeding to the two other types of analysis, I provide some phonetic details about the phonemes and a statement of their occurrences. The phonemes /u, o, w/ are characterized by considerable lip protrusion and rounding, which begins simultaneously with a preceding consonant.[5] In a similar fashion, the front position for the phoneme /y/ is also frequently assumed simultaneously with a preceding consonant. This anticipatory overlap of components W and Y calls for criteria 2 and 4 in §1.1; compare the treatment of the lagging overlap of Y and W in §1.31.

The back unrounded vowels /ə, ɔ, a/ are slightly centralized, respectively high, mid, and low; when short, /ə, ɔ/ are slightly lower than the corresponding cardinal vowels.[6] With some speakers, the vowel /ɔ/ has the following allophones when short: lower-mid back unrounded if the syllable is closed by a consonant; lower-mid back, slightly rounded (but without protrusion) if the syllable is open; an unrounded [o] when long. When preceded by the phoneme /y/, the allophone of /ɔ/ is considerably centralized, approaching [ə];[7] for many words, there are variants with /yɔ/ in one dialect corresponding to /ye/ or /e/ in another.

There is often some velarization with the phoneme /h/. The phoneme /q/ is characterized by glottal tension, beginning with a preceding consonant and continuing through the following vowel, producing a tense articulation throughout, in marked contrast with the usual lax articulation.[8]

The phonemes /m, n, ŋ, l/ are tenser than most other consonants, but lack the glottal tension characteristic of /q/.

Voicing is a conditioned quality.[9] Vowels are typically (e.g. in isolation) voiced, but often lose their voicing between voiceless consonants, or in the vicinity of /h/ or /s/. The nasals and the lateral are usually voiced, but occasionally lose at least a part of their voicing in the same environment.

The phonemes /p, t, c, s, k/ are typically voiceless, and lax except before /q/.[10] Between typically voiced phonemes, these consonants are sometimes voiced in rapid speech, but in somewhat slower speech the voicing is absent or

[5] To the contrary, with respect to /u/, Haguenauer 148: 'prononcé presque sans arrondir les lèvres'. This seems more like a description of /ə/.

[6] Somewhat loosely, the color of /ə/ and /ɔ/ may be described as unrounded [u] and unrounded [o] respectively.

[7] Cf. Haguenauer 150: 'Quant à yɔ, dans certains cas … il donne à l'oreille l'impression d'un yə.'

[8] The phonetic nature of /pq, tq, cq, sq, kq/ has been variously interpreted. Haguenauer (159 ff.) calls them 'quasi-geminées' and Polivanov considers them 'long' (La perception des sons d'une langue étrangère, TCLP 4.82 [1931]). On the other hand, the Korean phonetician Jung calls the sounds 'implosives' and the late eminent Japanese Koreanist Ogura writes them preglottalized (McCune 29 ff.). All observers seem to agree on the tenseness of the articulation, but differ in their evaluation of its nature and significance. Ramstedt (5–6) points out that the tenseness continues throughout the syllable, even raising the perceived pitch of the vowel. It is true that these sounds are of longer duration than a single consonant phoneme; so are /ph, th, ch, kh/. Although the sounds are not so heavily glottalized as many American Indian consonants, I hear distinct glottal tension. The interpretation as geminate consonants is perhaps influenced by the automatic alternations frequent in the morphophonemic structure.

[9] Cf. J. Lotz, Journal of the Acoustical Society of America 22.716 (1950).

[10] On the lax nature of these phonemes preceding /h/, cf. Haguenauer 159: 'Les aspirées du coréen sont en général sonores et plus douces qu'en chinois'. (The Peking aspirates are generally considered tense. So are the voiceless aspirates of most Chinese dialects which have hitherto been reported.)

very weak. When following a pause and not followed by /h/ or /q/, allophones of these phonemes are slightly aspirated, with the aspiration formed locally at the point of articulation, in contrast with the distinctly glottal aspiration represented by /h/. Between typically voiced phonemes, the phoneme /h/ is frequently voiced.

For many speakers, the phoneme /c/ is prepalatal when not followed by a back unrounded vowel /ə, ɔ, a/; for some speakers, this phoneme is prepalatal in all environments, for a few it is usually alveolar. The phoneme /s/ is palatalized by many speakers, especially before a front vowel. The sequences /cy/ and /sy/ do not occur.[11]

Syllable-final consonants are typically unreleased. Postvocalic syllable-initial /l/ is flapped, but otherwise formed in the same lateral manner as unreleased syllable-final /l/: the under-side of the tongue tip touches the alveolar ridge (and the upper teeth), with an opening on each side.

2.1. Stress is apparently not phonemic in Korean;[12] if there is, contrary to my view, a phoneme of stress, it belongs with the pitch components to the intonation system. There is a clear-cut syllable onset; but this may be described as conditioned, since the syllable can be defined and described wholly in terms of the phoneme sequences which compose it.[13] Table 2 illustrates the syllable structure:

Any occurrent syllable can be found in Table 2, each phoneme fitting into the appropriate vertical column. Within a given sequence, consonants are joined to a following vowel whenever possible; in the utterance /＊kɔŋ↑cheki↑isqəmni↑kqa＊/ 'Do you have a notebook?', the syllables are /kɔŋ, che, ki, i, sqəm, ni, kqa/. It is for this reason that /ŋ/ is put in the same box with /l, m, n, —/ in the chart, even though no morphs are observed to begin with /ŋ/.

Certain distributional limitations within the syllable are not apparent in the chart: not all sequences which can be plotted on the chart actually occur. The phoneme /y/ does not occur in syllables beginning with /t, c, s/ or including the vowel /i/; the semivowel /w/ does not occur before the vowels /ə, u, o/. The sequences /ny, ni/ and the phonemes /l, ŋ/ do not occur after pause. The positions of the phoneme of pause in the chart illustrate syllable environments (for further limitations see §2.3); it is probably best to consider the phoneme of pause as belonging to no syllable (cf. Bloch, Lg. 24.118).

2.2. Of more interest to morphophonemics, but of some relevance also to phonemics, is the list in Table 3 of occurrences of consonants and consonant clusters in morph-initial position before vowels. Occurrences of /ŏ/ are treated as equivalent to /we/; occurrences of the actual sequence /we/ beside /ŏ/ are distinguished by italicizing the vowel: /we/. Symbols in the first column (headed CV) represent the vowels which directly follow the consonant or consonant cluster shown at the left; those in the second column (headed CyV) represent the vowels which follow the indicated consonant or cluster plus /y/; those in the third column (headed CwV) represent the vowels which follow the indicated consonant or cluster plus /w/.

TABLE 2

	i e(ö) ε ə ɔ a u o	p t k m n ŋ l		
m, n			y	q, —
s			w	h, —
p, t, c, k				＊
l, m, n, ŋ, —				—
#				
—				

TABLE 3

	CV	CyV	CwV
p-	i e ε ɔ a u o	ɔ a	e
ph-	i e ε ɔ a u o	ɔ a o	e
pq-	i e ε ɔ a u o	ɔ a o	e
t-	i e ε ə ɔ a u o		i e ε ɔ a
th-	i e ε ə ɔ a u o		i e ε ɔ a
tq-	i e ε ə ɔ a u o		i e ε a
c-	i e ε ə ɔ a u o		i e ε a
ch-	i e ε ə ɔ a u o		i e a
cq-	i e ε ə ɔ a u o		e a
k-	i e ε ə ɔ a u o	ɔ a u o	i e ε ɔ a
kh-	e ə ɔ a u o	ɔ a u	i e ε ɔ a
kq-	i e ε ə ɔ a u o	ɔ a u	i e ɔ a
s-	i e ε ə ɔ a u o		i e ε ɔ
sq-	i e ε ə ɔ a o		i e ε
m-	i e ε ə ɔ a u o	ɔ a o	i e ɔ
n-	i e ε ə ɔ a u o	ɔ u o	i e ε ɔ
h-	i e ε ə ɔ a u o	a u o	i e ε ɔ a
l-	i e ε ə ɔ a u o	ɔ a u o	e

All the sequences in Table 3 occur after pause, except those beginning with /l, ny, ni/.

[11] The phoneme /c/ is considered an affricate by most writers; Jung, however, evidently thinks it is a palatal plosive (McCune 25)—unless, like Gim, he is using the IPA symbol for a palatal plosive to represent an affricate (258-8). Haguenauer describes the consonant as follows: 'le dos de la langue touche le bas des dents de la mâchoire supérieure pendant que l'apex est placé derrière les dents d'en bas. Il paraît bien y avoir occlusion synchronique du praedorsum. ... certains sujets placent la point de la langue à la base de la région alvéolaire de la mâchoire supérieure ...' He describes /s/ (156) as 'une fricative douce qui est prononcée la langue reposant à plat et sans tension; l'apex est en arrière de la face interne des incisives inférieures. L'expiration est moyenne; la bouche n'est qu'entr'ouverte.'

[12] For contrary findings, cf. E. D. Polivanov, Zur Frage der Betonungsfunktion, TCLP 6.80 ff. (1938): 'Und schliesslich hat im Koreanischen ein Wort innerhalb des Satzes Endbetonung, doch im Satzschluss sowie in isolierter Aussprache Anfangsbetonung.' This was paraphrased by N. S. Trubetskoy, Grundzüge der Phonologie, TCLP 7.246 (1939): 'Nach E. D. Polivanov soll im Koreanischen jedes Wort die Schlussilbe betonen, und nur das letzte Wort im Satze betont die Anfangsilbe.' This would seem to present a phonological criterion for defining the word. Unfortunately, my own data do not confirm Polivanov's findings, and accordingly my criteria for words must be primarily non-phonological.

[13] On phonetic and phonemic syllables, cf. JAOS 64.151-5 (1944), and SIL 3.46-50 (1945).

The list is perhaps not quite complete (especially if recent borrowings are to be included), so that not all blanks can be regarded as significant. The non-occurrence of /y/ after /t, c, s/ has already been noted. The non-occurrence of /ə/ after labials is parallel to its non-occurrence after /w/. Within a morph, there are occasional occurrences of /ə/ after a labial, e.g. in /kipqəta/ 'is happy', alongside a common (and expected) dialect variant /kipquta/ (the morph boundary is before the phoneme /t/).

2.3. When two syllables occur in uninterrupted succession, a limited number of consonant clusters occur. These are illustrated in Table 4. The horizontal line across the top shows the end of the prior syllable; the vertical line at the left shows the beginning of the following syllable. At a point of intersection, the symbol x indicates that the expected sequence occurs. A dyad in parentheses shows that the expected sequence does not occur, but is automatically replaced (when morphophonemically expected) by the given dyad.[14] In the last horizontal line, and in the fifth line from the end, the place of the hyphen indicates that a syllable begins with the consonant or cluster whenever possible; since this is just a reminder of a sub-phonemic phenomenon (embodied in the definition of the syllable as an automatically determined sequence of phonemes), no parentheses are used.

Examples of consonant clusters:

pt — haptoŋ 'merger'
pth — kopthal 'pillage'
ptq — naptqêm 'solder, pewter'
pc — sipcaka 'cross'
pch — chopchophi 'repeatedly, row on row'
pcq — ipcqilen 'squeamish, fastidious'
ps — sipsam 'thirteen'
psq — ipsqilam 'dispute, wrangle'
pk — sipku 'nineteen'
pkh — copkhal 'pocket-knife'
pkq — cipkqaci 'as far as the house'
kp — kakpyoli 'especially'
kph — mokphyo 'target, goal'
kpq — pqakpqakhan 'tight'
kt — siktaŋ 'dining room'
kth — mokyokthaŋ 'bathroom'
ktq — tqoktqok 'clearly'
kc — kakcu 'footnote'
kch — kakchu 'pyramid'
kcq — cqokcqoki 'in pieces'
ks — yuksip 'sixty'
ksq — sqiksqikhan 'brave, strong'
mp — tampi 'badger'
mph — tamphan 'negotiation, discussion'
mpq — tampquki 'in full'
mt — tamtaŋ 'charge, custody'
mth — samtheki 'dirt-carrier'
mtq — namtqon 'which had remained'
mc — namca 'man'
mch — simchwi 'fascination, infatuation'
mcq — namcqi 'remaining'
ms — simsin 'mind'
msq — namsqemnita 'remains'
mk — kámkak 'sense, sensation'
mkh — samkhinta 'swallows'
mkq — namkqo 'remaining'
mh — tamhwa 'conversation'
mm — namme 'brothers and sisters'
mn — namnyə 'men and women'
np — sînpôn 'social position'
nph — cinphûm 'curio'
npq — pqonpqonhan 'brazen, shameless'
nt — cîntôŋ 'vibration'
nth — cînthwê 'advance or retreat'
ntq — sintqon 'which had worn (on feet)'
nc — sincaŋ 'elongation, extension'
nch — anchi 'not existing'
ncq — sincqa 'let's wear (on feet)'
ns — sunsa 'policeman'
nsq — sinsqəmnita 'wears (on feet)'
nk — sinko 'hardships'
nkh — ankho 'not existing'
nkq — sinkqo 'wearing (on feet)'
nh — sinhó 'signal'
nm — sinmun 'newspaper'
nn — punno 'anger'
ŋp — koppu 'study'
ŋph — saŋphûm 'goods, commodities'
ŋpq — pqonpqoŋhan 'annoying, distressing'
ŋt — koŋtok 'charity'
ŋth — saŋthê 'condition, state'
ŋtq — koŋtqok 'good luck, windfall'
ŋc — koŋcak 'construction'
ŋch — saŋchi 'lettuce'
ŋcq — cqeŋcqeŋhan 'brilliant'
ŋs — koŋsik 'formality'
ŋsq — sqaŋsqaŋi 'in pairs; two by two'
ŋk — saŋkoŋ 'commerce and industry'
ŋkh — saŋkhwe 'exhilaration'
ŋkq — kqaŋkqeŋi 'fiddle'
ŋh — koŋhwa 'republic'
ŋm — koŋmû 'official business'
ŋn — myoŋnyon 'next year'
lp — kyolpiŋ 'freezing'
lph — kyolphip 'scarcity'
lpq — pqulpquli 'severally, respectively'
lt — talta 'is sweet'
lth — kyalthu 'duel, combat'
ltq — paltqal 'progress'
lc — kôlca 'let's hang up'
lch — silche 'substance, entity'
lcq — kyoloqon 'decision'
ls — chilsip 'seventy'
lsq — kyolsqan 'settlement of accounts'
lk — ôlkul 'face'
lkh — kyolkho 'absolutely'
lkq — ilkqun 'worker, coolie'
lh — solhwa 'story, narration'
lm — solmyoŋ 'explanation'
ll — sollip 'establishment'

3. Instead of speaking in terms of articulatory components, it is possible to analyze the phonemes in terms of AUDITORY QUALITIES. The terminology and the technique for such analysis are at best rudimentary, but the following attempt

	-p	-t	-k	-m	-n	-ŋ	-l	—[16]
p-	(pq)	(pq)	x	x	x	x	x	x
ph-	(ph)	(ph)	x	x	x	x	x	x
pq-	(pq)	(pq)	x	x	x	x	x	x
t-	x	(tq)	x	x	x	x	x	x
th-	x	(th)	x	x	x	x	x	x
tq-	x	(tq)	x	x	x	x	x	x
c-	x	(cq)	x	x	x	x	x	x
ch-	x	(ch)	x	x	x	x	x	x
cq-	x	(cq)	x	x	x	x	x	x
s-	x	(sq)	x	x	x	x	x	x
sq-	x	(sq)	x	x	x	x	x	x
k-	x	(kq)	(kq)	x	x	x	x	x
kh-	x	(kh)	(kh)	x	x	x	x	x
kq-	x	(kq)	(kq)	x	x	x	x	x
h-	ph-	th-	kh-	mh-	nh-	ŋh-	lh-	x
m-	(mm)	(nm)	(ŋm)	x	x	x	x	x
n-	(mm)	(nn)	(ŋn)	x	x	x	x	x
l-	(mm)	(nn)	(ŋn)	(mm)	(nn)	(ŋn)	(ll)	x
—[15]	p-	t-	k-	m-	n-	ŋ-	l-	x

TABLE 4

[14] These are the principal cases of fully automatic alternation in the morphophonemic structure. (Other cases involve similar reductions of consonant clusters which do not occur phonemically.) By fully automatic, I mean what Wells calls 'narrow static alternation', Lg. 25.107 (1949). The somewhat more complicated alternations of /l/ and /ny, ni/ are also cases of narrow static alternation after pause but not in other environments (e.g. word-initial within an utterance), which exhibit what Wells calls 'wide static alternation' (105–6). The difference is basically whether the automatic character is phonemically determined ('narrow alternation') or grammatically conditioned ('wide alternation').

[15] I.e. a syllable ending with a vowel.

[16] I.e. a syllable beginning with a vowel or with /y/ or /w/.

of the binary principle, I note that the technique of binary analysis, as it has been applied so far, seems to overextend its binary character in admitting both members of an opposing pair to be present in one phoneme. This device has at least the virtue of reducing the number of qualities which it is necessary to posit, in a way that makes Occam's razor seem dull indeed.[20]

To explore the possibilities of such a technique, I present here a binary analysis of the Korean phonemes (Table 6). Six distinctive oppositions are assumed: nasal/oral; front/back; high/low; labial/non-labial; tense/lax; contactual/fluid. In each pair, the first member is regarded as positive, on the basis of less frequent occurrence within the system,[21] and the second member as negative. In Table 6, the presence of a positive quality in a given phoneme is indicated by a plus sign. The presence of a negative member is not indicated overtly, but is implied by the absence of any mark.[22] When both members of an opposition are present in the same phoneme, the fact is indicated by the sign ±.

OPPOSITIONS	p	t	c	s	k	m	n	ŋ	h	q	l	y	w	i	e	ö	ɔ	e	ə	a	u	o
nasal (vs. oral)						+	+	+														
front (vs. back)						+						+		+	+	±		±		±		±
high (vs. low)												+	+	+							+	
labial (vs. non-labial)	+					+							+									
tense (vs. lax)		±	±	±						±		+										
contactual (vs. fluid)	+	+	±	±	+	+	+	+	±		±											

TABLE 6

The difficulty of the phoneme /l/ (§3) is somewhat less obtrusive in the binary analysis, since a difference between /m, n, ŋ, l/ and /q/ in the type of tenseness can here be indicated by taking advantage of the device referred to above: namely, by assuming the simultaneous occurrence of both members of an opposition. It is a question whether /p, m/ should not include the quality of frontness, since the absence of this quality presumably implies backness; and also whether highness should not be marked plus for all the consonants. Such questions re-

[20] Ibid.: '... in such a case we have to introduce either a complex middle term or allow trinary oppositions.' As a matter of fact, Jakobson and Lotz seem to admit still another contrast, that of applicability of a specific opposition to a particular phoneme. This may then be conceived as a double-level binary contrast: for a given phoneme, a specific opposition either occurs (i.e. is applicable) or does not occur; if it occurs, either (1) both members occur together, or (2) a secondary level of contrast is involved, that of the polarity of the two members. In other words, occurrence of either member or both members of the opposition is itself opposed to non-occurrence, and the differentiation within the opposition is relegated to a secondary level. I suspect this concept of the opposition theory may be in conflict with unstated assumptions on the part of some who support the theory.

[21] This principle of economy in the selection of positive entities is implied but usually not explicitly stated in analyses of phonemic systems.

[22] This represents a departure from the technique applied to French by Jakobson and Lotz (see fn. 18). Whereas, in their treatment, certain oppositions are not represented in certain phonemes at all (so that the number of distinctive features is not necessarily the same for all phonemes), I here assume that every one of the six oppositions is represented in every Korean phoneme, by its positive or its negative member, or by both together.

is made to illustrate the possibilities. (The pitch components are omitted from the analysis.)

It is assumed that there are nine distinctive auditory qualities in Korean, each of which is either present or absent in the occurrence of any phoneme. These qualities and their organization into the phonemic system are illustrated in Table 5. Where no symbol appears, the quality is absent from the phoneme written at the head of the column.

	p	t	c	s	k	m	n	ŋ	h	q	l	y	w	i	e	ö	ɔ	e	ə	a	u	o
Nasal						x	x	x														
Front	x	x	x			x						x	x	x	x							
High												x	x	x		x						
Mid[17]															x	x	x					x
Low																		x	x	x		
Labial	x					x							x								x	x
Tense		x	x	x	x					x												
Contactual	x	x	x	x	x	x	x	x	x		x											
Fricative				x	x				x													

TABLE 5

Other qualities (such as back, voiced, syllabic, lateral) are considered conditioned.

The principal difficulty in the auditory analysis is the treatment of /l/; short of setting up a distinctive quality of lateralness peculiar to the phoneme /l/, it is necessary in order to account for the difference between /t/ and /l/, to broaden the definition of tenseness to include that of the lateral and the nasals as well as the special glottal tension of /q/. This may seem inconsistent, in view of the overlapping nature of the phoneme /q/ itself, unless the criteria for handling different types of sequence (§1.1) are regarded as logically prior to the complete analysis of qualities.

4. Some analysts have attempted to deal with auditory qualities in terms of DISTINCTIVE OPPOSITIONS.[18] These linguists assume that a limited number of binary oppositions underlie the phonemic system: each phoneme is characterized by either or both of the opposing qualities, though not every opposition is necessarily represented in every phoneme.[19] Leaving aside the question of the validity

[17] It would be possible to eliminate the quality Mid by regarding the mid quality of /e, ö, ɔ, o/ as absence of both high and low qualities (just as the quality Back is treated as absence of front quality). This would define the phoneme /ɔ/ as having no distinctive qualities at all. While such a view is possible, it seems wiser to reserve the term 'back' for total absence of qualities for the phoneme of pause / # /.

[18] Cf. R. Jakobson and J. Lotz, Notes on the French phonemic pattern, Word 5.151-8 (1949); R. Jakobson, On the identification of phonemic entities, Travaux du Cercle linguistique de Copenhague 5.205-13 (1949). For clarity, where Jakobson and Lotz use the terms 'higher and lower saturation' I speak of 'back and front'; where they use the terms 'gravity and acuteness' I speak of 'low and high'.

[19] Cf. J. Lotz, Journal of the Acoustic Society of America 22.715-6 (1950): 'Thus it seems that speech in its distinctive aspect is built up entirely of features in accordance with a binary principle.'

POLARITY	p	t	c	s	k	m	n	ŋ	h	q	l	y	w	i	e	ŏ	ɛ	ɔ	a	u	o
+	2	2	1	1	1	2	2	2	1	0	1	1	1	2	1	2	1	1	0	0	2	1
±	0	0	1	0	0	2	2	2	0	0	2	0	0	0	1	1	0	0	1	1	0	1
−	4	4	4	5	5	2	2	3	6	5	3	5	5	4	4	3	5	5	5	5	4	4

TABLE 8

volve around the definition of the auditory qualities which our terms represent—a problem that remains to be adequately explored. One further difficulty is that the phoneme of pause / # / cannot be included in the table, since the absence of all positive qualities implies the presence of all negative qualities—and the definition 'oral, back, low, non-labial, lax, and fluid' is considered appropriate to the phoneme /h/.

5. It is interesting to compare the results of the three different kinds of componential analysis by investigating the internal organization of each componential system.

In the system of articulatory components, coextensive sequence is limited to two mutually exclusive groups: I, E, A, Y, W, defining the class of vowel phonemes; and P, T, C, S, K, N, L, defining the class of consonant phonemes. The components H and Q are always in overlapping sequence, defining a class of quasi-consonant phonemes. As for the syllabicity of I, E, and A, and the non-syllabicity of Y and W, when these components occur in other coextensive sequences—i.e. in the phonemes /ə, ɔ, a, y, w/—this is taken to be conditioned, so that the class of semivowels is not defined above the phonetic level. The components N and L are the only non-pitch components which always occur in coextensive sequence, defining the subclass of sonorant consonants and its negative counterpart, the subclass of non-sonorant consonants.

In the system of auditory components, the qualities High, Mid, and Low and the qualities Nasal, Tense, Contactual, and Fricative form two mutually exclusive groups, respectively defining vowel and consonant phonemes. The qualities Front and Labial are ambivalent, forming two structural groups which cut across the vowels and consonants.

In the system of distinctive oppositions, only the quality High defines the class of vowel phonemes. Otherwise, the internal structure is superficially similar to that of the auditory analysis.

It is possible to set up groups of phonemes according to their complexity, as determined by the number of coexistent qualities present within each phoneme. Table 7 compares the articulatory and auditory analyses on this basis.

NUMBER OF POSITIVE QUALITIES	IN ARTICULATORY ANALYSIS	IN AUDITORY ANALYSIS
0	#	#
1	p t c s k h q / y w e ə a	k h q y w e ə a
2	m n ŋ l / i e ɛ u o	p t s / i e ɛ u o
3	ŏ	c ŋ l ŏ
4		m n

TABLE 7

From the data shown in Table 8, several different kinds of structural arrangements are possible; I present three of them here. Table 9 groups the phonemes into three simple quantitative classes; Table 10 groups them into two classes based on combinations of polarity; Table 11 groups them into two classes based on a reduction of polarities.

POLARITY	OPPOSITIONS	PHONEMES
+	0	h c a
	1	c s k ŋ q l y w e ə
	2	p t m n i ŏ u
±	0	p t s k h q y w i e ə u
	1	c e ŏ ɔ a o
	2	m n ŋ l
−	2	m n
	3	ŋ l ŏ
	4	p t c i e u o
	5	s k q y w e ə ɔ a
	6	h

TABLE 9

Throughout these lists, there are five constant sets of phonemes which always occur together in like categories: (1) s k q y w e ə; (2) p t i u; (3) c e o; (4) m n; (5) ɔ a. These five sets include eighteen phonemes; the other four (h, l, ŋ, ŏ) are variable in their groupings.

POLARITY	OPPOSITIONS	PHONEMES
+ and ±	0	h
	1	s k q y w e ə a
	2	p t c i e u o
	3	ŏ l ŋ
	4	m n
− and ±	4	p t m n i ŏ u
	5	c s k ŋ q l y w e e e o
	6	h c a

TABLE 10

This kind of tabulation would be less meaningful for the system of distinctive oppositions, since here the negative qualities are structurally just as important as the positive. The raw quantitative data for this system are given in Table 8.

POLARITY	OPPOSITIONS	PHONEMES
+ minus ±	−1	ŋ l ɔ a
	0	c m n h e o
	1	s k q y w ö ɛ ə
	2	p t i u
− minus ±	0	m n
	1	ŋ l
	2	ö
	3	c e o
	4	p t i ɔ a u
	5	s k q y w ɛ ə
	6	h

TABLE 11

6. As a result of the comparisons made in the preceding section, it is possible to give objective reasons for preferring one of these three methods of analysis to the others. In many respects, the groups resulting from the articulatory analysis, as shown in Table 7, seem the most satisfactory. Although part of my preference may be based on a long-standing bias in favor of traditional phonetic classes, there is evidence from both the morphophonemic structure and the historical development of the phonemes that the groups resulting from the articulatory analysis are potentially more useful than the others. There are, however, some points favoring the other two analyses; the structural groups formed by the ambivalent qualities Front and Labial, cutting across vowels and consonants alike, have some useful correlations and seem to be handy categories. The mathematics of the polarity groups seems disappointingly irrelevant, but this might be a fault of the specific analysis undertaken, or of the quantitative approach in grouping, rather than of the oppositional technique itself. There is some relevance in the constant sets mentioned at the end of §5; the variability of the four phonemes /h, l, ŋ, ö/ is perhaps merely an indication that the specific oppositions chosen in §4 are inadequate.

THE METHOD OF DESCRIPTIVE MORPHOLOGY

FLOYD G. LOUNSBURY
Oneida Verb Morphology
Yale University Publications
In Anthropology No. 48—1953

In morphological analysis the two principal operations are the establishment of the basic formal units and the analysis of formal structure in terms of these units. These two aspects of analysis are currently known as morphemics and tactics respectively.

1.1. THE ESTABLISHMENT OF UNITS

Morphemics, in turn, also involves two operations. The first of these is the breaking up of forms into their minimal meaningful parts, while the second is the identification of semantically equivalent parts of this order. These two operations are known as segmentation and grouping.

Two general approaches to these problems may be recognized in the history of modern linguistics. One of these, the older of the two, has sometimes been known as the morphophonemic approach, because of the so-called 'morphophonemes' (see section 1.1.2) which are sometimes employed instead of ordinary phonemes in the identification of morphemes. This usage is confusing, however, for the term has other more common meanings in contemporary descriptive linguistics (Hockett, 1947: 342 ((241)), 1950:63 ((315)); Bloch, 1947:414 ((251)); Wells 1949:99–100). We shall call it, instead, the method of internal reconstruction, for whether the orientation be historical or avowedly synchronic, it is usually based on an operation which is similar to that of reconstruction from internal evidence. The other approach, which is the newer of the two, is the method of morpheme alternants.

We consider first the possible procedures under the method of morpheme alternants and then the method of internal reconstruction. Finally, we select a procedure which seems best suited to the task at hand.

1.1.1. The method of morpheme alternants

Following the method of morpheme alternants one divides or 'cuts' forms of actual utterances into minimal segments, or sequences of phonemes, to which it is possible to assign meanings. ('Sequence' is to be understood as including cases of one or of no phonemes, as well as of more than one, and also as including both continuous and discontinuous types.)[1] Such phoneme sequences or form-segments are known in current usage as morphs. Phonemically different morphs which have the same meaning (or the same range of different meanings sharing a common feature), and which are in complementary distribution, are said to constitute a class called a morpheme and are known as morpheme alternants, or allomorphs, of that morpheme.[2] The common meaning of the allomorphs is defined as the meaning of the morpheme.

The place to make a cut between two morphs may be obvious or obscure, and the business of segmenting may be correspondingly easy or difficult according as the data permit of but one manner of interpretation or of several. In agglutinating languages the matter is obvious and simple; it is settled immediately by the very nature of the data. A cut between two morphs can be made only in one place; a morpheme in such a language has in general but a single allomorph. In languages of the fusional type[3] this is not characteristically the case; the place to make the cut may often be decided upon only with difficulty and to some extent arbitrarily, and morphemes in general have many allomorphs. The Iroquoian languages are of this type.

The basic technique employed in segmenting forms is that of varying some part of the total meaning of a form while holding the remainder constant, and noting the correlated variable segments of the resulting forms as opposed to the constant portions of those forms. Repeated applications of the technique lead to irreducible segments of the forms. In agglutinating languages this simple technique of isolating constant from variable is sufficient and yields clear-cut segments which account for the totality of any form. In a fusional language if one seeks to arrive at constant segments in such a manner, conflicts arise in the placing of the cuts. One comparison of forms suggests one placement, while another comparison suggests another. Often, in fact, no constant segment can be isolated at all which corresponds to a given constant meaning. Situations of this kind often permit of more than one solution according to different manners of selecting and grouping environments. The locations of the cuts are not always uniquely determined.

[2] Cf. Hockett (1947) and Harris (1942). Hockett replaces the condition of complementary distribution by that of 'non-contrastive' distribution, so as to allow for grouping into a single morpheme such morphs as are in free variation in certain environments and in complementation otherwise. Here, however, we have avoided admitting allomorphs to be in free variation or in any distribution that involves it. It is too difficult to be sure of complete sameness of meaning.

[3] 'Agglutinating' and 'fusional' are used here in the senses in which Sapir used the terms (Sapir, 1921, Chap. VI).

[1] Cf. Harris's discussion of discontinuous morphemes (Harris, 1945).

THE METHOD OF DESCRIPTIVE MORPHOLOGY

It is agreed that an analysis of a linguistic form into segments must account for all the phonemes in that form.[4] In the manner of accounting for all the phonemes, different policies may be adopted. There are four possibilities. (α) One may decide that every phoneme shall belong to an allomorph of one and only one morpheme. Segmentation is carried as far as possible, and such morphemes (present in meaning) as have not been accounted for in the resulting segments are said to be represented by zero allomorphs. This is the convention followed by Bloch in his treatment of English verb inflection (Bloch, 1947). (β) One might instead proceed on a different policy, one which might be stated in the form: every phoneme shall belong to an allomorph of at least one morpheme. This allows for the possibility of a phoneme belonging either to an allomorph of only one morpheme or simultaneously to allomorphs of two (or more) different morphemes; i.e., it allows of overlapping morphs. A special case of such overlapping morphs is that in which they overlap completely. Such coincident morphs have been called portmanteau morphs by Hockett (1947:333 ((236))).[5] Another special case of overlapping morphs is that in which the whole of one coincides with a part of another. Morphs in this relationship we call included morphs and including morphs, respectively. (γ) Another possibility is the following: every phoneme shall belong to an allomorph of not more than one phoneme. As with (α) this does not allow of overlapping morphs or of portmanteau morphs in the analysis of a form. But it allows of empty morphs (Hockett, 1947:333 ((236))), which (α) and (β) do not; i.e., some phonemes are isolated as morphs which do not belong to any morpheme. This is often a convenience, as it cuts down the number of different allomorphs which must be carried for various given morphemes. Taken care of in this way are phonemes which have often been described (in a different methodology) as 'inorganic elements', 'meaningless elements', 'epenthetic phonemes', etc. (δ) The final alternative policy is one which allows of all the possibilities, viz., that a phoneme may be part of a morph which belongs to zero or to one or to more than one morpheme. Under this rule we have leeway to make use of empty morphs and overlapping or portmanteau morphs as well as of the ordinary ones and zero morphs.

According to the policy adopted, different solutions of the same data are possible. We may speak of α-morphs, β-morphs, etc., according as they result from the application of policy α, or of policy β,

etc. The choice of treatment accorded to any set of linguistic forms must be dictated by the nature of the case in hand, by the criterion of simplicity of final total solution, and by the particular purpose for which the analysis is being made (e.g., descriptive, historical, pedagogical, etc.).

1.1.2. The method of internal reconstruction

This method by-passes the problem of segmenting actual forms of a language of our type. In effect it sets up a fictitious agglutinating analog, such that a one-way transformation from the analog to the actual utterances is possible, and it segments that instead. This is a much easier job of segmentation— as easy as segmenting the forms of an actually agglutinating language. Forms of the analog are sometimes called morphophonemic forms (as contrasted with phonemic forms, which are actually occurring forms of the language). The relation of actual forms to those of the analog is expressed in transformation formulas called morphophonemic rules.[6] Different morphophonemic rules often have different domains of applicability within forms. The domain of applicability must be specified for each morphophonemic rule. Some linguists put this in a separate qualifying statement in connection with the rule. Others have built it into the orthography used in representing forms of the analog (Bloomfield, 1939; Hockett, 1948). In the latter case, separate morphophoneme symbols are set up to distinguish orthographically the instances where a given rule applies from those where it does not.

Three different conceptions of morphophonemic forms can be discerned in linguistic works. Some writers have explicitly ascribed to their morphophonemic units only the status of fictions devised by themselves for the facilitation of description. Such a treatment is Bloomfield's in his Menomini morphophonemics (1939) or Hockett's in his Potawatomi (1948). Others appear to have regarded them rather as 'ideal' morphemes, and true units of the language, which, however, when put together into constructions have changes wrought upon them so that they and their combinations are 'actualized' or 'realized' in an altered form. This attitude is implicit in many of the contributions to the Handbook of American Indian languages (Boas, ed., 1911, 1922, 1933). With this type of conceptualization, instead of morphophonemic rules we have 'phonological processes', as in the works of many of Sapir's students, or 'euphonic laws', as in some of Boas' works. Still others explicitly or implicitly consider their units to be historical prototypes of morphemes, and then we have 'phonetic laws' rather than morphophonemic rules

[4] Hockett's principle of 'total accountability' (Hockett, 1947:332 ((235))).

[5] Hockett, in discussing 'cuts' (1947:322((230))), mentioned the possibility of overlapping morphs, but in the section 'Morph and Morpheme' (1947:331 ff. ((235 ff.))) they are not included except for the special case of portmanteaus.

[6] Sometimes a complete application of this technique may not be possible and there is left over a residue of irregularities of unique types which cannot be accounted for by morphophonemic rules of this kind. Such are Bloomfield's 'morpholexical alternants' (Bloomfield, 1939).

or phonological processes. Such a treatment is Barbeau's analysis in his Classification of Iroquoian radicals (1915), where one of the purposes is historical and where internal evidence is made use of for this purpose. Some works show a mixing of the latter two points of view.

1.1.3. The relation of morphophonemic forms to historical forms

Morphophonemic constructs cannot be said to represent a previous state of the language. Although strictly agglutinating languages doubtless have existed (the Cuzco dialect of Quechua is nearly such a one) there are no grounds for supposing that every language has descended from such a forebear simply because it is possible to construct an agglutinating morphophonemic analog to it. But that the morphophonemic transformation formulas set up often correspond to actual historical sound changes of some variety cannot be doubted. Such an assumption is the basis for historical reconstruction from internal evidence.[7] The reason for the invalidity in considering morphophonemic constructs as historical forms lies in the fact that the morphophonemic rules correspond to historical changes of different types, which occurred during widely different periods of the history of the language. Some correspond to sound changes that have affected the phonetic pattern of the language as a whole and are of the type known as phonetic laws. Others correspond to analogical changes that never of themselves altered the phonetic pattern at large, but which were confined to specific morpheme combinations. Some represent changes (of either variety) which are relatively recent in history, whereas others represent changes which are, in comparison, extremely ancient. The net result of these circumstances is the differential applicability of the morphophonemic rules which can be set up. Some are of general applicability in going from morphophonemic construct to actual forms of a language and describe the so-called 'automatic' type of morphophonemic alternation. They express the manner of accommodation of morphemes and their combinations to the phonemic pattern of the language. Thus, the rules

(1) hCh > Ch (where C is any consonant), and
(2) $C_1C_2h > C_1C_2$ (C_1 and C_2 = any consonants),

and the rules

(3) VC?X > VCe?X (where C is any consonant, V any vowel, and X is word boundary or a consonant), and
(4) $V_1C?V_2 > V_1CV_2?V_2$ (where C is any consonant, and V_1 and V_2 are any two vowels, same or different),

in Oneida are of the automatic or general type for that language and are necessary conditions for the existence of its phonemic cluster pattern (see section 3.2). On the other hand, the rules

[7] Cf. Hoenigswald (1944, 1946).

(5) a + i > ʌ, and
(6) (w)a(?) + wa > u,

and the rules

(7) ? + w >˙h, and
(8) ? + y > ?

apply only to the domains of the pre-pronominal and pronominal prefixes and are not necessitated by the phonemic pattern of the language. The historical correspondences to these eight morphophonemic rules are various. Comparative evidence shows that the first four of these correspond to phonetic laws, though the changes were not all contemporaneous. The first two are among the changes which distinguish Oneida from Mohawk; the third and fourth are among those which distinguish Oneida and Mohawk from some of the other Northern Iroquoian languages. Comparative evidence from the extant or documented Iroquoian languages sheds no light on rules (5) and (6). If these rules correspond to real historical changes (and we assume that they do), then those changes are more ancient than the differentiation of the languages of the Iroquoian family. Their antiquity may be assumed to account for the limited domain of applicability of the morphophonemic rules to which they correspond: they would have ceased to be operative by the time later layers of formation developed. As for rule (7), comparative evidence confirms what internal evidence suggests, that it corresponds to an analogical change of very specific localization in the morphology. Rule (8) is open to more than one historical interpretation.

1.1.4. Validity of the methods

One may raise the question as to which of the methods outlined above is the more realistic procedure. It may be argued that the method of morpheme alternants is the more realistic procedure, since it deals with the segmentation of actual utterances rather than with constructs once removed from reality. This may indeed be considered a point in its favor. But opposing this is an equally legitimate contention that the resulting very discrete localizations of meaning associated with some of the procedures under the method of morpheme alternants are, or may be, highly unrealistic. We may approach the matter through an example, viz., the possible analyses of the Oneida prefix u- under the method of morpheme alternants.

The prefix u- occurs only with a certain class of bases (a-stems). E.g., compare:

katkáthos 'I see it'   wa?katkátho? 'I saw it'
watkáthos 'she sees it'   utkátho? 'she saw it'

Associated with its occurrence are the meanings which we designate as 'past tense' and 'third person singular feminine'. The procedure of α- or γ-morphemics requires one of the following two solutions:

'past tense' = u-, '3 sg F' = zero morph; or
'past tense' = zero morph, '3 sg F' = u-.

The procedure of β- or δ-morphemics allows of the solution:

'past tense' = u-, '3 sg F' = u-,
and one would mark the two listings of u- in some
way, e.g. [u]-, to show that as morphs they are
one, constitute an identity, and are non-additive.
(The solution according to the method of internal
reconstruction would be 'past tense' = WA?-,
'3 sg F' = WA-; WA? + WA > u.) It may be argued
that β-/δ-morphemics gives the more realistic
localization of meaning in this case; for it remains
a fact that it is the occurrence of the morph u- with
which both meanings are associated, since the occurrence of a zero morph cannot otherwise be perceived than through the occurrence of the morph
which implicates it.[8]

[8] We have used the word 'implicate' in accordance
with C. W. Morris's usage in his Foundations of a
Theory of Signs (1938). He defines three types of
sign-relations (or as we might call them, three types
of meaning): signs 'implicate' other signs, 'designate' or 'denote' their referents, and 'express' their
interpretants. These correspond to the syntactic, the
semantic, and the pragmatic dimensions of sign-
functioning or semiosis.
   Referring to the possible solutions of the Oneida
prefix u- which are given above, we say in the α-/γ-
solution that the morph u- is an allomorph of one
morpheme such as implies the presence of, or
implicates, a zero allomorph of the other morpheme.
(It implicates also a certain class of bases, viz.,
the a-stems.) In the β-/δ-solution, on the other
hand, we have a sign which is a sign simultaneously
of two designata. As long as we must depend upon
semantics, i.e., upon sign-to-designatum relations,
at certain crucial points in linguistic theory, it
seems well to avoid situations like the α-/γ-solution
whenever possible and to be as specific as possible
in the localization of meanings.
   The problem is not thus easily disposed of, however. Implication of this type happens not only to
zero morphs; the occurrence of any non-final morph
in an utterance implicates in some manner another
morph or morpheme or class of morphemes. This
is a logical consequence of structure in language.
One way of viewing it is as follows: at the point of
initiation of an utterance there is linguistically no
limitation on the 'direction' that the utterance may
take, except that it remain within the universe of
forms of the given language. After the occurrence
of the first morph there has already been a great
reduction in the possible 'moves' from that point on:
a class of forms smaller than the total universe of
forms of the language is already implicated. So, after
the occurrence of each additional morph, the range
of future possibilities is successively greatly nar-
rowed, and the end can often be guessed, or may
even be uniquely determined, before the final morph
of a word, or word of a sentence, has been reached.
From this point of view the problem of localization
of meaning is more complex. In Oneida, in utterance-
final forms of words, a final morpheme or two of a
word is sometimes represented by a zero morph.
There are cases where even the verb root is zero in
utterance-final forms. Such words are takná·jih.
'give me the kettle', jíten. 'let's go (you and I)',
jítow. 'let's go (we, plural inclusive)'. (Compare the
non-final forms: takná·jyu, jítne, jítwe, verb roots
-u 'give' and -e 'go'. The -i- of takná·jih. and the

1.1.5. Choice of a method
   The method of morpheme alternants is chosen
here, and of the possible alternatives under this
method, that which has been referred to as δ-morphemics is to be followed. This allows us to deal
always with actual phonemic forms, and it permits
more realistic localizations of meaning.
   The following rules will govern segmentation.
(1) A zero morph is never set up when the meaning
to be assigned would be implicated by the selection
of a particular allomorph of some one other morpheme. In such cases a portmanteau or included
morph is set up instead. (2) An empty morph is set
up only when a given phoneme or phoneme sequence
would otherwise have to be taken as identical fractions of the allomorphs of two or more different
morphemes. (3) Use of the principle of overlapping
morphs is restricted to the special cases where the
whole of one coincides with the whole or with a part
of another, i.e., it is restricted to portmanteau and
included morphs. The more general case of partially
overlapping morphs, which the procedure of δ-morphemics permits, is not utilized because of practical
difficulties of notation. The employment of portmanteau and included morphs is sufficient to avoid zero
morphs implicated solely by the selection of a particular allomorph of another morpheme.

1.2. THE ANALYSIS OF STRUCTURE
   The grammatical structure of a language may be
described in terms of its morphemes and their rules
of combination. The latter include rules of order, of
selection, and of derivation. This study deals not
with the whole of grammatical structure but with
only a single level within it, the morphology of the
verb. This limitation simplifies somewhat the formulation of a method for describing structure, since
the processes of deriving higher levels of structure
are eliminated from consideration.
1.2.1. Morphemes
   A morpheme, in the method of morpheme alternants, was defined above as a class of phonemically
different minimal meaningful segments, or morphs,
which are in complementary distribution and have
the same meaning (or the same range of different
meanings sharing a common feature). These are the
allomorphs of the morpheme. In the method of

-e- and -o- of jíten. and jítow. are automatic empty
morphs, phonologically determined, and in no way
dependent upon the verb roots -u and -e.) Whatever
type of analysis we employ, we have zero morphs,
i.e., nothing, for these verb roots in the utterance-
final forms. We may ask what then is the locus in the
forms, or for the hearer, of the meanings 'give' and
'go' in these examples? The answer is that it is in
the cumulative implication of the other morphs. It
remains a fact that the linguist's allocation of a
meaning corresponds to only a part of the native
hearer's source of derivation of a meaning, and the
correspondence is considerably less close for
fusional languages than for agglutinating languages.

internal reconstruction a morpheme is a minimal meaningful segment of the constructed agglutinating analog to actual linguistic forms. In both cases they are constructs. In general it is important to remember this, though in working with a strictly agglutinating language, where a construct (of either kind) always or nearly always coincides with a single segment of actual linguistic forms, the point tends to lose its significance. The allomorphs of a morpheme of the first variety, or the modified actualizations of a morpheme of the second variety, may be designated the phonemic forms of the morpheme.

A morpheme is said to occur when one of its phonemic forms occurs. Statements describing the occurrences of morphemes constitute the portion of a grammar called tactics (Hockett, 1947:321 ⟨⟨229⟩⟩). This includes both of the conventional divisions of grammar known as morphology and syntax. Tactics is not concerned with the phonemic forms of morphemes, whether they are constant or variable. Only the fact that some one of the phonemic forms occurs for a given morpheme is important; the question of 'which one' is not relevant. Such matters are regarded as sub-morphemic; the morphemic structure of forms can be described apart from their phonemic forms.

1.2.2. Order

A linguistic form may contain meaningful features that are not accounted for by the morphemes present. These are meaningful features of order (Bloomfield, 1933: 162-3).

In many utterances a given morpheme occurs more than once. Also, the relative order of occurrence of two given morphemes is sometimes different in different utterances, and sometimes this difference in order is meaningful. Within words, however, these two states of affairs are found much less frequently than in larger utterances such as phrases and sentences. It is possible, in fact, in the analysis of morphology, to proceed initially as if any given morpheme occurred only once, and as if the order of occurrence were fixed and therefore meaningless. That is, the method chosen may be one which is adapted to these conditions, and the few exceptions to these conditions may be given special treatment. It is, of course, desirable to have as general a method as possible, but it is also appropriate to recognize special cases within it. Thus, for the analysis of Iroquoian verb morphology we can choose a method which is a simple special case subsumable under a more general and complex method adapted to the analysis of grammar as a whole, to syntax as well as morphology. The basic method is that of the positional analysis of mutually substitutable morphemes. It is a special case of the more general method of positional analysis of mutually substitutable sequences of morphemes.

As a preliminary definition of a position class we may say that it is a class of morphemes which are mutually exclusive and which, when they occur, always occur in the same relative order with respect to other morphemes.[9] But there are two types of situations sometimes found in morphology which render this definition insufficiently flexible for general use. One of them is that sometimes different allomorphs of the same morpheme occur in different positions with respect to other morphemes. In Iroquoian this is infrequent, but it does happen. One way out of this difficulty would be to redefine the morpheme so that even if two morphs were in complementary distribution and had the same meaning, they would still not be considered members of the same morpheme unless they occurred in the same relative order with respect to other morphemes. The question is whether meaningless differences of order should be treated in the same manner as significant phonemic differences between allomorphs, or whether, in view of the usefulness of order as a dimension of analysis, differences of order might be put on a par with differences of meaning for distinguishing morphemes. A system can be developed on either basis; but current practise is to disregard differences of order unless they have contrastive value. Nevertheless, we should like to use sequential order as our chief dimension of analysis in this study, both because it is a convenient one in dealing with morphology, and because it furnishes an important tool in comparative morphology. A satisfactory way out, one which allows us to stay within our present system but still make use of position classes based upon order, is to define sub-classes of allomorphs within the morpheme on the basis of order, and to incorporate these into our definition of position class. So we define a morpheme partial as a sub-class consisting of the allomorphs of a morpheme which occur in the same relative order with respect to other morphemes or morpheme partials. And we can then redefine position class as a class

---

[9] It is to be noted that our position class is not the same as Harris's position class (1946, 1947). In our definitions position is always the relative order in which a morpheme occurs; in Harris's, position is a selected environment of other morphemes with which a morpheme may occur. Our classes will be order classes; his are substitution classes in which order is a subordinate consideration. When structures described in terms of the two different types of classes are put in the form of geometrical charts, certain differences become readily apparent. His chart represents certain features of selection in a convenient manner, which ours can represent only clumsily. On the other hand, our type of chart is better adapted for displaying features of order, while his sometimes necessitates violating order, a shortcoming which he comments on in his Delaware restatement (1947: 186, fn. 23). Our reason for emphasizing order rather than selection, and for developing a correspondingly different method, becomes apparent at the close of the section headed Selection.

of morphemes or morpheme partials which are mutually exclusive and which, when they occur, always occur in the same relative order with respect to other morphemes or morpheme partials.

The other of the two situations referred to is that in some cases a morph may be discontinuous (i.e., composed of a discontinuous sequence of phonemes) and hence cannot be confined within a single position with respect to other morphemes or morpheme partials but must of necessity occupy more than one position. To meet such cases we may define a morph fraction as any of the continuous or unbroken parts of a discontinuous morph, and similarly an allomorph fraction as any of the continuous or unbroken parts of a discontinuous allomorph of a morpheme. Then we can extend the application of the term morpheme partial and define it as a sub-class within a morpheme, consisting of allomorphs or allomorph fractions which occur in the same relative order with respect to other morphemes or morpheme partials. A new definition of position class is not necessary at this point, since the redefinition of morpheme partial is sufficient to accommodate the analysis of discontinuous allomorphs.

1.2.3. Derivation

The conditions of single occurrence and fixed order of morphemes within words are so prevalent in the polysynthetic languages known to the writer that they are tentatively assumed to have general validity. When they are found to be violated, it is assumed that the form involves more than one level of construction, and that a derived polymorphemic unit is present, which substitutes for a single morpheme within the pattern. This assumption receives substantiation when the semantics is examined, for in all such cases which have come to light, semantic specialization has been found.

Hence we may distinguish between purely linear constructions on a single level, and constructions in depth, involving successive levels, one within the other. The former or linear type is highly elaborated in Iroquoian morphology. For lack of a more suitable term we may extend the application of an older term and call it inflection. The second type, involving constructions within constructions, is confined to two positions in the Iroquoian morphological pattern. It may properly be called derivation.

The more general method must be one which can handle derivations as well as linear constructions. It may still be a method of position classes based upon order. The position class, however, must be redefined so as to include not only morphemes or morpheme partials, but also sequences of morphemes which, as units, satisfy the same conditions as are required of single morphemes.[10] A complete devel-

opment of this method is not necessary for our present purpose. What has already been said is sufficient to indicate the treatment of such types of derivation as may occur.

1.2.4. Selection.

Besides order of morphemes and manner of derivation of complex units in morphology, it is necessary to give the rules of selection which govern the combination of units. A positional chart of morphemes, for example, tells us only that if or when a certain combination of morphemes occurs, the morphemes will be in such and such a relative order, but it does not help in predicting what combinations of morphemes will occur unless indications of selection, as well as of order, are included with the chart.

The term selection is used to refer to phenomena on two different levels. On the submorphemic level one speaks of the selection of alternants, or allomorphs, of a morpheme, where the choice is governed by the phonemic or morphemic environments in which they occur. On the morphemic level one also speaks of selection, but here it refers to limitations upon combination of morphemes one with another. We shall be concerned with selection on both levels, but in general they will be treated separately.

Two kinds of selection may be recognized among morphemes: exclusions and linkages. Of exclusions, two types may be distinguished: those between morphemes belonging to the same position class, and those between members of different position classes. Linkages are of necessity between members of different classes. Further special types of linkage are mentioned below.

Morphemes occurring in different positions in the verb structure may be mutually exclusive because of incompatible meanings or for less 'logical' reasons. Thus, in Oneida the cislocative morpheme t- 'hither', of position class 6, is mutually exclusive with the translocative morpheme y- 'yonder', of position class 2. Similarly, the aorist tense morpheme partials w- and -a-, which are of position classes 3 and 7 respectively, are mutually exclusive with the future tense morpheme ʌ- of position class 5. These are examples of mutually incompatible meanings and of exclusions between members of different position classes.

On the other hand, mutual exclusions between members of the same position class are not necessarily or even typically cases of contradictory or logically exclusive meanings. Thus, the cislocative morpheme t- 'hither', of class 6, and the iterative morpheme s- 'again, re-, back', also of class 6, are mutually exclusive not because of incompatible meanings (note that the translocative, class 2, occurs freely with the iterative), but only because the structure of the verb is such that they happen to occupy the same position with respect to other morphemes and combine with them in the same way, and

---

[10] This is Harris's method (Harris, 1946) except for the priority here given to order of occurrence.

in a way which does not allow their combining with each other.

The simplest type of linkage is that of a morpheme with a morpheme, i.e., such that if one morpheme occurs another must also. A one-way linkage of this type is such that if morpheme A occurs then morpheme B must also occur, but that the converse is not true, i.e., morpheme B may occur without morpheme A. Two-way linkages between single morphemes might be considered a possibility, but the only examples we have of two-way linkages are those between morpheme partials which are better considered as fractions of discontinuous morphs. Other possible types of linkage are those of a morpheme to a class, of a class to a class, etc. Further contrasting types are internal and external linkages. For example, in the latter case a morpheme in a word may be linked in occurrence with another morpheme (or with any one of a class of morphemes) elsewhere in the phrase or sentence but outside of the given word.

We have chosen the positional chart as our device for representing as concisely as possible the features of order in the verb morphology. Features of selection are in general less conveniently represented. Cases of exclusions between members of adjacent position classes are represented very simply in the geometry of the chart. For representing other exclusions and linkages a system of indexing may be used, or the information can be given separately.

Comparative evidence shows that in Iroquoian morphology, at least, features of selection have been much more mutable and variable than features of order. The latter, in fact, have been immutable except for the cases of obsolescence and coalescence of positions, which are reducible to changes in features of selection; and cases of innovation through reinterpretation of segments of older morphemes brought about by severe phonological change and analogical creation. Coincident with these facts are the ease and clarity with which features of order may be represented and the relatively unsatisfactory portrayal of features of selection. Many features of selection, such as those connected with individual members of the noun-root and verb-root positions in the morphology, cannot be portrayed in our morphological charts but must be relegated to a separate lexicon. These coincidences may be advantageous or disadvantageous, depending on one's problem. Since structural features of order appear to be more enduring than those of selection, phonemic shape, and meanings of morphemes,[11] they furnish a convenient framework for description and comparison.

[11]Compare Sapir's opinions in Chapter IX of his Language (1921).

BIBLIOGRAPHY

Barbeau, C. M., 1915: Classification of Iroquoian Radicals with Subjective Pronominal Prefixes (Canada Department of Mines, Geological Survey, Memoir 46, Ottawa).

Bloch, Bernard, 1947: English verb inflection (Lang. 23.399–418) ⟪243⟫.

Bloomfield, Leonard, 1933: Language (New York).

———, 1939: Menomini morphophonemics (TCLP. 8.105–15).

Boas, Franz (ed.), 1911: Handbook of American Indian Languages, vol. 1 (Bureau of American Ethnology, Bulletin 40, pt. 1, Washington).

———, 1922: [the same] vol. 2 (the same, pt. 2).

———, 1933: [the same] vol. 3 (New York).

———, 1940: [the same] vol. 4, pt. 1 (New York). ⟦this 1940 item, not used above, listed here for clarity⟧

Harris, Zellig S., 1942: Morpheme alternants in linguistic analysis (Lang. 18.169–80) ⟪109⟫.

———, 1945: Discontinuous morphemes (Lang. 21.121–7).

———, 1946: From morpheme to utterance (Lang. 22.161–83) ⟪142⟫.

———, 1947: Structural restatements (IJAL, 13.47–58, 13.175–86).

Hockett, Charles F., 1947: Problems of morphemic analysis (Lang. 23.321–43) ⟪229⟫.

———, 1948: Potawatami (IJAL 14.1–10, 14.63–73, 14.139–49, 14.213–25).

———, 1950: Peiping morphophonemics (Lang. 26.63–85) ⟪315⟫.

Hoenigswald, Henry M., 1944: Internal reconstruction (SIL 2.78–87).

———, 1946: Sound change and linguistic structure (Lang. 22.138–43) ⟪139⟫.

Morris, Charles W., 1938: Foundation of a Theory of Signs (International Encyclopedia of Unified Science, vol. 1, no. 2, Chicago).

Sapir, Edward, 1921: Language: An Introduction to the Study of Speech (New York).

Wells, Rulon S., 1949: Automatic alternation (Lang. 25.99–116).

TWO MODELS OF GRAMMATICAL DESCRIPTION

CHARLES F. HOCKETT
Word 10.210–31—1954

1.1 By a 'model of grammatical description' is meant a frame of reference within which an analyst approaches the grammatical phase of a language and states the results of his investigations. In one sense, there are as many models as there are different descriptions ('grammars' in the sense of monographs). But in another, and very important, sense, most grammatical descriptions seem to cluster about a relatively small number of relatively distinct models; it is with these archetypical frames of reference that we are concerned here.

The bulk of the present paper was written between 1949 and 1951; at that time, the writer was under the erroneous impression that there were principally just two archetypes to be dealt with. If we confine our attention to monographs produced in the United States in the past half-century, this impression is not grossly inaccurate. One of the 'two models' which is well represented within those spatial and temporal limits is what we shall call item and process, or IP for short; the other we shall call item and arrangement, or IA. In most of what follows we shall have occasion to mention only these two.

But that limitation constitutes a defect in the paper—a defect which was recognized by the writer in 1951, and because of which the paper was long held unpublished. Quite apart from minor variants of IP or IA, or models that might be invented tomorrow, there is one model which is clearly distinct from either IA or IP, and which is older and more respectable than either. This is the word and paradigm (WP) model, the traditional framework for the discussion of Latin, Greek, Sanskrit, and a good many more modern familiar languages. It will not do to shrug this frame of reference off with the comment that it is obviously insufficiently general, incapable of organizing efficiently the facts of a language like Chinese. As yet we have no completely adequate model: WP deserves the same consideration here given to IP and IA. The writer offers his apologies for not having worked such consideration of WP into the present paper. However, lack of time prevented this, and the discussion as it stands may nevertheless be of some value.

1.2 As between IP and IA, the former is older. The key term in IP is 'process', as is evident from the following characterization by Harris (1944, p. 199):[1] "The difference between two partially similar

forms is frequently described… as a process which yields one form out of the other. Thus, when bases or themes have several vocalic forms, the various forms are said to be the result of vowel-change processes operating upon the base or theme. The difference between a base and a base-plus-suffix is described as a result of the process of suffixation. This is a traditional manner of speaking, especially in American Indian grammar. It has, of course, nothing to do with historical change or process through time: it is merely process through the configuration, moving from one to another or larger part of the pattern."

Rigorous work with historical linguistics, as everyone knows, preceded almost all rigorous descriptive work; the carry-over of 'process' terminology from historical discussion is natural enough. In this country Boas (1911, pp. 27 f.) established IP, and Sapir (1921, esp. ch. 4) elaborated it; the descriptive chapters of Sapir's Language are cast entirely in this mold. Grammars written largely under Sapir's aegis, such as Newman's Yokuts (1944; the specific aim of Harris's remarks quoted above), still stand as examples of IP in action.

1.3 As a further example of IP, consider the following paragraph from Haas's shorter treatment of Tunica (1946):

> The Tunica language is mildly synthetic in structure. In its technique of synthesis it is for the most part agglutinative, but it also employs a limited amount of fusion. The morphological processes used are juxtaposition, affixation (prefixation, infixation, and suffixation), reduplication, and suppletion. Of these, prefixation and suffixation, particularly the latter, are exploited to a greater extent than are the other processes.

There is no question about the meaningfulness of this characterization. Whether it is particularly relevant, either to a description of Tunica or to a proper placing of Tunica in the gamut of linguistic types, and whether, relevant or not, it is effectively phrased, are other matters.

1.4 The younger model, IA, has been formulated at least in part because of a feeling of dissatisfaction with the 'moving-part' or 'historical' analogy implicit in IP. At the very least, these analogies seem to imply the necessity of making certain decisions in a possibly arbitrary way. Critics of IP would prefer to circumvent such decisions altogether.

For example (cf. Hockett 1947a, pp. 282–3), if it be said that the English past-tense form baked is

---

[1] Reference is made by author and year of publication to the bibliography at the end of the article.

'formed' from <u>bake</u> by a 'process' of 'suffixation', then no matter what disclaimer of historicity is made, it is impossible not to conclude that some kind of priority is being assigned to <u>bake</u>, as against either <u>baked</u> or the suffix. And if this priority is not historical, what is it?[2] Supporters of IP have not answered that question satisfactorily.

Another objection which might be raised to IP as exemplified in the above quotation from Haas is that the wording tends toward personalization and teleology. The Tunica language 'uses' or 'employs' various techniques; it 'exploits' some of these more than others. The use of the term 'the Tunica language' as a subject with such verbs is personalization; the use of such verbs seems to imply teleology—the language has a purpose to accomplish, and it makes use of such-and-such means to the end. If any entity 'uses' the techniques, it is the speakers, not the language. This objection is pointless unless it can be shown that such a way of speaking leads its users into errors of fact. So long as it is merely a 'way of speaking', easier than some other way because English is an Indo-European language, we cannot object.

1.5 The essence of IA is to talk simply of things and the arrangements in which those things occur (Harris 1944, section 5, esp. end of page 203; Bloch 1947, introductory remarks; Harris 1945b; Harris 1942). One assumes that any utterance in a given language consists wholly of a certain number of minimum grammatically relevant elements, called morphemes, in a certain arrangement relative to each other. The structure of the utterance is specified by stating the morphemes and the arrangement. The pattern of the language is described if we list the morphemes and the arrangements in which they occur relative to each other in utterances—appending statements to cover the phonemic shapes which appear in any occurrent combination.[3]

The matter is not quite so simple as that. Some of the complexities will concern us later. Here it must be noted that there is some indeterminacy even in the apparently trivial matter of deciding what to subsume as 'item' and what to call 'arrangement'. In English, intonation phonemes can be taken as comprising parts of morphemes just as do vowels and consonants. There is then a set of morphemes composed entirely of intonation phonemes, and such intonation morphemes occur, not before or after other kinds of morphemes, but simultaneously with

[2] The possible criteria are examined by Pittman, 1948. But Pittman's discussion is cast in IA, and affords no obvious support for the IP approach.

[3] Floyd Lounsbury has suggested (private conversation) that we can profitably speak of the 'structure' of a word or utterance but of the 'pattern' of a language. This suggestion is followed here. (The contrast, of course, parallels one of those designated by the terms 'parole' and 'langue'.)

them. In <u>Come here!</u>, the segmental form and the /(2)31/ intonation morpheme occur at the same time. But this is not the only way to handle the matter. An alternative is to consider pitch as a second dimension in which (segmental) forms can be arranged, there being four possible positions along this dimension, in contrast to the infinite number along the time axis. For purposes of demonstration, we could then write

    (4)
    (3)   h
    (2)   come   e
    (1)   re

—where the numbers specify the pitch-levels. There would then be no intonation morphemes, but rather a two-dimensional space in which other types of morphemes are arranged relative to each other.[4] The four stress levels of English could be handled in the same way, giving three dimensions of arrangement. Bloomfield (1933, p.163) chooses this alternative when he speaks of taxemes of 'modulation'.

IA is present implicitly, though not with complete clarity, in Bloomfield's chapters on grammar; where traces of IP survive, he is sometimes a bit apologetic (1933, p.213 top; cf. Wells, 1949, p.102). It is certainly Bloomfield's systematization which has served as the main point of departure for the train of investigators who have been trying to develop IA—Harris and his students, Bloch, Wells, lately Nida, and others (see bibliography passim under these names, Nida only in 1948, 1949. Nida 1946 is cast essentially in IP). There are few full grammatical descriptions which illustrate IA in its purest form; Bloch's discussions of Japanese are probably the closest (1946: even more—work done under Bloch's direction— Gardner 1950, Yokoyama 1950).

1.6 There is partial translatability between IP and IA, but the results of translation are apt to seem somewhat strange. By way of demonstration, here is the passage from Haas's Tunica, recast in IA:

[4] The problem of dimensionality is confusing. Recognizing intonation morphemes, we have to accept simultaneity as one arrangement of morphemes relative to each other. This, in turn, suggests that there is a second dimension of arrangement in addition to time; but there are no contrasts between different 'arrangements' in this second dimension—the term 'superfix' is no more apt than 'subfix', and (the bad Latin) 'simulfix' might be even better. A dimension in which arrangements are not in contrast is rather thin. Lounsbury has suggested (private conversation) that it is better to speak of just one dimension, with simultaneity as one possible arrangement within it. If we treat intonations (or stresses) as features of arrangement instead of as morphemes, then clearly we have more than the one dimension time; but in this case, although two items can occur at different times on the same intonation level, two items cannot occur at the same time on different intonation levels. There is still something rather queer about the added dimensions.

The average number of morphemes per word in Tunica stands about midway between the highest and lowest averages known from various languages. The morphemes within a single word are for the most part relatively invariant in shape, but there are some cases of more alternations. Tunica morphemes fall into several position-classes: stems, prefixes, infixes, and suffixes; at least one affix [we are not told which kind or how many] is morphophonemically a chameleon. A single word may contain more than one stem. Suffixes are more numerous, both as a class and as regards the average number per word, than prefixes, and the latter in turn more numerous than infixes. In a few cases, morphophonemic alternations are between totally dissimilar forms.

The original, in all seeming, imparts relevant information about Tunica. The translation given above has little or no such impact—at least on this reader; it has the appearance, rather, of an assembly of prosaic facts, which have no particular reason for being given in the sequence in which they are here found, or, indeed, even for being given all at one place.

If this be true, then there must be more difference between the IP and the IA models than has yet been touched on; there must be major differences as to what features of a language are regarded as worthy of prominent mention and what features are prosaic —even if necessarily included somewhere in a reasonably complete description.

This last comment is offered not as a forerunner of greater elaboration to follow, but in lieu thereof. There are differences between IP and IA which will have to be ignored within the fairly formal framework that will shortly be built, and it would be wrong to ignore them altogether.

1.7 It seems to me that the current general preference for IA rather than IP—and such a prejudice is certainly observable—stems at least in part not from any great excess of merit of IA over IP, but rather from the following: (1) We like, nowadays, to be as formal as possible. (2) IA has been formalized, and IP has not. It is unfair to compare a formalized IA with an informal IP and conclude that the former is better just because it is formalized. If it could be shown that IA is capable of formalization but that IP is not, that would be another matter. But in what follows, I hope to demonstrate that no such claim can be made.

To do this, it is of course necessary to devise a formalized version of IP. This will be almost our last step. It will be preceded by: a general outline of IA, in broad enough terms to cover most, if not all, of its current varieties; a survey of some of the problems implicit in IA (in two parts: tactical and morphophonemic); an excursion into certain elementary notions of mathematics, seeking analogs for IA and other possibly useful analogs. Our formal version of IP will be derived from such an analog. We will then be in the position to assess the relative merits and defects of IA and IP.

II. ITEM AND ARRANGEMENT

2.0 The following outline of IA might be called 'semiformal'—not so formal as to qualify as 'postulates', but succinct rather than discursive. The model is familiar, so all but the most essential examples are eschewed.

2.1 A linguistic form is either simple or composite.[5]

2.2 A simple form is a morpheme.

2.3 A composite form consists of two or more immediate constituents standing in a construction and forming a constitute. Constituents and construction recur in other composite forms (save for an occasional unique constituent). Each IC (=immediate constituent) occupies a certain position in the construction; each is the partner of the other(s).[6]

2.4 Occasionally it is convenient to regard a morpheme not as participating in any construction, but rather as a marker of the construction in which nearby forms stand.

Any such concession necessitates a statement of the conditions under which the interpretation is to be accepted. Three such statements of conditions occur to me, the first being the trivial (but not unimportant) one of excluding the interpretation altogether.

The second is to allow the interpretation only where the marker indicates the boundary between partners in a construction, and nothing more. By this, the Peiping Chinese junctural morphemes /;/ and /,/ are allowable as markers, since in such an utterance as /ue3 lai2, ni3 zieu4 cy4./ 'When I come, you go right away', the /,/ tells us that the segmental sequence before it and that after it are partners in a construction—that is, that this division of the whole sequence, rather than any other, is the correct one—but it does not tell us what construction is involved (Hockett 1950, section 2).

This limitation, however, would not allow us to interpret men and women as a bipartite construction with marker and, since and quite obviously gives us more information than the maximum amount specified. A set of conditions which would allow the interpretation in this case would have to be along the following lines: there is a form ABC consisting of three smaller forms, where (1) one of the smaller forms, say B (it would not have to be the one in the middle) is a single morpheme; (2) the remaining two, A and C, are structurally similar to each other (in some appropriate sense) but not to B; (3) there is no evidence forcing either an interpretation as

[5] The term 'linguistic form' is here to be regarded as being defined by the other terms at least as much as they are by it. The outline assumes, without explicit statement, a certain amount of our linguistic common sense.

[6] The only new term is 'partner', which I venture to suggest to fill a hole in our terminology in which I have stumbled more than once.

A⌊BC or as AB⌊C.[7]

Even more liberal sets of conditions might be formulated. Our reason for including the present discussion will appear in the sequel.

2.5 The <u>tactical pattern</u> of a language is completely covered by a set of statements of the following form (or by any set of statements which can be transformed mechanically into this form):[8]

(1) A list of the constructions.
(2) Under each construction as heading,
    (2.1) Enumeration of the positions in that construction.
    (2.2) Specification of any marker for that construction.
    (2.3) For each position,
        (2.31) A list of the morphemes which occur there, and
        (2.32) A list of the constructions, composite forms belonging to which occur there.

2.6 A morpheme may appear in more than a single phonemic shape. A single shape of a morpheme is a <u>morph</u>; the various morphs which are the shapes or <u>representations</u> of one and the same morpheme are <u>its allomorphs</u>.

2.7 The alternations in shape of a morpheme are predictable in terms of the environments in which it occurs (plus, of course, the morphophonemic statements which one makes).

This necessitates a definition of 'environment': the environment of a morpheme-occurrence is the setting of that occurrence, insofar as that setting can be described in purely structural (i. e., nonsemantic) terms. Narrower definitions are possible; ours is intentionally wide.

2.8 All the phonemic material in an utterance is accountable for in terms of the morphemes which compose the utterance and the arrangement in which they occur relative to each other (plus, once again, one's morphophonemic statements).

2.9 Subject to the conditions just stated (2.6–8), it is possible to allow such devices as the following where they prove convenient:

[7] This incorporates Wells's specification of the conditions under which one resorts to a tripartite instead of a bipartite construction (Wells 1947, pp. 103 f. ((199))).

[8] Many different arrangements of descriptive statements are convertible into this form. In particular there is the contrast between beginning with the most inclusive constructions and working down the scale (large-to-small), which is perhaps the traditional way at least for syntax (exemplified, e. g., by the arrangement of the grammatical chapters in Bloomfield 1933), and beginning with the least inclusive constructions and working up the scale (small-to-large), the procedure proposed by Harris, 1946. These two ways have in common—despite Harris's disclaimer in section 3.7 and fn. 8—the recognition of IC or hierarchical structure, though Harris's procedure discovers that structure step by step, whereas the alternative seems to imply discovering it in advance.

(1) We may recognize phonemic zero as a possible morph shape. This requires carefully formulated supplementary criteria. At least two apparently consistent limitations have been proposed:

    (1.1) A morpheme does not appear everywhere as zero (Bloch, 1947, section 2.3 (3)).

    (1.2) A morpheme may appear everywhere as zero, providing it is a member of a tactically relevant class (under some suitable definition), other members of which are not (or not always) represented by zero (Nida 1948, 1949; the criterion is there by implication, though not overtly stated).

(2) We may recognize a morph which belongs to no morpheme (Hockett 1947b, p. 333 ((236))). Or, instead of this, we may simply classify some of the phonemic material in some utterances as <u>nonmorphemic</u> (Hockett 1950, fn. 8).

(3) We may recognize a morph which belongs simultaneously to two (or more) morphemes in a fixed arrangement (whether partners in a construction or not). If the morphemes involved appear, in other environments, in separable shapes, then the morph in question is a <u>portmanteau</u> representation of the morpheme-group (Hockett 1947b, p. 333 ((236))). If the morphemes involved appear only in such portmanteau representations, the usual terminology is a little different: the representations themselves are called 'morphemes', and the separate entities represented are called 'morphemic components' (Harris 1948, more extensively in 1951). This more usual, but deviant, terminology will not be used in the present discussion.

(4) We may allow a particular phoneme or sequence of phonemes to belong at one and the same time both to a morph which includes some preceding phonemes (and represents one morpheme) and to a morph which includes some following phonemes (and represents another morpheme)—<u>linked morphs</u>, the shared phoneme(s) being a <u>link</u> (Wells 1949, fn. 29, with credit to Lounsbury). Trivially different is the case in which one of the morphs, instead of both, contains phonemic material which is not part of the other.

2.10 The statement of shapes, alternations, and conditions of alternation describes the <u>morphophonemic pattern</u> of the language.

2.11 Morphophonemic and tactical pattern taken together constitute <u>grammatical pattern</u>. This, paired with <u>phonological pattern</u>, completes the synchronic pattern of a language. The cleavage between phonology and grammar is thought by some (including myself) to be more fundamental than that, within grammar, between morphophonemics and tactics, even though, for some purposes, other stratifications are possible. For example, it is sometimes convenient to class morphophonemic and phonological facts together, say as 'mechanics', in collective contrast to tactics (Hockett 1948, p. 185). Or, if the distinction between automatic and non-automatic morphophonemics is made (we have not taken the trouble to work it into the above outline), it also makes a good deal of sense to class automatic morphophonemic facts with phonology, non-automatic with tactics; I have no labels to propose for the resulting two divisions (this is the stratification which seems to be implied by certain of Sapir's discussions: 1933, 1930). In any case, there are indeed problems about the exact location of the lines of demarcation between levels, but we need not concern ourselves with them here because the formal version of IP to be presented later will solve them neither more nor less than does IA.

III. TACTICAL DIFFICULTIES WITH IA

3.0 A grammatical description built according to the plan outlined in II sets forth principles by which one can generate any number of utterances in the language; in this sense, it is operationally comparable to the structure of that portion of a human being which enables him to produce utterances in a language; i. e., to speak. It is also comparable to a cookbook. From the lists in the tactical description, choose any set of compatible ingredients. Put them together, two by two or few by few (ICs), until all have been tentatively assembled; then treat in accordance with the morphophonemic statements (in cooking, 'cream', 'blend', 'broil', etc.); remove traces of these operations (clean and put away the cooking utensils); and one has an utterance in the language. In cooking, a difference in the sequence in which ingredients are put together can make a difference in the end-product; if this were not so, manufacturers of processed foods would not announce, as they sometimes do on packages, both ingredients and proportions. But there can also be differences of sequence in cooking operations which make no discernible difference in the end-product. For the moment this second fact is of primary relevance for the analogy. There is, in linguistics, no guarantee that different sequences of operations, performed on the same ultimate constituents, may not produce the same, or what is ostensibly the same, end-product.

In fact, we can specify the conditions under which this will be the case. The conditions involve the constructions recognized in the tactical description and the forms listed under the various positions for the various constructions. Let there be four constructions, C_1, C_2, C_3, and C_4 (some of which may be the same). Let there be three forms F_1, F_2, and F_3. Suppose that F_1 and F_2 occur in that order in C_1; F_2 and F_3 in that order in C_2. Suppose that forms conforming to C_1 (hence F_1F_2) occur in the first position of C_3, and that F_3 occurs in the second position of C_3. Finally, suppose that forms conforming to C_2 (hence F_2F_3) occur in the second position of C_4, and that F_1 occurs in the first position of C_4. Under just these conditions, the composite form $F_1F_2F_3$ will be a case in point.

We may illustrate with English. C_1 and C_4 are the construction of adjective-attribute and nominal-head.

F_1 is <u>old</u>, F_2 is <u>men</u>. C_2 and C_3 are the marked construction <u>X and Y</u>; F_3 is <u>women</u>. Consequently we may build the composite form <u>old men and women</u> by either of two procedural sequences: putting <u>old</u> and <u>men</u> together by C_1, and then joining the result to <u>women</u> by C_2; or putting <u>men and women</u> together by C_2, and then putting <u>old</u> together with the result of C_2 in accordance with C_1.[9]

The converse of the cookbook nature of a grammatical description is that, when presented with an utterance in a language whose pattern has been determined, the analyst should be able to state its structure. Now it is clear that in any such case as that of <u>old men and women</u>, the analyst will be able to determine the ultimate constituents and the (linear) order of these constituents, but he will not necessarily be able to tell the order of association, the IC-structure or <u>hierarchical structure</u>, of the utterance. The fact that his description supplies more than a single procedural sequence which will build the composite form implies that when presented with the whole form the analyst cannot determine which procedural sequence was involved in its production.

We therefore have to make a decision. It was mentioned above that a grammatical description is an operational parallel to part of a speaker's internal apparatus. If we believe that this parallel extends to the matter of order of association, so that ambiguities in the description are matched (at least in some cases) by distinct internal chains of activity which produce identical linear sequences of morphemes, then we can regard the matter of hierarchical structure as an integral part of the structure of utterances even in ambiguous cases. But if we do not so believe, or if we feel that such a conclusion ought not to influence our development of analytical techniques, then we are forced to conclude that hierarchical structure is at most a convenient shorthand for description—not anything essential about the grammar of a language, but simply a way to make our description of a whole language less cumbersome—an intrusive artifact, like the dye on a bacteriologist's slide. For, obviously, it would be possible (save for lack of time) to specify all arrangements of ultimate constituents in utterances without resort to any intermediate groupings.

---

[9] Wells 1947, p. 93 ((193)). Since normal English orthography leaves out certain grammatically relevant features of utterances (e. g., intonations), any single English notation, such as 'old men and women', subsumes ambiguously a family of linguistic forms. Some members of this family are marked clearly as having one IC structure; some are marked equally clearly as having the other. But, at least for my own speech, there are also members of the family that are not marked in either way. In the context, it is of course one of the latter with which we are dealing; here, and in similar situations later, the reader must assume that this is the case.

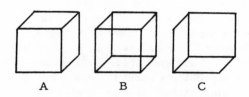

The IA picture is therefore potentially somewhat more complex than our original emphasis on the two notions ('item' and 'arrangement') would imply. There are more potentially independent factors than those two. Specifically, there are (1) forms, (2) [linear] order, (3) constructions, and (4) IC or hierarchical structure. We must investigate the status of these factors relative to each other. Are they all 'primitives' in the system, or are some derivable from others?

The independence of forms and order is clear almost without demonstration. Such a trivial example as John hit Bill versus John hit Dick demonstrates the independence of form from order; the former versus Bill hit John demonstrates the independence of order from form, since these two could be said to differ only as to order of ultimate constituents. But the status of constructions and of hierarchical structure needs further discussion.

3.1 Beginning with hierarchical structure, let us consider again Wells's case of hierarchical ambiguity, this time embedded in a longer utterance: The old men and women stayed at home. It is quite possible that if I say this to an audience, some hearers may conclude that I have referred to old males and all females, others may believe that I have spoken of all old people of both sexes; still others may believe that I am consciously being ambiguous (as I am!) or may simply be unable to decide the matter.

Wells adopts a very simple solution. He assumes that old men and women has one or the other hierarchical structure depending on the meaning. Since there are cases in which the hearer cannot tell what the meaning is, this must revert to a consideration of something like 'speaker's intention', which means that the step mentioned earlier is indeed being taken. Before we resort to such a drastic measure, let us look for further evidence.

We might apply the same technique by which we separate homophonous morphemes. Old men and women can be substituted for, say, old people, in one large set of environments (for example, old people belong at home and old men and women belong at home are both good English sentences); it can be substituted for women and old men in another, partly different, set of environments (The women and old men stayed at home while the young men went to war; The old men and women...). But old people and women and old men are not so freely interchangeable. It is by just this procedure that we would, in the first instance, separate The sun's rays meet and The sons raise meat. Having separated either pair of homophones, we can seek for correlated internal structural differences. In the latter pair, the differences lie in the ultimate constituents; in the former, the only difference is in the hierarchical organization.

But there is a deeper consideration. The hearer, confronted with The old men and women stayed at home, is in much the same position as the observer who sees a picture of a hollow cube and can, almost at will, see first one corner and then another as closer to him. There is a third way to see the picture: as an assemblage of straight lines on a flat surface, without depth. This third way is difficult without the special training which artists, whose task it is to produce such visual representations, have to get. The ordinary individual, looking at the three figures A, B, and C, can easily enough see that B is different from both A and C, but he will also see B now as more like A, now as more like C. Since most of our visual experience is with depth perception, we 'read' depth into many two-dimensional portrayals.

B, then, is ambiguous. An ambiguity cannot exist in the abstract; it must be between things. The alternatives in the visual case are not A and C; they are B's being like A or C respectively. 'Being like A' and 'being like C' are two distinct and mutually exclusive matters: B cannot at one and the same time be taken both as like A and as like C.

The same argument holds for hierarchical ambiguity. Our B is The old men and women stayed at home. For A and C, we can select respectively The women and old men stayed at home and The old men and old women stayed at home. B's 'being like' A is one hierarchical structure; B's 'being like' C is another. A hierarchical structure is a class of forms which are alike in a certain way; so is a construction. A single sequence of morphemes cannot be like two mutually exclusive other sequences at one and the same moment for a single hearer, but in some cases it may fluctuate between the two directions of likeness. Interpreting old men and women as merely a linear sequence of morphemes is highly unnatural; the linguist, for his special purposes, may have to develop the ability to do so, just as the artist has to develop the ability to see things without depth in order to represent them in such a way that others will report the presence of depth.

Our conclusion, then, is that hierarchical structure is a 'primitive' just as are forms and order. The demonstration turns necessarily on two considerations: (1) there must be many utterances in which the hierarchical structure in unambiguous, to afford a frame of reference; (2) there must be also at least a few in which the hierarchical structure is ambiguous, since otherwise the hierarchical structure would in every case be determined by forms and order, and hence not a 'primitive'.

3.2 One recently proposed type of morphemic analysis turns on the 'primitive' status of hierarchical structure in a way which has never been made clear. This is the utilization of discontinuous morphemes (Harris 1945a). For those to whom this type of analysis appeals, this dependence, to be demonstrated in a moment, may add weight to the desirability of recognizing IC-structure as a 'primitive'. But since there is no situation in which the analyst is actually forced to use discontinuous-morpheme analysis, its dependence on IC-structure cannot count in any sense as evidence for the status of the latter.

Consider the following two Latin sentences: (a) pater bonus filium amat; (b) pater bonum filium amat. The latter, though unusual, was certainly possible; it is easier to handle than more complex and more realistic examples that could be found.

According to the more customary procedure— rejecting discontinuous morphemes—the ultimate constituents of (a) include two occurrences of a morpheme that we may call {nominative} and one occurrence of {accusative}, while those of (b) include one of {nominative} and two of {accusative}.[10] The distribution of the two occurrences of {nominative} in (a) marks pater and bonus as going together as partners in a construction, while the distribution of the two occurrences of {accusative} in (b) mark bonum and filium in the same way. The hierarchical structure in each case is partly marked by the nature and location of these morpheme-occurrences. There is no need, in these examples, for hierarchical structure to be an independent primitive.

Using discontinuous morphemes, the results are different. The ultimate constituents of (a) in this case include one occurrence each of {nominative} and of {accusative}—and in (b) there will be found, also, just one occurrence of each of these morphemes. In (a), the one occurrence of {nominative} is an occurrence in discontinuous form, the separated representations coming at the ends of two successive words; in (b) similarly for the {accusative} morpheme.

Now when discontinuous morphemes are recognized, it is necessary not only for the particular shape of each representation of such a morpheme, but also for the number of representations involved in any one occurrence and the precise location of those representations, to be predictable on the morphophonemic level. It is not enough that we be able to predict that if the stem patr- and the nominative morpheme co-occur, the total form will be pater; we must also be able to predict that if the stem-sequence patr-...bon-... and {nominative} co-occur the total form will be pater bonus. Now assume that we have the partial patr-...bon-...fili-...amat and

one occurrence each of {nominative} and {accusative}. There is absolutely no way of knowing that the total form will be pater bonus filium amat, or pater bonum filium amat, or possibly something else, unless among the environmentally relevant facts it is given that patr- and bon- are partners, rather than bon- and fili-. The distribution of representations of discontinuous morphemes is not predictable in Latin unless hierarchical structure is allowed to count as part of morphophonemically relevant environment. When we make use of discontinuous morphemes, then Latin sentences (a) and (b), despite overt phonemic differences, are structurally the same as the two English phrases of shape old men and women.

The requirement of 2.7 was intentionally phrased broadly enough to allow this. However, it has not been customary to count IC-structure as relevant environment, and it may that the necessary added complication will be enough to turn some against the whole notion of discontinuous morphemes.

3.3 Next in line is the status of constructions.

Given verb-stem bake and the past-tense morpheme, with instructions that they are to go together, the only thing one can do is to put them together as baked. There is no problem of hierarchical structure since each constituent is ultimate. Linear order is determined.

Given John and saw to be put together, the result can be either John saw or saw John (either of which, partnered by an intonation, might occur as an utterance). Here there is a choice of procedure. If to John and saw we add a specification as to linear order, then there is no longer any choice between constructions: only John saw, which is the actor-action construction, is possible with one order specification, and only saw John (action-goal construction) is possible with the other. But instead of approaching the matter in this way, we can equally well regard the order as determined by the construction: John, saw, and subject-predicate construction result necessarily in one linear order, the same forms and action-goal construction result necessarily in the other. Whichever course we follow, it is clear that we are confronted with one more variable than the maximum number which can be regarded as independent: forms to be partners, order, and construction cannot in such a case all be independent of each other.

The nearest example to complete independence of these three matters that I have so far discovered is in Chinese. Given crau[3] 'to fry' and fan[4] 'rice', and the specification that the first is to precede the second, there is still a choice of construction—though it does not manifest itself in any overt way within the sequence itself. One possible construction is verb-object, giving crau[3] fan[4] 'to fry rice, fry rice'; the other is attribute-head, giving crau[3] fan[4] 'fried rice'. These are really different: the first is also the construction of cr[1] fan[4] 'to eat rice, eat rice',

---

[10] These morphemes, treated as discontinuous or not, are what Harris has called morphemic components, a fact which does not disturb the present argument (see 2.9 (3) of this paper).

unambiguously verb–object; the second is also the construction of hau³ fan⁴ 'good rice', which is unambiguously attribute–head.

From here on our argument about <u>old men and women</u> applies pari passu to crau³ fan⁴, and need not be repeated in detail. There are, of course, some larger contexts in which crau³ fan⁴ is marked unambiguously as one or the other construction, just as there are larger environments in which the hierarchical structure of <u>old men and women</u> is not ambiguous. But there are also larger contexts in which the ambiguity remains. The construction, then, cannot be derived from the forms and the order. The reverse is possible: given forms and construction, the order can be regarded as determined—it just so happens that either of two constructions, with the same two constituents, results in the same order.

The conclusion to which we are forced is that, at least in some cases in some languages, choice of construction is a primitive.

3.4 If a particular version of IA allows the recognition of marked constructions, then the question as to the primitive or derived status of constructions becomes trivial: at least such constructions as have markers must have primitive status. Consider <u>John and Bill</u>, a bipartite construction with marker <u>and</u>. This form contrasts with <u>Bill and John</u> only as to order, with <u>John and Mary</u> (or <u>Tom and Mary</u>) only as to form, and with <u>John or Bill</u> only as to construction—since <u>or</u> is the marker of a different construction. In this case, all three factors are independent. It immediately follows that in <u>old men and women</u> all four factors are independent, since in addition to the <u>X and Y</u> construction there is also the matter of hierarchical structure, already demonstrably independent of the other factors.

3.5 So the four factors, the status of which we set out to survey, all have to be recognized as potentially independent, and therefore as primitives. If there is a possible exception, it is, surprisingly enough, linear order—one of the two factors (the other being forms) which would seem so obviously primary. The only situation discussed above in which linear order had to be accepted as independent of all other factors was in the case of marked constructions like <u>John and Bill</u>, and it is possible to proscribe marked constructions altogether.

The survey also shows, however, that in the bulk of cases not all of this machinery is needed. In most cases, a determination of two or three of the factors leaves no choice for the remainder. It is this fact which gives rise to the most embarrassing tactical trouble inherent in IA: machinery which has to be in our workshop for use in certain marginal cases tends to obtrude itself where it isn't wanted.

Thus Bloch writes as follows (1947, p. 400 ⟨243⟩): "the preterit form <u>waited</u>... can be described as follows. It consists of two morphemes, /weyt/ and /ed/, occurring in that order. The meaning of the first morpheme is a particular action that we need not

specifically define here; that of the second is 'past time' or the like. The constructional meaning of the order in which the two morphemes occur is approximately 'perform a certain action at a certain time'." Bloch has cut down on the total amount of machinery by identifying 'construction' and 'order' (which, as we have seen, is in general questionable). But, still, entities are multiplied beyond necessity. Given the morphemes /weyt/ and /ed/ to be put together, actually nothing further need be said at all on the tactical level. There is no possible linear order save that of /weyt/ first and /ed/ second. Nor—if we separate order and construction—is there any choice of construction. Semantically, it is quite pointless to break down the meaning of the whole form <u>waited</u> into <u>three</u> parts: structurally, there are two and only two independent variables, and the only valid procedure is to assign, as the meaning of the second variable, everything which differentiates the meaning of <u>waited</u> from that of <u>wait</u>.

IV. MORPHOPHONEMIC TROUBLES WITH IA

4.1 Most morphophonemic problems find simple answers in IA, for there is available a wide variety of morphophonemic techniques all well within the bounds of the IA model. However, there is a refractory residue, troublesome not because no solution can be found, but either because a multiplicity of solutions present themselves, no one seeming much better than another, or because the intuitively best solution is clearly in violation of the fundamental orientation of IA. This residue includes such cases as <u>took</u>, <u>put</u> (past tense), <u>children</u>, French <u>bon</u> and <u>bonne</u>, Chinese <u>lia</u>³ and <u>liang</u>³ 'two'. We need deal in detail only with one of these, and <u>took</u> will do.

4.2 The following morphophonemic solutions have been proposed (or might be proposed) for <u>took</u> (we here follow, in the main, Bloch 1947, pp. 400–1 ⟨244⟩):

(1) <u>took</u> is a single morpheme, so that there is no morphophonemic problem.

(2) <u>took</u> is a portmanteau representation of the two-morpheme sequence <u>take</u> and /ed/.

(3) <u>took</u> is an allomorph of the morpheme which appears elsewhere as <u>take</u>, plus a zero allomorph of /ed/.

(4) <u>took</u> is a discontinuous allomorph /t...k/ of <u>take</u>, and an infixed allomorph /u/ of /ed/.

(5) <u>took</u> is <u>take</u> plus a <u>replacive morph</u> /u/←/ey/ (read '/u/ replaces /ey/').

Let us consider these one by one.

(1) is unacceptable because it controverts the tactical parallelism between <u>took</u> and <u>baked</u> and many other obviously composite forms.

(2) is the most general solution, since it avoids, in a sense, the problem of identification of partial similarity in shape. But this very avoidance is arbitrary: <u>took</u> and <u>take</u> are partly similar in phonemic shape just as are <u>baked</u> and <u>bake</u>, and similar in meaning also in the same way; the fact should not be obscured.

(3) is arbitrary because it assigns to something that isn't there phonemically—something that is 'there' only in the fact that it calls for a phonemically distinct allomorph of the accompanying morpheme—a meaning which would more naturally be assigned to some location within the overt form took. The same solution for the past tense put (or the plural sheep) is even more strained since there is not even this phonemic effect on the accompanying morpheme. Within the same special rules that allow (3), it would also be possible to propose that took be interpreted as an allomorph of /ed/ accompanied by a zero allomorph of take. I see no reason why (3) should be considered any more or less seriously than this alternative. (3), in effect, gains nothing at all over (2).

(4) is in some ways the most attractive (with some manipulation, this proposed solution can be derived from Nida's discussions in 1948, 1949; his 'replacive' terminology tends to obscure the matter). It meets the objections so far raised to the other alternatives, as well as that which will shortly be raised to (5). The most serious criticism so far offered is that we might be led to interpret take, also, as an allomorph /t...k/ plus an infixed allomorph /ey/; this is not justified because take, like bake, rake, catch, and so on, acts tactically like a single morpheme. This is not a very serious criticism, since we need not be so submissive to the proposed analogy. Within the IA framework, (4) is probably the best answer.

(5) is not valid within IA. It calls an 'allomorph' something which is not in conformity with the general definition of the term. A morph is composed wholly of phonemic material or (as the limiting case) of no phonemic material at all. A 'replacive', like '/u/←/ey/', is not by any stretch of the imagination composed of phonemic material.

The same comment applies to 'subtractives', which happen not to apply in the case of take. It is tactically convenient to regard French bon as more complex than bonne, Chinese lia³ 'two' as more complex than liang³ 'two'.[11] Bon is then, it is proposed, to be taken as bonne plus a 'subtractive' morph consisting of loss of final consonant (and nasalization of the vowel); lia³ is to be taken as liang³ plus a terminal 'subtractive'. A subtraction is no more composed of phonemic material than is a replacement.

4.3 Why is so much emphasis placed on this? Could we not modify our definition of 'morph' in such a way as to allow subtractives and replacives in those circumstances where they seem so clearly convenient? Of course we can do so. But such action seems to be equivalent—perhaps rather unexpectedly—to removing the keystone of the whole IA arch;

the model begins to collapse. All the criteria which have been so laboriously established as a basis for the selection of one morphophonemic treatment or another have to be supplemented by new clauses. Even the tactical picture tends to be modified. When we pick up the pieces and try to fit them together again—without restoring the keystone—we find that we are no longer dealing with anything that looks like IA; we have a new model on our hands. After a short intermission this new model will be put on exhibit.

V. MATHEMATICAL INTERLUDE

5.1 Mathematics is a good place to turn to for analogs of structures, since mathematicians and mathematical logicians have as their business the construction of structures of the greatest variety and generality. For our purposes, we shall only have to venture into the most elementary phases of their activity (see the more elementary and readable portions of Quine 1940, Birkhoff and MacLane 1944).

A good many mathematical systems are characterizable wholly or primarily as consisting of a set of elements for which certain relations are defined. One such system has as elements all the positive integers, and as one elementary relation, the relation of 'greater than': two is greater than one, five is greater than two, and so on. A relation ties together pairs of elements, or, in some cases (for example, the relation 'is between ... and ...'), more than two elements. A relation is also quite satisfactorily definable as a class of ordered pairs (or of ordered n-ads with n greater than 2) of elements. In this sense, the number-pairs (3, 2), (5, 1), (2, 1) are said to be members of the relation 'greater than', while the number-pair (1, 3) or (1, 1) is not. The two approaches to relations are equivalent: we can begin with some property such as 'greater than' and observe that some pairs of numbers bear this relation, or we can begin with any set of ordered pairs of numbers—selected, it may be, quite randomly—and define a relation simply by listing the ordered pairs that belong to it.

Now it is easy to show that a construction, in the linguistic sense (within IA), is a relation (this proposal has not been made in print, to my knowledge; Wells has incorporated it in an as yet unpublished report on linguistics and semantics). The constituents of a constitute are elements; they are in a particular arrangement (linear order). A construction, then, is a class of ordered n-ads of constituents, whereupon a construction is a relation.

There is one point at which this characterization seems (wrongly) to fall down. Two and three are numbers; 'three is greater than two' is not a number, nor is (3, 2) a number. Black and cat are forms; and black cat is a form too. It makes sense to say that black cat participates, as a whole, as an element in larger constructions; it certainly does not make sense to say that (3, 2) is greater than something or

11 This comment on 'subtractives' and 'replacives' is given by Bloch in fn. 3 of Nida 1948. The error discussed here crops up also in Hockett 1947b, pp. 339–40 ((239–40)); Hockett 1950, pp. 82–3 ((326–7)); Harris 1942, pp. 170–1 ((110)).

less than something. This apparent discrepancy is due to the perhaps overly simple nature of the particular mathematical system we have chosen. It is hardly possible to say that (3, 2) can be greater than some number, but it is perfectly possible to define—in the arbitrary way mentioned above—a relation which has as members not only ordered pairs of numbers such as (3, 2) and (3, 1) but also ordered pairs of elements one or both of which are in turn ordered pairs of numbers—such as ((3, 2), 1) or (3, (2, 1)), or even ((3, 2), (3, 1)). Most such invented relations would be trivial and uninteresting, but some might be fruitful, and all are perfectly acceptable logically. So there is nothing to keep us from recognizing a relation in linguistics which has as members both such ordered pairs as <u>black cat</u> and also such as <u>big</u>⌐<u>black cat</u>.

5.2 Another great class of mathematical systems are characterizable as consisting of a set of elements for which certain <u>operations</u> are defined. One such system has, as did our exemplification of a system with relations, the positive integers as its elements, and has, as one elementary operation, that of <u>addition</u>. Addition applies in the first instance to pairs of positive integers, and is therefore a <u>binary</u> operation: two plus two is four, three plus four is seven, and so on. Addition has certain further properties. For instance, it is <u>commutative</u>: we get the same result adding two and three whether we start with the two or with the three. There are operations which are not commutative; e. g., subtraction defined over the same set of elements, since five minus seven is not only not the same as seven minus five, but actually meaningless. Addition is also <u>associative</u>: $(2 + 3) + 6$ and $2 + (3 + 6)$ add up to the same total. By virtue of this property, parentheses can be dropped, and the operation takes on the appearance of not being binary at all, but of applying to any number of terms, two or more. Fundamentally, however, it is convenient to regard addition as binary.

It can be shown that operations are reducible to relations, so far as their logical status is concerned. Thus the binary operation of addition, by which $2 + 3 = 5$, can also be interpreted as a ternary relation holding between the ordered triad of numbers (2, 3, 5) and between any ordered triad of numbers (a, b, c) for which it is true that $a + b = c$. In general, any n-ary operation is logically reducible to an appropriate (n + 1)-ary relation.

Psychologically, however, this replacement leaves something out. Relations seem static, whereas operations seem dynamic—seem to generate something which we perhaps did not know was there. One use of mathematical systems is in computing; that is, in discovering implications that are not known, or not obvious, to the computer until the computation has been performed. Computing makes use of systems involving operations, not those characterized purely by relations, underscoring the importance of the dynamic or generative nature of operations. Logical

identifications are always achieved by leaving something out; the mathematical logician is willing to leave out this psychological difference between relations and operations, but the ordinary mathematician is not. For our purposes, we shall follow the inclination of the ordinary mathematician.

5.3 There are two features of operations which may render them useful to us in linguistics, in place of relations—despite the logical substitutability which has been demonstrated.

One of these is the fact that the result of applying an operation to a pair (or set) of elements, or to a single element, is also an element. 'Two is greater than one', whatever it may be, is certainly not the same kind of element as are 'two' and 'one'. But two plus three is the same kind of element as are two and three; indeed, it is specifically that element, another name for which is 'five'. So if we say that <u>black</u> and <u>cat</u> are joined by an operation, instead of by a relation, we shall be more comfortable about calling <u>black cat</u> a form too.

The other is the fact that there are singular operations, but no singular relations. We see this from the logical substitutability of operations and relations. An n-ary operation is equivalent to an (n + 1)-ary relation, so that the obvious existence of binary relations guarantees equally obvious singular operations; but if there were singular relations there would have to be nullary operations, and the one is as meaningless as the other.[12]

An example of a singular operation in mathematics is 'reciprocal of' or 'negative of'. The latter is undefined for positive integers, but is defined for the set of all integers, positive, negative, and zero: the negative of three is minus three; the negative of minus four is four; the negative of zero is zero. For that matter, given a binary operation, any number of singular operations can be devised. If addition is a binary operation, the addition of two to, addition of three to, and so on, are all singular operations.

The utility of a singular operation for linguistic analysis can be demonstrated with a form like <u>waited</u> where, as we saw in 3.5, it is pointless to isolate more than two factors. It may be advantageous to interpret <u>waited</u> as the result of a singular operation applied to <u>wait</u>, at least in that this gives us just two separate factors.

5.4 If 'relation' is our closest analog to 'construction', then certainly the linguistic analog to 'operation' is 'process'. A grammatical model constructed in terms of this analogy ought to differ from IA just as operations differ from relations: it should be dynamic instead of static. It was pointed out in 1.2–4 that this was one of the chief characteristics of the older unformalized IP model, and we shall see that it is retained in the formal version about to be presented.

[12] Since a relation is a class of ordered n-ads, the singular analog is a class of ordered monads; i.e., simply a class. What a nullary operation would be still escapes me entirely.

VI. ITEM AND PROCESS

6.0 The statements which follow parallel, as much as possible, those of II, and are abbreviated where reference to II can easily serve to fill them in; examples are left for VII.

6.1 A linguistic form is either simple or derived.

6.2 A simple form is a root.[13]

6.3 A derived form consists of one or more underlying forms to which a process has been applied. The underlying forms and the process all recur (save for occasional uniquenesses) in other forms. The underlying form or forms is (or are) the immediate constituent(s) of the derived form, which is also called a constitute; each underlying form is said to occupy a given position; each, if there are more than one, is the partner of the rest.

6.4 Some of the phonemic material in a derived form may be, not part of any underlying form, but rather a representation or marker of the process. (Such markers are not roots.)

As in the parallel statement for IA (2.4), this necessitates a statement of conditions; we defer this to VII.

6.5 The tactical pattern of a language is completely covered by a set of statements of the following form:

(1) A list of the processes.

(2) Under each process as heading,

   (2.1) Enumeration of the position or positions involved.

   (2.2) For each position,

      (2.21) A list of the roots which occur in that position, and

      (2.22) A list of the processes which produce forms which occur in that position.

There is no analog to statement (2.2) of section 2.5.

6.6 A root may appear in more than a single phonemic shape. A single shape of a root is a root-alternant.

A process may have more than one representation. A single representation of a process is a marker. A marker consists of the difference between the phonemic shape of a derived form and the phonemic shape(s) of the underlying form or forms. That is, a marker may consist of phonemic material in some specific position relative to the phonemic material which is identical with that of the underlying form, or it may consist of something present in the derived form in place of something else present in the underlying form, etc.

6.7 The alternations in shape of roots, and the choice in a particular instance of one or another marker of a process, are predictable in terms of

the environments in which they occur (plus, of course, one's morphophonemic statements). 'Environment' is definable as in 2.7.

6.8 All the phonemic material in an utterance is accountable for in terms of the roots which occur in the utterance and the processes to which they have been subjected.

6.9 Empty root-alternants, portmanteau root-alternants, and links are definable and allowable as in IA, should there be any need for them. Zero alternant roots and zero markers of processes are likewise allowable, under similar limitations.

6.10 The statement of shapes, alternations, and conditions of alternation describes the morphophonemic pattern of the language; further considerations remain as in IA (2.11).

VII. COMPARISONS

7.1 First we give examples of IP treatment.

(1) Baked is a derived form, with a single immediate constituent bake, which happens to be a root, subjected to a singulary process which we can simply label past-tense formation. This process has various markers; when applied to bake, the marker is a /t/ which follows the phonemes of the underlying form.

(2) Took is tactically like baked, with underlying form take. The morphophonemic difference is that here the singulary process in question has a marker consisting of replacement of the stem vowel /ey/ of the underlying form by /u/.

(3) John and saw, subjected to the binary process of predication, give John saw, necessarily with that order, and with zero marker unless the order be taken as a marker. The same forms, subjected to the binary process of resolution, give saw John, again with order determined and zero marker. As with IA, we could alternatively take the order as primary and the process as determined. In support of the first alternative, we can present comparable cases in mathematics. If we are concerned with positive integers only, then the operation of subtraction, if it is to apply to seven and three, necessarily requires the order $7-3$, since $3-7$ is undefined.

(4) Chinese crau³ and fan⁴, subjected to either the binary process of resolution or the binary process of modification, give crau³ fan⁴, respectively 'fry rice' and 'fried rice'. The difference in positions of occurrence in larger forms, and the difference in meaning, correlate with the difference in process.

(5) John and Bill is (perhaps) the underlying forms John and Bill, subjected to the process of addition, for which the only marker is and. Bill and John is a different derived form, involving the same underlying forms and the same process, but a different order—order in this case being separable from process. Note that this process, here called 'addition', does not have the properties of the mathematical operation of the same name; grammatical addition

---

13 The choice of terminology is difficult here; I do not recommend continued use of 'root' and terms stemming from it. 'Morpheme' would be preferable, but is avoided here in order better to contrast the two models.

is not commutative. Indeed, probably no grammatical processes will be found to be commutative.[14]

7.2 Our IP model differs, at least superficially, from anything to be found in the writings of Sapir.

This is partly because we have tried to incorporate into the more formalized version of IP some of the results of recent investigations carried on within the IA framework. Mainly this means the contrast between tactics and morphophonemics, which does not emerge at all clearly either in Sapir's writings or in Bloomfield's 1933 discussion. It would be a loss of ground to expunge this contrast during the reconstruction of IP.

But its retention leads us to use the term 'process' in a way different from Sapir's use. For Sapir, such matters as vowel-change, suffixation, reduplication, and the like, were 'processes'. For us 'vowel-change' refers to one possible canonical form of marker, a canonical form represented both in men, from man, and in took, from take, though the markers in men and took represent tactically different processes in our sense of the word; the marker in took and the marker in baked, representing the same process in our sense, are of different canonical forms and thus would be different 'processes' in the Sapir sense. Nida's (1946) earlier contrast (derived closely from Sapir) between 'phonological process' and 'morphological process' approaches closely our contrast between canonical forms of markers, on the one hand, and tactically relevant processes on the other.

All this would be easier to say, and at the same time perhaps less necessary, had we abandoned the term 'process' and simply imported 'operation' from mathematics, or had we used such a pair of terms as 'processeme' (tactical) and 'alloprocess' (morphophonemic), as a direct splitting-up of Sapir's more nebulous notion of 'process' in the light of recent developments.

7.3 The examples of 7.1 show that, by and large, grammatical descriptions cast in IP will run parallel to those cast in IA. There will be slight differences in terminology, and the wording certainly gives a

14 The inventors of mathematics, as speaking humans, distill mathematical notions out of the raw-material of everyday language. Their notions are derived by leaving something out of the nearest everyday-language analogs. A linguist analyzing English must assume that two plus three and three plus two are different forms. The mathematician chooses to ignore everything which differentiates the meanings of these two forms, and by so doing, he renders his 'addition' commutative. It may seem strange that we who are concerned with the total complexity of language should turn to mathematics for help, considering the ultimate source of mathematics. But the circle is not in fact closed: the mathematician derives his notions by abstraction from language, whereas we are deriving, not language itself, but a way of handling language, from mathematics.

'dynamic' rather than a 'static' feel to the statements. Apart from these matters, the main differences will be marginal—though perhaps crucial.

IP obviates the major tactical and the major morphophonemic difficulty of IA. We are not confronted with superfluous machinery in the case of baked or took: the process involved is singulary, so that the only factors are the respective underlying forms and the process. The morphophonemic difficulty which IA gets into with took is obviated, since the whole frame of reference is one in which the difference between took and take is just as acceptable as that between baked and bake.

On the other hand, IP makes for certain difficulties avoided by IA.

In the first place, a 'pure' IA approach (which bars the interpretation of any morphemes as markers of constructions) is clearly much more homogeneous than either a less pure IA, or IP. This homogeneity is not as simple as has been thought: 'items', true enough, are either morphemes or sequences of morphemes, but still one has to contend with the independent status of order, constructions, and hierarchical structure. Even so, there is a clear difference between taking some phonemic material as 'root' (= item) and some as 'marker' of processes, as IP requires, and the simple procedure of taking all phonemic material as either morphemic or else morphemically irrelevant and morphophonemically predictable.

The problem of priority, evaded by IA, comes back into the picture. How are we to tell under what conditions to interpret a derived form as involving two or more underlying forms and a binary or higher-order process, and under what conditions to interpret it as involving a single underlying form and a singulary process? In one sense, of course, this is an extension to the case of two versus one of a problem found in IA: when do we recognize three ICs rather than two, or, in general, n rather than n−1?

The answer probably lies partly in the cases which are solved more easily by IP than by IA. Baked and took are interpreted in terms of a singulary process because to do otherwise leads to tactical and semantic trouble in both cases, and to morphophonemic trouble in the second. Obviously cases will be found more difficult than these, and a full elaboration of the necessary criteria is not to be expected overnight. In this very connection, IP is sure to encounter its refractory residue, different in content from, but similar in implications to, that of IA.

7.4 Another contrast between IA and IP turns on the number of constructions one has to recognize for a language under IA, versus the number of processes necessary for the same language under IP. The criterion of economy seems never to be invoked in IA so far as the number of morphemes is concerned: there are in any case a great many morphemes, and a few more or less hardly matters. But economy enters the picture in reducing the number of classes of morphemes, or the number of major form-classes, or constructions, as much as possible. This is why, when confronted with the doublet plurals brothers and brethren, we are willing either to recognize two homonymous stem-morphemes brother requiring different allomorphs of the noun-plural morpheme (Hockett 1947b, p. 330), or, if need be, to recognize that the plural element in brethren is, after all, a different morpheme from that in brothers (Ibid., and Nida 1948, p. 415, by implication). It hardly occurs to us to suspect that the constituents are the same but the construction different.

The same tendency also manifests itself in the effort sometimes made to reduce, if not the total number of constructions, at least the total number of construction-types—that is, classes of constructions which manifest some similarity of behavior. Thus in Chinese there is no way in which one can call hau^3 fan^4 'good food' (stative verb followed by noun) and ie^3 lai^2 'also come' (adverb followed by verb) instances of a single construction; their privileges of occurrence in larger stretches of speech are quite different. But one can say that the two constructions exemplified by these forms are, in their turn, instances of a single construction-type, sharing the features of endocentricity and of head second rather than first. Without much bother, one can establish a classification of all the constructions in Chinese into eight construction-types. To do so is esthetically satisfying, probably just because of the psychological impact of the criterion of economy; in addition, it affords a useful basis for the organization of tactical statements about Chinese.

Perhaps it does not matter, but if we follow IP we are going to have to sacrifice some of this partly covert drive towards one form of 'economy'. The number of processes in a language, under IP, will probably in general be greater than the number of constructions in the same language under IA. For brothers and brethren, the interpretation of two homophonous underlying forms is still open to us, but loses much of its attractiveness. There is only one alternative: a single underlying form (brother) with two different singulary processes. And while the singulary process involved in brothers (normal noun-plural formation) is one which recurs widely, that in brethren, since it contrasts with that in brothers, is presumably also different from the one in boys, men, taxes, and so on; it is as forlorn as a process as the first IC (under either IA or IP) of cranberry is forlorn as an item. Uniquenesses under IP, in other words, may be unique constituents or unique processes. The only possible way to appease our parsimoniousness is to devise process-types on the cross-model analogy of construction-types.

7.5 Whether a grammatical description of a language is satisfactory or not depends in part of the use we want to make of it. Quite apart from esthetic or stylistic considerations, which can and do vary from one reader of grammars to another, and setting aside such matters as application to language pedagogy, there remains a number of properties which a grammatical description must have if it is to satisfy us for any scientific purpose. These properties have already been hinted at (particularly in 3.0). A grammatical description must be a guidebook for the analysis of material in the language— both material examined by the analyst before the description was formulated, and material observed after that. Lexically the coverage need not be complete, since new morphemes can turn up as one continues to record the language. Otherwise it must be prescriptive, not of course in the Fiddith sense, but in the sense that by following the statements one must be able to generate any number of utterances in the language, above and beyond those observed in advance by the analyst—new utterances most, if not all, of which will pass the test of casual acceptance by a native speaker.

If these are criteria for the evaluation of a grammatical description, what we need for the evaluation of models is a set of appropriately related metacriteria. The following list is perhaps not complete, and I am hesitant about the fifth, but no set would be complete which did not include the first four:

(1) A model must be general: it must be applicable to any language, not just to languages of certain types.

(2) A model must be specific: when applied to a given language, the results must be determined wholly by the nature of the model and the nature of the language, not at all by the whim of the analyst. It is not lack of specificity if the model requires us to subsume certain facts more than once, from different angles; it would be a lack of specificity if the model allowed us to take our choice in such cases, instead of forcing one choice or other or their joint option.

(3) A model must be inclusive: when applied to a given language, the results must cover all the observed data and, by implication, at least a very high percentage of all the not-yet-observed data. This is the analog of the 'guidebook' criterion (not metacriterion) mentioned earlier.

(4) A model must be productive: when applied to a given language, the results must make possible the creation of an indefinite number of valid new utterances. This is the analog of the 'prescriptive' criterion for descriptions.

(5) A model must be efficient: its application to any given language should achieve the necessary results with a minimum of machinery.

If we were confronted with two models, one of which fulfilled all the above requirements while the other did not, choice would be easy. If we were confronted with two, both of which fulfilled all the requirements, we would have to conclude that they differed only stylistically. Neither of these situations, of course, is at present the case. Neither any existing version of IA nor any existing version of IP meets all the metacriteria. Insofar as such matters can be felt quantitatively, it seems to me that IP, as constructed here, comes at least as close to satisfying the requirements as IA does, though perhaps no closer. In other words, what we have is two main types of model, neither completely satisfactory. Our course in this case is also clear. We must have more experimentation, as much with one model as with the other—and with the devising of further models too, for that matter—looking towards an eventual reintegration into a single more nearly satisfactory model, but not forcing that reintegration until we are ready for it.

BIBLIOGRAPHY

Birkhoff, Garrett, and Saunders MacLane, 1944: A survey of modern algebra. New York.

Bloch, Bernard, 1946: Studies in colloquial Japanese: I Inflection, JAOS 66.97–109; II Syntax, Lang. 22.200–48 ((154)); III Derivation of inflected words, JAOS 66.304–15.

———, 1947: English verb inflection. Lang. 23.399–418 ((243)).

Bloomfield, Leonard, 1933: Language. New York.

Boas, Franz, 1911: Introduction. Handbook of American Indian Languages, part 1, 1–83. Washington.

Gardner, Elizabeth F., 1950: The inflections of modern literary Japanese. Lang. Dissertation No. 46.

Haas, Mary, 1946: A grammatical sketch of Tunica. LSNA 337–66. VFPA 6. New York.

Harris, Zellig S., 1942: Morpheme alternants in linguistic analysis. Lang. 18.169–80 ((109)).

———, 1944: Yokuts structure and Newman's grammar. IJAL 10.196–211.

———, 1945a: Discontinuous morphemes. Lang. 21.121–7.

———, 1945b: review of M. B. Emeneau, Kota Texts; Part I. Lang. 21.283–9.

———, 1946: From morpheme to utterance. Lang. 22.161–83 ((142)).

———, 1948: Componential analysis of a Hebrew paradigm. Lang. 24.87–91 ((272)).

———, 1951: Methods in Structural Linguistics. Chicago.

Hockett, C. F., 1947a: review of E. A. Nida, Morphology[1]. Lang. 23.274–85.

———, 1947b: Problems of morphemic analysis. Lang. 23.321–43 ((229)).

———, 1948: review of LSNA. Lang. 24.183–8.

———, 1950: Peiping morphophonemics. Lang. 26.63–85 ((315)).

Newman, Stanley S., 1944: Yokuts language of California. VFPA 2, New York.

Nida, E. A., 1946: Morphology, the descriptive analysis of words[1]. Ann Arbor.

———, 1948: The identification of morphemes. Lang. 24.414–41 ((255)).

———, 1949: Morphology: the descriptive analysis of words[2]. Ann Arbor.

Pittman, R. S., 1948: Nuclear structures in linguistics. Lang. 24.287–92 ((275)).

Quine, W. V., 1940: Mathematical Logic. New York.

Sapir, Edward, 1921: Language. New York.

———, 1930: The Southern Paiute language. Proceedings, American Academy of Arts and Sciences 65:1 (1–296), 2 (297–536), 3 (537–730).

———, 1933: The psychological reality of phonemes. Journal de psychologie normale et pathologique 30.247–65; reprinted in D. G. Mandelbaum, editor, SWES (Berkeley and Los Angeles, 1949), 46–60.

Wells, R. S., 1947: Immediate constituents. Lang. 23.81–117 ((186)).

———, 1949: Automatic alternation. Lang. 25.99–116.

Yokoyama, M., 1950: The inflections of 8th-century Japanese. Lang. Dissertation No. 45.

READINGS IN
LINGUISTICS II

THE THEORY OF PHONEMES, AND ITS IMPORTANCE IN PRACTICAL LINGUISTICS

Daniel Jones

The idea of the phoneme is best seen from concrete illustrations. The *k*'s in *keep, call, cool* are different sounds, but belong to one phoneme. The voiceless *l̥* used in French when a word like *oncle* is final belongs to the same phoneme as the ordinary French *l*. The sound *ŋ* must be assigned to the *n*-phoneme in Italian: it "replaces" *n* before *k* and *g*.

h, *ç* and *φ* all occur in Japanese, but they must be regarded as members of one phoneme. *h* only occurs before *e*, *a* and *o*; *ç* only before *i*; and *φ* only before *u*.

DEFINITION OF A PHONEME

A family of sounds in a given language, which are related in character and are such that no one of them ever occurs in the same surroundings as any other in words. (The term "language" here means the pronunciation of one individual speaking in a definite style. "In the same surroundings" means surrounded by the same sounds and in the same condition as regards length, stress and intonation.)

The phoneme must be distinguished from the diaphone and from the variphone. The phoneme is a family of sounds occurring in the speech of a single person. The diaphone is a family of sounds heard when we compare the speech of one person with that of another. For instance, if we listen to a number of English speakers saying the word *coat*, we generally hear several varieties of vowel. The usual sound is diphthongal (*ou*), but with some speakers the initial element is closer and with others opener. With some, especially in the North of England, the *o* is near to a French or German *o*; in the South the sound is opener and has less lip-rounding; in London dialect the diphthong is actually *ʌu* or *ɐu*. On the other hand, in Scotland one often hears a mono-phthongal *oː*. These sounds *oː*, *ou* (several varieties), *ʌu*, *ɐu* are said to belong to the same diaphone, in such English words as *coat, road, home*.

The variphone is again different. It occasionally happens that a speaker uses one of two or more sounds absolutely indifferently and apparently at random. The Japanese *r* furnishes a good illustration. A single speaker will sometimes pronounce it very much like an English *r* and sometimes as a sound resembling *l*. But he does not do this according to a definite system as in the case of members of the same phoneme; when he says any particular word (say *mira*, to see), he sometimes says it with English *r* and sometimes with this *l*-like sound and sometimes with an actual *l*. He is unaware that his pronunciation varies. These three sounds may be said to constitute a variphone. Variphones are found in some varieties of German, where *p* and *b*, *ʃ* and *ʒ*, and other corre-sponding voiced and voiceless consonants are apparently used indifferently.

PRACTICAL IMPORTANCE OF THE PHONEME

The grouping of sounds into phonemes enables us to construct the simplest systems of phonetic transcription for every language. A system of transcription is unambiguous if one letter is provided for each phoneme of the language. It is not necessary to provide letters for subsidiary members of phonemes, since these values are determined by the surroundings.

Reformed orthographies should be based on this principle.

It follows from the definition that phonemes have a semantic function in language, but different sounds belonging to the same phoneme have no semantic function. (This is because the sounds of different phonemes can occur in identical situations, but sounds belonging to the same phoneme cannot occur in one word from another.) So the phoneme theory also has a bearing on practical language teaching. When a person is obliged to learn the elements of a language quickly, and has not time to master all the details of the pronunciation, he should concentrate on the principal members of each phoneme.

Reprinted from *Proceedings [First] International Congress of Phonetic Sciences*, 1932, pp. 23–24, with the permission of Hollandsche Maatschappij der Wetenschappen.

DAS MORDWINISCHE PHONOLOGISCHE SYSTEM VERGLICHEN MIT DEM RUSSISCHEN

N. S. Trubetzkoy

Die Frage, ob zwischen dem phonologischen System und dem grammatischen Bau einer Sprache ein innerer Zusammenhang besteht, kann nur nach eingehenden Untersuchungen entschieden werden. Dabei müssen vor allem Sprachen mit identischen oder ähnlichen phonologischen Systemen bei grundsätzlich verschiedenem grammatischem Baue mit einander verglichen werden. Ein lehrreiches Beispiel dieser Art bietet der Vergleich des Russischen mit dem Mordwinischen.[1] Diese zwei Sprachen sind in grammatischer Hinsicht grundsätzlich verschieden, da das Russische eine indogermanische, das Mordwinische dagegen — eine finnischugrische Sprache ist. Hiebei ist aber das Inventar der Sprachlaute in beiden Sprachen beinahe das gleiche.[2] Freilich besitzen gewisse gemeinsame Lautgegensätze im Mordwinischen nicht immer denselben phonologischen Wert, wie im Russischen.[3] Immerhin sind die phonologischen Systeme des Mordwinischen und des Russischen einander so ähnlich, daß die Mordwinen für ihre Sprache das russische Alphabet ohne irgendwelche Zusätze und Veränderungen verwenden, ohne dabei die geringste Schwierigkeit zu empfinden.

Die Ähnlichkeit besteht jedoch bloß im Phonemenrepertoire (gleiche Archiphoneme, gleiche Korrelationen.[4] In der phonologischen Funktions- und Kombinationslehre gehen beide Sprachen auseinander. Der Unterschied läßt sich so formulieren : — *der Verlust (oder die Neutralisierung) irgendeiner phonologischen Eigenschaft eines Phonems geschieht im Russischen unter dem Einfluße des folgenden, im Mordwinischen dagegen unter dem Einfluße des vorhergehenden Phonems* (bezw. der "Laut-Null"). Nach diesen Grundsätzen werden in beiden Sprachen sowohl die Stimmbeteiligungskorrelation[5] als auch die Mouillierungskorrelation,[6] und speziell im Mordwinischen auch noch die Annäherungskorrelation[7] behandelt. Man darf also sagen, daß die mordwinischen Lautregeln meistens *regressiv*, die russischen dagegen *progressiv* orientiert sind.[8] Im Zusammenhange mit dieser allgemeinen regressiven Orientierung der mordwinischen Phonologie steht die dem Mordwinischen eigene *Sonderstellung der ersten Wortsilbe*. Die fünf Vokalphoneme u, o, a, e werden nur in der ersten

---

Reprinted from *Charisteria V. Mathesio oblata*, pp. 21-24 (Prague: Cercle Linguistique de Prague, 1932), with the permission of Bohumil Trnka, secretary of Cercle Linguistique de Prague.

[1] Wir beschränken uns hier auf die mordwinische Schriftsprache, die auf den erza-mordwinischen Dialekte des Dorfes Kozlovka beruht. Vgl. die Beschreibung dieser Sprache bei Prof. D. V. Bubrich, Звуки и формы эрзанской речи (Moskau, 1930) vgl. ferner auch M. E. Evsevjev, Основы мордовской грамматики (Moskau, 1929).

[2] Vgl. die Äusserungen D. V. Bubrichs in *Sborník prací I. Sjezdu Slovanských Filologů v Praze 1929* (Praha, 1932) s. 455 ff.

[3] So ist der Gegensatz zwischen exspiratorisch starken ("betonten") und schwachen ("unbetonten") Vokalen im Russischen phonologisch gültig, im Mordwinischen dagegen nicht (vgl. Bubrich, Звуки и формы, S. 23, § 32). — Ebenso steht es mit dem Gegensatze zwischen mouillierten und nicht mouillierten Labialen, der im Mordwinischen rein äusserlich bedingt ist (vor und nach e, i sind alle Labiale mouilliert, in allen übrigen Stellungen — nicht mouilliert). — Das schriftmordwinische v steht in kombinatorischem Variantenverhältnis zu u, — indem v (bezw. v́ vor e, i) nur vor Vokalen, u (bezw. ŭ nach e, i) nur vor Konsonanten und im Auslaute auftreten, — und darf zu den Sonorlaut-Phonemen gerechnet werden, während das russische v/v́ ein Geräuschlaut (freilich, ein Geräuschlaut besonderer Art) ist. — Da das mordwinische č (im Gegensatz zum russischen) dieselbe Artikulationsstelle wie š/ž aufweist, und da neben das mordw. c auch ein mouilliertes ć besteht (was im Russischen nicht der Fall ist), so ist das Verhältnis s : c = š : č = ś : ć im Mordwinischen ein korrelatives ("Annäherungskorrelation") während im Russischen c, s disjunkte Phoneme sind. — Zu den Begriffen des "phonologischen Wertes", der "disjunktiven" und "korrelativen" Phoneme usw. vgl. unsere "Polabische Studien" (= *Sitzungsberichte der Akad. d. Wiss. in Wien, phil.-hist. Klasse*, 211/4) S. 111 ff, und "Die phonologischen Systeme" (in *Travaux du Cercle Linguistique de Prague* IV, S. 96 ff.).

[4] Und zwar : — Gemeinsame Archiphoneme sind U, O, A, E, I, P, T, K, F, S, Š, X, R, L, M, N, J; ausserdem besitzt das Russische noch Ṡ (щ, шч), Č (ч), C (die mordw. c, ć gehören zum Archiphonem S), und das Mordwinische — V (als Sonorlaut; die russ. v, v́ gehören zum Archiphonem F); — gemeinsame Korrelationen sind : die kons. Stimmbeteiligungskorrelation und die kons. Mouillierungskorrelation; ausserdem besitzt das Russische die vokal. Intensitätskorrelation (u : ŭ = a : ă = i : ĭ) und das Mordwinische — die Annäherungskorrelation (s : c = ś : ć = š : č).

[5] Bei der Verbindung mehrerer Geräuschlaute im Inlaute richten sich im Russischen alle Geräuschlaute hinsichtlich der Stimmbeteiligung nach dem letzten (kášit́ "mähen" ~ kážba "das Mähen", kálodá "grosser Holzblock" ~ kálotḱi "kleiner Holzblock, Leiste"). Im Mordwinischen geschieht dasselbe nur dann, wenn der folgende Geräuschlaut stimmlos ist (z.B. kuz "Tanne", ~ kustomo "ohne Tanne"); ist er aber von Haus aus stimmhaft, — so wird er nach stimmlosen Geräuschlauten selbst stimmlos (kudo "Haus", — Ablat. kudodo, kuz, "Tanne" ~ kuzdo, aber šokš "Topf" ~ Ablat. šokšto). Im Russischen sind die auslautenden Geräuschlaute hinsichtlich der Stimmbeteiligung neutralisiert und werden *vor* stimmhaften Geräuschlauten stimmhaft, in allen übrigen Stellungen stimmlos realisiert (naž dom "unser Haus" ~ naš ́ďec "unser Vater", nož d́ad́i "das Messer des Onkels", noš ́ďca "das Messer des Vaters"). Im Mordwinischen sind, im Gegenteil, die anlautenden Geräuschlaute hinsichtlich der Stimmbeteiligung neutralisiert und werden *nach* einer Pause und *nach* stimmlosen Lauten stimmlos, in den übrigen Stellungen stimmhaft realisiert (z. B. panar "Hemd", oŕak panar "ziehe ein Hemd an!" ~ ašo banar "weisses Hemd", od banar "neues Hemd", čoraň banarzo "ziehe das Hemd des Burschen"). — Nur in mehrsilbigen Wörtern werden im Mordwinischen auslautende Mediae stimmlos, jedoch nicht im Satzzusammenhange, sondern nur vor einer Pause. Diese Regel (deren Spielraum ohnehin schon sehr eng ist) kennt jedoch Ausnahmen : auslautendes ž bewahrt in mehrsilbigen Verbalformen auch vor der Pause seine Stimmhaftigkeit.

[6] In Hinsicht auf Mouillierung werden im Russischen die Konsonanten in gewissen Stellungen phonologisch neutralisiert : *vor* vortonigem ă werden alle Konsonanten, *vor* unmouillierten Dentalen alle Konsonanten ausser l, *vor* inlautendem u, ŭ alle Labiale immer unmouilliert, *vor* e alle Konsonanten immer mouilliert, *vor* v́ und *vor* mouillierten Dentalen die s-Laute mouilliert, die übrigen Konsonanten (ausser l) unmouilliert oder halbmouilliert gesprochen. Im Mordwinischen geschieht eine solche phonologische Neutralisierung des Eigentons nicht vor, sondern *nach* gewissen Phonemen. Und zwar werden alle Dentale ausser s, z, c, *nach* e, i und *nach* mouillierten Dentalen mouilliert und *nach* unmouillierten Dentalen unmouilliert gesprochen. Progressive Eigentonangleichung geschieht nur vor mouillierten l, ś und ź.

[7] Und zwar werden nach Dentalen nur die Affrikaten c, ć (bezw. dz, dź, die nur in dieser Stellung vorkommen) gesprochen. Empfunden werden sie aber als s, ś (bezw. z, ź), da die Spiranten s : c "merkmallosen" Glieder der Annäherungskorrelation sind.

[8] Der Vollständigkeit halber sei noch erwähnt, dass es im Mordwinischen auch eine nach beiden Richtungen orientierte Lautregel gibt : Geräuschlaute, die sich nicht unmittelbar mit einem Vokale berühren sind hinsichtlich der Stimmbeteiligung phonologisch neutral und werden stimmlos realisiert (daher z. B. andoms "nähren" ~ frequent. antnems usw.).

aber auch weiter, fügt ein Element an das andere, und die regressiv orientierten Lautregeln dehnen somit ihre Wirkung auf das ganze Wort aus. Der grammatische Bau des Mordwinischen ist rationell und regelmäßig. Er lässt keine Ausnahmen, keine unrationelle Mannigfaltigkeit der Paradigmen zu. Alles ist streng vorgeschrieben und der Spielraum der freien Wahl ist auf ein Mindestmaß eingeschränkt. Es gibt eine beschränkte Anzahl scharf umrissener, streng bestimmter grammatischer Schemen, in die jeder Gedanke hineingezwängt werden muß. Natürlich sind diese Schemen ziemlich grob gezeichnet, und lassen für feinere Nuancen wenig Raum. Dieser Art schematisch regelmäßigen Sprachdenkens entspricht auch die mordwinische Phonologie, die von der freien Ausnützung der Korrelations-Gegensätze wenig Gebrauch macht, und vorwiegend mit Archiphonemen operiert. Der phonologischen Eintönigkeit des Mordwinischen entspricht auch die Eintönigkeit des grammatischen Baues dieser Sprache. Somit zeigt das Mordwinische einen völligen Parallelismus zwischen dem phonologischen und dem grammatischen Sprachbau.

Wortsilbe als wirklich selbständige Phoneme behandelt. In den übrigen Silben ist das Auftreten der Vokallaute o, e, u rein äußerlich, und zwar durch regressiv orientierte Lautregeln bedingt, wobei o und e als kombinatorische Varianten eines einzigen Phonems betrachtet werden dürfen.[9] Somit ist der Vokalismus der ersten Silbe von dem der übrigen Silben grundsätzlich verschieden, und da auch die anlautenden Konsonanten eine besondere Behandlung aufweisen,[10] so bekommt die erste Wortsilbe überhaupt eine phonologische Sonderstellung. — Endlich fällt es auf, daß die *Korrelations-Gegensätze* im Mordwinischen im Vergleiche mit dem Russischen *verhältnismäßig wenig ausgenützt* sind. Die vokalischen Intensitätsgegensätze, die im Russischen eine so große Rolle spielen, sind dem Mordwinischen ganz fremd. Die Mouillierungskorrelation, die sich im Russischen auf Dentale und Labiale erstreckt, ist im Mordwinischen nur auf die Dentale beschränkt. Was die Stimmbeteiligungskorrelation betrifft, so bilden in der russischen Rede die stimmhaften (also merkmalhaltigen) Geräuschlaute 37%, die stimmlosen (also merkmallosen) 39% und die hinsichtlich der Stimmbeteiligung phonologisch neutralen (z. B. auslautenden usw.) nur 24%, während in der mordwinischen Rede die stimmhaften 18%, die stimmlosen 38,7% und die phonologisch neutralisierten 43,3% bilden.[11]

Alle diese Eigentümlichkeiten der mordwinischen Phonologie hängen aufs engste mit dem grammatischen Baue des Mordwinischen zusammen. Als typische "turanische" Sprache kennt das Mordwinische keine Präfixe. Die erste Wortsilbe ist somit immer eine *Wurzelsilbe*, wodurch ihre Sonderstellung auch vom grammatischen Gesichtspunkte berechtigt erscheint. Das Mordwinische kennt keine grammatisch verwertete Veränderung der Lautgestalt der Wurzel. Das einzige Mittel der Formbildung ist die Agglutination, d. i. das Anhängen, Anreihen formativer Elemente an die unveränderte Wurzel. Die regressiv orientierten Lautregeln verbürgen die maximale Unveränderlichkeit der Lautgestalt der Wurzel und dienen zugleich als ein Bindemittel, das die formativen Elemente fest mit der Wurzel vereinigt. Die Agglutination wirkt

---

[9] Und zwar darf o in nichterster Silbe nur nach unmouillierten Konsonanten stehen, dabei nur nach einer Silbe mit, u, o, a; dagegen kommt e nach mouillierten Konsonanten nur dann vor, wenn die vorhergehende Silbe e, oder i enthält; nach mouillierten Konsonanten tritt e ohne Rücksicht auf den Vokal der vorhergehenden Silbe auf. Somit ist der Gegensatz zwischen o und e, der in erster Wortsilbe Bedeutungsunterschiede bewirken kann (z. B. kov "Mond" ~ kev "Stein") in nichterster Silbe rein äußerlich, phonetisch bedingt. Der Vokal u kommt in nichterster Silbe nach unmouillierten Konsonanten zwischen einer Silbe mit u, o, a und einer mit o (aber nicht a, i vor (z. B. amal'ams "schöpfen", kulcuni "er hört"). In derselben Stellung darf auch o (aber nicht a) vor e stehen (z. B. kudoška "wie ein Haus"). — Vgl. unseren Aufsatz "Zur allgemeinen Theorie der phonologischen Vokalsysteme" (*Travaux du Cercle Linguistique de Prague* I, S. 39 ff.), besonders S. 58 f.

[10] Wie bereits erwähnt (s. oben Fussn. 5), sind die anlautenden Geräuschlaute hinsichtlich der Stimmbeteiligung neutralisiert. Der Gegensatz zwischen stimmhaften und stimmlosen Geräuschlauten, der im Inlaute und Auslaute Bedeutungsunterschiede bewirken kann (z. B. kozo "wohin" ~ koso "wo", lugaš "die Wiese" ~ lukaš "lukaš bewegte sich hin und her", ked' "Hand" ~ ket' "Hände", noldaź "noldaś gelassen" ~ noldaš "liess"), ist im Anlaute rein äußerlich, phonetisch bedingt (z. B. orčam panar "ich ziehe ein Hemd an" ~ orčak panar "ziehe ein Hemd an !"). Im Anlaute sind die Dentale ausser s, z vor e immer mouilliert, während im Inlaute vor e auch unmouillierte Dentale stehen dürfen (śeste "von dort").

[11] Diese Zahlen sind aus dem als Anhang zu D. V. Bubrichs "Звуки и формы эрзянской речи" abgedruckten mordwinischen Texte und seiner russischen Übersetzung gewonnen. Beide Texte sind nicht sehr umfangreich (der mordwinische enthält ca. 1120, der russische ca. 1180 Phoneme). Wir glauben aber, dass die Prozentverhältnisse auch in grösseren Texten ungefähr dieselben sind. Es wäre interessant eine genauere Statistik der Ausnützung mordwinischer Phoneme nach V. Mathesius's Methode durchzuführen.

DÉRIVATION LEXICALE ET DÉRIVATION SYNTAXIQUE (CONTRIBUTION À LA THÉORIE DES PARTIES DU DISCOURS)[1]

Jerzy Kuryłowicz

Il existe un rapport entre la valeur lexicale d'une partie du discours et ses fonctions syntaxiques. Ce rapport est reflété par la direction des procès de dérivation et semble indépendant des particularités individuelles des systèmes linguistiques.

Tout récemment, M. Slotty[2] a mis en relief le double caractère des parties du discours. D'après lui elles représentent des catégories (de mots) possédant d'une part une valeur lexicale (ou sémantique) très générale, et d'autre part une fonction syntaxique déterminée. Ainsi par exemple le substantif désigne un objet et fonctionne en même temps comme sujet et régime, l'adjectif désigne une qualité et fonctionne en même temps comme épithète, le verbe désigne un changement ou un état (transitoire) ou une action et fonctionne en même temps comme prédicat, etc. Mais d'autre part il y a par exemple des formes qui désignent une action et fonctionnent comme sujets ou régimes (abstraits verbaux) ; il y a les adjectifs " anaphoriques ", qui sont de véritables adjectifs quant à leur valeur lexicale, mais qui fonctionnent comme des substantifs au point de vue syntaxique ; il y a les participes, dont la valeur lexicale est celle du verbe personnel correspondant, mais qui pourraient aussi être qualifiés d'adjectifs en vue de leur fonction syntaxique ; etc. Par là même l'essai de M. Slotty d'établir une corrélation entre valeur lexicale et fonction syntaxique semble, *à première vue*, une de ces constructions philosophiques qui réclament une place d'honneur dans la grammaire générale, mais qui, n'étant directement applicables à aucune langue réelle, sont destinées à rester infécondes et sans portée pour la linguistique au sens propre. En effet, dira-t-on, si une valeur lexicale donnée peut être combinée avec n'importe quelle fonction syntaxique, n'y a-t-il pas là une preuve éclatante de l'indépendance des deux séries de valeurs ou fonctions grammaticales (valeurs lexicales ou sémantiques d'une part, valeurs syntaxiques de l'autre part) ? Si tel est le cas, s'il y a indépendance

de ces deux classes de fonctions, on pourra établir les parties du discours en partant de l'une ou de l'autre fonction, c'est-à-dire soit du point de vue lexical, soit du point de vue syntaxique. Suivant qu'on adopte l'un ou l'autre, on dira que dans des exemples comme : *le roi* (*est mort*) et (*Louis XIV*) *le roi* (*de France*) on a affaire à des parties du discours identiques ou différentes. La conclusion serait : 1º la distinction entre substantif, adjectif, verbe, adverbe ne peut être faite que d'un seul point de vue (le point de vue lexical étant celui qui importe, comme on verra plus bas) ; 2º il n'y a pas de rapport entre la valeur lexicale et la fonction syntaxique. La première conclusion serait aussi juste, mais contre la seconde affirmation la grammaire traditionnelle aussi bien que les linguistes praticiens vont protester et pour de bonnes raisons. Du fait qu'un mot désignant une qualité (c'est-à-dire un adjectif) peut fonctionner soit comme épithète, soit comme attribut (prédicat), il ne s'ensuit pas que toutes ces fonctions syntaxiques soient au même degré essentielles ou caractéristiques de la partie du discours en question. Autrement dit, le praticien s'en tiendra à la notion de *fonction syntaxique primaire* (*et fonctions syntaxiques secondaires*), qu'on trouve déjà chez M. Slotty *l. c.* Mais il va sans dire qu'un fondement *objectif* de la distinction entre fonction primaire et fonction secondaire doit être cherché d'abord dans la langue elle-même, c'est-à-dire dans *des critères formels*, et non pas en dehors de la langue, par exemple dans les conditions générales de la réalité ou de la vie psychique. Or la loi générale concernant le rapport de la fonction syntaxique primaire aux fonctions syntaxiques secondaires, est celle-ci :

Si le changement de la fonction syntaxique d'une forme (d'un mot) A entraîne le changement formel de A en B (la fonction lexicale restant la même), est fonction syntaxique primaire celle qui correspond à la forme-base, et fonction syntaxique secondaire celle qui correspond à la forme dérivée.

Exemples : entre lat. *amat* et *amans* il n'y a qu'une différence de fonction syntaxique. La valeur lexicale (action) est la même dans les deux cas. Mais comme c'est le participe qui est dérivé du verbe personnel et non pas inversement, on dira que chez les mots à valeur lexicale *action* (c'est-à-dire chez les verbes) la fonction prédicative est primaire et la fonction d'épithète, secondaire. De même, si par exemple en germanique l'adjectif faible est dérivé de l'adjectif fort, c'est la preuve que la fonction d'épithète est la fonction primaire de l'adjectif et que la fonction anaphorique en est une fonction secondaire. Les différences formelles entre fonction primaire et fonctions secondaires peuvent être inhérentes non pas aux mots, mais aux groupes dont le mot en question fait partie. Au lieu de parler d'une différence de forme il vaudra mieux se servir du terme différence d'entourage syntaxique ou de conditions syntaxiques. Ainsi dans la plupart des langues indo-européennes modernes l'adjectif attribut est dérivé de l'adjectif épithète moyennant le verbe *être*, par exemple *rouge : est rouge*. Dans la langue russe, où la forme simple (= non composée) de l'adjectif slave a été conservée dans l'usage prédicatif, cette forme simple est dérivée de la forme composée employée comme épithète. La direction du procès de dérivation a changé par suite du changement de l'emploi syntaxique des formes.

Reprinted from *Bulletin de la Société de Linguistique de Paris* 37 (1936) : 79–92, with the permission of the author and of M. Perrot of the Société de Linguistique de Paris.

[1] Communication présentée au Congrès Linguistique de Copenhague.
[2] Dans *Problem der Wortarten* (Forschungen und Fortschritte VIII [1932], p. 329–330).

un autre rôle syntaxique que la forme-base et par conséquent étant muni d'un morphème syntaxique ("Feldzeichen" chez M. Karl Bühler, *Sprachtheorie*, p. 35); par exemple flexion en *-n-* de l'adjectif germanique; place fixe du régime par rapport au verbe; article servant à "substantiver": τὸ νῦν, *das Hier und Jetzt*, etc. (on a vu plus haut que le *Feldzeichen* pouvait être inhérent au mot ou à une unité syntaxique supérieure). Il en résulte des formes qu'il semble, au premier coup d'œil, difficile de loger dans les classes traditionnelles. L'adjectif anaphorique (par exemple le type slave *dobrъ-jь*) est généralement classé parmi les adjectifs, de même un cas adverbial comme lat. *ferrō* n'est, à nos yeux, qu'une forme spéciale du substantif, les deux en vertu de leur sens lexical, tandis que par exemple un mot comme français *franchement* est considéré comme un adverbe à cause de sa fonction syntaxique, et que parfois on crée une classe spéciale pour caser le participe, lequel est un verbe au point de vue lexical et un adjectif au point de vue de sa fonction syntaxique primaire. Il est vrai que dans la grammaire on s'en tient plutôt à la fonction lexicale, ce qui est juste, et l'on groupe le participe avec le verbe personnel, et l'adjectif anaphorique, avec l'adjectif épithète. Toutefois on n'ose pas grouper avec les adjectifs les soi-disant adverbes en *-ment* et les formations analogues des autres langues, mais on s'en occupe dans le chapitre consacré aux véritables adverbes (de circonstance). Or il est clair que le morphème *-ment* est un morphème syntaxique ("Feldzeichen") ajouté à l'adjectif, non pas pour changer son sens lexical, mais pour en faire un déterminant syntaxique du verbe. On procède de manière analogue quand on ajoute la désinence d'accusatif à un substantif pour lui conférer la fonction de régime direct (déterminant du verbe transitif): le substantif ne devient pas pour cela un adverbe, il conserve sa valeur sémantique fondamentale, puisque la désinence n'est qu'un morphème syntaxique qui ne modifie guère cette valeur.

Dès lors il n'est pas difficile de comprendre en quoi la *dérivation syntaxique* diffère de ce qu'on pourrait appeler *dérivation lexicale* et qui est appelé *dérivation* tout court. Toute comme la dérivation syntaxique se déroule à l'intérieur d'un seule et même valeur lexicale (par exemple adjectif épithète → adjectif anaphorique, la valeur lexicale restant la même), tout ainsi la dérivation lexicale suppose que le mot-base et le dérivé sont identiques quant à leur fonction syntaxique primaire. Ainsi quand on bâtit un diminutif sur un substantif donné, ce diminutif, étant substantif, aura les mêmes fonctions syntaxiques que le mot-base. Même chose quand d'un verbe perfectif on dérive un verbe imperfectif. Mais l'état des choses n'est pas tellement transparent dans tous les cas. Dans un exemple comme français *rouge* (adjectif): (*le*) *rouge* (= crayon rouge) on distingue en même temps un changement de fonction syntaxique primaire (puisque la partie du discours est différente dans les deux cas), et un changement du contenu lexical (puisque *le rouge*, étant le nom d'un objet, implique encore d'autres qualités en dehors de la couleur rouge). On peut donc décomposer le procès de dérivation en deux étapes: 1° une étape de dérivation syntaxique: adjectif épithète → adjectif anaphorique; 2° une étape de dérivation lexicale:[3] adjectif anaphorique → substantif. Le mot-base de français (*le*) *rouge* (= crayon rouge) est donc en réalité l'adjectif anaphorique

[3] Cf. les termes *substantivation syntaxique* et *substantivation sémantique* (c'est-à-dire *lexicale*) de M. Jellinek (PBB XXXIV, p. 582).

La direction de la dérivation actuelle est donnée par la juxtaposition de couples comme

{*belyj* / *bel*} d'une part, {*malenkij* / *malenkij*} de l'autre,

la coexistence desquels suppose le rapport *belyj* (base) → *bel* (dérivé).

Dans le cas assez fréquent où il y a identité phonétique entre le cas sujet et le cas régime, il existe néanmoins un rapport de dérivation entre ces deux emplois syntaxiques du substantif, lequel peut être formulé de la manière suivante : On dérive le cas régime du cas sujet en lui attribuant une place déterminée par rapport au verbe (par exemple après le verbe ou immédiatement après le verbe). La place du cas-régime est *caractérisée* ou *motivée*, celle du cas sujet étant *non-caractérisée* ou *immotivée*. On voit que dans la dérivation syntaxique (autrement que dans la dérivation lexicale) on se sert non seulement d'éléments suffixaux, de désinences, etc. mais aussi de morphèmes inhérents au groupe et non pas au mot ("Gestaltqualitäten").

Il suit de ce qui précède que les mots possèdent une fonction syntaxique primaire en vertu même de leur sens lexical (*substantif: sujet, adjectif: déterminant-épithète du substantif, verbe: prédicat, adverbe: déterminant du verbe*), et que tout emploi dans une fonction syntaxique autre que la fonction primaire est un emploi *motivé* et *caractérisé* au point de vue formel. L'analyse structurale de la langue prouve donc que la doctrine "démodée" qui établissait des corrélations entre les fonctions syntaxiques et les parties du discours, ne manquait pas de fondement. L'objection qu'une partie du discours peut jouer n'importe quel rôle dans la structure syntaxique du groupe ou de la phrase, n'a pas tenu compte du fait qu'il existe une *hiérarchie* entre les différentes fonctions syntaxiques d'une partie du discours donnée, et que pour chaque partie du discours il existe une fonction-base ou fonction primaire. Bien que nous soyons d'accord avec M. Brøndal en postulant une distinction sévère des fonctions lexicales et des fonctions syntaxiques des mots et en soutenant le caractère foncièrement lexical des parties du discours (*L'autonomie de la syntaxe*, Journal de Psychologie XXX (1933), p. 217 ss.; *Ordklasserne*, p. 234–5), nous maintenons, d'autre part, que les fonctions syntaxiques primaires découlent des valeurs lexicales des parties du discours et en représentent en quelque sorte une transposition. C'est ce que nous enseigne la dérivation au sens large du terme, c'est-à-dire non seulement le fait que certains mots sont dérivés d'autres mots pour rendre une fonction syntaxique différente de celle du mot-base, mais aussi le fait que le même mot peut présenter des valeurs syntaxiques *secondaires* dans un entourage syntaxique *caractérisé*. Quant à la théorie de M. Slotty, nous admettons qu'il a eu raison d'attribuer aux parties du discours une valeur lexicale (sémantique) et une fonction syntaxique propre à chacune, mais il n'a pas souligné que la seconde découlait simplement de la première. Il introduit le terme *fonction syntaxique primaire* sans en donner une explication satisfaisante. M. Hjelmslev, *Principes de grammaire générale*, p. 331, parle d'une *fonction ordinaire* des parties du discours. Ce concept est sans doute identique à celui de fonction primaire de M. Slotty. Mais M. Hjelmslev ne le définit pas non plus.

La notion de dérivation syntaxique semble ainsi claire. Un dérivé syntaxique est une forme à contenu lexical identique à celui de la forme-base, mais jouant

le rouge (pouvant se rapporter à n'importe quel objet) et non pas l'adjectif épithète rouge. Si cette analyse de l'exemple français semble à première vue exagérée, c'est uniquement parce qu'en français l'emploi comme épithète et l'emploi anaphorique n'ont aucune influence sur la forme de l'adjectif lui-même et que par conséquent (le) rouge nous semble dérivé de l'adjectif tout court et non pas de l'adjectif employé dans telle ou telle autre fonction syntaxique spéciale. Mais déjà en allemand, ou l'ancienne distinction germanique entre l'adjectif épithète et l'adjectif anaphorique a été partiellement conservée (ein junger Mann, der junge Mann, mais seulement der Junge en fonction anaphorique que), un substantif comme der Junge, "le jeune homme"[4] et ein Junge "un jeune homme" se rattache, quant à son origine, à la forme anaphorique, qui est toujours un thème en -n-, tandis que l'épithète est un thème fort ou faible (dépendant de l'élément pronominal qui précède). Le fait qu'un substantif est dérivé de l'adjectif anaphorique et non pas de l'adjectif épithète est donc d'une importance capitale, bien qu'il n'entraîne des conséquences formelles que là où la langue distingue entre l'épithète et l'adjectif anaphorique. Un autre exemple instructif, ce sont les substantifs abstraits tirés d'adjectifs, comme français hauteur, all. Höhe, etc. Ce qui importe c'est que ces substantifs ne sont pas dérivés d'adjectifs épithètes, mais d'adjectifs attributs ("Prädikatsadjektiv"). On le sait par l'étude pénétrante de M. Porzig (Die Leistung der Abstrakta in der Sprache dans les Blätter für deutsche Philosophie IV (1930), pp. 66–77), d'après laquelle les abstraits servent à résumer une phrase en partant de son prédicat. Cela veut dire qu'ils reposent sur la substantivation syntaxique du prédicat, que ce prédicat soit un verbe ou un adjectif. Quand on dit : la hauteur de cette montagne, il ne s'agit pas de la qualité d'être haut, mais de la dimension verticale, et nous nous trouvons encore une fois en face d'une dérivation à deux étapes :

1° être haut → hauteur (= qualité d'être haut) représente la dérivation syntaxique ; 2° hauteur (= qualité d'être haut) → hauteur (= dimension verticale) représente la dérivation lexicale. Ici encore on va faire l'objection qu'étant donnée l'identité de l'adjectif épithète haut et de l'adjectif attribut (est) haut il est impossible de décider sur lequel des deux l'abstrait a été bâti. Mais ce ne sont pas seulement les langues qui différencient l'adjectif dans les deux fonctions syntaxiques en question, mais aussi le français lui-même, qui nous permet d'entrevoir la vérité : pour rendre le sens des abstraits proprement dits, on a dans cette langue recours à une locution analytique qui renferme la copule, comme : le fait d'être haut, la qualité d'être haut, etc., tirées de être haut (il est haut) et non pas de haut.

On voit dès maintenant comment en élargissant le domaine de la dérivation on peut se passer de la notion de la flexion. Ou bien, si en voulant sauver à tout prix cette notion, on tâche de lui créer une raison d'être, il faudra partir des notions fondamentales de fonction lexicale et fonction syntaxique, délimiter d'abord ces deux fonctions dans la forme "flexionnelle", et établir ensuite leur hiérarchie. P. ex. fonction lexicale de la marque du pluriel en tant qu'elle sert à indiquer une pluralité d'objets ; fonction syntaxique du même élément en tant qu'il sert à indiquer l'accord, c.-à-d. la détermination "attributive" ou prédicative.

[4] Exemple de M. Slotty, l.c.

Revenant à la dérivation syntaxique, nous tenons à rappeler encore une fois le lien existant entre la valeur lexicale et la fonction syntaxique, toute déviation de cet "ordre naturel" étant signalée soit par des morphèmes syntaxiques, soit par les conditions ou l'entourage syntaxique (dans le dernier cas on parlera de la fonction secondaire de la forme en question). Il reste maintenant à passer en revue les différentes parties du discours pour en indiquer les fonctions syntaxiques primaires. Le substantif est le support d'une détermination soit "attributive", soit prédicative. L'adjectif est le déterminant "attributif" du substantif, c'est-à-dire son épithète. Le verbe est le déterminant prédicatif du substantif. L'adverbe est le déterminant du verbe. Le rapport syntaxique de l'adverbe au verbe rappelle celui de l'adjectif au substantif; mais au point de vue lexical l'adjectif désigne une qualité, l'adverbe, une relation. On peut le prouver en appliquant grosso modo notre critère de dérivation à ces deux parties du discours. Il y a des procès de dérivation qui passent de l'adjectif à l'adverbe et d'autres qui passent de l'adverbe à l'adjectif. D'une part on bâtit des adverbes de qualité sur des adjectifs, d'autre part on bâtit des adjectifs sur les adverbes de lieu et de temps (par exemple all. hiesig, dortig, heutig, gestrig, etc.; pol. tutejszy, tamtejszy, dzisiejszy, wczorajszy, etc.). Les procédés productifs de dérivation nous enseignent vite qu'il y a un domaine sémantique particulier des adjectifs et un autre, différent, propre aux adverbes. Cf. aussi les composés verbaux, qui consistent en règle générale en un verbe précédé d'adverbe de relation spatiale et non pas de qualité. Les quatre parties du discours qu'on vient d'énumérer ont en commun deux caractéristiques : 1° leur fonction lexicale essentielle est une fonction symbolique ; 2° elles sont des mots au sens de la définition connue de M. Meillet.[5] Qu'on les appelle parties du discours ou non, les éléments suivants ne suffisent pas à une de ces deux conditions et ne sauraient être mis en opposition directe avec les quatre classes précitées :

1° Les interjections. Leur fonction consiste à exprimer et non pas à représenter.

2° Les pronoms. Ils sont des éléments qui représentent en montrant et non pas en symbolisant (K. Bühler).

Ces deux classes ne suffisent donc pas au premier critère. Comme le pronom ne se distingue des parties du discours précitées que par la technique de représentation (et non pas par l'objet de la représentation), il s'assimile, au point de vue syntaxique, au substantif, à l'adjectif, à l'adverbe, le moment même où il cesse d'être le simple compagnon d'un geste.

3° Les prépositions. Un tour prépositionnel comme par exemple sur la table est un mot et non pas un groupe de mots. S'il était un groupe, le membre régissant du groupe serait susceptible du même emploi syntaxique que le groupe lui-même. Or sur n'est pas susceptible d'un tel emploi. La préposition n'est pas donc un mot, mais un morphème (et parfois un sous-morphème formant une unité avec la désinence casuelle). Dans un exemple comme au-dessus de la table on a affaire à un groupe (au-dessus étant apte à jouer le même rôle syntaxique que le groupe), mais alors il s'agit d'un adverbe déterminé par un substantif et non pas d'un tour prépositionnel.

[5] "Un mot est défini par l'association d'un sens donné à un ensemble donné de sons, susceptible d'un emploi grammatical donné" (Linguistique historique et linguistique générale [1921], p. 30). Le terme sens équivaut ici à valeur lexicale, le terme emploi grammatical, à valeur (fonction) syntaxique.

langues indo-européennes modernes, par un tour à valeur verbale (*être* + *adjectif épithète*). L'adjectif employé en fonction d'un déterminant du verbe est remplacé par une forme à valeur adverbiale (par exemple par un cas concret ou par un tour prépositionnel), cf. les adverbes slaves en *-ě*, qui sont d'anciens locatifs (de substantifs abstraits) ou les adverbes romans en *-mente*, qui sont d'anciens instrumentaux. Le substantif employé comme déterminant d'un verbe est remplacé par un adverbe ou un tour adverbial, cf. les cas analytiques des langues modernes. Un verbe déterminant un autre verbe est remplacé par un mot ou un tour à valeur adverbiale (par exemple par un cas concret ou un tour prépositionnel), d'où l'infinitif, etc., etc.

Or on sait par *Études indoeuropéennes* I, p. 271 ss. que le remplacement partiel d'une forme *A* par une forme *B* conduit au rapport de dérivation entre *A* et *B*, pourvu que les deux formes soient apparentées (au point de vue étymologique). Le fait que *B* obtient une nouvelle base de dérivation *A* conduit à des rapports proportionnels entre la série *A* et la série *B*, ce qui peut entraîner une transformation partielle de la forme *B* (en *B'*). Tout en obtenant une nouvelle base de dérivation (*A*) la forme *B* acquiert une nouvelle fonction. Ainsi le type *blindan-* cesse d'être un substantif et devient un adjectif anaphorique dérivé de l'adjectif épithète. Les formes du type v. slave *pravě* ou français *franchement* cessent d'être des cas obliques et deviennent des "adverbes qualificatifs" bâtis sur les adjectifs (épithètes).

En cessant d'être un cas oblique du nom d'action l'infinitif devient le dérivé direct du verbe personnel. L'ancienne fonction ne transparaît plus que dans des conditions syntaxiques spéciales. Cf. un exemple comme *pour juger les bons et les mauvais*, avec valeur de substantif et non pas d'adjectif anaphorique.

Mais ce qui importe ici avant tout, c'est le fait du remplacement qui prouve encore une fois que chaque partie du discours a une fonction syntaxique non caractérisée propre à elle seulement, qui n'a pas besoin d'un signalement spécial. Ici se pose la question : pourquoi en est-il ainsi ? quel est le rapport intrinsèque entre la valeur lexicale (générale) et la fonction syntaxique ? La solution la plus simple est d'admettre que p. ex. la détermination "attributive" (= par épithèse) n'est qu'une transposition linguistique du procès psychique consistant à dégager des qualités dans les objets (réels ou imaginaires). Puisque les objets nous apparaissent définis (déterminés) par leurs qualités, les mots qui symbolisent les objets (*substantifs*) sont déterminés "d'une manière naturelle" par les mots qui symbolisent les qualités (*adjectifs*). Même chose pour le rapport des phénomènes et les circonstances qui les déterminent (verbes et adverbes), etc. Mais poursuivre cette idée serait dépasser les bornes d'une recherche purement linguistique et s'attaquer à la théorie générale du signe.

Si notre raisonnement est correct, il y a là une loi valable pour toutes les langues et en même temps un véritable fondement de la syntaxe générale. Car alors la description scientifique de la structure d'une langue quelconque, que ce soit le français, le chinois ou une langue athapaskane, aura à répondre à la question simple et claire (puisque ayant trait à la forme) : comment les fonctions syntaxiques secondaires sont-elles dérivées des fonctions primaires des parties du discours ? La réponse à cette question comprendra : 1° la description des formes à fonction syntaxique primaire, et 2° la description des procédés formels servant à caractériser soit le mot soit son entourage syntaxique

4° *Les conjonctions.* Leur rapport aux groupes de mots et aux phrases est analogue à celui des prépositions aux tours prépositionnels. Elles ne sont des mots capables de jouer un rôle syntaxique autonome que dans la mesure où elles gardent une valeur adverbiale (c'est-à-dire dans la mesure où elles ne sont pas de vraies conjonctions).

5° *Les noms de nombre (cardinaux).* Le vrai nom de nombre cardinal (non pas un substantif collectif) forme une unité sémantique avec la désinence de pluriel du substantif qu'il détermine. Un complexe comme *centum equites* s'analyse *centum [equit] -es*, c'est-à-dire que *centum* n'est pas le déterminant d'un morphème, donc un morphème lui-même. Le morphème composé *centum + -es* est ainsi comparable au morphème composé *in [urb] -em*, à ceci près que ce dernier est d'ordre syntaxique, le premier étant d'ordre lexical. Cet état de choses nous explique pourquoi les substantifs collectifs *tendent à perdre leur flexion* au moment où ils deviennent de vrais noms de nombre cardinaux.

6° *L'article (défini).* Il remplit des fonctions pronominales (anaphorique, anamnestique) ou bien il sert à la substantivation syntaxique : τὸ νῦν. Dans le premier cas il n'a pas de valeur symbolique, dans le second cas il n'est pas un mot autonome, mais un simple morphème syntaxique.

Nous n'affirmons pas que seules les quatre classes : substantif, adjectif, verbe, adverbe, méritent le nom de parties du discours. Une telle affirmation entraînerait des controverses infructueuses. Tout ce que nous voulons dire c'est que parmi les classes qu'on a jusqu'ici trouvées dignes de ce nom, il y a un groupe plus serré qui répond aux deux conditions indiquées ci-dessus et dont les membres ne diffèrent entre eux que sous un seul rapport : celui du contenu lexical. L'existence de ce sous-groupe prouve que les classifications faites jusqu'ici n'ont pas tenu compte de l'entrecroisement des facteurs, lequel rend impossible une division faite d'après un seul principe. Mais la seconde des deux conditions mentionnées plus haut conserve en tout cas sa valeur, puisque les parties du discours sont des *classes de mots* et non pas des classes de n'importe quelles formes linguistiques (morphèmes, groupe de mots, phrases). On pourrait tout au plus tâcher de remplacer la définition de M. Meillet, jusqu'ici la meilleure à ce qu'il nous semble, par une autre plus élastique (cf. par exemple K. Bühler, *Sprachtheorie*, p. 297).

Après cette digression passons à l'aspect diachronique de la question, à savoir le rapport des changements de fonction syntaxique aux changements formels, c'est-à-dire à la création de nouveaux phonèmes syntaxiques. Quand une forme *A* acquiert une valeur syntaxique secondaire dépendant de l'entourage syntaxique, elle est remplacée par une forme *B* (mot ou groupe de mots) dont cette fonction est la fonction primaire. Le remplacement de *A* par *B* équivaut donc au remplacement de l'entourage par la forme. Au lieu de caractériser une fonction syntaxique par l'ordre des mots, par l'accentuation du groupe, par le rythme (les pauses), etc., on se sert d'une forme dont la valeur lexicale implique déjà la fonction syntaxique en question. Ainsi l'adjectif employé en fonction de support de détermination est remplacé par un substantif apparenté au point de vue étymologique, d'où l'adjectif anaphorique, cf. germanique *blindan* "homme aveugle" pour *blinda-* "aveugle" ; le français ou le grec ancien ont eu recours à l'article (défini), originairement propre au seul substantif. L'adjectif attribut de l'indo-européen est remplacé, dans presque toutes les

pour conférer au mot une fonction syntaxique secondaire. Il paraît dès maintenant que c'est le degré de l'autonomie du mot, c'est-à-dire le fait de la
prépondérance, soit des morphèmes syntaxiques inhérents au mot, soit des
morphèmes syntaxiques inhérents aux unités supérieures, qui fera toute la
différence essentielle entre les langues humaines. Mais la circonstance que p. ex.
en anglais les différences entre les parties du discours sont, dans une large
mesure, rendues par le contexte syntaxique (*a doubt* : *to doubt*), n'entame en
rien le problème de la relation mutuelle des fonctions syntaxiques *à l'intérieur
d'une seule et même valeur lexicale* (p. ex. rapport du *doubt* "doute" employé
comme sujet à *doubt* "doute" fonctionnant comme régime).

NATURE DU SIGNE LINGUISTIQUE

Émile Benveniste

C'est de F. de Saussure que procède la théorie du signe linguistique actuelle-ment affirmée ou impliquée dans la plupart des travaux de linguistique générale. Et c'est comme une vérité évidente, non encore explicite, mais cependant incontestée en fait, que Saussure a enseigné que la nature du signe est *arbitraire*. La formule s'est immédiatement imposée. Tout propos sur l'essence du langage ou sur les modalités du discours commence par énoncer le caractère arbitraire du signe linguistique. Le principe est d'une telle portée qu'une réflexion portant sur une partie quelconque de la linguistique le rencontre nécessairement. Qu'il soit partout invoqué et toujours donné pour évident, cela fait deux raisons pour que l'on cherche au moins à comprendre en quel sens Saussure l'a pris et la nature des preuves qui le manifestent.

Cette définition est, dans le *Cours de linguistique générale*,[1] motivée par des énoncés très simples. On appelle *signe* "le total résultant de l'association d'un signifiant [= image acoustique] et d'un signifié [= concept]" … "Ainsi l'idée de " sœur " n'est liée par aucun rapport intérieur avec la suite de sons *s-ö-r* qui lui sert de signifiant; il pourrait être aussi bien représenté par n'importe quelle autre : à preuve les différences entre les langues et l'existence même de langues différentes : le signifié " bœuf " a pour signifiant *b-ö-f* d'un côté de la frontière et *o-k-s* (Ochs) de l'autre " (p. 102). Ceci doit établir que " le lien unissant le signifiant au signifié est arbitraire ", ou plus simplement que " le signe linguistique est arbitraire ". Par " arbitraire ", l'auteur entend qu'il n'a aucune attache naturelle dans la réalité " (p. 103). Ce caractère doit donc expliquer le fait même par où il se vérifie : savoir que, pour une notion, les expressions varient dans le temps et dans l'espace, et par suite n'ont avec elle aucune relation nécessaire.

Nous ne songeons pas à discuter cette conclusion au nom d'autres principes ou en partant de définitions différentes. Il s'agit de savoir si elle est cohérente, et si, la bipartition du signe étant admise (et nous l'admettons), il s'ensuit qu'on doive caractériser le signe comme arbitraire. On vient de voir que Saussure prend le signe linguistique comme constitué par un signifiant et un signifié. Or — ceci est essentiel — il entend par " signifié " le *concept*. Il déclare en propres termes (p. 100) que " le signe linguistique unit non une chose et un nom, mais un concept et une image acoustique ". Mais il l'assure, aussitôt après, que la nature du signe est arbitraire parce que il n'a avec le signifié " aucune attache naturelle dans la réalité ". Il est clair que le raisonnement est faussé par le recours inconscient et subreptice à un troisième terme, qui n'était pas compris dans la définition initiale. Ce troisième terme est la chose même, la réalité. Saussure a beau dire que l'idée de " sœur " n'est pas liée au signifiant *s-ö-r*; il n'en pense pas moins à la *réalité* de la notion. Quand il parle de la différence entre *b-ö-f* et *o-k-s*, il se réfère malgré lui au fait que ces deux termes s'appliquent à la même *réalité*. Voilà donc la *chose*, expressément exclue d'abord de la définition du signe, qui s'y introduit par un détour et qui y installe en permanence la contradiction. Car si l'on pose en principe — et avec raison — que la langue est *forme*, non *substance* (p. 163), il faut admettre — et Saussure l'a affirmé nettement — que la linguistique est science des formes exclusivement. D'autant plus impérieuse est alors la nécessité de laisser la " substance " *sœur* ou *bœuf* hors de la compréhension du signe. Or c'est seulement si l'on pense à l'animal " bœuf " dans sa particularité concrète et " substantielle " que l'on est fondé à juger " arbitraire " la relation entre *bœf* d'une part, *oks* de l'autre, à une même réalité. Il y a donc contradiction entre la manière dont Saussure définit le signe linguistique et la nature fondamentale qu'il lui attribue.

Une pareille anomalie dans le raisonnement si serré de Saussure ne me paraît pas imputable à un relâchement de son attention critique. J'y verrai plutôt un trait distinctif de la pensée historique et relativiste de la fin du XIXe siècle, une démarche habituelle à cette forme de la réflexion philosophique qu'est l'intelligence comparative. On observe chez les différents peuples les réactions que suscite un même phénomène : l'infinie diversité des attitudes et des juge-ments amène à considérer que rien apparemment n'est nécessaire. De l'uni-verselle dissemblance, on conclut à l'universelle contingence. La conception saussurienne est encore solidaire en quelque mesure de ce système de pensée. Décider que le signe linguistique est arbitraire parce que le même animal s'appelle *bœf* en un pays, *Ochs* ailleurs, équivaut à dire que la notion du deuil est " arbitraire ", parce qu'elle a pour symbole le noir en Europe, le blanc en Chine. Arbitraire, oui, mais seulement sous le regard impassible de Sirius ou pour celui qui se borne à constater du dehors la liaison établie entre une réalité objective et un comportement humain et se condamne ainsi à n'y voir que contingence. Certes, par rapport à une même réalité, toutes les dénominations ont égale valeur; qu'elles existent est donc la preuve qu'aucune d'elles ne peut prétendre à l'absolu de la dénomination en soi. Cela est vrai. Cela n'est même que trop vrai — et donc peu instructif. Le vrai problème est autrement profond. Il consiste à retrouver la structure intime du phénomène dont on ne perçoit que l'apparence extérieure et à décrire sa relation avec l'ensemble des manifestations dont il dépend.

Ainsi du signe linguistique. Une des composantes du signe, l'image acoustique, en constitue le signifiant; l'autre, le concept, en est le signifié. Entre le signi-fiant et le signifié, le lien n'est pas arbitraire; au contraire, il est *nécessaire*. Le concept (" signifié ") " bœuf " est forcément identique dans ma conscience à l'ensemble phonique (" signifiant ") *böf*. Comment en serait-il autrement ? Ensemble les deux ont été imprimés dans mon esprit; ensemble ils s'évoquent

Reprinted from *Acta Linguistica* 1 (1939) : 23-29, with the permission of the author and of the editorial board of *Acta Linguistica*.

[1] Cité ici d'après la 1ère éd., Lausanne–Paris, 1916.

en toute circonstance. Il y a a entre eux symbiose si étroite que le concept "bœuf" est comme l'âme de l'image acoustique *bœf*. L'esprit ne contient pas de formes vides, de concepts innommés. Saussure dit lui-même : "Psychologiquement, abstraction faite de son expression par les mots, notre pensée n'est qu'une masse amorphe et indistincte. Philosophes et linguistes se sont toujours accordés à reconnaître que, sans le secours des signes, nous serions incapables de distinguer deux idées d'une façon claire et constante. Prise en elle-même, la pensée est comme une nébuleuse où rien n'est nécessairement délimité. Il n'y a pas d'idées préétablies, et rien n'est distinct avant l'apparition de la langue." (p. 161). Inversement l'esprit n'accueille de forme sonore que celle qui sert de support à une représentation identifiable pour lui; sinon, il la rejette comme inconnue ou étrangère. Le signifiant et le signifié, la représentation mentale et l'image acoustique, sont donc en réalité les deux faces d'une même notion et se composent ensemble comme l'incorporant et l'incorporé. Le signifiant est la traduction phonique d'un concept; le signifié est la contrepartie mentale du signifiant. Cette consubstantialité du signifiant et du signifié assure l'unité structurale du signe linguistique. Ici encore c'est à Saussure même que nous en appelons quand il dit de la langue : "La langue est encore comparable à une feuille de papier : la pensée est le recto et le son le verso ; on ne peut découper le recto sans découper en même temps le verso ; de même dans la langue, on ne saurait isoler ni le son de la pensée, ni la pensée du son ; on n'y arriverait que par une abstraction dont le résultat serait de faire ou de la psychologie pure ou de la phonologie pure." (p. 163). Ce que Saussure dit ici de la langue vaut d'abord pour le signe linguistique en lequel s'affirment incontestablement les caractères premiers de la langue.

On voit maintenant et l'on peut délimiter la zone de l'" arbitraire ". Ce qui est arbitraire, c'est que tel signe, et non tel autre, soit appliqué à tel élément de la réalité, et non à tel autre. En ce sens, et en ce sens seulement il est permis de parler de contingence, et encore sera-ce moins pour donner au problème une solution que pour le signaler et en prendre provisoirement congé. Car ce problème n'est autre que le fameux : φύσει ou θέσει ? et ne peut être tranché que par décret. C'est en effet, transposé en termes linguistiques, le problème métaphysique de l'accord entre l'esprit et le monde, problème que le linguiste sera peut-être un jour en mesure d'aborder avec fruit, mais qu'il fera mieux pour l'instant de délaisser. Poser la relation comme arbitraire est pour le linguiste une manière de se défendre contre cette question et aussi contre la solution que le sujet parlant y apporte instinctivement. Pour le sujet parlant, il y a entre la langue et la réalité adéquation complète : le signe recouvre et commande la réalité ; mieux, il *est* cette réalité (*nomen omen*, tabous de parole, pouvoir magique du verbe, etc.). A vrai dire le point de vue du sujet et celui du linguiste sont si différents à cet égard que l'affirmation du linguiste quant à l'arbitraire des désignations ne réfute pas le sentiment contraire du sujet parlant. Mais, quoi qu'il en soit, la nature du signe linguistique n'y est en rien intéressée, si on le définit comme Saussure l'a fait, puisque le propre de cette définition est précisément de n'envisager que la relation du signifiant au signifié. Le domaine de l'arbitraire est ainsi relégué hors de la compréhension du signe linguistique.

Il est alors assez vain de défendre le principe de l'" arbitraire du signe " contre l'objection qui pourrait être tirée des onomatopées et mots expressifs (Saussure, p. 103-4), non seulement parce que la sphère d'emploi en est relativement limitée et parce que l'expressivité est un effet essentiellement transitoire, subjectif et souvent secondaire, mais surtout parce que, ici encore, quelle que soit la réalité dépeinte par l'onomatopée ou le mot expressif, l'allusion à cette réalité dans la plupart des cas n'est pas immédiate et n'est admise que par une convention symbolique analogue à celle qui accrédite les signes ordinaires du système. Nous retrouvons donc la définition et les caractères valables pour tout signe. L'arbitraire n'existe ici aussi que par rapport au phénomène ou à l'objet *matériel* et n'intervient pas dans la constitution propre du signe.

Il faut maintenant considérer brièvement quelques unes des conséquences que Saussure a tirées du principe ici discuté et qui retentissent loin. Par exemple il montre admirablement qu'on peut parler à la fois de l'immutabilité et de la mutabilité du signe : immutabilité, parce qu'étant arbitraire, il ne peut être mis en question au nom d'une norme raisonnable ; mutabilité, parce qu'étant arbitraire, il est toujours susceptible de s'altérer. "Une langue est radicalement impuissante à se défendre contre les facteurs qui déplacent d'instant en instant le rapport du signifié et du signifiant. C'est une des conséquences de l'arbitraire du signe" (p. 112). Le mérite de cette analyse n'est en rien diminué, mais bien renforcé au contraire si l'on spécifie mieux la relation à laquelle en fait elle s'applique. Ce n'est pas entre le signifiant et le signifié que la relation en même temps se modifie et reste immuable, c'est entre le signe et l'objet ; c'est, en d'autres termes, la *motivation objective* de la désignation, soumise, comme telle, à l'action de divers facteurs historiques. Ce que Saussure démontre reste vrai, mais de la *signification*, non du signe.

Un autre problème, non moins important, que la définition du signe intéresse directement, est celui de la *valeur*, où Saussure pense trouver une confirmation de ses vues : "...le choix qui appelle telle tranche acoustique pour telle idée est parfaitement arbitraire. Si ce n'était pas le cas, la notion de valeur perdrait quelque chose de son caractère, puisqu'elle contiendrait un élément imposé du dehors. Mais en fait les valeurs restent entièrement relatives, et voilà pourquoi le lien de l'idée et du son est radicalement arbitraire" (p. 163). Il vaut la peine de reprendre successivement les parties de ce raisonnement. Le choix qui appelle telle tranche acoustique pour telle idée n'est nullement arbitraire ; cette tranche acoustique n'existerait pas sans l'idée correspondante et vice versa. En réalité Saussure pense toujours, quoiqu'il parle d'" idée ", à la représentation de l'*objet réel* et au caractère évidemment non-nécessaire, immotivé, du lien qui unit le signe à la *chose signifiée*. La preuve de cette confusion gît dans la phrase suivante dont je souligne le membre caractéristique : "Si ce n'était pas le cas, la notion de valeur perdrait quelque chose de son caractère, puisqu'*elle contiendrait un élément imposé du dehors* ". C'est bien " un élément imposé du dehors ", donc la réalité *objective* que ce raisonnement prend comme axe de référence. Mais si l'on considère le signe en lui-même et en tant que porteur d'une valeur, l'arbitraire se trouve nécessairement éliminé. Car — la dernière proposition est celle qui enferme le plus clairement sa propre réfutation — il est bien vrai que les valeurs restent entièrement "relatives", mais il s'agit de savoir comment et par rapport à quoi. Posons tout de suite ceci : la valeur est un élément du signe ; si le signe pris en soi n'est pas arbitraire, comme on pense l'avoir montré, il s'ensuit que le caractère "relatif" de la valeur ne peut dépendre de la nature "arbitraire" du signe. Puisqu'il faut faire abstraction de la convenance du signe à la réalité, à plus forte raison doit-on ne considérer la valeur que comme un attribut de la *forme*, non de la substance. Dès lors dire que les valeurs sont "relatives" signifie qu'elles sont relatives *les unes aux autres*. Or n'est-ce pas là justement la preuve de leur *nécessité* ? Il s'agit ici, non plus du signe isolé, mais de la langue comme système de signes et nul n'a aussi fortement que Saussure conçu et décrit l'économie systématique de la langue. Qui dit système dit agencement et convenance des parties en une structure qui transcende et explique ses éléments. Tout y est si *nécessaire* que les modifications de l'ensemble et du détail s'y conditionnent réciproquement. La relativité des valeurs est la meilleure preuve qu'elles dépendent étroitement l'une de l'autre dans la synchronie d'un système toujours menacé, toujours restauré. C'est que toutes les valeurs sont d'opposition et ne se définissent que par leur différence. Opposées, elles se maintiennent en mutuelle relation de nécessité. Une opposition est, par la force des choses, sous-tendue de nécessité, comme la nécessité donne corps à l'opposition. Si la langue est autre chose qu'un conglomérat fortuit de notions erratiques et de sons émis au hasard, c'est bien qu'une nécessité est immanente à sa structure comme à toute structure.

Il apparaît donc que la part de contingence inhérente à la langue affecte la dénomination en tant que symbole phonique de la réalité et dans son rapport avec elle. Mais le signe, élément primordial du système linguistique, enferme un signifiant et un signifié dont la liaison doit être reconnue comme *nécessaire*, ces deux composantes étant consubstantielles l'une à l'autre. *Le caractère absolu du signe linguistique* ainsi entendu commande à son tour la *nécessité* dialectique des valeurs en constante opposition, et forme le principe structural de la langue. C'est peut-être le meilleur témoignage de la fécondité d'une doctrine que d'engendrer la contradiction qui la promeut. En restaurant la véritable nature du signe dans le conditionnement interne du système, on affermit, par delà Saussure, la rigueur de la pensée saussurienne.

PHONOLOGIE ET MÉLANGE DE LANGUES

Lucien Tesnière

Je ne sache pas que les phonologues aient jamais pris nettement position dans la question si controversée du mélange des langues. — A l'heure où, en France, la phonologie est en train de triompher des dernières résistances — car on ne triomphe jamais des premières —, il n'est peut-être pas sans intérêt de poser ce problème, dont la solution apparaît, comme la réaction en puissance dans les principes mêmes de la doctrine phonologique.

Des critères tout extérieurs invitent déjà à conjecturer que la phonologie ne saurait adopter, sur la question du mélange des langues, l'attitude parfaitement intransigeante qui fut celle des néo-grammairiens. Tout d'abord, sur bien des points, la phonologie a été amenée, par une réaction naturelle et salutaire, à prendre le contre-pied de la doctrine traditionnelle, dont les cadres étroits, suffisants à la rigueur pour intégrer une expérience linguistique livresque essentielle-ment alimentée par des textes écrits, devaient fatalement faire étouffer une génération de linguistes élevés dans la pratique directe, active et parlée des langues sur lesquelles ils opèrent. Aussi bien, les plus illustres non-conformistes de l'âge néo-grammairien étaient-ils parfois des partisans convaincus de la possibilité du mélange des langues. Tandis que Meillet proscrivait catégoriquement et le terme, et la notion de mélange,[1] Baudouin de Courtenay y voyait au contraire un procédé normal et courant dans l'histoire des langues,[2] Et Schuchardt exprimait la même thèse en termes explicites : " *Mischung durchsetzt überhaupt alle Sprachentwicklung. sie tritt in zwischen Einzelsprachen, zwischen nahen Mundarten, zwischen verwandten und selbst zwischen unverwandten Sprachen* ".[3] Dans quelle mesure ces vues sont-elles en harmonie avec les théories phonologiques ? C'est ce que nous voudrions examiner ici.

Un des axiomes essentiels de la phonologie est que tout, dans le mécanisme du langage, repose sur des oppositions. La phonologie procède par là directe-ment sur des oppositions. La phonologie procède par là, bien qu'on l'ait contesté, de la doctrine saussurienne, dont c'est une des idées maîtresses : " Deux signes comportant chacun un signifié et un significant ne sont pas différents, ils sont seulement distincts. Entre eux il n'y a qu'*opposi-tion*. Tout le mécanisme du langage...repose sur des oppositions de ce genre et sur les différences phoniques et conceptuelles qu'elles impliquent ".[4] Elles s'opposent entre elles et en arrivent à former de véritables systèmes organiques. De ce point de vue une langue apparaît comme un système d'oppositions. A y regarder de près, on constate même qu'il y a dans une langue plusieurs systèmes, le système

phonétique, le système morphologique, le système syntaxique, etc. Ce qui autorise à poser qu'une langue est un système de systèmes. La phonologie se trouve donc logiquement amenée à étudier ces systèmes. Et c'est bien effective-ment ce qu'elle fait, puisque l'objet qu'elle se propose est en dernière analyse la recherche empirique du schème psychologique selon lequel chaque langue ordonne ses phonèmes aux fins d'utilisation.

Si la phonologie a le mérite d'avoir intégré le caractère systématique des éléments du langage dans une théorie d'ensemble qui le fait ressortir en pleine lumière, elle n'est cependant pas la première à l'avoir reconnu. Il s'agit là d'un fait élémentaire d'observation courante, que l'on admet en général sans discus-sion. On sait que les linguistes allemands vont même parfois jusqu'à exprimer la notion d'analogie morphologique par le terme parfaitement adéquat de " Systemszwang ". En France, A. Meillet a toujours insisté avec force sur ce qu'il y a de systématique dans les langues : " Au point de vue de l'individu ", écrit-il,[5] " la langue est un système complexe d'associations inconscientes de mouvements et de sensations au moyen desquelles il peut parler et comprendre les paroles émises par d'autres individus. Ce système est propre à chaque homme...". Et ailleurs : " Chaque langue constitue un système "[6] ou encore : " La prononciation et la grammaire forment des systèmes fermés ; toutes les parties de chacun de ces systèmes sont liées les unes aux autres ".[7]

Mais un système est un organisme, un tout architecturé, dans lequel chaque partie s'harmonise avec l'ensemble. Vienne une de ces parties à disparaître, on ne saurait la remplacer indifféremment par une partie d'un autre ensemble. La pièce ainsi rapportée resterait hétérogène et ne ferait pas corps avec le système auquel on voudrait l'affecter. En d'autres termes on ne saurait refaire un système un et homogène avec deux moitiés de systèmes hétérogènes.

De là découlent les principes qui semblent devoir présider au mélange des langues. Une langue est d'autant plus rebelle aux mélanges qu'elle comporte des systèmes plus cohérents et mieux développés. Inversement une langue est d'autant plus sujette aux mélanges, que les systèmes qui la constituent sont plus relâchés. En d'autres termes : **La miscibilité d'une langue est fonction inverse de sa systématisation.**

Et c'est bien en effet ce que l'on constate. Là où l'on observe mélange, ce n'est jamais qu'entre des systèmes dissimilaires : système grammatical d'une langue avec système lexicographique d'une autre ; système phonétique d'une langue avec système morphologique d'une autre, etc. Par contre le mélange est impossible entre systèmes similaires de deux langues différentes : deux morphologies ne se mélangent pas ; elles ne peuvent que s'exclure. Quelques exemples suffiront à illustrer ces données.

Le cas de beaucoup le plus fréquent est celui du mélange d'une grammaire avec un vocabulaire d'autre origine. Les faits auxquels on peut se référer ici sont innombrables et bien connus.
Le grec présente une grammaire dont le caractère indo-européen est évident.

Reprinted from *Travaux du Cercle Linguistique de Prague* 8 (1939) : 83–93, with the permission of Bohumil Trnka, secretary of Cercle Linguistique de Prague.

[1] V. en particulier l'article intitulé " Le problème de la parenté des langues ", paru d'abord dans *Scientia*, XV, 1914, p. 403, et reproduit dans *Linguistique historique et linguistique générale*, 1921, p. 76.
[2] V. *Opyt fonetiky rezjanskich govorov*, pp. 120, 124 et 125, et l'article " sur le caractère mixte de toutes les langues " ; " O mešannom charakterě vsěch jazykov ", *Žurnal Ministerstva Narodnago Prosvěščenija*, 1901.
[3] Leo Spitzer, *Hugo Schuchardt-Brevier*, p. 171.
[4] V. F. de Saussure, *Cours de linguistique générale*, p. 174.

[5] *Introduction...*, pp. 17–18.
[6] *Scientia*, XV, cité ici d'après *Linguistique historique et linguistique générale*, p. 83.
[7] Ibid., p. 84.

Mais le vocabulaire est en grande partie "égéen" : "Il n'y a", dit Meillet, "qu'un petit nombre de mots grecs dont l'indo-européen fournisse une étymologie certaine".[8] "C'est sans doute qu'ils sont en grande partie empruntés à des langues non indo-européennes".[9] L'arménien allie à un système morphologique dont l'origine indo-européenne directe ne fait de doute pour personne aujourd'hui un vocabulaire si chargé d'éléments parthes et perses, qu'on a pu, pendant longtemps, y voir une langue iranienne. A son tour, "le tsigane arménien est purement de l'arménien pour la prononciation et la grammaire ; mais le vocabulaire n'a rien d'arménien ; ...les Tsiganes d'Arménie...ont gardé leur vocabulaire traditionnel".[10] De même l'albanais constitue par son système grammatical un rameau propre de l'indo-européen, mais le vocabulaire en est, pour la plus grande partie, composé de mots latins, italiens, grecs, slaves et turcs. On sait que le vocabulaire arabe de l'Islam s'est allié à une grammaire indo-européenne dans le persan et à une grammaire turco-tatare dans le turc. Schuchardt donne d'innombrables faits de ce type dans son livre intitulé *Slawo-Deutsches und Slawo-Italienisches*. Le slovène du nord est rempli de mots allemands, qui font bon ménage avec une grammaire foncièrement slave. On lira par exemple comme sous-titre du *Colemone-Shegen* la mention suivante :

v latinskzhei shprachi vrnkei dan.

Certaines phrases allemandes peuvent avoir un vocabulaire entièrement français, telle celle que cite J. Marouzeau : *"Die Dame kokketierte mit dem Militär-Attaché auf der Terrasse des Hotels".*[11] La chose est normale en alsacien, où l'on donne en exemple la phrase strasbourgeoise suivante : *"Geh mir aweck mit dere, sie isch wolasch in d'r Amitié, mer kann re kaan segré komfdiere"*. De même on trouve dans l'œuvre des frères Matthis, qui est en pur dialecte alsacien, une multitude de passages comme les suivants :

Vor em Bumbiéscommedant.[12]
Dort an d'r Mür glaenzt wie Cryschtall
E' Gasque van d'r Gard Nationnall.[13]

J. Vendryes cite,[14] pour le portugais de Mangalore, aux Indes, l'expression *governador's casa*, qui allie un morphème anglais à un vocabulaire purement portugais. On objectera qu'il s'agit ici, non pas d'anglais à vocabulaire portugais, mais de portugais à grammaire anglaise. La chose est d'importance au point de vue diachronique, mais elle ne change rien à la théorie. Que l'on verse à petites gouttes du vin dans de l'eau ou de l'eau dans du vin, le résultat finit toujours par être de l'eau rougie.

Ce qui importe bien davantage, c'est de noter que dans aucun des exemples précédents le mélange n'intéresse un vocabulaire dans sa totalité. Le grec est certes plein de mots égéens, mais il conserve quand même un certain fonds de mots indo-européens. De même les mots français de l'alsacien n'excluent pas,

loin de là, le contingent germanique. Il y a donc ici, à proprement parler, mélange de deux vocabulaires différents.

Loin d'infirmer le principe posé ci-dessus, cette observation en apporte au contraire une précieuse confirmation. C'est que le vocabulaire est loin de former un système aussi cohérent et aussi homogène que ceux de la phonétique et de la morphologie. Aussi, tandis que les systèmes proprement grammaticaux ne peuvent intervenir dans un mélange qu'en bloc et intégralement, les vocabulaires peuvent s'infiltrer lentement et progressivement. C'est aussi pourquoi l'origine du vocabulaire peut être multiple, comme nous l'avons vu par exemple ci-dessus pour l'albanais.

Il faut d'ailleurs se garder de penser que le vocabulaire, pour n'avoir pas l'armature solide d'un système grammatical, soit complètement inorganique. Il est en général beaucoup plus organisé qu'on ne l'imagine. Et l'on observe précisément que, dans la mesure même où il comporte des groupes compacts et cohérents, il est rebelle au mélange.

C'est le cas bien connu des noms d'animaux domestiques anglais, où le contingent des bêtes sur pied forme un groupe d'origine saxonne : *ox, calf, sheep, swine*, tandis que les mêmes servies sur table relèvent d'un bloc d'origine franco-normande : *beef, veal, mutton, pork.* "Tant que la bête est vivante et confiée à la garde d'un esclave saxon", dit Wamba dans *Ivanhoe*, "elle garde son nom saxon ; mais elle devient normande...quand on la porte à la salle à manger du château, pour y servir aux festins des nobles".[15] Il n'y a pas mélange, mais juxtaposition de deux groupes sémantiques avec des valeurs différentes.

L'impénétrabilité réciproque des systèmes apparaît en pleine lumière dès qu'il s'agit de phonétique et de morphologie. Deux phonétiques ou deux morphologies ne se mêlent pas. Mais la symbiose d'une phonétique et d'une morphologie d'origines différentes est parfaitement viable.

L'arménien présente un système morphologique dont l'indo-européanisme est indéniable. Mais il a une phonétique qui ressemble étrangement à celle des langues caucasiques voisines, et que l'on suppose pour cette raison être celle de la langue autochtone des inscriptions vanniques. "Ce n'est pas un hasard", écrit Meillet,[16] "que le système des occlusives de l'arménien soit identique à celui du géorgien, langue non indo-européenne". De même le germanique allie à une morphologie nettement indo-européenne un système phonétique d'origine différente, et qu'il est logique d'attribuer, toujours avec Meillet,[17] au type articulatoire d'une population dont la langue n'était pas l'indo-européen.

En vertu du même principe, un système morphologique donné peut s'allier à un système syntaxique tout différent. Schuchardt cite de bons exemples de ce type de mélange dans son *Slawo-Deutsches und Slawo-Italienisches*, ainsi : *nicht scheut er sich iḫn zu verleumden*,[18] dont le prototype syntaxique est le slovène *ne se sramuje ga obrekovati*.[18] Point n'est besoin, au demeurant, d'aller

[8] Meillet, *Aperçu d'une histoire de la langue grecque*, Chapitre III.
[9] Ibid.
[10] Meillet, *Linguistique historique et linguistique générale*, p. 95.
[11] Marouzeau, *La linguistique*, p. 141.
[12] Albert et Adolphe Matthis, *Fulefute* ; Strasbourg, 1937, p. 68.
[13] Ibid., p. 140.
[14] Dans *Le Langage*, 1921, p. 343 ; v. aussi Meillet, *Linguistique historique et linguistique générale*, p. 87.

[15] Voir tout le passage dans Walter Scott, *Ivanhoe*, chap. I.
[16] *Introduction...*,[7] p. 24 ; v. aussi Meillet, *Caractères généraux des langues germaniques*, Chap. I., La mutation consonantique.
[17] *Caractères généraux des Langues Germaniques*, ibid.
[18] Cité par Vendryes, *Le Langage*, 1921, p. 342.

chercher ses exemples si loin. Il suffit d'observer l'allemand des élèves de nos lycées, dont la syntaxe est parfois terriblement française : *Der Schüler in Frage ist krank gefallen*, d'après : *L'élève en question est tombé malade.*[19]

Quant à l'association d'un système phonétique avec un système syntaxique d'origine différente, il semble qu'on ne l'observe guère. C'est peut-être tout simplement parce que ces deux systèmes proviennent généralement l'un et l'autre de l'influence du substrat, qui est par définition le même.

Les conclusions qu'impose la structure systématique des langues quant à l'impénétrabilité des systèmes ont été formulées depuis longtemps par A. Meillet : "Les systèmes, grammaticaux de deux langues sont... impénétrables l'un à l'autre ".[20] "Le système phonétique et le système morphologique se prêtent donc peu à recevoir des emprunts. ...Au contraire les mots ne constituent pas un système ; ...Aussi peut-on emprunter à des langues étrangères autant de mots que l'on veut ".[21]

Comment se fait-il, dès lors, qu'en présence de tous les faits évidents de mélange que nous avons rappelés ci-dessus, Meillet se soit refusé avec tant d'insistance à admettre le principe même du mélange des langues, alors que d'autres, comme par exemple J. Vendryes, lui font sa juste place dans leur conception du langage ?[22]

Car ne nous y trompons pas : il ne s'agit pas seulement, dans l'esprit de Meillet, de l'impénétrabilité des **systèmes**, sur laquelle l'accord semble évident, mais bien de l'impénétrabilité des **langues** : "Certains linguistes parlent... de langues mixtes. L'expression est impropre. Car elle éveille l'idée qu'une pareille langue résulte du mélange de deux langues placées dans des conditions *égales* ".[23] Ou encore : "Les sujets bilingues qui ont le choix entre deux langues ne mêlent pas ces deux langues ".[24]

A y bien réfléchir, cette antinomie n'est pas insoluble. Et peut-être n'y faut-il voir qu'une différence de terminologie. Pour Meillet, la langue est un système de signes. Or le signe est par définition morphologique. Un phonème n'est pas par lui-même un signe. Il ne devient tel que lorsqu'il est associé à un sens, c'est-à-dire lorsqu'il prend une valeur morphologique. D'autre part la syntaxe n'existe, pour Meillet, qu'en tant que science des emplois des formes, c'est-à-dire seulement lorsqu'elle se réalise en morphologie. Quant au vocabulaire, s'il est bien composé de signes, par contre, il ne forme pas, à ses yeux, un système.

Il est facile de comprendre que, dans ces conditions, la langue se trouve en fait réduite à la morphologie, ou tout au moins que la morphologie y occupe une place privilégiée. C'est elle en tous cas qui est, dans l'esprit de Meillet, l'unique objet de la grammaire, d'où sont exclus par définition la phonétique et le vocabulaire : "Une langue est défini par trois choses : un système phonétique, un système morphologique et un vocabulaire, c'est-à-dire par une manière de prononcer, par une grammaire et par certaines manières de désigner les notions ".[25] L'égalité " morphologie égale grammaire " ressort à l'évidence de cette définition.

Aussi bien Meillet ne pouvait-il avoir que la morphologie en vue, lorsqu'il fondait le principe de la continuité linguistique sur la volonté consciente d'un groupe d'individus de parler telle langue plutôt que telle autre : "Une langue sera dite issue d'une autre langue si, à tous les moments compris entre celui où se parlait la première et celui où se parle la seconde, les sujets parlants ont eu le sentiment et la volonté de parler une même langue. ...Ainsi la parenté des langues résulte uniquement de la continuité du sentiment de l'unité linguistique ".[26] Car la continuité morphologique se réalise toujours par transmission directe, tandis que la continuité phonétique (et peut-être aussi syntaxique) emprunte le canal du substrat et la continuité du vocabulaire celui de l'emprunt.[27]

Aussi bien Meillet n'était-il pas sans faire état des faits de mélange, en particulier dans les périodes de bilinguisme : "Les sujets qui disposent à la fois de deux moyens d'expression distincts introduisent souvent dans l'une des deux langues qu'ils parlent des procédés appartenant à l'autre ".[28] Seulement, centrant toujours sa conception sur la morphologie, il ne voyait dans les éléments ainsi introduits dans une langue que des "emprunts". Une langue fût-elle essentiellement composée de mots latins, italiens, grecs, slaves et turcs, comme c'est le cas pour l'albanais, il n'y a point "mélange", mais seulement "emprunt". On voit la différence fondamentale avec Schuchardt, pour qui c'est tout un : "Ob von Mischung oder von Entlehnung, Nachahmung, fremdem Einfluss die Rede ist, immer haben wir wesengleiche Erscheinungen vor uns ".[29]

Si l'on écarte cette question de terminologie, le point de vue de Meillet n'est nullement en contradiction avec les principes énoncés ci-dessus. En effet, dès que l'on conçoit la langue comme étant essentiellement la morphologie, dire que deux langues ne peuvent se mélanger, c'est dire que deux morphologies ne peuvent se mélanger. Et cela se comprend aisément, puisqu'il s'agit de deux systèmes similaires et par conséquent, comme nous l'avons vu, impénétrables l'un à l'autre.

Il a été relativement facile de montrer que le mélange est possible entre systèmes dissimilaires d'origine différente. Les exemples positifs ne manquent

---

[19] Phrase entendue un jour d'examen.

[20] Meillet, *Linguistique historique et linguistique générale*, p. 82.

[21] Ibid., p. 84.

[22] J. Vendryes, *Le Langage*, 1921, pp. 345-347.

[23] *Linguistique historique et linguistique générale*, p. 83.

[24] Ibid., p. 83.

[25] *Linguistique historique et linguistique générale*, pp. 83-84. On notera dans cette énumération, volontairement incomplète, l'absence de la syntaxe, dans laquelle Meillet ne voyait qu'un appendice de la morphologie.

[26] Ibid., p. 81. Meillet écrit également au même endroit : "Entre la conquête de la Gaule par les Romains et l'époque actuelle, il n'y a eu aucun moment où les sujets parlants aient eu la volonté de parler une autre langue que le latin ". Ce point de vue, très fortement appuyé par Meillet, appelle d'ailleurs la discussion. Outre que, pour ma part, je n'ai jamais eu la volonté ou le sentiment de parler latin quand je parle français, l'affirmation ci-dessus présente, à mon sens, l'inconvénient de s'appliquer également à l'italien, à l'espagnol, etc. De ce qu'un Français et un Italien ont l'un et l'autre le "sentiment" ou la "volonté" de parler latin, il ne s'ensuit pas qu'ils parlent la même langue. Car le sentiment subjectif, évidemment erroné, des sujets parlants, ne saurait prévaloir contre la réalité objective, qui est que le français et l'italien sont bel et bien des langues différentes. (*Linguistique historique et linguistique générale*, p. 84.)

[27] "En somme, le vocabulaire est le domaine de l'emprunt ". (*Linguistique historique et linguistique générale*, p. 84.)

[28] Meillet, *Introduction...*, 7 p. 26.

[29] Leo Spitzer, *Hugo Schuchardt-Brevier*, 1922, p. 171.

pas. Il sera moins aisé de démontrer la proposition contraire, à savoir que deux systèmes cohérents similaires sont rebelles au mélange, car les exemples ne pourront par définition être que négatifs. Tout ce que l'on peut dire, c'est qu'on ne voit nulle part deux moitiés de systèmes morphologiques se souder pour former un nouveau système mixte. On n'arrive même pas à concevoir ce que pourrait être une déclinaison ou une conjugaison qui serait pour moitié latine et pour moitié arabe par exemple.

On objectera que la déclinaison latine s'accommodait fort bien des désinences grecques : *poesin*, *Socraten*, etc. Mais, outre qu'il ne s'agit pas là à proprement parler de formes latines, mais bien de formes grecques transcrites en latin, et senties comme telles, il ne faut pas oublier que le système de la déclinaison latine est au fond le même que celui de la déclinaison grecque, puisque toutes deux continuent un même prototype indo-européen qui a relativement peu évolué.

Quand il s'agit de deux systèmes vraiment différents, la pénétration est impossible. C'est ainsi que, quand par exemple l'argot militaire français emprunte le pluriel brisé arabe *toubib*, il en sent si peu la valeur dans le système morphologique de l'arabe, qu'il en fait un singulier auquel il redonne un pluriel conforme au système français : *des toubibs*. Le mot ne passe qu'à l'état isolé, et délesté de tout son système morphologique originel. Car la morphologie de l'arabe est inconciliable avec celle du français.

Certains affectent bien de dire : *un Targui, des Touareg*. Mais on ne les suit guère, quand ils ne font pas sourire. Le *Nouveau Larousse Illustré* enseigne qu'il faut accorder : *le costume targui et les armes touareg*. Mais il préconise en même temps : *une tribu targuie*, avec une forme de féminin essentiellement française. Et surtout il donne le mot sous la rubrique et à l'ordre alphabétique *Touareg*, s'infligeant par là à lui-même le plus éclatant démenti, puisqu'il n'est pas d'usage d'enregistrer sous la forme du pluriel les mots qui ont un singulier. De même lorsque le turc emprunte son relatif *-ki* au persan,[30] ce n'est qu'en le sortant complètement du système de la grammaire iranienne pour en faire un suffixe conforme à sa propre typologie. On invoquera également en faveur du mélange des morphologies le cas du pluriel allemand en *-s*, dont l'origine est, on le sait, française : *die Genes, die Kerls, die Fräuleins*. Mais on notera qu'il ne s'agit là que d'une désinence isolée, non d'un système. En outre, elle ne pénètre en allemand, si l'on excepte les mots français qui l'ont colportée (*die Genies*), que dans les mots en liquides (*die Kerls*) ou nasales (*die Mädchens, die Fräuleins*), dont la flexion est réduite à l'extrême, c'est-à-dire précisément dans la mesure où elle ne se heurte à aucun système morphologique hétérogène. Il y a d'ailleurs lieu de remarquer qu'elle ne fait que reprendre une place qui avait été occupée, quelques siècles auparavant, par la désinence parente germanique en *-s* qu'attestent l'anglosaxon *earmas* et même le vieux-saxon *armos* (en face de l'ancien-haut-allemand *arma*).

Ainsi nulle part on n'assiste au mélange de deux systèmes morphologiques. Mais cela ne veut pas dire que l'existence de deux systèmes morphologiques différents et par conséquent incompatibles soit jamais un obstacle au mélange des langues elles-mêmes. Si le brassage des populations est tellement intime que leurs langues ne puissent pas ne pas se mélanger, elles en sont quittes pour éliminer chacune leur système morphologique. Et l'on observe en effet que les langues très mélangées présentent une morphologie réduite à sa plus simple expression. "Les langues mixtes ont cet intérêt d'être aussi en général des langues très usées", constate I. Vendryes,[31] qui ajoute : "Déjà Grimm affirmait en 1819, que du conflit des langues résultait fatalement la perte de la grammaire. La conséquence n'est pas toujours fatale. Mais le fait est qu'on a souvent l'occasion de la constater".[32]

Tel est le cas pour le Caucase, où A. Dirr, cité par Vendryes,[33] constate que, là où les langues sont très mêlées, comme par exemple au Daghestan, "le résultat le plus remarquable est dans la simplification de la morphologie". Tel est également le cas de toutes les variétés de sabir, créole, petit nègre, pidgin-english, etc.

Ce serait une erreur de croire que ce qu'on appelle communément le petit nègre soit du français dont la morphologie et la syntaxe seraient ramenées au niveau élémentaire de la grammaire des noirs. La morphologie comme la syntaxe des langues des nègres, bantoues ou autres, est en effet loin d'être élémentaire. Et elle est au moins aussi difficile à acquérir pour un Européen que les nôtres pour un Africain. Ce qui est vrai, c'est que le petit nègre est le résultat d'un mélange où, chacun se révélant impuissant à assimiler le système de l'autre, les deux systèmes en présence disparaissent l'un et l'autre.

Quelques exemples montreront à quel point la grammaire est simplifiée dans ces langues mêlées :

Sabir : *Sbanioul chapar* (voler) *bourrico, andar labrizous* (prison). *Quand moi gagner drahem* (argent), *moi achetir moukère.*[34]

Créole de la Réunion : *Nous l'a çarré aussi ein bouteille rhum pour çauffe ein pé noat l'estoumac.*[35]

Créole de l'île Maurice : *Bien sir ça éne ptit banc qui li fine comande so domestique amène dans bord bassin pour mo capabe assisé, there* (quand) *mo bisoin tire quilotte pour alle bainqhe mo lécorps dans son dileau.*[36]

Aussi bien le petit nègre ne naît-il pas seulement dans nos rapports avec les nègres. Il apparaît spontanément dès que se trouvent en contact des langues différentes présentant des systèmes morphologiques ou syntaxiques compliqués. C'est en particulier ce qui s'est produit en 1914–1918 dans les camps de prisonniers d'Allemagne, où un savoureux sabir franco-russo-allemand a connu une floraison éphémère : *Moi nix bouffer, nix rabot.*[37]

Ainsi donc une langue mêlée est normalement une langue sans morphologie. On est en droit de se demander si la réciproque n'est pas vraie également, et si toute langue sans morphologie n'est pas le résultat d'un mélange récent, depuis lequel une nouvelle morphologie n'aurait pas eu le temps de se reconstituer.

[30] Meillet, *Linguistique historique et linguistique générale*, p. 87.

[31] Vendryes, *Le Langage*, p. 345.
[32] Ibid., p. 346.
[33] Ibid., p. 346.
[34] D'après Schuchardt, "De Lingua franca", *Zeitschrift für romanische Philologie*, XXXIII, p. 458.
[35] Héry, *Fables créoles*, Paris, 1883, p. 60.
[36] C. Baissac, *Le folklore de l'Ile-Maurice*, Paris, 1888, pp. 9-11.
[37] Du russe *rabota* "travail", *rabotat* "travailler".

Ce qui paraît en tous cas certain, c'est qu'une langue à système morphologique riche a toutes chances de ne pas provenir d'un mélange récent. Et comme la démonstration de la " parenté " linguistique ne peut guère être administrée que grâce à la morphologie,[38] on peut entrevoir là une possibilité d'expliquer l'état linguistique du monde, où, pour le plus grand désespoir des amateurs d'uniformité, à côté de grandes familles de langues aux rameaux nombreux et fournis, il subsiste une poussière de langues isolées que l'on ne rattache à aucune famille.

Une étude, même superficielle, de la question du mélange des langues à la lumière de la phonologie apparaît ainsi comme singulièrement instructive. Elle permet de prendre position entre les partisans et les adversaires de la théorie des mélanges. Certes, si l'on veut bien donner au mot langue toute son extension et ne pas en faire un simple synonyme de morphologie, il semble difficile de nier qu'il y ait des mélanges de langues. Et toutes les langues sont plus ou moins, à des titres et à des degrés divers, des langues mixtes. Mais tous les mélanges ne sont pas possibles, et ceux qui sont possibles ne s'opèrent pas n'importe comment. Ils obéissent à certaines lois, qu'il y aurait lieu de préciser dans le détail avant de songer à établir la théorie générale des mélanges de langues, dont la nécessité finira bien par s'imposer un jour.

Tout ce qui semble résulter pour le moment des brèves considérations qui précèdent, c'est que, dans cette théorie, les divers degrés de cohésion des systèmes en présence sont appelés à jouer un rôle capital. Aussi, si l'on arrive un jour à tirer au clair cette question complexe et délicate, ce ne sera qu'en tenant largement compte des méthodes et des résultats de la phonologie pragoise.

Qu'il me soit donc permis, en souvenir d'une amitié et d'une admiration qui datent de vingt-cinq ans, de dédier ces quelques pages à la mémoire du linguiste de grande classe dont la bienfaisante activité, prématurément interrompue, est à la source des théories de l'école de Prague, qui ont déjà tant fait pour renouveler la linguistique, et qui se relèvent d'autant plus fécondes qu'on les médite davantage.

[38] Meillet, *Linguistique historique et linguistique générale*, p. 97.

LE RAPPORT ENTRE LE DÉTERMINÉ, LE DÉTERMINANT ET LE DÉFINI

N. S. Trubetzkoy

Dans un recueil d'articles dédié à un des plus éminents représentants de l'école linguistique genevoise il est sans doute inutile d'insister sur la possibilité et la légitimité d'une étude linguistique comparative indépendante du principe généalogique. Tandis que la grammaire comparée des langues d'un groupe généalogique quelconque se pose pour but de découvrir l'origine de tel ou de tel autre phénomène observé dans chacune de ces langues et occupe par conséquent un point de vue diachronique, — l'étude comparative des langues non-apparentées se propose d'éclaircir les rapports synchroniques entre les faits d'une langue en les confrontant avec des rapports analogues existants dans une autre langue dans un contexte tout différent. Une telle étude ne peut partir que du point de vue synchronique.

Dans ce qui suit nous voulons exposer quelques idées sur les rapports du déterminé et du déterminant, du déterminé et du défini.

Le rapport de déterminé à déterminant est sans doute le plus répandu de tous les rapports syntagmatiques, mais nous sommes bien loin de l'envisager comme le seul rapport syntagmatique possible. Notamment, nous doutons fort que le sujet et le prédicat puissent être considérés comme déterminé et déterminant. Il y a beaucoup de langues qui possèdent un moyen unique pour marquer le rapport de déterminé à déterminant, — et dans la plupart de ces langues ce moyen ne s'applique pas au rapport entre le sujet et le prédicat. Ainsi dans les langues turques, mongoles et dans beaucoup de langues finno-ougriennes le déterminant précède le déterminé : l'adjectif précède le substantif ou le nom de nombre précédent le substantif ; un substantif au génitif précède le substantif auquel il se rapporte, l'adverbe précède l'adjectif ou le verbe auquel il se rapporte, enfin le complément direct ou indirect précède le verbe. Mais le prédicat (verbal ou nominal) suit son sujet, — ce qui prouve qu'il n'est pas considéré comme le déterminant du sujet. En gilyak (langue "palaeoasiatique" parlée dans le nord de l'île Sachalin et à l'embouchure de l'Amour) deux mots voisins se rapportant comme déterminant et déterminé subissent certaines altérations phonétiques (notamment la consonne initiale du second terme d'un tel syntagme devient une spirante). Ces altérations se produisent dans les groupes adjectif + substantif, "génitif" + substantif correspondant, complément + verbe, etc. Mais elles ne se produisent pas dans le groupe sujet + prédicat.[1] En ibo (langue "soudanaise" parlée en Nigérie), où l'on distingue trois tons, les tons fondamentaux des deux termes d'un groupe "déterminant + déterminé" ou "déterminé + déterminant" subissent certaines altérations : la dernière syllabe du premier terme et la première syllabe du second terme d'un tel groupe reçoivent un ton haut si elles ont un ton moyen ou bas dans d'autres positions.[2] Ces altérations peuvent être observées dans les groupes "adjectif + substantif", "nom (au génitif) + nom", "nom + démonstratif, nom de nombre, pronom relatif", "nom appartenant à la proposition principale + verbe de la proposition subordonnée se rapportant à ce nom." Mais l'altération de ton ne se produit jamais dans le groupe "sujet + prédicat". On aurait pu augmenter le nombre de ces exemples qui prouvent que dans les langues de structures les plus différentes le rapport entre sujet et prédicat n'est pas conçu comme un rapport entre déterminé et déterminant. Les exemples contraires sont rares et peu probants. Nous croyons donc distinguer les syntagmes déterminatifs (composés d'un déterminant et d'un déterminé) des syntagmes prédicatifs (composés d'un sujet et d'un prédicat).

Une troisième classe est représentée par les syntagmes sociatifs, dont les deux termes se trouvent toujours dans un rapport syntagmatique avec quelqu'autre membre du même énoncé. Nous entendons donc par syntagme sociatif deux sujets au même prédicat, deux prédicats au même sujet, deux déterminants se rapportant au même déterminé, etc.[3]

Les syntagmes déterminatifs présentent des types et des sous-types multiples dont le nombre dépend en partie de la structure grammaticale de la langue donnée. Certains de ces types se retrouvent dans un grand nombre de langues et ont reçu une dénomination commune traditionnelle : le déterminant d'un syntagme dont les deux termes sont des substantifs est d'ordinaire désigné du nom "génitif" ; dans un syntagme déterminatif dont l'un des termes est un substantif (ou un pronom) et l'autre une forme verbale, la forme verbale est appelée "participe" si c'est elle qui est le déterminant si, contraire, c'est le substantif ou le pronom qui est le déterminant, on les désigne comme "complément" et on distingue entre "complément direct" et "complément indirect". Toutes ces étiquettes ont une certaine raison d'être et sont parfois assez pratiques. Mais souvent elles donnent une idée fausse des rapports réels entre les différentes catégories grammaticales d'une langue donnée.

Tout verbe transitif employé comme prédicat suppose au moins deux substantifs (ou pronoms) dont l'un désigne l'auteur de l'action, l'autre, l'objet atteint par l'action. Des deux syntagmes formés par le verbe transitif et chacun

---

[1] Voir E. Krejnovič "Nivchskij (gil'ackij) jazyk", Jazyki i pis'mennost' narodov Severa III.

[2] Pour les détails voir Ida C. Ward, An Introduction to the Ibo Language, Cambridge 1936, ainsi que notre compte-rendu sur cet ouvrage dans Anthropos, XXXI, pp. 978 et suiv.

[3] Notons qu'en russe toutes les trois classes de syntagmes peuvent être exprimées par un groupe de deux substantifs, et dans ce cas la différence de sens est exprimée par l'intonation : čelovek-zvěŕ "l'homme bestial" (syntagme déterminatif) — sans aucune pause entre les deux termes et sans aucun accent sur le premier terme, — čelovek – zvěŕ "l'homme est une bête" (syntagme prédicatif) — avec une petite pause entre les deux termes, un accent ascendant sur le premier terme et un accent descendant sur le second, — čelovek, zvěŕ "(... ptica) "l'homme, la bête... "l'oiseau" (syntagme sociatif) — avec une pause assez grande entre les deux termes et un accent "d'énumération" (descendant) sur chaque terme.

Reprinted from Mélanges de linguistique, offerts à Charles Bally, pp. 75-82 (Geneva : Georg, 1939), with the permission of Bernard Gagnebin, dean, faculty of letters, University of Geneva.

de ces substantifs (ou pronoms) l'un est nécessairement un syntagme prédicatif, l'autre — un syntagme déterminatif. De là deux types de langues : les langues où le déterminant du verbe transitif est le nom de l'auteur de l'action, et les langues où le déterminant du verbe transitif est le nom de l'objet de l'action. Dans les celles du second type le nominatif (cas sujet) s'oppose à l'ergatif, dan celles du second type le nominatif s'oppose à l'accusatif. Le premier type est représenté par l'eskimo, le tibétain, les langues caucasiques du Nord, etc. ; le second type — par les langues soudanaises, sémitiques, indo-européennes, finno-ougriennes, turques, mongoles, etc. Certes, du point de vue de chacune de ces langues, les termes "nominatif et ergatif" ou "nominatif et accusatif" sont pratiques et commodes. Mais du point de vue de la grammaire générale il s'agit dans les deux types d'une opposition du "cas sujet" au "cas déterminant immédiat d'un verbe". Car, bien que l'ergatif soit juste le contraire de l'accusatif, ces deux cas jouent le même rôle dans les systèmes syntagmatiques des langues respectives : ce rôle consiste à déterminer immédiatement un verbe transitif (tandis que tout autre "cas déterminant" d'un tel verbe présuppose l'existence d'un déterminant immédiat).[4]

Si l'accusatif ou l'ergatif (selon le type de langue) est le cas déterminant adverbal immédiat, le génitif (selon le type de langue) peut être désigné comme le "cas déterminant adnominal". Ainsi s'explique la coïncidence (partielle ou totale) de l'accusatif ou de l'ergatif (selon le type de langue) avec le génitif dans beaucoup de langues. En arabe classique le génitif coïncide avec l'accusatif au duel et au pluriel ("régulier") de tous les substantifs et au singulier des noms propres ; dans les langues slaves (à l'exception du bulgare qui a perdu la déclinaison) les substantifs signifiant des êtres vivants masculins (aussi bien que les pronoms et les adjectifs se rapportant à de tels substantifs) emploient au singulier le génitif dans la valeur de l'accusatif ; dans certaines langues turques, p. ex. le balkar ou le karatchaï (au Caucase du Nord) le génitif coïncide toujours avec l'accusatif. D'autre part, dans certaines langues caucasiques orientales — notamment en lak (dans le Daghestan central) et dans la plupart des dialectes du kuri ou lesgi (au S.-E. du Daghestan) la forme du génitif coïncide avec celle de l'ergatif. Il est donc évident que du point de vue des langues telles que le balkar ou le lak il est faux de parler d'un cas génitif et d'un cas accusatif ou ergatif : il n'y a dans ces langues qu'un unique "cas déterminant immédiat", opposé d'une part à plusieurs cas déterminants non-immédiats et d'autre part à un cas non-déterminant ("nominatif"). De même l'arabe classique présente au duel et au pluriel non pas une opposition du "nominatif" au "cas non-déterminant" à un "cas déterminant". Ces exemples suffisent pour montrer quelles nuances multiples acquiert la notion de "déterminant immédiat" selon le contexte grammatical d'une langue donnée. Et il ne s'agit là encore que du type le plus simple des syntagmes déterminatifs.

La notion d'"article défini" est bien connue au monde de civilisation européenne. Mais les linguistes avertis savent que la même nuance de sens qui en grec, en français, en allemand ou en anglais est exprimée par l'addition de l'"article défini" s'exprime dans d'autres langues par d'autres moyens. Il y a donc lieu d'employer l'expression "forme définie" pour tout substantif qui, soit par l'addition d'un article, soit par quelqu'autre procédé morphologique, reçoit la nuance de sens que possèdent les substantifs munis d'un "article défini" en grec, en français, etc.

La notion du "défini" peut être exprimée par trois procédés : A) par un syntagme (déterminatif) composé du substantif en question et de l'"article défini", conçu comme mot ; B) par une forme spéciale du substantif en question (c'est-à-dire par une combinaison du thème de ce substantif avec un affixe spécial) ; C) par une forme spéciale d'un autre mot (substantif, adjectif, verbe) se rapportant au substantif en question, c'est-à-dire formant avec lui un syntagme (déterminatif ou prédicatif).

Il est parfois difficile de distinguer entre les procédés A et B. Une combinaison de deux mots doit être envisagée comme telle si ses membres peuvent être séparés par l'intercalation d'autres mots, tandis qu'un affixe ne peut être séparé du "thème" que par d'autres affixes à valeur formelle. Dans celles des langues de l'Europe moderne où l'article défini existe comme un mot séparable, il est toujours préposé (ainsi en grec, en italien, en français, en espagnol, en portugais, en anglais, en allemand, en hongrois). Par contre, dans celles des langues européennes où la notion du défini est exprimée par des affixes, ces derniers sont suffixés (ainsi en norvégien, en suédois, en danois, en albanais, en roumain, en bulgare et dans certains dialectes grand-russes). En étudiant les langues non-européennes les linguistes européens ont la tendance d'interpréter toutes les marques extérieures du défini comme articles — si elles sont préposées, et comme affixes — si elles sont postposées. Il est évident que c'est une erreur dont il faut se garder. Ainsi l'"article défini" de l'arabe n'est en réalité qu'un préfixe, — puisqu'il se trouve toujours immédiatement devant le substantif et ne peut être séparé de ce dernier par aucun autre mot. Au contraire le soi-disant "suffixe du défini" *r* en tcherkesse et en kabardi est en réalité un article, puisqu'il peut être séparé du substantif par des adjectifs et des noms de nombre : cf. tcherkesse *unedeǯešïr* "les (*r*) trois (*šï*) belles (*deze*) maisons (*une*)". — Quant au procédé C, il convient de mentionner que souvent il se combine avec l'un des deux autres. Ainsi en bulgare le défini est exprimé par un affixe qu'on ajoute au substantif, si ce dernier n'est pas déterminé par un adjectif (*čovekăt* l'homme) ou bien à l'adjectif qui détermine le substantif (*dobrïăt čovek* l'homme bon). En mordve le défini est toujours indiqué par un affixe ajouté au substantif, mais, en plus, les verbes transitifs possèdent des désinences différentes, selon que leur complément direct est défini ou indéfini : *raman kudo,* "j'achèterai une maison" ∼ *ramasa kudont'* "j'achèterai la maison" ∼ *ramat kudo* "tu achèteras une maison" ∼ *ramasak kudont'* "tu achèteras la maison" etc. Cf. les formes "fortes" et "faibles" de l'adjectif en allemand, etc.

Comme toutes les catégories grammaticales la notion du défini n'existe réellement qu'en tant qu'opposée à la notion contraire. Dans toutes les langues qui la possèdent, l'opposition entre défini et indéfini est neutralisée ou supprimée

[4] Cf. R. Jakobson, *Travaux du Cercle Linguistique de Prague* VI, p. 254.

dans certaines positions ou sous certaines conditions, qui diffèrent d'une langue à une autre. Il ne sera peut-être pas trop exagéré d'affirmer que dans la plupart des cas la neutralisation de l'opposition entre le défini et l'indéfini est liée au fonctionnement du système des syntagmes — prédicatifs ou déterminatifs.

Les syntagmes prédicatifs présentent des rapports très simples. Dans la plupart des langues l'opposition entre défini et indéfini conserve sa pleine vigueur pour tous les termes des dits syntagmes. Mais dans plusieurs langues cette opposition est supprimée pour les substantifs en fonction prédicative ; le contraire, c'est-à-dire la suppression de l'opposition entre défini et indéfini chez les substantifs en fonction de sujet (et sa conservation chez les substantifs en fonction prédicative) ne semble avoir lieu dans aucune langue du monde.

A l'intérieur des syntagmes déterminatifs les rapports sont plus compliqués et varient d'une langue à l'autre. Très souvent l'opposition entre défini et indéfini se trouve supprimée chez le déterminé, notamment dans deux groupes de cas : quand le déterminant est un démonstratif ou quand il est un possessif. Les substantifs déterminés par des démonstratifs se trouvent en dehors de l'opposition entre défini et indéfini presque dans toutes les langues.[5] Dans beaucoup d'autres langues il en est de même pour les substantifs déterminés par des possessifs-pronominaux (par exemple en français), par toute sorte de possessifs (par exemple, en vieux-slave, en tcherkesse, en abkhaz) ou par certains types de possessifs (par exemple en anglais, en allemand, en danois — par les possessifs pronominaux et par les génitifs en -s précédant leurs déterminés). Mais dans beaucoup de langues l'opposition entre défini et indéfini existe même chez les substantifs déterminés par des possessifs pronominaux (par exemple en grec, en italien, en arabe, etc.).

Quand le déterminant est un adjectif qualificatif, le déterminé conserve l'opposition entre défini et indéfini dans toutes les langues que nous connaissons. Il y a plus : dans certaines langues les substantifs déterminés par un adjectif qualificatif sont les seuls qui connaissent l'opposition entre défini et indéfini. C'est le cas en serbo-croate et en vieux-slave, où l'opposition entre défini et indéfini est exprimée par des formes spéciales de l'adjectif (" procédé C "). En français la même restriction existe par rapport aux noms propres qui n'admettent l'article que quand ils sont déterminés par des adjectifs : " il y avait parmi vos élèves un petit Jean, qui ne voulait pas apprendre ; et bien, le petit Jean paresseux — c'est moi ! "

En kabardi il n'y a à vrai dire que deux cas : le " cas déterminant " (= génitif, datif, locatif, et ergatif) et le cas " non-déterminant " (sujet des verbes intransitifs, complément direct des verbes transitifs et prédicat des phrases nominales), — les autres " cas " n'étant que des combinaisons avec des postpositions. Or dans cette langue l'opposition entre défini et indéfini n'existe que dans le " cas non-déterminant " et est supprimée dans le cas déterminant.[6]

Enfin, il y a des langues qui présentent des rapports directement contraires à ceux du kabardi, — des langues où l'opposition entre les notions du défini et de l'indéfini n'existent que chez les déterminants. Dans les langues turques le complément direct d'un verbe transitif (c'est-à-dire le déterminant nominal de ce verbe) peut être exprimé de deux manières selon qu'il est indéfini ou défini : dans le premier cas il ne reçoit pas de suffixe casuel, dans le second cas il reçoit le suffixe de l'" accusatif ". Pour la plupart des langues turques modernes c'est la seule situation syntaxique où les notions de défini et d'indéfini soient distinguées extérieurement. En russe moderne et peut-être dans quelques autres langues slaves les adjectifs possessifs dérivés de noms de personnes indiquent toujours l'appartenance à une personne définie, tandis que la tournure avec le génitif du nom de personne ne comporte pas cette nuance : *mal'nikova doč* veut dire toujours " fille du meunier ", tandis que *doč mel'nika* peut dire aussi bien " fille du meunier " que " fille *d'un* meunier ". C'est là le seul cas où le russe (du moins le russe littéraire) présente un germe de l'opposition entre les notions du défini et de l'indéfini, — et il est curieux de noter, qu'il s'agit du déterminant d'un syntagme déterminatif.

Nous voyons donc que l'opposition entre défini et indéfini peut être supprimée chez le déterminé (par exemple en français après les possessifs et les démonstratifs) ou chez le déterminant (par exemple en kabardi), mais qu'elle peut être limitée aussi uniquement au déterminé (par exemple en vieux-slave) ou au déterminant (par exemple en turc). Il serait utile d'étudier ces possibilités dans le contexte de l'ensemble du système grammatical de chaque langue donné.

---

[5] Mais en vieux-slave, où la notion du défini était exprimée par des formes spéciales de l'adjectif (" procédé C "), le défini pouvait être distingué de l'indéfini même en combinaison avec un pronom démonstratif. En mordve les substantifs déterminés par des démonstratifs présentent tantôt la forme définie tantôt la forme indéfinie, — mais il, est difficile de dire si, dans ce cas-là, il y a vraiment une opposition de sens.

[6] Le tcherkesse (ou bas-tcherkesse) qui est le parent le plus proche du kabardi diffère de ce dernier par le fait qu'il présente l'opposition entre le défini et l'indéfini dans les deux cas ; toutefois il emploie pour chacun des deux cas un autre article défini : pour le " non-déterminant " -r (comme le kabardi) et pour le " cas déterminant " -m (qui en kabardi sert de désinence casuelle sans distinction de défini et d'indéfini).

SPEECH AND WRITING [1]

H. J. Uldall

In his *Cours de linguistique générale*, Saussure said : "language is form, not substance". The meaning of this extraordinarily happy formulation is, of course, that the language, "la langue," as distinct from "la parole", is something apart from the substance in which it is manifested, an abstract system which is not defined by the substance, but which, on the contrary, forms the substance and defines it as such. Saussure himself did not live to draw the full theoretical consequences of his discovery, and it is a curious fact that it is only now, over twenty years later, that anyone at all has even begun to do this. It is even more curious when we consider that the practical consequences have been widely drawn, indeed had been drawn thousands of years before Saussure, for it is only through the concept of a difference between form and substance that we can explain the possibility of speech and writing existing at the same time as expressions of one and the same language. If either of these two substances, the stream of air or the stream of ink, were an integral part of the language itself, it would not be possible to go from one to the other without changing the language.

It is this concept of form and substance which underlies, also, the phoneme theory. The phoneme, which was also generally recognised in practice long before its theoretical discovery, can be briefly explained as follows : the infinite variety of sounds used in actual speech are seen to belong together in groups in such a way that the members of one and the same group can be exchanged without any change of meaning, while the interchange of two sounds belonging to different groups may lead to a change of meaning. In other words, there is a something which remains constant when you exchange within the same group, but which changes when you go from one group to another, and which, consequently, must be supposed to be common to all the sounds belonging to one group. This something is evidently not meaning : the meaning of the word " cat " cannot be dissected in such a way that a segment is ascribed

to the *k* which is recognisably the same in all words containing a *k*. Some people have tried to define the something in terms of phonic substance : all the different sounds belonging to a phoneme have some characteristic in common, which can be described physically or physiologically or both ; but as we have already seen that ink may be substituted for air without any change in the language, it is obvious that this explanation is not sufficient to establish our something as a fact belonging to *la langue*, although it is equally obvious that it is necessary in a description of *la parole*. Others have tried a psychological explanation—and then left it again rather hastily, because it was found that the " Sprachgefühl " is hard to get at, and too often vague and undependable when you do catch it.

In continuation of Saussure I would suggest that our something, that which is common to sounds and letters alike, is a form—a form which is independent of the particular substance in which it is manifested, and which is defined only by its functions to other forms of the same order. The form, then, will remain the same even if we change the substance, as long as we do not interfere with its function. When we write a phonetic or a phonemic transcription, we substitute ink for air, but the form remains the same, because the functions of each component form have not been changed : we have been careful that the number of graphemes should not be less than the number of phonemes, and that the order of forms should remain the same in the graphic manifestation as it was in the phonic one ; when these conditions are fulfilled, we have what is called an accurate transcription. We can distill from the phonic manifestation of a language an inventory of forms, which can be safely represented graphically or in any other way that may be found convenient, and of which we know that, in the combinations which we have registered, they are sufficient to express the language satisfactorily.

The substance of ink has not received the same attention on the part of linguists that they have so lavishly bestowed on the substance of air. We can see at a glance, however, that it behaves in much the same way : in writing we find a multiplicity of variants similar to the state of affairs in speech ; the shape of a letter varies according to the shapes of neighboring letters, according to position in the group (initial, final, or medial), according to individual taste and habit, and according to extrinsic factors such as the condition of the pen, in the same way that sound-quality varies for similar reasons. From a linguistic point of view, a bad pen is quite parallel to a sore throat or a cigar between the teeth of the speaker. In printing and typewriting we have standardised the shapes of letters to the exclusion of variants, so that there is only one shape per grapheme. To this there is nothing similar in speech, but, as shown by Menzerath's experiments with cutting a tonefilm to pieces and pasting it together again in a different order,[2] this is not due to any fundamental difference in the two substances : it would be quite feasible to produce standardised artificial speech of the same kind. If the technique of reproducing speech had happened to develop in another way, our broadcasting stations would have been sending out standardised one-variant-per-phoneme speech instead of employing live announcers.

Reprinted from *Acta Linguistica* 4 (1944) : 11-16, with the permission of Mrs. H. J. Uldall and of the editorial board of *Acta Linguistica*.

[1] Paper read to the linguistic section of the Congrès international des Sciences anthropologiques et ethnologiques, Copenhagen, 1938 (a resume is printed in the *Compte rendu* of the congress, Copenhagen, 1939). Dr. Josef Vachek has recently published a very interesting treatment of the same subject : *Zum Problem der geschriebenen Sprache* (*Travaux du Cercle linguistique de Prague* VIII, 1939) ; a comparison of the two brings out very clearly the difference between the phonological and the glossematic points of view.

[2] Cf. *Actes du quatrième Congrès international de Linguistes* (Copenhagen, 1938), pp. 72 ff.

From the graphic manifestation of a language we can distill, then, in the same way as from the phonic manifestation, an inventory of forms, defined by their mutual functions, which might equally well be represented phonically or in any other convenient way, and of which we know that in the combinations which we have registered, they are sufficient to express the language satisfactorily.

The extraordinary thing is that we shall often find that the forms derived from an analysis of the phonic manifestation differ from the forms derived from an analysis of the graphic manifestation of what is known as the same language. A moment's thought will show you that in almost any European language, English for choice, the number of phonemes does not tally with the number of graphemes. I shall take care not to give you my own count, because at the present stage of the game hardly two phoneticians agree as to the phonemic analysis of any language. But a striking fact which is enough to prove my contention, is that there are no graphemes in the orthography corresponding to the accents of the pronunciation, and that, conversely, the pronunciation has no phoneme corresponding to the spacing between words in the orthography.

The task which I have set myself in this paper is to find an explanation of the fact that two mutually incongruent systems can be used side by side to express the same language.

Before attempting this main problem, I should like to call your attention to two subsidiary problems, which might have a bearing on our inquiry: (1) can either of the two systems be said to be primary in relation to the other, and (2) what is the reason for the discrepancy between them?

(1) In my opinion it is illegitimate to consider either of them primary. They simply coexist. There is no indication, either systematically or historically, of any such relation between them, for although it is true that in the history of mankind generally, as far as we know it, speech preceded writing, it is not true that the present sound pattern preceded the present orthography, and influence of one upon the other, in matters of detail, seems to be about equal on both sides: if there have been cases of spelling-pronunciation, there have also been cases of pronunciation-spelling.

(2) As to the second question, it follows from what has already been said, that the reason for the difference between pronunciation and orthography is not to be sought in the difference between air and ink, since we can and do make graphic manifestations congruent with the usual phonic one—phonetic and phonemic transcriptions—and since we can, and some people do, make phonic manifestations congruent with the usual graphic one—in Denmark at least, you can hear people of scanty education carefully enunciating a sound for each letter and pausing between the words as they read aloud. The reason must be simply the well-known historical development: our alphabet was originally designed to be used for the manifestation of a structurally quite different language, the orthography is often more conservative than the pronunciation, and has further been artificially tampered with by printers and grammarians and sometimes even by politicians.

Now, to get back to the main question, let us first examine what is meant by saying that pronunciation and orthography express the same language.

A language consists of two planes, the plane of content, or meaning, and the plane of expression. The relation between these two planes is such that a unit belonging to one may call forth a unit belonging to the other. If I hear *kat* spoken or see "cat" written, it may call to my mind the idea of *felis domestica*, and conversely the idea of *felis domestica* may induce me to say *kat* or to write "cat". When we say that orthography and pronunciation are expressions of the same language, we mean simply that the orthographic units and the units of pronunciation correspond to, or, better, are functions of the same units of content: the fact that both *kat* and "cat" are functions of the idea *felis domestica*, as that idea is defined in relation to other English ideas, proves that they are expressions of the same language. It is this mutual function between two planes that constitutes a language: the units of content are defined as such by having an expression, and the units of expression are defined as such by having a content. If we keep the units of content constant, we shall have the same language whatever system is used to make up the corresponding units of expression, as we have seen. I don't want to take you too far away from the main inquiry into the details of this theory, but I should like to suggest in passing, that the same should logically hold true, if we keep the units of expression constant and change the corresponding units of content, or, in other words, if we took a dictionary and ascribed different meanings to all the words in it. As far as I know, this rather intricate experiment has never been carried out, but it has been done many times on a smaller scale, particularly with scientific terminology: we all know examples of familiar terms—units of expression—being used in an unfamiliar sense, i.e. with function to different units of content.[3] But this is merely a digression to show that the relation between content and expression is bilateral, not unilateral as has often been supposed.

The conclusion that is relevant to our inquiry, is that a system of any internal structure will do, provided that a sufficient number of units can be made up from it to express the units of content. Units of expression belonging to different systems unite into groups analogous to the groups of sounds which we call phonemes, and defined by all the members of one group being functions of the same unit of content. A group of this kind I shall call a *cenia*. Thus the speech-chain *kat* and the written chain "cat" belong to the same cenia, because they can be exchanged without a change of meaning, being functions of the same unit of content. But to the same cenia will belong also, it will be seen, any other unit from any other system of expression, if it is a function of the same unit of content. We can invent new pronunciations, or new orthographies, or new systems of expression manifested in any other way, such as flag-wagging or dancing,[4] and they will all be adequate, if they fulfil the single condition of providing a sufficient number of units to express the units of content.

The system of speech and the system of writing are thus only two realisations out of an infinite number of possible systems, of which no one can be said to

[3] Cf. e.g. "articulation" and "morphology", the meanings of which differ according as the context is linguistic or biological.
[4] Cf. G. K. Chesterton's almost glossematic story *The Noticeable Conduct of Professor Chadd*, in *The Club of Queer Trades*.

be more fundamental than any other. From a theoretical point of view it is therefore nonsense to talk about, for instance, the English graphic system being inadequate : we might just as well turn it around and say that the English phonic system is inadequate ; the truth must be that they are both equally adequate, and that any other system fulfilling the conditions would do just as well. Another thing is that for practical purposes it is probably more convenient to have one system than two, and as it is less difficult to change the orthography than the pronunciation, it might be an advantage to bring the graphic system into harmony with the phonic system.

The maximal system is the truly ideographic or ideophonic one, a system providing one element for each unit of content instead of a unit made up of elements which can be used over and over again in other combinations. The minimal system is the smallest one from which a sufficient number of units can be made up.

It is for the normative linguist—the standardiser of languages, and the inventor of artificial languages—to choose that system out of the infinite number of possible ones, which is best suited to his purpose.

SOME REMARKS ON WRITING AND PHONETIC TRANSCRIPTION

Josef Vachek

There is a more or less generally accepted belief among students of language that writing and phonetic transcription are to be regarded as two ways of recording speech utterances. The difference between the two is supposed to consist chiefly in the fact that transcription aims at the greatest possible accuracy in recording, whereas writing does not aspire to more than a rough-and-ready reproduction of the utterances. Transcription, it is usually asserted, can do far greater justice to the actual acoustic make-up of speech utterances because it does not shrink from using special symbols, one for each sound, instead of clinging to traditional letters used in the conventional way, as is done in writing. As traditional writing very often violates the " one-symbol-per-sound " principle, it cannot help lagging hopelessly behind transcription as far as both accuracy of record and adequacy of means are concerned.

However widespread the above views may be, they appear very doubtful if scrutinized from the functionalist and structuralist point-of-view. As is well known, the system is called the phonemic system and its units are known this, let us look more closely at the facts under discussion.

As regards phonetic transcription, it is useful to point out, at the very start, that it is, and should be, regarded as a primarily technical device. Its principal *raison d'être* is the optical embodiment of acoustic phenomena constituting a spoken utterance ; a projection of sounds, so to speak, on paper. This very intimate connection with the phonic make-up of the utterance should be regarded as the basic feature of phonetic transcription. As is well known, Daniel Jones goes so far as to believe that utterances of a language can be transcribed phonetically even if the transcribing person is totally ignorant of the language in question. The present writer believes he has shown, in another of his papers,[1] that Prof. Jones's thesis does not hold good on this point. What remains certain, however, is that in deciphering a text written in phonetic script one first of all undertakes the acoustic interpretation of the visual signs constituting the transcribed text, and only then proceeds to the semantic interpretation of the acoustic facts thus obtained. That is to say, the transcribed

text does not constitute the sign of the outside world, but the sign of the sign of the outside world (in other words, it is a sign of the second order).

The exact definition of what is called writing has hardly ever been attempted. Phoneticians have usually contented themselves with branding it as a kind of a highly unsatisfactory pseudotranscription, and other linguists have often confused writing with orthography. As a matter of fact, orthography is a kind of bridge leading from spoken sentences to their written counterparts. (Inversely, pronunciation is a kind of bridge leading from spoken to written sentences.) To stress the non-identity of writing and orthography is not, of course, the same as to solve the problem. It is essential to find out a positive answer as to the exact place of writing within the scale of the facts of language.

Any sound linguistic theory must be based on concrete utterances of speech. It is often overlooked, however, that speech utterances are of two different kinds, i.e. spoken and written utterances. The latter cannot be simply regarded as optical projections of the former. To difference of material existing between the two is added another difference, more profound and more essential, that is to say, a difference of functions. The function of the spoken utterance is to respond to the given stimulus (which, as a rule, is urgent) in a dynamic way, i.e. quickly, readily, and with equal attention to both the intellectual and the emotional factors of the situation that gave rise to the stimulus. On the other hand, the function of the written utterance is to respond to the given stimulus (which, as a rule, is not urgent) in a static way, that is to say, the response should be permanent (i.e. preservable), affording full comprehension as well as clear survey of the situation concerned, and stressing the intellectual factors of the situation. In another of his papers, the present writer has pointed out that each of the two kinds of utterances has its own standard, a standard which can be denoted as spoken language or written language, respectively.[2] It has been generally admitted that spoken language is based on a system of phonic oppositions capable of differentiating meanings in the given community. As is well known, the system is called the phonemic system and its units are known as phonemes. Analogously, written language must be based on a system of graphic oppositions capable of differentiating meanings in the given community. And it is this system, forming the basis of written language, which we call writing. The units of this system may be called graphemes.

As has been shown in another paper,[3] the phoneme is a member of a complex phonemic opposition, a member which is indivisible into smaller successive phonemic units. Analogously, the grapheme may be defined as a member of a complex " graphemic " opposition, a member which is indivisible into smaller successive graphemic units. " Graphemic " opposition is, of course, taken here as an exact counterpart of the phonemic opposition in the domain of spoken language—that is to say, it denotes such an opposition of graphic facts as is

Reprinted from *Acta Linguistica* 5 (1945–49) : 86–93, with the permission of the author and of the editorial board of *Acta Linguistica*.

[1] J. Vachek : *Professor Daniel Jones and the Phoneme. Charisteria Gu. Mathesio quinqua-genario... oblata*, Prague, 1932, pp. 25 f.

[2] For the theory of written language, see J. Vachek : *Zum Problem der geschriebenen Sprache, Travaux du Cercle linguistique de Prague* VIII (1939), pp. 94 f.—H. J. Uldall in his paper *Speech and Writing* (*Acta Linguistica* IV, pp. 11 ff.), full of interesting observations, does not seem to have stressed sufficiently the autonomous character of written language, as opposed to spoken language.—On the relations existing between written and printed language, see J. Vachek : *Written Language and Printed Language, Mélanges J. M. Kořínek*, Bratislava, 1949 (in print).

[3] J. Vachek : *Phonemes and Phonological Units. Travaux du Cercle Linguistique de Prague* VI (1936), pp. 235 f.

capable of differentiating meanings in the given language. It is hardly necessary to point out that the graphemes, being the smallest units of the written language, are characterized by some features analogous to those found in the phonemes, the smallest elements of the spoken language. The basic analogy lies in the fact that the graphemes of a given language—like its phonemes—remain differentiated from one another, i.e. that they do not get mixed up. The importance of this fact is promptly realized if a graphemic opposition comes to be neglected—thus, e.g. if a writing individual does not duly distinguish in written utterances his *a*'s from his *o*'s, his *h*'s from his *k*'s, his *s*'s from his *z*'s, etc.

To ascertain all consequences from the analogy existing between writing and the phonemic system, one must look down the scale of values as well as up the scale. Exactly as the phonemes of a given language are realized in concrete sounds and sound-attributes, so the graphemes become manifested in concrete letters and letter-attributes (diacritical marks, punctuation signs, etc.). These items make up what may be called the graphic inventory of the given language, which has, of course, its counterpart in the phonic inventory of the same language. It should be stressed, naturally, that these inventories are meant as materials only, without any regard to the functions of their component parts. On the other hand, these materials as wholes have their own peculiar distinctness of character. It is a well-known fact that even persons who do not speak a single word of English and French are able to tell the two languages from one another if they hear them spoken, and that they can perhaps give a kind of impressionist description of either of them. And it is equally true that even those who do not read English and French are able to tell English and French texts from one another by their looks, i.e. by the peculiar features typical of each of the two graphic inventories.

To turn again to the two ways of realizing utterances in the given language: they, again, differ not only in their respective materials but also in their immediate aims: the written realizations are intended for reading (i.e. for getting full, surveyable information, the wording of which can be easily controlled at any later time), whereas the spoken realizations are intended for listening (i.e. for getting quick, ready information, often coloured by emotional factors). It may sometimes happen that an utterance primarily intended for listening needs reading, and *vice versa*, an utterance intended for reading needs listening. In such cases, it must be pointed out, transposition from the one into the other material is not done with the intention of expressing the given content by means of other material; if it were so, the only possible accomplishment of the task would be to replace the spoken utterance by the written one, or *vice versa*. The actual task to be accomplished in such cases is a different one: to transpose, as accurately as possible, the component parts of the given utterance into the other material, i.e. (1) to express all phonic elements of a spoken utterance in writing, or (2) to express all graphic elements of a written utterance in speaking. A typical example of (1) is phonetic transcription, an every-day case of (2) is spelling (i.e. naming letters of which the words constituting the written utterance are composed).[4]

---

[4] Note that spelling keeps to the principle "one distinct phonic syllable for each letter", which is an interesting counterpart to the principle "one symbol for each sound", originally proclaimed by founders of phonetic transcriptions.

Thus an analysis of spoken and written utterances proves that the characterization of phonetic transcription as a primarily technical device is fully justified. It should be added that whereas a transcribed text is to be regarded as a sign of the second order (i.e. the sign of a sign of the outside world, see above), the text recorded in writing is to be taken, at least in advanced cultural communities, as a sign of the first order (i.e. the sign of an outside world). That is to say, in deciphering a text put down in writing no detour by way of spoken language is necessary to make out its content, as is the case in deciphering a phonetically transcribed text. A clear proof of this assertion is the well-known fact that there are many people who can, for instance, read English without having any idea of how the written text should be pronounced.

All that has been said here so far suffices to prove that writing is by no means the inferior pseudo transcription it has been taken for by the vast majority of scholars. The above developments amount to saying that writing occupies a higher place in the scale of the facts of language than phonetic transcription: the former is a system of elementary signs of language (or a system of the diacritica of language signs, to use Karl Bühler's terminology),[5] whereas the latter is a mere technical device for expressing, in graphic terms, the phonic materials manifesting such signs. Besides, of course, phonetic transcription undoubtedly belongs to the domain of spoken language, whereas writing pertains to the sphere of written language.

The above distinction is not to be interpreted as disparaging phonetic transcription. It simply aims at stressing the fact that writing and phonetic transcription cannot be efficiently compared unless the diversity of their respective functions is taken into account. As has been shown above, the function of phonetic transcription is to fix the phonic realizations of spoken utterances which respond to the given stimulus in a dynamic way; the function of writing, on the other hand, is to set up values which are at work in written utterances responding to a given stimulus in a static way. Thus writing should not be blamed for being inaccurate in recording the phonic make-up of spoken utterances—it lies outside the scope of its function to do this.[6] (Incidentally, if one tries to find out how writing and phonetic transcription fulfil their actual functions defined in the immediately preceding lines, it will be seen that writing cannot be branded as "lagging hopelessly behind" phonetic transcription, as its critics are often inclined to believe. On the contrary, writing is as well, or as badly, qualified to its task as phonetic transcription: the former can express, by primary or secondary means, the selected facts of the outside world which make up the content; the latter, faced with the overwhelming richness of phonic facts to be recorded, also has to make a selection of them by introducing the phonematic principle into its practice. In other words, phonetic transcription gives just as adequate—or just as inadequate—an idea of the phonic make-up of the utterance as that

---

[5] Cf. *Travaux du Cercle ling. de Prague* IV (1931), pp. 40 f.

[6] The diversity of functions mentioned above has been ignored by many students of language, from the pioneers of phonetic research (who, disgusted by the long decades of the "Buchstaben-gefängnis," endured by linguistic research, believed that the conventional ways of writing languages will sooner or later give way to phonetic transcription) to founders of modern linguistic thinking, such as F. de Saussure (*Cours de linguistique générale*, 2nd ed., Paris, 1922, p. 45 ff.) and L. Bloomfield (*Linguistic Aspects of Science*, Chicago, 1939, pp. 6 f.).

theory realized that the phonemic system is only one of the aspects of language considered as a system and that, therefore, the phonemic system cannot claim the exclusive right to being reflected in writing. The elements of writing, that is to say, should be such as to allow written utterances to perform their basic function with maximum efficiency, i.e. to express the content in the static way. This can generally be done in other ways than by giving an accurate phonemic transcription (i.e. by clinging to the correspondence of the "phoneme-grapheme" type). The present writer believes he has proved, in two of his earlier papers,[8] that Czech writing is built up on a correspondence which combines phonemic and morphemic considerations, and the same appears to be more or less true also of English, Russian, German, etc. Lack of space precludes a detailed explanation of the principle—two or three examples must suffice to give an idea of what it implies. There is a marked tendency in English to leave the graphemic make-up of written morphemes unchanged, however different may be, in various cases, the phonemic make-up of corresponding spoken morphemes.[9] Cf. *vari-ety*: ['veəri-əs, vəˈrai-iti]; *comfort*, *comfort-able*: [kʌmfət, kʌmft-əbl]; *want-ed*, *pass-ed*, *call-ed*: [wɒnt-id, pɑːs-t, kɔːl-d] etc. etc. Similar cases could be cited from Russian, German, etc.

The study of concrete writings and concrete written languages, as well as research in the theory of writing and of the written language, is still in its infancy. Only a few definite conclusions can therefore be presented at the present stage of research. At least one of them, however, seems certain: Writing cannot be flatly dismissed as an imperfect, conservative quasi-transcription, as has often been done up to the present day. On the contrary, writing is a system in its own right, adapted to fulfil its own specific functions, which are quite different from the functions proper to a phonetic transcription.

[8] J. Vachek: *Český pravopis a struktura češtiny.* *Listy filologické* 60 (1933), pp. 287 f.—J. Vachek: *Psaný jazyk a pravopis.* *Čtení o jazyce a poesii* I (1942), pp. 231 f.
[9] By the term "morpheme" is meant here the smallest element of the word, characterized by its own meaning (content), indivisible into smaller parts of the kind. Practically: morphemes include roots, all kinds of affixes, inflectional endings, etc.

which writing is able to give of the outside world—there is selection in both cases.)

Some more remarks are necessary in order that the mutual relations existing between writing and phonetic transcription may stand out with greatest possible clearness.

Even if writing in the cultural languages of to-day undoubtedly represents a more or less autonomous system (constituting a sign of the first order, as explained above), it is a well-known fact that it developed historically from a kind of quasi-transcription and was thus, indeed, originally a sign of the second order. This was regularly the case in the earliest stages of cultural languages, when members of their linguistic communities were trying hard to preserve fleeting spoken utterances by putting them down in writing. Soon, however, such a secondary system of signs became a primary one, i.e. written signs began to be bound directly to the content. Nevertheless, the tie existing between spoken and written utterances only became loosened, and was not lost altogether. It must be borne in mind that members of a cultural linguistic community are, as a matter of fact, something like bilinguals because they command two standards of language, the spoken and the written one. The coexistence of these two standards, as well as the complementariness of their functions (one of them is used for the static, the other for the dynamic response), necessarily result in mutual interdependence being felt between them. For this reason there is also a kind of correspondence between the written and the spoken standard, though the degree of the correspondence varies considerably in different linguistic communities.

The correspondence is more easily found in complex units of language than in simple ones. There is hardly any linguistic community in which a written sentence does not correspond to a spoken sentence. Somewhat less often, but still almost regularly, one can find a correspondence between spoken and written words (Chinese seems to be one of the exceptions). Much less numerous are, of course, linguistic communities which maintain consistent correspondence between phonemes and graphemes. This kind of correspondence appears to be most consistently observed in Serbo-Croatian and Finnish; in Czech, Polish and Russian it is valid in principle but subject to various limitations; still less consistently is the correspondence "phoneme—grapheme" observed in French and especially in English.

It may be of some interest to point out that in the early years of phonemic research a demand was voiced here and there for consistent phonemization of writing in this or that language (for Slovak, for instance, see L. Novák's paper *K problémům reformy československého pravopisu*).[7] This requirement can hardly surprise anyone; it was shown above that phoneticians, in their time, raised analogous claims. Still there was a notable difference between the respective attitudes of the phoneticians and the followers of the phoneme theory to such proposals. Whereas the phoneticians backed the demand for phonetization of writing practically to a man, those who asked for phonemization remained isolated, unsupported even by those who held the same theory of language as themselves. The vast majority of the followers of the structuralist

[7] *Sborník Matice Slovenskej* IX, 1931.

LA NATURE DES PROCÈS DITS « ANALOGIQUES »

Jerzy Kuryłowicz

L'opposition *mot-base* : *dérivé* permet de dégager, chez ce dernier, le morphème de dérivation. P. e. *fille* : *fill-ette* (suffixe), *fait* : *re-fait* (préfixe). Le morphème n'est pas toujours simple, il consiste parfois en deux ou plusieurs parties. Ainsi le diminutif allemand *Bäum-chen* est caractérisé, par rapport à *Baum*, non seulement par le suffixe (diminutif) *-chen*, mais encore par l'inflexion (« umlaut ») du vocalisme radical. Le morphème de dérivation y est donc bipartite et il se pose la question du rapport mutuel du suffixe *-chen* et du changement vocalique. Notons entre parenthèses qu'au point de vue de la langue moderne l'umlaut n'a pas un caractère phonétique, mais purement morphologique. Or ce rapport découle de l'étendue de l'emploi des deux morphèmes partiels. L'umlaut n'est propre qu'à une partie seulement de dérivés en *-chen* puisqu'il ne saurait apparaître qu'en cas de vocalisme radical postérieur (*a, o, u, au*). Si le suffixe *-chen* implique l'umlaut radical, l'inverse n'est pas vrai : l'umlaut de *Bäum-* n'entraîne pas nécessairement le suffixe *-chen* puisqu'il est aussi propre à *Bäum-e* ou à *Bäum-lein*. On se trouve ici en présence d'un rapport appelé par M. Hjelmslev *détermination.* (*Les fondements de la théorie linguistique* compte rendu de M. Martinet dans *BSL* XLII, p. 25.)

Au point de vue hiérarchique l'umlaut se trouve donc subordonné à la suffixation.

Dans le procès morphologique en question c'est l'application du suffixe *-chen* laquelle est fondamentale, et le changement vocalique y est ajouté après coup. Voici le schéma illustrant ce rapport : *Baum* > *Baum-chen > *Bäum-chen*.

Les imperfectifs (anciens itératifs) slaves en *-ajǫ* allongent la voyelle radicale en syllabe ouverte. On a *pekǫ : -pěkajǫ, bodǫ : badajǫ, mьrǫ : -měrajǫ, dъmǫ : -dymajǫ* etc. Par rapport à l'application de *-ajǫ* l'allongement radical se trouve restreint d'une double manière : il ne peut pas s'exercer auprès des racines à vocalisme long (p. e. *sypľǫ : -sypajǫ*) ; il n'est pas non plus possible en syllabe entravée (p. e. *tęgnǫ : -tegajǫ < *tengǫ*). Cette restriction de l'allongement par rapport à l'emploi du suffixe en fait la partie secondaire, subordonnée, ou marginale du morphème itératif, tandis que le suffixe en est la partie fondamentale, constitutive ou centrale. Ici encore la formule sera *pekǫ > -*pěkajǫ > -pěkajǫ*.

Reprinted from *Acta Linguistica* 5 (1945–49) : 121–38, with the permission of the author and of the editorial board of *Acta Linguistica*.

Le même phénomène se rencontre dans la flexion. Cf. p. e. la désinence *-er* de pluriel en allemand, laquelle entraîne l'umlaut d'un vocalisme radical postérieur : *Wald* > *Wälder, Huhn* > *Hühner.*

Mais le morphème composé peut être tripartite. Prenons comme exemple les dérivés v. indiens en *-á-* ou *-yá-* avec la vr̥ddhi de la syllabe initiale : type *bráhmaṇā-*. Il y en a aussi qui sont barytons, mais ceux-là constituent une série à part, différant de l'autre par sa valeur (sémantique). Le morphème consiste en trois éléments : suffixe, accentuation, vr̥ddhi. Quel en est l'ordre hiérarchique ? Tandis que le suffixe et l'oxytonèse sont constants, la vr̥ddhi, bien qu'apparaissant dans la majorité écrasante des exemples, est tout de même limitée par le fait que l'allongement ne s'opère pas dans le cas d'un *ā* de la syllabe initiale. La vr̥ddhi est donc subordonnée au suffixe et à l'accentuation. La question du rapport mutuel entre les deux derniers est plus délicate. On ne rencontre pas le suffixe (*-ya-, -a-*) sans l'accentuation, qui l'accompagne toujours, ni l'accentuation suffixale seule, laquelle ne saurait exister sans le support phonique du suffixe. Or l'accentuation suffixale est une *relation* entre racine et suffixe, elle n'est donc point imaginable sans l'existence préalable de ses fondements, *racine* et *suffixe*. De sorte que les trois éléments morphologiques en question se succèdent dans l'ordre suivant : *brahman-* (mot-base) > 1. *brahman-a-* (suffixation) > 2. *brahmán-a-* (accentuation suffixale) > 3. *brāhmaṇ-á-* (vr̥ddhi).

Le rapport de 2. à 1. est d'une autre nature que celui de 3. à 1. + 2. L'élément 2. est fondé sur 1. en tant que marque d'un complexe (*Gestaltqualität*) puisque la marque d'un complexe implique l'existence de ses éléments, tandis que 3. est fondé sur 1. + 2. par suite de la sphère de son emploi, plus restreinte que celle de 1. + 2.

On s'aperçoit dès lors que le fait tacitement mais généralement admis que les dérivés sont fondés sur les mots-bases repose aussi en dernière ligne sur le critère objectif de l'étendue de l'emploi. Un procédé de dérivation vivant, c'est-à-dire applicable à des cas nouveaux, prouve par là-même que l'aire des dérivés ne recouvre pas celle des mots-bases.

Autre est le rapport mutuel des formes flexionnelles formant un paradigme. En effet s'il est correct de dire que latin *lupulus* est fondé sur *lupus*, qu'il en est dérivé moyennant le suffixe diminutif *-olo-*, ce serait une grave erreur que d'analyser d'une manière analogue le gén. sing. *lupī* en le considérant comme tiré du thème (de la racine) *lup-* à l'aide de la désinence *-ī*. Car la notion du thème est postérieure aux formes concrètes composant le paradigme : on trouve le thème en dégageant les éléments communs à toutes les formes casuelles du paradigme (quand il s'agit de la déclinaison). P. e. *lup-us, -ī, -o, -um, -orum, -īs, -os* fondent le thème *lup-*. Le paradigme russe *trud-, -a, -u, -'om* etc. permet de dégager un thème *trud-* puisque l'oxytonèse est le trait commun de toutes les formes casuelles. Le rapport de fondement n'est donc pas *lup- > lup-ī*, mais *lup-us, -ī, -o* etc. > *lup-*. Il ne faut pas confondre le thème ainsi dégagé avec le thème apparaissant dans les premiers membres de composés. Là il revêt souvent une forme plus archaïque, qui peut rester longtemps à l'abri des changements ultérieurs du paradigme, cf. p. e. la voyelle *-a-* de got. *weina-basi*, la voyelle *-o-* du type slave *vodo-nosъ* etc. Il y a lieu de parler ici d'une voyelle de composition (*Fugenvokal*).

Le thème est donc une sorte d'abstraction destinée à résumer le paradigme. Quand on dit que *lupulus* est dérivé de *lupus* ou, d'une façon plus précise, que le thème *lup-ul-* est dérivé du thème *lup-*, cela signifie que le *paradigme* de *lupulus* est dérivé du *paradigme* de *lupus*. D'autant plus qu'en parlant du thème *lup-* ou *lupul-* nous sommes obligés d'ajouter que ces thèmes individuels régissent des désinences particulières (celles de la 2e déclinaison).

Le procès de dérivation de *lupulus* revêt un aspect concret que voici :

$$lupus, \text{-}i, \text{-}o, \text{-}um, \text{-}orum, \text{-}is, \text{-}os \quad \text{ou} \quad lup\text{-} \ (\text{-}us, \text{-}i, \text{-}o \text{ etc.})$$
$$\downarrow \qquad\qquad\qquad\qquad\qquad\qquad \downarrow$$
$$lupulus, \text{-}i, \text{-}o, \text{-}um, \text{-}orum, \text{-}is, \text{-}os \qquad lupul\text{-} \ (\text{-}us, \text{-}i, \text{-}o \text{ etc.})$$

Au point de vue de la dérivation le paradigme équivaut à un seul morphème, à savoir au thème. Les différentes formes casuelles constituent les éléments partiels qui contribuent à la structure de ce morphème. Dans une certaine mesure cet état des choses nous fait penser aux morphèmes composés dont on vient de parler. La question concrète est celle de savoir si certaines formes casuelles sont bâties sur d'autres de manière qu'une forme casuelle *A* nous fait prévoir la forme casuelle *B*, mais non pas inversement. Or il en est ainsi : Exemple : le nom. plur. grec du type τέχναι implique l'oxytonèse du gén. plur. en -ῶν (τεχνῶν), mais la règle inverse n'est pas valable, puisqu'il y a des gén. plur. en ῶν (τιμῶν) correspondant à des nom. plur. oxytons (τιμαί).

Une différence entre la structure du paradigme et celle d'un morphème composé consiste en ceci que ce dernier est *toujours* bâti sur le principe de hiérarchie, tandis qu'on ne peut pas affirmer la même chose pour le paradigme. Dans le cas où le principe trouve son application, par exemple dans τέχναι, τιμαί, on s'aperçoit que le fondement de *B* (gén. plur.) sur *A* (nom. plur.) repose sur l'étendue de l'emploi comme dans les exemples discutés plus haut. La forme du nom. plur. peut être barytonèse ou oxytone en face d'un gén. plur. restreint à la barytonèse. Le schéma τέχναι, τιμαί : -ῶν est ainsi tout à fait comparable à *Kind-chen, Bäum-chen,* où l'on rencontre *-chen* chez les mots à vocalisme antérieur et postérieur, tandis que l'umlaut ne se rencontre que chez les racines à vocalisme postérieur.

Le principe de hiérarchie fondé sur l'étendue de l'emploi des formes est d'ordre purement logique et non pas spécialement sémantique. Il concerne le rapport entre la forme et la fonction, le sens (sémantique) n'étant qu'un cas de fonction spéciale. Il y a en outre des fonctions syntaxiques, et la même bipartition existe pour les phonèmes : fonctions par rapport aux autres phonèmes d'une même classe et fonctions par rapport aux autres phonèmes de la même structure. Le principe s'applique donc aussi au domaine phonologique, cf. notre article sur *Le sens des mutations consonantiques,* publié dans la *Lingua* I, pp. 77–85. Ici nous avons vu qu'il en existe au moins une triple application :

1° pour le rapport mutuel des parties d'un morphème de dérivation (ou de flexion) composé ;
2° pour le rapport entre mot-base et dérivé ;
3° pour les rapports entre les formes d'un paradigme.

Dans le premier cas il s'agit des *morphèmes non-autonomes* et de leurs parties (éléments). Le deuxième cas concerne la relation entre des *mots* entiers. Le troisième, le plus intéressant, n'est qu'en apparence seulement un rapport

entre mots : il s'agit de mots en tant qu'éléments d'un paradigme lequel, à son tour, est une unité appelée thème. Par là-même le cas 3° est, dans une certaine mesure, comparable à 1°.

La différence entre 1° et 3° d'une part et 2° de l'autre présente encore un autre aspect. Les rapports sous 1° et 3° sont uniquement d'ordre formel. Il serait absurde de vouloir décomposer la diminution en éléments sémantiques plus petits correspondant aux éléments morphologiques *-chen* d'une part, et umlaut, de l'autre. Mais ce qui n'est pas aussi évident c'est que le rapport de fondation entre τέχναι et τεχνῶν n'a rien à faire avec les fonctions syntaxiques du nominatif et du gén., mais concerne ces formes en tant que réalisations *d'un seul et même thème.*

Dans 2° par contre le rapport est en même temps formel et sémantique, l'opposition entre mot-base et dérivé permettant de dégager et le morphème de dérivation et la modification sémantique dont il représente le support. Entre deux cas d'un paradigme un tel rapport est tout-à-fait exceptionnel ; il serait possible, si p. e. le gén. était le cas du régime direct partitif (par opposition à l'acc. représentant le cas régime normal), c.-à-d. si le gén. était sémantiquement subordonné à l'acc.

Passons maintenant à l'aspect diachronique de ces rapports.

Les *changements* de structure morphologique sont une conséquence de changements soit phonologiques soit sémantiques. Dans le premier cas les oppositions de formes altérées au point de vue phonique, dans le second cas les nouvelles oppositions causées par des déplacements fonctionnels (sémantiques), portent atteinte à l'équilibre du système morphologique, d'où la nécessité d'un réarrangement appelé " action analogique ". L'équilibre morphologique consiste dans la proportionnalité formelle entre les formes de fondation et les formes fondées, cf. le rapport formel constant entre mot-base et dérivé, lequel permet de prévoir la forme du dérivé d'une façon précise.

Par suite des actions phonétiques et sémantiques les lois de structure morphologique naissent, changent ou disparaissent. En v.-h.-a. ce sont soit des thèmes en -a- (*tag,* plur. *taga*) soit des thèmes en -i- (*gast,* plur. *gesti*), abstraction faite des restes de classes de thèmes en train de disparaître. L'apparition de l'umlaut dans *gesti* est un phénomène d'ordre phonétique : on n'a affaire qu'à la désinence -*i,* l'implication *a > e* n'est pas morphologique. Cet état des choses change au moment du passage, vers la fin de l'époque v.-h.-allemande, des voyelles finales (-*a,* -*i*) en -*e.* Les deux classes de thèmes coïncident alors, en ce qui concerne la désinence du pluriel, mais le pluriel des anciens thèmes en -*i-* comporte une implication : m.-h.-a. *gest-e,* en face de m.-h.-a. *tag-e,* où une telle implication n'a pas lieu. Le développement phonétique conduit à la genèse d'un morphème composé.

Mais ce n'est pas tout. On obtient un morphème -*e* servant à former le pluriel des substantifs masculins forts, et un morphème isofonctionnel (c.-à-d. servant lui aussi à former le pluriel des substantifs masculins forts) -*e* impliquant l'umlaut radical. Or ce qui nous semble d'importance capitale c'est l'extension de l'umlaut à la plupart des anciens thèmes en -*a-,* c.-à-d. des thèmes qui comportaient un pluriel en -*a* en v.-h.-a., p. e. *Bäume, Töpfe.*

I) *Un morphème bipartite tend à s'assimiler un morphème isofonctionnel consistant uniquement en un des deux éléments, c.-à-d. le morphème composé remplace le morphème simple.*

Il est important de souligner qu'une telle extension du morphème composé ne s'effectue pas d'une façon *nécessaire*. Ce que nous affirmons c'est que dans le cas d'une action "analogique" c'est le morphème composé qui l'emporte et non pas le morphème simple. Ainsi nous ne tâchons même pas de trouver la cause du fait qu'en allemand moderne il subsiste encore des pluriels en -e sans umlaut (*Tage*).

L'allongement vocalique chez les itératifs-imperfectifs slaves ne peut pas être de date indoeuropéenne. L'indoeuropéen ne connaît que l'allongement de la voyelle fondamentale e/o. Si l'on rencontre en balto-slave le degré long de i, u (ī, ū) c'est évidemment par suite du fait que des voyelles longues nouvelles s'y sont formées lors de la disparition de ə antéconsonantique. P. e. lit. gértì < *gérti < *gerəti, lit. pìntì < pìnəti < poⁿnəti-.

Or l'opposition -ēr-t-(forme-base) : -ēr-ajo (forme dérivée) = -er-t- (forme-base) : -er-ajo (forme dérivée) passe, après l'abrègement -ērt- > -ert-, à -er-t- : -ēr-ajo = -er-t : x (x = -ērajo). Les signes graphiques ont ici une valeur spéciale : e = voyelle quelconque, r = sonante quelconque, t (suffixal ou désinenciel) = consonne quelconque. L'implication (e > ē) est généralisée en vertu de la loi formulée plus haut.

Il y a des cas plus compliqués. Comme l'a démontré Wackernagel, l'accusatif pluriel des thèmes à hiatus (types εὐγενής, nom. plur. εὐγενέ-ες ; μείζων, nom. plur. * μείζο-ες etc.) suppose un remaniement consistant dans le remplacement de l'ancienne désinence -ας par -νς (sur le modèle des anciens thèmes vocaliques : πολλό-νς, τυμά-νς etc.). Or une forme * εὐγενεῖς nous fait attendre * εὐγενεῖς, avec accent aigu comme dans πολλούς, τυμάς. La forme εὐγενεῖς avec circonflexe est expliquée comme étant due à l'influence du nominatif, où le circonflexe est phonétique (-έ-ες > -εῖς). Mais le mécanisme de la transformation nous a échappé jusqu'à présent.

Voici notre explication. Les désinences du pluriel sont en grec, comme dans toutes les autres langues indoeuropéennes, des signes *globaux*. Le morphème sémantique de la pluralité et le morphème syntaxique du cas s'y confondent en un tout inanalysable. Il en est autrement qu'en turc (osmanli) et en arabe (classique), où le morphème plus central du pluriel se détache nettement des désinences casuelles. Le morphème -ες du nom. plur. εὐγενεῖς se décompose donc non seulement au point de vue formel (désinence -ες plus intonation), mais aussi au point de vue fonctionnel. Il a une fonction centrale de pluralité plus une fonction marginale casuelle. L'intonation du nom. plur. pénètre dans l'acc. et non pas inversement puisque l'intonation aigue ne représente que le manque de l'intonation (circonflexe).

À première vue notre explication peut paraître artificielle et recherchée, mais elle est confirmée par la coïncidence du nom. et de l'acc. plur. masc. en slave septentrional (polonais, tchèque, russe). La disparition des yers finaux (-ъ, -ь) y a engendré l'opposition entre les consonnes dures et les consonnes mouillées (palatales) : -tъ/-tь > t/t'. Ensuite les consonnes suivies de voyelles palatales ont été identifiées aux consonnes mouillées implosives. En gros l'état du russe moderne a été atteint. A ce moment la différence phonologique entre i et y cessa d'exister ; c'est que la différence entre ti et ty fut remplacée par t'i : ti. Les voyelles i et y devinrent des variantes combinatoires d'un seul phonème i réparties en fonction du caractère palatal ou dur de la consonne précédente. La voyelle fondamentale était i parce que i seul apparaissait en absence de consonne précédente, c.-à-d. à l'initiale du mot.

Cette coïncidence phonologique de i et y a entraîné l'identification des désinences du nom. et de l'acc. plur. des thèmes masculins en -o-. Or si les formes trudi (nom. plur.), trudy (acc. plur.) coïncident en ce qui concerne les désinences (nom. trudĭ, acc. trudŭ), la différence phonologique entre elles se maintient par suite du caractère de la consonne finale de la racine (palatal : dur). Mais le caractère dur de la consonne finale dans trudĭ (acc.) est une *implication* parce que normalement la voyelle i suppose la palatalité de la consonne précédente. Cette implication est surajoutée à la désinence -i du nom. plur., d'où le passage de trudĭ à trudĭ (identification du nom. et de l'acc. plur.). Cet exemple prouve non seulement la justesse de notre explication de l'acc. plur. εὐγενεῖς, il est aussi la preuve du fait que les fonctions syntaxiques du nom. et de l'acc. ne sont pour rien dans cette évolution. Car tandis qu'en grec c'est l'ancienne forme du nominatif qui l'a emporté (εὐγενεῖς), c'est le cas inverse pour le slave septentrional. La raison repose donc dans la structure des morphèmes en question. En grec c'est le nominatif qui présente le morphème composé, dont la partie centrale seulement apparaît à l'accusatif. En slave c'est juste le contraire.

L'extension du morphème composé dans le domaine de la dérivation équivaut à la création d'une *opposition polaire* entre le mot-base et le dérivé. En effet la distance entre A et A plus suffixe est plus grande que la distance entre A et A plus suffixe plus implication. L'extension de l'allongement chez les itératifs-imperfectifs slaves en est un bon exemple. Cette polarisation formelle entre mot-base et dérivé est un pendant à la polarisation sémantique. Mais notons qu'inversement le sens du dérivé tend à rejeter le mot-base vers un sens diamétralement opposé. C'est ainsi que le mot-base d'un diminutif revêt, par opposition au sens de ce dernier, une valeur augmentative, ou que le mot-base d'une formation féminine adopte le sens d'un être mâle (vrĭka- par opposition à vrĭkī-), bien qu'à l'origine la valeur du mot-base ait été neutre.

Ce qu'on appelle "conglutination" (fusion) d'éléments suffixaux n'est souvent qu'un phénomène de polarisation mettant en relief le dérivé par rapport au mot-base. D'une façon schématique on a

$$B \longrightarrow B + s_1$$
$$\downarrow$$
$$B + s_2 \qquad B + s_1 + s_2$$

où B désigne le mot-base (thème), s_1 étant un suffixe plus central et s_2 un suffixe plus marginal. S'il y a coïncidence sémantique entre B et $B + s_1$, c.-à-d. si la valeur du suffixe s_1 se perd, la généralisation de B (= évincement de $B + s_1$ par B) aura pour contrecoup le choix non pas de $B + s_2$, mais de $B + s_1 + s_2$ comme forme dérivée, parce que s_2 n'est qu'une partie du complexe $s_1 + s_2$. Le suffixe nouveau $s_1 + s_2$ aura naturellement la valeur de l'ancien suffixe s_2. Cf. allemand -lein < -l + -īn-, -chen < -k + -īn- etc.

Jusqu'ici nous avons pu constater que l'"analogie" consistait dans l'extension de morphèmes composés aux dépens de morphèmes isofonctionnels simples. Ce changement se laisse représenter par des proportions, tout à fait claires en cas de dérivation. P. e. dromǫ : dymajǫ = pekǫ : pēkajǫ etc. La base (le fondement) de la proportion est formée par le rapport mot-base : dérivé. Pour embrasser tous les cas qui entrent en ligne de compte il nous faut élargir la formule en introduisant les notions *forme de fondation* et *forme fondée*.

II) *Les actions dites "analogiques" suivent la direction : formes de fondation → formes fondées, dont le rapport découle de leurs sphères d'emploi.*

On voit le progrès que représente cette formule quand on la compare avec le principe de fréquence statistique qu'on a jadis voulu appliquer aux phénomènes de l'"analogie". Non seulement les sphères d'emploi sont autre chose que les fréquences numériques mais, ce qui est important, elles se laissent déterminer de façon rigoureuse.

Soit le paradigme de l'adjectif grec. Les accentuations du nom. gén. plur. fém. δικαιαι, δικαίων, propres seulement à l'adjectif, trouvent leur explication dans le fait que le féminin est bâti (fondé) sur le masculin. La sphère de la forme masculine déborde celle du féminin puisqu'il y a des adjectifs du type χρυσόθρονος ou εὐγενής dont la forme masculine fait double emploi. D'autre part, ce qui est essentiel, la fonction primaire[1] du masculin est le sens personnel "commun" parce que c'est le masculin qui est employé là où le sexe est sans importance. Ceci nous fait attendre que les changements d'ordre phonétique seront compensés par des proportions agissant dans le sens masculin → féminin, ce qui a en effet eu lieu lors du passage de δικαίων à *δικαιῶν. C'est à ce moment qu'est déclenché le mécanisme ἀγαθῶν (masc.) : ἀγαθῶν (fem.) : : δικαίων (masc.) : x (x = δικαίων au lieu de *δικαιῶν). L'accentuation δίκαιαι, plus ancienne, doit s'expliquer d'une manière semblable (ἀγαθοι : ἀγαθαι = δικαιοι : x = δικαιαι au lieu de *δικαιαι).

L'extension de l'umlaut dans le type Bäume, celle du circonflexe dans l'acc. plur. εὐγενεῖς, celle de la consonne dure dans le type trudy (nom. plur.) s'explique justement par le fait qu'il s'agit de formes du pluriel, donc de formes fondées (sur le singulier).

Le rapport des formations védiques vṛkíḥ et deví repose 1° sur l'identité de leur fonction : elles sont isofonctionnelles en tant que formations féminines tirées de mots-bases masculins. Leur répartition a un caractère mécanique, le suffixe -ī́/-iy- (du type vṛkíḥ) étant réservé aux mots-bases thématiques et le suffixe -ī́/-yā- (du type devī́) s'appliquant plutôt aux mots-bases athématiques (devī́ lui-même constitue une exception) ; 2° sur la sphère de leur emploi : vṛkíḥ se rencontre chez les thèmes substantifs, devī́ comprend en même temps des substantifs et des adjectifs.

De cette sorte le type vṛkíḥ n'occupant qu'une partie de la sphère d'emploi du type devī́ lui est subordonné ou, ce qui revient au même, est fondé sur lui. Les actions "analogiques" prendront donc le chemin devī́ → vṛkíḥ.

Dans le RV les deux types sont encore très bien distingués. Il y a un certain nombre de formes casuelles communes héritées, à savoir l'instr. plur. vṛkíbhiḥ, devíbhiḥ, le dat.-abl. plur. vṛkíbhyaḥ, devíbhyaḥ, l'instr. plur. vṛkíṣu, devíṣu et l'instr.-dat.-abl. duel vṛkíbhyām, devíbhyām (il s'agit des cas appelées "moyens"). Quant au reste du paradigme il y a différence :

	sg. nom.	acc.	dat.	gén.	plur. nom.	acc.	gén.	duel nom.-acc.	sing. instr. -loc.	duel gén.
devī́	devī́	devím	devyái	devyā́ḥ	devī́ḥ	devī́m	devīnā́m	devī́	devyā́	devyóḥ
vṛkíḥ	vṛkíḥ	vṛkíyam	vṛkíye	vṛkíyāḥ	vṛkíyaḥ	vṛkīṇā́m	vṛkíyā(u)	vṛkíyā		vṛkíyoḥ

La cause phonétique qui déclenche l'action assimilatrice de devī́ sur vṛkíḥ c'est le passage de -iy + voyelle à -(i)y + voyelle à svarita, d'où, dès l'Atharva, -(i)y + voyelle à udātta. L'instr. sing. vṛkíyā, le gén.-loc. duel vṛkíyoḥ deviennent vṛkíyā, vṛkíyoḥ en s'identifiant complètement, au point de vue flexionnel, aux formes correspondantes de devī́. Étant donné que vṛkíḥ est subordonné à devī́, cette identification entraîne l'assimilation complète de vṛkíḥ à devī́ et non pas inversement. Du paradigme de vṛkíḥ il ne reste que deux formes dont la conservation a permis de différencier les formes casuelles faisant double emploi : à côté de la forme nouvelle de l'acc. plur. vṛkíḥ l'ancienne forme vṛkíyaḥ, tout en cédant sa fonction d'accusatif à vṛkíḥ, retient l'ancienne fonction de nom. plur. ; la forme nouvelle vṛkí ne l'emporte que sur l'ancien nom. sing. (vṛkíḥ), tandis que l'ancien nom.-acc. duel vṛkíyā(u) > vṛkyáu ne lui succombe pas en se différenciant ainsi de la forme correspondante du sing. Ces deux différenciations s'imposent aussi à devī́ [nom. plur. devyáḥ, nom.-acc. duel devyā(u)]. Le type tanúḥ, parallèle de toutes pièces au type vṛkíḥ, en suit fidèlement les transformations. Donc vṛkíyam : vṛkím = tanúvam : tanúm, vṛkíye : vṛkyái = tanúve : tanvái etc.

Mais le fondement découlant du rapport des sphères d'emploi n'est pas l'unique possible. Il y a un autre entre une structure et son membre constitutif.

III) *Une structure consistant en membre constitutif plus membre subordonné forme le fondement du membre constitutif isolé, mais isofonctionnel.*

Il y aura donc polarisation formelle des racines dépourvues de suffixe par rapport aux racines plus suffixes ; des racines dépourvues de préfixes par rapport aux racines précédées de préfixes ; des racines munies de désinence zéro par rapport aux racines plus désinences syllabiques ; des morphèmes monosyllabiques (que ce soit des racines ou des désinences) par rapport aux morphèmes isofonctionnels polysyllabiques.[2]

Cette loi ne se rapporte pas à l'opposition de deux formes dont la hiérarchie résulterait de leurs sphères d'emploi. Ici c'est l'opposition entre une structure et son membre constitutif qui se trouve à la base du fondement. Ce qui vaut pour une structure vaut aussi pour son membre constitutif.

[1] La fonction primaire n'a rien à faire avec le sens étymologique de la forme, mais se rapporte à la valeur déterminée par le système et indépendante de l'entourage sémantique.

[2] Ce dernier rapport (morphèmes polysyllabiques : morphèmes isofonctionnels monosyllabiques) joue un rôle lorsqu'il s'agit de l'accentuation. Un morphème monosyllabique accentué ne contient que la syllabe accentuée (= constitutive au point de vue de l'accent), tandis qu'un morphème polysyllabique présente en outre une ou plusieurs syllabes inaccentuées (= subordonnées au point de vue de l'accent).

On se pose la question si les formules II) et III) sont compatibles. En effet si d'après II) un dérivé muni d'un suffixe ou préfixe est fondé sur le mot-base correspondant (p. e. grec λύω : ἀναλύω), la formule III) semble postuler juste l'inverse (ἀναλύω : λύω). Cette contradiction n'est qu'apparente. Les rapports entre les morphèmes (au sens large du terme) sont d'une double nature. D'une part le morphème contraste avec d'autres morphèmes appartenant à la même classe, d'autre part il s'oppose aux morphèmes avec lesquels il coexiste dans un même complexe (= morphème plus compliqué). Cela veut surtout clair pour le morphème. Il appartient à une classe sémantique (= partie du discours) et en même temps il joue un rôle syntaxique dans une phrase ou dans un groupe de mots. Mais tandis que pour le mot on se sert d'une double terminologie en parlant d'une part du verbe, du substantif, de l'adjectif etc., d'autre part du prédicat, du sujet, de l'épithète (attribut) etc., il n'en est pas de même pour les morphèmes plus petits, comme p. e. une racine ou un suffixe. Ce manque de terminologie est apte à nous masquer la différence entre II) et III) dans beaucoup de cas concrets. Notons cependant que si ἀνα-λύω est fondé sur λύω en tant que son dérivé, λύω de son côté n'est pas fondé sur ἀνα-λύω, mais sur *préfix-* + λύω, c.-à-d. ἀνα-λύω, κατα-λύω, παρα-λύω etc. *simultanément*. Cela veut dire que les valeurs individuelles de tous ces préfixes n'y sont pour rien, et qu'il s'agit uniquement de la forme pleine (développée) du verbe en face de laquelle le verbe simple apparaît comme une réduction. C'est que tandis que la fonction *sémantique* primaire est celle qui est indépendante de l'entourage sémantique (p. e. des suffixes), la fonction *syntaxique*[3] primaire est constituée par l'opposition du morphème avec les morphèmes qui l'accompagnent à l'intérieur d'une structure.

Passons maintenant aux exemples ayant trait à III).

La conjugaison française du moyen âge est bâtie sur trois éléments : 1o les désinences ; 2o la place de l'accent ; l'accent vieux français est encore mobile, quoique dans une mesure restreinte : le mots en -e y sont soit oxytons soit barytons, tous les autres n'étant qu'oxytons ; 3o l'alternance vocalique radicale. Ces trois éléments jouent un rôle aussi bien dans les conjugaisons dites irrégulières (IIb : type *tenir* ; III ; IV) que dans la conjugaison régulière I). P. e. *il leve : nous lavons ; il leve : nous levons*.

La structure du paradigme de la 1re conjugaison est donc la suivante : *certaines désinences contenant e impliquent l'accentuation radicale ; ces désinences plus accentuation radicale impliquent de leur côté le vocalisme radical (accentué)*. On a p. e. 2e p. sing. *levo-es > *leves > *lèves*. En pratique il s'agit des désinences -e, -es, -e (au singulier) et -ent (3e p. plur.) de l'indicatif et du subjonctif et de la désinence -e de la 2e p. sing. de l'impératif. Par suite de l'amuissement de l'e " féminin " (= e muet final) la catégorie phonologique de l'accent disparaît en français vers le milieu du XVIᵉ siècle. Toutes les désinences en question deviennent des désinences à vocalisme zéro ou plutôt des désinences zéro. Du coup l'alternance vocalique disparaît : c'est le vocalisme inaccentué qui est généralisé ; *avalons : avales = levons : leves* (au lieu de *lièves*) = *lavons : laves* (pour *lèves*). Dès le moment de la disparition de *l'e* muet les formes verbales à désinence quelconque présentent un vocalisme (jadis celui de la

syllabe inaccentuée) qui devient obligatoire pour les formes à désinence zéro. La généralisation du vocalisme *accentué* est exceptionnelle et suppose toujours une raison d'ordre particulier.

L'alternance vocalique s'est maintenue chez les verbes irréguliers IIb, III, IV. Là en effet la structure des formes était tout autre. Le vocalisme (accentué) y était d'avance propre non seulement aux formes à désinence *e* inaccentuée (3e p. plur. *meurent*, subjonctif *meure(s)*), mais aussi aux formes à désinences non-syllabiques (*meurs, meurt*), lesquelles n'existaient pas dans la première conjugaison. Mais, ce qui est essentiel, l'alternance *consonne/zéro* (p. e. *meus, meus, meut*) venait compliquer les rapports mutuels des formes du paradigme. Par rapport à *mouv-ons* les formes à désinence zéro sont *meu-*, ce qui empêche l'application de la loi parce que le vocalisme de *meu-* semble lié à l'absence de la consonne *v*.

Notons que les formes personnelles à désinence zéro sont isofonctionnelles par rapport aux formes à désinence pleine : dans les formes en question le zéro contrastant avec les désinences pleines représente une valeur déterminée à l'intérieur du système. Le rapport des formes à désinences pleines aux formes à désinence zéro est celui d'une structure pleine à la structure isofonctionnelle réduite à son membre constitutif (dans notre cas : à la racine verbale dépourvue de désinence ou plutôt munie de désinence zéro).

L'accentuation du verbe personnel en ancien grec s'explique par la même loi de fondement des membres constitutifs sur des structures. À une époque préhistorique la fusion du verbe personnel avec l'adverbe précédent (devenu préverbe) a privé le verbe de son accent. Comme c'était le cas pour n'importe quel préverbe, le verbe simple (c.-à-d. non précédé de préverbe) a dû suivre la structure *préverbe + verbe* ce qui équivalait à la perte de l'accent chez le verbe personnel. On a p. e. ἀπολεῖπον (participe neutre) : λεῖπον = ἀπολιπον' (1re p. sing. aoriste) : x (x = λίπον inaccentué). La même chose s'est passée en indien. Il n'est pas permis de penser à un héritage commun puisque la réunion du préverbe et du verbe s'effectue indépendamment dans chaque langue indoeuropéenne. Le lien étroit entre le manque de l'accent et la genèse des composés verbaux engage plutôt à poser des développements parallèles mais indépendants. On sait grâce à Wackernagel que la limitation de l'accent en grec a fait remplacer le manque de l'accent par l'accentuation récessive, devenue caractéristique du verbe personnel. On verra d'autre part que des faits analogues démontrant la dépendance du verbe simple par rapport au composé se sont produits en baltique.

Voici à son tour un exemple montrant la dépendance des racines monosyllabiques non intonables (= consistant en une seule more) par rapport aux racines monosyllabiques intonables (= consistant en deux mores).

Les thèmes indoeuropéens de *suésor- " sœur " et *dhugatér- " fille " se confondent partiellement en baltique par suite du recul des accents internes ayant lieu dans des conditions jusqu'ici mal définies (il semble qu'un accent interne reposant sur une voyelle ou une diphtongue brève est remplacé par un accent initial). En tout cas les formes fortes *dukterį, dùkter(e)s du lituanien historique, tandis que l'oxytonèse des cas faibles *dukt(e)rį, *dukt(e)rs (gén. sing.), *dukt(e)rū (gén. plur.) est continuée dans la langue moderne. Il y a donc coïncidence partielle entre

---

[3] Au sens large du terme.

les oxytons et les barytons, laquelle s'étend sur les cas forts : *duktéri, dúkteres* comme *sèserị, sèseres*, tandis que le changement phonétique ne touche aucunement l'opposition entre *sèseres* (gén. sing.), *sèserṇ* (gén. plur.) et les formes oxytones *dukteréṣ, duktérṇ*. Or quelles sont les conséquences ultérieures de cette identification partielle des deux paradigmes ?

1º Identification complète des paradigmes de *sesuô* et de *duktē* conduisant à un seul paradigme mobile ;

2º imposition de cette mobilité à tous les paradigmes vocaliques à vocalisme radical bref (c.-à-d. comportant l'intonation douce).

La première modification s'explique par le fait qu'il s'agit de thèmes immotivés à racine non intonable. Par là-même ils sont subordonnés, dans leur structure, aux thèmes immotivés à racine intonable. Ces derniers sont les rudes immobiles. Les thèmes *duktē/sesuô* sont donc sujets à la loi de réarrangement laquelle exige que le morphème composé *duktē* l'emporte sur le morphème simple. Tandis que le paradigme de *duktē* implique dans le rapport *dúkteri, dúkteres : dúkteres, dukteréṣ* un déplacement de l'accent, il n'en est rien dans le cas de *sesuô* (*sèserị, sèseres : *sèseres, *sèserṇ*). Le surplus morphologique représenté par le saut de l'accent déborde les anciennes limites morphologiques en s'étendant sur les paradigmes barytons, d'où gén. sing. *sèserẹs*, plur. *sèserṇ*.

L'influence des thèmes consonantiques (en -r-, -n-, -nt-, peut-être en -s-) sur les thèmes vocaliques ne consiste en somme que dans l'extension ultérieure du même phénomène d'"analogie". Le rapport *mótē : duktē* (ou *sesuô*) l'emporte sur le rapport *vỵ́ras* (rude immobile) : *vṛkás* (doux immobile : doux mobile). La même chose se passe dans une opposition double comme *vṛkás* (doux immobile : doux mobile). La mobilité historique de *vṛkás* est ainsi une conséquence de sa polarisation par rapport à *vỵ́ras*.

Un dernier exemple. Les neutres de la 3e déclinaison grecque présentent l'accentuation récessive (ἔρεβος, ὄνομα, ἄλειφαρ). À la suite des contractions certains neutres dissyllabiques devinrent des monosyllabes à intonation circonflexe, p. e. φάος > φῶς. Le monosyllabisme de certains neutres de la 3e déclinaison impliquant ainsi l'intonation (intonation circonflexe), les monosyllabes neutres hérités (comme *κῆρ) adoptent la même implication, d'où *κῆρ. La même chose se passe pour les formes personnelles du verbe, lesquelles aussi exigent l'accentuation récessive. Les formes monosyllabiques circonflexes résultant des contractions (p. e. σττέε > σττᾱ) imposent le circonflexe aux formes monosyllabiques héritées (δέ, βῆ). Il y a enfin des vocatifs monosyllabiques du type Ζεῦ dont le circonflexe (cf. nom Ζεύς) s'explique de manière identique. L'extension du circonflexe impliqué par ces différentes catégories est due au fait que les monosyllabes s'opposent aux polysyllabes, sur lesquels ils sont fondés.

Le procès du réarrangement peut être enrayé par la tendance à la différenciation. On a déjà vu, à propos de l'exemple *vṛkīḥ/devī́*, que les désinences attendues a priori, *-īḥ* au nom. pluriel, *-ī* au nom.-acc. duel (d'après le type *devī́*) ont cédé la place aux désinences correspondantes du type *vṛkīḥ* [*-(v)yāḥ, -(v)yāu* respectivement] pour des raisons de différenciation. La forme *devī́* joue un double rôle : elle est en même temps le nom. sing. et le nom.-acc. duel. De même la forme *devī́ḥ* représente en même temps le nom. sing. plur. La différenciation engendre une opposition entre *-ī* (nom. sing.) et *-(v)yāu*

(nom.-acc. duel), entre *-(v)yāḥ* (nom. plur.) et *-īḥ* (acc. plur.). Cette répartition s'explique par le fait que les désinences de fondation sont transformées suivant la nouvelle loi de structure, tandis que les désinences fondées retiennent l'ancienne structure en se différenciant ainsi des désinences de fondation. Car le nom.-acc. duel est fondé sur le nom. sing. ("déterminé" par le nom. sing.) puisque sa désinence *-a(u)* correspond en même temps au nom. sing. des thèmes en *-a* et en consonne ; de même la désinence *-ī* s'oppose soit à *-ȧḥ*, soit à *-ā*, la plur. en *-ȧḥ* est fondé sur l'acc. plur., puisqu'il correspond non seulement à l'acc. plur. en *-aḥ* des thèmes consonantiques, mais aussi à d'autres désinences de l'acc. plur. Le nom. sing. et l'acc. plur. obtiennent donc les désinences de *devī́*, le nom.-acc. duel et le nom. plur. retiennent celles de *vṛkīḥ*.[4]

IV) *Quand à la suite d'une transformation morphologique une forme subit la différenciation, la forme nouvelle correspond à sa fonction primaire (de fondation), la forme ancienne est réservée pour la fonction secondaire (fondée).*

La différenciation n'a lieu que dans le type *vṛkīḥ*, où elle devient possible grâce à l'évincement des anciennes désinences par celles de *devī́*. Ensuite seulement elle s'étend aussi sur l'ancien paradigme de *devī́*.

La différenciation joue un rôle capital dans les actions "analogiques". On constate des différenciations entre nom propre et nom commun, entre adjectif et diminutif, entre cas et adverbe, entre les bahuvrīhi et les tatpuruṣa etc. La différenciation comporte parfois un caractère spécial dont voici un exemple.

Il s'agit de la déclinaison romane, où le système casuel a été abandonné en faveur de la différenciation des nombres. Le système latin sing. *panis, panem* ; plur. *panēs, panēs* est transformé en roman occidental, à cause de la disparition de la nasale et de la coïncidence de ǐ, ē en ẹ, en *panẹs, panẹ : panẹs, panẹs*. La coïncidence phonétique entre le nom. sing. et le nom. plur. abolit une distinction sémantique, celle du nombre. Cette distinction est restituée aux frais de la distinction des cas, laquelle, étant syntaxique, occupe une position plus marginale que la distinction des nombres. Sur le modèle (acc.) plur. *panẹs* : (acc.) sing. *pane* on refait le nom. sing. ; (nom.) plur. *panẹs* : (nom.) sing. *pane*.

L'évincement du nom. sing. en *-s* a eu lieu en ibéroroman (esp. *pan*, port. *pão*), tandis que le v. français, bien qu'appliquant le même principe, s'est servi d'une autre proportion. Pour parer à la confusion des nombres dans la 3e déclinaison (*pains* de *panẹs* et de *panẹs*, *flours* de *floris* et de *flores*) il a tout simplement refait le nom. plur. sur la 2e déclinaison (lorsqu'il s'agissait des masculins) ou le nom. sing. sur la 1re d. (pour le féminin). Pour le masculin on obtient donc (nom.) sing. *murs* : (nom.) plur. *mur* = (nom.) sing. *pains* : (nom.) plur. *pain*. Féminin (nom.) plur. (déjà refait) *terres* : (nom.) sing. *terre* = (nom.) plur. *flours* : (nom.) sing. *flour*. Il faut ici remarquer que les féminins du type *flour* présentent, chez Chrétien de Troyes, un *s* au nom. sing. dont l'archaïsme fait objet de discussion.

La proportion employée en français n'était pas applicable en ibéroroman.

[4] Quand on dit que les désinences *-(v)yāḥ, -(v)yāu* de *devī́* évincent les désinences correspondantes de *devī́* grâce à leur "transparence", on formule d'une façon moins précise ce que nous venons de dire.

Un *maros, *mare (< *marus, mari) ou un *terra, terre (< terra, terrae) n'aurait pu aucunement, pour de simples raisons phonétiques (différence de vocalisme final), influer sur *panes etc. Le remplacement du nom. *panes par l'acc. pane en ibéroroman y déclenche l'extension de l'acc. aux frais du nom. dans la 1re décl. (esp. tierras) et dans la 2e décl. (muro, muros).

En roman oriental (roumain, italien) le résultat est différent à cause de la disparition prélittéraire de l's final. Mais le principe y maintient toute sa force. Les trois déclinaisons représentées par murus, terra et panis revêtent en italien l'aspect suivant :

nom.	terra	terre	muro	muri	*pani	pani
acc.	terra	*terra	*muro	muro	pane	pani

Il n'est pas nécessaire d'insister sur le mécanisme évident de la différenciation étant à la base de l'état historique.

Ces exemples romans nous enseignent que

V) *Pour rétablir une différence d'ordre central la langue abandonne une différence d'ordre plus marginal.*

Les cinq formules qu'on vient d'illustrer par des exemples concernent

1o les *bases* des réarrangements réalisés par des proportions. Ces bases sont constituées d'une part par le rapport du général au spécial, rapport objective-ment donné par les zones d'emploi respectives (formule II), d'autre part par le rapport de la structure à son membre constitutif isofonctionnel (formule III). Cette dichotomie correspond aux deux grandes classes de rapports existant dans le système de la langue : les rapports de dérivation et les rapports syntaxiques, c.-à-d. les rapports entre les éléments appartenant à une même classe, et les rapports entre les éléments entrant dans une même structure ;

2o le *résultat* des réarrangements consistant dans la généralisation de mor-phèmes complexes aux dépens de morphèmes simples (partiels ; formule I) ;

3o *la différenciation* en tant que résultat d'un réarrangement incomplet amenant le scindement d'une forme A en deux formes A' et A, dont la nouvelle représente la fonction primaire de A, la nouvelle forme secondaire étant réservée à l'ancienne forme A (formule IV). L'extension de la différenciation peut entraîner la suppression de différences marginales lorsqu'il s'agit de soutenir les différences centrales (formule V).

Or si les formules en question jettent une lumière sur le mécanisme des changements dits « analogiques », elles n'écartent pas pour cela le caractère de contingence qu'on a toujours attribué à ces transformations. La circonstance que le réarrangement peut être soit complet soit incomplet (dans le cas de différenciation) nous fait attendre qu'il peut ne pas s'effectuer du tout. Une preuve ultérieure en est fournie par les dialectes étroitement apparentés qui, partant du même changement phonétique, ont subi des transformations « analogiques » d'étendue différente. Nous allons analyser un exemple de ce genre.

En ancien scandinave la différence entre la 2e et la 3e p. sing. du présent de l'indicatif est abolie. Les désinences primitives des verbes forts étaient *-iz dans la 2e, *-iþ dans la 3e p. La syncope de la voyelle crée un contact de -z, -þ avec la consonne finale de la racine. Si cette consonne est l ou n, il y a assimila-tion de -lz > -ll, -lþ > -ll ; -nz > -nn, -nþ > -nn. De cette façon certains

verbes forts ont identifié les deux personnes au présent de l'indicatif. L'action « analogique » a étendu l'identité des deux personnes sur tous les verbes forts et faibles. On a donc en anc. islandais þú býþr et hann býþr, þú dǿmer, et hann dǿmer, þú kallar et hann kallar etc. Le scandinave occidental s'en tient là. En ancien suédois, par contre, cette identité continue à s'étendre en pénétrant finalement dans tous les paradigmes, celui du prétérit aussi bien que ceux des deux subjonctifs. Tandis que l'anc. islandais a kallar pour les deux personnes du présent (indicatif), et distingue entre (þú) kallader et (hann) kallade au prétérit, l'anc. suédois fait coincider les deux formes en kallade.

Le même germe phonétique a donc eu des conséquences morphologiques inégales en scandinave occidental et en scandinave oriental. En ouestique l'action « analogique » s'étendit d'abord sur les verbes forts, puis sur les verbes faibles, mais exclusivement à l'intérieur du présent de l'indicatif. En estique le présent de l'indicatif influe sur le prétérit de l'indicatif et le subjonctif. Il va sans dire que l'identification des formes de la 2e et de la 3e p. sing. est accompagnée de l'extension de l'emploi obligatoire du pronom personnel þú lequel seul permet de distinguer la 2e p. de la 3e.

Pourquoi la coincidence des deux formes a-t-elle envahi des zones d'étendue différente en ouestique et en estique ? A notre avis la cause n'en peut être qu'extérieure, c.-à-d. indépendante du système linguistique donné. La zone de l'action analogique, plus grande en estique qu'en ouestique, nous semble démontrer que l'extension de la forme nouvelle (c.-à-d. de l'identité des deux personnes) y a duré plus longtemps en surmontant des résistances sociales plus grandes.

Le mécanisme de l'extension des formes nouvelles se laisse représenter par le schéma suivant : que A constitue le centre ou le point de départ de l'innovation, B₁, B₂ etc. les milieux sociaux (classes, professions, générations, territoires etc.) dans lesquels cette innovation pénètre par étapes successives.

$$
\begin{array}{c|ccc|cc}
 & A \longrightarrow A_1 \longrightarrow A_2 & & & B_1 & B_2 \\
\hline
\text{Ind.} & r & r & r & r & r \\
 & þ & þ & þ & þ & þ \\
 & er & er & er & er & er \\
 & e & e & e & e & e \\
\text{Subj.} & r & r & r & r & r \\
 & e & e & e & e & e
\end{array}
$$

Dès que B₁ adopte l'identification des personnes effectuée dans le milieu A, la désinence -r est généralisée suivant la proportion -þ (milieu B₁) : -r (milieu A) dans les 3es personnes sing. du présent de l'indicatif. A un individu appartenant au milieu B₁, lequel distingue les désinences -r et -þ dans son propre parler, leur coincidence paraît une marque caractéristique de la langue A : il l'imite en exagérant (généralisant) la différence entre A et B₁, en l'étendant aux cas où elle n'a pas jusqu'ici existé et en créant des formes hypercorrectes, c.-à-d. introduisant partout la désinence -r à la place de -þ au présent de l'indicatif. Si la langue A continue à se répandre sous cet aspect modifié (A₁) en pénétrant

p. e. dans le milieu B_2, elle peut devenir le fondement de polarisations ultérieures et de formes hypercorrectes nouvelles. Par un individu appartenant au milieu B_2 l'identité des deux personnes est conçue comme une marque du parler A_1, ce qui conduit à la coincidence de ces personnes au présent du subjonctif (dans A_2) en face de leur différence dans B_2 (-er, -e).

La langue A (il s'agisse de langue commune, officielle, littéraire etc.) subit donc lors de sa pénétration dans les milieux sociaux successifs B_1, B_2 des changements conditionnés par l'opposition du parler (au sens large de ce terme) et de la langue A dans l'esprit du parlant. Si les parlers B_1, B_2 s'accordent à l'origine dans le détail morphologique en question (désinences verbales en l'espèce), l'innovation "analogique" (la coincidence de la 2e er la 3e p.) a des chances de s'imposer au système tout entier (ici: les deux temps et les deux modes).

2e 3e p. sing.	prés. ind.	prés. subj.	prét. ind.	prét. subj.
anc. islandais	-ar, -ar	-er, -e	-er, -e	-er, -e
anc. suédois	-ar, -ar	-e, -e	-e, -e	-e, -e

Autrement dit l'extension de la forme nouvelle dans le système de la langue est en rapport direct et étroit avec son extension à l'intérieur de la communauté linguistique. On en trouve la preuve non seulement dans la morphologie, mais aussi dans le vocabulaire. Ainsi la richesse des nuances sémantiques d'un mot, sa polysémie reflètent son emploi plus ou moins étendu à l'intérieur des différents milieux sociaux, professions, territoires etc. Mais plus une communauté est homogène, plus il y a des chances pour que l'innovation se répande sans déborder la zone primitive de son emploi. A cet égard la différence entre le scandinave occidental et le scandinave oriental est instructive. Il semble que le premier ait été un milieu plus homogène et par conséquent plus perméable aux changements linguistiques que le dernier.

Mais la chose présente encore un autre aspect. L'extension de l'identité de la 2e et la 3e p. sing. en scandinave oriental équivaut à l'emploi du pronom personnel de la 2e p. *þú*, p. e. *þú kallaþe* en face de la 3e p. *kallaþe* (se rapportant habituellement à un substantif). Les milieux adoptant la forme nouvelle de la 2e p. la conçoivent comme un remplacement de l'ancien tour "synthétique" *kallaþ-er* "clamavisti" par un tour "analytique" *þú kallaþe* *"tu clamavit"*. Or l'imitation de cet aspect de l'innovation conduit au remplacement du tour synthétique par le tour analytique dans la 1re sing., d'où au lieu de *kallaþa* la construction *ek kallaþe*. Ainsi l'innovation se répand dans deux directions: paradigme de l'indicatif → autres paradigmes, 2e p. sing. → 1re p. sing. Le résultat final est l'identité de toutes les trois personnes sing. dans les paradigmes verbaux du scandinave oriental.

Les phénomènes morphologiques scandinaves trouvent un pendant sur le territoire allemand. En v. saxon (et en anglofrisien) il n'existe au pluriel des deux temps et des deux modes qu'une seule désinence: *gēbath*; *gēben*; *gāþun*; *gābin* en face du franconien ind. prés. *wērthan, wirthit, wērthant* etc. Ce trait morphologique du saxon et de l'anglofrisien est dû à la disparition, propre à ces langues, des consonnes nasales devant les spirantes *f, þ, s*. Les désinences -*aþ* de la 2e p. plur. et -*anþ* de la 3e p. plur. y aboutissent au même résultat puisque l'allongement compensatoire de la voyelle précédente (cf. *ûs* < *uns*, *fîf* < *fimf*)

est annulé par l'abrègement des voyelles inaccentuées (-*anþ* > -*áþ* > -*aþ*). Cette coincidence, phonétique chez les verbes en -*an* et -*jan*, est généralisée: dans les langues historiques elle est obligatoire pour tous les verbes et pour tous les quatre paradigmes. De plus la construction analytique devenue nécessaire dans la 2e p. plur. (p. e. v. saxon *gi gēbath* "vous donnez") se communique à la 1re p. plur. En v. saxon et en anglofrisien les choses se sont donc passées, pour le pluriel, exactement de la même manière que pour le singulier du scandinave oriental:

a) coincidence de la 2e et la 3e p. prés. ind. de certains verbes (singulier en scandinave oriental, pluriel en v. saxon);

b) envahissement du prét. ind. et des deux subjonctifs (singulier en scandinave oriental, pluriel en v. saxon);

c) envahissement de la 1re p. de tous les paradigmes (singulier en scandinave oriental, pluriel en v. saxon).

Un troisième exemple d'une coincidence des trois personnes est fourni par les dialectes alemaniques, où la désinence commune du pluriel est -*et* (*gebet*). A l'origine il n'y avait identité que de la 2e et la 3e p. plur.: cet état des choses est attesté non seulement par Notker (*wir gēben, ir gēbent, sie gēbent*), mais aussi par le parler moderne de Wallis (-*e*, -*et*, -*et*).

On voit par ces trois exemples que la construction analytique (pronom personnel plus verbe à la 3e p.) se généralise à l'intérieur du nombre (singulier ou pluriel). La direction de l'action "analogique" est soit 2e p. sing. → 1re p. sing., soit 2e p. plur. → 1re p. plur., jamais 2e p. sing. → 2e p. plur. ou inversement. La construction analytique du type *tu amat au lieu de *amas peut déclencher *ego amat pour amo, tandis que *vos amat pour amatis est impossible parce que le système grammatical exige au pluriel *amant et non pas *amat. Le développement *vos amat ne serait possible que si le sing. et le plur. de la 3e p. étaient d'avance identiques comme c'est le cas p. e. en lituanien.

Les mêmes dialectes alemaniques fournissent des exemples encore plus clairs de formes hypercorrectes résultant de la réaction du parler envers la langue commune (littéraire). A Bâle[5] la désinence commune des trois personnes du pluriel est -*e* (< -*en*). Elle provient d'une proportion dont les termes de fondation sont dialectaux et les termes fondés littéraires:

formes de fondation:	gebe(t), gebet, gebet
formes fondées:	gebe(n), gebet, gebe(n)

Le rapport *gebet* : *gebe* à la 3e p. plur. entraîne *gebet* : *x* (*x* = *gebe*) aussi dans la 2e p. plur.

Des réactions semblables ont lieu sur les territoires représentant la transition de l'alemanique au franconien:

formes de fondation:	gebet, gebet, gebet
franconien et littéraire:	geben, geben, geben
territoire de transition:	geben, geben, geben
	gebet : *geben* (1re, 3e p. plur.) = *gebet* : *x* (*x* = *geben*).

Le trait caractéristique des proportions étant à la base de ces changements c'est que leurs membres sont des termes *identiques* appartenant à deux

[5] D'après Behaghel, *Geschichte der deutschen Sprache*[5], p. 168 s.

systèmes différents. Elles représentent un cas spécial, apte à illustrer que le fondement *interne* défini par les formules II) et III) est en même temps un fondement *externe*.

VI) *Le premier et le second terme d'une proportion appartiennent à l'origine à des systèmes différents : l'un appartient au parler imité, l'autre au parler imitant.*

Retournant à notre point de départ nous constatons que l'*étendue* d'une action " analogique " ne peut être prévue d'avance (cf. scandinave occidental : oriental). L'extension de changements morphologiques est en même temps *externe* (à l'intérieur d'une communauté linguistique) et *interne* (à l'intérieur du système grammatical). Car d'une part un système défini est propre à un grand nombre d'individus, d'autre part l'individu représente un point de croisement de plusieurs systèmes (de parlers, dialectes, langues). En ce qui concerne ce croisement il a été appelé par Schuchardt *Sprachmischung*, mais il serait plus juste de parler du *fondement* du système *A* sur le système *B* (v. schéma ci-dessus) déclenchant des effets d'opposition, de polarisation etc. parce que les différences existant entre deux systèmes apparentés sont normalement généralisées par le sujet parlant (formes hypercorrectes). Les phénomènes de ce genre ont été mis en lumière et décrits en détail par le maître de la géographie linguistique J. Gilliéron.

Somme toute les choses se présentent de la façon suivante : Il résulte d'un système grammatical concret quelles transformations " analogiques " sont possibles (formules I–V). Mais c'est le facteur social (formule VI) qui décide si et dans quelle mesure ces possibilités se réalisent. Il en est comme de l'eau de pluie qui doit prendre un chemin prévu (gouttières, égouts, conduits) *une fois qu'il pleut*. Mais la pluie n'est pas une nécessité. De même les actions prévues de l'" analogie " ne sont pas des nécessités. Étant obligée à compter avec ces deux facteurs différents la linguistique ne peut jamais prévoir les changements à venir. A côté de la dépendance mutuelle et de la hiérarchie d'éléments linguistiques à l'intérieur d'un système donné elle a affaire à la contingence historique de la structure sociale. Et bien que la linguistique générale penche plutôt vers l'analyse du système comme tel, les problèmes historiques concrets ne trouvent une solution satisfaisante que si l'on tient compte des deux facteurs simultanément.[6]

---

[6] Le présent article fut envoyé aux *A. L.* en avril 1947. Dans l'entretemps l'auteur a entrepris des recherches sur l'accentuation balto-slave qui lui ont fait voir le rapport des paradigmes *doux mobiles : rudes immobiles* (v. p. 14–15) dans une lumière nouvelle. Mais le fait essentiel de la *polarisation* résultant du rapport de fondement, n'en est pas touché.

SOUNDS AND PROSODIES

J. R. Firth

The purpose of this paper is to present some of the main principles of a theory of the phonological structure of the word in the piece or sentence, and to illustrate them by noticing especially sounds and prosodies that are often described as laryngals and pharyngals. I shall not deal with tone and intonation explicitly.

Sweet himself bequeathed to the phoneticians coming after him the problems of synthesis which still continue to vex us. Most phoneticians and even the "new" phonologists have continued to elaborate the analysis of words, some in general phonetic terms, others in phonological terms based on theories of opposition, alternances, and distinctive differentiations or substitutions. Such studies I should describe as paradigmatic and monosystemic in principle.

Since de Saussure's famous Cours, the majority of such studies seem also to have accepted the monosystemic principle so succinctly stated by Meillet: "chaque langue forme un système où tout se tient". I have in recent years taken up some of the neglected problems left to us by Sweet. I now suggest principles for a technique of statement which assumes first of all that the primary linguistic data are pieces, phrases, clauses, and sentences within which the word must be delimited and identified, and secondly that the facts of the phonological structure of such various languages as English, Hindustani, Telugu, Tamil,[1] Maltese,[2] and Nyanja[3] are most economically and most completely stated on a polysystemic hypothesis.

In presenting these views for your consideration, I am aware of the danger of idiosyncrasy on the one hand, and on the other of employing common words which may be current in linguistics but not conventionally scientific. Nevertheless, the dangers are unavoidable since linguistics is reflexive and introvert.

Reprinted from *Papers in Linguistics, 1934–1951* (London: Oxford University Press, 1957), with the permission of Oxford University Press, publisher of the volume under the auspices of the School of Oriental and African Studies, London University. Originally published in *Transactions of the Philological Society* 1948, pp. 127–52.

[1] At one of the 1948 meetings of the Linguistic Society of America, Mr. Kenneth Pike suggested that in certain Mexican Indian languages it would be convenient to hypothecate a second or phonemic sub-system to account for all the facts. Taking part in the discussion which followed, I pointed out my own findings in Tamil and Telugu for both of which languages it is necessary to assume at least three phonological systems: non-brahman Dravidian, Sanskrito-dravidian, and Sanskritic.

[2] See J. Aquilina: *The Structure of Maltese, A Study in Mixed Grammar and Vocabulary*. (Thesis for the Ph.D. degree, 1940. University of London Library.)

[3] See T. Hill: *The Phonetics of a Nyanja Speaker*, With Particular Reference to the Phonological Structure of the Word. (Thesis for the M.A. degree, 1948. University of London Library.)

That is to say, in linguistics language is turned back upon itself. We have to use language about language, words about words, letters about letters. The authors of a recent American report on education win our sympathetic attention when they say "we realize that language is ill adapted for talking about itself". There is no easy escape from the vicious circle, and "yet", as the report points out, "we cannot imagine that so many people would have attempted this work of analysis for themselves and others unless they believed that they could reach some measure of success in so difficult a task". All I can hope for is your indulgence and some measure of success in the confused and difficult fields of phonetics and phonology.

For the purpose of distinguishing prosodic systems from phonematic systems, words will be my principal isolates. In examining these isolates, I shall not overlook the contexts from which they are taken and within which the analyses must be tested. Indeed, I propose to apply some of the principles of word structure to what I term *pieces* or combinations of words. I shall deal with words and pieces in English, Hindustani, Egyptian Arabic, and Maltese, and refer to word features in German and other languages. It is especially helpful that there *are* things called English words and Arabic words. They are so called by authoritative bodies; indeed, English words and Classical Arabic words are firmly institutionalized. To those undefined terms must be added the words *sound, syllable, letter, vowel, consonant, length, quantity, stress, tone, intonation*, and more of the related vocabulary.

In dealing with these matters, words and expressions have been taken from a variety of sources, even the most ancient, and most of them are familiar. That does not mean that the set of principles or the system of thought here presented are either ancient or familiar. To some they may seem revolutionary. Word analysis is as ancient as writing and as various. We A.B.C. people, as some Chinese have described us, are used to the process of splitting up words into letters, consonants and vowels, and into syllables, and we have attributed to them such several qualities as length, quantity, tone and stress.

I have purposely avoided the word *phoneme* in the title of my paper, because not one of the meanings in its present wide range of application suits my purpose and *sound* will do less harm. One after another, phonologists and phoneticians seem to have said to themselves "*Your* phonemes are dead, long live *my* phoneme". For my part, I would restrict the application of the term to certain features only of consonants and vowels systematically stated *ad hoc* for each language. By a further degree of abstraction we may speak of a five-vowel or seven-vowel phonematic system, or of the phonematic system of the concord prefixes of a Bantu language,[4] or of the monosyllable in English.[5]

By using the common symbols c and v instead of the specific symbols for phonematic consonant and vowel units, we generalize syllabic structure in a new order of abstraction eliminating the specific paradigmatic consonant and vowel systems as such, and enabling the syntagmatic word structure of syllables with all their attributes to be stated systematically. Similarly we may abstract

[4] See T. Hill: *The Phonetics of a Nyanja Speaker.*

[5] Miss Eileen M. Evans, Senior Lecturer in Phonetics, School of Oriental and African Studies, has work in preparation on this subject, as part of a wider study of the phonology of modern English.

those features which mark word or syllable initials and word or syllable finals or word junctions from the word, piece, or sentence, and regard them syntagmatically as prosodies, distinct from the phonematic constituents which are referred to as units of the consonant and vowel systems. The use of spaces between words duly delimited and identified is, like a punctuation mark or "accent", a prosodic symbol. Compare the orthographic example "Is she?" with the phonetic transcript iʒiy? in the matter of prosodic signs. The inter-word space of the orthography is replaced by the junction sequence symbolized in general phonetic terms by ʒJ. Such a sequence is, in modern spoken English, a mark of junction which is here regarded as a prosody. If the symbol i is used for word initial and f for word final, ʒJ is fi. As in the case of e and v, i and f generalize beyond the phonematic level.

We are accustomed to positional criteria in classifying phonematic variants or allophones as initial, medial, intervocalic, or final. Such procedure makes abstraction of certain postulated units, phonemes, comprising a scatter of distributed variants (allophones). Looking at language material from a syntagmatic point of view, any phonetic features characteristic of and peculiar to such positions or junctions can just as profitably and perhaps more profitably be stated as prosodies of the sentence or word. Penultimate stress or junctional geminations are also obvious prosodic features in syntagmatic junction. Thus the phonetic and phonological analysis of the word can be grouped under the two headings which form the title of this paper—sounds and prosodies. I am inclined to the classical view that the correct rendering of the syllabic accent or the syllabic prosodies of the word is anima vocis, the soul, the breath, the life of the word. The study of the prosodies in modern linguistics is in a primitive state compared with the techniques for the systematic study of sounds. The study of sounds and the theoretical justification of roman notation have led first to the apotheosis of the sound-letter in the phoneme and later to the extended use of such doubtful derivatives as "phonemics" and "phonemicist", especially in America, and the misapplication of the principles of vowel and consonant analysis to the prosodies. There is a tendency to use one magic phoneme principle within a monosystemic hypothesis. I am suggesting alternatives to such a "monophysite" doctrine.

When first I considered giving this paper, it was to be called "Further Studies in Semantics". I had in mind the semantics of my own subject or a critical study of the language being used about language, of the symbols used for other symbols, and especially the new idioms that have grown up around the word "phoneme". Instead of a critical review of that kind, I am now submitting a system of ideas on word structure, especially emphasizing the convenience of stating word structure and its musical attributes as distinct orders of abstractions from the total phonological complex. Such abstractions I refer to as prosodies, and again emphasize the plurality of systems within any given language. I think the classical grammarians employed the right emphasis when they referred to the prosodies as anima vocis. Whitney, answering the question "What is articulation?" said: "Articulation consists not in the mode of production of individual sounds, but in the mode of their combination for the purposes of speech".[6]

[6] Amply illustrated by the patterns to be seen on the Visible Speech Translator produced by the Bell Telephone Laboratories.

The Romans and the English managed to dispense with those written signs called "accents" and avoided pepperbox spelling. Not so the more ingenious Greeks. The invention of the written signs for the prosodies of the ancient classical language were not required by a native for reading what was written in ordinary Greek. They were, in the main, the inventions of the great scholars of Alexandria, one of whom, Aristarchus, was described by Jebb as the greatest scholar and the best Homeric critic of antiquity. The final codification of traditional Greek accentuation had to wait nearly four hundred years—some would say much longer—so that we may expect to learn something from such endeavours.[7] It is interesting to notice that the signs used to mark the accents were themselves called προσωδίαι, prosodies, and they included the marks for the rough and smooth breathings. It is also relevant to my purpose that what was a prosody to the Greeks was treated as a consonant by the Romans, hence the "h" of hydra. On the relative merits of the Greek and Roman alphabets as the basis of an international phonetic system of notation, Prince Trubetzkoy favoured Greek and, when we talked on this subject, it was clear he was trying to imagine how much better phonetics might have been if it had started from Greek with the Greek alphabet. Phonetics and phonology have their ultimate roots in India. Very little of ancient Hindu theory has been adequately stated in European languages. When it is, we shall know how much was lost when such glimpses as we had were expressed as a theory of the Roman alphabet.

More detailed notice of "h" and the glottal stop in a variety of languages will reveal the scientific convenience of regarding them as belonging to the prosodic systems of certain languages rather than to the sound systems. "h" has been variously considered as a sort of vowel or a consonant in certain languages, and the glottal stop as a variety of things. Phonetically, the glottal stop, unreleased, is the negation of all sound whether vocalic or consonantal. Is it the perfect minimum or terminus of the syllable, the beginning and the end, the master or maximum consonant? We have a good illustration of that in the American or Tamil exclamation ʔaʔa! Or is it just a necessary metrical pause or rest, a sort of measure of time, a sort of mora or matra? Is it therefore a general syllable maker or marker, part of the syllabic structure? As we shall see later, it may be all or any of these things, or just a member of the consonant system according to the language.

We have noticed the influence of the Roman and Greek alphabets on notions of sounds and prosodies. The method of writing used for Sanskrit is syllabic, and the Devanagari syllabary as used for that language, and also other forms of it used for the modern Sanskritic dialects of India, are to this day models of phonetic and phonological excellence. The word analysis is syllabic and clearly expressive of the syllabic structure. Within that structure the pronunciation, even the phonetics of the consonants, can be fully discussed and represented in writing with the help of the prosodic sign for a consonant closing a syllable. For the Sanskritic languages an analysis of the word satisfying the demands of modern phonetics, phonology, and grammar could be presented on a syllabic basis using the Devanagari syllabic notation without the use of the phoneme concept, unless of course syllables and even words can be considered as "phonemes".

[7] See "A Short Guide to the accentuation of Ancient Greek", by Postgate.

In our Japanese phonetics courses at the School of Oriental and African Studies during the war, directed to the specialized purposes of operational linguistics, we analysed the Japanese word and piece by a syllabic technique although we employed roman letters. The roomazi system, as a system, is based on the native Kana syllabary. The syllabic structure of the word—was treated as the basis of other prosodies perhaps over-simplified, but kept distinct from the syllabary. The syllabary was, so to speak, a paradigmatic system, and the prosodies a syntagmatic system. We never met any unit or part which *had* to be called a phoneme, though a different analysis, in my opinion not so good, has been made on the phoneme principle.

Here may I quote a few of the wiser words of Samuel Haldeman (1856), first professor of Comparative Philology in the University of Pennsylvania, one of the earlier American phoneticians, contemporary with Ellis and Bell. " Good phonetics must recognize the value for certain languages ' of alphabets of a more or less syllabic character ', in which ' a consonant position and a vowel position of the organs ' are regarded ' as in a manner constituting a unitary element ' ".[8] Sir William Jones was the first to point out the excellence of what he called the Devanagari system, and also of the Arabic alphabet. The Arabic syllabary he found almost perfect for Arabic itself—" Not a letter ", he comments, " could be added or taken away without manifest inconvenience ". He adds the remark, " Our English alphabet and orthography are disgracefully and almost ridiculously imperfect ". I shall later be using Arabic words in Roman transcription to illustrate the nature of syllabic analysis in that language as the framework for the prosodies. Sir William Jones emphasized the importance as he put it of the " Orthography of Asiatic Words in Roman Letters ". The development of comparative philology, and especially of phonology, also meant increased attention to transliteration and transcription in roman letters. Sir William Jones was not in any position to understand how all this might contribute to the tendency, both in historical and descriptive linguistics, to phonetic hypostatization of roman letters, and theories built on such hypostatization.

In introducing my subject I began with sounds and the Roman alphabet which has determined a good deal of our phonetic thinking in Western Europe—as a reminder that in the Latin word the letter was regarded as a sound, *vox articulata*. We moved east to Greek, and met the prosodies, i.e. smooth and rough breathings, and the accents. The accents are marks, but they are also musical properties of the word. In Sanskrit we meet a syllabary built on phonetic principles, and each character is **akṣara**, ultimate, permanent, and indestructible. Any work I have done in the romanization of Oriental languages has been in the spirit of Sir William Jones, and consequently I have not under-estimated the grammatical, even phonetic, excellence of the characters and letters of the East where our own alphabet finds its origins. On the contrary, one of the purposes of my paper is to recall the principles of other systems of writing to redress the balance of the West.

And now let us notice the main features of the Arabic alphabet. I suppose it can claim the title " alphabet " on etymological grounds, but it is really a

[8] Cf. " English School of Phonetics ", *Trans. Phil. Soc.*, 1946.

syllabary.[9] First, each Arabic letter has a name of its own. Secondly, each one is capable of being realized as an art figure in itself. Thirdly, and most important of all, each one has syllabic value, the value or *potestas* in the most general terms, being consonant plus vowel, including vowel zero, or zero vowel. The special mark, *sukuun*, for a letter without vowel possibilities, i.e. with zero vowel, or for a letter to end a syllable not begin it, is the key to the under-standing of the syllabic value of the simple letter not so marked, and this is congruent with the essentials of Arabic grammar. Like the **helent** in Devanagari, **sukuun** is a prosodic sign. The framework of the language and the etymology of words, including their basic syllabic structure, consist in significant sequences of radicals usually in threes. Hence a letter has the potestas of one of these radicals plus one of the three possible vowels **i**, **a**, or **u** or zero. Each syllabic sign or letter has, in the most general terms, a trivocalic potentiality, or zero vowel, but in any given word placed in an adequate context, the possibilities are so narrowly determined by the grammar that in fact the syllable is, in the majority of words, fully determined and all possibilities except one are excluded. The prosodies of the Arabic word are indicated by the letters if the context is adequate. If the syllabic structure is known, we always know which syllable takes the main prominence. It is, of course, convenient to make the syllabic structure more precise by marking a letter specially, to show it has what is called zero vowel, or to show it is doubled. Such marks are prosodic. And it is even possible to maintain that in this system of writing the diacritics pointing out the vowels and consonants in detail are added prosodic marks rather than separate vowel signs or separate sounds in the roman sense; that is to say, generalizing beyond the phonematic level, **fatḥa**, **kasra**, **ḍamma**, **sukuun**, **alif**, **waw**, **ya**, **tafdiid** and **hamza** form a prosodic system.

In China the characters, their figures and arrangement, are designs in their own right. Words in calligraphy are artefacts in themselves of high aesthetic value, for which there is much more general respect than we have in England for the Etonian pronunciation of the King's English. For my purpose Chinese offered excellent material for the study of institutionalized words long since delimited and identified. With the help of Mr. K. H. Hu, of Changsha, I studied the pronunciation and phonology of his dialect of Hunanese.[10] Eventually I sorted out into phonological classes and categories large numbers of characters in accordance with their distinguishing diacritica. Diacritica were of two main types, phonematic and prosodic. The prosodic diacritica included tone, voice quality, and other properties of the sonants, and also yotization and labio-velarization, symbolized by **y** and **w**. Such diacritica of the monosyllable are not considered as successive fractions or segments in any linear sense, or as distributed in separate measures of time.[11] They are stated as systematized abstractions from the primary sensory data, i.e. the uttered instances of monosyllables. We must distinguish between such a conceptual framework

[9] Or rather Arabic writing is syllabic in principle. Professor Edgar Sturtevant has stated this view and recently confirmed it personally in conversation.

[10] See my " The Chinese Monosyllable in a Hunanese Dialect (Changsha) ", *BSOS*, vol. viii, pt. 4 (1937) [with B. B. Rogers].

[11] In the sending of Japanese morse ak = ka, the first signal being the characteristic sonant. (Joos, *Acoustic Phonetics*, L.S.A., pp. 116–126, and conclusions on segmentation.)

which is a set of relations between categories, and the serial signals we make and hear in any given instance.[12]

Before turning to suggest principles of analysis recognizing other systems of thought and systems of writing outside the Western European tradition, let me amplify what has already been said about the prosodies by quoting from a grammarian of the older tradition and by referring to the traditional theory of music.

Lindley Murray's English Grammar (1795) is divided in accordance with good European tradition,[13] into four parts, viz. Orthography, Etymology, Syntax, and Prosody. Part IV, Prosody, begins as follows: "Prosody consists of two parts: the former teaches the true PRONUNCIATION of words, comprising ACCENT, QUANTITY, EMPHASIS, PAUSE, and TONE; and the latter, the laws of versification. Notice the headings in the first part—ACCENT, QUANTITY, EMPHASIS, PAUSE, and TONE".

In section 1 of ACCENT, he uses the expression the *stress of the voice* as distinguishing the accent of English. The stress of the voice on a particular syllable of the word enables the number of syllables of the word to be perceived as grouped in the utterance of that word. In other words, the accent is a function of the syllabic structure of the word. He recognizes principal and secondary accent in English. He recognizes two quantities of the syllable in English, long and short, and discusses the syllabic analysis and accentuation of English dissyllables, trisyllables, and polysyllables, and notices intonation and emphasis.

The syntagmatic system of the word-complex, that is to say the syllabic structure with properties such as initial, final and medial characteristics, number and nature of syllables, quantity, stress, and tone, invites comparison with theories of melody and rhythm in music. Writers on the theory of music often say that you cannot have melody without rhythm, also that if such a thing were conceivable as a continuous series of notes of equal value, of the same pitch and without accent, musical rhythm could not be found in it. Hence the musical description of rhythm would be "the grouping of measures", and a measure "the grouping of stress and non-stress". Moreover, a measure or a bar-length is a grouping of pulses which have to each other definite interrelations as to their length, as well as interrelations of strength. Interrelations of pitch and quality also appear to correlate with the sense of stress and enter into the grouping of measures.

We can tentatively adapt this part of the theory of music for the purpose of framing a theory of the prosodies. Let us regard the syllable as a pulse or beat, and a word or piece as a sort of bar length or grouping of pulses which bear to each other definite interrelations of length, stress, tone, quality—including voice quality and nasality. The principle to be emphasized is the *interrelation*

[12] See also N. C. Scott, "A Study in the Phonetics of Fijian", *BSOAS.*, vol. xii, pts. 3–4 (1948), and J. Carnochan, "A Study in the Phonology of an Igbo Speaker", *BSOAS.*, vol. xii, pt. 2 (1948). Eugénie Henderson, Prosodies in Siamese, in *Asia Major*, N.S. Vol. I, 1949.
[13] Cf. "Arte de Escribir", by Torquato Torio de la Riva, addressed to the Count of Trastamara, Madrid, 1802. The four parts of grammar are etimología ó analogía, syntaxis, prosódia, or [sic—Ed.] ortografía. Prosódia teaches the quantity of syllables in order to pronounce words with their due accent. There are three degrees in Spanish, acute or long, grave or short, and what are termed *común* or *indiferentes*.

of the syllables, what I have previously referred to as the *syntagmatic relations*, as opposed to the *paradigmatic or differential relations* of sounds in vowel and consonant systems, and to the paradigmatic aspect of the theory of phonemes, and to the analytic method of regarding contextual characteristics of sounds as allophones of phonematic units.

A good illustration of these principles of word-analysis is provided if we examine full words in the spoken Arabic of Cairo, for which there are corresponding forms in Classical Arabic. Such words (in the case of nouns the article is not included) have from one to five syllables. There are five types of syllable, represented by the formulae given below, and examples of each are given.

SYLLABIC STRUCTURE IN CAIRO COLLOQUIAL [14]

(i) CV: open short. C + i, a, or u.
  (a) fíhim nízil
  (b) zálamu ſitláxam qárabit
  (c) ſindáhaʃu (cvv-cv-cv-cv)

(ii) CVV: open medium. C + i, a, or u, and the prosody of vowel length indicated by doubling the vowel, hence VV—the first V may be considered the symbol of one of the three members of the vowel system and the second the mark of the prosody of length. Alternatively y and w may be used instead of the second i or u.
  (a) fáahim fíʔulah nóobah*
  (b) muʃíibah ginéenah* misóogar*
  (c) ſiʃtaddéenah* (cvv-cvv-cvv-cvc)
  (d) ſistafáad náahum

(iii) CVC: closed medium. C + i, a, or u.
  (a) ſáfham dúrguh
  (b) yistáfhim dúxtilhum
  (c) mistalbáxha (cvv-cvc-cvc-cv)

(iv) CVVC: closed long. C + i, a, or u and the prosody of vowel length—see under (ii).
  (a) naam guum ziid
    baat ʃiil xoof*
  (b) kitáab yiʃíil yiʃtúum
  (c) ſistafáad yistafíid yifhamúuh
  (d) ſistalbaxnáah tistalbaxtíih

(v) CVCC: closed long. C + i, a, or u and the prosody of consonant length in final position only, the occurrence of two consecutive consonants in final position.
  (a) jadd bint
  (b) qarábt yimírr
  (c) ſistaʔádd yistaʔídd (cvc-cv-cvcc)

In the above words the prominent is marked by an accent. This is, however, not necessary since prominence can be stated in rules without exception, given the above analysis of syllabic structure.

[14] See also Ibrahim Anis, *The Grammatical Characteristics of the Spoken Arabic of Egypt.* (Thesis for the Ph.D. degree, 1941. University of London Library.) ṭ ḍ ṣ ẓ = t d s z (I.P.A.)

There is a sort of vowel harmony and perhaps consonant harmony, also involving the so-called emphatic or dark consonants.

I think it will be found that word-analysis in Arabic can be more clearly stated if we emphasize the syntagmatic study of the word complex as it holds together, rather than the paradigmatic study of ranges of possible sound substitutions upon which a detailed phonematic study would be based. Not that such phonematic studies are to be neglected. On the contrary, they are the basis for the syntagmatic prosodic study I am here suggesting. In stating the structure of Arabic words, the prosodic systems will be found weightier than the phonematic. The same may be true of the Sino-Tibetan languages and the West African tone languages.

Such common phenomena as elision, liaison, anaptyxis, the use of so-called "cushion" consonants or "sounds for euphony", are involved in this study of prosodies. These devices of explanation begin to make sense when prosodic structure is approached as a system of syntagmatic relations.

Speaking quite generally of the relations of consonants and vowels to prosodic or syllabic structure, we must first be prepared to enumerate the consonants and vowels of any particular language for that language, and not rely on any general definitions of vowel and consonant universally applicable. Secondly, we must be prepared to find almost any sound having syllabic value. It is not implied that general categories such as vowel, consonant, liquid, are not valid. They are perhaps in general linguistics. But since syllabic structure must be studied in particular language systems, and within the words of these systems, the consonants and vowels of the systems must also be particular to that language and determined by its phonological structure.

Let us now turn to certain general categories or types of sound which appear to crop up repeatedly in syllabic analysis. These are the weak, neutral, or "minimal" vowel, the glottal stop or "maximum" consonant, aitch or the pulmonic onset—all of which deserve the general name of laryngals. Next there are such sounds as $ħ$ and $ʕ$ characteristic of the Semitic group of languages which may also be grouped with "laryngals" and perhaps the back **y** and **w**. Then the liquids and semi-vowels **l, r, n** (and other nasals), **y** and **w**.

Not that prosodic markers are limited to the above types of "sound". Almost any type of "sound" may have prosodic function, and the same "sound" may have to be noticed both as a consonant or vowel unit and as a prosody.

First, the neutral vowel in English. It must be remembered that the qualities of this vowel do not yield in distinctness to any other vowel quality. The term neutral suits it in English, since it is in fact neutral to the phonematic system of vowels in Southern English. It is closely bound up with the prosodies of English words and word junctions. Unlike the phonematic units, it does not bear any strong stress. Its occurrence marks a weak syllable including weak forms such as **wəz, kən, ə**.

Owing to the distribution of stress and length in Southern English words, it is often final in junction with a following consonant initial. Two of the commonest words in the language, *the* and *a*, require a number of prosodic realizations determined by junction and stress, **ðə, ði, 'ðiy, ə, ən, ey, æn.**

Though there are five types of syllable, they divide into three quantities short, medium, and long. When vowel length is referred to, it must be differentiated from syllabic quantity—vowels can be short or long only. The two prosodies for vowels contribute to the three prosodies for syllables.

The special case of ee and oo.

In most cases Colloquial **ee** and **oo** correspond to Classical *ay* and *aw*, often described as diphthongs. There are advantages, however, in regarding *y* and *w* as terms of a prosodic system, functioning as such in the syllabic structure of the word. **xawf** and **xoof** are thus both closed long, though *cvvc* is replaced by *cvvc*. Similarly **gináynah** and **ginéenah, náy** and **née** are both medium, one with *y*-prosody and one with vowel length. Though the syllabic quantities are equivalent, the syllabic structure is different. Two more vowel qualities must be added to the vowel system, **e** and **o**, different from the other three in that the vowel quality is prosodically bound and is always long.

There are other interesting cases in which, quite similarly, colloquial C + **ee** or **oo** with the prosody of length in the vowel in such words as **geet** or **ʃuum,** correspond to equivalent classical monosyllables **jiʃt, ʃuʕm.** The phonematic constituents of the pairs of corresponding words are different, but the prosody of equipollent quantity is maintained. Many such examples could be quoted including some in which the prosodic function of **ʕ** (glottal stop) and "**y**" are equivalent.

Classical.	Cairo Colloquial.
ðiʕb	diib
qaraʕt	ʕareet
[Cyrenaican : garayt]	
faʕs	faas
daaʕim	daayim
naaʕim	naayim
maaʕil	maayil
qaraaʕib	qaraayib

The prosodic features of the word in Cairo colloquial are the following:—

In any word there is usually such an interrelation of syllables that one of them is more prominent than the rest by nature of its prosodies of strength, quantity, and tone, and this prominent syllable may be regarded as the nucleus of the group of syllables forming the word. The prominent syllable is a function of the whole word or piece structure. Naturally therefore, the prosodic features of a word include:—

1. The number of syllables.
2. The nature of the syllables—open or closed.
3. The syllabic quantities.
4. The sequence of syllables.
5. The sequence of consonants } [radicals and flexional elements separately treated.]
6. The sequence of vowels.
7. The position, nature, and quantity of the prominent.
8. The dark or clear qualities of the syllables.

In other positions, too, the neutral vowel often, though by no means always, marks an etymological junction or is required by the prosodies of word formation, especially the formation of derivatives. The distribution of the neutral vowel in English from this point of view would make an interesting study. The prosodic nature of ə is further illustrated by the necessity of considering it in connection with other prosodies such as the so-called "intrusive" r, the "linking" r, the glottal stop, aitch, and even w and y. Examples: *vanilla ice, law and order, creʹation, beʹhind, pa and ma, to earn, to ooze, secretary, behave, without money.* The occurrence of Southern English diphthongs in junctions is a good illustration of the value of prosodic treatment, e.g.:—

(i) The so-called "centring" diphthongs, iə(r), eə(r), ɔə(r), uə(r).
(ii) What may be termed the "y" diphthongs, iy,[15] ey, ay, oy.
(iii) The "w" diphthongs uw, ow, aw.

It may be noted that e, æ, ɔ do not occur finally or in similar junctions, and that ɔ:, a:, and ə: all involve prosodic r.

Internal junctions are of great importance in this connection since the verb *bear* must take *-ing* and *-er*, and *run* leads to *runner up*. Can the r of *bearing* be said to be "intrusive" in Southern English? As a prosodic feature along with ə and in other contexts with the glottal stop, aitch and prosodic y and w, it takes its place in the prosodic system of the language. In certain of its prosodic functions the neutral vowel might be described temporarily as a pro-syllable. However obscure or neutral or unstressed, it is essential in *a bitter for me* to distinguish it from *a bit for me*. In contemporary Southern English many "sounds"[16] may be pro-syllabic, e.g. tsnʹapl, tstuwʹmatʃ, sekrtʹtri or sektʹtri, sʹmain, sʹtruw. Even if *'s true* and *strew* should happen to be homophonous, the two structures are different: cʹcvv and 'cvv. "Linking" and "separating" are both phenomena of junction to be considered as prosodies. In such a German phrase as ʔvn ʔeinem ʔalten '*Buch*, the glottal stop is a junction prosody. I suppose Danish is the best European language in which to study the glottal stop from the prosodic point of view.[17] Unfortunately, I am not on phonetic speaking terms with Danish and can only report. The Danish glottal stop is in a sense parallel with sounds said to be originally long, and in final position only in stressed syllables. If the word in question loses its stress for rhythmical or other reasons, it also loses the glottal stop. It is therefore best considered prosodically as a feature of syllabic structure and word formation. The glottal stop is a feature of monosyllables, but when such elements add flexions or enter compounds, the glottal stop may be lost. In studying the glottal stop in Danish, the phonematic systems are not directly relevant, but rather the syllabic structure of dissyllabic and polysyllabic words

[15] It is, I think, an advantage from this point of view to regard English so-called long i: and u: as y-closing or w-closing diphthongs and emphasize the closing termination by writing with Sweet iy or iʸ, and uw.
[16] In the general phonetic sense, not in the phonematic sense.
[17] See Sweet, "On Danish Pronunciation" (1873), in *Collected Papers*, p. 345, in which he makes a prosodic comparison with Greek accents. (On p. 348 he uses the term "tonology".)

and compounds. In Yorkshire dialects interesting forms like 'fɔʔti occur. Note however 'fəwər and 'fəwəʹtiyn. A central vowel unit occurs in stressed positions in these dialects, e.g. 'θəʔti, 'θəʔtiyn.

There may even be traces of a prosodic glottal stop in such phrases as t 'θəðʔdɛɛ, t 'θəðʔtaym. Junctions of the definite article with stressed words having initial t or d are of interest, e.g. ɔntʔtɛɛbl, itʔtɛɛbl, tətʔtɛxtʃə, fətʔdɔktə, witʔtawil. These are quite different junctions from those in 'gud 'dɛɛ or 'bad 'taym. Compare also Yorkshire trɛɛn (cvvc) tʔreen (cʹcvv), tətʹʃɔp, tə 'tʃɔp, also witʔtak (*with the tack*) and wid 'tak (*weʹd take*), also witəʹtak (*wilt thou take*). In London one hears 'θəːʔtsiyn and 'θəːtʔʔiyn, where the two glottal stops have somewhat different prosodic functions.

The glottal stop as a release for intervocalic plosives is common in Cockney, and is a medial or internal prosody contrasting with aspiration, affrication, or unreleased glottal stop in initial or final positions. Such pronunciations as 'kɔpʔʔə, 'sapʔʔə, 'wintʔʔə, dʒampʔʔə are quite common. I would like to submit the following note of an actual bit of conversation between two Cockneys, for prosodic examination: i 'ʔɔːʔ ʔə 'ʔɛv iʔ 'ʔɔːf, baʔ i 'waw ʔ ʔɛv iʔ ɔːf.

I have already suggested the y and w prosodies of English, including their effect on the length prosody of the diphthongs and their function in junctions when final. After all, human beings do not neglect the use of broad simple contrasts when they can combine these with many other differentiations and in that way multiply phonetic means of differentiation. In the Sino-Tibetan group of languages the y and w element is found in a large number of syllables—there are many more y and w syllables than, say, b or d or a syllables. In the many Roman notations used for Chinese, these two elements are variously represented and are sometimes regarded as members of the paradigm of initials, but, generally as members of the paradigm of finals. They can be classified with either, or can be simply regarded as syllabic features. Sounds of the y or w type, known as semi-vowels or consonantal vowels, often have the syllable-marking function especially in initial and intervocalic position. In Sanskrit and the modern languages affiliated to it, it is clear that prosodic y and w must be kept distinct from similar "sounds" in the phonematic systems. The verbal forms **aya, laya, benaya** in Hindustani are not phonematically irregular, but with the y prosody are regular formations from **a-na, la-na,** and **bena-na.** In Tamil and other Dravidian languages y and v prosodies are common, as markers of initials, for example, in such Tamil words as **(y)enna, (y)evan, (y)eetu, (v)oor, (v)oolai, (v)ooṭṭu.** However, the prosodies of the Dravidian languages present complicated problems owing to their mixed character.

Other sounds of this semi-vowel nature which lend themselves to prosodic function are r and l, and these often correspond or interchange with y or w types of element both in Indo-European and Sino-Tibetan languages. Elements such as these have, in some languages, such pro-syllabic or syllable-marking functions that I think they might be better classified with the syntagmatic prosodies rather than with the overall paradigmatic vowel and consonant systems. Studies of these problems in Indo-European and Sino-Tibetan languages are equally interesting.

TABLE I

h

Hindustani, Eastern, careful.	Hindustani, Western, quick.	Panjabi, (Gujranwala).
pehyle	peyhle	pə̃ylle
behwt	bewht	bə̃wt
pehwŋena	pewhŋena	pə̃wŋe
bhei		bə̃i
ker reha hey	kerraheyh	rə̃ynda
rehta (rẽhta)		

In **pehyle** we have a three-syllable word in which h is phonematic (*cvcvcv*). In **peyhle** there are two syllables by a sort of coalescence in which **ayh** indicates an open " h "-coloured or breathy vowel of the æ-type (*cvhcv*). Similarly in the phrase **behwt‿eccha** there are four syllables (*cvcv‿vcv*), in **bewht‿eccha** three, the vowel in the first of which is open back and " h "-coloured (*cvhcvcv*).

In Panjabi **pə̃ylle** the open vowel carries a compound high falling tone and the structure is prosodically quite different (*cvcv*) which, I think, is equipollent with *cvhcv* (**peyhle**). **bə̃wt** similarly is *cvc*, reduced to a monosyllable with initial and final consonant and a tonal prosody. In Hindustani verbal forms like **rehna, rehta ; kehna, kehta ;** the **ə** vowel in the h-coloured syllable immediately followed by a consonant is open with a retracted æ-like quality. **yih** is realized as **ye, vwh** as **vo,** in both of which there is a similar lowering and potential lengthening in emphasis.

TABLE II

ARABIC ʕ IN URDU LOAN-WORDS

Spelling Transliterated.	Transcription of Realization in Speech.
maʕlum	malum
baʕd	bad
defaʕ	defa
manʕ	mena
maʕni	meani, mani
ystaʕmal	ystemal

In all these cases the vowel realized is open and fairly long. In Maltese, words which in Arabic have h and which still retain h in the spelling are pronounced long with retracted quality, e.g. **he, hi, ho, eh, ehe,** as in **fehem, fehmu, sehem, sehmek, qalbhom.** These long vowels may be unstressed. Similarly all the **gh** spellings (transliterated **ɣ**) are realized as long slightly pharyngalized vowels which may also occur in unstressed positions, which is not possible with vowels other than those with the Semitic **h** and **gh** spellings. E.g. **ɣa, aɣa, yo, oɣ, oyo, ɣi (ɣey), ɣe, ɣu (ɣew)** in such words as **ghidt, ghuda maghmul, balagh.** In the phrase **balagh balgha** (he swallowed a mouthful) the two forms are pronounced alike with final long **a** (for form, cf. **hataf hatfa,** he snatched) the **h** and **gh** are often realized in spoken Maltese as a prosody of length.

The rough and smooth breathings are treated as prosodies or accentual elements in the writing of Greek. It is true that, as with accents in other languages, the rough breathing may imply the omission of a sound, often **s,** or affect the quality and nature of the preceding final consonants in junction. " h " in French is similarly connected with junction and elision. Even in English, though it has phonematic value in such paradigms as *eating, heating ; eels, heels ; ear, hear ; ill, hill ; owl, howl ; art, heart ; arming, harming ; anchoring, hankering ; airy, hairy ; arrow, Harrow ;* and many others, it is an *initial signal* in stressed syllables of full words having no weak forms. English **h** is a special study in weak forms, and in all these respects is perhaps also to be considered as one of the elements having special functions, which I have termed prosodic. In English dialects phonematic " h " (if there is such a thing) disappears, but prosodic " h " is sometimes introduced by mixing up its function with the glottal stop. I have long felt that the aitchiness, aitchification, or breathiness of sounds and syllables, and similarly their creakiness or " glottalization " are more often than not features of the whole syllable or set of syllables. Indeed, in some of the Sino-Tibetan languages, breathiness or creakiness or " glottalization " are characteristic of prosodic features called tones. In an article published in the *Bulletin of the School of Oriental and African Studies,* Mr. J. Carnochan has a few examples of aspiration and nasalization in Igbo as syntagmatic features of a whole word, rather like vowel harmony, which is prosodic.

Apart from the fact that nasals such as *m, n, ŋ* are often sonants—that is to say, have syllabic function—they are also quite frequently initial or final signals, and in Bantu languages such signals have essentially a syntagmatic or syllable or word-grouping function. In a restricted prosodic sense, they can be compared with the glottal stop in German.

In bringing certain types of speech sound into consideration of the prosodies, I have so far noticed the neutral or weak vowel, the minimal vowel, which often becomes zero; the glottal stop, the pulmonic onset, and the liquids and nasals. The first two, I suggest, deserve the name of laryngals, and perhaps h. There remain such sounds as **h, ʕ, ɣ,** and **x,** characteristic of the Semitic group of languages. But in the dialects they are often replaced in cognate words by the prosody of length in change of vowel quality, generally more open than that of the measure of comparison.

When words containing these sounds are borrowed from Arabic by speakers of non-Semitic languages, they are usually similarly replaced by elements of a prosodic nature, often with changes of quality in the vowels of the corresponding syllable.

Hindustani and Panjabi provide interesting examples of phonematic units in one dialect or style being represented in another by prosodies. Instances of interchanges in cognates between phonematic units of the vowel system and units of the consonant system are common, and examples and suggestions have been offered of interchanges and correspondences between phonematic units of both kinds and prosodies. The following table provides broad transcriptions to illustrate these principles.

hope that some of the notions I have suggested may be of value to those who are discussing laryngals in Indo-European, and even to those engaged in field work on hitherto unwritten languages. The monosystemic analysis based on a paradigmatic technique of oppositions and phonemes with allophones has reached, even overstepped, its limits! The time has come to try fresh hypotheses of a polysystemic character. The suggested approach will not make phonological problems appear easier or oversimplify them. It may make the highly complex patterns of language clearer both in descriptive and historical linguistics. The phonological structure of the sentence and the words which comprise it are to be expressed as a plurality of systems of interrelated phonematic and prosodic categories. Such systems and categories are not necessarily linear and certainly cannot bear direct relations to successive fractions or segments of the time-track of instances of speech. By their very nature they are abstractions from such time-track items. Their order and interrelations are not chronological.

An example is given below of the new approach in sentence phonetics and phonology [18] in which the syntagmatic prosodies are indicated in the upper stave and the phonematic structure in the lower stave, with a combination text between. Stress is marked with the intonation indicated.

```
                     . ˊ . ̲ ˉ . ˋ ˊ . ̲ . _

Prosodies        {   cy   cvc   cvc   cvz ̮mvvʃ ̮bvcɔ   vy   cvvc
                     ðy   ʌðə ¹⁹   ɔfə   wɛz   mʌtʃ   betə   aɣ   θiŋk

Phonematic       {   ð—ʌð—ɔf—w–z      mʌtʃ       bet—ə—θiŋk
Structure


                     _ ̲ ˊ . ̲ . ˋ ˊ . _

Prosodies        {   cvy   hvz ̮ʃvy   ɛcvccic   cvc   cvc
                     waɣ   hæz ʃiy   əkseptid   ðis   wʌn

Phonematic       {   wa   æz   ʃi   ksept   d   ðis   wʌn
Structure
```

It is already clear that in cognate languages what is a phonematic constituent in one may be a prosody in another, and that in the history of any given language sounds and prosodies interchange with one another. In the main, however, the prosodies of the sentence and the word tend to be dominant.

To say the prosodies may be regarded as dominant is to emphasize the view that syntax is the dominant discipline in grammar and also with the findings of recent American research in acoustics. The interpenetration of consonants and vowels, the overlap of so-called segments, and of such layers as voice, nasalization and

[18] For a fuller illustration of the scope of sentence phonology and its possible applications, see Eugénie Henderson's *Prosodies in Siamese*.
[19] The use of ə as a prosodic symbol in such final contexts implies potential r or ʔ according to the nature of the junction.

In Turkish the Arabic ʕ in loan-words is often realized as a prosody of length in such pronunciations as **fiil** (*verb, act*), **saat** (*hour*), and similarly Arabic ʕ, in **iblaa** (*communicate*), and Turkish ğ in **uultu** (*tumult*). We are reminded again of Arabic ʕ which is also realized as a prosody of length in the colloquials, e.g. Classical **jiʕt** is paralleled by **geet** in Cairo, **jeʕt** in Iraqi, and **ʒiit** in Cyrenaican Saʕadi. In Cairo and Iraqi the prosody of length is applied to an opener vowel than in Classical, but this is not always the case.

The study of prosodic structures has bearing on all phonological studies of loan-words, and also on the operation of grammatical processes on basic material in any language. Taking the last-mentioned first, elision or anaptyxis in modern Cairo colloquial are prosodically necessary in such cases as the following: **misikt + ni = misiktini**, where the anaptyctic i is required to avoid the junction of three consonants consecutively which is an impossible pattern. The prominence then falls on the anaptyctic vowel by rule. Pieces such as **bint + fariid** are realized as **bintifariid**. With the vowels **i** and **u**, elision is possible within required patterns, e.g.: **yindihʃ + u = yindihʃu, titlixim + i = titlixmi**, but not with **a**, **ʕitlaxam + it = ʕitlaxamit**.

Amusing illustrations of the effect of prosodic patterns on word-borrowing are provided by loan-words from English in Indian and African languages and in Japanese. Prosodic anaptyxis produces **sekrul** in Panjabi and prothesis **iskrul** in Hindi or Urdu. By similar processes **seʈeʃen** in Panjabi and **isʈeʃen** for *station*. In Hausa *screw-driver* is naturalized as **sukuru direba.** Treating **skr** and **dr** as initial phonematic units, English *screw-driver* has the structure 'cvcv-cvyca, the prosodies of which Hausa could not realize, hence cvcvcvcvcvcv, a totally different structure which I have carefully expressed in non-phonematic notation, to emphasize the fallacy of saying Hausa speakers cannot pronounce the "sounds"; and to point to the value of studying prosodic structure by a different set of abstractions from those appropriate to phonematic structure.

It is not implied that there is one all-over prosodic system for any given language. A loan-word may bring with it a new pattern suited to its class or type, as in English borrowings from French, both nominals and verbals. When completely naturalized the prosodic system of the type or class of word in the borrowing language is dominant. In Japanese strange prosodic transformations take place, e.g. **bisuketto** (biscuit), **kiromeetoru, kiroguramu, supittohwaia, messaasyumitto, arupen-suttoku, biheebiyarisuto, doriburusuru** (to dribble).

Linguists have always realized the importance of the general attributes of stress, length, tone, and syllabic structure, and such considerations have frequently been epoch-making in the history of linguistics. Generally speaking, however, the general attributes have been closely associated with the traditional historical study of sound-change, which, in my terminology, has been chiefly phonematic. I suggest that the study of the prosodies by means of ad hoc categories and at a different level of abstraction from the systematic phonematic categories, may enable us to take a big step forward in the understanding of synthesis. This approach has the great merit of building on the piece or sentence as the primary datum. The theory I have put forward may in the future throw light on the subject of Ablaut which, in spite of the scholarship expended on it in the nineteenth century from Grimm to Brugmann, still remains a vexed question and unrelated to spoken language. I venture to aspiration, in utterance, are commonplaces of phonetics. On the perception side, it is improbable that we listen to auditory fractions corresponding to uni-directional phonematic units in any linear sense.

Whatever units we may find in analysis, must be closely related to the whole utterance, and that is achieved by systematic statement of the prosodies. In the perception of speech by the listener whatever units there may be are prosodically reintegrated. We speak prosodies and we listen to them.

HOMONYMIE ET IDENTITÉ

Robert Godel

On peut voir dans l'homonymie un simple accident dont toute langue fournit plus ou moins d'exemples et qui ne présente guère d'intérêt pour le linguiste. L'existence ou l'absence d'homonymes paraît sans conséquence pour la structure de la langue, et l'on peut même admettre, avec M. Buyssens,[1] que "l'homonymie est un défaut de perspective qui ne se produit que lorsqu'on isole artificiellement le signe du discours". Mais on peut y voir aussi l'un des aspects d'une question générale dont Saussure a marqué l'importance et la difficulté : la délimitation et le classement des unités synchroniques. "La langue, observe-t-il, a le caractère d'un système basé complètement sur l'opposition de ses unités concrètes. On ne peut ni se dispenser de les connaître, ni faire un pas sans recourir à elles ; et pourtant leur délimitation est un problème si délicat qu'on se demande si elles sont réellement données".[2] Ce qui est donné, en effet, ce sont des combinaisons d'unités ; le système que supposent ces combinaisons ne peut être décrit, l'inventaire des unités qui le constituent ne peut être dressé que si l'on a d'abord analysé correctement les différents types de combinaisons en usage. Or l'analyse — j'entends l'analyse synchronique — n'atteint pas toujours des unités absolument simples, ni surtout absolument invariables. L'unité simple, le *monème*, comme M. Frei a proposé de l'appeler,[3] ne se présente pas avec la même forme et la même signification exactement dans toutes les combinaisons où il entre : le signifié comme le signifiant peut varier dans une certaine mesure sans que soit compromise l'identité du signe. Dans quelle mesure, voilà ce qu'il faudrait préciser pour pouvoir établir, dans un système donné, le tableau des monèmes comme on établit celui des phonèmes ; cela suppose que, dans l'un et l'autre cas, les faits synchroniques se prêtent à une analyse objective. La question, dans son ensemble, dépasse mon propos : les remarques qui suivent ne visent qu'à déterminer la situation des homonymes dans un système linguistique.

Les variations du signifiant n'affectent pas l'identité du signe tant qu'elles

sont strictement combinatoires, c'est-à-dire déterminées par le seul contact des signifiants voisins. Tel est le cas des variations dues au sandhi, comme *mwa / mwaz* (= mois), pour reprendre un exemple donné par Saussure.[4] Il en est de même, en turc, pour les variations des suffixes causées par l'harmonie vocalique et l'assimilation des consonnes : les adjectifs verbaux *ezgin* "écrasé", *yorgun* "fatigué", *küskün* "vexé, fâché", etc. contiennent tous un suffixe identique -GIn. En revanche, lorsque la différence entre les signifiants ne relève pas d'une règle combinatoire, on ne peut parler d'identité : les préfixes *co-* (cohéritier, copropriétaire) et *con-* (concitoyen) ne sont pas deux variantes, mais deux monèmes distincts, d'ailleurs synonymes, comme le sont les suffixes -*able* et -*ible*. En turc, il n'y a pas d'alternance régulière entre les voyelles A et I dans les suffixes ; il faut donc considérer comme distincts les suffixes -GAn et -GIn dont les valeurs, au surplus ne coïncident pas toujours (*dargın* "fâché" : *darılgan* "irascible").[5]

Ainsi, malgré la similitude des signifiés, on n'hésitera pas à reconnaître des unités distinctes dans tous les cas où les signifiants sont différenciés, le critère de différenciation étant fourni par la phonologie.

En est-il de même dans le cas inverse ? Autrement dit, étant donné deux signifiés associés au même signifiant, y a-t-il des raisons valables pour affirmer qu'il s'agit d'unités distinctes, ou des variations de sens d'une unité qui reste identique ? A première vue, la situation est claire : il existe d'une part des homonymes ; d'autre part, un signe peut, sans se dédoubler, élargir sa valeur par extension de sens, figure ou emploi technique.[6] Si l'on s'en tient à la définition classique des homonymes et à l'emploi qu'on a coutume d'en faire, aucune question ne se pose. Mais c'est précisément sur la notion même d'homonymie qu'il conviendrait d'abord de s'entendre. La grammaire traditionnelle ne reconnaît pour homonymes que des mots. M. Marouzeau dit, avec plus de rigueur étymologique : "Sont homonymes, des noms (gr. ónoma) de prononciation identique et de sens différents".[7] Avec ou sans cette restriction, les homonymes ainsi définis ne sont qu'un groupe particulier de faits, qu'il serait logique de remplacer dans l'ensemble des faits de même nature ; et c'est ainsi que bien des linguistes ont été amenés à un usage beaucoup plus large de cette notion.[8] Non seulement les divers types d'unités, mais les syntagmes, les phrases même fournissent des exemples d'homonymie. Tous ces faits appartiennent-ils également à la langue ? Leur caractère commun a-t-il plus d'importance que ce qui les distingue ? C'est ce qu'il faudra voir, après avoir signalé une autre difficulté.

Entre les homonymes et les unités à signification variable, le contraste n'est vraiment net que dans la perspective diachronique. L'historien de la langue,

Reprinted from *Cahiers Ferdinand de Saussure* 7 (1948) : 5-15, with the permission of *Cahiers Ferdinand de Saussure*.

[1] *Les langages et le discours*, Bruxelles 1943, § 60-61.
[2] *Cours de linguistique générale* (CLG), 2me éd. Paris 1922, p. 149.
[3] *Qu'est-ce qu'un dictionnaire de phrases ?* dans *Cahiers F. de S.* 1, p. 51. La célèbre définition du "mot", qu'a proposée Meillet (*Linguistique historique et linguistique générale*, 2me éd. Paris, 1926, p. 30) serait celle du monème si elle comprenait l'indivision du signifiant.

[4] *CLG*, p. 147. M. Buyssens voit aussi dans les deux prononciations de *ces, des, des* (devant consonne ou devant voyelle) des "variantes combinatoires" d'un même mot (*Leuvense Bijdragen*, 1948, 1-2, p. 3).
[5] Je rectifie ici ce que j'ai dit de ces suffixes dans ma *Grammaire turque* (Genève, 1945), § 9 et 176. Un doublet comme : *alışkan/alışkın* "accoutumé" est exceptionnel et ne prouve pas l'identité (cf. franç. *herbeux / herbu*).
[6] *CLG*, p. 151 : adopter un enfant, une mode.
[7] *Lexique de terminologie linguistique*, 2me éd. Paris, 1948, p. 108.
[8] Voir par ex. tout le chapitre de Bally, *Linguistique générale et linguistique française* (LGLF) 2me éd. Berne, 1944, p. 172-178.

attentif à l'évolution sémantique, ne met pas en doute l'identité du signe dont il décrit et classe les significations successives ou coexistantes, de même qu'il ne cesse de considérer comme distincts deux signes étymologiquement différents dont l'évolution phonétique a rendu semblables les signifiants. La définition de l'homonymie semble, il est vrai, n'avoir qu'une portée synchronique ; mais il est sous-entendu (comme l'indiquent les exemples habituels) que le fait synchronique résulte d'un événement diachronique particulier : la convergence phonétique des signifiants. Si, par exemple, en arménien moderne (dialecte occidental), *kayl* "pas", et *kayl* "loup", sont homonymes, c'est que les phonèmes différenciateurs se sont confondus (cf. arm. classique : *khayl / gayl*).

Il y a là, pour le dire en passant, une donnée utile en phonologie : de l'homonymie de deux unités, on peut inférer l'identité d'un phonème (dans l'exemple cité, *k*, noté par les lettres *ke* et *kim*). On range dans la série homonymique : *pois, poids, poix*, l'interjection *pouah !* qui a un *p* aspiré et un accent expressif : c'est qu'en français ces particularités phonétiques ne sont pas des traits pertinents.

Mais on sait que l'événement inverse, soit la divergence et la dissociation des signifiés, engendre aussi des homonymes (*dessein / dessine* ; *voler / voler*) qu'on peut appeler, avec Bally,[9] des "homonymes sémantiques". Or, du point de vue synchronique, rien ne distingue ces deux classes d'homonymes. Il suffirait qu'on ignorât l'histoire et les antécédents des couples homonymiques pour que le cas des deux verbes : *louer* (de *locāre*) / *louer* (de *laudāre*) se confondît avec celui de *voler / voler*, continuant l'un et l'autre le même *volāre*. On ne connaît pas d'étymologie vraiment sûre au latin *tempus* "temps" ; il est donc impossible de déterminer s'il est homonyme étymologique ou sémantique de *tempus* "tempe".

D'ailleurs, même les comparatistes considèrent comme distincts, dans le système de telle langue, des suffixes ou des désinences de forme semblable, aussi bien dans les cas de différenciation des signifiés que dans ceux de convergence des signifiants : dans la flexion nominale du latin, le *-a* de *vuga* est homonyme et distinct de celui de *domina, equa*, bien qu'ils soient sans doute originellement identiques, alors que les désinences du datif et de l'ablatif singulier, dans le type *dominō*, sont issues de finales différentes (lat. arch. *-ōi̯ / -ōd*). Envisagé du point de vue synchronique, le fait d'homonymie se définit par la coexistence, dans un même système, de deux ou plusieurs signes distincts, quoique phonologiquement semblables. Et ceci nous ramène à la question posée plus haut : comment savoir si ces signes sont réellement distincts, ou s'il s'agit d'un même signe à signification variable ?

A la question : identité ou homonymie ? il n'est pas certain qu'une réponse précise puisse être donnée dans chaque cas particulier. On en conclura, simplement qu'un dénombrement exact des monèmes d'une langue donnée n'est pas possible. Cependant, le sentiment de l'identité ou, au contraire, de l'homonymie, existe souvent chez ceux qui parlent leur propre langue : je sens, par exemple, l'identité du verbe dans : *recevoir* un ami, une lettre, un coup ; celle de l'adjectif *épais*, qualifiant un papier, une forêt, un liquide. Dire, avec Bally,[10]

[9] *Traité de stylistique française*, 2me éd. Heidelberg et Paris, s. d. I § 50 ; *LGLF* § 284.
[10] *LGLF* § 274. Bally indique plus loin (§ 278) qu'il entend par cette expression l'absence de rapports associatifs.

que dans les homonymes les signifiés sont "hétérogènes", c'est user d'un critère un peu vague : qu'on se rappelle les observations de Saussure[11] sur la *valeur* du signe linguistique, distinguée de sa signification.

Pour déterminer la place des homonymes dans un système linguistique, il conviendrait d'abord de considérer les faits sous les deux aspects indiqués par Saussure :[12] dans le plan syntagmatique, d'une part, et dans le plan associatif. On verrait peut-être mieux, alors, pourquoi certains nient l'existence même des homonymes alors que d'autres en découvrent d'innombrables.

Dans le syntagme, les unités ne se distinguent pas seulement par leur forme et leur sens, mais aussi par leurs caractères grammaticaux (classe, fonction). Ainsi les verbes "terminer, finir, achever", pris au sens propre, sont synonymes : dans la plupart des contextes, ils peuvent se remplacer, et les nuances de sens que signalent les dictionnaires sont souvent négligées dans l'usage courant. En revanche, leurs emplois sont délimités par des caractères grammaticaux différents : "terminer" n'admet pour complément qu'un substantif : "finir" comporte l'emploi intransitif. Ces caractères font partie de la valeur du signe — donc du signifié ; mais en se réalisant dans les syntagmes, ils différencient indirectement les signifiants. Selon la définition de M. Marouzeau, un "nom" ne peut être homonyme d'un signe d'une autre classe. Il est exact que deux signes de catégories différentes ne sont pas, l'un à l'égard de l'autre, dans la même situation que deux signes de même catégorie. Dans le premier cas, la question d'identité ne se pose pas : *si* (adverbe) et *si* (conjonction) sont des unités distinctes, de même que les suffixes *-eur* (f. *-euse*) et *-eur* (f. ex. : blancheur), dont le premier se joint à des radicaux de verbes, le second à des adjectifs. La différence des sens est accusée par celle des fonctions : les deux signes ne peuvent jamais figurer dans des syntagmes de même type. Dans le cas où les homonymes appartiennent à la même classe, la différence de sens peut se trouver combinée avec une distinction indirecte des signifiants : l'homonymie de *poêle* (m.) et *poêle* (f.) ne se manifeste, dans le syntagme, que si la différence de genre ne trouve pas à s'exprimer. Les conditions sont en somme les mêmes que pour les radicaux *fond-* (de fondre) et *fond-* (de fonder) : les deux paradigmes coïncident en partie (fondons, fondant, etc.).

Or, des coïncidences semblables peuvent se produire entre des syntagmes ou des fragments de phrase qui ne contiennent pas d'unités homonymes : ainsi *kilèm*, dans : celui qui l'aime / qu'il aime. Il y aurait peut-être avantage, du moins pour la question traitée ici, à désigner d'un autre terme que celui d'homonymie les accidents syntagmatiques de ce genre, et à parler de groupes ou de segments *homophones*. En effet, l'homophonie n'implique nécessairement ni le même nombre d'unités de part et d'autre, ni le même agencement. En turc, les verbes *yenmek* "vaincre" et *yenmek* "être mangé" ont le même radical ;[13] il ne s'agit pas d'unités homonymes, car *yen-* "vaincre" est un monème, tandis

[11] *CLG*, p. 160-161.
[12] *CLG*, p. 187-188. Les termes saussuriens (syntagmatique et associatif) ont été critiqués ; l'accord n'étant pas encore fait sur ceux qui devraient les remplacer, je ne vois pas d'inconvénient à m'en servir ici.
[13] Les deux paradigmes coïncident entièrement, sauf au présent indéfini : *yener* "il vainc" / *yenir* "il se mange". Un cas du même genre est signalé par Bally, *Traité de stylistique franç.* I, § 41 : *représenter / re-présenter*.

que *ye-n*, passif de *ye-* "manger" est formé de deux unités. Dans cette même langue, il existe deux types d'adjectifs en *-lī* : l'un dérivé nominal (ex. *sislī* "brumeux"), l'autre adjectif verbal (ex. *serlī* "étendu", *dayalī* "appuyé"). les deux formations peuvent donner le même produit apparent ; mais dans : *pərinç kilitli bir sandək* "un coffre à serrure de cuivre", *kilitli* s'analyse en *kilit* "serrure" + *-lī* "muni de", alors que dans : *sandək kilitli ıdı* "le coffre était fermé à clé", il s'agit de l'adjectif verbal de *kilitlemek* "fermer à clé", où *-lī* contient, par superposition, le suffixe du dénominatif (*-le-*) et celui de l'adjectif verbal. Ce sont deux syntagmes homophones, et de cohésion différente ; le type : substantif + *-lī* appartenant à la syntaxe libre, il serait même inexact de parler de "mots" homonymes.

L'homonymie, d'autre part, exclut l'identité ; en revanche, deux groupes homophones peuvent contenir des éléments identiques, ou même être composés des mêmes unités placées dans le même ordre. C'est ainsi qu'en turc *hasta-lar* signifie, selon le contexte, "les malades" ou "ils (sont) malades" (cf. *evler-de* "dans les maisons" / *ev-de-ler* "ils (sont) à la maison").

Normalement, dans le discours, la signification de chaque unité se trouve fixée par le contexte et la situation, de façon à exclure non seulement les homonymes éventuels, mais encore les autres acceptions de la même unité. Il y a bien, il est vrai, des phrases à double sens ; mais l'équivoque, involontaire ou voulue, ne suppose ni ne prouve l'existence d'homonymes.[14] elle peut tout aussi bien résulter d'une double acception du même signe ("Philopoemen, le *dernier* des Grecs") ou de quelque autre cause : il m'est arrivé, par exemple, de ne pas reconnaître le mot *partage* dans le contexte suivant : "un enclos où les cowboys procèdent au triage, partage et marquage du bétail".

C'est donc seulement dans le système des rapports associatifs ou mémoriels qu'on peut tenter de faire le départ entre signes homonymes et variations sémantiques d'un signe identique. Il suffit de comparer les unités non pas isolément, mais en tenant compte des familles de signes auxquelles elles appartiennent. Par familles de signes, j'entends, d'accord avec M. Frei,[15] les classes de dérivés (ex. les noms d'action en *-ment* : *enseignement, changement...*) et les séries paradigmatiques et dérivationnelles, ces deux dernières réunies dans l'exemple donné par Saussure : *enseignement, enseigner, enseignons....*[16] Sont homonymes, deux ou plusieurs signes ayant même signifiant, mais appartenant à des familles différentes. Ainsi les suffixes *-esse* (*maîtresse, tigresse*) et *-esse* (*tristesse, faiblesse*) sont homonymes, car les dérivés des deux types forment deux classes distinctes. De même, les radicaux *fond-* (fondre) et *fond-* (fonder), dont les séries paradigmatiques divergent, ainsi que les dérivés (*fondeur / fondateur*, etc.) ; ou encore, en latin, *ser-* (*serō, sēvi, satum ; sator, satio, sēmen...*). Il y a en français, deux adjectifs *poli* homonymes, avec des familles différentes : *poli, polir, dépolir, polissage... / poli, impoli, poliment, politesse*, etc. De cette constatation, on ne peut toutefois déduire que l'homonymie soit

[14] Frei. *La grammaire des fautes*, 1929, p. 65, 69-70 ; Buyssens, au passage cité dans la note 1.
[15] *Ramification des signes dans la mémoire, Cahiers F. de S. 2*, p. 15-16.
[16] *CLG*, p. 175.

exclue entre signes de même famille ; seulement, en ce cas, elle se prouve indirectement par la confrontation de séries parallèles. L'ordonnance en séries parallèles (plusieurs déclinaisons, singulier et pluriel, conjugaison) est peut-être une caractéristique des paradigmes. Ainsi, en latin, il y a homonymie entre la désinence de 1re p. sg. *-am* au futur de l'indicatif et *-am* au subjonctif présent dans le type : *dīcam, audiam*, puisqu'on a, d'une part, les séries *-am, -ēs, -et, ēmus /-am, -ās, -at, -āmus*, et d'autre part : *amābō / amem, ībō / eam*, etc. en regard de : *dīcam / dīcam*. Pareillement, dans les substantifs du type *dominus, iugum*, l'homonymie des désinences *-ō* (dat. sg.) et *-ō* (abl. sg.) est garantie par le contraste des désinences de ces deux cas dans les autres paradigmes : *dominae / dominā, ducī / duce, mihi / me*, etc. Si, dans toutes ces dernières séries, les signifiants cessaient d'être distingués, il n'y aurait plus qu'un seul cas. C'est ce qui est arrivé, en latin, pour l'ablatif et l'instrumental : la valeur de l'ablatif latin est simplement plus étendue que celle, par exemple, de l'ablatif arménien, qui s'oppose à un instrumental. Il est frappant que les écrivains romains traduisent toujours l'ablatif latin par le datif grec, même dans les emplois où l'on aurait en grec un génitif (= ablatif) : ἐξ συνδέσμου. Inst. or. I, 4, 18) en face du grec : ἐχ συνδέσμου.

Ces remarques ne prétendent pas à épuiser ni à résoudre en bloc le problème complexe des syncrétismes de cas, auquel j'espère revenir dans une étude sur le système des cas en arménien moderne. Je souscrirais volontiers, en tout cas, aux critiques qu'adresse M. Bazell à ce propos à R. Jakobson.[17]

Si l'on admet ce qui précède, on exclura du domaine de l'homonymie toutes les différences entre signifiés qui relèvent de la transposition sémantique — plus exactement, de la transposition implicite ou alternance des signifiés.[18] Si, par exemple, *louer* (louange, louangeur) est homonyme[19] de *louer* (location, locataire, sous-louer), ce dernier, en revanche, est identique dans ses deux acceptions (donner / prendre en location) : la même alternance se retrouve dans une série d'autres verbes : *apprendre, mettre* ou *ôter* (un vêtement), et familièrement *évier marier* (épouser / donner en mariage). En effet, si les faits d'homonymie sont toujours singuliers, l'alternance des signifiés suppose des procédés susceptibles d'applications nouvelles. Il y a transposition libre, et non homonymie, entre les suffixes *-ier* (*-ière*) ou *-eur* (*-euse*) désignant un agent (laitier, fournisseur) et les mêmes suffixes dénotant un instrument (sucrier, compteur), car il existe un nombre indéfini d'exemples.

Il y aurait lieu d'étudier les alternances qui peuvent être considérées comme régulières, et généralement les procédés de transposition usités dans une langue donnée ; car, n'étant pas les mêmes partout, ils contribuent à caractériser les systèmes. Le turc n'a pas — ou n'avait pas, avant l'élaboration du nouveau vocabulaire — d'adjectifs de relation du type : *familial, républicain*, sauf les emprunts à l'arabe. En arménien (en turc aussi), un nom abstrait ou de matière se transpose couramment en adjectif : *ken* "rancune / brouillé (avec quelqu'un)", *šuk* "ombre / ombragé", *medals* "soie / en soie", etc. En français,

[17] Ch. Bazell. *On morpheme and paradigm*, Istanbul, 1948, p. 2.
[18] Cette expression m'est suggérée par M. Bazell (lettre du 29. 5. 1948). Cf. l'article de M. Frei, dans *Cahiers F. de S. 2*, p. 18-19.
[19] On peut, pour abréger, appeler verbes homonymes les verbes à radicaux homonymes et de même conjugaison.

la chose est exceptionnelle (colère, chagrin, chic). Cet exemple soulève la question des classes de signes : en français, où l'adjectif et le substantif constituent deux classes bien distinctes, la transposition est dirigée ; type régulier : *riche* → *un riche* ; type irrégulier : *la colère* → *un homme colère*. En arménien, elle semble libre dans un grand nombre de cas (*ken*, *šuk*). En revanche, la transposition, libre ou dirigée, entre nom d'action et nom de lieu est régulière en français : *cuisine, poste, arrêt, dépôt, garage, parc* (parc pour autos / parc autorisé) ; l'arménien, à ma connaissance, n'en a aucun exemple. En latin, beaucoup d'adjectifs comportent une alternance de sens actif-passif (grātus, sollicitus, caecus, dubius...). Si Lucrèce (R. N. VI v. 394) et Salluste (Cat. 39) ont employé *innoxius* avec une valeur passive, c'est qu'une pareille transposition n'était pas étrangère ou contraire au système de la langue.

Concluons. Même du point de vue synchronique, on peut constater l'existence de signes homonymes : ce sont des monèmes, phonologiquement semblables, mais distingués par leur place dans les rapports associatifs. C'est dans ces conditions qu'il y a lieu de discerner les cas d'homonymie et ceux d'identité, et la confrontation des séries mémorielles fournit un critère moins subjectif que le sentiment linguistique des individus.

L'homonymie des unités se rencontre-t-elle dans d'autres systèmes de signes ? Dans l'alphabet, les lettres forment une seule série d'unités, et chacune reste identique dans ses divers emplois : dans l'orthographe française, il n'y a qu'une lettre s, notant alternativement les phonèmes s et z, ce qui ressemble à la transposition sémantique (p. 13). La même combinaison, par exemple *eu*, peut avoir des valeurs différentes (ex. *jeu* / *j'eus*) : cas comparable à celui du turc : *hasta-lar* (p. 11). En revanche, il y a homonymie réelle entre les lettres majuscules *I*, *V*, *X*, *C* et les chiffres romains un, cinq, dix, cent, etc. Dans la typographie des textes anglais, ce sont les minuscules qui sont homonymes des chiffres romains : les risques d'équivoque sont nuls, alors qu'il y en aurait si le chiffre " un " était noté *I*. Le clavier des machines à écrire fait bien voir la situation des homonymes : la série des chiffres occupe (en partie) le registre supérieur, et les lettres sont distribuées sur les autres. L'absence d'un chiffre dans la série, à la place où il devrait figurer, signifie que ce chiffre a un homonyme parmi les lettres : *l* minuscule pour " un ", et *O* majuscule pour " zéro " sur les claviers français ; *Z* majuscule pour " trois " sur les claviers russes.

Les couleurs du blason forment deux séries (émaux et métaux) ; toutes leurs combinaisons sont différenciées, et c'est seulement en l'absence des autres éléments (disposition, figures) que bleu et blanc, sur une cocarde ou une banderolle, par exemple, peuvent faire penser, si la situation ne fournit pas d'indice, à l'écusson de Lucerne ou de Zoug aussi bien qu'à celui de Zurich : simple équivoque, qui n'implique aucune homonymie véritable.

ON THE NEUTRALISATION OF SYNTACTIC OPPOSITIONS

C. E. Bazell

Four types of non-paradigmatic relation, each applicable to the planes of content and of expression, have some bearing on our subject:

(i) The relations in a given chain, i.e. *in praesentia*.

(ii) The relations in the system which these manifest, so far as they are relevant. For instance in the expressive chain *ab*, *a* and *b* are successive. But this succession of speech-units need not answer to anything in the system. To prove that it does we must show that the reverse sequence *ba* stands in distinctive contrast, i.e. that the reversal of phonemes is capable of calling forth a difference in content. If in principle it can, then the relation "before/after" corresponds to an opposition in the system, in the same right as the relevant features of the phonemes themselves.

(iii) The syntagmatic functions, e.g. "selection".[1] These are faculties for combination in the chain, and hence cannot of course be applied to the relations in any given chain.

(iv) The relations between the terms in a pattern, e.g. subordination. If in the pattern of which the combination of attributive adjective and substantive is an example, the functions of one member (e.g. the substantive) alone are similar to the functions of the whole group, this member is said to be super-ordinate. The same relations may hold between phonemes in the chain. They might in some sense be called relations *in praesentia*, but they are clearly of quite a different kind from that of succession. For the relation of succession is given in the chain in question, whereas that of subordination can only be determined through the behaviour of the units in other environments.

It is to be noted that the relations under the second heading themselves form paradigms. Whereas one term preceding another in the chain is in syntagmatic relation with it, the relation "before", regarded as a relevant unit in the system, is paradigmatically opposed to "after". The sequence *ab* contrasts, *in absentia*, with the sequence *ba*.

In some languages the order of units within the morpheme has no distinctive function. In North Chinese (Mandarin) the phonetic order of consonants is fixed, except for *n*; of the other consonants *r* is always final, while the remaining consonants within the syllable is entirely fixed; this is not common in European dialects, but Old Slavonic, before the loss of the "reduced vowels", may probably be cited.[2] In other languages the orders of one class of unit could be regarded as distinctive, while the sequence of the other units would follow automatically. For instance, it would often suffice to describe consonants as final or non-final, from which all other relations would ensue.[3] But where the sequence of units is in principle unfixed, and is regulated only in certain environments or in the case of certain phonemes, it is still unusual to speak of neutralization.

For this fact there are doubtless two reasons. These neutralizations have few morphological effects. Only rarely the replacement of one order by the other, i.e. "implication"[4] in the domain of sequence, involves a morphological transposition, a reversal in the order of phonemes expressing a morpheme. But many neutralizations of phonemic oppositions are also incapable of entailing alternations of morphemic expression. This is true for instance of the neutralization of the opposition *m/ŋ* in final position in Greek, as contrasted e.g. with Finnish. Inversely, implications of order occasionally entail morpheme-alternations: for instance in Hungarian, where the opposition of order is suspended for the combination of *r* and *h* within the morpheme, inflected forms from the stem *teher* "burden" are of the type *terh-* (for **tehr*). No fusion in the expression of plerematic units is here involved, similar to that of Russian *rod-* "race" and *rot-* "mouth",[5] since by chance a noun **tereh* in distinctive opposition is lacking. But it is clear that this fact is irrelevant to the principle.

The second reason has still less relevance. This is the common tendency to treat terms and relations in the light of quite different criteria. That this tendency is unjustified follows from the fact that the distinction between term and relation is not "given": it is the result of an interpretation. The fact that a reversal of expressive units is capable of calling forth a difference in content implies that their order answers to something in the system, but it does not follow that this feature in the system is the relation of order. For order in the chain, even if relevant, could be replaced by some non-relational substance without the system being affected. Let us suppose order replaced

Reprinted from *Travaux du Cercle Linguistique de Copenhague* 5 (1949) : 77–86, with the permission of the author and of the Linguistic Circle of Copenhagen.

[1] Cf. Hjelmslev, *Omkring Sprogteoriens Grundlæggelse*, pp. 21–37. Cited here as *OSG*.

[2] According to one view, supported by Trubetzkoy, *ŋ* could occur in syllabic final as well as initial position. Trubetzkoy based his opinion mainly on the use, in the Glagolitic script, of a distinct graphy for the nasal where most modern dialects show a nasal vowel. Since, however, this sign is distinct from that for initial *n*, a separate phoneme can probably be posited. This may well be the best structural interpretation of final nasal in Chinese, the increase in number of phonemes thus entailed being compensated by the simpler formulation of the principle of the irrelevance of position.

[3] This would seem to be the position in most Tibeto-Burman dialects. Trubetzkoy (*Grundzüge*, p. 220) gives a different account of Burmese, according to which "Konsonanten ... im Wortauslaut nicht geduldet werden". It is difficult to see how the system could bear this interpretation. But if it were correct, it would follow that order could not be a phonological feature within the Burmese word, a consequence he did not draw.

It is to be noted that in a system with only two orders distinguished in their actualization by position relative to a unit regarded as itself without order, we should not have to do with a feature answering to the functional definition of order implied below.

[4] Cf. Hjelmslev, *Note sur les oppositions supprimables*, TCLP VIII, p. 55, and *OSG*, p. 81.

[5] Cf. *Note sur les oppositions supprimables*, loc. cit.

the first and third phonemes as a phonemic syntagma. In other words the "structural order" would not be so different from that of English as the actual order. That it nevertheless would be different derives from the fact that the actual order also has structural relevance, and would have to be taken into consideration like every other feature of the system. For this reason the term "structural order", which we keep here for want of a better, is not very fortunate. The difference is that between a syntactic relation of the second, and of the fourth, type; that is to say that "structural order" belongs to the same level as subordination. Whereas relations of the second type appear from an inspection of the individual chain, providing only that we know how they are manifested in the substance in question, those of the fourth type are only discovered through a comparison of different chains, even after such comparisons as are necessary for the establishment of the relevant features have been undertaken. The latter we call pattern-relations. Relations of the second type will be termed in contrast overt relations.

The overt relations are directly manifested in the actual chain-relations, or at least in some features of la parole, capable of calling forth a distinction upon the other plane. For the pattern-relations on the other hand the question of relevance cannot arise: they are relations between types of relevant features, or rather the schemes into which these may enter. An expressive pattern has no content, though it may be necessary to recognize the pattern before we can recognize the meaning; for semantic oppositions may be expressed by the position of an expressive feature in the pattern, which, though not itself having content, provides the framework without which position could not be conceived. The patterns are, as it were, the chess-boards on which the game of meaning is played; though to render the analogy more close one would have to imagine that the board, in chess, could only be guessed through the arrangement of the chess-pieces. In some artificial systems, such as that of mathematical symbolism, the pattern is necessarily deducible from the units and their arrangement, and this is often true of part-systems in natural languages, e.g. within the phonology of the word. But more often this is not so, which in practice means that even when each term in the chain can be unambiguously interpreted, the chain as a whole may remain ambiguous.

There is a natural though not a necessary correspondence between the pattern-relations and the overt relations, and again between these and the actual relations in the chain. The latter correspondence derives from the fact that, though logically form precedes substance, historically substance precedes form. This form may afterwards be manifested in new substances, but the tension between the old form and the new substance [10] is always plain. We shall assume below that the overt relations answer to their manifestation in the chain, since it is outside the scope of this note to define them. It is rather the pattern-relations with which we are concerned.

The pattern-relations of subordination and cohesion have in common that they presuppose structural order: the latter can be concluded from either. Cohesion

by pitch: a given order in the chain would be replaced by a given absolute degree of pitch, and the actualization of the phonemes could then take place in a given random sequence. Now the pitch of each phoneme may be determined without reference to its environment; hence the relations in the actual chain would count for nothing.

It seems likely that, presented with such a norm, the analyst would be inclined to interpret the various degrees of pitch as features of the phonemes rather than as relations between them. And yet the pitches are mere substitutions of the orders, and as such must manifest the same system. The characteristics of order would of course be kept in the new substance (pitch): i.e. pitch 3 would presuppose pitches 1 and 2, and so on. This is all that is meant by order, and if we have decided to treat it as a relation the new substance will not affect the analysis. But we could have decided otherwise.[6]

So far we have taken order as our example of a syntactic relation. In the plane of expression three levels have been mentioned. Firstly phonetic order. Secondly phonemic order, i.e. order of which the relevance has been proved but which, so to speak, is still tainted with the substance: its definition is of the same sort as that which the Prague School would give for vowel or consonant. Thirdly order in the system, which must be given the sort of definition which glossematics would demand for vowel[7] or consonant. At this third stage "after" and "before" are mere labels for a relational opposition. If we were to substitute one member of the opposition for another (that is to say, in practice, if we were to reverse all chain-sequences) the system would remain the same.[8] But this does not exhaust the levels of order, since there remains another type of order which rightly enjoys this name, the so-called structural definition[9] though in a different field. This is the so-called "structural order", as when it is said that German wird kommen können has the structural order "wird — können — kommen", or better "wird-können/ kommen". By this it is meant that the syntactic system of German forces us to take wird können and not wird kommen as a unit in this case despite the ostensible sequence. It is true that this also answers to the relations in content, but that is not the same fact. The distinction may easily be illustrated from the purely expressive level. Let us suppose that we transposed the first two phonemes in all English words and presented the result to a phonologist for analysis, as though it were the material of an actual language. He would soon discover that the combinatory rules in this new language often favoured treating

---

[6] It is usual to interpret the prosodic features as qualities of units (prosodische Eigenschaften), though in the chain they are actualized as relations between units, as is peculiarly obvious with the "Anschlussarteigenschaften". It may well be here that the system would better be interpreted in agreement with the substance.

[7] The present writer is unable to agree in detail with the definitions of vowel hitherto offered in glossematics, so far as they are familiar to him; and believes that the ultimate definition is more likely to be in terms of subordination than of determination. But the principle stands.

[8] It is sometimes forgotten that such substitutions can only be carried out with minimal features. We could not substitute p for k, in a language possessing b and g, without affecting the system. Still less could we substitute one word-meaning for another, as has recently been suggested; the minimal units of content alone provide the basis for such an operation.

[9] This definition would not entail that order be taken as a relation. If it is, then an isolated term cannot be said to have order; whereas if it were chosen to call order a feature of the unit, an isolated unit would be said to be "first": a mere difference of convention, but one which might well be suggested by the morphological system of the language concerned.

[10] There is for instance an obvious tension between the graphic substance and the system of a natural language, which was never intended for actualization in two-dimensional space; though in a limited degree the form is already influenced by its new mode of manifestation, cf. the possibility of a new "taxeminventar" or new categories (OSG, p. 92).

is the degree with which two units combine to make the equivalent of a single unit : for instance if of the two groups *en* and *ne* the former may unite with much the same preceding and following elements as a simple vowel, or may combine with supra-segmental features such as the tones in the manner of a single vowel-phoneme, whereas the latter cannot, then *en* has closer cohesion than *ne*. If in both these combinations the combinatory possibilities of the whole group are more similar to the vowel's than to the consonant's, then the vowel is superordinate, and the consonant subordinate.

But these relations only hold on condition they are characteristic of the pattern to which the group belongs. When a group is not characteristic of its pattern, i.e. when one at least of its members is used in a " marked " function, the relations are those which customarily hold between the members of the pattern. Thus *ai* may be equally commutable with *a* or *i*, but if *ai* belongs to the same pattern as *al*, *ar*, *at*, *as* etc. and if *a* is superordinate in these groups, it is also superordinate in the group *ai*. Since the superordinate is the unmarked term of the opposition *super-/subordinate*, it may be replaced by the term " central " and this used when there is only one member as well.

The natural equivalents of cohesion and subordination among the *overt* relations are juncture and relative prominence. Two units in close cohesion tend to unite more closely in the chain. The central element tends to be more prominent. But there is no necessary association. Two units in close cohesion may not even be adjacent in the chain, whereas the central unit, as above defined, may be less prominent than the subordinate.

When two units are simultaneous in the structural order, the opposition of subordination is neutralized, i.e. there is co-ordination. This answers to the obvious fact that when two features (e.g. vowel-quality and nasality) are simultaneous in overt order, no distinctions of prominence (e.g. syllabic/asyllabic) can be made, as between the two features.

The fact that two groups belong to the same pattern cannot be determined by the fact that the interior relations (e.g. cohesion or subordination) are the same, since this would involve circularity : it is the general characteristics of the pattern which determine the relations posited for a given group, and the question of identity of pattern is the mutual substitution of two groups, and the question of interior relations comes after.

This is of special importance for another pattern-relation, that of determination. By determination we understand, with the glossematicians, presupposition, but apply the term here not to a syntagmatic function but to the general relations in the pattern. One unit will be said to determine the other if the bulk of elements having the same position in the same pattern presuppose a member of the class to which the other element belongs, but not vice versa. In this we follow the conventional usage whereby a substantive is said to determine another substantive if it fills that place in the pattern which normally falls to an adjective or other semanteme whose " unmarked " function it is to accompany a substantive. On the pure plane of expression the determinant is normally also subordinate, e.g. the fact that the functions of *ba* are in general the functions of *a* is due to the fact that *a* may, like the whole combination, stand alone, i.e. it does not determine *b*. But in morphology it is common that an element should show all the characteristics otherwise associated with a

superordinate while remaining determinant. That verbs are the determinants of their subjects is evident, at least on the side of content. At the same time the verb combines, in the expression, with those inflections which embrace the whole nexus [11] inclusive of subject, i.e. is treated as central in the nexus. Again morphemes commutable [12] with nexus, e.g. the impersonals, are verbal rather than nominal. Thus the verb in predicative function, although determinant, is that member of the group whose characteristics are more nearly the characteristics of the whole group. Hence its final position in the phrase in those languages in which the subordinate, with normal word-order, always precedes.

Unlike the other pattern-relations, determination can have no overt equivalent, for the simple reason that one unit could not be " seen " to presuppose another in the actual chain unless the latter were in fact necessary, so that the relation between the two units would be irreversible and hence irrelevant. This objection does not apply to determination itself, since a pattern in which one set of terms, taken in general, presupposes another, may be filled in a given chain by two terms in the inverse relation.

It is comparatively rare that the three relations of cohesion, subordination and determination should be all completely independent of one another, but an instance is provided by the combination of verb and noun in European languages :

(i) The verb may be either central or subordinate with respect to the noun without alteration of cohesion or determination : cf. verb with object and participle with superordinate noun.

(ii) The verb may have different relations of cohesion with the noun, without alteration of subordination or determination : object and subject are both subordinate determinata but with different degrees of cohesion (cf. above).

(iii) The verb may have different relations of determination vis-à-vis the noun, without alteration of cohesion or subordination, cf. the use with object and that with noun in " adverbial " function.

With reference especially to the last of these three possibilities, it must be added that the comparison of almost any two groups will yield differences of cohesion. When however these are as small as is compatible with the other differences of relation, they may be regarded as irrelevant.

The oppositions between pattern-relations could be regarded as neutralized whenever two morphemes can enter into only one of two given relations with each other. But in practice it is not profitable to speak of neutralization except when all members of the paradigms in question stand to each other in a fixed relation. The most obvious instance is the relation of most inflectional morphemes to the stem they determine. The inflections of tense, for example, are naturally always determinants of the verbal semanteme ; they have a fixed cohesion with the latter and are always subordinate, i.e. the stem is

[11] Cf. Hjelmslev, *Essai d'une théorie des morphèmes* (Actes du IVe congrès des linguistes), p. 143, and *Mélanges...J. Marouzeau*, p. 276.

[12] This commutability applies of course only to the third person, which is one reason why the cohesion of subject and verb must be regarded as looser than that of object and verb, which has wide commutability with intransitive stems. Indeed the cohesion of subject is the loosest compatible with the role of determinatum to a unit adjacent in structural order.

decisive for the functions of the whole group. The degrees of cohesion vary from one inflection to another, and are less close by definition than for basic affixes, but within a given paradigm they are generally constant. Not all inflections have a subordinate character: the inflections of case and mood are decisive for the functions of the word-complex; but their relation to the stem is clearly incapable of being reversed in this respect.

To such morphemes as the last the notion of determination is hardly applicable at all on the level of content. For the determination of noun by transitive verb, where three morphemes (verb, noun, accusative) are concerned, means that the verb presupposes a noun in a given relation; and it is precisely this relation which the accusative expresses. In other words the content of the inflectional morpheme is here the relation involved in the fact of determination. It is thus meaningless to speak of this relation as holding between the accusative and the stem-morphemes.

This is even more obvious for the morphemes of congruence, such as adjectival gender or number. Here the morphemes express not a given relation but the fact of relation to a given other unit alone. They answer, on the plane of content, to the relations of structural order themselves; while the relations they bear to other expressive units correspond to nothing in content.

The fact that within the limits of the word syntactic oppositions are often either neutralized or, in special cases, inapplicable, was the structural basis of the old convention according to which relations in the word did not come under the heading of syntax at all. This convention was less harmful than the assumption, which it usually accompanied, that syntactic relations hold between words considered as wholes. This assumption could never be carried to its logical conclusion in any description of language; for the rest the traditional notion of inflection as opposed to formative affix depends precisely on the fact that the former does not, or does not necessarily, unite with a stem to form a unit in the chain. That syntactic relations cut across word-boundaries was therefore implicitly recognized in traditional grammar, though it coexisted with the incompatible view of the word as fundamental unit in the chain of discourse. Its importance on the level of expression cannot be denied, in the same right as that of syllable or phoneme;[13] but like the latter it has no necessary correspondence with any unit or complex in the content.

Why then should there be a correspondence, however rough, between the expression of units within the word and the neutralization of syntactic oppositions? Partly no doubt because it is precisely the role of the word-cliché to assume responsibility for the arrangement of elements, thus removing the burden of choice from the speaker. Historically, the causes which operate

towards the unification of different elements in the body of a single word are the same as those which operate towards neutralization in general. It is therefore not surprising that the oppositions of relations within the word are often fewer than the features of content expressed could explain.[14] It is not however the relations of content as such between which the oppositions are neutralized; we have rather to do with a limitation to the possibilities of expressing these relations within the boundaries of given types of syntagma. It is possible to examine an expressive unit such as the word from the stand-point of content, but the results will inevitably be coloured by the choice of a given expressive unit, of which the limits do not coincide with those of the semantic units. Such results cannot be regarded as valid except in relation to their arbitrarily chosen starting-point. Though it has now become axiomatic that either plane must be judged with reference to the other, a real equality of treatment remains an ideal still far from fulfilment. At the present stage it is probably enough to demand that the preferential treatment of one level, usually that of expression, should arise from the nature of our material and never be imposed by the linguist.

[13] In many languages the word might be defined as the maximal unit within which there are no oppositions of juncture, just as the syllable might be defined as the maximal unit in which there are no oppositions of prominence and the phoneme as the maximal unit in which there are no oppositions of order, i.e. the phonemic features are necessarily simultaneous. In other languages there are different degrees of juncture in the word, e.g. looser junction for composition than for inflection, or different degrees of prominence within the syllable, in relevant opposition (at least if the "Silbigkeitskorrelation" [Trubetzkoy, *Grundzüge* 139] answers to the same functional definition within the syllable as the "Betonungskorrelation" for the relations as between one syllable and another). It seems likely that the same relations may be repeated at different stages of the hierarchy, so that the former cannot be used to define the latter.

[14] For instance in Turkish a reversal of the suffixes *-il-* (passive) and *-dir-* (causative) would answer to a distinction of meaning: *sev-dir-il-mek* "to be caused to love", *sev-il-dir-mek* "to cause to be loved". But the latter form, though cited in several general works on linguistics, is unknown to Osmanli Turkish, where the meaning required must be expressed by a periphrasis. Where order within the Turkish verb is free, a reversal is not generally accompanied by a change in content.

ON THE PROBLEM OF THE MORPHEME

C. E. Bazell

The common definition of the morpheme as " minimum formal unit ", and the usual interpretation of this definition in the sense of " minimal *signifiant* ", are open to several objections. Some of these objections are trivial, since they no longer apply as soon as the brief primary definition is expanded. Unfortunately a trivial objection often bears some resemblance to a relevant criticism with which in fact it has little to do, and when the grounds for this objection have been removed it is imagined that the criticism has been answered. The chances of confusion may be reduced if the trivial and relevant objections are set side by side, or even given the same verbal form :

(i) " The definition starts from expression rather than from meaning. But the morpheme is a sign in the sense of de Saussure, an association of a *signifiant* and a *signifié* upon equal terms ".[1] This objection may be merely pedantic, since it matters little whether we start from the expression or from the meaning so long as we pay equal attention to both. If the unit is as a whole the same, it is indifferent whether we think of it as an expression with meaning or as a meaning with expression. But if the definition leads us to judge the two levels by different criteria, and if it is this practice against which the objection is aimed, a real weakness in current morphemic theory is implied.

(ii) " There are formal features other than the morphemes, e.g. features of arrangement. These presuppose the morphemes but are none the less minimal, and share with the morphemes the expression of distinctive functions ". The objection is obvious if it means simply that the primary definition must be taken in rather a narrow sense. Such distinctions as that of morpheme and " tagma ", as the constituents of the syntagm provide the necessary correction. But there is a different sense in which morpheme and tagma may share in the expression of the meaning of a syntagm : a feature of meaning may be distributed over both. This is usually expressed by saying that the morpheme concerned has a given meaning only in certain syntactic patterns, but it would be truer to say that neither the morpheme nor its place in the pattern here have meaning in their own right : their combination constitutes the *signifiant*.

Reprinted from *Archivum Linguisticum* 1 (1949) : 1–15, with the permission of the author and of I. M. Campbell of *Archivum Linguisticum*.

[1] " de Saussure does not always adhere strictly to this definition ... more often he lapses into 'l'usage courant' according to which 'ce terme désigne généralement l'image acoustique seule '99c ". (R. S. Wells, *De Saussure's System of Linguistics*, *Word*, III 7–8.)

(iii) " The interpretation as minimal *signifiant*, i.e. as ' smallest meaningful unit ' or ' the smallest linguistic unit charged with its own meaning ',[2] implies a consistency of meaning which is not a necessary feature of the morpheme ". If contextual variations are referred to here, the objection is irrelevant, since a range of meaning however wide does not affect the essential unity of value within the system. But there are semasiological variants within the limits of a single morpheme which are purely conventional, i.e. they resemble the differences of meaning expressed by distinct morphemes ; just as there are variant expressions of the morpheme (the so-called morpheme-alternants) which may resemble the expressions of distinct morphemes in so far as they have no phonemes in common. The notion of morpheme as meaningful unit is often taken to imply a unity of meaning incompatible with this sort of variation, especially in the domain of inflectional morphemes.[3]

(iv) " The morpheme serves less to express a meaning than to express a distinction of meaning ". This may merely conceal the tedious old view that units smaller than the word cannot have meaning as such, or possibly the view, not less tedious, that stems have their meanings in a sense in which inflections do not. It may however mean this, that the method by which we arrive at the morpheme is the method of substitution with the proof that this substitution can systematically call forth distinctions of meaning. By adding that the morpheme " has meaning " we are saying something not implied by the methods used for its determination, and which may, in any given instance, be right or wrong.[4]

The relevant objections as opposed to the trivial ones have this in common that they arise from the nature of the languages with which we have to deal and would not necessarily apply in the case of a language of exceptionally simple structure. In such a language all variations in morpheme-meaning might in fact be referable to the context and the functions of morpheme and tagma be quite distinct or the latter unit be lacking.[5] All one could object to in the definition of morpheme so far as this language was concerned, would be that it was unnecessary, since the morpheme would be identical with the sign. The sign is by definition minimal, since higher units are to be regarded as combinations of signs, not as complex signs. But in the languages with which we have

[2] R. Jakobson in *Rapports sur les questions historiques* ... (*Actes du 6e Congrès international des linguistes*, p. 7.)

[3] For the category of case for example there are the studies of the Russian system by Jakobson, *Beitrag zur allgemeinen Kasuslehre* (*TCLP*, I, VI, 240), of the early Georgian system by H. Vogt, *Norsk Tidsskrift for Sprogvidenskap*, XIV, 99 ff., and of the *Finnish and Hungarian Case-systems* by Sebeok (Stockholm, 1944), all based on the assumption that each case expresses a single semantic feature or bundle of features.

[4] It would seem that the function of the morpheme in expressing distinctions of meaning is felt to characterise it insufficiently as against the phoneme. But the phoneme does not express distinctions of meaning, nor does it even " distinguish between meanings "; it distinguishes between the expressions of meanings, i.e. between " forms ", in the popular sense of " being a distinctive feature ".

[5] It goes without saying that the arrangement of morphemes would always keep the function of showing which meanings " went together "; but this is a natural not a conventional function and therefore belongs to speech rather than to language.
In his *La langue et la société* (Instituttet for sammenlignende kulturforskning A, XVII) Sommerfelt has described an Australian language that he holds to possess a simple structure of this kind. Unfortunately the assumption is the easier to make the less we know of the language or culture concerned.

to deal the sign is not co-extensive with the morpheme : the justification for the latter term lies in an asymmetry between expression and content which a system of signs does not necessarily presuppose.

The first and third of the objections above are in so far related as the refusal to recognise the inner-linguistic status of semantic variants within the morpheme implies that expression and meaning do not play corresponding roles in its determination, since the expressive variants of a morpheme are obviously units within *la langue*, so far at least as they do not simply reflect the rules of phonemic syntax.

The notion that a morpheme must have a single value underlying all its uses in speech, a value perhaps highly abstract or difficult to ascertain but always accessible to patient research, would seem partly to depend upon a comparison between phoneme and morpheme. Two comparisons are familiar, the one between the allophones of a phoneme and the alternants of a morpheme,[6] the other between the allophones and the semantic variants of the morphemic *Gesamtbedeutung*. The former of these comparisons is absurd, since allophones are identified as members of the same phoneme through their intrinsic characteristics, and belong to speech, whereas the morpheme-alternants are recognised as members of the same morpheme by the functions which they serve, and belong to language. The second comparison is false, since the units of meaning which underlie semantic variants stand in no necessary relation to the morphemes.

Yet both these comparisons have contributed to the view of the morpheme as a semantic unit. The fact that the morphemic alternants as such have nothing in common has suggested the conclusion that their relation is only assured by a single common value which they express ; and the analogy of the allophones and the semantic variants implies that when all contextual and situational variations have been allowed for there will remain some one common feature or bundle of features common to all examples.[7]

This is to reverse the error of the earlier grammarians, who were often tempted to take as linguistic distinctions differences of meaning easily attributable to the force of the context. The infinity of contextual meanings—of "things meant" [8]—must answer to a limited number of values in *la langue*, but this number has no relation to the number of morphemes.

The unity of a morpheme is guaranteed less by its uniform meaning than by the systematic irrelevance of any distinctions of meaning to its expressions. This systematic irrelevance may characterise either the morpheme as such, or the language. In the latter case, there is a real identity of value : the variations in meaning are merely contextual. But when the semantic oppositions are only suspended at a given point of the system, to reappear elsewhere, we have to do with a difference of value which morphemic identity cannot affect.

For example it would be clearly erroneous to put such distinctions as that of "directive" and "passive" (object-) accusative in early IE languages on the same level as that of the "affected" and "effected" object. The latter distinction has no formal repercussions : it is not a matter of linguistic meaning but belongs to the sphere of the "thing meant". On the other hand the categories of passive and directive have linguistic expression ; the fact that the accusative may be used for both means merely that the distinction is suppressed at this point. Should this lead us to suppose that there is something in common between the two meanings, and that it is this common feature that the accusative expresses ? The supposition would not necessarily be wrong, but it is surely not logically cogent.

Jakobson argues : [9] "Wenn die Einzelbedeutungen eines Kasus wirklich 'nichts Gemeinsames miteinander hätten', so wäre auch der Kasus unvermeidlich in mehere homonyme, miteinander nicht verknüpfte Formen zerfallen". But what shows that the cases do not in fact constitute each a set of homonymous forms ? The grammarian excludes the possibility at the start : if two "cases" are invariably identical, then they constitute a single case. He does the same for every small paradigm, holding rightly that, other things equal, the importance of an identity is in inverse proportion to the number of members in the class. Where the class is a large one, such as those of noun or verb, mere formal identity is trivial, and to such trivial identities he restricts the term homonym. This is a commonplace of method, from which no semantic conclusions can be drawn.

This method is justified by the facts of language. Identity of form within a small paradigm creates a stronger associative link than within a large paradigm, and thus at the same time provides more favourable conditions for analogical extensions of the expressive association. Semantic relations will support this association, but they need not be so close as to enable a single value to be posited.[10]

There are two opposite dangers, that of taking merely logical distinctions to be linguistic, and that of taking linguistic distinctions to be merely features of *la parole* because they are neutralised within the limits of some morphological category. It is the latter danger to which the structural linguist, whose task it is to show the unity that underlies diversity, is more exposed. It should go without saying that if this danger is not avoided, real relations will be missed :

[6] In his recent article, *Problems of Morphemic Analysis* (*Language*, XXIII, 321 ff.), C. F. Hockett even makes this comparison a basis for his new term *morph* for "morphemic alternant", on the valid analogy (*allo*)*phone* : *phoneme* :: *morph* : *morpheme*" (p. 322, footnote 7).

[7] The allophones of a phoneme do not necessarily show common phonetic features in the strictest sense, but the variations must be such that common "neuremes" may be supposed (cf. Martin Joos, *Acoustic Phonetics*).

[8] "Thing meant" is understood in Gardiner's sense : whatever the speaker has intended shall be understood by the listener (*Speech and Language*, 82). The thing meant is not to be confused with the "object referred to" : the meaning is in language, and the object referred to is outside language, before the utterance, whereas the thing meant has no independence of the utterance. The object or situation referred to has no interest as such for the linguist, but the thing meant is the "matter" of the semasiologist in the same sense as sounds are the matter of the phonematician, without being his subject.

[9] Beitrag, p. 241, cf. footnote 2, p. 2 [footnote 3, p. 217 above].

[10] Jakobson (*loc. cit.*) remarks that there may be systematic formal relations between e.g. a case of one number and a different case of another number ; nobody would think of positing a single morpheme here, and therefore the notion of case-identity must imply something more than systematic formal relations. Indeed ; but the "more" implied is of syntactic rather than semantic nature, cf. below. Actually his argument tells in the opposite direction ; since if there may be systematic relations of identity between categories clearly quite different semantically, may there not also be such relations between categories where the postulation of a common meaning is just conceivable—*but, in fact, not valid* ? To assume the contrary is to fall into a logical error similar to that of the "conservative editor" who admits evident corruptions in his text but insists on defending the manuscript whenever the reading will "just make sense".

the features common to different morphemes will be overlooked through false identifications within the boundaries of a single morpheme.[11]

Since the morpheme has variants on both the linguistic levels, it would be preferable to abandon the term "morpheme-alternant" and to speak of expressive and semantic alternants according to the level concerned. On both planes the alternants proper, of which the choice depends upon their position in the chain, can be distinguished from the free variants. For morphemic unity it is necessary, in the first place, that the limit between one expressive variant and another should not answer to the limit between one semantic variant and another, i.e. that no variation in the expression should be accompanied by a variation in content.

The expressive alternants are usually determined by the other morphemes within the same word, whereas the semantic alternants are usually determined by morphemes outside the word in which the semantic alternant of the morpheme is found. Typical examples are the variants of "case-form"[12] in different declensions, and the variations of "case-value"[12] with different verbal or prepositional rection. This is a consequence of the fact that the expressions of morphemes combine in an expressive unit, the word, whereas their meanings combine in a unit of meaning, which is not the word.[13]

The mutual indifference of expressive and semantic variants is a necessary, but not of course a sufficient, criterion of the unity of a morpheme. Let us suppose for instance that we have a set of distinct prepositions each identical with a perfectivising prefix; the prefixes cannot be distinguished in meaning but depend upon the verbal stem in question. Then we may either posit a single perfectivising morpheme of which these forms are expressive alternants, and which is distinct from any of the prepositions, or we may posit a set of morphemes of which the prepositional and prefixal meanings are variants, thus referring each prefix to a different morpheme. Either will be a legitimate analysis, since within the boundaries of a single unit no difference of meaning answers to a different expression.

But for any given system the question must be asked: which units show greater cohesion? Is there a tendency to transplant any expressive variant of the prepositions into the corresponding prefixal form, or a tendency to extend any new meaning of a prefix to the other prefixes?[14] In the former case we shall prefer to allot the expressively similar elements to one morpheme, in the latter case we must be prepared to allow two contradictory systems.

This is not "to introduce diachronic criteria into synchronic grammar", since an analogy does not effect a change in the system but merely presupposes a given arrangement of the elements in this system, alike whether it gives rise to a "new form" or simply maintains an old one.[15] The criterion of tendency is confessedly often difficult to apply; but it should carry weight not only in otherwise doubtful cases but act also as a brake on merely ingenious analyses. An analysis which has no consequences for speech has no purpose. For instance a recent synchronic description of French includes such divisions as aîné into a "prefix" é "before", and né "born".[16] It is hardly probable that the author thinks that the historical relation can have any further relevance in French: he would doubtless agree that if the participle né should ever be replaced by a analogical form it is not only unlikely, but practically inconceivable, that aîné would be affected. But he would hold, perhaps, that such an opinion is subjective. It cannot indeed be immediately put to the test. But knowledge of a wide range of dialects over long periods can tell us what sort of analyses are likely to be relevant to speech as productive or preservative patterns. Such as are not may surely be held superfluous. It would however be wrong to demand with another American scholar that productivity in the usual sense (i.e. the ability of the morphemic expression to enter new combinations) should be taken as sole criterion.[17]

[11] The appeal to a "pre-logical mentality" in which the "different meanings" are in fact one meaning is here irrelevant, since the distinctions under discussion are such as to receive expression at some point in the system, and which therefore are real for the "pre-logical mentality", whatever this may mean. Moreover the ground for assuming a given mentality in such cases are usually linguistic, so that the argument is circular. It is unfortunate that such empirical tests as can be applied are seldom resorted to. For instance, can the morpheme in question have the two "meanings" simultaneously? In Latin, the same accusative can combine with two verbs, which one entails an "affected" and the other an "effected" object, but not with two verbs of which one entails a directive and the other an objective accusative. There is such general agreement between European languages in this respect that often rules need not be given; but it would be valuable to know how far they apply in exotic forms of speech, while one would willingly dispense with the information, more often given, that for the speaker of such and such a dialect, two concepts distinct for us are "identified" or "felt as the same".

[12] For example the dative in German expresses the unmarked member of the opposition static : kinetic in many prepositional combinations, in minimal contrast to the accusative; whereas the accusative expresses the unmarked member of the opposition direct : indirect in many verbal combinations, in minimal contrast to the dative. It is such oppositions, and not the oppositions of the morphemes conceived as wholes, which are the semantic equivalent of the phonemic oppositions. The semantic oppositions like those of the phonemes, reappear in different morphemes without implying identity in any other respect.

[13] For instance, on the semantic level an inflectional morpheme is one member of a syntagm whose other member is not merely the "sememe" with which it combines in the word, but this semanteme together with most or all of the subordinate morpheme-groups, e.g. it is the whole nexus, not the verb as such, with which the tense-morpheme combines. Cf. L. Hjelmslev, Essai d'une théorie des morphèmes, Actes du IV Congrès, p. 143. But it is untrue to say that the morphemes of voice combine with the whole nexus, for their function is to show the relation of subject to predicate, not to qualify the sentence as a whole. Similarly, preposition and case form an immediate constituent as opposed to the noun-stem.

[14] In the exceptionally simple instance chosen "any subsequently developed variant of meaning (or expression)" must be meant, since we have assumed that there is no variation at the stage posited. But the assumption of semantic variants of the perfective which are not common to all the prefixes would not change the principle, so long as no two prefixes could combine with the same verb-stem in distinctive functions.

[15] Tendency must be understood in a wide sense, since it includes the tendency to maintain relations. For example an English strong past like ground is not simply traditional, since it owes its survival to the analogy of semantically similar "circular-action" verbs (bound, wound) and thus presupposes the analysis of models which might have survived in their own right.

[16] R. A. Hall, French, "Structural Sketches", I [Language Monographs, No. 24, p.3. supplement to Language, 1948). Against the analysis is the obsolescence of (pyine), the indivisibility of the opposite (kade), the absence of monophonemic nominal prefixes in French with exception of the semi-learned ə (eu-) etc.

[17] For the view of D. L. Bolinger, Word, IV, 18–24. It would be justified if we could call preservative analogy a sort of concealed productivity.

It is a logical conclusion from the relevance of tendency to the interpretation of the system that two identical forms of speech, taken over a small period, might correspond to two different systems. This conclusion has been drawn by Isačenko, Zur phonologischen Deutung der Akzentverschiebungen in den slavischen Sprachen (TCLP, VIII, 173–83), for the phonematic system.

It is the fault of "mechanistic" descriptions of language that they fail to account for speech-tendencies. For instance a description of the phonemic structure of a vocabulary as of little interest if no distinction is made between those combinations which tend to be altered as soon as the words in which they occur enter into everyday usage and those which remain constant

Now the definition of a linguistic unit or category, to be generally applicable to different languages, must be in terms of nuclear features. It would be false to suppose that the characteristic features of a class must necessarily all be shown by every member of the class defined. A more rigid conception of category is bound to do violence to the facts of any new system to which it is applied. For example every definition of "case" will necessarily include the notion of relation as a specific feature of the category.[18] But traditionally the vocative is allowed as a case, although it does not express a relation in the same sense as the others. Must we therefore, with some very ancient as well as very recent grammarians, exclude the vocative from the case-paradigm; or must we instead widen the definition of case to allow the vocative entry into the category in its own right? To adopt the former solution is to run counter to the system of the languages concerned, in which a large number of common features favour case-status; to adopt the latter is to render the definition so wide that other morphemes not sharing the case-features would have to be classed as cases.[19]

These are the horns of a false dilemma. A definition in linguistics should be merely the starting-point for classification while the fuller contours of the category are left to be filled in as the system dictates. Starting from the oblique cases as nuclear members of the case-category we regard the vocative as peripheral within the class of cases, to which it belongs by virtue of common expressive features (syncretism with other cases, cumul with number, etc.) and common "scope".[20]

What applies to a paradigmatic class applies *mutatis mutandis* to the morpheme as such. The nuclear type is represented by the "unambiguous signs", i.e. signs which are neither homonymous nor synonymous with others, and which are not suspect either of being divisible into signs or of being only parts of signs. Other morphemes are in various manners peripheral.[21] Morphemes with alternants are in so far similar to unambiguous signs as the variations in expression do not call forth differences in meaning nor the semantic variants differences in expression. In other words within the limits of such morphemes the variations in expression and meaning resemble variations in irrelevant phonetic qualities and in "things meant" respectively, differing from the latter only by their functional relevance outside the limits of the morpheme in question. A morpheme is thus a member of the class of elements converging upon the nucleus of unambiguous signs. Some applications may now be considered.

It is commonly said that certain historically independent signs have in given constructions become "mere grammatical tools" or "of purely syntactic function" and the like, phrases which constant use has not endowed with any very clear meaning. An extreme example would be English *do* in negative constructions. Have we to speak of different morphemes in *do not do*? The content of *do* in its first occurrence is plainly zero, but zero is no less acceptable as a semantic alternant of the morpheme than zero-phoneme as an expressive alternant.

Semantic form is different both from meaning in *la parole* and from morphemic form. When Hjelmslev writes that Danish *jeg ved det ikke* and Finnish *en tiedä* have the same meaning but different forms,[22] we have rather a contrast between morphemic form and semantic matter that still leaves room for the distinction of semantic form. In both languages there is a privative opposition between positive and negative, there is no intermediate term, nor does either entail the suspension of a semantic opposition which the other allows. In these respects the semantic forms are the same, and this fact is not altered by the appearance of the expression of the negative at different points of the morpheme chain (in Danish as verbal determinant, in Finnish as verb-stem). A real difference of semantic form would be shown by a language with a third term "dubitative" opposed at once to positive and negative; this happens not to be true of the languages we know, in which "dubitative" may itself combine with either positive or negative. Another sort of difference is actually shown by those languages which combine negation with another semantic opposition which is neutralised in the positive; of such languages classical Greek, so far as the variation of negative particles is not automatically regulated, is the best-known example. These are real distinctions of semantic form, and, have nothing to do with those differences in form which the contrast between verbal and adverbial rendering in Finnish and Danish respectively is fit to illustrate.[23]

(cf. F. Hintze's criticism of Twaddell's account of German word-form in *Studia Linguistica*, II, 45 ff.). It is true that if the system concerned is that of a modern language and the word in question of recent accession, there is a risk of error: it is possible that the system may have widened to allow room for the new forms. But the risk must be taken.

[18] The sense in which other nominal morphemes express relation does not concern us here. There are also nominal morphemes that express the same sort of relation as the cases, but are differently orientated, e.g. the *status constructus* in Hebrew expresses a relation to the subordinate, whereas the cases express a relation to a superordinate.

[19] For instance the adverb could be regarded as a case of the adjective, as has been proposed, the relation expressed being that between two sentence-elements and not, as with the vocative, between speaker and hearer (a very dubious interpretation of the vocative, but the only way to save it as a relating morpheme, cf. de Groot, *Lingua*, I, p. 462). But the adverb differs from a combination of noun and case by a strong tendency to lexicalisation, by rough functional equivalence to simple morphemes—the synchronic interpretation of these as isolated cases of defective nouns being highly artificial—absence of concord, etc. etc., all features which cannot a priori be regarded as less important. These differences do not of course all apply in every language: e.g. Turkish adverbial *-ce* may very well be regarded as a case.

[20] The scope of a morpheme is the semantic equivalent to its order in the expressive chain, e.g. the scope of a case embraces the noun inclusive of number and gender, that of a number gender only, etc. In Latin case, while having the same expressive order as that of the numbers, has the same scope as that of the prepositions, whereas in languages of "agglutinative" structure there tends to be symmetry between scope and order. The fact that in a combination of preposition and case it may often be impossible to distinguish the meanings of each separately, is the converse of *cumul*, i.e. distinct members of the *signifiant* are cumulated upon one *signifié*, while in *cumul*, as usually employed, distinct *signifiés* are cumulated upon one *signifiant*.

[21] A given morpheme may of course be nuclear qua morpheme and yet peripheral in its paradigm or *vice-versa*.

[22] *Omkring Sprogteoriens Grundlæggelse*, pp. 47–8. Form with the glossematicians does not mean *expressive* form, so that the statement is not obvious in *this* sense.

[23] A glossematician would certainly consider that his theory had been misrepresented in several ways here, since it is the merit of this school to have insisted on the equipollence of expression and content. The above argument implies that practice has not followed theory. This view cannot be justified in detail here, but it is not unfair to remark that the primacy of expression over content was an earlier tenet of this school (cf. Hjelmslev, *op. cit.*, 68, footnote 2). Few who have followed Hjelmslev's work can have failed to be struck by the meagre practical results of the change in attitude. The new theory has mainly been used—whether rightly or wrongly—to justify old practices.

At the same time one misunderstanding which might arise from the over-simplified account

If, for example, Finnish possessed two contrasting negative constructions of which the one cited would, in fact, be normally that chosen to render the negative in the example given, then indeed we should have an identity of meaning which concealed a distinction of semantic form. If North German *suchte* and South German *hat gesucht* are different in semantic form even where they have the same meaning, this is not because the morpheme-structure is entirely different but because the South German construction does not stand in opposition to a form with the meaning of North German *hat gesucht*. A Greek negative construction might well have been chosen to illustrate the coincidence of similar meaning with different form; whereas the comparison of Danish and Finnish[24] phrases serves merely to obscure the issue.

It would lie outside the scope of this note to discuss the very complex question of how semantic form is to be determined. This problem is not the problem of the morpheme. Thus in order to decide whether French "partitive *du*" is the same morphemically as the combination of preposition and article, we do not need to decide whether the two meanings may be both referred to some more abstract value, or whether partitive *du* stands in minimal semantic opposition to *un*. The latter fact is doubtless the reason why the two are traditionally given quite separate places in the French morpheme-system. The relevant reasons in favour of one or the other solution are that there is a systematic expressive identity of partitive with prepositional combination but a systematic syntactical parallel between *du* and *un* which does not apply to normal prepositional combinations.[25]

A very different problem is presented by such morphemes as Hungarian -*nál* (adessive), -*tól* (ablative), -*hoz* (allative). Here the expressive data have been responsible for the monomorphemic interpretation. A division of the phonemic chain in respect of function is not possible, though the semantic division into two features, one of "adhesion" which the three elements have in common, and one of direction which each has in common with a pair of other suffixes, is apparent. Now this is not enough to justify a morphemic division. But the features of direction have their separate expression in other combinations, e.g. *mellett* "beside", *mellé* "to beside", *mellöl* : "from beside",

whereas the features of adhesion may be shown by a common phoneme even in the suffixes (the suffixes of interiority have all initial *b*). The syntactic parallel between suffixes and "postpositions" is very close in Hungarian.[26] One should therefore be prepared to recognize a morpheme-division in the Hungarian suffixes.

The divisibility of the Latin case-number suffixes rests on different criteria, since the case-features never receive distinct expression. On the other hand that of the syntactic distinction of case and number in Hungarian is far more marked than that of adhesion and direction in Hungarian, since the two series of features may be governed by entirely different sets of morphemes, e.g. the prepositions and numerals respectively. But this is a characteristic of distinct signs.[27] There is therefore something to be said in favour of regarding the cases and numbers as morphemes rather than as "morphemic components".

In a syncretic system it may not always be possible to draw a fast line between syncretism proper and the neutralisation of a morphemic opposition. In the traditional grammar of the classical languages the nominative and accusative neuter are regarded as distinct morphemes, whereas it is not usual to speak of a 1st person dual active of a Greek verb, but rather to say that the plural is used where the dual of other persons would be normal; i.e. there is syncretism in the former case but neutralisation in the latter. The choice of the classical grammarians in such cases was doubtless usually the appropriate one. The extreme view of Bloomfield[28] that a distinction in however few paradigms implies homonymy in all those in which the distinction is not made, would involve denial of the privative nature of oppositions expressed by morphemes, and could of course not be carried to its logical conclusion in any grammatical description.

The definitions of sub-classes of morphemes, such as stem and inflection, semanteme and morpheme in the older sense, free and bound forms, or again constituents and exponents, must be subject to the same provisos. For instance the criterion of word-boundaries, which plays some part in each, will, if rigidly interpreted, lead to the separation of features which go together in the language concerned. Where the lines of division which the criterion of the word would lead to, do not tend to coincide with other dividing-lines,[29] then the unit defined should

---

above is worth countering. The semantic form might be identical even if the meaning were entirely different, e.g. the opposition of positive and negative in one language might answer to the oppositions of tense in another language, if the relations within the system as a whole were the same, just as (phonetically) the consonantal system of one language might answer to the vowel-system of another. It is not the semantic opposition as such, but its place in the network of relations, which is relevant to form. This point is not considered above, but its neglect implies no difference of principle.

[24] The statement that Finnish *en tiedä* contains a verb meaning "not", while correct so far as it goes, might awaken the false impression that this form has the same place in Finnish as an ordinary negative verb, e.g. "fails to do". In fact the Finnish negative verb is syntactically unique, not, as *fail* in English, a "verb like any other".

[25] The parallel is of course far from complete, since *un* may combine with all prepositions whereas *du* cannot combine with the historically identical preposition. That a minimal semantic opposition may not be morphemically minimal is—for common sense—illustrated by the pair "A killed X" and "A was killed by X", where the semantic contrast is minimal but where the second of the pair differs from the first by several morphemes. The tendency is to escape this conclusion by saying that the second construction is to be differently interpreted: the "thing meant" is minimally different but the speaker expresses it in terms of quite other value. But the evidence for this seems simply to be that the morpheme-structure is indeed quite different, which was obvious at the start. The argument, if made explicit, would be seen to be circular.

[26] Cf., e.g. *abban a házban, a mellett a ház mellett* "in", resp. "beside that house", in which *mellett* like -*ban* takes part in the agreement of noun and demonstrative. This is one reason why the postulation of a nominative morpheme with zero-suffix (cf., e.g. J. Lotz, *Das ungarische Sprachsystem*, p. 63) will not fit the system: there is no more reason to say here that *ház* has a zero-suffix when an independent word with *mellett* than when a stem with -*ban*. In either case we have simply the stem with following overt morphemes. Similarly in the Turanian linguistic type. On the other hand one cannot go so far as to deny, with some American scholars, that a morpheme can consistently be expressed by a zero-suffix; if there is reason to attribute a positive meaning to zero a morpheme must be assumed.

[27] It might be objected that syntagms function like signs within the framework of larger syntagms. The theory of the immediate constituent is based on this simple fact. But a resemblance which is valid for an infinite number of units is naturally without significance for the determination of a minimal unit. The cases and numbers belong to a limited class of elements concerning which it is desirable to make the same sort of statements as we make about separate morphemes, rather than about morpheme-features or classes of morphemes.

[28] Bloomfield, *Language*, p. 224.

[29] An example has been given from Hungarian (cf. footnote 2, p. 13) [i.e. footnote 26 above]. Lotz (*op. cit.*, p. 99) deals with the postpositions as "unselbständige Adverbien", as though

not be sought in the system in question, which will doubtless have other units clustering round different nuclei.

The morpheme of current grammatical description is a compromise between two different units, of which the one is that with which this note is concerned, whereas the other might be described as the " minimal complex of semantic features capable of receiving distinct expression ". Up to a point the two units may stand in a one-one relation, and it is only good method to assume that they do when there is no cogent argument to the contrary. But there is no necessary relation. The morpheme, as the central unit of language, bridges the asymmetry of content and expression, but stands itself in a relation of " reduced " asymmetry to each of these two levels. These asymmetries are in their turn covered by intermediate units, for instance the morphoneme as link between the phoneme and morpheme, and—though still to be named—some unit between the morpheme and the semantic elements. Not all these units may be needed for every language, and more will be needed for some systems. Each of these intermediary units must be defined by its functions as systematic link between different levels, and can carry no further implications. If so interpreted, the definition of the morpheme as minimum formal unit may be allowed.

---

there were less relation between -*ben*, *benne* and the parallel *mellett*, *mellette* than between the latter and a morpheme such as *túl* " beyond ", which cannot take suffixes, governs itself a " case-suffix ", and may, though less commonly, precede the noun.

LINGUISTIQUE ET THÉORIE DU SIGNE

Jerzy Kuryłowicz

Malgré son étymologie, le terme *sémantique* ne se rapporte habituellement qu'à la science qui s'occupe des sens (de la signification, de l'acception) des formes linguistiques.[1] Pour donner un nom à la théorie générale du signe, F. de Saussure,[2] éprouvant le besoin d'un terme nouveau, a proposé celui de *sémiologie*. En face de la linguistique et des autres sciences sociologiques, elle serait ce que la physique est pour les sciences naturelles. Les différents théorèmes de la linguistique résulteraient de l'application de la sémiologie au cas concret et spécial du langage humain.

Pour dégager la couche fondamentale relevant de la théorie générale du signe, il faudrait confronter la sémantique avec d'autres sciences traitant de n'importe quelle fonction (pas nécessairement symbolique). Mais en réalité de telles comparaisons ne sauraient en l'état actuel des recherches, être fructueuses. La linguistique elle-même, la mieux systématisée parmi les sciences sociales, n'a pas encore, malgré Bühler et les mises au point de Laziczius, de Lohmann et d'autres, établi une hiérarchie transparente de ses axiomes. Non seulement les différences de méthode existant entre les sciences spéciales, mais surtout les divergences entre les matériaux analysés, ayant tantôt un caractère massif et continu, tantôt fragmentaire et isolé, contribuent à décourager, de prime abord, toute tentative de comparaison.

Au cours de ces vingt dernières années, les progrès de la phonologie ont donné un essor nouveau à la théorie du signe. Le mérite principal de la phonologie à cet égard est d'avoir développé les concepts d'*opposition* et de *corrélation*, identiques à ceux qui, depuis longtemps, avaient eu cours dans le domaine sémantique (morphologique). Remarquons seulement qu'ici c'est le terme *dérivation* qui désigne le rapport *neutre-négatif : positif* d'une opposition (par exemple, *château : châtelet*), correspondant ainsi de toutes pièces au terme *corrélation* employé en phonologie (par exemple, *p* sourd : *b* sonore). Si l'autre grand trait commun aux deux domaines, sémantique et phonique, à savoir la relation entre les éléments d'une même structure (= complexe) ou la *syntaxe* au sens large du mot, n'a pas d'abord attiré l'attention des linguistes, c'est que

la phonologie ne lui a pas consacré assez d'attention. Mais l'esquisse de *glossématique*, présentée par MM. Hjelmslev et Uldall au Congrès Linguistique de Copenhague (1936), a déjà le mérite de souligner le parallélisme profond des deux domaines (appelés plérématique et cénématique), justement en fait de structures.

Ce dont on ne s'est pas rendu compte, du moins de manière explicite, c'est qu'une théorie générale du signe servant de base à une théorie du signe linguistique n'a pas besoin de quitter le domaine de la langue. C'est que le domaine phonique et le domaine sémantique, indépendamment de la relation qui les unit et qui constitue l'essence même de la langue, représentent, *chacun*, un système de signes, et, ce qui plus est, représentent des systèmes *hétérogènes* en ce qui concerne la forme, le contenu et la fonction des signes.

Dans le domaine phonique, il y a certains sons-types élémentaires dont la forme peut être arrêtée et décrite par des méthodes relevant de la physique et de la physiologie. Leur fonction n'est pas du tout, il faut insister sur ce point, d'ordre sémantique, c'est-à-dire qu'ils ne servent pas directement de symboles. Ils servent, par contre, à bâtir des unités sémantiques, telles que les racines, les affixes, etc. Dans le domaine sémantique, ce sont ces unités qui fonctionnent comme éléments à l'intérieur de structures à fonction sémantique : les mots et les structures plus compliquées (groupes de mots, propositions). Autrement dit, ces dernières, de leur côté, entrent comme éléments dans des structures sémantiques. Entre le découpage d'une structure sémantique en unités (éléments) sémantiques et l'analyse phonique de ces dernières, il y a abîme qui nous fait bien sentir les natures hétérogènes de la phonologie et de la sémantique. C'est la même distance qui existe, par exemple, entre les éléments d'un style d'architecture et les propriétés physiques et chimiques de la pierre employée dans la construction. Si, malgré tout, les systèmes phoniques et sémantiques montrent des affinités profondes, voire même des traits identiques dans leur structure, il faut y reconnaître des lois propres, non pas à *un* système, mais à des systèmes remplissant certaines conditions générales.

Pour mettre en lumière ces affinités, nous allons citer une loi valable dans les deux domaines, phonique et sémantique, la loi bien connue (de la logique élémentaire) concernant le contenu et l'emploi (la fonction) d'un concept : plus étroite est la zone de son emploi, plus riche est son contenu (son sens) ; plus large est son emploi, plus pauvre est son contenu. Cette loi est familière aux linguistes. La généralisation et la spécialisation du sens d'un mot, d'un suffixe, etc., sont en rapport étroit avec l'élargissement et le rétrécissement de son emploi. Or cette loi a un pendant dans la système phonique ; nous avons essayé de le démontrer dans notre article *Le sens des mutations consonantiques*.[3] On sait, grâce au regretté Trubetzkoy,[4] que l'opposition de phonèmes dite privative, c'est-à-dire celle qui, dans certaines conditions, est supprimée, crée un lien étroit entre deux phonèmes, dont l'un, appelé *positif*, n'apparaît que dans l'opposition, l'autre, *négatif-neutre*, apparaissant soit dans l'opposition (négatif), soit en dehors d'elle (neutre). L'exemple le plus connu, c'est le rapport

Reprinted from *Journal de Psychologie* 42 (1949): 170–80, with the permission of the author and of *Journal de Psychologie*.

[1] C'est dans ce sens que nous emploierons le terme *sémantique* ici. Il comprend le lexique et la grammaire, la morphologie au sens étroit du mot aussi bien que la syntaxe.

[2] *Cours de linguistique générale*,[2] 1922, p. 33.

[3] *Lingua*, I, 1, 1947, p. 77–85.

[4] *Journal de Psychologie*, XXX, 1933, p. 227–246.

p : *b*, *t* : *d*, etc., lequel, dans beaucoup de langues, fonctionne comme un rapport de *sourde* à *sonore*. En face de *t*, *p*, etc., les phonèmes *d*, *b*, etc., présentent la marque de la *sonorité*, laquelle fait défaut pour *t*, *p*. Le caractère sourd de ces dernières n'est pas perçu comme une marque positive, mais comme un *manque* de sonorité. D'une part, *p* se définit donc comme une occlusive labiale ; d'autre part, *b* comme une occlusive labiale sonore. Le contenu, c'est-à-dire la somme des caractères pertinents, de *b*, est plus riche que le contenu de *p*. Or, cette différence se reflète dans leurs emplois respectifs. Ainsi, dans des langues comme le polonais, le russe ou l'allemand du Nord, l'opposition *p* : *b*, *t* : *d*, etc., se trouve supprimée, à la fin du mot, au profit de la sourde. Au commencement de la syllabe, cette opposition, au contraire, est toujours possible. Il y a donc des positions communes aux sourdes et aux sonores, et d'autre part des positions où les sourdes seules sont admissibles. Il en résulte que la zone d'emploi des sourdes débord celle des sonores, et que le rapport entre le contenu et l'emploi (la fonction) vaut aussi bien pour le domaine des sons que pour celui du sens. L'ancienne formule, qui ne se rapportait qu'aux concepts ou aux unités sémantiques, s'applique désormais aussi à d'autres signes, tels les phonèmes.

La loi logique (sémantique) du contenu et de l'emploi des *concepts* devient ainsi une loi *sémiologique* concernant le contenu et l'emploi des *signes*. Il se pose ainsi la question de savoir sur quelles identités foncières des deux systèmes repose cette loi valant aussi bien en phonologie qu'en sémantique (morphologie). Le tableau ci-dessous résume ce qui précède :

TABLEAU SYNOPTIQUE DES DEUX SYSTÈMES (ISOMORPHES)

Domaine	Sémantique	Phonique
Forme	Phonèmes	Sons
Contenu	Sens	Phonèmes
Emploi (fonction)	Opposition à l'intérieur d'une structure ou d'une classe	
Structures	Propositions, groupes de mots	Syllabes
Classes	Parties du discours, groupes de dérivés	Voyelles, consonnes avec leurs sub-divisions

Le trait commun le plus important, c'est le double groupement des éléments, d'une part en structures, de l'autre en classes. Dans le domaine sémantique, les propositions sont composées de mots, mais ces derniers appartiennent à des classes appelées *parties du discours*. La sémantique se sert d'une double série de termes, l'une syntaxique par exemple *prédicat, sujet, attribut, détermination circonstancielle* ; l'autre proprement sémantique : *verbe substantif, adjectif, adverbe*. La première vise les fonctions à l'intérieur des structures que sont les propositions et les groupes de mots, la seconde se rapporte au contenu sémantique à l'intérieur des classes. Or, ce qui est de première importance, c'est le fait que les contenus ne sont qu'un reflet des fonctions syntaxiques d'abord, de certaines fonctions sémantiques spéciales ensuite. C'est parce que le verbe est prédicat, et que c'est-à-dire une détermination *in statu nascendi*, qu'il désigne l'action, et que l'adjectif épithète, qui en est une aussi, mais une détermination qui est donnée d'avance, désigne une qualité ; le substantif servant de support à la détermina-tion désigne l'objet, etc. Les traits essentiels du système sémantique de la

langue se résument ainsi dans la thèse suivante : les fonctions syntaxiques fondent des classes caractérisées par des contenus sémantiques généraux ; à l'intérieur d'une classe, il y a des groupes et des sous-groupes de members unis par un sens plus spécial (p. ex. les diminutifs en -*et* dans la classe des substantifs).

Nous croyons, dans cette synthèse pouvoir passer sous silence certaines questions ayant, du reste, une importance considérable pour la linguistique. C'est d'abord le problème de la dérivation, mis à l'ordre du jour du VIᵉ Congrès international des Linguistes (Paris, juillet 1948), où l'on parlera des fondements syntaxiques de la dérivation. Il y a ensuite la question d'*éléments* et de *structures* sémantiques. S'ils équivalent, chez nous, aux *mots* et aux *propositions* respectivement, ce n'est là qu'*une* des solutions possibles, bien que la plus importante. Le mot lui-même est, de son côté, une structure composée d'une partie radicale (autosémantique) et de parties affixales (synsémantiques), dont les rapports fonctionnels posent aussi des questions d'ordre "syntaxique" et sémantique. Mais, pour passer de la structure la plus complète, qu'est la proposition, aux sémantèmes élémentaires, que sont les racines et les affixes, on ne peut pas brûler l'étape *mot*.

Passant au domaine phonique, nous constatons d'abord que les classements faits jusqu'ici soit par la phonétique traditionnelle, soit par la phonologie, surtout en ce qui concerne les consonnes, ont manqué de principes généraux. La bipartition *voyelles* : *consonnes* est fondée sur la fonction "syntaxique" de ces éléments à l'intérieur de la syllabe, ce qui a été admis toujours quoique tacitement. Or, le même principe de la fonction nous permet de pousser le classement plus en avant en établissant des sous-groupes de consonnes isofonc-tionnelles, dont les contenus, par là-même, se recouvrent en partie (identité de certaines marques articulatoires). Un essai de ce genre a été publié récemment par l'auteur dans *Bulletin de la Société linguistique polonaise*.[5]

Faisant abstraction du contenu et ne s'en tenant qu'à la fonction, on peut dresser, par exemple, le tableau de correspondances que voici :

proposition	syllabe
prédicat	voyelle
sujet	groupe consonantique initial
détermination circonstancielle	groupe consonantique final, etc.

Dans l'article qu'on vient de citer, le lecteur trouvera l'explication de la différence fonctionnelle entre le groupe consonantique initial (explosif) et le groupe consonantique final (implosif) par rapport au centre vocalique.

Dans les deux systèmes, sémantique et phonique, les éléments ou plutôt les classes des éléments, sont fondés sur les structures. C'est là un fait primordial qu'on s'explique par les données immédiates de la parole. La langue se réalise toujours sous la forme d'énoncés, dont les propositions ne sont qu'un cas spécial et sous une forme syllabique. Ce sont, en un mot, les structures et non pas les éléments qui constituent nos données protocolaires.

Le trait essentiel commun aux systèmes phonique et sémantique, c'est donc la fondation des classes d'éléments isofonctionnels sur la base de structures. Si

[5] Contribution à la théorie de la syllabe, *Bulletin de la Société linguistique polonaise*, VIII, 1948.

la science parcourt le chemin en sens inverse, en partant des éléments (p. ex. phonèmes) pour arriver aux structures (p. ex. syllabes), c'est que, par un procès préalable d'analyse *non explicite*, elle a dégagé les éléments. Ce qu'on attend de la linguistique de nos jours, c'est justement une analyse rigoureuse et *explicite* des structures, et la déduction des classes ancrées, par leurs fonctions syntaxiques, dans les structures.

Il faut distinguer entre deux éléments *commutables*, appartenant à la même classe, par exemple entre deux substantifs, et deux éléments entrant dans une structure, par exemple *substantif + verbe* formant une proposition. Dans le premier cas, le rapport entre les deux éléments, s'il y en a un, est celui de la subordination (logique), par exemple, *château : châtelet, oiseau : rossignol.* Il y a, comme on l'a vu plus haut, un membre *neutre (-négatif)* et un membre *positif*, le premier pouvant *toujours* remplacer le dernier, sans que l'inverse soit possible. Le rapport entre les membres d'une phrase, par exemple *l'oiseau chante*, est d'une autre nature. Le prédicat y est le membre constitutif (central d'après MM. Hjelmslev et Uldall), le sujet est complémentaire (marginal suivant les mêmes auteurs), parce que le prédicat à lui seul présente la même valeur syntaxique qu'une proposition complète.[6] Dans le domaine phonique, la voyelle est la partie constitutive de la syllabe, parce qu'elle peut à elle seule fonctionner comme syllabe ; les groupes consonantiques n'en sont que des parties complémentaires.

Il y a ainsi deux sortes d'oppositions : entre les membres d'une même classe et entre les membres d'une même structure. Tout comme le membre positif se définit par le membre neutre (-négatif), le membre neutre (-négatif) étant le *definiens*, le membre positif, le *definiendum*, de même le membre complémentaire d'une structure (par exemple le sujet d'une proposition ou les complexes consonantiques d'une syllabe) se définit par l'opposition (syntaxique cette fois) au membre constitutif.

La loi sémantique du contenu et de la zone d'emploi s'est révélée comme un cas spécial d'une loi sémiologique. Cette loi concerne les éléments commutables s'opposant l'un à l'autre à l'intérieur d'une seule et même classe, dont les uns sont plus généraux, les autres, subordonnées aux premiers, plus spéciaux. On se demande s'il existe aussi une loi sémiologique correspondante concernant les éléments parties d'une structure.

Dans un article sur *Les lois des procès dits " analogiques "*[7] nous avons tâché de déterminer les chemins par lesquels se propagent les innovations linguistiques attribuées à l'" analogie ". Or, les matériaux empiriques en indiquent deux : l'un du général au spécial, par exemple, ce qui vaut pour le mot-base vaut aussi pour le dérivé (principe II). L'autre de la structure pleine à son membre constitutif (principe III). Pour illustrer ce dernier cas : dans plusieurs langues indo-européennes le verbe simple adopte l'accentuation du verbe composé. Si, dans *tous* les verbes composés, par suite de la fusion du préverbe avec le verbe, quel que soit le préverbe, le thème verbal se trouve accentué (ou inaccentué) d'une certaine manière, le verbe simple, qui ne comporte aucun préverbe, présentera la même accentuation (ou le même manque d'accentuation).

Des structures isofonctionnelles (ici les verbes) apparaissent donc tantôt sous une forme développée (pleine) *préverbe + thème*, tantôt sous une forme réduite à la partie constitutive seule (= le thème). Puisque ces formes sont isofonctionnelles, la même fonction verbale s'étend une fois sur *préverbe + thème*, l'autre fois sur le *thème* seul. On peut donc dire que, dans le dernier cas, elle occupe une zone plus étroite que dans le premier ; mais les zones d'emploi sont ici mesurées de tout autre manière que dans le théorème logique précédent.

Les deux chemins par lesquels se propagent les innovations linguistiques dites *analogiques*, du général au spécial, et des structures pleines aux structures réduites, nous font donc entrevoir la structure des systèmes phonique et sémantique. Ajoutons que ces deux chemins correspondent aux deux procédés de raisonnement humain : le premier, la déduction, procédant du général pour aboutir au spécial (*ce qui vaut pour le concept général A vaut aussi pour le concept spécial a*) ; le second, l'induction, partant du spécial pour aboutir au général (*ce qui vaut pour le membre constitutif plus le membre complémentaire* $a_1, a_2, a_3, \ldots, a_n$, *où n épuise toutes les possibilités, vaut aussi pour le membre constitutif plus zéro*).

Dans le système de la langue, que ce soit le domaine phonique ou le domaine sémantique, une double hiérarchie gouverne les rapports mutuels de ses membres. L'une est identique à la loi logique de la subordination du spécial au général. L'autre, ignorée jusqu'ici, mais formant un pendant exact à la première, c'est la subordination des structures réduites aux structures pleines isofonctionnelles. C'est sans doute l'opinion erronée que les propositions se fondent sur des mots isolés qui est responsable du fait que la logique traditionnelle, émanation de la grammaire, ne s'est pas aperçu de la loi générale concernant les structures. Mais la grammaire moderne ne la codifie pas non plus, ce qui entraîne des conséquences fâcheuses en phonologie aussi bien qu'en morphologie ou en syntaxe. Ainsi, par exemple, il arrive encore qu'on traite les propositions impersonnelles du type lat. *pluit* " il pleut ", comme des prototypes de propositions, ou formes élémentaires servant de base aux formes développées. Or, suivant le théorème en question, ce sont au contraire des formes *motivées* qui s'appuient sur les propositions dichotomes, à (*groupe ed*) *sujet* + (*groupe de*) *prédicat*. La question de la *genèse* des différents types de propositions ne saurait nous intéresser ici.

La sémiologie dont il est question ici ne saurait devenir une théorie *générale* du signe. Ce sera une sémiologie dégagée de deux domaines hétérogènes, il est vrai, mais qui présentent des ressemblances de structure frappantes, en particulier les classes de signes basées sur les fonctions " syntaxiques ". Mais si la grammaire a engendré la logique, il faut refaire l'œuvre d'Aristote pour dégager une sémiologie qui corrigerait deux défauts essentiels de sa logique. L'un c'est le point de vue traditionnel qui semble considérer le *contenu* comme donné d'avance. Or, le contenu, par exemple la somme des marques articulatoires d'un phonème, le contenu sémantique d'un morphème, n'est qu'une condensation de ses emplois, c'est-à-dire découle des oppositions phoniques ou sémantiques respectivement, dans lesquels le phonème ou le morphème figure. Le contenu est fondé sur la zone de l'emploi, et non inversement. L'argument phonologique cité plus haut, concernant les membres neutre (-négatif) et positif d'une corrélation phonologique, est péremptoire à cet égard. Toute proportion gardée, le

---

[6] On en trouvera la preuve formelle dans notre article : Les structures fondamentales de la langue : groupes et propositions, *Studia Philosophica*, III, 1948, p. 203–209.
[7] Les lois des procès dits " analogiques ", *Acta Linguistica*, V.

théorème du *contenu* et de l'*emploi* nous rappelle le célèbre théorème de la masse et de l'énergie.

L'autre défaut grave de la logique traditionnelle est de considérer les concepts comme quelque chose qui préexiste aux jugements, c'est-à-dire de considérer les propositions comme fondées sur les mots simples. Or, le fait que les classes sémantiques sont ancrées dans les fonctions syntaxiques, le théorème des structures réduites fondées sur les structures pleines, plaident en faveur d'un état de choses contraire.

Nous laissons de côté les changements chronologiques du système. Dans l'article précité des *Acta Linguistica*, V, auquel nous renvoyons le lecteur intéressé, nous nous sommes servi de quelques concepts se rapportant à la diachronie, tels la *différenciation* et la *polarisation*. Ce qui importe avant tout, c'est de reconnaître la hiérarchie et l'interdépendance des structures et des éléments, lesquelles se maintiennent et se rétablissent à travers et malgré les changements. Nous ne pouvons non plus discuter ici les notions de *fonction primaire* (ou *valeur*) et de *fonctions secondaires*, lesquelles sont d'une importance capitale, tant pour l'aspect diachronique que pour l'aspect synchronique.

Ce n'est pas tout. Le facteur *social*, qui semble au premier coup d'œil extérieur au *système* de la langue, lui est en réalité organiquement lié. L'expansion d'un signe à l'intérieur du système n'est qu'un contre-coup de son expansion dans la communauté linguistique.[8] Or, ce rapport possède non seulement un côté dynamique, mais aussi un aspect statique. La sphère d'emploi d'un signe à l'intérieur du système correspond à la sphère de son emploi dans la communauté linguistique. C'est-à-dire que plus le contenu est général, plus large est l'emploi du signe dans la communauté parlante ; plus le contenu est spécial, plus aussi l'emploi, non seulement interne (= à l'intérieur du système), mais aussi externe (= à l'intérieur de la communauté) est étroit. Pour le domaine *séman-tique*, cette dépendance entre le système et le facteur social a été dès longtemps signalée par Meillet.[9] D'autre part, M. Twaddell[10] a souligné la nature sociale du *phonème*. Mais le caractère social intrinsèque des systèmes étudiés ici, et par conséquent aussi du système sémiologique qui est à leur base, découle surtout de considérations générales. Les essais occasionnels pour saisir le système de la langue à travers ses réalisations sont toujours parties de la supposition, plus ou moins tacite, mais justifiée, que la fonction de représentation ou la fonction symbolique (*Darstellungsfunktion* de Bühler) était la seule qui méritât l'attention. C'est cette fonction qui résume le côté social du langage, c'est-à-dire la *langue*, tandis que les fonctions expressive et appellative, dans la mesure où elles ont un caractère spontané et non conventionnel, n'apparaissent que dans la *parole*, et relèvent d'une théorie des activités humaines plus que d'une théorie des *signes*. Et ce qui vaut pour la nature sociale des symboles garde sa force pour les éléments phoniques qui servent à bâtir ces symboles, c'est-à-dire pour les phonèmes, dont le caractère social est non moins assuré.

[8] Toute innovation "analogique" repose sur une proportion dont les termes appartiennent à deux parlers différents (cf. le principe VI de notre article des *Acta Linguistica*, V).
[9] Comment les mots changent de sens, *Année sociologique*, 1905-6, et *Linguistique historique et linguistique générale*, I, 1921, p. 230.
[10] On defining the phoneme, *Language Monographs*, XVI, 1935.

ON THE SIMPLICITY OF DESCRIPTIONS

Henning Spang-Hanssen

The object of glossematics is to provide a procedure by means of which linguistic texts may be described exhaustively and without contradiction.[1] If several procedures prove to lead to this goal that procedure must be chosen which ensures the simplest possible result of the description.

While it is hardly difficult, neither theoretically nor practically, to decide how far a description of linguistic texts is contradictionless and exhaustive, the decision which of the several procedures is the simplest gives rise to special problems. Such a decision will on the one hand presuppose an objective standard for what is simplicity. More important, however, is the fact that the simplicity of a description (i.e. the result of a description) is not only dependent on the description itself (the descriptive result). Simplicity in ordinary usage is a notion bound up with processes, not with "things"; if a thing is said to be simple, it will always be conceived as being part of a process,[2] and since "one and the same thing" may be connected with various processes (e.g. be the result of one process, or have the function of an instrument in another process) it is impossible to regard simplicity as an independent and permanent quality of the thing. Simplicity in the terminology of linguistic theory cannot in this respect be different from simplicity in ordinary vague usage. The simplicity of a description (i.e. of the result of a description) is dependent on the process of which the description is a part. If the description is regarded as the final result of an analytical procedure then its simplicity will be measurable by the simplicity of the procedure; if, on the other hand, the description is taken as a means of predicting certain relations in texts other than those that are the subject of the analysis, then the simplicity of the description will be measurable by the simplicity of the prediction process.

Since descriptions may aim at different aspects of the texts, it is further to be expected that a description which in one respect is relatively simple will prove to be less simple in other respects. An estimate of the simplicity of a description used as a means of predicting presupposes that the special goal of the prediction is known. Simplicity is a relative concept just as expediency.

It is not necessary here to discuss what precisely may be taken as the standard of the simplicity of a certain process. In vague speech it may be said that, of several processes with the same final result, that one is simplest which requires least exertion in attaining the result. The difficulty is to say precisely what exertion means. There is no doubt that in many processes it will be a question of physically or psychologically defined exertion. Only further investigations can show whether it will be possible with regard to the processes relevant for the description of linguistic texts (i.e. the analytical procedure and the prediction process) to formulate criteria which are formal in a glossematic sense,[3] and which can serve as a standard for simplicity, that is criteria which present an exact standard, and which are at the same time related to the ordinary concept of simplicity.[4] Neither for the preceding nor the following argument is it essential whether the simplicity of a description applied to a given prediction goal can be measured by means of formal criteria or whether it is necessary to measure the simplicity by means of psychological and/or physical units. The essential thing here is that the simplicity of a description—taken as a means—is a relative concept, which has significance only if the purpose to which the description is applied is indicated.

This circumstance is important for the concrete formulation of descriptions of linguistic texts. The following remarks are intended to illustrate this by means of a few instances taken from the analysis of the expression plane, with special regard to the inventory of expression taxemes (phonemes).

The phoneme inventory of a language is ascertained by applying the commutation test to the phoneme variants found in the analysis of a text. It must be a rule that commutation tests are applied to all variants in the expression signs which the examined text material contains.[5] If a single commutation test gives a positive result, i.e. if the substitution of an examined variant for another examined variant in a given sign expression results in a change of content then each of the two examined variants is an invariant: in other words we are dealing with two different phonemes. But if a single commutation test is negative, if the substitution of variants does not result in a change of content, we are not therefore entitled to conclude that the variants belong to the same phoneme. The commutation test in individual cases will only help to establish phonemic difference, not phonemic identity. Not until the commutation test has been applied to the entire material is it possible to ascertain groups, each containing a number of variants among which the commutation test everywhere in the material has given a negative result, i.e. a number of replaceable variants. The variants of such a group therefore do not exhibit any phonemic difference, in other words they are instances of one and the same phoneme.

Every concrete application of the commutation test requires that it is

Reprinted from *Travaux du Cercle Linguistique de Copenhague* 5 (1949): 61–70, with the permission of the author and of the Linguistic Circle of Copenhagen.

[1] cf. Louis Hjelmslev: *Omkring sprogteoriens grundlæggelse* (Copenhagen 1943; in the following shortened to *OSG*) par. 6.

[2] This is only an instance that "things" on the whole can only be conceived in their reciprocity, i.e. they are only defined by being linked with others, cf. *OSG* par. 9.

[3] I.e. they belong to the pattern of the language. The term "formal" is convenient but may be misunderstood, since "form" in other contexts is often used as the opposite of "real", or as belonging to the "form" as contradistinct from the "content". In the terminology of glossematics "form" (and "formal") is a relative concept. Cf. *OSG* par. 15.

[4] It may be laid down, e.g., that the number of units in the inventories is the inverse ratio of simplicity if otherwise everything—including the purpose of the description—remains unchanged (cf. *OSG* par. 14).

[5] More precisely: to all variants of one and the same category; e.g. in the case of a vowel variant the commutation test is only applied to vowel variants; cf. *OSG* par. 14.

possible, with an objectively controllable motivation, to maintain that we are dealing all the time with the same variant, after an examined variant in the sign expression in which it was found has been shifted to a given place in another examined sign expression. This means that it must be possible by means of some criterion to characterize the variant. If the sign expressions in question e.g. occur in a spoken text, the acoustic character of the variants may be used. Explicitly or implicitly, this acoustic criterion has been used in phonemics. It has also been used in glossematic analyses of the expression system of spoken languages. But while this criterion in phonemics enters into the very notion of the phoneme the fundamental distinction of glossematics between pattern and usage necessitates an intrinsically different valuation of the part played by the acoustic quality in ascertaining the expression taxemes of the spoken language.[6] In glossematics, the pattern of a language is independent of usage, in so far as a usage presupposes the pattern, but not vice versa. The pattern of a language is therefore not necessarily bound up with a definite usage, more particularly with a definite manifestation. One and the same pattern can be manifested in different "substances"; the expression plane may among other things be manifested through the acoustic substance and the graphic substance. It follows from this view that a characterization of variants by means of acoustic qualities is not the only theoretically possible procedure in ascertaining the inventory of expression taxemes in a language.

If it is the aim of a linguistic description, as is normally the case, to predict both the pattern and certain aspects of usage in hitherto not examined texts, it will be practical, however, in the description to seek the closest possible contact with the pertinent aspects of usage. If the indication of the pronunciation of a text is among the aims, it will thus be practical to make the pronunciation criteria characterize the variants. This presupposes an independent forming in usage, in this case the sound substance. Many formings of this kind are possible; the sound substance may be analyzed on a physical, articulatory or auditory basis, and there are probably within each section various possible procedures. But no such independent forming in the usage can be expected to agree entirely with the pattern of the language, i.e. to be perfectly congruent with the latter; different formings in usage can only be more or less affinitive to the pattern, i.e. they are more or less congruent with it. In principle therefore no particular forming in usage is superior to others. The choice between them is determined exclusively by the question what aspects of usage are to be described together with the pattern of the language. Furthermore, among several possibilities that refer to the same aspect, that one will be chosen which makes the desired prediction simplest.

It may also be desirable to have regard to other aspects than the pronunciation of a language—or more exactly certain features of the pronunciation—in making a description of a language. It may be expedient, e.g. to operate with as few elements as possible;[7] if the description is intended to serve as a basis of a graphic system it is essential to remember that the number of letter symbols should for practical reasons be kept low, an aim that has played an important part in working out orthographies, as in those cases where the Latin alphabet was made to serve in languages with a greater number of phonemes. It is always possible in principle to reduce the number of taxemes by regarding commutable variants as made up of unequal numbers of repetitions of one and the same taxeme. Thus in glossematic analyses which aim at establishing contact with the pronunciation in languages with commutable long and short vowel variants the long vowels will be regarded as repeated short vowels, by which means the number of different vowels is diminished. Theoretically it is possible by such a procedure to reduce the number of taxemes until only one is left which may be repeated a greater or smaller number of times. The Morse alphabet works analogously with two taxemes (written · and —); seen from a phonetic point of view this alphabet is arbitrary, i.e. there is no connexion between the formation of the Morse letters and the customary sound value of the letters described phonetically. A description of the expression system of ordinary languages by means of a very few taxemes (repeated a greater or smaller number of times) will from a phonetic point of view probably always be arbitrary, since it is hardly possible to arrange the sounds of a language unambiguously in one or a very few dimensions.[8] But it must be remembered that arbitrariness—just as simplicity—is a relative concept; non-phonetic criteria can be pointed out by means of which a reduction to few taxemes can be carried out, so that the description is not arbitrary in another respect. Ascertained phonemes might e.g. be reduced to repetitions of one and the same element, so that the number of repetitions is determined by the place of the phoneme in the set of phonemes arranged according to progressively diminishing frequency. Such a principle has been made the basis of the formation of the Morse alphabet.

In graphic systems the desire for a low number of elements is usually accompanied by a desire for parallelism of graphic elements and phonemes, a factor that may also work in the opposite direction. According to what is the dominating regard the number of elements may be different. But it may be interesting also from a theoretical point of view to examine the various possibilities which present themselves when different points of view are made the basis for the arrangement of expression systems. By way of illustration we shall take the short vowels in Danish.

There are among others the y- and $ø$-phonemes, manifested in the pronunciation by [y] and [ø] respectively, [ø] being more open than [y].[9] This phonemic difference is apparent in a great number of twin words, but in some words both vowels occur without any difference as to content.[10] Further, a phonemic difference is found between ø and ö, the latter being pronounced [ö] which is more open than [ø],[9] and also a phonemic difference between y and ö. These last two phonemic differences occur exclusively in such pairs of words in which the vowel is followed by n; some instances: synder [sønər] "sins",—sønner [sønər] "sons"; brynde [brynə] "passion",—brønde [brönə] "wells". There

[6] The term "phoneme" in itself indicates connexion with sound. Glossematics, however, uses the term "expression taxeme" which is neutral as to substance.

[7] This must not be confused with the well-known principle that of several descriptions otherwise identical the one is called simplest that lists the smallest inventory (cf. note 2, p. 62) [i.e. note 4, p. 235]. In the text above, however, we are dealing with the purpose of making the inventory small.

[8] The concept of sonority represents a—hardly practicable—attempt to arrange the sounds of language in one dimension.

[9] See e.g. A. Martinet: *La phonologie du mot en danois* (BSLP 38, 2; 1937) par. 2–2.

[10] *Ibid.* par. 2–14, 2–16, 2–17.

description. But as regards the simple description of inflexion and derivation paradigms, another reduction of *ú* and *ou* will be preferable (the number of taxemes remaining unchanged). In the numerous cases in which in such paradigms an alternation takes place between short and long vowels in the stem (or root), *o* alternates with *ó* (not with *ú*, which occurs only in foreign words), and *u* with *ou* or (only initially) with *ú* (but not with *ů*); e.g.

Nominative sing.	hrách	"pea"	chléb	"bread"	dům	"house"
Genitive sing.	hrachu		chleba		domu	
Nominative sing.	kráva	"cow"	trouba	"pipe"		
Genitive plur.	krav		trub			
Diminutive	prach	"dust"	bok	"hip, side"	zub	"tooth"
	prášek		buček		zoubek	
Infinitive	hájiti	"defend"	chýliti	"bend"	hloubiti	"deepen"
Iterative infinitive	hajovati		chylovati		hlubovati	

It will be possible to formulate the alternations more simply—contrary to the simplest possible phonetic description of the expression taxemes—by reducing *ú to oo* and by reducing both *ou* and *ú* to *uu*; since *ou* is not commutable with *o*, and *ú as uu* there will be no ambiguity in regarding both *ou* and *ú as uu* (in dialects, by the way, the pronunciation [ou] for *ú* occurs). Thus [u:] becomes the manifestation of two different taxemes: of *uu* initially, and of *oo* in other positions. The differentiation of Czech orthography between *ú* and *ů* has its origin in precisely this circumstance: *ú* is written in the cases in which there is alternation with *o* (and where earlier stages of the language had long *o*), which is always the case except initially. The graphic symbol of *ů* is a fusion of *u* and *o*.

It will be necessary to emphasize that the problem of listing the inventory of taxemes which we are dealing with here and which the mentioned instances have illustrated is fundamentally different from the question of a definition of the individual taxemes, a question that has been treated in monographs by several authors. For several languages it has been shown (first for English by *Bloomfield*) how the individual phonemes may, without regard to their phonetic character, be defined on the basis of their possible combinations or alternations. In glossematics a further analysis of the taxemes is carried out by observing their syncretisms. But every definition or further analysis presupposes that the inventory of taxemes has been completely listed; a definition of Czech *u* e.g., on the basis of possible combinations, may turn out differently in proportion as graphic *ou* is reduced to *oo* or *uu*. All of the mentioned monographs have—implicitly or explicitly—presupposed that the inventory of taxemes or phonemes has been listed in the closest possible contact with the phonetic description, i.e. by applying exclusively acoustic criteria in the characterization of the variants in the commutation test.[12]

For us, however, the question is how far is it possible, and under given conditions expedient, to replace the phonetic characterization of the variants in the commutation test by other forms of characterization, e.g. certain aspects of inflexion and derivation.

Morphonologic or morphemic monographs have no direct bearing on this subject either, since they also presuppose that the phoneme inventory has

[12] Stated explicitly by Hans Vogt (*Norsk tidsskrift for sprogvidenskap XII* (1942) p. 7).

exists, however, no pair of words in which *y* and *ø* are commutable before *n*; in this position *y* is rare and does not occur as phonemically different from *ø*.[11]

If now the mentioned part of the vowel inventory is to be arranged in such a way that phonetically identical variants, which have proved to be interchangeable, are regarded as belonging to one and the same expression taxeme, we must acknowledge three taxemes: *y*, *ø*, and *ö*. If, on the other hand, the preponderant idea is to reduce the inventory, it is possible to give an unambiguous description by means of only two taxemes, which might be spelt *y* and *ø*. The manifestation of these in the pronunciation may then be described in such a way that *y* is pronounced [y], before *n* however [ø] or (rarely) [y], *ø* is pronounced [ø], but before *n* [ö]. Roughly speaking, the matter might phonetically be described like this: that the pronunciation of both taxemes before *n* inclines towards a greater degree of opening (a similar tendency in the same direction is well known as regards the pronunciation of *y* and *ø* before *r*). From a phonetic point of view the description by means of three taxemes is simplest, but if it is a question of reducing the inventory, the description by means of two taxemes is simplest. It may be added that Danish spelling likewise has only the two letters *y* and *ø*; their distribution, however, is determined by several additional factors.

Both from a theoretical and from a practical point of view, considerable importance is attached to the possibility of attaining a simpler description of inflexional and derivative paradigms—more precisely of their expression plane—by a suitable arrangement of the inventory of expression taxemes. Here the problem is to reach a simpler description of certain aspects of the pattern of language, whereas the regard to a simple phonetic description concerns certain aspects of usage. The cases of alternation that occur frequently in paradigms may, at any rate for a part, be eliminated by a suitable arrangement of the inventory of the expression taxemes, by means of which a simpler description of the expression plane of the paradigms is attained. This will be done at the cost of the simplicity of the description as regards the phonetic aspect of the expression taxemes, and the choice between the possibilities is therefore determined by the question which of the different aspects shall be made the subject of a simple description. Instances taken from the vowel inventory of Czech may illustrate these remarks.

Corresponding to the vowels *a*, *e*, *i* (or *y*), *o*, and *u*. There are, further, the short vowels *u* and *o*, together with long *u*, written *ú*, or *ů*; the graph *ú* is only used initially, *ů* in all other positions (long *o*, written *ó*, occurs only in foreign words and will not be considered in the following). Of several diphthongs only *ou* is mentioned here.

All the vowels and diphthongs that occur can be described by means of the taxeme inventory: *a*, *e*, *i* (or *y*), *o*, and *u*. The long vowels may be regarded as monosyllabically repeated short vowels, e.g. *á as aa*, long *u* (*ú* and *ů*) as *uu*. The diphthongs also may be reduced, written e.g. *ou*, to the taxemes *ou*. Such a description effects the simplest possible contact with an ordinary phonetic

[11] We emphasize that the illustration comprises only the *short* vowels *y*, *ø*, *ö*. It is moreover a moot question whether it is necessary to regard long *ó* as phonemically different from long *ø*, and it is thus seen that both the short as well as the long *ó* have special positions among the Danish vowels.

description of the manifestation of the expression taxemes in the pronunciation has been a dominant factor, which, however, at several points was counteracted by other regards. In practice, attention to the pronunciation will play an important part in every description of the expression system of a spoken language. My observations are not intended to deny this principle: they are intended to point out that a description on the basis of this view is not the only possible one for a glossematic consideration, nor in all cases the most expedient one. It is of fundamental importance to analyse these questions and one of the reasons is that analogous problems will appear in the content analysis where the problems are less familiar and where the wider aim of the description is not necessarily entirely analogous with the customary aim of descriptions of the expression plane. "En examinant de plus près les faits particuliers qu's'observent ou bien dans la langue en général, ou bien dans telle langue particulière, on se rend compte qu'il y a certains faits qui s'observent plus facilement dans l'un des deux plans, d'autres qui s'observent plus facilement dans l'autre ".[15]

[15] Louis Hjelmslev: *Note sur les oppositions supprimables* (*TCLP VIII* (1939) p. 52).

already been established. On the other hand, the traditional orthographies offer material to elucidate the problem, this not only appears from the above-mentioned instances, but mention may also be made of the principle—well known from many orthographies—that a stem or a root within certain limits retains its spelling unchanged independent of phonematic changes in the inflexion and derivation. Glossematics seems on the whole to be a fertile soil for the study of the independent principles of written languages.

A special form is to work with *latent* units where it is possible in the listing of the inventory of expression taxemes, to attain a simple description for a special purpose. A taxeme in a sign expression is thus under certain conditions regarded as forming a reductible syncretism with a taxeme whose manifestation is zero.[13] The syncretism is reduced by introducing in its place the taxeme (or more precisely the taxeme variety) with a manifestation other than zero, which under changed conditions may be found in the sign expression under investigation. The principle is known from traditional orthographies that employ " silent letters ", which are accounted for by the fact that the " silent letter " of a word reassumes its usual sound value when the word is subjected to inflexion or derivation.

The object of operating with latent expression taxemes may be to attain a small inventory. Thus by assuming a latent *d* in Danish, *Louis Hjelmslev* has been able to describe the glottal stop as a signal for certain syllabic structures, a method which eliminates the introduction of a latent *d* in certain words, e.g. *mand* " man ", *vand* " water ", is the fact that in adjectival derivatives in *-ig* (e.g. *mandig* " manly ", *vandig* " watery ") a *d* occurs which is manifested in the pronunciation.[14] The aim may also be to effect a simpler description of inflexion and/or derivation paradigms, e.g. the inflexion as to the gender of substantives and adjectives in French. A latent *d* in Danish *mand, vand*, and others also simplifies the description of derivatives in *-ig*, compare e.g. *vand—vandig* with *luft* " air "—*luftig*, in which there is no latent expression taxeme.

The introduction of latent units is a particularly practical means to simplify descriptions with special aims, for latent units can never be in direct opposition to a description that aims at affinity with the pronunciation. But the description becomes less simple with respect to the prediction of the pronunciation in not investigated texts, as it is necessary—by way of supplement—to indicate under what conditions the taxemes are latent. Where it is desirable to retain a comparatively simple contact with the pronunciation, which will be mostly the case, rather narrow bounds are fixed for how many latent units may be expediently introduced.

The object of the foregoing remarks and illustrations has been to throw light on the general principle that in the choice between several contradictionless and exhaustive descriptions of texts the wider aim of the description must be the decisive factor, and that among several descriptions, each of which is expedient in certain respects, the simplest must be preferred. In all these instances the desire for a simple

[13] cf. *OSG* par. 18.
[14] There is however no *necessity* to reckon with the latent *a*; *-dig* may be regarded as a derivative.

ACTIF ET MOYEN DANS LE VERBE

Émile Benveniste

La distinction de l'actif et du passif peut fournir un exemple d'une catégorie verbale propre à dérouter nos habitudes de pensée : elle semble nécessaire — et beaucoup de langues l'ignorent ; simple — et nous avons grande difficulté à l'interpréter ; symétrique — et elle abonde en expressions discordantes. Dans nos langues même, où cette distinction paraît s'imposer comme une détermination fondamentale de la pensée, elle est si peu essentielle au système verbal indo-européen que nous la voyons se former au cours d'une histoire qui n'est pas si ancienne. Au lieu d'une opposition entre actif et passif, nous avons en indo-européen historique une triple division : actif, moyen, passif, que reflète encore notre terminologie : entre l'ἐνέργεια (= actif) et le πάθος (= passif), les grammairiens grecs ont institué une classe intermédiaire, "moyenne" (μεσότης), qui semblerait faire la transition entre les deux autres, concepts que la particularité d'un certain état de langue. Mais la doctrine hellénique ne fait que transposer en "voix" n'a rien d'organique. Elle prête certes à une étude de synchronie linguistique, mais pour une période donnée de l'histoire du grec. Dans le développement général des langues indo-européennes, les comparatistes ont établi depuis longtemps que le passif est une modalité du moyen, dont il procède et avec lequel il garde des liens étroits alors même qu'il s'est constitué en catégorie distincte. L'état indo-européen du verbe se caractérise donc par une opposition de deux diathèses seulement, active et moyenne, selon l'appellation traditionnelle.

Il est évident alors que la signification de cette opposition doit être tout autre, dans la catégorisation du verbe, qu'on ne l'imaginerait en partant d'une langue où règne seule l'opposition de l'actif et du passif. Il n'est pas question de considérer la distinction "actif-moyen" comme plus ou comme moins authentique que la distinction "actif-passif". L'une et l'autre sont commandées par les nécessités d'un système linguistique, et le premier point est de reconnaître ces nécessités, y compris celle d'une période intermédiaire où moyen et passif coexistent. Mais à prendre l'évolution à ses deux extrémités, nous voyons qu'une forme verbale active s'oppose d'abord à une forme moyenne, puis à une forme passive. Dans ces deux types d'opposition, nous avons affaire à des catégories différentes, et même le terme qui leur est commun, celui d'"actif", ne peut avoir, opposé au "moyen", le même sens que s'il est opposé au "passif". Le contraste qui nous est familier de l'actif et du passif peut se figurer — assez grossièrement, mais cela suffit ici — comme celui de l'action agie et de l'action subie. Par contre, quel sens attribuerons-nous à la distinction entre actif et moyen ? C'est le problème que nous examinerons sommairement.

Il faut bien mesurer l'importance et la situation de cette catégorie parmi celles qui s'expriment dans le verbe. Toute forme verbale finie relève nécessairement de l'une ou de l'autre diathèse, et même certaines des formes nominales du verbe (infinitifs, participes) y sont également soumises. C'est dire que temps, mode, personne, nombre ont une expression différente dans l'actif et dans le moyen. Nous avons bien affaire à une catégorie fondamentale, et qui se lie, dans le verbe indo-européen, aux autres déterminations morphologiques. Ce qui caractérise en propre le verbe indo-européen est qu'il ne porte référence qu'au sujet, non à l'objet. A la différence du verbe des langues caucasiennes ou amérindiennes par exemple, celui-ci n'inclut pas d'indice signalant le terme (ou l'objet) du procès. Il est donc impossible, devant une forme verbale isolée, de dire si elle est transitive ou intransitive, positive ou négative dans son contexte, si elle comporte un régime nominal ou pronominal, singulier ou pluriel, personnel ou non, etc. Tout est présenté et ordonné par rapport au sujet. Mais les catégories verbales qui se conjoignent dans les désinences ne sont pas toutes également spécifiques : la personne se marque aussi dans le pronom ; le nombre, dans le pronom et dans le nom. Il reste donc le mode, le temps, et, par-dessus tout, la "voix", qui est la diathèse fondamentale du sujet dans le verbe ; elle dénote une certaine attitude du sujet relativement au procès, par où ce procès se trouve déterminé dans son principe.

Sur le sens général du moyen, tous les linguistes s'accordent à peu près. Rejetant la définition des grammairiens grecs, on se fonde aujourd'hui sur la distinction que Pāṇini, avec un discernement admirable pour son temps, établit entre le *parasmaipada* "mot pour un autre" (= actif) et l'*ātmanepada* "mot pour soi" (= moyen). A la prendre littéralement, elle ressort en effet d'oppositions comme celle dont le grammairien hindou fait état : skr. *yajáti* "il sacrifie" (pour un autre, en tant que prêtre) et *yájate* "il sacrifie" (pour soi, en tant qu'offrant).[1] On ne saurait douter que cette définition réponde en gros à la réalité. Mais il s'en faut qu'elle s'applique telle quelle à tous les faits, même en sanskrit, et qu'elle rende compte des acceptions assez diverses du moyen. Si on embrasse l'ensemble des langues indo-européennes, les faits apparaissent souvent si fuyants que, pour les couvrir tous, on doit se contenter d'une formule assez vague, qu'on retrouve à peu près identique chez tous les comparatistes : le moyen indiquerait seulement une certaine relation de l'action avec le sujet, ou un "intérêt" du sujet dans l'action. Il semble qu'on ne puisse préciser davantage, sinon en produisant des emplois spécialisés où le moyen favorise une acception restreinte, qui est ou possessive, ou réflexive, ou réciproque, etc. On est donc renvoyé d'une définition très générale à des exemples très particuliers, morcelés en petits groupes et déjà diversifiés. Ils ont

[1] Nous avons utilisé dans cet article, à dessein, les exemples qui sont cités dans tous les ouvrages de grammaire comparée.

Reprinted from *Journal de Psychologie* 43 (1950) : 119-27, with the permission of the author and of *Journal de Psychologie*.

certés un point commun, cette référence à l'*ātman*, au " pour soi " de Pāṇini, mais la nature linguistique de cette référence échappe encore, à défaut de laquelle le sens de la diathèse risque de n'être plus qu'un fantôme.

Cette situation donne à la catégorie de la " voix " quelque chose de singulier. Ne faut-il pas s'étonner que les autres catégories verbales, mode, temps, personne, nombre, admettent des définitions assez précises, mais que la catégorie de base, la diathèse verbale, ne se laisse pas délimiter avec quelque rigueur? Ou serait-ce qu'elle s'oblitérait déjà avant la constitution des dialectes? C'est peu probable, à voir la constance de l'usage et les correspondances nombreuses qui s'établissent d'une langue à l'autre dans la répartition des formes. On doit donc se demander par où aborder le problème et quels sont les faits les plus propres à illustrer cette distinction de " voix ".

Les linguistes se sont jusqu'à présent accordés à juger, explicitement ou non, que le moyen devait être défini à partir des formes — et elles sont nombreuses — qui admettent les deux séries de désinences, telles que skr. *yajati* et *yajate*, gr. ποιεῖ et ποιεῖται. Le principe est irréprochable, mais il n'atteint que des acceptions déjà restreintes, ou une signification d'ensemble assez lâche. Cette méthode n'est cependant pas la seule possible, car la faculté de recevoir les désinences actives ou les désinences moyennes, si générale qu'elle soit, n'est pas inhérente à toutes les formes verbales. Il y a un certain nombre de verbes qui ne possèdent qu'une série de désinences; ils sont les uns seulement actifs, les autres seulement moyens. Personne n'ignore ces classes des *activa tantum* et des *media tantum*, mais on les laisse en marge des descriptions.[2] Ils ne sont pourtant ni rares, ni insignifiants. Pour n'en rappeler qu'une preuve, nous avons dans les déponents du latin, une classe entière de *media tantum*. On peut présumer que ces verbes à diathèse unique étaient si caractérisés ou comme actifs ou comme moyens qu'ils ne pouvaient admettre la double diathèse dont les autres verbes étaient susceptibles. Au moins à titre d'essai, on doit chercher pourquoi ils sont restés irréductibles. Nous n'avons plus alors la possibilité de confronter les deux formes d'un même verbe. Il faut procéder par comparaison de deux classes de verbes différents, pour voir ce qui rend chacune inapte à la diathèse de l'autre.

On dispose d'un certain nombre de faits sûrs, grâce à la comparaison. Nous allons énumérer brièvement les principaux verbes représentés dans chacune des deux classes.

I. — Sont seulement actifs : être (skr. *asti*, gr. ἐστι); aller (skr. *gachati*, gr. βαίνει); vivre (skr. *jīvati*, lat. *vīvit*); couler (skr. *sravati*, gr. ῥεῖ); ramper (skr. *sarpati*, gr. ἕρπει); plier (skr. *bhujati*, gr. φεύγει); souffler (en parlant du vent, skr. *vāti*, gr. ἄησι); manger (skr. *atti*, gr. ἔδει); boire (skr. *pibati*, lat. *bibit*); donner (skr. *dadāti*, lat. *dat*).

II. — Sont seulement moyens : naître (gr. γίγνομαι, lat. *nascor*); mourir (skr. *mṛiyate*, *marate*, lat. *morior*); suivre épouser un mouvement (skr. *sacate*, lat. *sequor*); être maître (av. *xšayete*, gr. κτάομαι; et skr. *patyate*, lat. *potior*); être couché (skr. *śete*, gr. κεῖμαι); être assis (skr. *āste*, gr. ἧμαι, lat. *dat*).

état familier (skr. *nasate*, gr. νέομαι); jouir, avoir profit (skr. *bhuṅkte*, lat. *fungor*, cf. *fruor*); souffrir, endurer (lat. *patior*, cf. gr. πένομαι); éprouver une agitation mentale (skr. *manyate*, gr. μαίνομαι); prendre des mesures (lat. *medeor*, *meditor*, gr. μήδομαι); parler (*loquor*, *for*, cf. φάτο), etc. Nous nous bornons dans cette classe et dans l'autre à relever ceux des verbes dont l'accord d'au moins deux langues garantit la diathèse ancienne et qui la conservent dans l'usage historique. Il serait facile d'allonger cette liste à l'aide de verbes qui sont dans chaque langue spécifiquement moyens, comme skr. *vardhate* " croît "; *cyavate* (cf. gr. σεύομαι) " s'ébranler "; *prathate* " s'élargir "; ou gr. δύναμαι, βούλομαι, ἔραμαι, ἔλπομαι, αἴδομαι, ἄζομαι, etc.

De cette confrontation se dégage assez clairement le principe d'une distinction proprement linguistique, portant sur la relation entre le sujet et le procès. Dans l'actif, les verbes dénotent un procès qui s'accomplit à partir du sujet et hors de lui. Dans le moyen, qui est la diathèse à définir par opposition, le verbe indique un procès dont le sujet est le siège ; le sujet est intérieur au procès.

Cette définition vaut sans doute à l'égard de la nature sémantique des verbes considérés ; verbes d'état et verbes d'action sont également représentés dans les deux classes. Il ne s'agit donc nullement de faire coïncider la différence de l'actif au moyen avec celle des verbes d'action et des verbes d'état. Une autre confusion à éviter est celle qui pourrait naître de la représentation " instinctive " que nous nous formons de certaines notions. Il peut nous paraître surprenant par exemple que " être " appartienne aux *activa tantum*, au même titre que " manger ". Mais c'est là un fait et il faut y conformer notre interprétation : " être " est en indo-européen, comme " aller " ou " couler ", un procès où la participation du sujet n'est pas requise. En face de cette définition qui ne peut être exacte qu'autant qu'elle est négative, celle du moyen porte des traits positifs. Ici le sujet est le lieu du procès, même si ce procès, comme c'est le cas pour lat. *fruor* ou skr. *manyate*, demande un objet ; le sujet est centre en même temps qu'acteur du procès ; il accomplit quelque chose qui s'accomplit en lui, naître, dormir, gésir, imaginer, croître, etc. Il est bien intérieur au procès dont il est l'agent.

Dès lors supposons qu'un verbe typiquement moyen tel que gr. κοιμᾶται " il dort " soit doté secondairement d'une forme active. Il en résultera, dans la relation du sujet au procès, un changement tel que le sujet, devenant extérieur au procès, en sera l'agent, et que le procès, n'ayant plus le sujet pour lieu, sera transféré sur un autre terme qui en deviendra objet. Le moyen se convertira en transitif. C'est ce qui se produit quand κοιμᾶται " il dort " fournit κοιμᾷ " il endort (quelqu'un) " ; ou que skr. *vardhate* " il croît " passe à *vardhati* " il accroît (quelque chose) ". La transitivité est le produit nécessaire de cette conversion du moyen à l'actif. Ainsi se constituent à partir du moyen des actifs qu'on dénomme transitifs ou causatifs ou factitifs et qui se caractérisent toujours par ceci que le sujet, posé hors du procès, le commande désormais comme acteur, et que le procès, au lieu d'avoir le sujet pour siège, doit prendre un objet pour fin : ἔλπομαι " j'espère " > ἔλπω " je produis espoir (chez un autre) " ; ὀρχέομαι " je danse " > ὀρχέω " je fais danser (un autre) ".

Si maintenant nous revenons aux verbes à double diathèse, qui sont de beaucoup les plus nombreux, nous constaterons que la définition rend compte ici aussi de l'opposition actif : moyen. Mais cette fois, c'est par les formes du

---

2 À ma connaissance seul Delbrück, *Vergl. Synt.*, II, p. 412 sq., les met à la base de sa description. Mais il a morcelé les faits en petites catégories sémantiques au lieu de viser à une définition générale. — En procédant ainsi, nous n'impliquons pas que ces verbes à diathèse unique préservent nécessairement un état plus ancien que les verbes à double diathèse.

même verbe et dans la même expression sémantique que le contraste s'établit. L'actif alors n'est plus seulement l'absence du moyen, c'est bien un actif, une production d'acte, révélant plus clairement encore la position *extérieure* du sujet relativement au procès ; et le moyen servira à définir le sujet comme *intérieur* au procès : δῶρα φέρει "il porte des dons" : δῶρα φέρεται "il porte des dons qui l'impliquent lui-même" (= il emporte des dons qu'il a reçus) ; — νόμους τιθέναι "poser des lois" : νόμους τιθέσθαι "poser des lois en s'y incluant" (= se donner des lois) ; — λύει τὸν ἵππον "il détache le cheval" ; λύεται τὸν ἵππον "il détache le cheval en s'affectant par là-même" (d'où il ressort que ce cheval est le *sien*) ; — πόλεμον ποιεῖ "il fait la guerre" : πόλεμον ποιεῖται "il produit la guerre (= il en donne l'occasion ou le signal) : πόλεμον ποιεῖ "il prend part", etc. On peut diversifier le jeu de ces oppositions autant qu'on le voudra, et le grec en a usé avec une extraordinaire souplesse ; elles reviennent toujours en définitive à situer des positions du sujet vis-à-vis du procès, selon qu'il y est extérieur ou intérieur, et à le qualifier en tant qu'agent, selon qu'il affecte, dans l'actif, où qu'il effectue en s'affectant, dans le moyen. Il semble que cette formulation réponde à la fois à la signification des formes et aux exigences d'une définition, en même temps qu'elle nous dispense de recourir à la notion, fuyante et d'ailleurs extra-linguistique, d'"intérêt" du sujet dans le procès.

Cette réduction à un critère purement linguistique du contenu de l'opposition entraîne plusieurs conséquences. L'une ne peut être qu'indiquée ici. La présente définition, si elle vaut, doit conduire à une nouvelle interprétation du passif. Dans la mesure même où le passif dépend du "moyen" dont il représente historiquement une transformation, qui à son tour contribue à transformer le système qui l'accueille. Mais c'est là un problème qui ne saurait être discuté en passant. Pour rester dans les limites de celui-ci, nous n'avons à indiquer quelle place cette diathèse tient dans le système verbal indo-européen et à quelles fins elle est employée.

Si forte est la suggestion qui émane de la terminologie traditionnelle, qu'on a peine à se représenter comme nécessaire une opposition fonctionnant entre une forme "active" et une forme "moyenne". Même le linguiste peut avoir l'impression qu'une pareille distinction reste incomplète, boiteuse, un peu bizarre, gratuite en tout cas, en regard de la symétrie réputée intelligible et satisfaisante entre l'"actif" et le "passif". Mais, si l'on convient de substituer aux termes "actif" et "moyen" les notions de "diathèse externe" et de "diathèse interne", cette catégorie retrouve plus facilement sa nécessité dans le groupe de celles que porte la forme verbale. La diathèse s'associe aux marques de la personne et du nombre pour caractériser la désinence verbale. On a donc, réunies en un même élément, un ensemble de trois références qui, chacune à sa manière, situent le sujet relativement au procès et dont le groupement définit ce qu'on pourrait appeler le champ positionnel du sujet : la personne, suivant que le sujet entre dans la relation de personne "je-tu" ou qu'il est non-personne (dans la terminologie usuelle "3e personne") ; [3] le nombre, suivant qu'il est individuel ou pluriel ; la diathèse enfin, selon qu'il est extérieur ou intérieur au procès. Ces trois catégories fondues en un élément unique et constant, la

désinence, se distinguent des oppositions modales, qui se marquent dans la structure du thème verbal. Il y a ainsi solidarité des morphèmes avec les fonctions sémantiques qu'ils portent, mais en même temps il y a répartition et équilibre des fonctions sémantiques à travers, la structure délicate de la forme verbale : celles qui sont dévolues à la désinence (dont la diathèse) indiquent le rapport du sujet au procès, alors que les variations modales et temporelles propres au thème affectent la représentation même du procès, indépendamment de la situation du sujet.

Pour que cette distinction des diathèses ait eu en indo-européen une importance égale à celle de la personne et du nombre, il faut qu'elle ait permis de réaliser des oppositions sémantiques qui n'avaient pas d'autre expression possible. On constate en effet que les langues de type ancien ont tiré parti de la diathèse pour des fins variées. L'une est l'opposition, notée par Pāṇini, entre le "pour un autre" et le "pour soi", dans les formes, citées plus haut, du type skr. *yajati* et *yajate*. Dans cette distinction toute concrète et qui compte un bon nombre d'exemples, nous voyons, non plus la formule générale de la catégorie, mais seulement une des manières dont on l'a utilisée. Il y en a d'autres, tout aussi réelles : par exemple la possibilité d'obtenir certaines modalités du réfléchi, pour signaler des procès qui affectent physiquement le sujet, sans que toutefois le sujet se prenne lui-même pour objet ; notions analogues à celles de fr. *s'emparer de, se saisir de*, aptes à se nuancer diversement. Enfin les langues ont effectué à l'aide de cette diathèse des oppositions lexicales de notions polaires où un même verbe, par le jeu des désinences, pouvait signifier ou "prendre" ou "donner" : skr. *dāti* "il donne" : *ādāte* "il reçoit" ; gr. μισθοῖ "donner en location" : μισθοῦσθαι "prendre en location" ; — δανείζειν "prêter" : δανείζεσθαι "emprunter" ; lat. *licet* "(l'objet) est mis aux enchères" : *licetur* "(l'homme) se porte acquéreur". Notions importantes quand les rapports humains sont fondés sur la réciprocité des prestations privées ou publiques, dans une société où il faut s'engager pour obtenir.

Ainsi s'organise en "langue" et en "parole" une catégorie verbale dont on a tenté d'esquisser, à l'aide de critères linguistiques, la structure et la fonction sémantiques, en partant des oppositions qui les manifestent. Il est dans la nature des faits linguistiques, puisqu'ils sont des signes, de se réaliser en oppositions et de ne signifier que par là.

---

[3] Cette distinction est justifiée dans un article du *Bull. Soc. Lingu.*, XLIII, 1946, p. 1 sq.

ON THE DEFINITION OF PHONEME CATEGORIES ON A DISTRIBUTIONAL BASIS [1]

Eli Fischer-Jørgensen

I. PREVIOUS TREATMENTS

Sapir was probably the first to suggest that phonemes might be grouped into categories according to their possibilities of combination with other phonemes in the speech chain.[2] Bloomfield goes much farther. He maintains[3] that this is the only definition of phoneme categories which is structurally relevant, whereas the classification by distinctive features is irrelevant, because it is in reality a physiological description. This statement is probably too categorical. At any rate it may be maintained that the distinctive features are also found by commutation and can be defined by their mutual combinations, that they must accordingly be considered as linguistic units, and that it is only the next step, the analysis of these features, which is concerned with pure substance.[4] Both classifications would in that case be structurally relevant, and in a complete description of a language phonemes should be classified in both ways: (1) according to their constituent parts (their distinctive features) and (2) according to their possibilities of combination (their distribution or relations in the speech chain). But this article is only concerned with the second problem, the establishment of phoneme categories on a distributional basis.[5]

Bloomfield did not only demand a distributional definition, he gave a complete analysis of the English phonemic system as an example of his method.

Reprinted from Acta Linguistica 7 (1952): 8–39, with the permission of the author and of the editorial board of Acta Linguistica.

[1] This paper was read at a meeting of the Cercle linguistique de Copenhague on the 18th of May, 1951. Part of the material had been presented at the Nordisk Filologmøde, Helsingiørs-Åbo, August, 1950. I am grateful to Louis Hjelmslev for many discussions of the problems involved.

[2] E. Sapir, *Sound Patterns in Language* (Language I, 1925, p. 37–51).

[3] L. Bloomfield, *Language* 1933, p. 129–30.

[4] cp. A. Martinet, *Où en est la phonologie?* (*Lingua* I, p. 34–58); Roman Jakobson, *On the Identification of Phonemic Entities* (*TCLC* V, 1949, p. 205–213); Roman Jakobson and J. Lotz, *Notes on the French Phonemic Pattern* (*Word* V, 1949, p. 151–158).

[5] Fritz Hintze (*Zum Verhältnis der sprachlichen "Forme" zur "Substanz"* (*Studia Linguistica* III, 1949, p. 86 ssq.)) uses the terminology "internal" and "external" for these two ways of establishing categories. Knud Togeby (*Structure immanente de la langue française* (*TCLC* VI, 1951, p. 47 and 89 sqq.), which I have been able to utilize for this last version of the present paper) uses the terminology "synthetic" and "analytic".

But it is a striking fact that in spite of the enormous influence which Bloomfield has had on American linguistics, there have been very few to follow him on this particular point. Not that there have been objections to his method: many American linguists quote this point in Bloomfield's book with approval,[6] but they do not apply his method in their actual language descriptions. G. L. Trager is one of the few exceptions.[7] But it may nevertheless be due to Bloomfield's influence that most American linguists, even in short phonemic descriptions (such as the numerous descriptions of American Indian languages in the International Journal of American Linguistics), give a rather detailed statement of the syllabic structure of the language, and in this way present the material on the basis of which the phoneme categories may be established.

In contradistinction to Bloomfield, Trubetzkoy considers the internal description of phonemes as consisting of a definite number of distinctive features and their classification according to these features as the most important task. But he mentions the classification based on different possibilities of combination as a desirable supplement, and gives a classification of Greek consonants along these lines.[8] He emphasizes, however, that it is not possible in all languages to give each phoneme a unique definition in this way. This is certainly true,[9] but it should not be used as a reason for rejecting the method.[10] On the contrary, the different possibilities of establishing subcategories show interesting differences in linguistic structure.

In general the Prague phonologists do not pay much attention to this problem but like the American phonemicists they very often describe the syllabic structure of the language in question, whereas the London school of phonetics is distinguished by its almost complete disregard of syllabic structure.

But other scholars, chiefly in Scandinavian countries, have tried to find methods for a classification of phonemes in this way, partly under direct influence from Bloomfield. H. Vogt has given a detailed analysis of phoneme categories in Norwegian.[11] Hjelmslev has repeatedly called for a relational definition and suggested methods which he found appropriate for this purpose,[12] and he has applied his method to Danish[13] and French.[14] A. Bjerrum has described the categories of the Danish dialect in Fjolde,[15] Ella Jensen has mentioned some possible classifications in the dialect of Houlbjerg,[16] K. Togeby has given a complete description of French combined with a theoretical discussion of the method employed.[17] And J. Kuryłowicz has given original

[6] e.g., B. Bloch and G. L. Trager, *Outline of Linguistic Analysis*, 1942, p. 45; Ch. F. Hockett, *A System of Descriptive Phonology* (*Language* XVIII, 1942, p. 3–21).

[7] *La systématique des phonèmes du polonais* (in this review. I, 1939, p. 179–188).

[8] *Grundzüge der Phonologie*, TCLP VI, 1939, p. 219.

[9] Although his Burmese example, l.c. p. 220 was not correct, cp. e.g. Togeby. *l.c.* p. 15.

[10] As I have done *Nordisk Tidsskrift for Tale og Stemme*, VII, 1945, p. 92.

[11] H. Vogt, *The Structure of the Norwegian Monosyllables* (*Norsk Tidsskrift for Sprogvidenskap*, XII, 1942, p. 5–29).

[12] e.g.: *Langue et parole* (*Cahiers Ferd. de Saussure*, II, 1942, p. 29–44) and *La structure morphologique* (*Ve Congrès int. des ling.* 1939, *Rapports*, p. 66–93); but his basic point of view is different, since he attempts a purely formal analysis.

[13] *Grundtræk af det danske udtrykssystem med særligt henblik paa stødet* (Selskab for nord. Filologi, Arsberetning for 1948–49–50, p. 12–23).

[14] *Bulletin du Cercle Linguistique de Copenhagen* 1948–49 (in preparation).

[15] A. Bjerrum, *Fjoldemålets lydsystem*, 1944, p. 118 ff. and 228 ff.

[16] Ella Jensen, *Houlbjergmaalet*, 1944, p. 46.

[17] *Structure immanente de la langue française* (*TCLC* VI, 1951), p. 44–88, particularly p. 79 ff.

contributions to the methodological discussion.[18] But these various descriptions have been made according to so widely divergent principles that a comparison between the languages described is hardly possible, and it seems therefore highly desirable to take up a general discussion of this question.

II. THE PURPOSE AND METHODOLOGICAL BACKGROUND OF THE PRESENT TREATMENT

The purpose of this paper is to propose a method for establishing distributional categories of phonemes which will give a sound basis for comparisons between languages. This purpose may come into conflict with the endeavour to classify the phonemes of a particular language in the simplest possible way. There will generally be several possible ways of grouping the phonemes of a language, and most authors have chosen one of these ways as the most simple, or as that characterizing the language in the best way, or as the one which has the most evident affinity to the phonetic classification. But for these purposes it has often been necessary to choose criteria of classification which are too specific to allow of any comparison with other languages. This conflict is, however, only real when it is maintained that a language should only be described in one way. When on the other hand it is required (as in the glossematic method) that a description of a language should be exhaustive in the sense that all possible classifications should be registered, the conflict is reduced to the observation that different classifications may be preferable for different purposes.

The methodological background of this paper is that of conventional phonemics. This means above all that the procedure is not purely formal, and particularly that identifications (including the identification of units belonging to different languages) are made on the basis of phonetic substance.

The terms "form", and "substance" which were introduced by F. de Saussure and have been employed by several European linguists since then, particularly by Hjelmslev, are perhaps not very happy, because they may suggest all sorts of metaphysical implications which need not interest us here, but it is mostly in these terms that the problem has been treated. Form is here taken to mean a complex of specific linguistic functions (or relations), comprising both the important relation between the two planes (content and expression), which allows the establishment of a restricted number of distinctive units in each plane (e.g. the relation between the expression [stiːm] and the content "steam-") and these relations between the distinctive units within one plane, e.g. between s and t in [stiːm]. These relations cannot be derived from the system of functions of other sciences.—But the end points of the relations may also be described in terms of other sciences, e.g. physics or physiology, and this is the "substance" point of view.

In a previous paper [19] I have discussed the possibility of establishing the inventory of distinctive elements of the expression without taking the phonetic substance into account. The result was that the linguistic analysis cannot start

[18] *Contribution à la théorie de la syllabe* (*Bull. de la Soc. pol. de ling.*, 1948), p. 107 ff.; and *La notion de l'isomorphisme* (*TCLC V*, 1949, p. 48–60).

[19] *Remarques sur les principes de l'analyse phonémique* (*TCLC V*), particularly p. 231.

from pure form without taking the substance into consideration. The number of commutable elements in each position (or paradigm) is found through an analysis of the interrelations between sound and meaning (in the case of spoken languages), which presupposes the recognition of differences (as yet perhaps unspecified) in these substances. And the identification of elements in different paradigms (e.g. p before i and before u; initial and final p) must in many cases take phonetic facts into account. If it does not, the reduction will be either impossible or completely arbitrary (e.g. initial p identified with final k), which would complicate the description of the phonetic manifestation of the elements and thus be in contradiction to the principle of simplicity. In the above-mentioned article the problem was simplified by treating commutation and identification as two consecutive steps. But as a matter of fact the statement that p and t are commutable in pin and tin presupposes the identification of the in of pin with the in of tin.[20] This means that these two operations must take place simultaneously, and that the problem of dissolving the chain into phonemes consists in deciding which phonetic differences have to be considered as distinctive and which as automatic. The decision must be based on an interpretation having the purpose of describing all the facts (including the phonetic manifestation) in the simplest way.[21]

Commutation and identification form the basis for the establishment of the categories. A consonant cannot be considered as both initial and final until these two variants have been identified. But when this has been done, it must be possible to define the categories on a purely functional basis, and this whole formal structure may be transferred into another substance without any change in the definitions. It is the merit of glossematics to have emphasized this possibility.

It must also be possible to compare various languages on a purely formal basis, identifying the categories by reference to a general system of formal definitions. This is however not the generally adopted method which consists in identifying expression units in different languages on a phonetic basis.[22] It must be emphasized that these two methods will yield quite different results. From a traditional phonemic point of view it is, for instance, perfectly legitimate to compare the syllabic structures of French, Russian, and Finnish, stating the differences in consonant clusters, etc. But from a purely formal point of view it may be different. Starting, for instance, from glossematic definitions, the so-called syllables in these languages are of completely different kinds, since in French their combination is free, whereas in Russian and Finnish some categories of syllables presuppose others. In glossematic terminology the latter type is called direction-syllable, the French type pseudo-syllable. The direction can be shown by further analysis to take place between smaller parts of the syllables. These parts are called accents. But these accents are stresses in Russian

[20] As emphasized by Buyssens (*Cahiers Ferd. de Sauss.*, VIII, 1949, p. 49 ff.).

[21] The point of view adopted here, i.e. that commutation and identification must involve substantial considerations if the analysis is to be of any use, is not incompatible with Hjelmslev's theory in its present form. His "purely formal analysis" is not meant as a preliminary linguistic operation, but as a final control of the results gained in this way by trial and error.

[22] Even Togeby (*Structure immanente de la langue française*), who claims to give a purely formal description, employs this traditional method.

and vocoids [23] in Finnish. The Finnish contoids are therefore not consonants, but unspecified constituents. In other languages accents may be manifested by tones, but tones may also formally be constituents (e.g. parts of vowels) if there is no direction between them.—Consonants are defined as presupposing vowels, and vowels as presupposed by consonants. If a language has only the syllabic type cv, not v alone,[24] it can consequently not be said to have vowels and consonants in this sense. And even if two languages possess consonants both in the traditional and in the glossematic sense, their subcategories may be differently defined by the two methods. Suppose e.g. that one language has the syllabic types V, CV, CVC (i.e. final position presupposing initial position), another V, VC, CVC (initial position presupposing final position—this combination, by the way, has hardly ever been found), and a third V, CV, VC, CVC (with free combination between the positions), and all have the consonants p, t, k occurring exclusively in initial position : then, when the categories of consonants are defined by their positions, p, t, k will belong to the same category in the three languages if the positions are identified on a phonetic basis, but from a formal point of view p, t, k will belong to differently defined categories in all three languages.

This means that it is necessary to distinguish between the two methods of comparison. The purely formal method is the most consistent one, and it is an important task to attempt a description along these lines ; but it requires a complete system of general definitions. Such a system is being elaborated by glossematics, but it has not yet been published in detail. The traditional procedure, which is followed here, is in a certain sense a hybrid method, since the elements and the relations are chosen, for the purpose of comparison, on the basis of phonetic similarity. This method may, however, lead to interesting observations, e.g. concerning the affinities between the phonetic qualities of a sound and its syllabic position, and concerning the frequency in actual languages of the theoretically possible categories. Finally the tendencies to free combination or to definite restrictions between different parts of the syllable seem to be more easily formulated when the parts of the syllable are identified on a phonetic basis.

The designation "phoneme", then, is also used here in a conventional sense. It has been defined in many ways, but all definitions have aimed at the same object, namely the first class of distinctive units of the expression (meaning the first class of units met with in a division of the speech chain into smaller and smaller units), of which most members (e.g. English s) are not capable of any further decomposition into successive distinctive units (some members may, however, be capable of such a decomposition, in English ph could be dissolved into the successive units p and h, but ph belongs nevertheless to the same level as s, not to the level of e.g. pr, because it cannot be dissolved into units of which both are capable of functioning in the same environments as the larger unit (ph, p, and h are not distinctive in the same environment, but $pr-$, p, and r are)). This is not meant as a new definition but simply as a description of what is

[23] It may sometimes be convenient to use Pike's terminology "vocoids" and "contoids" for phonetic units, "consonant" and "vowel" for formal units.

[24] c and v symbolize two different classes of elements, manifested chiefly by vocoids and contoids respectively. C and V symbolize consonants and vowels in the formal sense of the words.

generally termed a phoneme.[25] It is usual to distinguish between segmental and suprasegmental phonemes. The latter class (comprising stress and tone) is characterized by not being able to enter into relations of sequence with members of the first class. We shall restrict our discussion to the relations between segmental phonemes.

III. THE BASIC UNIT

The first difficult problem is the choice of the unit which is to be taken as the basis within which the relations operate.

The minimal sign (the "morpheme", according to the American and the Prague terminology) may be discarded at once as not suitable for this purpose,[26] because its internal structure is much too variable : it may, for instance, contain a series of syllables (e.g. French *pantalon*) or consist of a single consonant (s) or a group of consonants (e.g. *est* in German). The same is true of the "word", which, moreover, is a unit of a more dubious kind. This does not mean that the phonemic structure of words and minimal signs should not be described, but only that they should not be chosen as the general frame for the definition of the phoneme categories.

This frame must be some sort of phonemic "syllable". Most linguists who have treated this problem, simply speak of the syllable without giving any definition. K. L. Pike describes the "phonemic syllable" as "the basic structural unit which serves best as a point of reference for describing the distribution of the phonemes in the language in question",[27] and according to Pike this may be a unit of tone-placement or a unit of stress-placement or of length, or a "morpheme" or it may simply be the phonetic syllable. This point of view is not very different from that held by Togeby, who gives different structural definitions of the syllables of different languages;[28] and there is probably no escape here : the unit serving as the best basis for describing the relations between phonemes will hardly be structurally the same in all languages. The most suitable method will probably be to choose the structural unit presenting the closest affinity to the phonetic syllable.[29] This implies the possibility of an identification between phonetic syllables in different languages, and such a possibility can in effect be maintained to a very large extent, notwithstanding the fact that the phonetic syllable has been defined in many different ways, and that its very existence has been denied. A discussion of the various definitions will not be attempted in this place. It is considered for this purpose as a unit of speech containing one relative peak of prominence. The

[25] Trubetzkoy (*Grundzüge*, p. 34) defines phonemes as "phonologische Einheiten, die sich nicht in noch kürzere aufeinanderfolgende phonologische Einheiten teilen lassen". The restriction "first" introduced here is necessary to exclude the distinctive features. Without this restriction the term "aufeinanderfolgend" is superfluous. If the features are not recognized as distinctive phonemic units, the phoneme will simply be the minimal distinctive unit. Trubetzkoy did not recognize the distinctive features as "phonologische Einheiten", but had taken over the term "successive" from Vachek, who did.

[26] It has been employed by Trubetzkoy, *Grundzüge*, p. 224 ff.

[27] K. L. Pike, *Phonemics*, 1947, p. 144.

[28] *Structure immanente de la langue française*, p. 47 and 48.

[29] This is also the common feature of all Pike's different phonemic syllables.

division of the chain of speech into syllables may be due simply to the inherent loudness of the successive sounds, but the peaks may be reinforced or altered by arbitrary changes of loudness, and this means may also be used to give a clear delimitation of the units. The rhythmic impression may be reinforced by what Pike calls syllable-timing,[30] i.e. the peaks occur with equal intervals of duration as in Romance languages and in Japanese, where this seems to be a predominant feature.[31] It is in all probability particularly the rôle played by the inherent loudness of sounds (creating a certain similarity of internal structure) which makes the phonetic syllable a practical point of reference for describing the distribution of phonemes. But it is evident that from a phonetic point of view there will be borderline cases, perceived differently by different people, and such cases will then have to be decided on the basis of the corresponding structural unit in the particular language.

In many languages the syllable can be defined as a unit of tone or stress-placement. But if we seek a basis for the definition of categories of segmental phonemes, it is not the syllable as a whole, but the syllable minus tones and stresses, i.e. the syllabic base, which must be chosen as the basic unit. In most languages this syllabic base may be defined structurally as the class of the smallest units, of which each (in connection with stress, tone, and intonation, if such units are distinctive in the language in question) is capable of constituting an utterance by itself. "Utterance" is taken to mean the same as Hjelmslev's term "lexia",[32] e.g. the first unit met with in the analysis, the parts (i.e. the immediate constituents) of which cannot all function as the whole unit.—"Capable of" does not imply that all members of this class are actually found as utterances (e.g. in French most syllables can be found as utterances, but not $p\bar{a}$), but it implies that the fact that some are not found must be due to accidental gaps in the inventory of signs, and cannot be explained by structural laws of the language preventing particular types from having this function. This means that if the syllabic bases can be divided into two categories with different internal structure, one capable of constituting an utterance, the other not, then the class of syllabic bases as a whole cannot be said to have this function. But this case seems to be very rare. It is often found that one type of syllables, e.g. the unaccented syllables, cannot be found alone, but the syllabic bases of the unaccented syllables will generally be the same as those found in accented syllables. Cases might be adduced where the vowel ə is only found in unaccented syllables, but normally this ə will not be a separate phoneme but will be identifiable with one or more of the vowels found in accented syllables. There are, however, some real exceptions to which we shall return below.

The fact that the syllabic base is capable of constituting an utterance base is important, because this makes it possible to decide the number of syllables in a chain and to fix the boundaries between them on the analogy of the phonemes found initially and finally in utterances. There may be cases presenting more than one possibility of division; then the choice will be of interest for the

interpretation of the concrete words or phrases under consideration,[33] but it cannot have any influence on the establishment of the syllabic types or the possibilities of combination of phonemes, since this double possibility presupposes that both combinations have already been found.

But the opposite case, i.e. that some medial clusters cannot be dissolved into actually occurring final and initial clusters, is relevant to our problem. This is e.g. the case of *vr* in Italian; and many examples may be adduced from the descriptions of American Indian languages in IJAL;[34] and although some may be due to restrictions in the material used, it is evident that the phenomenon is not rare. But generally these cases are exceptions, even within the system of the language in question, and if the descriptions of medial clusters were formulated not in terms of particular phonemes, but in a more general way, the exceptions would often disappear.

But there are very extreme cases of this phenomenon, which may require a different interpretation. Finnish constitutes a good example. In Finnish the only consonants admitted finally are *n, r, l, t, s*, and initially genuine Finnish words have only one consonant; but medially a great diversity of clusters is found, e.g. *ks, rst, mp*, etc. The type *kansa* may be dissolved into *kan* and *sa*, both having a structure permitted initially and finally in an utterance, but the type *maksa*, which is very common, cannot be dissolved in the same way. In Finnish, then, there is discrepancy between the syllabic base (which may be identified on a phonetic basis, and which, in Finnish, may receive a structural definition based on vowel harmony) and the minimal unit capable of constituting an utterance. And in this case it appears to be the best solution that the description of the phoneme categories on a relational basis should be founded on the syllabic base (the division of medial clusters may be undertaken on the analogy of the structure found initially, i.e. before the last consonant), but the fact that a whole class of consonants are only found finally in the syllabic base within the utterance, should not be completely neglected, but must be taken into account in the classification of the consonants.[35] A somewhat similar case would be a

connection between the particular structure of Finnish syllabic bases and the fact that Finnish has vowel harmony. As already mentioned, the Finnish vocoids are, according to Hjelmslev's terminology, accents (because of their heterosyllabic relations), and the contoids are unspecified constituents (neither consonants nor vowels) which are submitted to the same rules of combinations as consonants in other languages.—This might also be formulated by saying that in Finnish there is a more intimate connection between the syllables within a word than in most other languages. This appears at two points: (1) vowel harmony, according to which certain categories of vocoids in the final syllable(s) presuppose the presence of certain categories in the first syllable ; and (2) the fact that certain initial syllables cannot form utterances alone, but presuppose a following syllable. There is thus presupposition both ways.—A tendency to a similar cohesion is found in languages with distinctive stress (which, according to Hjelmslev, have the same type of syllables as Finnish, if there is presupposition) : the weak syllable cannot be found alone as an utterance, it may have particular syllabic bases containing special phonemes (ə), and often there seem to be particular rules for the occurrence of medial consonants and clusters before such weak syllables with ə, e.g. in German.

---

[30] *Phonemics*, 1947, p. 73 a.

[31] B. Bloch, *Studies in Colloquial Japanese IV, Phonemics* (*Language* XXVI, 1950, p. 90 ff.).

[32] *Grundtræk* ...; cp. note 13, p. 300, above. And the syllabic base corresponds roughly to Hjelmslev's "syllabeme", ibid. p. 15.

[33] For a discussion of methods determining the choice, see F. W. Twaddell, *A Phonological Analysis of Intervocalic Consonant Clusters in German* (*Actes du IVe Congr. int. de ling.* 1936, p. 218–225), and J. Kurylowicz, *Contribution a la théorie de la syllabe* (*Bull. de la Soc. pol. de ling.*, 1948, p. 80–114).

[34] E.g. H. P. Aschmann, *Totonaco Phonemics* (*IJAL* XII, 1946, p. 37–42) ; Viola Waterhouse and May Morrison, *Chontal Phonemics* (*IJAL* XVI, 1950, p. 35–39) ; A. M. Halpern, *Yuma I : Phonemics ; II : Morphophonemics* (*IJAL* XII, 1946, p. 25–33 and 147–151) ; Paul L. Garvin, *Kutenai I : Phonemics* (*IJAL* XIV, 1948, p. 37–42).

[35] Hjelmslev has suggested a connection between the particular structure of Finnish syllabic

language like Keresan,[36] in which no utterance can end or begin with a vowel (the minimal monosyllable being cvc, but which nevertheless has words of the structure cvcvc and cvcvcvc, which, according to the author, should be decomposed into the syllables cv-cvc and cv-cv-cvc (the other theoretically possible decomposition cvc-vc would not be better). The syllabic type cv cannot form an utterance alone, but presupposes a following syllabic base. An exception of a different kind is formed by languages of the Mixteco-type. In Mixteco[37] the minimal utterance is cvcvc or cvv, containing two syllabic bases.

The difficulty, then, is this, that in languages where there is no coincidence between the syllabic base and the minimal unit capable of constituting an utterance, there is no safe means of dissolving medial clusters and delimitating the syllabic bases. A way out of this difficulty would be to choose the (phonemically) minimal utterance as the frame of reference and not the syllabic base, and classify the consonants according to their occurrence and combinations initially, finally, and medially in such utterances. But this involves a definition of vowels and consonants on the basis of the utterance (e.g. vowels being capable of forming an utterance alone), which might give some more problems than the definition within the syllable (e.g. in languages where vcv is found, but not v alone). And, in practice, the procedure would not differ much from that proposed here, for it would only be advisable to describe medial clusters in minimal utterances, not dissolvable into smaller parts which in principle might occur alone, and that means that only few languages would have medial clusters. Taking all utterance-medial clusters into account would complicate the description needlessly, since all combinations of final-initial clusters will normally be found, and restricting "medial clusters" to those found in "words", means the introduction of a rather dubious concept.

IV. THE TECHNIQUE

When the basic unit has been determined the next problem will be how to establish the categories. Two different procedures have been employed: (1) overlapping structural sets and (2) a hierarchy of categories and subcategories. Bloomfield employs the former method, Hjelmslev, Togeby, and Bjerrum the latter. The methods of Vogt and Trager present a mixture of these two procedures.

Structural sets means classes of phonemes having in some respect or other the same relations. In Bloomfield's description of English[38] the consonants form 38 different sets. Thus [ŋ] and [ʒ] form a set, because they are not found initially, [p, t, k, f, m, n] form a set, because they occur after [s], and for the same reason [s] forms a set of its own; [s] and [h] form a set because they never occur before [r] etc. The same phoneme may belong to different sets, so that there is mutual overlapping, but different phonemes will generally not all be members of the same sets. The sets have arbitrary numbers, and one phoneme may thus be defined by being a member of sets 1, 5, 8 and 9, another by being a member of sets 3, 5, 7, 10 and so on. In its present form this method can hardly be recommended. It is much too complicated, and it does not allow of any comparison with other languages.—The method might be used for comparisons, if only a few sets based on criteria found in various languages (e.g. four different positions) were employed, and if the numbering were undertaken according to a definite principle.

The hierarchic method may proceed by pure dichotomies (this is the form employed by Trubetzkoy), or it may be modified in such a way to as allow a class to be divided into more than two subclasses; there may be not only one subcategory having a definite relation, and another having an opposite relation, but also two other possibilities: both-and and neither-nor (this is the form employed by Hjelmslev). In both these forms the hierarchic procedure is superior to the procedure based on overlapping sets, it is simpler, and it permits of comparisons between different languages, provided that an appropriate order of the criteria is chosen. There may of course be overlapping in a certain sense, since the same criterion may be used in different branches of the hierarchy at the same level, and the members of the last subcategories must be defined by their membership of this and all the preceding classes, but the hierarchic order and the categories should be respected.

A particular problem concerning the general procedure is the use of statistical considerations. Bjerrum[39] divides the consonants into two groups having in most, but not in all, cases different relations; and Kuryłowicz[40] employs the same method, speaking of primary and secondary functions. This can hardly be recommended; it is difficult to tell just how common the relation must be.

V. THE CRITERIA AND THEIR ORDER

If we want to divide the phonemes of particular languages into as many subcategories as possible, the use of very specific criteria, different in different languages, can hardly be avoided. This, however, need not impair the possibilities of comparison, provided that these criteria are used at the last stages of the hierarchy to establish the smallest subcategories. But it is important that the criteria used for the larger categories should be such that they can be employed in a very great number of languages.

The descriptions given e.g. by Trubetzkoy, Vogt, and Trager of Greek, Norwegian, and Polish respectively[41] do not satisfy this requirement. It is evident that they have chosen their criteria and arranged the procedure in such a way as to obtain a close affinity between the classes established on a relational basis and the phonetic classification of phonemes. It is of course interesting that this can be done, but it can only be done by choosing very specific criteria, employed in a rather unsystematic order.—On the whole, any procedure starting with relations between particular phonemes will be of a very limited application, whereas a procedure which, apart from the distinction between consonants and vowels, is mainly based on position, will be of a much more general application.

36 Robert E. Spencer, *The Phonemes of Keresan* (*IJAL* XII, 1946, p. 229–236).
37 K. L. Pike, *Tone Languages*, 1948, p. 77–94.
38 *Language*, p. 130 ff.
39 *Fjoldemålets lydsystem*, 1944, p. 230.
40 *La notion de l'isomorphisme* (*TCLC* V), p. 56–57.
41 op. footnotes 8, 11, and 7.

B. SUBCATEGORIES OF CONSONANTS

(1) *Position as the chief criterion.* The most general criterion for classifying the consonants must be position. This phenomenon, position or sequence, may be considered from different aspects. Bazell [46] has emphasized that formally it need not be considered as a relation. It might be replaced, for instance, by a definite pitch combined with each phoneme without affecting the system. In this he is certainly right (and that is why the term position is preferred here to order or sequence). Position is here considered as a phonetic feature which, like other features, may be distinctive or not. It is usually said that the difference in meaning between e.g. *tap* and *pat* is due to the permutation of the initial and final consonants, but this is only a particular consequence of two facts: (1) that in the language considered, initial and final positions are distinctive (cp. *tea/eat*); (2) that in this language both *p* and *t* (as well as other consonants) are commutable in initial position (*pin, tin*), and also in final position (*hat, hap*). And it would not be impossible to consider position as a distinctive feature belonging to the phonemes. If initial and final position are designated I and II respectively, we would then have two commutable consonants t^I and t^{II}, and we might write *ta, at, tap, pat* as $t^I a$, $t^{II} a$, $t^I p^{II} a$, $t^{II} p^I a$ and consider position as automatic, but this would complicate the inventory of phonemes enormously, and it is therefore preferable to consider *t* as one phoneme which may be combined with both I and II, but these two elements must somehow be considered as belonging to the phonemic system of the language. And if position is also distinctive within clusters, these positions must also belong to the system.

(2) *The hierarchic order.* The general principle should be to start with the criteria applicable to the greatest number of languages. In languages possessing only the syllabic type cv (and v) there is no possibility of subdivision of the consonants, but this is possible in languages having in addition the types cvc or ccv, if not all consonants occur in all positions. It may be subject to discussion whether it would be most practical to start with the difference between initial and final consonants or with the difference between their positions in clusters. The occurrence of the types cv + cvc (i.e. many languages have no final consonants), but it gives a simpler procedure to start with the difference between initial and final consonants.

The first step should therefore be a classification of the consonants according to their possibility of occurring initially and finally, or, in other words, according to their possibility of combination with position I or position II. These two positions seem always to be distinctive, when both occur in a language. There will be three possibilities: only initial, only final, both initial and final.

The next step should be a division of the categories found at the preceding step according to their capacity of entering into clusters. There will be two possibilities: entering into clusters, and not entering into clusters. It may be asked why we have not proposed a similar step before the classification into

[46] *On the Neutralisation of Syntactic Oppositions* (*TCLC* V, 1949, p. 77–86), particularly p. 78–79.

A. VOWELS AND CONSONANTS

It will probably be possible in nearly all languages to divide the phonemes into two classes, in such a way that the members of each class are mutually commutable (i.e. are distinctive in a common environment), whereas members of the two different classes are not commutable (i.e. are not found in the same environment) but may be combined in the syllable.[42] If we find, for instance, the syllables *pi, ti, ki, pu, tu, ku, pa, ta, ka*, we may, on this basis, establish a class of mutually commutable members (*p, t, k*) which may be combined with another class of mutually commutable members (*i, a, u*). Theoretically there would be a possibility of identifying members of the two classes in pairs as variants of the same phoneme (e.g. *p* with *a, t* with *i*, etc.). This is not done, because there is generally no phonetic motivation for doing it in one definite way rather than in another,[43] but in some cases the phonetic relationship is evident and the identification is made (ǐ/j, u̯/w). In this case we get a third class, whose members are commutable with members of both of the other classes.

If members of one of the two (or three) categories can constitute a syllabic base by themselves (e.g. *i, a, u*), there is an old tradition for calling members of this category vowels, and members of the other category consonants.[44] And in so far "vowels" and "consonants" are defined formally. This is a very common case. But it is not rare that no one phoneme can constitute a syllabic base by itself (i.e. cv is found, but not v). In this case we may follow the traditional procedure and call one of the categories vowels, and the other consonants, giving the name vowels to the category covering roughly the same phonetic zone as the vowels of other languages. This can be done because it has been found that the category capable of standing alone will always cover approximately the same phonetic zone, and in any case include the vocoids.—It is often said that the category forming the syllabic peak is called vowels, but this amounts to the same thing, considering that the phonetic zone normally covered by the vowels (e.g. the zone of the vocoids) has more inherent loudness than the zone covered by the consonants, and the vowels will therefore be perceived as the peak of the syllables. (This is not a formal definition, as Bloomfield [45] and others seem to believe, but it differs from the point of view taken here by considering the phonetic differences in each syllable taken separately.)

Vowels and consonants can be divided into smaller subcategories. Generally the consonants present more possibilities of categorizing than the vowels. They will therefore be treated first, and in more detail.

[42] cp. Vogt, *The Structure of the Norwegian Monosyllables* (*Norsk Tidsskrift for Sprogvidenskap*, XII, 1942, p. 11).
[43] *Remarques* . . . (*TCLC* V), p. 227–228.
[44] Later these terms have also been employed for classes of sounds, i.e. for the sounds functioning as vowels and consonants in well-known languages, particularly Latin; according to this terminology *l* would be called a consonant, even in Czech, although functionally it belongs here to the class both-and.—It is in order to avoid this ambiguity that Pike has proposed the terms vocoids and contoids for the phonetic classes.
[45] *Language*, 1933, p. 130 ff.

initial and final consonants, i.e. a division of the consonants into those which can be combined with other consonants in the combination initial-final, i.e. which cannot be combined with other consonants in the same syllabic base, and those which can. The answer is that probably nothing would come out of such a division. If the language has only initial consonants, it is evident that none of these can be combined with final consonants, and if it has both initial and final consonants, it is very improbable that some of the initial consonants should not be able to combine with any final consonants. I do not know of any such language, but the possibility that such a language may be found can of course not be denied, and it would then be possible to introduce such a preliminary criterion of classification.

As the third step we propose a subdivision of the consonants entering into clusters according to their possibilities of entering into initial or final clusters. This division can only be applied to the consonants found both initially and finally, and there will be three possibilities: entering into initial clusters only, entering into final clusters only, and entering into both.

As a further criterion we may use the position of the consonants in clusters. Kuryłowicz[47] starts his classification of Greek consonants with clusters of three consonants as a basis. This may give a simple description of Greek, but it precludes comparison with the numerous languages having clusters of two consonants only. It will be better to start with position of consonants in two-consonantal clusters. Here two positions may be distinguished: the position immediately adjoining the vowel (in the following called position 1) and the position not immediately adjoining the vowel (called position 2). It is practical to start the numbering from the vowel, because then it can be continued for clusters of more than two consonants. The three possible classes at this fourth step will thus be: consonants only occurring in position 1, consonants only occurring in position 2, and consonants occurring in both positions.

The first four steps of the classification as proposed here may be represented schematically as follows (I meaning initial, II: final, cl.: entering into clusters, ÷ cl.: not entering into clusters, 1: adjoining the vowel, 2: not adjoining the vowel).

CONSONANTS

	I		II		I–II		
(1)	I		II		I–II		
(2)	÷ cl.	cl.	÷ cl.	cl.	cl.		
(3)		I cl.		II cl.	I cl.	II cl.	I–II cl.
(4)		1 · 2 · 1–2		1 · 2 · 1–2	1 · 2 · 1–2	1 · 2 · 1–2	1 · 2 · 1–2

Kuryłowicz maintains that the classification of consonants should always be based on the distribution of consonants in initial clusters, the distribution in final clusters serving only as a corollary.[48] This may be a good method to use for Greek or for the Slavonic languages, but there seems to be no reason for establishing it as a general procedure. But the last column in the diagram (i.e.: consonants entering into both initial and final clusters, and both adjoining the vowel and not) might be further subdivided according to position of the consonants in initial and final clusters respectively. This might be done by choosing arbitrarily the position in initial clusters as the first criterion, and the position in final clusters as the second criterion, or it would be possible to establish four overlapping sets.

In languages containing clusters of more than two consonants, these may be employed for further subdivisions. Bjerrum[49] is of the opinion that clusters containing two consonants will be a sufficient basis for the classification, since more comprehensive clusters are nearly always composed of clusters of two already registered. This argument is hardly tenable. In the first place the rule formulated the "empirical law" that clusters of three consonants can always be dissolved into two clusters of two consonants $(1 + 2 + 3$ dissolved into $1 + 2$ and $2 + 3)$ already found in the language. But there are exceptions, e.g. in Russian, where *mgl-* and *mgn-* occur initially, but *mg-* does not, and *mzd-* is found, whereas *mz-* is not. And a good many of the clusters of 3 and 4 consonants in Kutenai, as described by Garvin[51] cannot be dissolved.—But perhaps the rule is valid in a more general form, namely that consonants adjoining the vowel in clusters of more than two consonants are also found adjoining the vowel in clusters of two, and that consonant number 2 (counting from the vowel) is also found as first consonant in clusters of two, e.g. the group *sgv-* would involve that *v-* is found in groups like *kv-*, *sv-*, and *g-* in *gr-*, *gl-*, but not necessarily *gv*.[52]—But even if the rule is valid in this form, it cannot be used as an argument against undertaking further classifications on the basis of clusters of 3 consonants, on the contrary: it would mean that the number of clusters consisting of more than two consonants is more restricted than the number of clusters consisting of two. It might therefore be possible to divide the given subcategories further according to the function of the consonants in clusters of more than two members.

(3) *The actual occurrence of the categories.* There are some interesting differences in the actual occurrence of corresponding categories at different steps. This concerns particularly steps 1 (initial and final consonants) and 4 (consonants adjoining and not adjoining the vowel) as compared with the first division into consonants and vowels.

In most languages the phonemes can be divided into two rather comprehensive classes: consonants and vowels, whereas the class "both-and" is usually

[47] *La notion de l'isomorphisme* (TCLC V), p. 56.
[48] *Contribution à la théorie de la syllabe* (Bull. Soc. pol. ling., 1948), p. 107 ff.
[49] *Fjoldemålets lydsystem*, p. 218.
[50] *Proceedings of the 2nd Int. Congr. of Phon. Sc.* 1935, p. 53.
[51] *l.c.*, IJAL XIV, 1948, p. 37 ff.
[52] This is the case in Danish, but as *k* is not found after *s*, it would also be possible to interpret *sg-* as *sk-* and *sgv-* as *skv-*, and then there would not be any exception, since *kv-* occurs. Cf. Uldall, *Proc. 2nd Congr. Phon. Sc.*, p. 57.

of weakenings and assimilations.[54] But these affinities are only slight and cannot form any basis of identifications of categories between different languages. Such identifications must be based on position in the syllable.

Corresponding to the three possible categories at step 1 (initial, final, both-and) we find at step 4 the three categories: only occurring in position 1 (adjoining the vowel), only occurring in position 2 (not adjoining the vowel), and occurring in both positions. But the actual occurrences of these categories are different. As stated above, it is extremely rare to find the categories " only initial " and " only final " in one and the same language ; but the corresponding categories " only in position 1 " and " only in position 2 " are often found together. This does not, however, imply that (as in the case of vowels and consonants) some of them might be reduceable to variants of one and the same phoneme, for they may all occur separately with mutual commutation, and so cannot be reduced.— The frequency of the two extreme categories means that position in clusters is often distinctive for only few consonants. But if it is distinctive in one case, the other distributions can be regarded as defective, and it is perfectly legitimate to define the consonants by their possibilities of combination with positions 1 and 2. If there is no case of distinction, it may nevertheless be possible to distinguish two categories on the basis of their possibilities of mutual combination (e.g. if the only clusters are pr, tr, kr, pl, tl, kl, there is a category p, t, k, and a category r, l), but if these categories are identified with the categories occurring in positions 1 and 2 in other languages, then a feature (position) which is only phonetic in one language has been identified with one that is phonemic in another.

The affinity between the two classes " only in position 1 " and " only in position 2 " with certain types of sounds will be greater than was the case with the corresponding classes of initial and final consonants. It is not rare that the former comprises nasals and liquids, and the latter mostly stops and fricatives ; thus the type pr- is common initially and -rp finally. This has the well-known phonetic explanation that the shifting between peaks and valleys of prominence (or crests and troughs in Pike's terminology) will be smoother if the consonants immediately adjoining the vowel have more inherent loudness than the consonants farther away from the peak. But it should not be forgotten that this is only essential in languages which do not use other phonetic means of delimiting the phonetic syllables (e.g. the Germanic languages). In languages with a fresh stress-onset before each syllable or with syllable-timing, the rules need not be so strict ; sometimes such languages (e.g. the Romance languages) also prefer the above-mentioned type, which from a phonetic point of view may perhaps be called the optimal type of syllable ; but others do not, and this " optimal " type of syllable is by no means so common as it appears from the classical textbooks of phonetics (Jespersen, Sievers, etc). It is not at all rare to find particularly nasals entering into the category of phonemes never adjoining

[54] The specific power of resistance of dentals must be due to their place of articulation (an organ which can be moved with great precision (the tongue tip) articulating against a hard and fixed object). The nasals on the other hand may perhaps be protected by a partial fusion with the preceding vowel, and perhaps by their rôle as part of the tonal basis (the languages quoted are all tone languages).

small when it exists at all. Contrariwise with the initial and final consonants, where it will often be found that the class " both-and " comprises most of the consonants of the language, supplemented by small classes of purely initial or purely final consonants ; or the class " both-and " may be the only class.—It is also frequently found that the class " only initial " comprises most or all of the consonants, supplemented by a small class of " both-and ". A third possibility is this that the two classes " only initial " and " both-and " are of equal importance.—But the class " only final " is generally small, and it seems never to be the only class found. Moreover it is very rare to find the two classes " only initial " and " only final " in the same language. The only wellknown example always quoted is h/η in English and German and in some other languages, but even this exception may perhaps be discarded, since η may be considered $= n + g$. Yuma seems to present both categories, but the facts might be interpreted differently.[53] Anyhow the phenomenon is rare. This means that normally all consonants are mutually commutable either initially or finally (and the same is true—mutatis mutandis—of the vowels), and that the further division of consonants (and vowels) into subcategories is only a further redistribution of elements which all belong to the same analytical level.

Looked at from the phonetic aspect this fact may be formulated like this : sounds found initially and finally in the marginal parts of the syllable are generally so closely related phonetically that they may be reduced two by two as variants of the same phoneme. A phonetic explanation of this may be that it is of no importance for the syllable as a phonetic unit that initial and final consonants should be phonetically of different types (excepting their particular way of pronunciation as " explosive " and " implosive ", " releasing " and " abutting " in Stetson's terminology—pronunciations which may be combined with all types of sounds), whereas it is of importance that there is a distinct peak in the syllable and therefore the classes of vowels and consonants are normally phonetically rather different. A consequence of this is that whereas it is mostly possible to identify two categories called vowels and consonants in different languages on the basis of their phonetic type, this is not possible for the subcategories of consonants.

There are, however, certain affinities between position and phonetic type : the sound h is often found exclusively in initial position, and it is not rare that voiced consonants, as distinguished from unvoiced, are found only initially (e.g. in some Germanic and Slavonic languages). And if the class of phonemes occurring finally (generally it will be the class of " both-and ") is very small, it happens very often that it comprises exclusively dentals (e.g. Greek, Italian, Finnish) or nasals (e.g. Mandarin Chinese, Mixteco, and various African languages). It is hardly accidental that precisely these types show a particular power of resistance in sound history. They are evidently more capable than others of standing in the final part of the syllable, which, as shown by Grammont and verified by others, is weaker than the initial part and exposed to all sorts

[53] A. M. Halpern, Yuma I, Phonemics (*IJAL* XII, 1946, p. 25–33). There are 6 consonants found only initially in words (but 4 are velarized or palatalized and may perhaps be considered as clusters), and 3 found only finally ($\mathfrak{z}$, $\mathfrak{v}$, $\mathfrak{v}'$); but these latter are found initially in unaccented syllables within words.

the vowel in clusters (position 2, type *nta*); this is the case e.g. in Terena,[55] and Cuicateco,[56] where the affinity is therefore opposite, or there may be no affinity at all.

C. SUBCATEGORIES OF VOWELS

The vowels may be classified according to similar principles. Corresponding to the first stage in the classification of the consonants, it would be possible to start with a classification into vowels found only initially in syllables, only finally, and both initially and finally. But the type vc is often of restricted frequency, and it seems in these cases to be accidental which vowels are found in this position and which not; on the other hand, the possibility of occurring finally or not seems to yield a good basis for a classification, e.g. in German and Dutch. So it would perhaps be preferable to divide the vowels into categories according to their possibilities of occurring : only before final consonants, only alone finally, or/and in both positions. Step 2 should be a classification according to their possibilities of entering into clusters (diphthongs and triphthongs), or not, and step 3 a classification according to their positions in these clusters.

D. DISCUSSION OF FURTHER GENERAL CRITERIA

It is questionable whether any further general rules can be given. This does not mean that the classification in each particular language should necessarily stop here. Further subdivisions may be made according to the particular phonemes entering into mutual combinations. But a comparison between different languages at these stages would be difficult. In languages containing not dissolvable medial clusters further subdivisions should take this fact into account.

Togeby [57] has given a complete classification of the phonemes of French according to a procedure which is intended to be general, and he makes an interesting attempt to continue the general procedure two steps further. After having divided the phonemes into consonants and vowels, he proceeds in much the same way as proposed here,[58] establishing categories of consonants on the basis of their position initially or finally in the syllable and of their adjoining the vowel or not. But there are some differences in detail. The latter division is for instance, not restricted to the occurrence in clusters, so that all consonants are registered as adjoining the vowel.

Togeby's next stage is a subdivision on the basis of syncretisms. The class containing ʃ, ʒ, m, is thus divided into ʃ (not entering into syncretisms), m (entering into syncretism with n), and ʒ (entering into syncretism with s).—A purely practical difficulty involved by this criterion is the general disagreement about syncretisms (neutralizations). Most American

phonemicists do not distinguish between syncretisms and defective distribution. In Europe this distinction is generally made, but according to divergent principles. But apart from this practical difficulty it might be asked why syncretisms are considered as more fundamental than defective distribution in general. Togeby does not give any reason for his preference, but it might be argued that syncretisms seem to constitute a very stable part of the system of a language, normally extended to foreign words, even when other new combinations are adopted. But at any rate the subdivision on the basis of syncretisms with particular other phonemes does not allow of any comparison between different languages; it would probably be better to divide according to the criterion: entering into syncretisms or not. (On the whole syncretisms may probably be described more simply on the level of the distinctive features.)

The last stage in Togeby's division is called " extension ". Here the phonemes of the last classes are further subdivided according to their mutual relations as " intensive " or " extensive ". These terms are used in a rather vague sense, " extensive " meaning : capable of entering into more combinations compared with the other(s), depending on syncretisms or defective distributions or, perhaps simply on frequency. The idea of establishing this as a general criterion is ingenious, but it might be objected that the concept is somewhat too vague to allow of a precise comparison, and that it may be rather accidental whether phonemes entering into an evident opposition as extensive and intensive will be found together in the last subdivisions. In many cases, by the very reason of the difference in distribution, they will belong to different subcategories.

When a phoneme has received a unique definition, Togeby refrains from any further characterization on the basis of the criteria of later stages. The possibility of continuing in such a way that all phonemes are characterized (as far as possible) according to all criteria should however be taken into consideration.

VI. STRUCTURAL LAW OR ACCIDENTAL GAPS [59]

A. THE GENERAL PROBLEM.

Most linguists who have attempted to arrive at a specific definition of each phoneme (in so far as this has been possible in the particular language) by utilizing all differences of distribution. Hjelmslev seems to be the only exception. After having divided the consonants on the basis of the two criteria 1) initial or final, 2) adjoining the vowel or not, he refrains from further subdivisions. One reason has been that further criteria would be too particular to allow of comparisons between languages. This is perhaps true, but provided that the first criteria have been such that the existing possibilities of comparison have been utilized, this consideration should not prevent us from attempting an exhaustive categorizing of the phonemes of the particular language. Another reason has been the fear of getting beyond the limit between structural laws and accidences of utilization

[55] Margaret Harden, *Syllable Structure in Terena* (*IJAL XII*, 1946, p. 60–63).
[56] Doris Needham and Marjorie Davis, *Cuicateco Phonology* (*IJAL XII*, 1946, p. 139–146).
[57] *Structure immanente de la langue française* (*TCLC VI*, 1951), p. 79–88.
[58] We have both been influenced by Hjelmslev.

[59] I am indebted to H. Spang-Hanssen for some improvements of the formulation of this chapter.

in the given stock of words. This indeed is a very difficult problem.[60]—Generally one has a vague feeling that there is a difference, and there would be general agreement in the extreme cases: anyone would probably admit that *prust* would be a possible monosyllable in English, although it does not exist, whereas *mlqapmt* would not. The question is whether we can find valid arguments in the particular language, and whether it is possible to find general rules for all languages.

Many linguists have mentioned this problem briefly without attempting any analysis of it.[61] others have implicitly fixed such a limit; it is for instance evident from the examples given by V. Mathesius[62] that he considers combinations between consonants in clusters as submitted to rules, whereas combinations between vowels and consonants are considered as accidental. Bloomfield,[63] on the other hand, defines the English vowels by means of their possibilities of combination with the following consonants, and consequently he must consider these combinations as submitted to rules. Vogt[64] defines the Norwegian vowels by means of their combinations with the preceding consonant clusters, and somewhat hesitatingly, and he emphasizes that restrictions here may be accidental and that the vague feeling one has for such differences can probably be stated by linguistic means in terms of structural rules, articulatory patterns and statistical frequency.[65] These very brief remarks at the end of Vogt's article seem to include the essential aspects of the problem. In the following pages a somewhat more detailed analysis will be attempted.[66]

First it must be emphasized that it is theoretically impossible to fix a non-arbitrary borderline between law and accident. Laws may be stated as deviations from accidental distribution; and there are many degrees of deviation. But not all cases are equally dubious.

In the first place it should be kept in mind that a gap—e.g. the non-occurrence of a specific cluster—may be due to rules having a different place in the hierarchy of categories. And as this hierarchy has been established in such a way as to begin with the more general classes, it follows that the higher the rule is placed in the hierarchy the greater is the number of particular cases which it will generally cover, and the safer it is. An example may illustrate this: the fact that the cluster -*sp* is not found in a certain language may be due to a very general rule (covering many other gaps) that the language in question has no final consonants; it will also be due to a very general rule, if final consonants

are found, but no clusters; it will be due to a somewhat more specific, but still comprehensive, rule if clusters are found but no final clusters, and to a still more specific rule if final clusters are found but none with *s* adjoining the vowel, and none with *p* not adjoining the vowel, and the rule may be somewhat more restricted, if only one of the two consonants does not occur in this position, but this rule might still comprise the non-occurrence of e.g. *st* and *sk*. In all these cases we may maintain with relative certainty that the lack of the cluster *sp* is due to structural laws of the language. But if the only explanation which can be alleged is the very fact that *sp* has not been found, then the chance that we are on the borderline between structural law and contingency is very great.

In these cases it is necessary to consider the relative frequency of the phonemes in the given position (not the frequency in a text, but the frequency in the material of words). In German *j* is not found before *æ*. This may be due to pure accident, for initial *j* is relatively infrequent compared with other initial consonants, and the diphthong *æ* is also relatively rare in other combinations. The probability of their occurring together is therefore not very great, and the non-occurrence need not be due to a specific law preventing this particular combination. On the other hand, there does not seem to be a similar explanation of the lack of e.g. *tl-* in English. And the systematic nature of this gap seems to be corroborated by the lack of *dl-*. One would probably, on the whole, be more inclined to recognize a law if the occurrence or the non-occurrence can be formulated in terms of phonetically similar groups of phonemes (e.g. dentals, high vowels, etc.) and think of an accidental gap if this is not the case. Psychologically this is of course of importance. Structurally it might be motivated by the fact that in the former case the rule could be formulated in a more general way in terms of distinctive features. But this is dubious.

It is evident that if not only combinations of two, but of three, four, or more elements are considered, then the chance of finding all possible combinations realized within the (always-restricted) word-stock of the language will be smaller. It is not very probable that all combinations of *str-* with different final clusters will be found, and consequently it cannot be proved that the non-occurring combinations are excluded by a structural law.

It is perhaps this consideration which is behind Twaddell's remark about English.[67] "We find, in American English, that all fundamental characteristics involving the absence of (presumably potential) distinctive forms can be correlated with immediately preceding or following phonetic fractions, including the omnipresent factor of stress". And he gives the example that *fet* is a possible syllable in English, because the combinations *fe-* and *-et* occur. But in this general form (i.e. if we find x + y and y + z, then x + y + z is possible) the rule is not valid, either in English or in other languages.

B. EMPIRICAL RULES CONCERNING THE CONNEXION BETWEEN DIFFERENT PARTS OF THE SYLLABLE.

Twaddell's assertion might be true if the syllabic base consisted simply of a series of phonemes and did not allow of any further division into parts or units.

[67] *On Defining the Phoneme* (Language Monographs XVI, 1935), p. 50.

[60] It is presupposed in this argument that the aim of the description with which we are concerned is not simply an enumeration of the combinations of phonemes found in the given syllables and words, but the formulation of general laws governing these combinations, allowing for possible combinations not utilized in the given vocabulary.
[61] e.g. A. Martinet, *Phonologie du mot in danois* (BSL, 1937), p. 6; A. W. de Groot, *Structural Linguistics and Phonetic Law* (Archives néerlandaises XVII, 1941), p. 92; A. Bjerrum, *Fjoldemålets lydsystem*, p. 117; K. L. Pike, *Phonemics* 1947, p. 73 ff. and 81 ff.
[62] *TCLP* I, 1929, p. 67–89.
[63] *Language*, 1933, p. 134.
[64] *The Structure of the Norwegian Monosyllables* (Norsk Tidsskrift for Sprogvidenskap, XII, 1942), p. 25.
[65] *l.c.*, p. 29.
[66] The same problems arise for the descriptions of word structure, cp. Uhlenbeck, *De Structuur van het Javaanse Morpheem*, 1949, p. 5–10. He distinguishes between negative and positive structural laws. But if these positive laws include simply the possibility of combination, it is only a reversal of the negative laws.

But the division into central and marginal units (comprising vowels and consonants) and into initial and final clusters prove to be significant from this point of view. —It is not a theoretical necessity, but it is an empirical fact that in most languages there are relatively strict rules for the combinations within the units, but not for the combinations at the limits, i.e. between phonemes belonging to different units. The consonantal and vocalic clusters actually found in a language will normally be of a restricted number (compared to the theoretical possibilities), and the phonemes found in the different positions in these clusters will be still more restricted, so that the clusters found can normally be said to belong to a few frequently recurring types, and thus it will not be possible to maintain that the non-occurring clusters are simply accidental gaps. —It is true that there are languages possessing a very great number of different clusters of various types (e.g. some American Indian languages) and in these languages it might be possible to assume that the non-occurrence of some of the clusters were simply due to accidental gaps. But in most languages there are laws not only for the combination of two adjoining phonemes, but also for the combinations of three and more if such occur. It is however very rare that there are any rules for the connexion between initial and final consonants, or consonant clusters (that is why Twaddell's example *fet* is tenable), although a certain tendency to avoid the same consonants or the same phonetic types of consonants immediately before and after the vowel has been discovered in various languages;[68] but generally it is only a tendency.

It seems also to be very rare to find rules for the combination between the initial consonantal unit and the central unit, not only so that the combination of the first and last member in groups of three members can be said to be free (i.e. if *pr* and *ri* are found, then *pri* is a possibility), but also so that even the combination of two phonemes (a single initial consonant and a following vowel) seems to be free. Normally all theoretically possible combinations are found, and if not, the non-occurrence can often be explained by the fact that one or both of the phonemes are relatively rare in this position, so that it is statistically justified to speak of an accidental gap. In the combinations of three phonemes, for example *pri*, the probability of finding accidental gaps, and consequently the justification of considering non-occurrence as accidental, is greater, since more elements are involved, and some clusters or vowels may be rare.[69]

The connexion between the central unit and the final consonantal cluster seems also to be relatively free, i.e. there are less strict rules than for combinations within the units, but often it is not so free as the connexion between the initial consonant and the central unit. There may be some restrictions, which can hardly be accidental. Twaddell mentions the occurrence of vowels before r in English; in Danish the short vowels *i*, *y*, *u* do not occur before final

nasal consonant; and before *r* there is no distinction between *i*, *y*, *u* and *e*, *ø*, *o* (the pronunciation varies).[70] There may also be restrictions concerning the combinations of groups: in German and Dutch diphthongs are not found before *r*,[71] and there are also definite restrictions to the consonantal clusters found after diphthongs; in the Germanic languages long vowels do not occur before *ŋ* (and it is possible that both long vowels and *ŋ* should be interpreted as clusters). And there are certainly languages where consonant clusters do not occur at all after long vowels (in Germanic languages a certain tendency to avoid this is obvious.) This means that in many languages there is a more intimate connection between the central unit and the final one than between the central unit and the initial one. And this might serve as a further argument for the analysis of the syllabic base proposed by Kuryłowicz,[72] namely C + (V + C). (This is an analytical operation and does not prevent the establishment of vowels and consonants as the two main categories of phonemes. The establishment of categories is based upon the analysis, but does not coincide with it.)

The empirical rules concerning accidence or law in the combination of different parts of the syllable mentioned on the preceding pages, seem in any case to be valid for well-known languages. This means that Vogt goes too far, when he establishes categories of vowels in Norwegian defined by their possibilities of combination with preceding consonant clusters, and that Trnka[73] goes too far when he describes English vowels in terms of their ability to combine with preceding or following consonants and consonant clusters. The same thing can be maintained of Abrahams' definition of Danish consonants,[74] particularly of his definition of the difference between *t* and *d*, consisting in the restrictions of combination between the cluster *dj* and a following vowel. —On the other hand, it will often be possible to go farther than Hjelmslev, who does not use combinations between particular phonemes within the clusters to define smaller sub-categories. And it should not be forgotten that the assumption of accidental gaps has consequences for the commutation. When the gap is accidental, the commutation in question is possible, and it does not matter for the commutation that a word-pair with a minimal difference is not found, provided that it can be constructed without breaking the laws of the language. The border between law and contingency should be established for each language, and the accidental gaps should be utilized for the commutation, and all structural laws for the establishment of subcategories of phonemes.

It should be possible to verify the validity of the empirical rules concerning the relations between the different parts of the syllable, and of the hierarchy of more or less general laws, established above, by an inquiry into the treatment of loanwords containing combinations of phonemes not occurring in the receiving

---

[68] W. F. Twaddell, *Combinations of Consonants in Stressed Syllables in German* (*Acta Linguistica* I, p. 189–199 and II, p. 31–50); H. Vogt, *l.c.*, p. 22 (Norwegian); E. M. Uhlenbeck, *De Structuur van het Javaanse Morpheem*, 1949, p. 10 (in Javanese the types clvl and crvr do not occur); Trnka, *Die Phonologie in čechisch und slovakisch geschriebenen Arbeiten* (*Archiv für vergleichende Phonetik* VI, 1943, p. 65–77), mentions that repetition of the same phoneme before and after the vowel in English shows foreign origin or expressiveness.

[69] In German the gaps after clusters of three consonants concern particularly the rare vowels *ō* and *ū* (e.g. *ō*: is not found after *gl-*, *gn-*, and others). Among the clusters of three consonants, some are relatively rare and are consequently only found before few vowels (*špl* e.g. only before *i:*, *i*, *ai* (and in foreign words *e*)). These gaps are accidental.

[70] In the Danish dialects described by Ella Jensen and Bjerrum (cp. p. 300, notes 15 and 16), the combination between vowel and final consonant seems also to be submitted to certain rules.

[71] In the historical development this has been avoided in two different ways: in Dutch by not diphthongizing long *i:*, *u:*, *y:* before *r* (e.g. *vuur*); in German by inserting an *ə* and developing a new syllable (*Feuer*). These particular rules before *r* may be explained phonetically, cp. L. L. Hammerich, *Tysk Fonetik*, pp. 140–141.

[72] *TCLC* V, p. 50 ff.

[73] *A Phonological Analysis of Present-Day Standard English* (*English Studies*, 1935).

[74] *Tendances évolutives des consonnes occlusives du germanique*, 1949, p. 96.

language. If the non-occurrence was due to an accidental gap, the introduction of the foreign word should not make any difficulties, e.g. the introduction of a word " *prust* " in English. But the more general the law forbidding this combination, the more difficult it would be to introduce the word without any change.—Thus the word *sklerose* has been introduced into Danish without too many difficulties (although the group *skl-* is not found in Danish words), since clusters of the type *spl, skr,* etc., exist, i.e. clusters with *s, k,* and *l* in the positions required, and the combinations *sk-* and *kl-* exist. The same thing is true about the group *pn-* (*pneuma*), since *pl, pr* and *kn, gn* occur, *ps-* is more difficult, since *s* is not found elsewhere as a second member of an initial group, and the *p* is therefore usually left out. A language having initial clusters but no final clusters, should then have more difficulty in introducing a final cluster than an unknown initial cluster (and still more if final single consonants were also unknown).—But only the relative difficulty of assimilation would be of interest in this connection, not the absolute difficulty, for this depends also on social and psychological factors : many European languages are more inclined to take over foreign words without alterations nowadays than some centuries ago. In Finnish all initial clusters were simplified in older loanwords; but in recent loanwords clusters can be found. And this is not simply a question of time, but of social attitude.—There are linguistic communities where the " correct " pronunciation of foreign words is considered very important (German is a typical example), others where this pretension does not exist. These social differences must be taken into account in an evaluation of the material.

The above observations, and also the proposals concerning a fixed procedure for the classification of phonemes for comparative purposes are of a preliminary nature and do not pretend to give definitive solutions. Many questions need further discussion.—And it should not be forgotten that for other purposes other classifications may be preferable. Position seems to be a useful basis for comparative purposes, but for the description of a single language the relations between particular phonemes might be considered equally essential, e.g. the fact that in English *p, t, k* adjoining the vowel are only found after *s*.[75]

Finally we want to emphasize that the result of such a classification depends on the way the phoneme inventory has been established. The more the inventory is reduced, the greater will be the uniformity of distribution, and the more restricted the possibilities of classification on distributional grounds. These two aims of the analysis (to get few phonemes, and many categories), seem to a certain extent to be in mutual contradiction.

[75] For an interesting description of English consonant clusters from this point of view, cp. the article by Mel Most (to appear in *Word*).

THE GRAPHEME

C. E. Bazell

A graphemics parallel in every way to phonemics is rendered infeasible by several familiar considerations, such as (i) the partial dependence of graphies on phonemic form, (ii) the fact that graphic systems are of many different kinds, while all phonemic systems are of essentially the same kind, (iii) the relative artificiality of graphic systems.

One consequence of the first consideration is that the term *allograph* is ambiguous. According to one linguist,[1] "the graphic shape of an allograph is dependent on its graphic surroundings". On the other hand according to the authors[2] of a recent study of Old English graphies in relation to phonemics, two graphs are allographs of the same grapheme if they represent the same phoneme, whether or not they stand in relations of complementary distribution, as they confess that the two "allographs" with which they are concerned do not (despite a general tendency in this direction). Presumably also for them, graphic resemblance would not count as a criterion; for instance the two forms of Greek sigma would be regarded as allographs whether or not one held there to be some similarity.

The first use of *allograph* is parallel to the use of *allophone*, while the second is more nearly parallel to the use of *allomorph*. Indeed it would be exactly parallel if (i) the identification of allomorphs is held to be a semantic rather than a purely distributional procedure, and (ii) phonemics is regarded as the "semantics" of graphemics. But this of course will not do. There is nothing for which morphemes "stand" in the way that letters stand for sounds, as morphemes are normally used. (There is indeed a set of morphemes which are exceptional in normally "standing for" something: namely the names of letters, which may stand either for letters or for sounds, and as abbreviations also for words. But such morphemes are semantically marginal.)

But the same consideration has also another consequence. We should not be interested, for its own sake, in the distribution of phonemes if this were normally dependent on written language: for then it would suffice to study the distribution of graphs and to record that oral speech followed the same pattern. This would answer to the method of excluding from the normal material for phonemic analysis that part of the vocabulary which is notoriously under graphic influence, e.g. proper names and especially surnames. Even linguists who would include these as ordinary material through a reluctance to leaving any part of the investigated utterances out, would draw the line at *foreign* proper names. It is true that the objection would be based not on graphic motivation but rather on derivation from a different language-system. But this objection would then remain invalid if the pronunciation of the foreign proper names was based on the spelling of these names and not on their phonemic form in the other system. Actually the objection to taking in foreign material and the objection to taking in graphically motivated material, despite the fact that some linguists might allow the former without allowing the latter, have one and the same source. All *exterior* influence disqualifies, to some extent, the status of a unit—whether this is the influence of another language system, or the influence of another level within the same language. (What is called the "artificiality" of graphic systems may be treated as another form of "exterior influence"—it is difficult to take too seriously a convention which is subject to the whims of a minister of education or a rich spelling-reformer. Phonemics is a subject apart by virtue of the fact that the opportunities for interference are far more restricted.)

Hence *in so far as* spelling is influenced by its representative function, it is not a matter of "graphemics" at all. A pure graphemics would study the conventional relations between graphies; e.g. the relation of *q* and *u* in English such that the former is invariably followed by the latter. Whereas the fact that *p* never follows *f* would have no graphemic interest; it would be parallel to the fact that the morpheme "snow" never follows the morpheme "green", which is not due to a distributional convention but rather to the fact that there is no occasion for the sequence. In either case, if occasion arose, the sequence would be used. (Experiments could readily be devised to call forth the sequence, without interfering with linguistic conventions.)

Up to the present point we have spoken as though the nearest equivalent on the graphic level to the phoneme is the letter. All writers on the subject seem to have assumed this. Yet once the question is raised, the assumption is easily seen to be wrong.

By definition the phoneme cannot contain smaller distinctive features unless these are simultaneous. The corresponding graphic unit should equally have no smaller features except such as are spatially superimposed. But letters are normally distinguished from each other by features (dots, curves etc.) located in different positions, these positions themselves being relevant (e.g. b/d). Hence it is, for instance, the bar and loop of *b* and *d*, not these whole letters, that answer to phonemes. (In *b* and *p* the vertical dimension is used; instinctively one feels that there is something like "simultaneity" here; but the instinct derives of course just from the fact that the linear sequence of letters is horizontal. A Chinaman might have the opposite "instinct".)

An equivalent to the simultaneous features of the phoneme is rare on the graphic level, but not impossible. The best example is probably the distinction of *thin* and *thick* in the Pitman shorthand system. It matters little that this system is "artificial", since this is a general property of graphs as opposed to phones. But if one asks for an example from a "natural" language, the distinction of small and capital letters will serve. The only reason for not putting

Reprinted from *Litera* (Istanbul) 3 (1956): 43–46, with the permission of the author.

1 Ernst Pulgram, "Phoneme and Grapheme: a Parallel", *Word* 7, 15.
2 R. S. Stockwell and C. W. Barritt, *Some Old English Graphemic-Phonemic Correspondences* (Washington 1951).

it first, is that it bears some resemblance to the phonemic feature of " prominence ", which is regarded as prosodic rather than inherent.

Hence what one is at first sight inclined to look on as a " feature " turns out to be the equivalent (very roughly) of the phoneme. And the letter, which one took to be the equivalent (very roughly) of the phoneme, turns out to be more similar—to the morpheme. This conclusion was vaguely anticipated above, and will be returned to immediately. But it may be added that the graphic *word* also has similarities to the spoken *sentence* (spacing resp. pause). In other words the graphic categories, as compared with the phonic categories are shifted each time one unit along the hierarchy. It was a mistake to suppose that they occupied the same position in the hierarchy as the units they stand for.

The letter, we have said, answers to the morpheme; it is the " minimal meaningful unit " in the graphic form, though its meaning consists in its rendering of phonemes, immediately, not in its share in expressing ordinary linguistic meaning, which it does via the in themselves meaningless phonemes. Of course in traditional writing-systems individual letters do not always represent phonemes; but then, neither do individual morphemes always have a meaning. It is merely a general characteristic that they should have. Just as no " phonemic meaning " can be attributed to the individual letters *e* and *a* in English *read*, so also no meaning can be attributed to the individual morphemes in fossilised groups. (True, one might refuse to analyse the group into morphemes when one cannot attribute meanings to them individually; but a parallel example in which two ostensive letters are taken to be a single letter is given below.)

At the same time it must be stressed that graphemics is not important in the *same* way as phonemics.

The important questions in matters of graphy are historical, practical or aesthetic, not questions of synchronic analysis. It is to be hoped that nobody will ever write a paper on " One Grapheme or Two ? ", for the answer in each individual case is within wide limits up to the printing-house or the private writer. (Compilers of Czech dictionaries [3] choose to treat *ch* as a single letter, and since a dictionary is also a text, in some sense they thereby *make* it a single letter.) At the same time the second consideration leaves open the possibility that a graphematic analysis might be far more serious a task for one system than for another.

The renewed interest in the graphic side of language is in itself welcome. But the idea should not be encouraged that we have just another " substance " of language, which should be submitted to the same processes of analysis [4] as the " phonic substance ". And if the methods of phonemics cannot simply be transferred to the graphic level, the notion, prevalent in some circles, that they will finally be transferable to non-linguistic planes of culture (e.g. that social events will be sliced up into their component " behaviouremes " by application of the principles of intrinsic similarity and complementary distribution) should be recognised for what it is.

[3] It might be objected that a dictionary is a meta-text rather than a normal text. But this is its function only in relation to semantics; obviously it could not be used along with normal texts in a semantic study; but since it is not in any sense *about* graphemes, the graphic conventions it uses belong with other graphic conventions.

[4] Hjelmslev's ideas on the subject have been put into practice by H. Spang-Hanssen in a study for the Copenhagen Circle.

LA POSITION LINGUISTIQUE DU NOM PROPRE

Jerzy Kurylowicz

On s'est toujours rendu compte du fait que tant dans la lexicologie que dans la grammaire, les noms propres semblent jouer un rôle plutôt marginal. On se propose ici d'analyser leur position dans le système de la langue, en insistant sur les critères formels qui conjointement avec leur valeur sémantique spéciale, de tout temps reconnue, leur assignent une place à part parmi les autres catégories nominales.

Tout nom commun (appellatif) a un contenu et une zone d'emploi étant en raison inverse du contenu : plus riche le contenu sémantique et plus restreint l'emploi d'un mot donné. Ainsi le terme *lévrier* comporte un contenu plus spécial et détaillé que le terme *chien*, mais la sphère d'emploi du dernier déborde celle de *lévrier*. Le rapport intrinsèque entre le contenu et l'étendue d'un concept intéresse surtout le logicien. Mais le linguiste, quand il parle des fonctions sémantiques du mot, recourt au fond aux mêmes notions. En vertu de son contenu, l'appellatif possède une signification, tandis que les objets qu'il est apte à désigner, constituent la sphère de son emploi.

Si parmi les substantifs les noms concrets représentent la catégorie sémantique centrale, c'est justement grâce au fait qu'ils jouissent de la double faculté de *signifier* et de *désigner*. Ils ont un contenu sémantique définissable et ils sont en même temps applicables à des objets réels. Ils ont une structure sémantique pleinement développée.

Mais dans la langue il existe toujours, à côté de structures pleines, d'autres qui sont défectives. Il y a des substantifs qui manquent soit de contenu soit de zone d'emploi. Le premier cas est celui des pronoms, p. ex. le démonstratif *celui-ci*, applicable à n'importe quel objet et limité par le seul critère de genre grammatical. De l'autre côté c'est justement l'*applicabilité* qui est réduite au minimum dans le nom propre. En effet, les noms comme *Cervantes, Napoléon, Mont-Blanc*, représentent, par opposition à *loup, arbre*, ou *ville*, des " classes à un seul individu ". Les cas extrêmes du pronom et du nom propre confirment la règle du rapport logique entre le contenu et l'étendue. Le contenu sémantique du pronom *celui-ci*, étant commun à tous les substantifs (de genre masculin), est infiniment pauvre : il ne connote aucune qualité en dehors de celle d'être un objet. Un nom propre comme *Cervantes* a, au contraire, un contenu infiniment riche, de sorte qu'attaché à un seul individu il n'est pas en principe transmissible. Au lieu de simplement désigner, comme fait le nom commun, il *nomme*.

Les logiciens sont tentés de considérer les substantifs abstraits comme des noms ayant une zone d'applicabilité *zéro*. Ces noms comportent sans doute un contenu sémantique, c.-à-d. un sens. Mais on a eu tort de les confronter directement avec les noms concrets (communs et propres). Les abstraits, de même que les adjectifs ou les verbes, n'appartiennent pas à la couche lexicale primaire. Ce sont des mots d'un ordre linguistique supérieur. Pour apprécier d'une manière exacte la position de l'adjectif ou du verbe, il faut partir de leur fonction syntaxique *primaire*, c.-à-d. des fonctions d'épithète (pour l'adjectif) ou de prédicat (pour le verbe). Un adjectif comme *rouge*, à l'état isolé, est dégagé de complexes comme *rose rouge, couleur rouge*, etc. C'est le groupe entier *rose rouge*, qui se rapporte à la réalité *directement*, tandis que *rouge* ne la vise qu'à travers le complexe syntaxique. *Mutatis mutandis* la même considération vaut aussi pour le verbe personnel. Pour ce qui est des abstraits, c'est le mérite de M. Porzig d'avoir démontré, il y a un quart de siècle,[1] que leur fonction primaire consiste à ramasser une proposition en un groupe syntaxique, p. ex. *le roi est mort > la mort du roi*. Le prédicat devient le membre déterminé d'un groupe nominal. Or, puisqu'il y a lieu de distinguer entre *abstraits déverbatifs* et *abstraits dénominatifs*, on peut préciser la position de ces sous-espèces à l'intérieur de la langue par le schéma suivant :

proposition (ou groupe)-base	*les vieilles coutumes dépérissent ; ses cheveux blancs*
groupe dérivé	*le dépérissement des vieilles coutumes ; la blancheur de ses cheveux*
nom abstrait (dégagé du groupe)	*(le) dépérissement*[2] *(la) blancheur*

Autrement que les noms appellatifs, qui sont autonomes, les abstraits représentent le troisième étage du bâtiment linguistique en ce qui concerne le mot. Mettre en opposition les noms abstraits et les noms concrets est une erreur méthodique à peu près comparable à la confusion d'un prosodème avec un trait pertinent du phonème.[3]

On arrive ainsi à la conclusion que les appellatifs concrets et les noms propres constituent le noyau de la catégorie du substantif, tandis que l'adjectif (substantivé) ou les abstraits relèvent d'abord de complexes syntaxiques et ne joignent le vrai substantif que par un détour. Cette constatation vaut pour le point de vue synchronique aussi bien que diachronique. Dans la couche

---

[1] *Die Leistung der Abstrakta in der Sprache*, Blätter für deutsche Philosophie IV, 1930, p. 66–77.

[2] On passe ici sous silence les fonctions *secondaires* des noms abstraits. Ainsi la fonction secondaire de *blancheur* est de servir d'abstrait à *être blanc* (*ses cheveux sont blancs*). Et, vice versa, *dépérissement* peut se rapporter, en fonction secondaire, à *dépérissant* (*les coutumes dépérissantes*). Le raisonnement ci-dessus n'est d'abord applicable qu'aux abstraits motivés, mais il peut être étendu aux abstraits immotivés (comme p. ex. *chance, malheur*), grâce à l'équivalence sémantique des deux groupes.

[3] Ainsi p. ex. η contraste en grec (ionien-attique) avec ε en tant qu'un ξ (ouvert) avec un ẹ (fermé). Mais le contraste entre η (inaccentué) et η (accentué) se fonde sur une confrontation de complexes au moins dissyllabiques.

Reprinted from *Esquisses linguistiques*, pp. 182–92 (Wroclaw-Krakow : Wydawnictwo Polskiej Akademii Nauk, 1960), with the permission of the author.

constitutive du nom, consistant d'appellatifs et de noms propres,[4] c'est donc le rapport entre ces deux groupes qui arrête l'attention du linguiste. Y a-t-il un pendant linguistique de la distinction, faite par les logiciens, entre les noms génériques et les noms individuels? La réponse à cette question sera positive si l'on réussit à déterminer l'exposant formel qui différencie les deux catégories ou plutôt, puisqu'il ne s'agit pas d'une langue concrète, mais de considérations générales, si l'on arrive à formuler le rapport entre les noms communs et les noms propres de telle manière que les moyens de leur différenciation formelle, dans n'importe quelle langue, en découlent d'une façon automatique.

Pour simplifier notre exposé nous nous bornons dans la suite aux problèmes onomastiques. C'est là que ressortent avec clarté les rapports entre nom commun et nom propre *ne de personnes.*

L'intérêt linguistique du rapport entre ces deux groupes de substantifs concrets commence qu'au moment où s'établit une différence formelle, comme p. ex. une différence d'accentuation, des divergences dans l'usage de l'article, des particularités de flexion, etc. Tous ces morphèmes ont un caractère *actif* lorsqu'ils sont les seuls supports de la différence formelle entre les noms propres et les noms communs dont ceux-ci adoptent le thème. P. ex. all. *der (ein) Wolf: Wolf* (nom propre). Les mêmes morphèmes sont *passifs* et pour ainsi dire pléonastiques, quand il s'agit de noms propres immotivés, obscurs au point de vue étymologique, p. ex *Schubert, Schubart, Schuchardt* (sans article) < v.-h.-a. *scuoh-wurho* "cordonnier".

La variabilité d'emploi des appellatifs, capables de désigner des objets différents, est abolie dans les noms propres, qui par définition ne sauraient viser qu'un objet individuel déterminé. Cette réduction singulière d'emploi crée entre le nom commun et le nom propre un rapport de fondation, l'appellatif étant la forme-base, le nom propre, la forme fondée (cf. *Acta Linguistica* V, p. 15-37).

1. Lorsqu'un appellatif est aussi employé comme un nom propre (cf. un sobriquet), son renouvellement formel (morphologique) peut amener un scindement entre la forme nouvelle, restreinte à la seule valeur appellative, et la forme ancienne dévolue au nom propre (*l.c.*, p. 30).

2. Le rapport *forme nouvelle: forme ancienne,* chargé de la différence sémantique *appellatif: nom commun,* peut rester improductif (dans ce cas on ne parlera que des résidus de la forme ancienne), ou bien tendre à se généraliser en donnant naissance à un procédé nouveau de la formation des noms propres.

3. Dans le dernier cas tout se passe comme si l'appellatif était le mot-base, et le nom propre, le dérivé. Le principe de la proportionnalité ($a_1 : a'_1 = a_2 : a'_2 = a_3 : a'_3 \ldots$) y joue un rôle aussi important que celui de la polarisation formelle, c.-à-d. du choix de la différence (formelle) maxima fournie par le système de la langue (*ibid.*, p. 20).

4. Une fois installés, les traits morphologiques caractérisants les noms propres (surtout de personnes) peuvent être appliqués, pour des buts stylistiques (d'expression), à des noms communs.

Voici quelques exemples historiques illustrant ces tendances générales. En v. indien les composés bahuvrihi sont accentués sur le premier membre.

En insistant sur la valeur adjective du composé, on recourt souvent au suffixe accentué *-á-* (qui reste latent lorsque le deuxième membre comporte déjà la voyelle thématique). Ainsi *vadhri-aśvá-* "qui a des chevaux châtrés", *vṛṣan-aśvá-* "dont les chevaux sont des étalons", à côté de bahuvrihi normaux comme *hári-aśva-* et *áśu-aśva-*.[5] Le composé *śruta-sena-* "dont l'armée est célèbre" apparaît en indien sous la forme oxytone: *śruta-sená-*. Mais l'ancienne forme accentuée sur le 1er membre subsiste dans le nom propre d'un démon (*śrutá-sena-*). On a de même *bṛhad-rathá-* "dont le char est grand" en face de *bṛhád-ratha-*, nom propre. Le renouvellement morphologique des bahuvrihi n'a pas donc envahi tous leurs usages. Employés comme noms propres ils ont conservé, ici et là, leur forme ancienne en représentant, au point de vue formel, *les résidus d'un état morphologique dépassé.*

Mais les résidus peuvent servir d'amorce pour créer une série productive de noms propres. Cela n'arrive que si l'opposition entre la forme nouvelle (nom commun) et la forme ancienne (conservée, à titre de résidu, dans quelques noms propres) devient un procédé morphologique, permettant de dériver d'un appellatif donné le nom propre correspondant. En grec prélittéraire l'accent libre et mobile, hérité de l'indo-européen, a été limité au *complexe final* consistant des deux dernières mores plus la syllabe précédente (XX‿, X‿). En même temps la langue a éliminé, à peu d'exemples près, l'accentuation récessive du vocatif, en la remplaçant par l'accentuation *columnale* propre aux autres cas du paradigme, p. ex. ὦ πομήν, βασιλεῦ; βασιλέως, ἐλπί, αἰδοῖ, πειθοῖ, etc. Les exceptions πομένος, πομένι, πομένα, πομένα concernent surtout les noms de personnes: ὦ πάτερ, μῆτερ, θύγατερ, ἄνερ. Dans certains appellatifs employés, en fonction secondaire, comme noms propres (ou plutôt comme sobriquets), le vocatif s'est soustrait à ce réarrangement, p. ex. Ἕλπι en face de ἐλπί. L'opposition a fini par s'étendre sur tout le paradigme Ἕλπιδος: ἐλπίδος, Ἕλπιδα: ἐλπίδα... Ensuite, autrement qu'en indien, le contraste accentual du type ἐλπίς: Ἕλπις est devenu productif en grec historique. On trouve καρπός "fruit": Κάρπος (nom propre), ἀστήρ "étoile": Ἀστήρ, φροντίς "soin": Φρόντις, Γραικός et Τευκρός (noms ethniques): Γραῖκος, Τεῦκρος (noms de personnes). Par l'intermédiaire de l'adjectif substantivé on arrive à bâtir des noms propres sur des adjectifs, ainsi γλαυκός "luisant, bleuâtre": Γλαῦκος, ξανθός "blond": Ξάνθος, γελῶν "riant": Γέλων, ἀργεστής "brillant": Ἀργέστης, ἀγακλεής "célèbre": Ἀγακλέης. L'accentuation récessive des noms propres continue donc, de manière indirecte, l'accentuation récessive du vocatif indo-européen, abandonnée en grec historique.

La genèse et l'extension de l'article défini en français, comme d'ailleurs dans toutes les langues romanes, est en grande partie un fait prélittéraire. Lorsque l'article devint obligatoire chez les noms communs, il s'est effectué un scindement entre la fonction primaire (appellative), dont l'exposant était l'article, et la fonction secondaire, celle de nom propre, caractérisée par son absence. De cette façon on est à même de distinguer deux couches chronologiques de noms propres provenant d'appellatifs:

1. sans article: *Barbier, Chapelain, Charpentier, Meunier...*
2. avec article: *Lefèvre, Lemoine, Lenormand, Leverrer...*

---

[4] Le fait que le pronom est perçu comme une catégorie distincte du nom prouve que la fonction sémantique constitutive de celui-ci est la *signification* et non pas la faculté de *désigner* (qu'il partage avec le pronom). Dans le nom propre cette dernière est restreinte à sa limite extrême.

[5] *L'accentuation des langues indo-européennes*, 1952, p. 87.

Les deux groupes contrastent avec les appellatifs respectifs de la manière suivante :

Mercier	le mercier	Lemercier
de Mercier	du mercier	de Lemercier
à Mercier	au mercier	à Lemercier (point de contraction de *de* à + *le*)

Une évolution analogue a eu lieu en arabe. Dans cette langue l'article défini ancien est représenté par la nounation, l'article défini récent, par le préfixe *al-*. Il y a donc d'une part une couche ancienne de noms propres, caractérisée par zéro en face de la nounation des noms communs, p. ex. *'akrabu* (nom propre) mais *'akrabun* " scorpion " ; *zufaru* (nom propre) mais *zufarun* " un personnage puissant " ; *zawnabu* (nom de femme), mais *zawnabun* " espèce d'arbre " ; *miṣru* " Égypte, le Caire ", mais *miṣrun* " pays, territoire, (grande) ville ". Il y a, de l'autre côté, un groupe de noms propres plus récent à nounation comme *hasanun* (" beau "), *sa'dun* (" heureux "), *muhammadun* (" célébré "), *murâdun* (" voulu "). Mais le rôle de la nounation est différent dans *hasanun* " beau ", où elle est entretemps devenue un signe d'indétermination, et dans *hasanun* " Hassan ", où l'ancienne valeur d'article défini est inhérente au nom propre.

La couche la plus récente des noms propres ce sont les substantifs ou les adjectifs munis de l'article *al-* : *al-ḥariṯu* (" laboureur "), *al-ja'du* (" qui a les cheveux crépus ").

La langue arabe a profité du bouleversement causé par le remplacement des anciens pluriels réguliers en *-ûna* (masc.) et *-âtun* (fém.) par des formes collectives, pour délimiter d'une façon encore plus nette les appellatifs et les noms propres. En ce qui concerne les derniers, le pluriel " sain " est continué tant par les féminins que par les masculins [8] *hasanun* " Hassan " : plur. *hasanûna*, mais *hasanun* " beau " : plur. *ḥisânun* ; *faṭîmatun* " Fatima " : plur. *faṭîmâtun*, mais *faṭîmatun* " sevrée " : plur. *fuṭumun*. Dans les cas des anciens noms propres et les appellatifs homonymes diffèrent par le thème de pluriel.

Mais ce n'est pas tout. Les noms propres sans nounation (type *'akrabu* v. plus haut) se sont différenciés des noms communs aussi au singulier en devenant diptotes, c.-à-d. en faisant coïncider le génitif et l'accusatif en une seule forme.

al-'akrabu " le scorpion " (nom.) : *'akrabu* " Akrab " (nom propre)
al-'akrabi " du scorpion " (gén.) } : *'akraba* = gén. et acc.
al-'akraba " le scorpion " (acc.)

Le diptotisme des noms propres sans nounation est probablement dû à l'influence des pluriels " sains ", diptotiques de provenance.[9]

Dans tous les exemples précités le renouvellement morphologique du nom commun entraîne un scindement formel entre l'appellatif comme tel et l'appellatif employé en fonction secondaire. Au point de vue du mécanisme linguistique, ces exemples sont comparables aux cas comme *tailleur* remplaçant *sartre* (> *Sartre*) ou *le forgeron* succédant à *le fevre* (> *Lefèvre*). Mais ceux-ci sont

d'un ordre purement *lexical*, tandis que nous visons ici les aspects *grammaticaux* de l'évolution.

Un trait morphologique particulier des noms propres ce sont les procédés *hypocoristiques* étant en relation génétique avec les procédés de *diminution* des noms communs. Le même suffixe employé auprès un appellatif et un nom propre exprime des modifications de sens différentes, cf. *maison : maisonnette* et *Anne : Annette*. Il en suit qu'un renouvellement des procédés diminutifs est apte à conduire à une différenciation entre le suffixe nouveau, diminutif, et l'ancien suffixe, sortant d'usage comme suffixe diminutif et limité désormais à la fonction hypocoristique. Autrement dit : les suffixes hypocoristiques spéciaux représentent en principe des suffixes diminutifs devenus obsolètes.

On sait que la base du procédé hypocoristique est souvent constituée non pas par le nom propre sous son aspect normal, mais par une forme abrégée et modifiée provenant du langage enfantin et adoptée par les adultes. Son caractère spontané se perd quand on la soumet à une règle morphologique rigoureuse. En anglais les formes *Bess* (< *Elisabeth*), *Bill* (< *William*), *Dick* (< *Richard*), *Ned* ou *Ted* (< *Edward*), *Nell* (< *Eleanor*), sont des formes hypocoristiques originales acceptées par la langue des adultes. A part cela il y a un procédé d'abréviation conventionnelle rigoureusement appliqué, consistant à dégager la syllabe initiale du mot pour obtenir une espèce de " racine hypocoristique ". Munie de suffixe *-ie* (*-y*) ou zéro, elle sert de forme hypocoristique conventionnelle :

forme pleine	" racine hypocoristique "	forme hypocoristique usitée
Edward	*Ed*	*Eddie*
William	*Will*	*Willie*
Joseph	*Joe*	*Joey*
Louis	*Lou*	*Louie* [10]

En v.-h.-a., où les noms pleins de provenance germanique sont composés, la " racine hypocoristique " est habituellement représentée par le 1er membre (*Werinher* > *Werin*, *Arnold* > *Arn*), rarement par le deuxième. Elle peut être élargie par les suffixes hypocoristiques *-o* (impliquant parfois la gémination de l'occlusive finale de la racine) ou *-zzo* :

forme pleine	" racine hypocoristique "	forme hypocoristique usitée
Eberhart	*Eb(er)*	*Ebero, Eppo*
Heimrâch	*Heim*	*Heimo, Heinzo (Heinz)*
Uodalrâch	*Uod(al)*	*Uozzo*

Cf. aussi *Fritz, Kunz, Diez* (< *Frizzo, Kuonzo, Diezzo*), etc. La suppression occasionnelle de *r* est peut-être due au langage enfantin : *Benno* < *Bernhard*, *Geppa* < *Gerbirga*. En polonais une déformation systématique du nom plein consistait jadis à détacher le commencement du mot (= le consonantisme initial + la voyelle

---

[6] Ancien morphème de détermination et non d'indétermination (v. *La mimation et l'article en arabe*, Archiv Orientální XVIII, 1-2, 1950, p. 323-328).

[7] Pour les grammairiens arabes le nom propre est *mu'arrafun binafsihi* " déterminé par lui-même ".

[8] V. plus loin pour ce qui concerne la fonction du pluriel des noms propres.

[9] *Le diptotisme et la construction des noms propres en arabe*, Word VII, 1951, pp. 222-226.

[10] Cf. la syllabation *Ed-ward, Wil-liam, Jo-seph, Lou-is.* On trouve du reste aussi *Davy* < *Daviḍ* (*Da-viḍ*).

suivante) et à y ajouter les éléments hypocoristiques *-ch, -sz, -ś*, éventuellement élargis d'autres suffixes:

forme pleine	"racine hypocoristique"	forme hypocoristique usitée
Jan	Ja-	Jaś, Jasiek
Paweł	Pa-	Paszek, Paś
Stanisław	Sta-	Stach, Staszek, Staś
Barbara	Ba-	Basia
Katarzyna	Ka-	Kasia, Kachna

Autrement qu'en anglais ou en allemand, la "racine hypocoristique" n'y est pas employée à l'état nu.

Tandis que la réduction de la forme pleine, due à des facteurs externes (langage enfantin), ne devient un phénomène morphologique qu'à condition d'être normalisée, les suffixes hypocoristiques qui s'y ajoutent, comme v.-h.-a. *-zzo*[11] ou pol. *-ch*, posent toujours des problèmes historiques. D'après tout ce qui précède, il faut les regarder comme des *suffixes diminutifs sortis d'usage*.

Parfois les diminutifs des noms de personnes, communs ou propres, loin d'être hypocoristiques, se chargent d'une fonction tout à fait différente. Ils servent à désigner le *descendant* de la personne portant le nom originaire:

noms de famille (polonais)			sens primitif
Kowalczyk	le petit forgeron	(kowal)	= fils du forgeron
Ślusarczyk	,, serrurier	(ślusarz)	= ,, serrurier
Stolarczyk	,, menuisier	(stolarz)	= ,, menuisier
Szklarczyk	,, verrier	(szklarz)	= ,, verrier
Tokarczyk	,, tourneur	(tokarz)	= ,, tourneur
Mikołajczyk	,, Nicolas	(Mikołaj)	= ,, de Nicolas
Stańczyk	,, Stanislas	(Stan)	= ,, Stanislas

Et ainsi de suite, pour toute une série de suffixes diminutifs (*-czak, -czuk, -yk, -uk, -ek*, etc.).

Dans d'autres langues le même procédé peut aussi revêtir une forme "analytique": fr. *Petitjean*, all. *Kleinhans*, etc.

L'adjonction de suffixes hypocoristiques ou patronymiques aux noms communs a d'abord une valeur expressive. En partant des noms propres ils pénètrent dans les noms de personnes communs, dans les noms d'animaux et même dans ceux d'objets inanimés. P. ex. lit. *brôlis* < *brôtê*, pol. *brach* < *brat(r)*, all. *Spatz* < v.-h.-a. *sparo*, *Petz* (*Bätz*) < *Bär*, pol. *brzuś* (< *brzuch*, pol. *brzuch* "ventre") "petit (cher) ventre", *pysio* "petite (chère) bouche" (< *pysk* "gueule"), *kuś* (< *kutas* "membrum virile"), etc.

Il semble donc, à première vue, que les deux domaines de l'appellatif et du nom commun s'enchevêtrent et s'influencent *mutuellement* de manière qu'on ne saurait parler d'une subordination des uns aux autres. Mais il ne faut pas être dupe des apparences. Grâce aux procès de renouvellement et de différenciation, les procédés hypocoristiques et patronymiques sont constamment nourris de la part de la suffixation diminutive ordinaire. Mais l'inverse n'est pas vrai. L'emploi de ces procédés expressifs en dehors du nom propre est toujours

restreint et ne conduit point à la constitution d'une catégorie suffixale non-expressive. Privés de leur expressivité, les suffixes respectifs deviennent des morphèmes vides.

La hiérarchie qui règle les rapports des deux catégories principales des noms concrets, nous permet de déterminer l'origine de certains groupes importants de suffixes. Pour trouver le point de départ d'une formation hypocoristique ou patronymique, on cherchera parmi les formations diminutives apparentées subsistantes ou hypothétiques (préhistoriques). De l'autre côté, on attribuera sans hésitation aux formes comme *soliculus* (français *soleil*) ou *aviculus* (*oiseau*) une provenance expressive hypocoristique. Il y aura naturellement, comme partout ailleurs, des cas spéciaux limitrophes difficiles à trancher, dont voici un exemple. En slave les dérivés en *-ętjo-* (v. slave *-ištь*, s.-cr. *-ěč*, russe *-č*, pol. *-ič*) fournissent des noms de jeunes animaux et aussi des noms patronymiques. P. ex. slovène *ogьr* "anguille": *ogьrič* "petite ou jeune anguille", *gǫs* "oie": *gǫsič* "jeune oie", s.-cr. *vran* "corbeau": *vranič* "jeune corbeau", *vъk* "loup": *vъčič* "jeune loup"; s.-cr. *králjević* = russe *korolěvič* = pol. *krôlewic* "fils du roi", s.-cr. *Petrović* = russe *Petrovič* = pol. *Piotrowic* "fils de Pierre", et ainsi de suite.

On se demande si *-ętjo-* est un suffixe patronymique autonome (provenant d'un suffixe diminutif préhistorique, transformé ou non, mais enfin autonome à date historique), dont l'emploi pour former les noms de jeunes animaux est secondaire et expressif, ou bien s'il s'agit d'un suffixe diminutif vivant, le sens patronymique n'étant qu'une variante sémantique commandée par la racine (nom de personne).[12]

Tout comme les suffixes hypocoristiques et expressifs, le nom propre tout fait connaît aussi l'emploi expressif: *Lazarus* > *ladre*, *Metze* (forme hypocoristique de *Mechtilde*) "fille". Dans ce cas encore le procédé est sporadique, tandis que l'emploi des appellatifs au sens de noms propres ne connaît presque pas de limites. On comprend cette asymétrie en confrontant les contenus sémantiques de l'appellatif et du nom propre. Employé comme nom propre l'appellatif apporte un contenu relativement pauvre, qui est loin d'épuiser la richesse infinie du nom. De l'autre côté, la charge sémantique du nom propre déborde celle de l'appellatif qu'il remplace, ce qui explique son expressivité.

Ce rapport sémantique entre les deux catégories est accompagné d'une certaine différence formelle constante. Le nom propre, qui ne désigne qu'un seul individu, n'a pas de pluriel[13] au sens courant du terme (= ensemble d'individus ayant des qualités communes). Quand je dis *tous les Pierres célèbrent aujourd'hui la fête de leur patron*, je parle d'un ensemble de personnes de sexe mâle qui n'ont rien de commun en dehors du nom. Le pluriel dit elliptique, qu'on constate pour les noms propres, p. ex. pol. *Jankowie* "Jean et sa femme", est aussi attesté dans le domaine de l'appellatif (type esp. *padres* "les pères" au sens de "parents" = père et mère). Mais cet usage est conditionné et exceptionnel. Enfin dans un exemple comme: *nous n'aurons plus*

[11] On y voit la continuation tantôt d'un *t* germanique (= *d* indo-européen), tantôt de *s* combiné avec une consonne dentale de la racine.

[12] Aucune de ces deux hypothèses n'échappe à des difficultés. Les noms de jeunes animaux se retrouvent en lituanien (*ungurýtis, žąsýtis, varnýtis, vilkýtis*), il paraît donc difficile d'admettre un emploi expressif de *-ętjo-* en slave. Mais d'autre part un usage purement diminutif laisse inexpliqué l'absence de noms inanimés en *-ętjo-*.

[13] Nous ne parlons ici que de noms d'individus. Les noms de groupes (p. ex. ethniques) apparaissent surtout au pluriel.

de Catons, le nom propre s'approche par son sens de l'appellatif: "hommes ayant les qualités de Caton".

En formant le pluriel d'un nom propre on est donc obligé de recourir soit à un emploi métonymique, soit à un emploi métaphorique (basé sur les qualités caractéristiques de l'individu), en faisant ainsi tomber son caractère de nom propre.[14]

Les remarques précédentes ont le but de poser le problème *grammatical* du nom propre en le dégageant de la richesse déconcertante de points de vue et de considérations d'ordre non-linguistique, qui tendent à occuper le premier plan dans les recherches onomastiques. Les faits externes de l'histoire en général, de l'histoire de la civilisation en particulier, sont souvent décisifs lorsqu'il s'agit d'établir l'étymologie du nom propre. Mais son intérêt *linguistique* véritable repose dans les particularités qu'il présente par rapport aux autres catégories du substantif. Le reste relève en grande partie de sciences limitrophes : ethnologie, sociologie, histoire politique, histoire de civilisation, etc.

[14] Tout récemment, dans la Revista Brasileira de Filologia I, 1, 1955, pp. 1–16, M. E. Coseriu a consacré des remarques judicieuses au pluriel des noms propres. A son avis il faut d'abord écarter 1) le type *les Andes*, qui n'a pas de singulier ; 2) le type *Μῆδοι* qui, en tant que nom ethnique, n'a point de singulier, mais en tant que pluriel de *Μῆδος* (+ *Μῆδος* + *Μῆδος* + ...) est le pluriel d'un nom *commun* (contenu = " ayant les qualités ethniques d'un Mède "). Dans la première acception le singulier est aussi admissible : ital. *il Turco*, pol. *Hiszpan na zamku zatkuął sztandary.*

Quant aux formes *Claudii, los Sánchez*, l'auteur les considère à juste titre comme des noms de *familles* ou de *lignées*, et non comme des pluriels de noms individuels (*Claudius, Sánchez*): "*los Sánchez, Claudii*, a pesar de ser plurales, no son los plurales de *Claudius et Sánchez*".

Enfin un pluriel comme *los Sánchez* est en réalité un nom *commun* (appellatif) quand il désigne:
1. des individus *appelés* Sánchez ;
2. les oeuvres de Sánchez ;
3. des hommes comme Sánchez ;
4. les manières d'être de Sánchez ("le Sánchez d'aujourd'hui n'est pas le Sánchez d'hier ").

ARBITRAIRE LINGUISTIQUE ET DOUBLE ARTICULATION

André Martinet

Parmi les nombreux paradoxes qui sont, tout ensemble, un des attraits de la glossématique et la source de bien des réserves à son égard, le principe de l'isomorphisme[1] occupe une place de choix. Ce principe implique le parallélisme complet des deux plans du contenu et de l'expression, une organisation foncièrement identique des deux faces de la langue, celles qu'en termes de substance on désignerait comme les sons et le sens. Poser ce principe, c'est certainement outrepasser de beaucoup les implications de la théorie saussurienne du signe. Mais il n'en est pas moins vrai que c'est la présentation du signifiant et du signifié comme les deux faces d'une même réalité qui est à la source du principe hjelmslévien de l'isomorphisme.

Comme tous les paradoxes glossématiques, la théorie de l'isomorphisme est riche d'enseignements. Jerzy Kuryłowicz en a bien dégagé la fertilité tout en en suggérant, en passant, les limites.[2] Ce qui paraît généralement critiquable dans l'isomorphisme, c'est le caractère absolu que lui prête la glossématique. On lui reproche volontiers de méconnaître la finalité de la langue : on parle pour être compris, et l'expression est au service du contenu ; il y a solidarité certes, mais solidarité dans un sens déterminé. Les analogies qu'on constate — et que personne ne nie — dans l'organisation des deux plans, ne changent rien à ce rapport de subordination des deux plans, ne changent rien à ce rapport de subordination des sons au sens qui semble incompatible avec le parallélisme intégral que postule la théorie. On répondra, peut-être, que cette subordination ne prend corps que dans l'acte de parole, et qu'elle n'affecte pas la langue proprement dite en tant que réalité parfaitement statique. Mais quelle que soit l'issue du débat, il demeure que la pensée glossématique se heurte ici à des résistances sourdes, à une incompréhension récurrente dont il n'est peut-être pas impossible de dégager les causes. Avant de pouvoir constater le parallélisme des deux plans, il faut s'être convaincu qu'il y a effectivement deux plans distincts. Il faut avoir identifié un plan de l'expression qui est bien celui où les phonologues rencontrent les phonèmes, mais celui aussi où le glossématicien

retrouve les signifiants qui forment les énoncés : appartiennent au plan de l'expression non seulement les unités simples /m/, /a/ et /l/, mais, au même titre, le signifiant /mal/, la suite de signifiants /ž e mal o dã/, la face phonique (/mal/) ou graphique (*mal*) de tous les énoncés passés, présents ou futurs dont l'ensemble forme la réalité accessible de la langue. Il faut, ensuite, avoir identifié un plan du contenu d'où sont exclus les phonèmes (/m/, /a/ ou /l/), mais également les signifiants simples (/mal/) ou complexes (/ž e mal o dã/), où, par conséquent, ont seuls droit de cité les signifiés "mal", "j'ai mal aux dents" et d'autres plus vastes. Ces signifiés existent, certes, en tant que tels, mais ils ne peuvent que parce qu'ils correspondent à des signifiants distincts. Mais ils ne peuvent figurer sur le plan du contenu que dans la mesure où on les conçoit comme distincts des signifiants. En glossématique, l'opposition de base est entre phonèmes (ou mieux "cénèmes") et signifiants d'une part, signifiés d'autre part selon le schéma suivant :

$$
\left.
\begin{array}{l}
\text{/m/} \\
\text{/mal/} \\
\text{/ž e mal o dã/} \\
\text{etc.}
\end{array}
\right\}
\quad\sim\quad
\left\{
\begin{array}{l}
\text{"mal"} \\
\text{"j'ai mal aux dents"} \\
\text{etc.}
\end{array}
\right.
$$

Pour le linguiste ordinaire, l'unité du signe linguistique est une réalité plus évidente que sa dualité : /mal/ et "mal" sont deux aspects d'une même chose. On veut bien se convaincre que le signe a deux faces, mais on n'est pas prêt à fonder toute l'analyse linguistique sur un divorce définitif de ces deux faces. S'opposant au signe, unité complexe, certes, puisqu'elle participe à ce qu'on nomme traditionnellement le sens et la forme, mais considéré comme un tout, on reconnaît le phonème, unité simple dans la mesure où elle participe à la forme, mais non au sens. L'opposition de base est ici entre phonèmes d'une part, signifiants et signifiés d'autre part, selon le schéma suivant :

$$
\left.
\begin{array}{l}
\text{/m/}
\end{array}
\right\}
\quad\sim\quad
\left\{
\begin{array}{l}
\text{/mal/ — "mal"} \\
\text{/ž e mal o dã/ — "j'ai mal aux dents"}
\end{array}
\right.
$$

Le linguiste ordinaire conçoit bien qu'il puisse exister de profondes analogies entre les systèmes de signes et les systèmes de phonèmes, et que le groupement de ces unités dans la chaîne puisse présenter de frappantes similitudes, encore que les tentatives pour pousser un peu loin le parallélisme se heurtent vite à la complexité bien supérieure des unités à deux faces et à l'impossibilité où l'on se trouve d'en clore jamais la liste. Mais ce même linguiste se trompe s'il s'imagine que ces analogies correspondent exactement et nécessairement à celles que suppose le parallélisme des deux plans hjelmsléviens de l'expression et du contenu, puisque ce parallélisme est entre signifiants et signifiés et que les analogies constatées sont entre signes et phonèmes. On note constamment, chez ceux qui, sans être glossématiciens déclarés, font un effort pour se représenter la réalité linguistique dans le cadre hjelmslévien, qu'ils se laissent aller à confondre, dans une certaine mesure, les deux plans, sans s'apercevoir que ce ne sont plus des unités de contenu qu'ils vont opposer à des unités d'expression, mais bien des signes, qui participent aux deux plans, à des phonèmes, qui n'appartiennent qu'à un seul.

Cet état de choses, qu'on peut déplorer, s'explique évidemment par la

Reprinted from *Cahiers Ferdinand de Saussure* 15 (1957) : 105-16, with the permission of the author and of *Cahiers Ferdinand de Saussure*.

[1] Le mot est employé par J. Kuryłowicz dans sa contribution aux *Recherches structurales* 1949, *TCLC* 5 (Copenhague), p. 48-60.

[2] *Ibid.*, p. 51.

difficulté qu'on éprouve à manipuler la réalité sémantique sans le secours d'une réalité concrète correspondante, phonique ou graphique. Il faut noter d'ailleurs que nous ne disposons pas des ressources terminologiques qui pourraient nous permettre de traiter avec quelque rigueur des faits sémantiques indépendamment de leurs supports formels. Il n'y a, bien entendu, aucune discipline paralinguistique qui corresponde à la " phonétique " (par opposition à la " phonologie ") et qui nous permette de traiter d'une réalité psychique antérieure à toute intégration aux cadres linguistiques. Mais, même en matière d'examen de la réalité psychique intégrée à la structure linguistique, on n'a rien qui soit le pendant de ce qu'est la phonologie sur le plan des sons. On dispose heureusement du terme " sémantique " qu'on emploie assez précisément en référence à l'aspect signifié du signe et qui nous a permis, on l'espère, de nous faire entendre dans ce qui précède. On possède, en outre, le terme " signifié " qui, n'existant que par opposition à " signifiant ", est d'une clarté parfaite. Mais toute expansion terminologique est interdite à partir de ce participe passif. Quant à " sémantique ", s'il a acquis le sens qui nous intéresse, il n'en est pas moins dérivé d'une racine qui évoque, non point une réalité psychique, mais bien le processus de signification qui implique la combinaison du signifiant et du signifié. La sémantique est peut-être autre chose que la sémiologie ; mais on voit mal de quelle série terminologique " sémantique " pourrait être le départ ; on emploie, en tout cas, ne saurait être autre chose qu'une unité à double face.

Il n'entre pas dans nos intentions de rechercher ici s'il est possible et utile de combler ces lacunes. On renverra à l'intéressante tentative de Luis Prieto,[3] et l'on marquera simplement que cette absence de parallélisme dans le développement de l'analyse sur les deux plans n'est pas fortuite : elle ne fait que refléter ce qui se passe dans la communication linguistique où l'on " signifie " quelque chose qui n'est pas manifeste au moyen de quelque chose qui l'est.

Les modes de pensée qui font échec à la conception hjelmslévienne des deux plans parallèles ont été fort mal explicités. Ceci s'explique du fait de leur caractère quasi général : on ne prend conscience de l'existence d'une chose que lorsqu'on ne la trouve plus là où on l'attendait. C'est, en fait, dans la mesure où l'on saisit exactement l'originalité de la position glossématique, qu'on prend conscience de l'existence d'un autre schème, celui selon lequel les faits linguistiques s'ordonnent dans le cadre d'articulations successives, une première articulation en unités minima à deux faces (les " morphèmes " de la plupart des structuralistes), une seconde en unités successives minima de fonction uniquement distinctive (les phonèmes). Ce schème forme sans aucun doute le substrat ordinaire des démarches de la plupart des linguistes, et c'est ce qui explique que l'exposé qui en a été fait dans Recherches structurales 1949[4] ait généralement dérouté les recenseurs du volume qui estimaient n'y retrouver que des vérités d'évidence et ne discernaient pas les rapports antithétiques qui justifiaient l'inclusion de cet exposé parmi les " interventions dans le débat glossématique ".

Présentée comme un trait que l'observation révèle dans les langues au sens ordinaire du terme, la double articulation fait donc aisément figure de truisme. Ce n'est guère que lorsqu'on prétend l'imposer comme le critère de ce qui est langue ou non-langue que l'interlocuteur prend conscience de la gravité du problème. Et pourtant, s'il est évident que toutes les langues qu'étudie en fait le linguiste s'articulent bien à deux reprises, pourquoi hésiter à réserver le terme de langue à des objets qui présentent cette caractéristique ? Regrette-t-on d'exclure ainsi de la linguistique les systèmes de communication qui articulent bien les messages en unités successives, mais ne soumettent pas ces unités elles-mêmes à une articulation supplémentaire ? Le désir de faire entrer la linguistique dans le cadre plus vaste d'une sémiologie générale est certes légitime, mais en perdra-t-on rien à bien marquer, dès l'abord, ce qui fait, parmi les systèmes de signes, l'originalité des langues au sens le plus ordinaire, le plus banal du terme ?

Les avantages didactiques de la conception de la langue comme caractérisée par une double articulation se sont révélés à l'usage et se sont confirmés au cours de dix années d'enseignement. Ils apparaissent plus considérables que ne le laisserait supposer l'exposé un peu schématique de 1949. Ils comportent notamment l'établissement d'une hiérarchie des faits de langue qui n'est pas sans rapport avec celle qu'on aurait pu probablement dégager des exposés saussuriens relatifs à l'arbitraire du signe si l'on s'était attaché plus aux faits fonctionnels et moins aux aspects psychologiques du problème. Noter, en effet, que rien dans les choses à désigner ne justifie le choix de tel signifiant pour tel signifié, marquer que les unités linguistiques sont des valeurs, c'est-à-dire qu'elles n'existent que du fait du consensus d'une communauté particulière, tout ceci revient à marquer l'indépendance du fait linguistique vis-à-vis de ce qui n'est pas langue. Mais relever le caractère doublement articulé de la langue n'est-ce pas indiquer, non seulement comment elle parvient à réduire, au fini des " morphèmes " et des phonèmes, l'infinie variété de l'expérience et de la sensation, mais aussi comment, par une analyse particulière à chaque communauté, elle établit ses valeurs propres, et comment, en confiant le soin de former ses signifiants à des unités sans face signifiée, les phonèmes, elle les protège contre les atteintes du sens ? Qu'on essaye, un instant, d'imaginer ce que pourrait être une " langue " à signifiants inarticulés, un système de communication où, à chaque signifié, correspondrait une production vocale distincte, en bloc, de tous les autres signifiants. D'un point de vue strictement statique, on a pu se demander si les organes humains de production et réception seraient capables d'émettre et de percevoir un nombre suffisant de tels signifiants distincts, pour que le système obtenu rende les services qu'on attend d'une langue ".[5] Mais notre point de vue est, ici, surtout dynamique : à condition que se maintiennent les distinctions entre les signes, rien ne pourrait empêcher les locuteurs de modifier la prononciation des signifiants dans le sens où, selon le sentiment général, l'expression deviendrait plus adéquate à la notion exprimée ; l'arbitraire du signe serait, dans ces conditions, vite immolé sur l'autel de l'expressivité. Ce qui empêche ces glissements des signifiants et assure leur autonomie vis-à-vis des signifiés est le fait que, dans les langues réelles, ils sont composés de phonèmes, unités à face unique, sur lesquels le sens du mot n'a pas de prise parce que chaque réalisation d'un

---

[3] Dans son article " Contributions à l'étude fonctionnelle du contenu ", Travaux de l'Institut de Linguistique 1 (Paris 1956), p. 23-41.

[4] P. 30-37.

[5] Cf. Economie des changements phonétiques, Traité de phonologie diachronique (Berne, 1955), § 4-2.

phonème donné, dans un mot particulier, reste solidaire des autres réalisations du même phonème dans tout autre mot ; cette solidarité phonématique pourra, on le sait, être brisée sous la pression de contextes phoniques différents ; l'important, en ce qui nous concerne ici, est que, face au signifié, cette solidarité reste totale. Les phonèmes, produits de la seconde articulation linguistique, se révèlent ainsi comme les garants de l'arbitraire du signe.

Les Néogrammairiens n'avaient pas tort de placer au centre de leurs préoc-cupations ce que nous appellerions le problème du comportement diachronique des unités d'expression. De leur enseignement relatif aux "lois phonétiques", il faut retenir le principe que, dans les conditions qu'on doit appeler "normales" le sens d'un mot ne saurait avoir aucune action sur le destin des phonèmes dont se compose sa face expressive. Ces linguistes ont eu tort de nier l'existence d'exceptions : il y en a, on le sait.[6] Mais il est important qu'elles restent conçues comme des faits marginaux qui, par contraste, font mieux comprendre le caractère des faits proprement linguistiques : une formule de politesse peut se réduire rapidement à quelques sons, une gémination ou un allongement expressifs peuvent arriver à se fixer dans des circonstances favorables. Mais ces cas, très particuliers, où l'équilibre entre la densité du contenu et la masse phonique des significants a été rompu dans un sens ou dans un autre, ne font que mettre en valeur le caractère normal de l'autonomie des phonèmes par rapport au sens particulier de chaque mot.

La théorie de la double articulation aboutit à distinguer nettement parmi les productions vocales entre des faits centraux, ceux qui entrent dans le cadre qu'elle délimite, et des faits marginaux, tous ceux qui, en tout ou en partie échappent à ce cadre.

Les faits centraux ainsi dégagés, signes et phonèmes, sont ceux dont le caractère conventionnel, arbitraire au sens saussurien du terme, est le plus marqué ; ils sont d'une nature qu'après les mathématiciens on nomme "discrète", c'est-à-dire qu'ils valent par leur présence ou leur absence, ce qui exclut la variation progressive et continue : en français où l'on possède deux phonèmes bilabiaux /p/ et /b/, toute orale bilabiale d'un énoncé ne peut être que /p/ ou /b/ et jamais quelque chose d'intermédiaire entre /p/ et /b/ ; bière avec un b à moitié dévoisé n'indique pas une substance intermédiaire entre la bière et la pierre ; le signe est-ce-que, défini exactement comme /ɛsk/, marque une question et jamais rien de plus ou de moins ; pour le nuancer il faudra ajouter à la chaîne un nouveau signe, également discret, comme peut-être.

Les faits marginaux sont en général, par nature, exposés à la pression directe des besoins de la communication et de l'expression ; certains d'entre eux, tels les tons, peuvent participer au caractère discret constaté pour les unités des deux articulations ; mais la plupart gardent le pouvoir de nuancer le message par des variations dont on ne saurait dire si elles sont ou non des unités nouvelles ou des avatars de l'ancienne : c'est le cas de l'accent qui, certes, participe au caractère discret lorsqu'il contraste avec son absence dans des syllabes voisines, mais dont le degré de force peut varier en rapport direct et immédiat avec les nécessités de l'expression ; c'est plus encore le cas de l'intonation où même un

trait aussi arbitrarisé que la mélodie montante de l'interrogation (il pleut ?) comporte un message qui variera au fur et à mesure que se modifiera la pente ou que s'esquisseront des inflexions de la courbe.

Pour autant qu'il est légitime d'identifier "linguistique" et "arbitraire", on dira qu'un acte de communication est proprement linguistique si le message à transmettre s'articule en une chaîne de signes dont chacun est réalisé au moyen d'une succession de phonèmes : /il fɛ bo/. On posera, d'autre part, qu'il n'est pas d'acte de communication proprement linguistique qui ne comporte la double articulation : un cri articulé n'est pas, en son essence, un message ; il peut le devenir, mais il ne différa pas alors sémiologiquement du geste ; il pourra s'articuler dans le sens qu'il se réalisera comme une succession de phonèmes existants dans la langue du crieur, comme dans l'appel /ɔla/ ou l'interjection /aj/ ; il ne frappera plus, dans ces conditions, comme phono-logiquement allogène dans un contexte linguistique ; mais n'ayant pas été soumis à la première articulation, celle qui réduit le message en signes successifs, il ne pourra jamais s'intégrer pleinement à l'énoncé, ou, du moins, il faudrait pour cela qu'il reçût le statut d'unite de la première articulation, c'est-à-dire de signe linguistique.

Chacune des unités d'une des deux articulations représente nécessairement le chaînon d'un énoncé, et tout énoncé s'analyse intégralement en unités des deux ordres. Ceci implique que tout fait reconnu comme marginal parce qu'échappant, en tout ou en partie, à la double articulation, ou bien sera exclu des énoncés articulés, ou n'y pourra figurer qu'à titre suprasegmental. En d'autres termes, les faits marginaux que l'on peut trouver dans les énoncés pleinement articulés sont ceux que l'on nomme prosodiques. On tend à con-sidérer les faits prosodiques comme une annexe des faits phonématiques, et à les ranger dans la phonologie, ce qui ne se justifie que partiellement. Certaines unités prosodiques, les tons proprement dits, sont des unités distinctives à face unique comme les phonèmes : la différence mélodique qui empêche la confusion des mots norvégiens /¹bɔnr/ "paysan" et /²bɔnr/ "haricots" a exactement la même fonction que la différence d'articulation glottale qui oppose en français bière à pierre. Mais d'autres traits prosodiques, maints faits d'intonation par exemple, sont, comme les signes, des unités à double face qui combinent une expression phonique et un contenu sémantique : l'intonation interrogative de la question il pleut ? a un signifié qui équivaut généralement à "est-ce-que" et un signifiant qui est la montée mélodique. Il en va de même de faits dynamiques comme l'accent d'insistance qui peut frapper l'initiale du substantif dans c'est un polisson ; dans ce cas, le signifié pourrait être rendu par quelque chose comme "je suis très affecté" ; le signifiant s'identifiant avec l'allongement qui affecte /p/. Ceci veut dire que le caractère suprasegmental vaut aussi bien sur le plan sémantique que sur celui des sons, et que les faits auxquels la double articulation confère un caractère marginal ne se limitent point au domaine phonologique.

Les faits prosodiques, dont l'aire est ainsi précisée, se trouvent si fréquemment au centre des préoccupations linguistiques, qu'on hésitera peut-être à n'y voir qu'une annexe du domaine linguistique proprement dit. Le diachroniste, par exemple, ne peut oublier que c'est dans ce domaine que se manifestent et s'amorcent les déséquilibres qui entretiendront une permanente instabilité dans

6 Ibid., §§ 1-19 à 21.

déterminé. Mais on n'en pourra guère nier le caractère généralement facultatif. Et, puisqu'en dernière analyse nous sommes à la recherche de ce qui caractérise constamment tout ce que nous désirons appeler une langue, il est normal que nous retenions la double articulation et écartions les faits prosodiques.

Comme sans doute bien des œuvres dont la publication n'a pas reçu la sanction de leur auteur, le *Cours de linguistique générale* doit représenter, sous une forme durcie, un stade d'une pensée en cours d'épanouissement. Le structuraliste contemporain, qui y a appris l'arbitraire du signe et qui a laissé sa pensée se cristalliser autour de ce concept, est frappé, à la relecture de l'ouvrage, du caractère un peu dispersé de l'enseignement relatif aux caractères conventionnels de la langue qui apparaissent au moins sous les deux aspects de l'arbitraire du signifiant et de la notion de valeur. Il attendrait une synthèse qui groupe sous une seule rubrique tous les traits qui concourent à assurer l'autonomie de la langue par rapport à tout ce qui n'est pas elle, en marquant ses distances vis-à-vis des réalités extra-linguistiques de tous ordres. C'est au lecteur à découvrir que l'attribution "arbitraire" de tel signifiant à tel signifié n'est qu'un aspect d'une autonomie linguistique dont une autre face comporte le choix et la délimitation des signifiés. En fait, l'indépendance de la langue vis-à-vis de la réalité non linguistique se manifeste, plus encore que par le choix des signifiants, dans la façon dont elle interprète en ses propres termes cette réalité établissant en consultation avec elle sans doute, mais souverainement, ce qu'on appelait ses concepts et ce que nous nommerions plutôt ses oppositions : elle pourra s'inspirer du spectre pour dégager les qualités des objets qu'on appelle "couleurs" ; mais elle choisira à sa guise ceux des points de ce spectre qu'elle nommera, opposant ici un bleu, un vert et un jaune, se contentant là de la simple opposition de deux points pour le même espace. Les implications de tout ceci dépassent de loin celles qui découlent de l'enseignement relatif au signifiant. Nous mesurons jusqu'à quel point c'est la langue que nous parlons qui détermine la vision que chacun de nous a du monde. Nous découvrons qu'elle tient sans cesse en lisière notre activité mentale, que ce n'est pas une pensée autonome qui crée des mythes que la langue se contentera de nommer, tel Adam nommant les bêtes et les choses que lui présentait le Seigneur, mais que les mythes bourgeonnent sur la langue, changeant de forme et de sexe aux hasards de ses développements, telle la déesse *Nerthus* que l'évolution de la déclinaison germanique a virilisée sous la forme du *Njord* scandinave.

Ce sont les conditions et les implications de l'autonomie de la langue que groupe et condense la théorie de la double articulation et, à ce titre seul, elle mériterait de retenir l'attention des linguistes.

le système des phonèmes : les modifications des inventaires phonématiques semblent, en effet, en dernière analyse, toujours se ramener ou se rattacher à quelque innovation prosodique. Le synchroniste dira que c'est par la structure prosodique que commence l'identification par l'auditeur des énoncés entendus, de telle sorte qu'en espagnol *pasó* "je passai" est perçu comme distinct de *paso* (/páso/) "je passe" parce qu'appartenant à un autre schème accentuel, — ⏑ —, et non — ⏑ —, sans que le pouvoir distinctif des phonèmes des deux formes entre jamais réellement en ligne de compte.[7]

Tout ceci n'enlève rien au caractère plus central des unités de première et de deuxième articulation. Si les déséquilibres pénètrent jusqu'aux systèmes phonématiques par la zone prosodique, c'est que, précisément, cette zone est plus exposée aux atteintes du monde extérieur du fait de son moindre arbitraire. Il y a bien des raisons pour que les faits prosodiques s'imposent plus immédiatement que les faits phonématiques à l'attention des auditeurs. Mais la plupart d'entre elles se ramènent au fait qu'ils sont de nature moins abstraite, qu'ils évoquent plus directement l'objet que représente en ... ce détour que représente en fait la double articulation. Ce détour, certes, est indispensable au maintien de la précision de la communication et à la préservation de l'outil linguistique, mais l'homme tend à s'en dispenser et à en faire abstraction lorsqu'il peut arriver à ses fins à l'aide d'éléments moins élaborés et plus directs que signes et phonèmes. Ces éléments sont physiquement présents dans tout énoncé : il faut toujours une certaine énergie pour émettre une chaîne parlée ; toute voix a nécessairement une hauteur musicale ; toute émission, de par son caractère linéaire, a nécessairement une durée. Pour quiconque n'interprète pas automatiquement tous les faits phoniques en termes de pertinence phonologique, la présence inéluctable dans la parole de l'énergie, de la mélodie et de la quantité semble imposer ces traits comme les éléments fondamentaux du langage humain. En fait, ils sont si indispensables et si permanents qu'on peut tendre à ne plus les remarquer ; Et quel usage linguistique peut-on faire d'un trait qu'on ne remarque pas ? De sorte qu'on serait tenté de dire qu'ils sont fondamentaux dans le langage, plutôt que dans la langue. Mais comme c'est la langue, plutôt que le langage, qui fait l'objet de la linguistique, il est justifié d'énoncer que les faits prosodiques sont moins foncièrement linguistiques que les signes et les phonèmes.

Toutes les langues connues utilisent des signes combinables et un système phonologique. Mais il y en a, comme le français, qui, pourrait-on presque dire, n'utilisent les latitudes prosodiques que par superfétation ou par raccroc. On peut toujours, dans une telle langue, arriver à ses fins communicatives sans avoir recours à elles. On dira "C'est moi qui …" là où une autre langue accentuerait le pronom de première personne, et, en disant *est-ce qu'il pleut ?* ou *pleut-il ?*, on évitera l'emploi distinctif de la mélodie interrogative dont d'autres langues, comme l'espagnol, ne sauraient s'affranchir. Ceci ne veut naturellement pas dire qu'en français comme ailleurs le recours aux marges expressives ne permette, très souvent, d'alléger les énoncés et de rendre plus alertes les échanges linguistiques. A propos d'une langue de ce type, on pourra peut-être discuter de l'importance du rôle des éléments prosodiques dans un style ou un usage

[7] *Ibid.*, § 5-5.